The Cultural Industries

The Cultural Industries

3rd edition

David Hesmondhalgh

Los Angeles | London | New Delhi
Singapore | Washington DC

Los Angeles | London | New Delhi
Singapore | Washington DC

SAGE Publications Ltd
1 Oliver's Yard
55 City Road
London EC1Y 1SP

SAGE Publications Inc.
2455 Teller Road
Thousand Oaks, California 91320

SAGE Publications India Pvt Ltd
B 1/I 1 Mohan Cooperative Industrial Area
Mathura Road
New Delhi 110 044

SAGE Publications Asia-Pacific Pte Ltd
3 Church Street
#10-04 Samsung Hub
Singapore 049483

Editor: Mila Steele
Editorial assistant: James Piper
Production editor: Imogen Roome
Copyeditor: Audrey Scriven
Proofreader: Dick Davis
Marketing manager: Michael Ainsley
Cover design: Francis Kenny
Typeset by: C&M Digitals (P) Ltd, Chennai, India
Printed and bound by CPI Group (UK) Ltd,
Croydon, CR0 4YY

Library of Congress Control Number: 2011945432

British Library Cataloguing in Publication data

A catalogue record for this book is available from
the British Library

MIX
Paper from
responsible sources
FSC® C013604
www.fsc.org

ISBN 978-1-4462-0925-7
ISBN 978-1-4462-0926-4 (pbk)

To Helen, again
More cultural blah blah blah

Our lives shall not be sweated from birth until life closes
Hearts starve as well as bodies; give us bread, but give us roses.

James Oppenheim

The more the antagonisms of the present must be suffered, the more the future is drawn upon as a source of pseudo-unity and synthetic morale.

C. Wright Mills

Things are more like they are now than they've ever been before.

Attributed to Dwight D. Eisenhower

Contents

Boxes, tables and figures   xiv
Preface to the Third Edition (2012)   xvii
Preface to the Second Edition (2007)   xix

**Introduction: Change and Continuity, Power
    and Creativity**   1
An overview of some changes – and the importance
    of continuity   2
Why do the cultural industries matter?   4
    The cultural industries make and circulate texts   4
    The cultural industries manage creativity and
        knowledge   6
    The cultural industries are agents of economic,
        social and cultural change   8
Outline of the argument   10
Matters of definition   16
    Borderline and problem cases   18
    Some objections to the definitions and assumptions
        employed here   20
Alternative terms   22
From 'The Culture Industry' to the cultural industries   23
Industries that make texts: the distinctive features   26
    Risky business   27
    Creativity versus commerce   28
    High production costs and low reproduction costs   29
    Semi-public goods   29
    Misses are offset against hits by building a repertoire   30
    Concentration, integration and co-opting publicity   30
    Artificial scarcity   31
    Formatting: stars, genres, serials   31
    Loose control of symbol creators; tight control of
        distribution and marketing   32
Author to reader   33

PART ONE   ANALYTICAL FRAMEWORKS   35

1   Theories of Culture, Theories of Cultural Production   37
Media and cultural economics   38
Communication studies   40
Critical political economy approaches   42
Which political economy?   44
   Contradiction   45
   The specific conditions of cultural industries   45
   Tensions between production and consumption   46
   Symbol creators   46
   Information and entertainment   46
   Historical variations in the social relations of
     cultural production   47
Sociology of culture and organisational and
   management studies   47
Radical media sociology/media studies   48
The problem of texts   50
Some achievements and limitations of cultural studies   51
Cultural studies approaches to media industries and
   media production   54
   Industry produces culture, culture produces industry   55
   'Production studies': the cultural studies of media
     industries approach   55
   Digital optimism   56
   Creative industries analysis   57
   Cultural economy   58
The approach taken here   58

**2   Cultural Industries in the Twentieth Century:
   The Key Features**   64
The place of cultural production in economies
   and societies   66
A question of commodification   68
Business ownership and structure   71
Organisation, management and creative autonomy   77
   Creativity and commerce relations   81
The quality of cultural work   83
Internationalisation and domination by the USA   85
Dominant technologies   87
Textual change   88

Choice, diversity, multiplicity   88
Quality   89
Texts, social justice and the serving of interests   89

3   **Why the Cultural Industries Began to Change in
    the 1980s**   **93**
How not to explain change: three forms of reduction   93
Contexts for change and continuity in the cultural
    industries, 1945–1990   95
Political-economic change: the Long Downturn   97
Political and regulatory change: the rise of neo-liberalism   99
Changing business strategies   102
    Investment shifts towards service industries   102
    Internationalisation   105
    Organisational innovation and restructuring   107
Sociocultural and textual changes   109
Technological change: information technology
    and consumer electronics   112

PART TWO   POLICY CHANGE   **119**

4   **Marketisation in Telecommunications and Broadcasting**   **121**
Deregulation, re-regulation and cultural marketisation   126
Telecommunications and broadcasting – why was the
    state so involved?   128
    Telecommunications as a public utility   129
    Broadcasting as a national resource and a limited one   129
    The power of broadcasting   130
The 1980s: the rationales are dismantled and
    marketisation follows   131
    Challenge to the telecoms as utility rationale   131
    Challenge to the broadcasting as scarce, national
        resource rationale   131
    Challenge to the power of broadcasting rationale   132
Four waves of marketisation   132
The first wave: changes in communications policy in
    the USA, 1980–1990   134
The second wave: changes in broadcasting policy in
    other advanced industrial states, 1985–1995   137
    Defining characteristics of public service
        broadcasting systems   137

Variations in public service systems   138
The social and cultural role of PSB   140
PSB under attack: case studies of change   140
   The UK   142
   France   143
   Germany   144
   Australia   144
   Japan   145
   Summary of PSB under attack   146
The third wave: transitional and mixed societies,
   1989 onwards   146
   India   147
   Russia and Eastern Europe   149
   China   149
   Latin America   150
   Summary of marketisation in transitional societies   150
The fourth wave: towards convergence and
   internationalisation, 1992 onwards   151
   Convergence   151
   International policy bodies   153

5   Further Changes in Policy: Copyright and the Cult
    of Creativity   158
Copyright   159
   Longer, bigger, stronger copyrights   160
Cultural policy: the creative industries moment   165
   The Greater London Council and leftist cultural
      industries policy   166
   Local and urban cultural industries policy   167
   The creativity cult: cities, clusters and classes   170
   Contradictions of national creative industries policy   174
   Creative industries policy goes global   177

PART THREE   CHANGE AND CONTINUITY IN THE
              CULTURAL INDUSTRIES, 1980 TO 2012   183

6   Ownership, Structure and Size   185
1990s merger mania – and early twenty-first
   century reverses   187
A new generation of mega-corporations: the big get
   very big indeed   192
Conglomeration: from synergy to convergence   195
Vertical integration   200

Is ownership becoming more concentrated? And
   does it matter?   204
The continuing presence of small companies   209
Interdependence, inter-firm networks and alliances   212
Are the cultural industries getting bigger?   216
   Cultural industries in modern economies   216
   Cultural industries in global business   219
Continuing commodification   221

7   **Creativity and Commerce, Organisation and Labour**   **228**
Managing cultural production: loose control of
   creativity, tight control of circulation   229
The increasing importance of marketing and
   market research   233
   Audience research and autonomy in film,
      advertising and television   236
   A note on audience research in the digital age   242
Control of creativity: tighter or looser?   243
   Journalistic autonomy   243
   Creativity, commerce and control in popular
      music and theatre   248
Division of labour and working conditions   253
   Characteristics of cultural labour   253
Terms and conditions of cultural work in different roles 258
   'Unskilled' and semi-skilled workers   259
   Technical workers   260
   Creative managers   260
   Symbol creators   261

8   **Internationalisation: Neither Globalisation Nor**
   Cultural Imperialism   **269**
Factors behind cultural domination by the USA   270
   Size and nature of the domestic market for leisure
      in the USA   270
   Active role of the US state in promoting its
      industries abroad   271
Neither cultural imperialism nor globalisation   272
Television and geo-cultural markets   277
   Reversing cultural flows? The case of Latin
      American drama   280
   Transnational TV transmission and reception:
      post-national broadcasting?   284
   The rise of East Asian television   287

The international film industry: Hollywood power 293
Other film industries, other texts: India and Hong Kong 295
Cultural imperialism and popular music 301
  Authenticity versus hybridity 302
  Western cultural products can be interpreted
    in different ways 302
  Spread of ownership 304

9 Digitalisation and the Internet **310**
'New media' and digitalisation: beyond the hype 310
The digital optimists and their key claims 313
  A more sophisticated digital optimism? Benkler,
    Jenkins and Castells 317
Criticisms of digital optimism – and three dilemmas 321
  1. Digital divides: inequalities in access, skills and activity 323
  2. Control of circulation and concentrations of attention 327
  3. Commercialisation, surveillance and 'free labour' 330

10 The Impact of the Internet and Digitalisation on
**   Existing Cultural Industries** **341**
The music industry in crisis: distinguishing hype
  from reality 341
  File-sharing 343
  'Legitimate' digital distribution 343
Television: meaningful consumer control? 348
Newspapers, periodicals and books 356
The digital games industry 358

11 Texts: Diversity, Quality and Social Justice **364**
Choice, diversity and multiplicity 365
  How might we measure diversity? The case of
    popular music 367
  It's all the same: assertions of homogeneity 369
  Is television offering a greater diversity of experiences
    and perspectives in the 'post-network' era? 371
  Diversity or otherwise in the powerful UK press 373
Social justice and changes in texts 375
  Advertising, promotion, commercialism 375
  The politics of entertainment 381
  Has news journalism become less questioning
    of power? 385
  Social fragmentation and market segmentation 388

Has quality declined?   392
    Short attention spans, shock and cultural authority:
        reality televsion   392
    Comparing quality: book publishing   395
    Quality, independence and niche markets: indie cinema
        in the 1990s   398

Conclusions: A New Era in Cultural Production?   **402**
    The extent of change   402
    Evaluating change/continuity   407
    Explaining change/continuity   410
    Implications for future study   411

Glossary   414
References   421
Index   451

Boxes, Tables and Figures

Every effort has been made to trace the copyright holders but if any have been inadvertently overlooked the publisher will be pleased to make the necessary arrangement at the first opportunity.

BOXES

0.1	The core cultural industries	17
0.2	Summary of distinctive features of the cultural industries	26
2.1	Understanding transitions	67
2.2	The Hollywood oligopoly across the complex professional era	73
2.3	'Stages' of cultural production	80
3.1	The information society	100
4.1	Defining policy in communications, media and culture	122
4.2	How policy works	124
4.3	The peculiarities of broadcasting regulation in the USA	135
4.4	Main international policy agencies	154
5.1	The WTO enters the field	161
5.2	What is cultural policy?	166
5.3	Creativity: business with feeling	170
5.4	The role of creativity in the new economy	173
6.1	Vertical integration in US television	202
6.2	Depth versus breadth in defining cultural industries	218
7.1	Effects of marketing on creativity: the high concept movie	235
7.2	Media moguls and control of news	245
7.3	Contracts, copyright and cultural work	257
7.4	The post-punk intervention	263
8.1	Herman and McChesney: globalisation as cultural imperialism	273
8.2	Arabic television and Al-Jazeera: the export of journalistic professionalism?	292

8.3   Opening up world cinema?   299
8.4   K-pop and the Korean Wave: a counter to
      cultural imperialism?   303
9.1   Early forms of digitalisation in cultural production   311
9.2   Web 2.0   317
9.3   The internet: different uses, varied elements   322
9.4   Do (digital) audiences work for the cultural industries? 336
10.1 YouTube: a new hybrid cultural form   351
10.2 The rise of digital television   353
11.1 Cross-media promotion and dubious secondary texts   378
11.2 The HBO model: high-quality television in the USA,
      but not for everyone   391

TABLES

2.1   Aspects of cultural production
      and questions about change and continuity   65
3.1   Comparing the post-war boom and the Long Downturn   98
3.2   The shift to services   103
3.3   Increases in advertising expenditure, 1980–1990   106
4.1   Changes in television funding systems in the 1980s
      and 1990s   139
4.2   Marketisation interest groups in Europe   141
6.1   Some major cultural industry mergers and acquisitions   190
6.2   The 'Magnificent Seven' cultural industry corporations 195
6.3   Conglomeration in the Magnificent Seven, c 2003   196
6.4   Media concentration in Western Europe in the 1990s   208
6.5   The largest corporations with cultural industry interests 222
8.1   Change in worldwide TV revenue, 2006 onwards   288
8.2   Domestic films' share of box office receipts, 2004   295
8.3   Most prolific feature film-producing nations in the 1990s 296
8.4   The world's best-selling albums, 2009   305
9.1   Internet use in developed and developing countries,
      2000–2010   326
9.2   Proportion of households with internet access,
      by region, 2010   326
9.3   Market share of the 4 main search engine companies   329
10.1 Average hours of television viewing per day in the
      UK, 2001–2010   349
10.2 Audience share by terrestrial channel, 2001–2010   350
10.3 Hours per week spent watching television by 'platform',
      USA 2010   351

FIGURES

4.1	Four waves of marketisation	133
6.1	Worldwide mergers and acquisitions in the media and telecoms industries, 1984–2008	187
6.2	A web of collaboration between corporations	214
6.3	Key interlockings between media and internet corporations	215
6.4	Sectors of US communications	220
7.1	A typology of creative organisations	230

published since the last edition, and to work I hadn't discovered at the time I was writing it. Nevertheless, I'm still conscious of the many valuable contributions I've had to leave out, or didn't get round to reading.

Thank you to Mila Steele at Sage, and to Ralitsa (Ali) Padelska and Christiaan De Beukalaer for research assistance. I have so many great colleagues at the Institute of Communications Studies at the University of Leeds that I can't possibly name them all here. I'm grateful to Judith Stamper, for taking on the role of Acting Head of Institute while I took some research leave to prepare this edition.

I hope the people thanked in the two earlier editions of this book will forgive me if I don't repeat their names here, but I must mention Jason Toynbee again because he was so (typically) generous with help and advice on both of them.

Helen Steward, Rosa Hesmondhalgh and Joe Hesmondhalgh are delightful people to live with. I suspect I'm not. They influence what I write more than they know.

The Accrington diaspora and its honorary members, in Beeston, St Albans, Brighton, Bulgaria, and elsewhere, continue to make me laugh and think. And so too do the conference party posse known collectively as the Northerners, even though none of them actually is from the North of England apart from me. I miss my and Helen's Oxford friends, and I still mourn the late Gary Conway. I'm proud of my sister Julie and her lovely husband Ian Kershaw. Twenty editions of this book wouldn't be enough to thank my Mum and Dad, or to express my appreciation of their love and resilience.

Preface to the
Third Edition (2012)

In the second half of the first decade of the twenty first century, claims about the transformation of cultural production were heard as never before. We were in the era of 'web 2.0'. Academics wrote of the urgent need to develop 'Media Studies 2.0' or even '3.0' because the old versions were now hopelessly outdated. (Versions 1.1, 1.2 and so on were never mentioned for some reason). History was bunk. Digital networks had democratised cultural production, and had made the world a better place, or were just about to do so: it wasn't always clear whether the digital optimists were making predictions or describing what they thought was current reality. Such claims appeared to be based on a democratically-motivated critique of concentrations of power in the 'old media'. Their proponents were rightly interested in the democratising and emancipatory potential of YouTube, blogging and Wikipedia. But they were curiously uncritical of what cultural production as a whole was going to look like in the supposed utopia that had either just arrived, or was just over the horizon. There was little sense even in the more sophisticated versions of digital optimism of the profound economic and social contradictions that triggered the global recession that began in 2008, and a global tide of protest in 2010–11.

I'm not a pessimist, and this book does not aim to show that everything you thought was good is in fact bad. It simply aims to provide a balanced historical account of how cultural production has changed, and why. It points to the continuing existence of cultural artefacts that are challenging, enlightening, enthralling and so on, and ways in which the internet may have made our cultural lives richer. But it also makes clear that concentrations of power in cultural production have not gone away. They may just be appearing in new guises. What looks like a challenge to the established order might be based on new orthodoxies.

As with the second edition, I've significantly revised, expanded and updated the book for this third edition, especially Chapters 6 to 11 (Part Three). Among many other changes, two chapters are now devoted to the onset of digital networks, one of them on the impact of these networks on existing cultural industries. There are hundreds of references to works

Preface to the
Second Edition (2007)

This book gives an account of how and why cultural production has changed since the early 1980s. The first edition was written in 2000–2001 and appeared in 2002. Since then, there have of course been numerous further changes in the cultural industries. New phrases representing new phenomena have appeared, including blogging, i-Pods, podcasting, the HBO model, social networking sites and digital rights management. Other processes, already under way when I was writing at the turn of the century, have intensified, with significant implications for our cultural lives, whether we are conscious of them or not. Television and radio channels continue to multiply. Many of us gain more and more of our information from the web. The dot.com bubble had already burst in 2000 and fewer commentators now speak of 'a new economy', but more and more policymakers and academics claim that culture, information, creativity and intellectual property are going to be, and/or should be, an increasingly important part of future economies and societies. Since I finished writing the first edition, China – already a growing market for the products of cultural industries – has joined the World Trade Organisation, signalling that its integration with global capitalism is beginning in earnest.

I deal with these various terms, concepts and processes in what follows, but, as with the first edition of *The Cultural Industries*, my aim has been to think about these and other developments in the context of long-term historical currents – in economics, in politics and culture. My argument is that cultural production and consumption haven't changed quite as much as some commentators would have us believe. Why write an academic book about this? Because only through a careful consideration of the long term can we understand change and continuity in culture and such consideration takes some time and effort. The media themselves produce a constant babble and chatter about transformations in the way that cultural products are made and experienced. There is little time in the frenetic rush of everyday journalism to consider the long-term historical context. This is one of the reasons academic study of the cultural industries can be valuable.

As well as updating the book, I've dealt with some issues that were neglected or underemphasised in the first edition. A new chapter addresses two vital aspects of policy: changes in copyright and in the relationship between cultural and urban policy on the one hand, and the cultural industries on the other. That chapter includes an assessment of the increasing use of the terms 'creativity' and 'creative industries' in policy and business. Not only in that chapter but also throughout the book, there is more material on intellectual property and the crucial but dubious concept of the 'information society'. Linked to this, the concept of commodification of culture is given the greater billing it deserves. There is much more explicit treatment of the question of the extent to which the cultural industries are an increasingly important component of modern economic life (see Chapters 2 and 6). Throughout, I've tried to learn more and think more about non-Anglophone cultural industry systems.

I've made hundreds of other smaller changes – adding references to old and new sources that I've encountered since the first edition, cutting out unnecessary detail and the odd sloppy phrase that made me wince, and making arguments more concise where possible. In spite of all these many changes, my main goal has remained the same: to provide a research-driven overview of this fascinating area based on my own particular view of things, but one that students and teachers might also use if they wish.

Introduction: Change and Continuity, Power and Creativity

An overview of some changes – and the importance
of continuity 2
Why do the cultural industries matter? 4
The cultural industries make and circulate texts 4
The cultural industries manage creativity and
knowledge 6
The cultural industries are agents of economic,
social and cultural change 8
Outline of the argument 10
Matters of definition 16
Borderline and problem cases 18
Some objections to the definitions and assumptions
employed here 20
Alternative terms 22
From 'The Culture Industry' to the cultural industries 23
Industries that make texts: the distinctive features 26
Risky business 27
Creativity versus commerce 28
High production costs and low reproduction costs 29
Semi-public goods 29
Misses are offset against hits by building a repertoire 30
Concentration, integration and co-opting publicity 30
Artificial scarcity 31
Formatting: stars, genres, serials 31
Loose control of symbol creators; tight control of
distribution and marketing 32
Author to reader 33

AN OVERVIEW OF SOME CHANGES – AND THE IMPORTANCE OF CONTINUITY

Nearly all commentators accept that the cultural industries have undergone remarkable transformation since the early 1980s. Here are some of the major changes I intend to deal with in what follows.

- The cultural industries have moved closer to the centre of the economic action in many countries and across much of the world. Cultural industry companies can no longer be seen as secondary to the 'real' economy where durable, 'useful' goods are manufactured. Some of these companies are now vast global businesses and are among the most discussed and debated corporations on the planet.
- The ownership and organisation of the cultural industries have changed radically. The largest companies no longer specialise in a particular cultural industry, such as film, publishing, television or recording; they now operate across a number of different cultural industries. These conglomerates compete with each other, but, more than ever before, they are connected – with each other and with other companies – in complex webs of alliance, partnership and joint venture.
- Despite this, there are also more and more small- and medium-sized companies in the business of culture and there are increasingly complex relationships between large, medium and small cultural companies.
- Digitalisation, the internet and mobile telephony have multiplied the ways in which audiences can gain access to content, and have made small-scale production easier for millions of people. They have also enabled powerful corporations from the information technology sector to compete with more established cultural-industry and consumer electronics businesses. Microsoft, Google, Apple and Amazon are now as significant as News Corporation, Time Warner and Sony for understanding cultural production and consumption.
- Cultural products increasingly circulate across national borders. Images, sounds and narratives are borrowed and adapted from other places on an unprecedented scale, producing new hybrids but also, for some, reaffirming the value of cultural authenticity. The long-standing domination of cultural trade by the USA may be diminishing.
- The way that the cultural industries conceive of their audiences is changing. There is greater emphasis on audience research, marketing and addressing 'niche' audiences.
- Government policy and regulation have altered drastically. Longstanding traditions of public ownership and regulation have been dismantled. Key policy decisions are increasingly carried out at an international level. At the same time, the cultural industries have become more and more significant in local urban and social policy, as a means of regenerating economies and providing a competitive advantage over other cities and regions.

- There has been a huge boom in the amount of money that businesses spend on advertising, only partially interrupted by the economic crash of 2008–2009. This boom helped to fuel the spectacular growth of the cultural industries.
- *Texts*[1] (in my view, the best collective name for content and for cultural 'works' of all kinds: the programmes, films, records, books, comics, images, magazines, newspapers and so on produced by the cultural industries) have undergone a radical transformation. There is an increasing penetration of promotional and advertising material into previously protected realms. There is more and more product of all kinds, across a wider range of genres, across a wider range of forms of cultural activity than before. Various forms of cultural authority are increasingly questioned and satirised.

To what extent, though, do such changes really represent major, epochal shifts in the way that culture is produced and consumed? After all, alongside these changes, there are many continuities that might be obscured by an overemphasis on change. For example, television continues to play a huge role, as a source of information and entertainment, in people's lives; stars continue to be the main mechanism via which cultural industry companies promote their products; the USA is still thought of, across the globe, as the world centre for popular culture; and copyright remains fundamental to how companies and successful producers make money. Because continuities such as these are entangled with the above changes, I refer throughout this book to **patterns of change and continuity in the cultural industries**. The interweaving of change and continuity is its central theme.

Many commentators go much further than I have above in pointing to change. Some claim, for example, that digitalisation has transformed cultural production beyond recognition. The internet and the mobile phone have triumphed. The music industry is dying or already dead, they say. Television is over. Book publishing as we knew it is finished. Yet these industries continue to pour out huge amounts of product, employ tens of thousands of people, produce considerable amounts of revenue, and occupy vast amounts of our time. Some optimistically see a new age where distinctions between producers and audiences disappear, and 'users' become the new creators. Commentary of this kind often implies, and sometimes explicitly states, that all the old notions and models need to be thrown out, and the history of cultural production is irrelevant because we are now living in an 'information age' rather than an 'industrial age' (or some other term that serves to simplify the past). Others see transformation just over the horizon. In many cases, it is unclear whether we are reading analysis of what is happening now, or a prediction of the future.

---

1 Throughout this book, I use **bold italics** to denote key concepts on their first major occurrence, **bold** to highlight key phrases, and *italics* for titles and ordinary emphasis. The key concepts are defined in the Glossary at the end of the book and usually on their first appearance, too.

A more balanced assessment is required, and one that is grounded in a longer-term historical perspective than many of the celebrations of a new digital age. We need, for example, to understand that the cultural industries have always been in competition with (and yet often also in collaboration with) other neighbouring sets of industries. The most notable historically have been the telecommunications and consumer electronics industries. The information technology industries have now joined this group of interlinked industries. The development of the internet and the web, and the entry of IT firms into cultural markets, has certainly brought about considerable change in the everyday cultural experiences of billions of people. But has it altered the fundamental underlying dynamics of cultural production and consumption? To address such issues of change and continuity, we need to understand what these fundamental dynamics are. Starting with this chapter, this book provides such an understanding. As a basis for this, we must first think about the distinctive role of the cultural industries in modern societies, and the best way to do this is to ask the question, why do the cultural industries matter? The answers all involve their actual or potential **power**.

WHY DO THE CULTURAL INDUSTRIES MATTER?

The importance of the cultural industries in modern societies rests on three related elements: their ability to make and circulate products that influence our knowledge, understanding and experience (texts); their role as systems for the management of creativity and knowledge; and their effects as agents of economic, social and cultural change. I shall deal with each of them in turn now.

The cultural industries make and circulate texts

The cultural industries are involved in the making and circulating of products that, more than the products of any other kind of industry, have **an influence on our understanding and knowledge of the world**. Debates about the nature and extent of this influence comprise, in the words of a valuable survey of the concept, 'the contested core of media research' (Corner, 2000: 376). The best contributions to such debates suggest the complex, negotiated, and often indirect, nature of media influence, but of one thing there can be no doubt: the media do have an influence. We are influenced not only by informational texts, such as newspapers, broadcast news programmes, documentaries and analytical books, but also by entertainment. Films, TV series, comics, music, video games and so on provide us with recurring representations of the world and so act as a kind of reporting. Just as crucially, they draw on and help to constitute our inner, private lives and our public selves: our fantasies, emotions and identities.

Collectively, informational and entertainment texts contribute strongly to our sense of who we are, of what it means to be a woman or a man, an

African or an Arab, a Canadian or a New Yorker, straight or gay. They shape our sense of how we might live together in modern societies, of how democracy, justice and rights might operate.[2] They are the way in which we come to form our opinions about the rights and wrongs of consumerism, and the prospects for the future of the planet. For these reasons, the products of the cultural industries are more than just a way of passing time – a mere diversion from other, more worthwhile things. All the same, the sheer amount of time that we spend experiencing texts, however distractedly we might do so, in itself makes the cultural industries a powerful factor in our lives.

So, studying the cultural industries might help us to understand how texts take the form they do and how these texts have come to play such a central role in contemporary societies. Importantly, most texts that we consume are circulated by powerful corporations. As we shall see, this is just as true in the age of the internet as it was in the decades before its emergence. These corporations, like all businesses, have an interest in making profits. They want to support conditions in which businesses in general – especially their own – can make profits. This raises a crucial issue: do the cultural industries ultimately serve the interests of their owners and their executives and those of their political and business allies?

We must avoid simplistic answers to this vital question. Throughout this book, I argue for a view of the cultural industries and the texts they produce as **complex, ambivalent and contested**. (Some influential analyses of the cultural industries have downplayed these aspects – see Chapter 1.) In societies where the cultural industries are big business, cultural industry companies tend to support conditions in which large companies and their political allies can make money: conditions where there is constant demand for new products, minimal regulation by the state outside of general competition law, relative political and economic stability, workforces that are willing to work hard and so on. Yet, in contemporary societies, many of the texts produced and disseminated by the cultural industries do not simply support such conditions. Very often (not just occasionally) they tend to orientate their audiences towards ways of thinking that do not coincide with the interests of capitalism or of structured domination by men over women or institutional racism. (I address this issue further in Chapters 2 and 11.)

If this is true, why does it happen? Partly, it is for the simple economic reason that cultural companies have to compete with each other, as well as maintain the general conditions in which to do business, and so they attempt to outstrip each other to satisfy audience desires for the shocking, the profane and the rebellious. It is also because of social and cultural factors deeply embedded in many societies regarding what we expect of art and entertainment. This takes us to a second argument for the importance

---

2 See the interesting and valuable theorisations of 'mediatisation' collected in Lundby (2009). Mediatisation is the process by which the media become more and more involved in other institutions, such as politics, sport, family, religion, and so on, but also become institutions in their own right (see Hjarvard, 2008).

of the subject of this book and into a domain that has been neglected in academic and public debate in recent years.

The cultural industries manage creativity and knowledge

The cultural industries are concerned, fundamentally, with the management and selling of a particular kind of work. Since the Renaissance – and especially since the Romantic movement of the nineteenth century – there has been a widespread tendency to think of 'art' as one of the highest forms of human creativity. Sociologists and Marxists have argued in response that artistic work is not so different from other kinds of labour, in that both are orientated towards the production of objects or experiences (Wolff, 1993, Chapter 1, provides an excellent summary of these debates). This view helps to counter the idea that 'artists' are different from the rest of us, that they are involved in some mystically special form of creativity. Nevertheless, there is something distinctive about that area of human creativity often called 'art'. The invention and/or performance of stories, songs, images, poems, jokes and so on, in no matter what technological form, involves a particular type of creativity – the manipulation of symbols for the purposes of entertainment, information and perhaps even enlightenment. Instead of the term 'art', with all its connotations of individual genius and a higher calling, I want to use the more cumbersome term *symbolic creativity*[3] and, instead of the term 'artists', I prefer the phrase *symbol creators* or symbol makers for those who make up, interpret or rework stories, songs, images and so on. This is a more inclusive term, and that means it also incorporates the work of those involved in the production and sharing of knowledge as well as of art and entertainment.

So the terms 'symbol creators' and 'symbolic creativity' are intended to cover the work of actors, writers (journalists, book authors, screenwriters, poets, bloggers, advertising copywriters), comedians, musicians, painters, photographers, cinematographers, camera operators, sculptors, dancers – and a whole set of terms that mean different things in different industries such as television, film, theatre and music: directors, producers, and designers.[4]

Symbol creators were for many years ignored or at best marginalised in academic research on the cultural industries. This was perhaps because of an understandable, but excessive, reaction against the fetishisation of their work as extraordinary. Sociologists emphasised systems or rituals of production,

---

3 My use of this term is borrowed from Willis (1990), but I differ from him in focusing on industrialised symbolic creativity, whereas he is concerned with the creativity of young people as consumers.

4 Cultural production is centred on symbol making, but involves a complex division of labour encompassing many other kinds of workers besides symbol creators. See Chapters 2 and 7.

rather than genius. In the academic fields of media studies and cultural studies in the 1980s, many researchers began, quite rightly, to examine the pleasures and interpretative activities of audiences much more assiduously than
in previous analysis. But this led to a shift in fashion, away not only from
analysis of symbol creators, but also from cultural production in general.
Some strongly implied that audiences trumped producers, because they had
the freedom to make of texts pretty much whatever they wanted, and therefore the study of cultural production and cultural industries was irrelevant,
or at least far less pressing than some had argued it to be (Fiske, 1987).

The study of cultural and media industries never went away entirely (see
Chapter 1) but much of it paid little attention to the question of how symbol making was organised and circulated. In the 1990s, a new generation of writers began
to put symbol creators back in the picture (Born, 1993; Toynbee, 2000). This was
a good thing. After all, symbol creators are the primary workers in the making of
texts. Texts, by definition, would not exist without them, however much they rely
on industrial systems and a complex division of labour for the dissemination of
their work. This does not mean that we should romantically celebrate the work
of musicians, authors, film-makers and so on. Symbolic creativity *can* enrich people's lives, but often it is banal or mediocre. Sometimes it meekly serves power,
or it promotes commercialism over creativity and knowledge.

Other traditions of study, for example of literature or fine art, have focused
on especially talented or fêted symbol creators, at times hardly referring to
the means by which authors, musicians and so on have reached their audiences, how their work was funded, supported or suppressed. Some widely
disseminated versions of such thinking offer a pious and complacent celebration of the achievements of Western civilisation (Clark, 1969). Instead,
we need better ways of historicising symbolic creativity, and understanding
the relationships between culture, society and commerce. Writers such as the
Welsh cultural studies analyst Raymond Williams and the French sociologist Pierre Bourdieu offer better models (see Bourdieu, 1996; Williams, 1981).
They and others show how such creativity has been a more or less permanent
presence in human history, but how its management and circulation have
taken radically different forms in different societies. In Europe, for example,
systems of patronage gave way in the nineteenth century to the organisation
of symbolic creativity around the market. It was at this point that the cultural
industries began to emerge. From the early twentieth century, this market
organisation began to take a new, complex form (see Chapter 2). Examining
changes in the cultural industries allows us to think about how symbolic
creativity has been organised and circulated in our own lifetimes and – the
key theme of this book – how this might be changing.

Again, we need to understand the cultural industries as fundamentally
ambivalent. The way the cultural industries organise and circulate symbolic
creativity reflects the extreme inequalities and injustices (along class, gender,
ethnic and other lines) apparent in contemporary capitalist societies. There
are vast inequalities in access to the cultural industries – and these persist in
the era of digitalisation. Those who succeed in having their work circulated

widely are often treated shabbily and many people who want to create texts struggle to earn a living. Failure is far more common than success. There are great pressures to produce certain kinds of texts rather than others and it is hard to come across information about the existence of organisations and texts that attempt to do things differently. Some types of text are made much more available than others. These are bleak features of the cultural industry landscape, yet, because original and distinctive symbolic creativity is at a premium, the cultural industries can never quite control it. Owners and executives make concessions to symbol creators by granting them far more *autonomy* (self-determination) than they would to workers of equivalent status in other industries and to most workers historically. Paradoxically, this freedom – which is, in the end, a limited and provisional one – can then act as a form of control because it makes the scarce and poorly-paid jobs offered by the cultural industries highly desirable; as we shall see, especially in Chapter 7, there is a massive oversupply of potential workers to the cultural industries, and this helps to keep wages low. However, the relative autonomy of symbol makers may also help to explain the ambivalence in texts referred to above, because it provides a certain amount of freedom for at least some symbol creators to make strange, funny, pleasing work.

Cultural industry companies face another difficulty, too. They have to find audiences for the texts that symbol creators produce. Usually, this is not a matter of finding the greatest possible mass audience for a product. Different groups of people tend to have different tastes, so much of the work of cultural industry companies attempts to match texts to audiences, to find appropriate ways of circulating texts to those audiences and to make audiences aware of the existence of texts. This is a risky business. Many texts fail, even those that companies expect to succeed. The upshot of these processes is that cultural industry companies keep a much tighter grip on the *circulation* of texts than they do on their production.

The importance of symbolic creativity helps to explain the fact that the main focus of this book is on patterns of change/continuity in the cultural industries, as opposed to, say, change/continuity in the texts produced by those industries or in how audiences understand texts. As I should have made clear by now, however, this does not mean that I am interested only in the cultural industries as systems of production. In fact, my primary interest is **how production relates to human experience of culture and knowledge**. But all writers, given their limited time and energy, must make decisions about where to concentrate their attention and, rather than focusing on the texts themselves and then working backwards from there to the industries, my primary topic is production.

The cultural industries are agents of economic, social and cultural change

A third and final reason for the importance of examining change and continuity in the cultural industries is that they are increasingly significant sources of wealth and employment in many economies. Measuring the relative size of these industries is difficult and there are controversies, occasionally useful but sometimes tedious, about how best to do so (see Chapter 6). Much depends on how we define the cultural industries, an issue discussed in the next section of this Introduction. It seems fair to say, though, that the economic role of cultural production is growing, but not nearly as much or as quickly as some commentators and policymakers claim.

That the cultural industries might be providing more wealth and employment is, of course, significant in itself, but it also has implications for how we understand **the relationships between culture, society and economy**. Many of the most important debates about these relationships over the last few decades have concerned what we might call theories of transition. Have we moved from industrial societies to post-industrial or information societies, based on a much greater emphasis than before on knowledge? This was a line of thought initiated in the 1960s and 1970s by the work of, among others, Daniel Bell (for example, 1974) and maintained by writers such as Manuel Castells (such as, 1989, 1996) in the 1980s and 1990s. Have we moved from societies best characterised as 'modern', because of their increasing ephemerality, fragmentedness and flux, to a situation better characterised as 'postmodern', where these features become so accentuated that rationality and meaning seem to break down (Harvey, 1989; Lyotard, 1984)? In one version of such debates, some analysts (notably Castells, 1996; and Lash and Urry, 1994) suggested that symbolic creativity and/or information were becoming increasingly central in social and economic life. An implication of this, drawn out more fully by Lash and Urry than by Castells, was that the cultural industries therefore increasingly provided a model for understanding transformations in other industries. Others claimed that the cultural industries themselves were becoming more like other industries and losing their distinctiveness as an economic sector (Padioleau, 1987).

Academic study was echoed by business and management analysts, who placed increasing emphasis on firms' non-tangible assets, especially the value of these businesses' brand names (see Wolf, 1999, for a popularising version). Brands can only be made valuable as a result of massive amounts of work being put into product names and logos and how they are represented and circulated. Cultural industry companies such as Disney, because they were considered so experienced in developing brands (in a sense, every film, every star, every book is something like a brand), were often named alongside companies such as Nike and more traditional firms such as Coca-Cola as leaders in this field.

Brands, however, were only one part of the hype about the increasing role of information, culture and knowledge in modern economies. In the late 1990s and early 2000s, the rise of the internet and the world wide web fuelled these debates and sent them off in new directions. There was a seemingly unstoppable flow of books about 'the weightless world' (Coyle, 1999), about how, in the future knowledge economy, we would be 'living on thin air' (Leadbeater, 2000) rather than on material goods. There was much talk of 'the new economy' (see Henwood, 2003, for a critique of this idea) in which the traditional business cycles of boom and slump would be replaced by continuous growth; communication technologies, branding, information and culture were all seen as central to this new configuration. For a number of writers, the concept of creativity was particularly significant. In the 'creative economy' (Howkins, 2001), economic life would be based on a new centrality for creativity and innovation, of many different kinds.

The bursting of the so-called dot.com bubble in 2000–2001 provided only a temporary respite. The hype took off with unprecedented power in the mid-2000s, propelled by a potent mixture of credit-based economic growth and digital optimism. Some claimed that creativity would 'be the driver of social and economic change during the next century' (Hartley, 2005: 1). Leading US news magazine *Newsweek* devoted the 2006 version of its annual special issue preview of the forthcoming year to 'The Knowledge Revolution', including much discussion of the magical new buzzword 'creativity' (see also Florida, 2002, 2005). In one of the most over-quoted journalistic events of the twenty first century, carried away by celebrations of 'user-generated content', *Time* magazine made 'you' its annual 'person of the year' for 2006. The digitalising cultural industries were supposedly leading the way into an economy based on the provision of goods and services to niche markets, rather than mass markets; this would enable small companies to challenge big business (Anderson, 2006). More serious analysts wrote of a 'networked information economy' (Benkler, 2006) and of a culture now based on a democratisation of participation enabled by 'convergence culture' (Jenkins, 2006).

If the cultural industries are playing a central part in these supposed transitions – to the information or knowledge society, to economies based on brands, on signs and meanings, on creativity and culture – it is surprising how rarely systematic, historically informed analysis of changes in these industries has been carried out by those involved in such debates. This book seeks to offer such analysis. A key aim is to cast light on these various notions and on whether they exaggerate change at the expense of continuity.

OUTLINE OF THE ARGUMENT

Two questions seem to me to be of particular importance in relation to patterns of change/continuity in the cultural industries, both involving a set of subsidiary questions. First, **how might we *explain* them**? What were the forces driving change and ensuring continuity? Which groups of people made the key decisions in bringing about new patterns of change and continuity? What interests did they represent?

Second, **how might we *assess* change and continuity**? This involves two further moves: considering the *extent* of change and *evaluating* it. Which phenomena represent fundamental transformations in cultural production and consumption and which are merely superficial changes? What political and ethical principles can we draw on to think about what is right and wrong in the way that the cultural industries are structured, governed and organised in the late twentieth century and at the beginning of the twenty first?

The rest of this introductory chapter lays out the working definition of the cultural industries I am using in this book. It explains the etymology of the term and my reasons for preferring it over other alternatives. It outlines the distinctive features of the cultural industries. These features are important for the argument in the rest of the book because they help to explain changes and continuities in the way that the cultural industries are structured, organised and regulated.

Following the Introduction, Part One consists of three chapters that establish the analytical frameworks for the rest of the book and begin the story of change and continuity in the cultural industries since, roughly, 1980. Chapter 1 prepares the ground for assessment and explanation by considering **the main approaches that serious analysts have taken to understanding the cultural industries and the concept of culture more generally**. It argues for an approach based on a fusion of various approaches, involving

- an understanding of the complex intermeshing of economic, political and cultural power, which I mainly draw from a particular version of the critical political economy of culture, but also from the sociology of culture and communication studies;
- a sociological analysis of the relations between cultural production and texts, of what actually happens 'inside' culture-producing organisations, and how this might help shape the different kinds of cultural experience that different groups might have;
- the understanding that social theory and some versions of cultural studies can provide of the complexity and importance of culture itself, including its relationship to power, inequality and social justice.

The main purpose of the chapter is to explain a number of assumptions that underlie the analysis and argument in the rest of the book, and to lay out how my approach differs from, but also draws upon, other people's research.

Chapter 2 deals with how we might **assess** patterns of change/continuity in the cultural industries. In order to do so, it provides an outline of the key aspects of what, adapting Raymond Williams, I call **the complex professional era of cultural production**. The complex professional form of production took shape in advanced industrial societies in the early twentieth century and, by the middle of the twentieth century, had become the dominant form. The key aspects are discussed in terms of the following categories:

- What is the place of cultural production in modern economies and societies?
- Who owns cultural industry businesses and how they are structured?

- How is production organised? (This includes questions concerning the autonomy or independence of creative workers from commercial and state control, and the relationships between creativity and knowledge, on the one hand, and commerce on the other).
- What is the nature of cultural work and what are the rewards for it?
- Which countries and regions dominate global and international cultural production?
- Which communication technologies have been used, and with what effects?
- How might we characterise the texts produced by the cultural industries?

This is not just a set of abstract arguments. The aim is actually to provide a historical outline of what industrialised cultural production looked like up to the 1970s, *before* the changes discussed in this book began to take place. This historical outline allows us to ask two types of questions about change and continuity, and these are then laid out in the rest of the chapter.

First, there are questions about the **extent** of changes since 1980, about how much things have changed. A key objective of the book is to assess whether changes since 1980 have seen the emergence of a completely new era of cultural production or whether these changes represent shifts *within* the complex professional era and therefore a relatively limited (though still potentially significant) set of transformations. But they crucially raise further questions about the **evaluation** of changes and continuities. Which changes are good for people, for culture, society and democracy, and which are not? A set of principles for how we might evaluate cultural production is laid out, building on the approach advocated in Chapter 1 and on my summary, earlier in this Introduction, of why I think the cultural industries matter.

Chapter 3 discusses how we might **explain** change, assessing the rival claims of approaches that emphasise economic, political, technological and sociocultural factors. Again, although there is some necessary abstraction here, as I discuss how we should understand these factors, the chapter also has a strongly concrete dimension: it begins the story of recent change/continuity in the cultural industries. It does so, first of all, by examining how various economic, political, technological and sociocultural factors interacted to produce a set of intertwined crises in Western societies in the late 1960s and 1970s. These crises initiated many of the key changes discussed in the book. What some writers have called The Long Downturn in advanced industrial economies from the late 1960s onwards is a vital context for understanding the four decades that followed. For the crises helped bring about a huge change in how governments across the world thought about how to govern many aspects of societies. From the 1970s onwards, governments increasingly adopted public policies based on a set of ideas that can usefully be grouped together under the name *neoliberalism*.

Linked to this, this period also saw the rise of a particular way of thinking about the future of knowledge, culture and economy, which had a considerable influence on public policy on business, communication and culture. I call this way of thinking *information society* **discourse**. However, neoliberalism and information society discourse do not explain everything that happened in the cultural industries. The chapter also discusses three other forms of change that drove changes in cultural production and consumption: changes in business strategy; sociocultural and textual changes; and technological change. By stressing these multiple factors, I avoid a problem that haunts some accounts of change in the cultural industries: reductionism.

Chapters 4 and 5 constitute Part Two of the book. The various factors discussed in Chapter 3 provide a basis for understanding a number of policy changes in relation to telecommunications, broadcasting and computing that were fundamental in bringing about many of the changes examined later. I show how governments altered their telecommunications and broadcasting policies in the 1980s and 1990s to encourage the development of the commercial cultural industries by privatising public corporations and 'loosening' the regulation of media and culture. Governments also encouraged the growth of IT and telecommunications sectors in such a way that would eventually exacerbate tensions and contradictions between these different sectors. The story of this privatisation and 'deregulation' may seem familiar to some readers in media and communication studies. My account is different from existing ones, though, because of its international emphasis and its periodisation of change. I outline four overlapping waves of change in the communications policies of national governments:

- The first in the USA in the 1980s.
- The second in other advanced industrial countries from the mid-1980s to the mid-1990s.
- The third in transitional and mixed societies after 1989.
- The fourth, which continues today, across all these regions/polities, involving the increasing convergence of the cultural industries with telecommunications and computers sectors.

Chapter 5 then examines changes in two other key domains of policy, cultural policy and copyright law, that were also crucially affected by neoliberalism, information society discourse, and the other factors discussed in Chapter 3. Again, these policy changes have been a very important basis for other changes. They represent shifts in how creativity and cultural production are conceived in relation to commerce and capital.

Part Three then builds on the foundations established in Parts One and Two to examine changes and continuities in the various aspects of cultural production outlined. To reiterate, a key underpinning idea is whether the features of the complex professional era of cultural production outlined in Chapter 2 still hold. In line with the framework established in Part One, each chapter not only examines the extent of change but also addresses how we might evaluate events.

In Chapter 6, I examine changes and continuities in business ownership and structure, and in the place of the cultural industries in modern economies. I trace the massive wave of mergers and conglomeration that occurred in the 1990s and 2000s. These produced a new generation of vertically-integrated, conglomerated titans, sitting above two lesser tiers of big and smaller companies. I also note a counter-tendency, from the mid-2000s, towards de-conglomeration as over-extended corporations partially withdrew from some areas of the sector. I examine whether cultural production really has become more concentrated in terms of ownership, and the degree to which this matters. A major development has been the entry of IT giants such as Microsoft and Google into cultural-industry terrain. This requires an understanding of dynamics of competition and collaboration between cultural-industry companies, on the one hand, and those in neighbouring sectors, such as consumer electronics, telecommunications and information technology, on the other. Finally, I address the question of the extent to which the cultural industries are a key part of national economies and global business. I argue that the steadily growing significance of these industries needs to be understood as a phase in the long-term commodification of culture and I outline the ambivalent consequences of this.

Chapter 7 deals with changes and continuities in **the organisation of cultural production** and in **cultural work**.[5] Perennial questions about how to control risk and manage creativity were being answered in new ways from the 1980s onwards. Notably, there was an increasing focus on marketing and market research. I then analyse some evidence about the degree to which control of creative outputs on the part of cultural-industry businesses in pursuit of profit might be becoming tighter and more restrictive, in journalism, theatre and advertising, and whether commercialisation might be affecting creative autonomy. The final section discusses changes in the terms and conditions of cultural work. Did such changes represent a fundamental shift in the social relations of cultural production? Did the conditions of cultural workers improve as the cultural industries expanded?

One of the main ways in which firms tried to compete in the new business environment created by governmental and business response to The Long Downturn and by various sociocultural changes of the period was by internationalising their operations. The consequences of this for the cultural industries are assessed in Chapter 8. *Internationalisation* in the cultural industries has helped lead to a much greater complexity of international flows of culture than before, but it has also meant the increasing global presence of vast corporations. So, the chapter considers whether

---

5   These and other dimensions of the cultural industries are sometimes labelled 'micro' factors as opposed to 'macro' ones such as ownership, conglomeration and so on. The macro/micro dualism can be used poorly, but I think it is valuable. I use it as shorthand from time to time in this book.

or not we should think of the new state of play in the cultural industries internationally as a new stage of cultural imperialism or as a sign of a new global interconnectedness with democratising possibilities. The chapter also asks if this duality between imperialism and interconnectedness is an adequate conceptual basis for addressing the key issues. It provides assessments of changes in three industries in particular: television (looking at Latin American and Arabic television); film (looking at Hollywood power, and at the Indian and Hong Kong industries); and music.

Chapter 9 focuses on what is generally agreed to be the key technological development of the last 20 years – *digitalisation* – and, closely associated with it, the rise of the internet. I begin by discussing the key tenets of *digital optimism* in relation to cultural production and consumption: that digitalisation and the internet allow for substantially greater levels of control, creativity and participation on the part of non-professional 'users' and/or audiences; and that, because of this, the power of industrial, professional and institutionalised cultural production is eroding, and a more democratic and vigorous system of communication has either arrived, or is just over the horizon. I then outline some major criticisms that have been made of this type of thinking, which in turn generates a set of problems about how to evaluate the effects of digitalisation and the internet on cultural production, as follows. To what extent do inequalities in access and skills undermine claims about democratisation? How do new centralisations of power (for example, the control of search engines by very few companies, and the use of particular search protocols) affect cultural production? How might we interpret the presence of intensified commercialism and surveillance in digital networks? While recognising that the internet and digitalisation have brought cultural and political benefits, I argue that we need to be sceptical about the claims of even the most sophisticated digital optimists – but this does not mean that we have to be pessimistic.

Chapter 10 then examines the impact of digitalisation and the internet on a number of cultural industries, building on the discussion in Chapter 9. It analyses the major crisis undergone by the recording industry in the first decade of the twenty first century, and the increasing control of distribution by new entrants from the information technology industry, notably Apple and Amazon. It also asks whether the digitalisation of television in many countries has really led to an increase in meaningful consumer choice and control and examines the impact so far of digitalisation on newspapers, magazines and books. I close the chapter by examining how video games or digital games emerged as a new medium of culture and communication in the 1990s and 2000s, and what the implications are for understanding digitalisation.

Chapter 11 deals with the effects of all these patterns of change/continuity at the point where the cultural industries arguably have their most profound impacts on social and cultural life: **texts**. In what significant ways have cultural texts and their consumption by audiences changed (or not) during the period covered by this book (essentially 1980 to 2012)? And in what ways has this then had reciprocal effects on the institutions, organisation and economics of the cultural industries? I deal with three particularly important but tricky issues in assessing texts: diversity, quality, and the extent to which texts serve the interests of cultural industry businesses and their political allies.

Finally, a concluding chapter summarises the arguments of the book and outlines its importance for understanding changing relationships of power and social justice in relation to cultural production.

MATTERS OF DEFINITION

The cultural industries are difficult to define, and many researchers have demonstrated great confusion in trying to do so. One vital step is to take the concept of culture seriously.

If we define culture, in the broadest anthropological sense as a '"whole way of life" of a distinct people or other social group' (Williams, 1981: 11), it is possible to argue that all industries are cultural industries in that they are involved in the production and consumption of culture. For by this definition, the clothes we wear, the furniture in our houses and workplaces, the cars, buses and trains we use for transport, the food and drink we consume are all part of our culture and they are nearly all produced industrially, for profit.

The term 'cultural industries' has tended to be used in a much more restricted way than this, based implicitly on a definition of culture as 'the *signifying system* through which necessarily (though among other means) a social order is communicated, reproduced, experienced and explored' (Williams, 1981: 13, original emphasis). To put this a little more simply, the cultural industries have usually been thought of as those institutions (mainly profit-making companies, but also state organisations and non-profit organisations) that are most directly involved in **the production of social meaning**. Therefore, nearly all definitions of the cultural industries would include television (cable and satellite, too), radio, the cinema, newspaper, magazine and book publishing, the music recording and publishing industries, advertising and the performing arts. These are all activities the primary aim of which is to communicate to an audience, to create texts.

All cultural artefacts are texts in the very broad sense that they are open to interpretation. Cars, for example, signify: they have meanings. Every car involves significant design and marketing inputs. However, the *primary* aim of cars as a category is not to provide a set of meanings to customers, or to look nice, but transport. What defines a text, then, is a matter of degree, a question of balance between its functional and communicative aspects (see Hirsch, 1990/1972 for a similar argument). Texts (songs, narratives, performances) are heavy on signification and tend to be light on functionality and they are created with communicative goals primarily in mind. Box 0.1 presents the core cultural industries that are the main focus of this book. They are cultural industries because **they deal primarily with the industrial production and circulation of texts**.

Box 0.1 The core cultural industries

The following industries are centrally concerned with the industrial production and circulation of texts and they therefore constitute what I want to call the core cultural industries for the purposes of this book:

- *Broadcasting*: the radio and television industries, including their newer cable, satellite and digital forms.
- *Film industries*: this category includes the dissemination of films on video, DVD and other formats and on television.
- *Music industries*: recording (which, of course, includes the recording of sounds other than music, but is for the most part centred on music) publishing[6] and live performance.
- *Print and electronic publishing*: including books, online databases, information services, magazines and newspapers.
- *Video and computer games* or digital games as many commentators now prefer to call them.
- *Advertising, marketing and public relations*: compared with other cultural industries, advertisements and marketing artefacts tend to have a greater functional element as they are intended to sell and promote other products. Nevertheless, they are centred on the creation of texts and require the work of symbol creators (see Chapter 2 for a further discussion of how marketers fit into the cultural industries).
- *Web design*: most internet industries involve high-functionality dynamics, but the strong aesthetic element in web design arguably makes it part of the cultural industries sector.

All of these core cultural industries have their own dynamics and I discuss these at various points in the book, but one of the most salient contributions of work on 'the cultural industries' has been to see that these industries interact and interconnect with each other in complex ways. Largely, this is because they compete with each other for the same resources. The most significant of these resources are as follows (see Garnham, 1990: 158):

- A limited pool of disposable consumer income.
- A limited pool of advertising revenue.
- A limited amount of consumption time.
- Skilled creative and technical labour.

It is because of this competition for the same resources, as well as their shared characteristics as producers of primarily symbolic artefacts, that the cultural industries can be thought of as a sector or a linked production system (there are arguments in economic and business analysis about which term might be better, but these need not concern us here). This point is not always clearly understood, even by academic analysts.

---

6 While this term might seem to be about the printing of sheet music, music publishing concerns much more than this as it involves the ownership and control of the rights to musical compositions.

There is another set of cultural industries that I shall call 'peripheral'. These are important industries, and the term 'peripheral' is in no way intended to marginalise the benefits they can bring to a society, or the creativity of those involved in such work. There are two analytical reasons why I call them peripheral, and so deal with them somewhat less than the core industries. The first is that these industries reach fewer people in modern societies and therefore, other things being equal, are of lesser social and cultural influence than the core cultural industries. A reason for this lesser reach and potential influence can be found in the second factor for my categorisation of these industries as 'peripheral'. Like the core cultural industries, these more peripheral cultural industries are centrally concerned with the production of texts. But the reproduction of these symbols is based mainly on semi-industrial or non-industrial methods. Theatre, for example, has only recently begun to take on what might be called industrial forms of production and reproduction (see Chapter 7). The making, exhibition and sale of works of art (paintings, installations, sculptures) generate enormous amounts of money and commentary each year, but reproduction is limited, where it exists at all. The art prints industry limits reproduction artificially and uses laborious methods in order to add value to the prints.

I refer, in passing, to some of these industries, and I discuss theatre in Chapter 7. But in order to make this book readable – and writable – I have had to focus on a limited number of industries: the core cultural industries listed in Box 0.1. I recognise that the core and peripheral industries interact with each other in various significant ways. Actors and writers might work in television and theatre, for example, and art schools produce artists who might move in and out of various forms of commercial production, including film direction, advertising and music.

Borderline and problem cases

What kinds of industrial and business activity does my definition not include? As with all definitions of complex phenomena, there are several significant borderline cases.

- *Consumer electronics/cultural industry hardware* Making television programmes is based on an intentional act of cultural communication and would be included as a cultural industry in all definitions. But does the making of television *sets* constitute a cultural industry? The consumer electronics industries develop and make the machines through which we can experience texts. These industries are extremely important for understanding change and continuity in the cultural industries because they provide the hardware on and through which texts are reproduced or transmitted (hi-fi, television sets, MP3 and DVD players). These goods and others (fridges, microwave ovens) rely on the crucial input of designers and of often poorly paid assembly-line workers, but they are not centred on the production of primarily symbolic goods in the way that the cultural industries are and so they fall outside what I consider to be a useful definition.

- *Information technology* The software industry has some notable parallels with the cultural industries. Creative teams work together to try and create distinctive outcomes, but the actual presentation of the software does not take the form of a text as defined above. Its functional aspects – to carry out certain computerised tasks – outweigh the aesthetic dimensions of its design. Engineers rather than artists and designers dominate. Computer hardware design and manufacture is more akin to the consumer electronics industry, and is excluded from my definition of the cultural industries for similar reasons.
- Some of the most difficult definitional issues surround *the internet industries*. Eli Noam (2009: 274–89) differentiates seven sub-industries, some of which are closely related to the IT and telecommunications industries: internet backbone infrastructure; internet service providers; broadband service; navigational software; search engines and web directories; web portals; internet telephony applications; and media player software. I follow Noam in treating these as separate from the cultural industries. But, for reasons explained above, I think it is valid to see web design as a cultural industry.

Noam treats media, information technology (which for him includes consumer electronics, though I would call this a separate industry), telecommunications and internet industries as inter-related parts of 'the information sector' (Noam, 2009: 5). This is a sensible move. Throughout this book, I shall consider the changing relationships between these groups of industries, and their complex dance of competition and collaboration.

To make this discussion more concrete, let me discuss how the IT and internet giants relate to the cultural industries. Is Google a cultural-industry company? My answer is no, because it is not really involved in the production of content or texts. All the same, like other institutions, it is extremely important for understanding the cultural industries. Google increasingly acts as a crucial gateway for content produced by cultural businesses. Its Google Books project makes available enormous amounts of cultural content that would otherwise be much more difficult to find. It is impossible to understand the contemporary advertising environment without knowing about search engines (see Chapter 9). But none of this means that it is a cultural industry organisation. Nor is Apple. Apple designs and markets devices that have affected the cultural industries profoundly, but it does not produce texts in the usual sense of the term discussed earlier. Microsoft is slightly different, because it commissions digital games – but this is only a tiny part of what it does. Amazon has become a crucial retailer for cultural industry products, and so, to a lesser extent has Apple (with its i-Tunes store). But Amazon is now a retailer of many products besides the cultural-industry products with which it built its brand.

Let me deal with one or two other borderline cases now.

- *Fashion* Fashion is a fascinating 'hybrid' of a cultural industry, in the sense that I use the term here, and a consumer goods industry. The high degree of balance between functionality and signification makes this a complex special case, made all the more interesting by distinctive forms of organisation (see McRobbie, 1998, for a valuable study).
- *Sport* Industries such as football (soccer) and baseball arrange for the performance of live spectacles that are, in many respects, very like the live entertainment sector of the cultural industries. People pay to be entertained in real time in the co-presence of talented or not-that-talented performers. But there are notable differences, even from live entertainment in the cultural industries. Sport is fundamentally competitive, whereas symbol making isn't. Texts (in the sense in which I use the term in this book) tend to be more scripted or scored than in sports, which are essentially improvised around a set of competitive rules.

I could go on for pages more, dealing with borderline cases, which share features with the cultural industries, but which are, I think, sufficiently different to merit separate treatment. I would hope though that by now my point will be clear enough: that I am focusing here on industries that are based on the industrial production and circulation of texts and centrally reliant on the work of symbol creators.

Some objections to the definitions and assumptions employed here

In this section, I deal with some problems that have been raised with the definition of the cultural industries that I and other analysts employ. For some analysts, the focus on symbolic creativity represents a problem. Keith Negus (2006: 201–2) has objected to my focus on symbolic creativity as the basis of a definition of the cultural industries on the grounds that creativity and the circulation of potentially influential meanings are just as much a feature of industries such as 'food, banking, tobacco, insurance' as, say, music and television. Negus is right to say that the cultural industries are not the only place where symbolic creativity takes place and I agree that symbol makers should not be fetishised as more special than the rest of us. And it is certainly true that cigarettes and bank accounts, like television programmes and songs, have cultural meaning.[7] Yet, if we blur the distinction, it seems to me that we miss something vital. In order to understand cultural production adequately, we need to get at the *specificity* of the cultural industries. This means appreciating the difference between activities *centrally* involved with the production of artefacts that are *primarily* composed of symbols and other types of social

---

7   See also Mato (2009) for a particularly confused version of the argument that 'all industries are cultural'.

activity. Bankers, after all, are not like musicians, and the differences seem to me to be vital (see 'Why do the cultural industries matter?', above).

Another objection to the focus on symbol creators is that it marginal-ises the importance of other cultural workers. In its accounting practices, Hollywood traditionally differentiated 'above the line' workers (symbol cre-ators) from 'below the line' craft and technical workers. Some have implied that 'above the line' workers are privileged, perhaps even 'bourgeois' while 'below the line' craft and technical workers suffer by comparison, and there-fore to focus on symbol creators is to reproduce a version of class inequality (Mayer, 2011). But the situation is more complex than this. Many symbol cre-ators are under-rewarded, under-employed, oppressed and exploited, and many un-named technical workers face relatively good conditions – partly because they tend more often to be unionised. The reason for the focus on symbolic creativity does not derive from any desire on my part to highlight a pampered creative elite and ignore oppressed technical and unskilled workers. It is based on the decision to understand conditions of cultural work in relation to the particular nature of that work, as the production of *culture*. In Raymond Williams's words, a sociological understanding of culture must concern itself with 'the social relations of its specific means of production' and 'with the ways in which, within social life, "culture" and "cultural pro-duction" are socially identified and distinguished' (Williams, 1981: 30–1). Objections to definitions of the cultural industries based on symbol making need to address debates about the definition and importance of culture in modern societies.

A leading cultural economist, David Throsby, has recently offered what he calls a 'concentric circles' model of cultural industries. This differs in funda-mental ways from my model and definition, and I want to explain why I think it does not work. In a sense, my own definition is based on concentric circles too, with, at the centre, those industrialised forms of production that account for most cultural activity in modern societies, and, outside these, those semi-industrialised forms that account for less cultural experience. Throsby and I differ on what we put in the centre, and what we put on the periphery. Throsby puts in the centre those activities which, in his view, have the great-est ratio of creative to commercial goals. These are what he calls 'the core crea-tive arts' (2010: 26): 'music, drama, dance, visual art, literature' (p. 91). These are then surrounded by another ring: other 'core industries' such as film, museums and galleries. The next layer out is 'the wider cultural industries of the media, publishing and so on' (p. 26), and then on the outside are cul-tural industries where the commercial content is highest, such as fashion and advertising. The idea is that 'creative ideas and influences in the core diffuse outwards through the concentric circles' (p. 26). This is based on the assump-tion that putting 'the pure creative arts at the centre provides a direct means of representing the core role of the arts in motivating and sustaining the entire cultural sector' (p. 27). Throsby gives the example of television scriptwriters, who are located at the core of the model, and sell their work to broadcasters located in the broader cultural industries circle.

I find this model, as presented in Throsby's book, sociologically strange. It is not at all clear to me why the 'pure arts' might be thought of as the principal source of creativity for the broader cultural industries. (Nor am I at all sure what the term 'pure' might mean in this context). The arts are one potential source of creative ideas, alongside many others, including not only symbol makers' own life experiences, but also existing products from commercial texts. So television scriptwriters may draw experiences from their childhood, their present life, and from the drama and the visual arts that are at the core of the model. But they are surely just as likely, in the contemporary world, to draw on ideas from industries and products that Throsby defines as 'commercial' and which therefore should be on the outside of the model. This might include existing television programmes, recent films the screenwriter may have seen, or even songs that they hear on the radio.

Nor is it clear to me why, in Throsby's characterisation, screenwriters are at the 'core', which is supposed to be occupied by drama, dance, the visual arts and literature. Aren't even freelance screenwriters, in a key sense, part of the broadcasting industry that Throsby places further out? To compound the problem, most of the industries that he puts at his core are divided between sectors that emphasise commercial goals and those which emphasise creative goals. This is well established in sociology of culture (Bourdieu, 1996, and Thompson, 2010, are just two of hundreds of examples). Some screenwriters might be operating in a highly subsidised 'arts' world, perhaps working on an avant-garde film project. Others might be employed by a major commercial institution and could be given a story idea to work on. Throsby seems to assume that creativity can only come from 'outside' commercial industries – surely an overly polarised conception of creativity and commerce.

Throsby makes clear that his intention is to defend the arts against what he sees as a marginalisation of them in work on the cultural industries. This is understandable, and I would absolutely want to defend public funding of the arts (see Chapter 5). But Throsby's model, which has been taken up by policymakers in the UK, seems to be based on some curious (mis)understandings of cultural production.[8]

ALTERNATIVE TERMS

Clearly, the term 'cultural industries' is a contested, difficult one and, as I have implied, its problems derive from the difficulty of defining 'culture'

---

8   According to Throsby, my division of core and peripheral industries is based on the idea that the peripheral industries are seen 'as a reflection of the tastes of a hegemonic cultural elite and hence are of less policy concern' (2010: 90, 104). But I simply don't see them in that way; my conceptualisation is not based on this populist conception of the arts as elitist. It is based on an understanding of the greater size and reach of the core cultural industries, not of their political, social or artistic value.

(not to mention 'industry'). Given all these problems of definition, why not abandon the term 'cultural industries' altogether in favour of an alternative? A number of alternative possibilities can be discussed here:

- The cultural industries are often referred to interchangeably with the 'media industries', and my focus in this book is primarily (but by no means exclusively) with what might validly be called media industries. But the concept of media is not without its problems of definition either.
- Some analysts have used the term 'information industries' but in its most developed form, in a recent groundbreaking book by Eli Noam (2009), this concept of the information sector has been used to refer not only to the media industries (close to what I am defining as the cultural industries here) but also to the telecommunications, internet, and information and communication technology (ICT) sectors. In the way in which Noam develops the concept, this is a valuable move, because his analysis delineates the various industries that should be included in these categories, and outlines how the four sectors are related (though still separate).
- An informative book on *The Leisure Industries* (Roberts, 2004) deals with sport and tourism alongside what I am calling the cultural industries here.
- Business analysts often use the term 'entertainment industries' – especially in the USA.
- Without doubt, though, the most often preferred alternative to 'cultural industries' is **creative industries**. Many policymakers and some academic analysts now use this term. Chapter 5 provides an account of some of the problems associated with it. This includes a discussion of the ways in which policy labelled 'creative industries' has generally differed from policy labelled 'cultural industries'.

Leisure, information, entertainment, media and creativity are all addressed in this book, but I prefer to use the term 'cultural industries' than the alternatives. The use of the term 'culture' draws attention to the historical importance of the cultural industries in affecting relations between culture and economics, texts and industry, meaning and function. What's more, 'cultural industries' not only refers to a type of industrial activity, it also invokes a certain tradition of thinking about this activity. As my own approach draws on that tradition of thought (along with others) I outline it in the next section.

FROM 'THE CULTURE INDUSTRY' TO THE CULTURAL INDUSTRIES

The concept of cultural industries has its origins in a chapter by two German-Jewish philosophers associated with the Frankfurt School of Critical Theory, Theodor Adorno and Max Horkheimer (1977[1944]). Although the term may have been used before, 'The Culture Industry' was part of the title of a chapter in their book *Dialektik der Aufklärung* (*Dialectic of Enlightenment*), which they wrote in the USA in the 1940s while in exile from Nazi Germany. The book was born out of a conviction that life in the capitalist democracy of the USA was, in its own way, as empty and superficial, if not quite as brutal and horrific, as life in the Germany they had fled. 'Culture Industry' was a concept intended to shock. Adorno and Horkheimer, like many other users of the term 'culture' in the nineteenth and twentieth centuries, equated culture in its ideal state with art, with special, exceptional forms of human creativity. For them, and for the tradition of Hegelian philosophy of which they were a part, art could act as a form of critique of the rest of life and provide a utopian vision of how a better life might be possible. In Adorno and Horkheimer's view, however, culture had almost entirely lost this capacity to act as utopian critique because it had become commodified – a thing to be bought and sold. Culture and Industry were supposed, in their view, to be opposites but, in modern capitalist democracy, the two had collapsed together. Hence, Culture Industry.[9]

By the late 1960s, it was clear that culture, society and business were becoming more intertwined than ever as transnational corporations invested in film, television and record companies and these forms took on ever greater social and political significance. Adorno, Horkheimer and other present and former members of the Frankfurt School became internationally prominent as left-wing students and intellectuals turned to their ideas to make sense of these changes. The term 'Culture Industry' became widely used in polemics against the perceived limitations of modern cultural life and was picked up by French sociologists (most notably Huet et al., 1978; Miège, 1979; Morin, 1962), as well as by activists and policymakers[10], and converted into the term 'cultural industries'.

So why prefer the plural to the singular form? The distinction is revealing and more significant than may at first appear to be the case. The French 'cultural industries' sociologists rejected Adorno and Horkheimer's use of the singular term 'The Culture Industry' because it suggested a 'unified field' where all the different forms of cultural production that coexist in modern life are assumed to obey the same logic. They were concerned, instead, to show how *complex* the cultural industries are and to identify the different logics at work in various types of cultural production – how, for example, the broadcasting industries operated in a very different way from the press or from industries reliant on 'editorial' or publishing models of production, such as book publishing or the recording

---

9 Steinert (2003: 9) clarifies that Adorno and Horkheimer used the term in two different senses: 'Culture Industry' to refer to 'commodity production as the principle of a specific form of cultural production' and the culture industry to refer to a specific branch of production.

10 Internationally, the term was disseminated in policy circles through the United Nations Educational, Scientific and Cultural Organization (UNESCO), based in Paris. UNESCO sponsored a large-scale comparative international programme on the cultural industries in 1979 and 1980, which culminated in a conference in Montreal in June 1980, the proceedings of which were published in English as UNESCO (1982).

industry (see Miège, 1987). As a result, they preferred the plural term 'industries culturelles'.[11]

The cultural industries sociologists rejected the approach of Adorno and Horkheimer on other grounds, too, as the leading writer in this tradition, Bernard Miège (1989: 9–12), made clear in the foreword to a translated collection of his work.[12] First, they rejected Adorno and Horkheimer's attachment to pre-industrial forms of cultural production. Following other critics of the Frankfurt School, including Adorno's friend and contemporary Walter Benjamin, Miège argued that the introduction of industrialisation and new technologies into cultural production did indeed lead to increasing commodification, but that it also led to exciting new directions and innovations. The commodification of culture, then, was a much more *ambivalent* process than was allowed for by Adorno and Horkheimer's cultural pessimism. (As we shall see in the next chapter, this is an insight shared by some cultural studies approaches.) Second, rather than assuming that the process of commodification of culture has been a smooth, unresisted one, the cultural industries sociologists were concerned with the limited and incomplete nature of attempts to extend capitalism into the realm of culture. They saw the cultural industries, in other words, as *contested* – a zone of continuing struggle – whereas there is a constant sense in Adorno and Horkheimer that the battle has already been lost, that culture has been already subsumed both by capital and by an abstract system of 'instrumental reason'.

These modifications of Adorno and Horkheimer's Culture Industry thesis are real advances. The point here is not simply to show that two German intellectuals writing in the middle of the twentieth century got it wrong. Adorno and Horkheimer are interesting, amongst other reasons, because they provided a highly sophisticated version of a mode of thinking about culture that is still common today. Newspaper commentators can often be read or heard dismissing industrialised culture as debased. Writers, teachers and students often lapse into a pessimism similar to that of the Culture Industry chapter, even while they enjoy and feel enriched by many of the products of the cultural industries. Adorno and Horkheimer provide the fullest and most intelligent version of the extreme, pessimistic view of the industrialisation of culture. For Miège and others, however, even this intelligent version of cultural pessimism is lacking. Abandoning extreme pessimism is not the same thing as complacently celebrating the cultural industries as they are. The key words, to repeat, are *complex*, *ambivalent* and *contested*. These terms drive my efforts to explain and assess the cultural industries in what follows. Using the term 'cultural industries' signals not only an awareness of the problems of the industrialisation of culture, but also a refusal to simplify assessment and explanation.

---

11 Many writers (such as Lash and Urry, 1994, and Garnham, 2000 – though not Garnham, 1990) use the term 'culture industries'. The difference is trivial, but I prefer 'cultural industries' because it symbolises the move beyond the Frankfurt School approach.

12 This poorly edited translation forms the most important source in English of Francophone sociological work on the cultural industries, but see also Lacroix and Tremblay (1997).

INDUSTRIES THAT MAKE TEXTS: THE DISTINCTIVE FEATURES

In light of the work by Miège and others – including, most notably, Garnham (1990) – it is possible to outline the distinctive features of the cultural industries, as compared with other forms of capitalist production. These are summarised in Box 0.2.[13] The first four features are the distinctive *problems* faced by the cultural industries and the next five features are the most common *responses*, or attempted solutions, undertaken by cultural industry businesses. These distinctive features have key implications for the rest of the book. They help to explain recurring strategies of cultural industry companies in terms of how they manage and organise cultural production. They indicate potential causes of change. They help us to understand the constraints facing those who want to work as symbol creators or set up their own independent and/or alternative cultural organisations. They also provide a way of understanding the differences *between* cultural industries, in that certain features are more apparent in some industries than in others, or the same features take somewhat different forms.

Box 0.2   Summary of distinctive features of the cultural industries

Problems:

- Risky business.
- Creativity versus commerce.
- High production costs and low reproduction costs.
- Semi-public goods; the need to create scarcity.

Responses:

- Misses are offset against hits by building a repertoire.
- Concentration, integration and co-opting publicity.
- Artificial scarcity.
- Formatting: stars, genres and serials.
- Loose control of symbol creators; tight control of distribution and marketing.

---

13 A number of other writers have attempted to define the characteristics of those industries that are involved primarily in the production and circulation of symbolic goods, even if they do not use the term 'cultural industries'. Many of these are ultimately consistent with the terms used by Garnham in his classic outline of the terrain (Baker, 2002, Caves, 2000, and Grant and Wood, 2004, are notable examples). My own outline here is distinctive in presenting these characteristics as a set of problems and attempted solutions or responses.

Risky business

All business is risky, but the cultural industries constitute a particularly risky business (the title of a book on the film industry by Prindle, 1993 – presumably named in homage to the enjoyable 1983 film starring Tom Cruise) because they are centred on the production of texts that can be bought and sold. For Garnham, influenced by Bourdieu (1984), this *risk* derives from the fact that audiences use cultural commodities in highly volatile and unpredictable ways, often in order to express the view that they are different from other people (Garnham, 1990: 161).[14] As a result, fashionable performers or styles, even if heavily marketed, can suddenly come to be perceived as outmoded and, equally, other texts can become unexpectedly successful. These risks, which stem from consumption, from the ways in which audiences tend to use texts, are made worse by two further factors related to production. First, as we saw earlier, companies grant symbol creators a limited autonomy in the hope that the creators will come up with something original and distinctive enough to be a hit. But this means that cultural companies are engaged in a constant process of struggle to control what symbol creators are likely to come up with. Second, any particular cultural industry company (Company A) is reliant on other cultural industry companies (B, C, D, and so on) to make audiences aware of the existence of a new product or of the uses and pleasures that they might get from experiencing the product. Even if Company A actually owns Company B or F, they can't quite control the kind of publicity the text is likely to get because it is difficult to predict how critics, journalists, radio and television producers, presenters, and so on are likely to evaluate texts.

All these factors mean that cultural industry companies face special problems of risk and unpredictability. Here are some statistics:

- Nearly 30,000 albums were released in the USA in 1998, of which fewer than 2 per cent sold more than 50,000 copies (Wolf, 1999: 89).
- Eighty eight hits in 1999 – 0.03 per cent of releases – accounted for a quarter of US record sales (Alderman, 2001).
- Neuman (1991: 139) quotes a rule of thumb in publishing that 80 per cent of the income derives from 20 per cent of the published product.
- Bettig (1996: 102) claims that, of the 350 or so films released each year in the USA at the time of his study, only 10 or so will be box office hits.
- Driver and Gillespie (1993: 191) report that only one-third to one-half of UK magazines break even and only 25 per cent make a profit.
- According to figures cited by Moran (1997: 444), about 80 per cent of the 50,000 book titles published in the USA each year in the mid-1980s were financial failures.

Nevertheless, across the cultural industries as a whole, this risk is successfully negotiated by the larger companies:

---

14 Even if we do not think of the problem in this way, it is clear that the consumption of texts is likely to be highly subjective and arational.

- Television profits have traditionally run at a rate of 20 per cent of sales, according to Neuman (1991: 136).
- Compaine (1982: 34, cited by Neuman, 1991: 136) claims that profits from motion pictures tend to run at 33 to 100 per cent higher than the US average.

Profits, though, are highly variable, depending on the degree of competition within and across industries:

- Dale (1997: 20) samples figures from 1992 showing the following profit margins (operating income divided by sales) in different industries:
- cable, 20 per cent;
- broadcast television, nearly 17.5 per cent;
- the press and books, around 12 per cent;
- music, network television and magazines, just under 10 per cent;
- film and advertising agencies, in the high single digits.
- Film industry profits fell from an average of 15 per cent in the 1970s to about 10 per cent in the early 1980s, then to around 5–6 per cent in the late 1980s, before making a recovery in the early 1990s (Dale, 1997: 20).
- In the early 2000s, the majors that dominate the cultural industries showed either very high temporary losses, reflecting the huge costs of mergers or investment, or poor profit rates: less than 5 per cent at Disney and less than 3 per cent at Viacom in 2002 (Grant and Wood, 2004: 100).

The cultural industries, then, can be highly profitable in spite of the particularly high levels of risk many businesses face, but it may be difficult to achieve high levels of profit for individual companies.

Creativity versus commerce

The account in the previous section may have made it sound as though symbol creators work under relatively autonomous conditions in the cultural industries because this relative autonomy is generously granted to them by companies. The reality, however, is more complicated. Such autonomy is also a product of historical understandings of the nature of symbolic creativity and knowledge, in particular, the view that they are not readily compatible with the pursuit of commerce. Romantic conceptions of art in 'Western' societies established the idea that art is at its most special when it represents the original self-expression of a particular author. At one level this is a mystification, so to set creativity too strongly against commerce – as a great deal of romantic and modernist thought about art did – is wrong. Creators need to be paid and some of the most eye-opening, thought-provoking, funny and lovely works have been produced as part of a commercial system. However dubious the romantic conception of opposing creativity and knowledge to commerce may be, it has had the long-term effect of generating a set of tensions which are vital to understanding the cultural industries. The creativity/commerce dialectic helps to generate the relative and provisional autonomy that many symbol makers attain. It also adds to the uncertainty and difficulty of the environment in which cultural businesses work. Parallels exist in other fields. There are tensions in science and engineering, for example, between the goal of making knowledge publicly available and gaining financial advantage from that knowledge. But it is impossible to understand the distinctive nature of cultural production without an understanding of the commerce/creativity dialectic. I explore these issues further in Chapters 2 and 7.

High production costs and low reproduction costs

Most cultural commodities have high fixed costs and low variable costs: a record can cost a lot to make because of all the time and effort that has to go into composition, recording, mixing and editing to get the right sound for its makers and their intended audience, but once 'the first copy' is made, all subsequent copies are relatively cheap to reproduce. Digitalisation has only amplified this feature. The key point here is the *ratio* between production and reproduction costs: nails, for example, have a low design input, making the first copy cheapish to produce and each further copy costing not much less. This produces a very different kind of market from that which prevails in the cultural industries. Cars are more like the texts that the cultural industries produce, but are still substantially different. The prototype of a car is extremely expensive, with enormous amounts of design and engineering input, and the costs of each new car built from the prototype are very expensive, too, because of the materials and safety checks required. So, even though the fixed costs are high, the ratio of fixed costs to variable costs is relatively low. The much higher ratio of fixed costs to variable costs in the cultural industries means that big hits are extremely profitable. This is because, beyond the break-even point, the profit made from the sale of every extra unit can be considerable,[15] compensating for the inevitably large number of misses that come about as a result of the volatile and unpredictable nature of demand. This leads to a very strong orientation towards 'audience maximisation' in the cultural industries (Garnham, 1990: 160).

Semi-public goods

Cultural commodities are rarely destroyed by use. They tend to act like what economists call 'public goods' – goods where the act of consumption by one individual does not reduce the possibility of consumption by others. If I listen to a CD, for example, that doesn't in any way alter your experience of it if I pass it on to you. The same could certainly not be said of my eating a pie. Using a car diminishes its value for another user much more than watching

---

15 Those cultural industries that do not sell goods directly to customers, most notably broadcasting and, increasingly, internet content, work in different but related ways. In them, the extra unit is that of audiences, which are then 'sold' on to advertisers. See Chapter 9 for a discussion of some of the implications of this for digital media.

a DVD does the DVD. What is more, the means of industrial reproduction of cultural goods are relatively low in cost. This means that firms have to achieve the scarcity that gives value to goods by limiting access to cultural goods and services by artificial means (see below).

How, then, do cultural industry businesses attempt to respond to the particular set of issues facing them as they attempt to make profit and generate capital from the production of culture?

Misses are offset against hits by building a repertoire

This extra emphasis on audience maximisation means that, in the cultural industries, companies tend to offset misses against hits by means of 'over-production' (Hirsch, 1990[1972]), attempting to put together a large catalogue or 'cultural repertoire' (Garnham, 1990: 161) or, to put it another way, 'throwing mud' – or other similar substances – 'against the wall' to see what sticks (Laing, 1985: 9; Negus, 1999: 34). If, as Garnham suggests, one record in every nine is a hit and the other eight are misses, then a company issuing five records is less likely to have sufficient hits to keep it afloat than another company with a repertoire or catalogue of 50 record releases. This is one of the pressures towards achieving greater size for cultural companies, though there are countervailing tendencies that favour smaller companies. Much has been made in recent years of the idea of *the 'long tail' thesis* (Anderson, 2006): the idea that commerce will be increasingly oriented towards providing goods for niche products with a relatively small demand, but which collectively sustain businesses, because digitalisation allows for lower distribution costs. In fact, as we shall see in Chapter 9, there is evidence that the 'long tail' thesis is faulty. Attention and revenue still tend to be heavily concentrated in hits, or the most successful and popular cultural products.

Concentration, integration and co-opting publicity

Cultural industry companies deal with risk and the need to ensure audience maximisation by using strategies that are also apparent in other sectors.

- *Horizontal integration* They buy up other companies in the same sector to reduce the competition for audiences and audience time.
- *Vertical integration* They buy up other companies involved in different stages of the process of production and circulation. Companies might buy 'downstream', such as when a company involved in making films buys a DVD distributor, or 'upstream', which is when a company involved in distribution or transmission (such as a cable television company) buys a programme-maker.
- *Internationalisation* By buying and partnering other companies abroad, corporations can sell massive amounts of extra copies of a product they have already paid to produce (though they will have to pay new marketing costs, of course).

- *Multisector and multimedia integration* They buy into other related areas of cultural industry production to ensure cross-promotion.
- Also important is the attempt to 'co-opt' (Hirsch, 1990[1972]) critics, DJs and various other people responsible for publicising texts, by socialising with them and sending them gifts, press releases, and so on.

Such forms of integration have led to the formation of bigger and more powerful companies. Nearly all major industries – from aluminium to biochemicals to clothing – are dominated by large companies. There is only limited evidence that the cultural industries have higher degrees of industry *concentration* than other industries. Arguably, though, the consequences of not succeeding in growth and integration are greater in the cultural industries than in many other industries because there is a very high failure rate for smaller companies. This, in turn, is explained by the fact that small cultural companies are unable to spread risk across a repertoire. Crucially, the consequences of this size and power are unique to the cultural industries because of the ability of the goods they produce – texts – to have an influence on our thinking about their operations, about all other industries and, indeed, potentially, about all aspects of life.

Artificial scarcity

Garnham (1990: 38–9, 161) identified a number of ways in which scarcity is achieved for cultural goods (which, as we saw above, because they often show public good features, tend not to be scarce). Primary among them is vertical integration. The ownership of distribution and retail channels allows companies to control release schedules and ensure the adequate availability of goods. Just as central, however, are:

- advertising, which limits the relative importance for profits of the *sale* of cultural goods;
- copyright, which aims to prevent people from freely copying texts;
- limiting access to the means of reproduction, so that copying is not easy.

Formatting: stars, genres, serials

Another way for cultural industry companies to cope with the high levels of risk in the sector is to minimise the danger of misses by *formatting* their cultural products (Ryan, 1992).[16] One major means of formatting is **the star**

---

16 The term 'format' is widely used in the television industry to refer to the concept of a particular programme, such as *Who Wants to be a Millionaire?*, *Big Brother* or *Jeopardy*. This is often developed in an initial market and then sold as a copyrighted idea (rather than as a programme) in overseas markets (see Moran and Keane, 2004). That is not the sense in which Ryan uses the term, but this strategy can be understood as a way of attempting to spread the high fixed costs associated with developing a programme idea and reaping the reward from the relatively low variable costs.

system – associating the names of star writers, performers and so on with texts. This involves considerable marketing efforts, in order to break a writer or performer as a new star or ensure the continuation of a star's aura. This type of formatting is reserved for privileged texts that cultural industry companies hope will become big hits. The importance of the star system can be indicated by the following statistic: of the 126 movies that made more than US$100 million at US box offices in the 1990s, 41 starred one or more of just seven actors: Tom Hanks, Julia Roberts, Robin Williams, Jim Carrey, Tom Cruise, Arnold Schwarzenegger and Bruce Willis (Standard & Poor's *Movies and Home Entertainment Industry Survey*, 11 May 2000: 14).

Another crucial means of formatting is the use of **genre**, such as 'horror film', 'hip hop album', 'literary novel'. Genre terms operate as labels, not unlike brand names, that suggest to audiences the kinds of satisfaction and reward they might attain by experiencing the product. The terms might not be universally understood and also might not even be explicitly used, but the key thing here is that a type of cultural product is suggested and associated with particular uses and pleasures. Many cultural products promoted and publicised primarily via the use of genre also carry author names, but until the author becomes a star, genre is paramount.

Finally, the **serial** remains a major type of formatting, especially where authorship and genre are less significant. This has been an important aspect of publishing – popular fiction, comics, and so on. Hollywood relies more than ever on sequels and prequels: 27 sequels and prequels were listed in the US cinema release schedule for 2011 as it stood in January of that year – more than in any previous year (Gray, 2011).

Loose control of symbol creators; tight control of distribution and marketing

In discussing symbol creators earlier, I pointed out that symbol creators are granted considerable autonomy within the process of production – far more, in fact, than most workers in other forms of industry. There are cultural reasons for this (namely, long-standing assumptions about the ethical desirability of creative autonomy, which derive from the romantic conception of symbolic creativity, and traditions of free speech) as well as economic and organisational ones. Managers assume that major hits and the creation of new genre, star and series brands require originality. Symbol creators are usually overseen from a certain distance by 'creative managers' (Ryan, 1992), such as editors or television producers, who act as intermediaries between the creators and the commercial imperatives of the company. Those symbol creators who become stars – their names promising certain experiences – are rewarded enormously, but most creative workers exist in a vast reservoir of underused and under-resourced talent, picking up work here and there. In many cases, production will actually take place under the auspices of a separate, independent company. Such 'independents' – often, in fact, tied to larger companies by financing, licensing and distribution deals – are to be found in abundance in the cultural industries, mainly because symbol creators and some audiences are suspicious of the bureaucratic control of creativity, again reflecting ingrained cultural assumptions about art and knowledge. In order to control the risks associated with managing creativity, senior managers exert much tighter control over reproduction, distribution and marketing – what I will call **circulation** – than they do over production. In many cases this is achieved by means of vertical integration.

An objection might be made to a characterisation of the distinctive features of the cultural industries, such as the one above, that some of these features will be shared with other industries. Such an objection entirely misses the point: it is the *collective* nature of these characteristics that matters.[17] Nor, as I stressed earlier, does the fact that cultural industry businesses are linked to other sets of industries and other businesses invalidate the idea that there are useful if provisional and porous boundaries to be drawn around the sector. Analysing these distinctive features collectively helps us to understand the production and consumption of culture. The key point, however, is that whether they do so successfully or not, **cultural industry companies respond in particular (though variable) ways to perceived difficulties of making profits** and these distinctive dynamics play an important role in the account of change and continuity in this book.

AUTHOR TO READER

I outlined at the beginning of this Introduction why I think the cultural industries matter: the power they have to influence people, the varied ways in which they manage the work of symbol creators and their role in bringing about more general industrial, social and cultural change. Relating the fundamental concerns of the book to my own personal background may help to make them more concrete. I hope this will provide some context for the particular approach I take to the cultural industries, the approach developed in this book.

As a teenager, I was infuriated by what I perceived as the lies and distortions of television, and of the ultraconservative newspapers my parents read (typically for a certain section of the Northern English, working class/ lower middle class). *The Daily Mail* and *Sunday Express* seemed constantly to be attacking anyone who was trying to achieve social justice in Britain in the late 1970s – trade unions, feminists, anti-racist activists. They wrote as if the British role in Northern Ireland was one of making peace between tribal

---

17 Other industries have been analysed for their distinctive characteristics and Caves (2000: 1) usefully summarises some examples, such as the pharmaceuticals industry, which is marked by the particular intensity of competition over innovation; chemical process industries, by rivalry over the installation of new capacity; and food processing, by product differentiation and the rise of dominant brands.

factions. Even at 15, I knew enough about Irish history to find this difficult to accept. These newspapers were also decidedly lukewarm in their condemnation of far-right neo-Nazi groups, whose graffiti was all over the town where I grew up, directed at the British South Asian community there. It seemed to me, right from my teens, that the cultural industries had a role in maintaining power relations and distorting people's understanding of them.

My other main relationship to the media and popular culture was as a fan, and a fan I remain. Even if some media seemed to take a stance against most of the people and political positions I respected, there was plenty of exciting, interesting and funny popular culture around. I still find this to be the case today, so I cannot accept the view of the cultural industries to be found in some writing on the subject – that they are simply a monstrous system for the maintenance of conformity. In the late 1970s and early 1980s, the musical genre of punk seemed to me to embody the most remarkable creative energy. Suddenly, the emotional range of my small record collection was massively expanded: music could be shocking or coolly detached; intelligent or belligerent; hilarious or deadly serious. Punk musicians were always talking about the music industry and were often arguing that it could be changed, to make creativity more widespread and to make sure that more of the money went to those creating the music.

My sense of the importance (and ambivalence) of media and popular culture eventually led me to a career in teaching, where I was fortunate enough to meet dozens of students who were prepared to share their perspectives with me. My love of US popular culture (particularly classical and Movie Brat Hollywood cinema, black music and Jewish comedy) and my fascinated loathing for the US government's role in global geopolitics took me to the outskirts of Chicago for a postgraduate degree. Teaching and learning provided the impulse to write this book, but it's also informed by my experience, over the last few years, of researching and writing about the cultural industries. There is an assumption among many academics that the most prestigious books will necessarily be more or less incomprehensible to students. I've worked hard to make this book interesting and useful for other teachers and researchers, but I've also endeavoured to make it accessible for students, by explaining difficult concepts as they arise and trying to get across why I think the issues I'm dealing with matter. I've had to assume some knowledge of and interest in the topic, but I've also tried not to assume too much.

PART ONE
ANALYTICAL FRAMEWORKS

1

Theories of Culture, Theories of Cultural Production

Media and cultural economics	38
Communication studies	40
Critical political economy approaches	42
Which political economy?	44
Contradiction	45
The specific conditions of cultural industries	45
Tensions between production and consumption	46
Symbol creators	46
Information and entertainment	46
Historical variations in the social relations of cultural production	47
Sociology of culture and organisational and management studies	47
Radical media sociology/media studies	48
The problem of texts	50
Some achievements and limitations of cultural studies	51
Cultural studies approaches to media industries and media production	54
Industry produces culture, culture produces industry	55
'Production studies': the cultural studies of media industries approach	55
Digital optimism	56
Creative industries analysis	57
Cultural economy	58
The approach taken here	58

How have researchers approached the cultural industries? Which research traditions provide the most useful tools for addressing the central themes of this book – explaining and assessing patterns of change/continuity in the cultural industries since the late 1970s? The search is for approaches that address the fundamental issues outlined in the second section of the Introduction ('Why do the cultural industries matter?'). We need, in other words, perspectives that are sensitive to the potential power of the cultural industries, as makers of texts, as systems for the management and marketing of creative work, and as agents of change. We also need a combination of approaches that are able to provide analysis of the two parts of the term 'the cultural industries': the 'culture' part and the 'industries' part. I'll begin with two traditions of analysis that promise, at first sight, to make valuable contributions to such an analysis, but are in fact compromised by their lack of attention to issues of power.

MEDIA AND CULTURAL ECONOMICS

Cultural economics is the branch of economics devoted specifically to culture and to the arts, while media economics employs economic concepts to analyse the media. Both have been relatively marginal within the field of economics as a whole. However, in recent years, they have experienced something of a boom, especially media economics (see, for example, Doyle, 2002; Hoskins et al., 2004). This may partly be explained by the fact that the influence of the 'dismal science' of economics on government policy has been profound, as we shall see in Chapter 4.

Since it developed in its modern form in the late nineteenth century, economics has been dominated by particular conceptions of its assumptions and goals that have come to be known as 'neoclassical', to distinguish them from the 'classical' economics of the eighteenth century. *Neoclassical economics* claimed to offer a scientific basis for the study of economic affairs and cut itself off from the roots of the discipline in moral philosophy. It 'presented capitalism as a network of markets, regulated by rational self-interest, whose organization and outcomes could be modelled mathematically' (Murdock, 2011: 13). This dominant form of economics is not concerned with determining human needs and rights, nor with intervening in questions of social justice. Instead, it focuses on how human wants might be most efficiently satisfied. Even though its language and procedures are often very specialist and esoteric, neoclassical economics claims to be a practical social science, aimed at understanding how and under what conditions markets best function. It equates the well-being of people with their ability to maximise their satisfactions. It provides methods for calculating how such satisfaction might be maximised, and this shows its roots in utilitarianism – the philosophy of happiness maximisation (see Mosco, 1996: 47–8). Given our concerns, as outlined in the Introduction, with the way that public and everyday life are affected by the products of the cultural industries, such a bracketing of questions concerning power and justice is limiting, to say the least. The equation of human well-being with the optimising of economic satisfactions, an underlying assumption that many media and cultural economics writers too often implicitly inherit from neoclassical economics, provides a limited basis on which to proceed in assessing the cultural industries.

In spite of this, it would be a serious mistake to think that economic concepts are irrelevant or useless to the present analysis of cultural production. And economics should not be equated with the neoclassical paradigm. There are numerous heterodox varieties and, as in any discipline, there are more and less sophisticated applications of the analysis.[1] A crucial issue in the context of this book is whether or not and, if so, in what ways and with what implications, analysts recognise the specificity of the realm of culture, symbols and information, as opposed to other forms of activity in society. Some early cultural economists (such as Mark Blaug, William Baumol and William Bowen) recognised the distinctive nature of media, culture and the arts and incorporated this into their analysis. Such work has influenced the way in which other more critical traditions of analysis have understood the distinctive nature of the cultural industries (notably Miège, 1989, and Garnham, 1990 – see below). The breakdown of distinctive features in the Introduction drew on such work and used economic concepts, such as the distinction between private and public goods, the relationship between production and reproduction costs, and the creation of artificial scarcity.[2]

The problem is that many economists who are concerned to analyse the distinctive nature of media and cultural products often fail to recognise the implications of these characteristics and the limitations of the fundamental economic concepts underpinning their approaches. There is no space here to explore these limitations fully.[3] The key point concerns the way in which economics as a discipline has played a pivotal role in generating forms of public policy. In its most invidious forms, mainstream economics has helped to fuel a *neoliberal* approach to culture, which plays an important part in the story of change and continuity told in this book (see especially Chapter 3).

---

1 Winseck (2011: 25–6) rightly points to the influence of the Austrian historian Joseph Schumpeter on economics, and, indirectly, on various approaches to the cultural and information technology industries. Schumpeterian analysis is by no means neoclassical, and recognises the 'creative destruction' in capitalism. But it assumes the impossibility of managing the 'creative destruction' of capitalism, and therefore can fit well with strands of neo-liberalism.

2 Later media and cultural economists have continued to recognise the distinctive nature of cultural production, for example, Caves (2000, 2005), Doyle (2002: 11–15) and Picard (2002: 9–18).

3 Good critiques are provided by the following, in ascending order of technical difficulty: Grant and Wood (2004: 56–61); Gandy (1992); Garnham (2000: 45–54); Baker (2002). None of these writers is an economist, but all use good economic concepts to criticise bad economics. While some economists recognise the limitations of neoclassical models of rational actors pursuing utility maximisation, many media and cultural economics textbooks remain more or less untouched by that recognition.

Underpinning the neoliberal approach to culture is the idea, derived from neoclassical theory, that 'free', unregulated competition will produce efficient markets. *Neo-liberalism* takes this a stage further by assuming that the production of efficient markets should be the primary goal of public policy. In some cases, this has involved downplaying or marginalising the specificity of media and culture and arguing that economic models can be used to analyse cultural goods (such as television, books, newspapers) in the same way as other goods. As one major media economist, Ronald Coase (1974: 389) put it, there is 'no fundamental distinction' between 'the market for goods and the market for ideas'. Perhaps the most famous expression of such a view was made by Mark Fowler. After being appointed by the ultraconservative US president Ronald Reagan to run the Federal Communications Commission in 1981, Fowler observed that television was 'just another appliance ... a toaster with pictures' (cited, for example, by Baker, 2002: 3) – provocatively implying that there was no difference between television and a toaster, they were both simply economic goods to be bought and sold.

Only the most extreme neo-classical economists would deny that the symbol-laden nature of cultural goods offers a distinctive set of problems for economics, and for regulation. But even economic analysis that recognises the specificity of media and culture, and some of the limitations of traditional forms of economic analysis, tends to downplay the severity of the problems of cultural markets. The work of Richard Caves (2000, 2005) would be an example of this in my view. Another example would be the way in which the economic concept of 'market failure' has been used to justify continued public intervention in broadcasting markets, but potentially at the cost of relegating non-economic goals, such as democratic and civic participation, to secondary, residual features of market systems (see Hardy, 2004, for criticism of the use of this concept of market failure).

Economic concepts, then, provide an important lens through which to view culture and the cultural industries, but the nature of economics as an academic discipline and as a form of policy intervention means that it needs careful handling.[4]

COMMUNICATION STUDIES

From the 1930s onwards, researchers began to investigate mass communication media using sociological methods. By the 1950s in the USA, there was

---

4   Terry Flew (2009) thinks that I and other writers such as Des Freedman (2008) are setting up a straw figure in assessing mainstream economics in this way, but I disagree. See Jackson (2009) for a powerful critique of the failure of orthodox and much heterodox economics to incorporate the concept of culture adequately into explanations of economic life.

an established discipline of communication studies. The subject continues to thrive today and has spread to Europe and elsewhere. It has tended to neglect cultural production, and downplay questions of power and social justice.

For many years, the dominant concern of this field was the 'effects' of media messages on audiences, with a tendency to conceive of those effects as limited and difficult to prove (see Lowery and DeFleur, 1995). This tradition was strongly influenced by behaviourism, the belief that society is best understood by observation of the outward behaviour of individuals, rather than by efforts to understand (in psychology or philosophy) mental processes and events or (in sociology) issues of social power and status. In this tradition of research, analysis of cultural consumption was cut off from any consideration of cultural production and organisation. This mainstream of communication studies reinvented itself in the 1970s and 1980s via a functionalist focus on what people got out of the media (see Curran, 2002: 135). A sophisticated sociological variant of this 'liberal functionalism' (Curran, 2002: 134–6) saw the media primarily as agencies of social integration and emphasized ritual and continuity (Dayan and Katz, 1992).

The politics underlying this mainstream tendency in communications research tend to be liberal and pluralist. By 'liberal', I do not mean economically liberal, as in the term 'neo-liberalism' – which emphasises the virtues of unregulated markets. Nor do I use this term in the way it is sometimes used in North America, to mean something like 'leftist', in contrast with 'conservative'. Rather, I mean a form of politics that emphasises the freedom and autonomy of individuals over other conceptions of the good; liberals in this sense can be egalitarian or libertarian, leftist or conservative. By 'pluralism' I mean a view of society that takes power to be highly dispersed, and believes governments can, with relative ease, counteract inequalities of power. Other traditions of thought place greater emphasis on collectivities, conflicts and concentrations of power than does liberal-pluralism (see Marsh, 2002, for a useful critique of this form of political thought). Partly as a result of this underlying politics, communication studies failed for many decades to offer any systematic account of how the cultural industries relate to more general economic, political and sociocultural processes.[5]

It needs to be recognised that some communication studies that might broadly be characterised as 'liberal-pluralist' has been much more concerned with the issues of power and social justice in relation to cultural production, which are the fundamental concerns of this book. For example, an important tradition has examined the way that the impact of the media has transformed political communication. This emphasised the dangers for modern societies of the way that democratic processes were being affected by the broadcast

---

5 Some more critical accounts came from communication researchers who positioned themselves against these dominant tendencies in the discipline, aligning themselves instead with approaches coming from other fields, such as sociology and politics. One particularly important set of approaches will be addressed in the next section.

and press media. Jay Blumler and Michael Gurevitch (1995), for example, have written convincingly about a 'crisis of civic communication' and the difficulties of sustaining participatory citizenship in a society where most people will gain their knowledge of politics from television. Other writers in this tradition have attempted to develop normative models to assess how well (and how badly) the media perform in fostering democracy (such as Christians et al., 2009; McQuail, 1992). The work of the Euromedia Research Group (see, for example, Euromedia,1997; McQuail and Siune, 1998; Trappel et al., 2010) and its individual associates (such as the prolific Jeremy Tunstall) has provided helpful information about changes in media policy and cultural-industry organisations. There has been increasing dialogue with other approaches, such as cultural studies (see below), in sophisticated analyses of public engagement and the uses by children and young people of new media (see Livingstone, 2010, for example). Throughout these strands of communication studies and sociological work, there is a crucial concern, from an ultimately liberal–pluralist political perspective, with how the cultural industries affect democratic processes and public life.

CRITICAL POLITICAL ECONOMY APPROACHES

Political economy approaches have more to offer than cultural and media economics and liberal-pluralist communication studies in terms of analysing power in relation to cultural production. Political economy is a general term for an entire tradition of economic analysis at odds with mainstream economics, in that it places much greater emphasis on ethical and normative questions, reflecting the roots of the discipline in moral philosophy. The term 'political economy' has been claimed not only by those on the political left who are critical of the sidelining of questions of power and conflict in mainstream economics. There are strong conservative traditions, too. Therefore some writers use the term **critical political economy** to distinguish their perspective from the work of classical political economists such as Adam Smith and David Ricardo and their later heirs.[6]

Critical political economy approaches to culture (or media or communications – the terms are often used indiscriminately in labelling this tradition) developed in the late 1960s among academic sociologists and political scientists concerned about what they saw as the dubious role of large corporations and states in cultural production. Critical political economy approaches to culture are often misunderstood, simplified or dismissed. Because such approaches are so heavily critical of media and cultural corporations and their allies in government, it is no surprise that many who work in media

---

6   See Mosco (1996: 22–69) for a detailed and informative analysis of political economy
    approaches in general, as a background to understanding critical political economy of
    communication.

institutions might be dismissive or hostile. More surprising perhaps is the animosity of many elsewhere to the left of them. (From now on, I shall use 'political economy' as shorthand to refer to 'critical political economy'; this is common in analysis of cultural industries).

One common misunderstanding among some analysts is to see political economy approaches as a version of orthodox cultural and media economics. In fact, political economies explicitly aim at challenging the lack of an adequate ethical perspective in the neoclassical paradigm discussed in the earlier section on economics. Peter Golding and Graham Murdock (2005: 61–6) distinguish political economy approaches to the media from mainstream economics approaches in four respects:

- Political economy approaches to the media are **holistic**, seeing the economy as interrelated with political, social and cultural life, rather than as a separate domain.
- They are **historical**, paying close attention to long-term changes in the role of state, corporations and the media in culture.
- They are 'centrally concerned with **the balance between capitalist enterprise and public intervention**' (p. 61).
- Finally, 'and perhaps most importantly', they go 'beyond technical issues of efficiency to **engage with basic moral questions of justice, equity and the public good**' (p. 61).

Golding and Murdock's is a significant definition of political economy approaches and they certainly clarify the difference between such approaches and cultural and media economics, but two further features will help to delineate the distinctiveness of this analytical tradition even more clearly.

- Political economy approaches see the fact that culture is produced and consumed under capitalism as a fundamental issue in explaining inequalities of power, prestige and profit. This emphasis in political economy work on capitalism and its negative effects should make it clear that, while you don't have to be a Marxist to work here, it helps.
- A major area of contribution from political economy approaches to the study of the cultural industries has been to put on to the intellectual agenda debates about the extent to which the cultural industries serve the interests of the wealthy and powerful. As a result, a central theme in political economy approaches has been the ownership and control of the cultural industries (see Chapters 2 and 6). Does ownership of the cultural industries by the wealthy and powerful ultimately, through their control of cultural industry organisations, lead to the circulation of texts that serve the interests of these wealthy and powerful owners and their governmental and business allies? This has been such an important debate that some writers, teachers and students tend, wrongly, to equate political economy approaches with the view that cultural industry organisations do indeed serve the interests of their owners in this

way when, in fact, many political economy writers are concerned precisely with addressing the difficulties and complexities surrounding
this issue.

WHICH POLITICAL ECONOMY?

It should be clear that the focus within political economy approaches on
ethical and political issues in relation to culture means that they will have
key contributions to make to this study, given the concerns outlined in the
Introduction. However, certain versions of the political economy of culture
provide much more scope for understanding what drives change/continu-
ity in the cultural industries than others. At this point, we need to delineate
political economy more carefully. This will also help us to counter some simplifications and misunderstandings surrounding the term.

   Proponents and opponents of a political economy of culture often portray the field as a single, unified approach. Vincent Mosco (1996: 82–134) has
provided a detailed account of the differences between the kinds of political
economy work developed in three geographical and political settings: North
America, Europe and 'The Third World' – that is, developing countries in
Asia, Latin America and Africa. I shall deal with important work from this
last bloc, on cultural dependency and media imperialism, in Chapter 8. Here,
though, I want to build on Mosco's useful division by discussing the tensions
between two particular strands of North American and European political
economy approaches.

- A tradition within North American political economy work exemplified by the work of Herbert Schiller, Noam Chomsky, Edward Herman
  and Robert McChesney. This **Schiller-McChesney tradition** has been
  extremely important in cataloguing and documenting the growth in
  wealth and power of the cultural industries and their links with politi-
  cal and business allies.
- The **cultural industries approach**, initiated in Europe by Bernard
  Miège (1989; see also Miège, 2000, for a more recent statement) and
  Nicholas Garnham (1990), among others, and continued by other
  European writers and writers based in other continents (Aksoy and
  Robins, 1992; Bolaño et al., 2004; Bouquillon and Combès, 2007;
  Bustamante, 2004; Driver and Gillespie, 1993; Ryan, 1992; Straw, 1990;
  Toynbee, 2000;).[7]

---

7 This division leaves out many important contributions to critical political economy
   work, such as those of James Curran, Michael Curtin, Peter Golding, Armand Mattelart, Eileen Meehan, Vincent Mosco, Graham Murdock, Thomas Streeter and Janet
   Wasko. The best work of these writers, cited at numerous points in this book, shares
   many of the major strengths of the cultural industries approach, while also pursuing
   distinctive agendas.

In the Introduction, I referred to the work of Bernard Miège, who helped to popularise the plural term 'cultural industries' (as opposed to Adorno and Horkheimer's singular 'The Culture Industry') as an example of an approach that allowed for complexity, contestation and ambivalence in the study of culture.[8] As my praise for Miège and Garnham's work there suggests, I think that the cultural industries approach has more to offer in terms of assessing and explaining change/continuity in the cultural industries than the Schiller-McChesney tradition. In my view, the cultural industries approach is better at dealing with the following elements, each of which I address below:

- Contradiction.
- The specific conditions of cultural industries.
- Tensions between production and consumption.
- Symbol creators.
- Information and entertainment.
- Historical variations in the social relations of cultural production.

Brief explanations of each now follow.

Contradiction

The Schiller-McChesney tradition emphasises strategic uses of power. There is no doubt that such strategic uses of power by businesses are common and it is wrong to dismiss the approach of Schiller and others as 'conspiracy theory' (an accusation sometimes levelled at political economy approaches in general). But in emphasising concerted strategy, this tradition underestimates the contradictions in the system. The cultural industries approach's emphasis on problems and contradictions, on the partial and incomplete process of commodifying culture, provides a more accurate picture of cultural production. It allows for contradiction *within* industrial, commercial cultural production, rather than assuming a polarity *between* corporations and non-profit 'alternative' producers, as in the Schiller-McChesney tradition.

The specific conditions of cultural industries

The cultural industries approach's greater ability to deal with contradiction stems from another important advantage: its ability to combine an interest in relations between general economy and cultural industries (which is a key concern in the Schiller-McChesney tradition) with an analysis of what

---

8 Some teachers and students tend to equate the cultural pessimism of Adorno and Horkheimer and some of their Frankfurt School colleagues with political economy, defining one by the other. However, as we saw in the Introduction, Miège founds his particular approach on a critique of Adorno and Horkheimer. For many in the Schiller-McChesney tradition, the theoretical concerns of the Frankfurt School seem to be more or less irrelevant.

distinguishes industrial cultural production from other forms of industrial production (which isn't). It was work within the cultural industries approach that provided the breakdown of the specific conditions of cultural production laid out in the Introduction.

Tensions between production and consumption

Although, as its name suggests, the cultural industries approach focuses on the supply side – on cultural production and circulation and their social and political contexts – it does not ignore the activity of audiences and users, which is a charge that is often levelled at political economy approaches and certain versions of media sociology. Instead, the cultural industries approach sees the business of cultural production as complex, ambivalent and contested largely because of certain problems derived from the way audiences behave. Production and consumption are not seen as separate entities, but as different moments in a single process. The connections and tensions between production and consumption are discussed only rarely in the Schiller-McChesney tradition.

Symbol creators

The processes of concentration, conglomeration and integration catalogued by the Schiller-McChesney tradition are significant (see Chapter 6 for further discussion), but key researchers rarely comment on how such issues of market structure affect the *organisation* of cultural production and the making of texts on an ordinary, everyday level. The cultural industries approach puts symbol creators – the personnel responsible for the creative input in texts, such as writers, directors, producers, performers – in the picture, whereas they are often absent in the Schiller-McChesney tradition. The cultural industries approach has emphasised the conditions facing cultural workers as a result of these processes.[9] Its attention to this important issue makes the cultural industries approach better equipped than the Schiller-McChesney tradition to assess the degree to which cultural production is organised in a socially just manner (see Chapter 2).

Information and entertainment

In the Schiller-McChesney tradition, as in liberal-pluralist communication studies, the primary concern is with information media. The cultural industries

---

9   Miège (1989), Garnham (1990) and Ryan (1992) were for many years unusual in paying serious attention to this issue. In the late 1990s, cultural studies writers, such as McRobbie (1998) and Ross (1998), began to address these questions. In the 2000s, there was a 'turn to cultural work' in the social sciences and humanities (see Banks, 2007; and Chapter 7, below).

approach has been more successful in the difficult task of addressing both information and entertainment.

Historical variations in the social relations of cultural production

Finally, both approaches are concerned very much with history (see, for example, McChesney, 1993) but the cultural industries approach is often more sensitive than the Schiller-McChesney tradition to historical variations in the social relations of cultural production and consumption – a concern that some of its writers derive from Raymond Williams's interventions in the historical sociology of culture (see Chapter 2).

SOCIOLOGY OF CULTURE AND ORGANISATIONAL AND MANAGEMENT STUDIES

On the basis of my comments above, and in the Introduction to this book, it should be clear by now that I find political economy approaches to culture useful, especially the cultural industries approach. However, even within the cultural industries approach, which is much more interested in the organisational dynamics of cultural production than the Schiller-McChesney tradition, there has been a lack of empirical attention to what happens in cultural industry *organisations*. A certain tradition of work in the sociology of culture (primarily based in the USA, and drawing on Weberian and interactionist traditions of analysis), the 'production of culture' perspective, has made important contributions in this respect. Recent years have seen a notable growth in the intertwined academic fields of management, business and organisational studies and some researchers in these fields have paid attention to cultural industries (see, for example, Lampel et al., 2006). Cultural industries research in these burgeoning disciplines has inherited this interest in organisations.

Some of this work can provide a valuable complement to political economy work on the cultural industries. One of the most useful contributions of the production of culture perspective was to enrich our notions of symbolic creativity. Instead of understanding culture as the product of supremely talented individuals, writers such as Howard Becker (1982) and Richard Peterson (1976) helped to make it clear that creative cultural and artistic work is the product of collaboration and a complex division of labour. Particularly useful in the present context is the work of Peterson and Berger (1971), Hirsch (1990[1972]) and DiMaggio (1977) on the distinctive characteristics of the cultural industries. There is important concordance with work in the cultural industries approach on the distinctive strategies of companies that produce texts. Hirsch's work, for example, informed my outline of the distinctive features of the cultural industries in the Introduction. Also valuable are detailed studies of particular industries, such as Coser et al.'s (1982) study of book publishing.

The work of these sociologists in the USA, developed in parallel to that of the French cultural industries writers already mentioned, was groundbreaking, but it is only when it is synthesised into a more comprehensive vision of how cultural production and consumption fit into wider economic, political and cultural contexts that an analysis of specific conditions of cultural production really produces its explanatory pay-off. The cultural industries are treated implicitly by some of the US organisational sociologists and their management studies heirs as isolated systems, cut off from political and sociocultural conflict. Issues of power and domination are sidelined. The conditions of creative workers are hardly registered, other than the admittedly important fact that they are granted more autonomy than workers in other industries. The world of the rip-off, the shady deal, the disparity between the glass skyscrapers of the multinational entertainment corporations and the struggle young artists and musicians endure to stay afloat financially is scarcely considered. As with communication studies, I think that these problems derive from the political perspectives underlying the work of these writers. There is undoubtedly a democratising impulse at work. The aim is to demystify creativity and to understand and question hierarchies of taste and value. Sociologists such as Howard Becker show an admirable interest in the resourcefulness of cultural producers in their everyday lives. However, while this is a valuable counter to easy, glib assumptions about our powerlessness in the face of giant cultural industry corporations, much of the sociology of culture and management studies seems, at times, insufficiently concerned with questions of power. As Paul Hirsch (1990[1972]: 643) put it in an article that has been highly influential in subsequent management and organisational studies, his organisational approach 'seldom enquires into the functions performed by the organization for the social system but asks, rather, as a temporary partisan, how the goals of the organization may be constrained by society'.[10] Acting as temporary partisans of media organisations would be a form of false objectivity for political economists.

RADICAL MEDIA SOCIOLOGY/MEDIA STUDIES

So, if the concerns of political economy with 'macro' questions of power need complementing by other approaches more attuned to the 'micro' level of what happens in the worlds of cultural production – both 'inside' culture-producing organisations and outside – we need to look elsewhere. Research that is more attuned to issues of power at the 'micro' level than those considered so

---

10 See Hirsch (2000) for his reflections on how influential this piece has been.

far can be found in radical media sociology and media studies, and also in cultural studies approaches (I shall come back to the latter approach shortly). I mean 'radical' here in the sense that these approaches see pernicious forms of power and inequality as being rooted in the very structure of contemporary societies rather than resulting from correctable aberrations, as in liberal–pluralist perspectives. From the early 1970s onwards, radical media sociology in the USA and the emergent discipline of media studies in Europe provided approaches that were complementary to the political economy work developing in parallel with them.

Some of the most significant work in the USA grew out of a Weberian sociological tradition and concentrated on how news programmes did not so much report reality as reflect the imperatives of news organisations (see, for example, Gans, 1979; Tuchman, 1978). According to this perspective, journalists worked autonomously, but their work was structured by bureaucratic requirements and routines. These routines were seen as producing texts that failed to address existing power relations adequately. The thrust of such work was echoed in important British studies of news (such as Schlesinger, 1978). Studies of entertainment were rarer, but, at their best, provided real insight into cultural industry dynamics. Todd Gitlin's book *Inside Prime Time* (1983), for example, showed, via interviews with television executives and reconstructions of the histories of these organisations, how the commercial imperatives of the networks led to conservatism in the texts produced.

One major contribution from radical sociology to analysing cultural production was that of the French sociologist Pierre Bourdieu (1930–2002). His work is useful to analysis of the cultural industries for a number of reasons, including his account of the development of the tensions between creativity and commerce noted in the Introduction. In *The Rules of Art* (1996), Bourdieu showed how, in the nineteenth century, the idea developed that painters and writers should be autonomous of political power and commercial imperatives. According to Bourdieu, this gradually created a particular structure of cultural production – one divided between large-scale production, for primarily short-term commercial products, and 'restricted' or small-scale production, where artistic success was the main goal (and where, for businesses, the hope was that artistic success would lead to long-term financial rewards). Bourdieu hardly dealt with popular culture at all and failed to show how the rise of the cultural industries affected the structure of the field of cultural production in the twentieth century, but his work has provided the fullest analysis available of the complex relations between creativity and commerce in cultural production.[11]

Radical sociological work, such as that of Gitlin and Bourdieu, is, to some extent, compatible with political economy approaches to culture. However, political economies attempt an overall understanding of the place of cultural

---

11 There is no space here to assess Bourdieu's work on cultural production adequately. See Hesmondhalgh (2006a) for futher discussion.

production within contemporary capitalism and empirical studies of cultural industry organisations have not been central to this tradition. The great benefit of such radical sociology is that, at its best, it links dynamics of power in the cultural industries with questions of meaning – questions regarding the kinds of texts that are produced by cultural industry organisations. The next section considers this question of texts and meanings in more detail.

THE PROBLEM OF TEXTS

Up until now I have been explaining why we need to find approaches to the cultural industries that adequately deal with questions of *power* in relation to cultural industry organisations. In the Introduction, I outlined a view of the cultural industries that placed a central emphasis on the particular products that they create, products that have an especially strong potential to influence our knowledge and understanding of the world. For example, do the products of the cultural industries serve the interests of powerful groups in societies, and therefore help to entrench existing inequalities? What approaches and theories might help us best to understand this aspect of the cultural industries? Liberal-pluralist communication studies has, for the most part, operated with a deficient view of texts. There is a branch of the discipline that analyses cultural outcomes using the methods of quantitative **content analysis**. The aim is to produce an objective, verifiable measure of meaning (Hesmondhalgh, 2006b). As John Fiske (1990: 137) points out, 'this can be a useful check to the more subjective, selective way in which we normally receive messages'. There is, however, an understanding of cultural content as a *message* or set of messages in the effects research that dominated the discipline for many years. A considerably more complex notion of *meaning* needs to be put into operation, one which recognises **polysemy** – that is, the ability of texts to be interpreted in a number of ways. We also need to take into account the aesthetic experiences brought about by texts – their capacity to engage or bore, please or alienate. To think about meaning, aesthetic experience and emotion means addressing questions of form as well as content. By 'form', I mean how texts look and sound, their stylistic properties as well as the stories they tell and the assertions they make. (In practice, form and content are never really separate as the one always affects the other.)

While liberal-pluralist communication studies has generally had a limited understanding of texts as 'content' or 'message', the production of culture perspective, with some exceptions (see Peterson, 1997), ignored the issue of textual meaning. Richard A. Peterson, for example, in outlining the production of culture perspective, was frank in admitting the approach's lack of interest in the form and content of cultural artefacts, but he claimed that an interest in production can complement such concerns (1976: 10). This suggests that the study of production has no effect on the study of texts – that the two are separate, autonomous domains of analysis. The challenge of the cultural industries, though (if my claims in the Introduction are correct) is to consider these relationships rather than ignore them. We need to think, for example, about how historical transformations in the way that culture is produced and consumed relate to changes in texts.

There is a lack of attention to textual analysis and meaning among writers drawn to political economy approaches to culture. For all its strengths, the work of Miège barely mentions questions of textual meaning and pleasure. Many of the essays in Garnham's *Capitalism and Communication* (1990) attack the tendency within media studies to 'privilege the text' and 'focus on questions of representation and ideology' (p. 1).[12] In the Schiller-McChesney tradition, the underlying assumption is that most texts produced by the cultural industries are conformist and conservative, but little systematic evidence is marshalled to support this assumption (for a problematic exception, see the 'propaganda model' of Herman and Chomsky, 1988). Indeed, the assumption is rarely made explicit. Texts, and the experiences, values, meanings and pleasures they afford their audiences, are an issue addressed much more by the set of approaches that I consider next.

SOME ACHIEVEMENTS AND LIMITATIONS OF CULTURAL STUDIES

Cultural studies is a diverse and fragmented field of study, but at its core is **the attempt to examine and rethink culture by considering its relationship to social power**. In the past, there was some hostility towards this interdisciplinary field from many of the approaches discussed above. In turn, some cultural studies writers were very negative about the above approaches, including political economy and radical media sociology. Yet cultural studies approaches, at their best, have much to offer in terms of aiding our understanding of meaning and cultural value. This can help fill gaps left by other approaches to the cultural industries – especially when it comes to questions of culture, creativity and texts, which are obviously central to the cultural industries. I begin by discussing some of the main contributions that cultural studies has made to understandings of culture and power, as well as some of the limitations of approaches that have sometimes (often inaccurately) been labeled as 'cultural studies'. I then turn to discuss some recent approaches to media production and media industries that have claimed to draw on cultural studies.

First, cultural studies has argued convincingly that **ordinary, everyday culture needs to be taken seriously**. This has meant questioning hierarchical ways of understanding culture to be found in public debate and in the more established humanities and social science disciplines. Cultural studies resists

---

12 Garnham's *Emancipation, the Media and Modernity* (2000) addressed the study of texts and symbolic forms in much greater detail than did his work in the 1980s and 1990s.

this focus on consecrated, 'high culture' texts. This has resulted in some analysts associated with cultural studies celebrating popular culture in an uncritical way (see below). However many others chose not to do so, and it may be that the term 'cultural studies' should not have been applied to such uncritical researchers: they were more like naïve sociologists or cultural commentators. Cultural studies at its best has insisted that we need to think broadly about all the different elements in a culture in relation to each other rather than decide in advance which parts need to be analysed and which do not. This broader conception of culture has an international dimension as well. As cultural studies became internationalised in the 1980s and 1990s, writers who were originally from outside the Euro-American cosmopolitan heartlands, including diasporic intellectuals such as Edward Said (1994) and Gayatri Spivak (1988), addressed the concept of culture in ways that recognised the complex legacy of colonialism. Because of this, the best cultural studies approaches can be seen as a considerable improvement on the often dismissive attitude to popular and non-Western culture to be found in some political economy and liberal-pluralist communication research. The best cultural studies work has achieved an in-depth, serious consideration of a much wider range of cultural experience than had been recognised in other traditions of writing about culture. Other anthropological and sociological approaches (including the empirical sociology of culture) had this democratising impulse, but cultural studies deals more fully with questions of symbolic power.

Second, **cultural studies has provided considerable refinement of what we might mean by that difficult term 'culture'**. In particular, it has put forward powerful criticisms of essentialist notions of culture that see the culture of a particular place and/or people as 'one, shared culture' (Hall, 1994: 323), as a bounded, fixed thing rather than as a complex space where many different influences combine and conflict. Again, work by writers outside the Euro-American metropolitan centre and migrants from former colonies to such centres has been vital in developing this understanding. Such challenges to traditional ways of thinking about culture have important implications in what follows. Through its richer understanding of the concept of culture, cultural studies has greatly advanced thinking about texts. Political economy writers and their allies in media studies and radical media sociology have been much concerned with the question of whose interests might be served by the texts produced by the cultural industries. Cultural studies, however, has extended this conception of interests beyond economic and political ones to include a strong sense of the politics involved in issues of recognition and identity. It has pointed out how certain texts and representational practices, while seemingly progressive, (further) serve to exclude and marginalise the relatively powerless.

Third, **cultural studies has raised vital political questions about representation, about 'who is speaking?', and about who has the authority to make pronouncements on culture**. Importantly, these questions are often applied with equal vigour to those who seek to criticise capitalism, patriarchy, heterosexism, white supremacy, imperialism and so on, as to those who defend them. Throughout much cultural studies writing, there is a relentless probing of authority in culture. Anthropologists working in cultural studies, for example, have scrutinised the apparent objectivity of the traditional ethnographer who observes the culture of indigenous, 'primitive' peoples from a relatively privileged position (see Clifford, 1988). In some respects, this echoes the questioning of positivism and objectivism in the 'interpretative turn' in social thought since the 1960s. At its worst, it involves a naïve constructivism and suspicion of anyone's right to say anything at all about any less powerful social group. Other fields of enquiry, such as black studies, queer studies and women's studies, have brought new voices into cultural studies and raised serious and important questions about the politics of speaking from one particular subject position (for example, white, private school-educated, male) about the cultural practices of others.

Fourth, **cultural studies has forefronted issues of subjectivity, identity, discourse and pleasure in relation to culture**. It has enormously enriched our understanding of how judgements of cultural value might relate to the politics of social identity, especially class, gender, ethnicity and sexuality. This is not just a matter of saying that taste is a product of social background (which is the approach that the empirical sociology of culture has tended to take). Rather, cultural studies explores the complex ways in which systems of aesthetic value feed into cultural power. Whose voices are heard within a culture and whose voices are marginalised? Which (and whose) forms of pleasure are sanctioned and which (whose) are felt to be facile, banal or even dangerous? These are questions about discourse, about the way that meanings and texts circulate in society. They also concern subjectivity and identity and the often irrational and unconscious processes by which we become who we are. These questions – sidelined in many of the approaches to the cultural industries discussed above – have been investigated with great vigour by cultural studies writers, who have pointed out that the most dismissed and reviled forms of culture are still those consumed by relatively powerless groups in society. Feminist work on such forms as soaps (Geraghty, 1991) and women's magazines (Hermes, 1995) was significant in this respect. There was a strong interest in understanding the experiences and interpretations of audience members: **active audiences**, including the study of fans and fandom, became a central theme in one type of cultural studies.[13]

Cultural studies, at its best, offers potentially valuable tools for the analysis of culture in relation to social power. Nevertheless, some analysis of media and popular culture, which has either claimed to be taking a cultural studies perspective or has been labeled in this way by others, has developed highly problematic conceptions of culture, and of cultural production. In analysing the rich political potential of popular culture, and the ability of 'ordinary people' to engage with the media on terms outside the control of the cultural industries,

---

13 This was sometimes closer to the interests of mainstream communication studies than some authors seemed to realise.

some analysts, in the 1980s/1990s heyday of postmodernist cultural theory, undoubtedly risked lapsing into an uncritical celebration of contemporary popular culture (such as Fiske, 1987; see also McGuigan, 1992, for a critique of such 'uncritical populism'). This was hardly the same kind of cultural studies as that practised by writers such as Raymond Williams, Stuart Hall and Edward Said.

The legacy of such populist analysis can be found in various writing on the media and popular culture today. The intention is often a good one – to complicate simplistic dismissals of commercial culture, whether from audiences, journalists, or other researchers. Such commercial culture may, the neo-populists suggest, be considerably more fruitful, empowering and enriching than its critics make out. Some of the research at least makes an effort to talk to audiences about their experiences of, for example, reality television (Hill, 2005). But other contributions risk massively overstating the democratization of the media that was made possible by the expansion of the cultural industries and by associated developments in information technology. John Hartley, for example, has written provocatively about a process of 'democratainment' in the proliferation of media and the increasing presence of 'ordinary' people in their products (see Hartley, 1999: Chapter 12). As Graeme Turner (2010: 16) has noted, the democratic part of Hartley's neologism is 'an occasional and accidental consequence of the "entertainment" part and its least systemic component'.[14] Perhaps the main legacy of postmodernist cultural populism is to be found in a more recent generation of cultural studies writers who celebrate the emancipatory effects of digital technologies (for example Jenkins, 2006). These cultural studies writers are part of a powerful movement of **digital optimism**, along with researchers from other disciplines, such as management and business studies (Shirky, 2008), law (Benkler, 2006) and sociology (Castells, 2008).

CULTURAL STUDIES APPROACHES TO MEDIA INDUSTRIES AND MEDIA PRODUCTION

In spite of its potential contributions to understanding culture, the application of cultural studies approaches to cultural industries or even to cultural production was relatively sparse until the 2000s. Recently, however, a number of new approaches have emerged, with a variety of different relationships to cultural studies, and a mix of potential contributions and drawbacks.

---

14 Graeme Turner may himself be described as a cultural studies researcher, and his excellent critique of 'the demotic turn' in research on media and popular culture (Turner, 2010) suggests that some of the best critiques of uncritical cultural populism may come from those who have engaged most fully with cultural studies debates, from within.

Industry produces culture, culture produces industry

One older strand of research ably stressed reciprocal relationships between cultural industries and broader currents of culture within a society. Keith Negus (1999) developed a perspective that claimed that while it was true that 'an industry produces culture' it was also the case that 'culture produces an industry' (p. 14).[15] For example, this perspective assumed, in Simon Frith's words (2000: 27), that

> popular music isn't the effect of a popular music industry; rather, the music industry is an aspect of popular music culture ... [T]he music industry cannot be treated as being somehow apart from the sociology of everyday life – its activities are culturally determined.

A cultural studies approach of this kind, then, might involve examining how prevailing patterns of cultural behaviour and power are reflected in the cultural industries themselves. The perspective is a sociological one, and there is some overlap here with the sociology of culture work discussed earlier, such as that of Howard Becker. But there is more emphasis than in sociology of culture on questions of power and inequality, especially ethnicity and gender. For example, Negus, in his (1992, 1999) studies of the recording industry in the UK and USA, showed how prevailing concepts of gender and 'race' in society at large affected the operations of recording-industry companies, and therefore shaped what recordings were made available to the buying public, and how they were marketed.

'Production studies': the cultural studies of media industries approach

A major development in recent media industries research has been the arrival of a new generation of research that is consistent with this 'culture produces industry' approach, but which builds on it using other theories and takes it in new directions. It has already produced some rich studies (see, for example, Caldwell, 2008; Havens, 2006; Mayer et al., 2009). Some indication of the approach is provided by the introduction to Mayer, Banks and Caldwell's introduction to their collection of essays on 'cultural studies of media industries'. **Production studies** – by which they mean the cultural studies approach that they are advocating – 'borrow theoretical insights from the social sciences and humanities, but, perhaps most importantly, they take the lived realities of people involved in media production as the

---

15 Negus is using the term 'culture' here in its broader anthropological sense. See my discussion of definitions in the Introduction for some of the problems associated with this interpretation of the term.

subjects for theorizing production as culture' (p. 4). According to Mayer, Banks and Caldwell, the empirical data gathered by such studies include routines and rituals, and also the political and economic forces that shape roles and technologies, as well as the distribution of resources according to cultural and demographic differences. Yet the research questions all this boils down to are rather narrower, and fundamentally concern *representation*: 'How do media producers represent themselves given the paradoxical importance of media in society? How do we, as researchers, then represent those varied and contested representations?' (p. 4) These questions of representation are important, and have been a central issue in cultural studies, as mentioned above (see Hall, 1997). The focus on representation is what distinguishes this new cultural studies of media industries approach from sociological approaches more generally. But to make representation the main object of inquiry in the way that Mayer, Banks and Caldwell suggest they want to do may ultimately serve to marginalise the 'lived realities' that the authors claim are also central to their approach. Moreover, like Caldwell's otherwise extremely impressive study of the narratives and rituals of film and television workers in Los Angeles (2008), this account of cultural studies of production leaves us wondering how we are ultimately supposed to *evaluate* what is being observed.

I should make clear that my point is not aimed against ethnography or sociological fieldwork. This is emphatically not an argument for privileging the macro over the micro. The present book has primarily macro aims, given that it tries to cover historical change in the cultural industries. But macro and micro need to be integrated in studies of the cultural industries. In other research I have observed and interviewed workers, and I draw on ethnographic research by others at various points in this book. The issue is how a particular research project – such as cultural studies of media industries – might articulate theory and evidence, the micro and the macro, the empirical and the normative.[16] These are difficult questions, and it may be that the cultural studies of media industries approach will develop answers to them in the future. This is, after all, a new (and welcome) addition to analysis of cultural industries and cultural production.

Digital optimism

Another very different strand of cultural studies research on production inherits the emphasis on audience activity in 1980s and 1990s communication and cultural studies and applies it to the digitalising media of the early twenty first century. The most able exponent of this approach is Henry Jenkins, whose earlier work examined the activities of fans. In his book, *Convergence Culture*, Jenkins analysed a wide range of practices made

---

16 The easy answer to this is to invoke the idea of 'middle range theory'. See Alford (1998) for an explanation of why this is inadequate.

possible by new digital technologies and which are 'enabling new forms of participation and collaboration' (2006: 256).

In this respect, Jenkins is one of a number of intelligent digital optimists who celebrate the democratising possibilities of digital technologies. As indicated earlier, this digital optimism now extends way beyond cultural studies. The populists and optimists have been joined by a powerful army of journalists, authors, bloggers and academics from other disciplines, all of whom have inherited the countercultural belief that computers have the potential to liberate knowledge and creativity. This makes digital optimism a formidable cultural force (see Chapter 2 and especially Chapter 9, where I shall discuss this at much greater length).

Creative industries analysis

In the 1990s, cultural studies in Australia took a particular turn. Researchers influenced by the French historian Michel Foucault began to apply critical analysis to policymaking in the field of culture. The approach derived from Foucault's analysis of what distinguished modern forms of government from previous forms. There was a particular interest in the way in which concepts and phenomena such as citizenship and therapy, seemingly benign, were bound up in distinctively modern forms of power. The approach claimed to offer a distinctive model of power, which saw it as more dispersed and less concentrated than did Marxist theory. The leading exponent of this approach in cultural studies was Tony Bennett, who, to give just one example of his research, analysed the historical development of museums in Foucauldian terms.[17] Unusually for cultural studies, this approach was pragmatic in that it sought dialogue with policymakers, and was explicitly committed to programmes of reform.

In the early 2000s, followers of this approach (though not Bennett) turned their attention to new forms of government policy which sought to expand the role of the cultural industries. These policies were often rebranded 'creative industries' for reasons that we shall explore in Chapter 5. This new generation of quasi-Foucauldian researchers (by this I mean that they were influenced by the French historian Michel Foucault but in a strange and rather uneven way) combined postmodernist cultural populism with the concepts and language of digital optimism(see Hartley, 2005). This school has tended to pay considerably more attention to pragmatism and policy than to the critique of modern forms of power associated with Foucault and many of his followers. The result has been a distinctive and controversial form of cultural studies analysis which has contributed to the increasing popularity of the term 'creative industries', as discussed in Chapter 5. (See also Hesmondhalgh, 2007: 148–9, 2009a).

---

17 See Bennett (1998) for a major collection of essays and McGuigan (1996) for a critique of this kind of approach as applied to cultural policy.

Cultural economy

Finally, an interesting cultural studies perspective on economic life known as 'cultural economy' (Amin and Thrift, 2004; du Gay and Pryke, 2002) is sometimes understood as an analysis of the cultural industries, but, in fact, most of the researchers who employ this term have broader ambitions than this. Their aim is to apply post-structuralist cultural studies insights to production and to economic life in general; Foucault was an influence here too. Cultural economy, in this sense, sees the realm of economic practice – in all its various forms, such as markets and economic and organisational relations – as formatted and framed by economic discourses (du Gay and Pryke, 2002: 2), and makes this the starting point for analysis rather than placing it as a supplement to existing economic or political-economic analysis. This certainly does not preclude analysis of the cultural industries and some work has been published under this banner, but there has been rather too little of such work to constitute a distinctive approach to the cultural industries (as opposed to an approach to production or the economy in general). However, cultural economy raises issues about how to ground critique of developments in the cultural industries. The cultural economy approach encourages us to question the easy dichotomies that some political economists and sociologists of culture draw between the realm of culture and the increasing encroachment of economics on that realm. However, the deconstruction of such binary oppositions can neglect important political and ethical questions with regard to relations between culture and commerce. For example, are there potentially harmful effects to commodification? All societies reserve some aspects of the world – nature, personhood or culture, for example – from commodification. What aspects of culture might contemporary societies shelter from exchange and private ownership and on what grounds? (These issues are fruitfully pursued, for example, by John Frow, 1997, himself a cultural studies analyst. I return to them in relation to cultural production in Chapter 2.)

THE APPROACH TAKEN HERE

In the respects discussed above, and others too, cultural studies has made an enormous though at times problematic contribution to our understanding of culture and power, and more recently to studies of cultural production. In the 1980s and 1990s, cultural studies was attacked not only by conservatives who questioned its emphasis on respect for cultural difference, but also by liberals and radicals. In fact, some of the strongest attacks on cultural studies came from fellow leftists in political economy and radical media sociology who often accused it of a secret complicity with conservatism (see, for example, Gitlin, 1998; Miller and Philo, 2000, and others). Cultural studies gave as good as it got and, again, the main targets were often potential allies on the political left. The result was a series of polemics, which helped to create a perception, at least in the research fields of media, communication and cultural studies, that critical analysis was evenly divided between two camps – political economy and cultural studies. This idea was reproduced not only in published books and articles but also in countless everyday references in seminar rooms, conference bars and so on, along the lines of 'political economy does X, cultural studies does Y'. Even when some writers claimed that they want to move beyond the split, they then proceeded to attack, from a position strongly identified with one camp, a caricatured version of the other, thus maintaining the myth (such as Grossberg, 1995).

In the two previous editions of this book, I took issue with this polarisation, as a way of explaining my own synthesis of approaches to culture and power. My claim was that **political economy versus cultural studies was neither an accurate nor useful way to characterise approaches to the media and popular culture**. The opposition simplified a whole web of disagreements and conflicts between the various different approaches to culture that we might take down to just two players. Contrary to some naïve misperceptions, political economy is not the same thing as 'studies of production' and cultural studies does not consist of 'empirical studies of audiences' or 'studies of texts'. All this should be apparent from the above discussions. In fact, the issue was never really cultural studies versus political economy – as if the field of enquiry was divided neatly between two approaches. The real goal of discussions about theory and method in relation to media and popular culture, I pointed out, should be to understand the potential contributions and limitations of the key approaches, and to synthesise the best aspects of them. Discussions organised around simple dichotomies such as political economy versus cultural studies were never likely to achieve this goal.

Thankfully this crude opposition now appears to have faded. Its prominence in the 1980s and 1990s perhaps reflected the tensions between two different kinds of leftist politics, one based primarily on issues of social identity, such as gender, ethnicity and sexuality, the other on economics, internationalist politics and the redistribution of resources (the latter sometimes portrayed as Marxist when it could just as easily be social-democratic).[18] For some, this concern with social identity was a retreat from the project of building coalitions to resist the economic and political forces that bring about oppression in the first place.

We now live in different times, where many analysts recognise the central importance of geopolitical and financial power (issues almost entirely neglected by the best-known versions of cultural studies) *and* social identity. The fading of the dichotomy may also reflect that people interested in the study of the media and popular culture might now divide their sense of the field more by topic than by (often caricatured) theoretical approach: political communication, media industries, media and gender/sexuality, international communication, journalism, internet studies, television studies, film studies, and so on.

---

18 See Hall (1992) for an account of cultural studies that portrays it as a reaction by the left against certain forms of Marxism, especially those influenced by Stalinism.

The political economy versus cultural studies dichotomy was discussed in some detail in the previous two editions, but I have cut this here, and any readers who may be interested are referred to either of those previous editions (Hesmondhalgh, 2002, 2007). Instead, I deal more briefly with some longstanding tensions and dilemmas arising from differences in approach to culture and the cultural industries. I try to dispel one or two persistent confusions relevant to analysis of cultural industries, and indicate my own theoretical and methodological approach in this book.

- Analysts have often identified a number of moments or processes that are particularly relevant to the study of media and popular culture. The most often used terms are: production, audiences, texts (sometimes the terms 'representation' or 'content' are used instead), and policy/ regulation. Nearly everyone emphasises the significance of seeing these moments or processes in relation to each other (see du Gay et al., 1997 on 'the circuit of culture' – reproduced and discussed in Hesmondhalgh, 2002: 43), even if they believe that certain moments or processes have more causal effect on media in general (see Toynbee, 2008). Nearly everyone recognises that the best way of understanding the media and popular culture is to address all these different moments and processes, even if analysts choose to focus on a particular one or two.
- Studies of cultural, media and creative industries tend to focus on dynamics of production and the way in which government policy and regulation might shape production. Some focus on these dynamics in relation to texts as well. This is the approach taken in the present book.
- The cultural industries have a dual role – as 'economic' systems of production and 'cultural' producers of texts. Production is profoundly cultural and texts are determined by economic factors (among others). If we want to criticise the forms of culture produced by the cultural industries and the ways that they produce them, then we need to take account of both the politics of *redistribution*, focused on issues of political economy, and the politics of *recognition*, focused on questions of cultural identity (Fraser, 1997).
- Some theoretical and methodological dilemmas can't easily be reconciled, however. A significant split between different types of research concerns epistemology – the understandings of how we gain knowledge that underlie our attempt to seek understanding – and method. Put crudely, some analysts, including political economy writers, tend in questions of epistemology towards realism: the 'assumption that there is a material world external to our cognitive processes which possesses specific properties ultimately accessible to our understanding' (Garnham, 1990: 3). This view is crucially linked to the view that we can achieve objective knowledge of that independent reality. Cultural studies writers take a variety of more constructivist and subjectivist epistemological paths, in some cases aiming to gain greater objectivity by recognition of the effect of the observer on the observed (see Couldry, 2000: 12–14, on feminist epistemology), while in other cases, there is

a radical scepticism about truth claims. This is especially true in post-structuralist and postmodernist approaches. The approach in the present book is built on a critical realist perspective (see Hesmondhalgh and Toynbee, 2008; Sayer, 2000).

• Another difficult theoretical problem concerns explanation and the problem of economic *reductionism* – the attribution of complex cultural events and processes, such as the form of the Hollywood film industry or the nature of television soap operas or the development of television as a medium of communication, to a single political-economic cause, such as the interests of the social class that controls the means of production or the requirement within capitalism for owners and executives to make profits. There are indeed such economically reductionist accounts, which fail to do justice to the complex interplay of factors involved in culture, but the fact that some political-economic accounts are reductionist is no argument against political-economic analysis per se. An important concept has been *determination*, generally used in the Marxist tradition to refer to the process by which objective conditions might fix causally what happens. There are dubious Marxist accounts of determination, which portray forces as leading inevitably to something happening; and there are more useful accounts that examine how certain conditions might set limits and exert pressures on events and processes (see Williams, 1977: 83–9, for an exposition of this distinction). A good analysis will set processes of economic determination alongside other processes and pressures in culture and think about how they interact. Debates about economic determination and reductionism have produced the most significant tensions between political economy and other approaches. An eclectic methodology, allied to a radical social-democratic recognition of the existence of structures of power, inequality and injustice, might provide the possibility of building on the already greater convergence between different critical approaches. The more pragmatic option advocated here involves identifying particular moments where economic factors are strongly determinant and moments where other factors, such as those listed above, need to be stressed more. This, as we shall see, will be a crucial aspect of Chapter 3, which sets about explaining change and continuity in the cultural industries.

* * *

In this chapter, I have concentrated on identifying the achievements and pinpointing the limitations of the main approaches relevant to study of the cultural industries. I have done so by considering how these approaches might best help us to understand the issues identified in the Introduction as central to the book as a whole: the relationships between culture/creativity and power, and between change and continuity. I also outlined my approach, which might be summarised as **a sociological version of political economy, heavily informed by certain aspects of cultural studies and media studies**.

RECOMMENDED AND FURTHER READING[19]

The approach outlined in this chapter relies on an understanding of the importance of the relationships between culture, society and democracy that has been articulated in different ways by a number of writers. There is only space to mention some of them here.

Raymond Williams remains a key inspiration for anyone concerned about the relationships between culture, society and power. His early work such as *Culture and Society* (1958) and *The Long Revolution* (1961) is most often cited, but I often suggest starting with the late essays, such as *Towards 2000* (1983) and *What I Came to Say* (1989). Paul Jones's *Raymond Williams's Sociology of Culture* (2004) is a good though formidable overview.

James Curran has synthesised approaches from political economy, communication studies and sociology of culture, while also being attentive to cultural studies. His books *Media and Power* (2002) and *Media and Democracy* (2011) collect some notable interventions. The collection Curran edited with the late Michael Gurevitch, called *Mass Media and Society* in its first four editions and retitled *The Media and Society* for its 5th edition (2010) is, in my view, the best introductory collection of serious writing about the media.

C. Edwin Baker was a legal scholar, highly influenced by the political economy approach, who wrote a brilliant series of books on key issues related to the cultural industries and their role in contemporary societies: *Advertising and a Democratic Press* (1994), *Media, Markets and Democracy* (2002), and *Media Concentration and Democracy* (2007).

Amongst the most rewarding contemporary cultural studies writers on questions relevant to the cultural industries are Graeme Turner (such as *Understanding Celebrity*, 2004, and *Ordinary People and the Media*, 2010); Andrew Ross (*No Collar*, 2003; *Nice Work If You Can Get It*, 2009); and Angela McRobbie (*The Aftermath of Feminism*, 2008, but see also early and important essays on cultural labour, such as McRobbie, 2002). The best introduction to cultural studies I know is still Nick Couldry's *Inside Culture* (2000). Don Robotham's *Culture, Society and Economy* (2005) offers a trenchant critique of how cultural studies and social theory have failed to analyse economic power.

A very good recent collection of work in the political economy tradition is Dwayne Winseck and Dal Yong Jin's *The Political Economies of Media* (2011). This has an excellent introductory essay by Winseck (2011). Janet Wasko, Graham Murdock and Helena Sousa's *The Handbook of Political Economy of Communications* (2011) contains a number of good pieces. A good book-length overview of the political economy approach is Vincent Mosco's *The Political Economy of Communication* (1st edition, 1996), though I found the (2009) second edition's treatment of more recent developments a little disappointing.

---

19 Full bibliographical details of works suggested in the Selected and Further Reading section that follows each main chapter can be found in the References at the end of the book.

Peter Golding and Graham Murdock have provided a series of vital contributions to analysis of the media and culture, both individually and together. These go back to essays published in the 1970s (Murdock and Golding, 1974, 1977) and an overview of the changing communications field in 1977 (Murdock and Golding, 1977). In 1991, they published a substantially new version ('Culture, communications and political economy') of their 1977 essay, which they then revised three times, in 1996, 2000 and 2005 (see Golding and Murdock, 2005). Changes in the agenda of the critical political economy tradition can be traced across these contributions.

Although my preference is clearly for the 'cultural industries' variants of political economy, the Schiller-McChesney school (or, as Winseck (2011: 21–3) has it, the 'monopoly capital and digital capitalism' schools) has a great deal to offer the analysis of cultural industries. Examples include McChesney's book on *The Political Economy of Media* (2008).

A good textbook sympathetic to the new cultural studies of media industries is Timothy Havens and Amanda Lotz's *Understanding Media Industries* (2011). Jennifer Holt and Alisa Perren's *Media Industries: History, Theory and Method* (2009) and Vicki Mayer, Miranda J. Banks and John Thornton Caldwell's *Production Studies* (2009) are good collections. The focus of all these books is very much on television and film.

For general introductions to the study of media, see Gillespie (2006) on audiences, Gillespie and Toynbee (2006) on *Analysing Media Texts*, and Hesmondhalgh (2006b) on media production.

2

Cultural Industries in the Twentieth Century: The Key Features

The place of cultural production in economies
    and societies   66
A question of commodification   68
Business ownership and structure   71
Organisation, management and creative autonomy   77
  Creativity and commerce relations   81
The quality of cultural work   83
Internationalisation and domination by the USA   85
Dominant technologies   87
Textual change   88
  Choice, diversity, multiplicity   88
  Quality   89
  Texts, social justice and the serving of interests   89

This chapter begins the story of how the cultural industries have changed by analysing how the cultural industries developed in the twentieth century. It lays out a number of key features of the cultural industries between the end of the first world war and the 1970s.

Laying out these key features provides a framework that will allow for the assessment of changes and continuities in the cultural industries in the rest of the book, for the discussion of each aspect generates two types of question to be answered in Part Three.

- The first concerns the *extent* of change. Do changes in the major aspects of cultural production in the period that mainly concerns us (1980 onwards) represent fundamental alterations or are they merely surface changes, underpinned by continuity?
- The second type of question concerns the *evaluation* of change and continuity in these different aspects.

Table 2.1 Aspects of cultural production and questions about change and continuity

Aspects of cultural production in the twentieth century	Questions concerning extent of change since 1980	Questions concerning evaluation of change	Chapter in which aspects and questions are discussed
Business ownership and structure	To what extent have changes in conglomeration and integration led to recognisably new and distinct forms of ownership and structure?	What are the effects of the growth in size and power of cultural industry corporations on cultural production and wider society?	6
The place of cultural production in economies and societies	To what extent have the cultural industries become increasingly important in national economies and global business?	What are the implications of a further commoditisation of culture?	6 (but Chapter 5 on copyright is an important introduction)
Organisation and creative autonomy	To what extent have the dynamics of the distinctive organisational form of cultural production changed?	Has creative autonomy been expanded or diminished? What changes have there been in the extent to which creative workers within the cultural industries determine how their work will be edited, promoted, circulated?	7
Cultural work and its rewards	To what extent have the cultural labour market and systems of reward for cultural workers changed?	Have the rewards and working conditions of creative workers – and, indeed, other workers in the cultural industries – improved during this time?	7
Internationalisation and domination of cultural trade by USA	To what extent have international cultural flows changed sufficiently for us to speak of a new era in cultural production and circulation? To what extent has the USA retained its international cultural dominance?	Does the increasingly global reach of the largest firms mean an exclusion of voices from cultural markets? What opportunities are there for cultural producers from outside the 'core' areas of cultural production to gain access to new global networks of cultural production and consumption?	8
Dominant technologies	To what extent have digitalisation and the internet transformed cultural production and consumption?	Have digitalisation and the internet opened up access to the means of cultural production and circulation? Are barriers between production and consumption breaking down?	9 and 10
Texts	To what extent are the texts produced by the cultural industries growing more or less diverse?	Has the overall quality of texts declined? Do the cultural industries increasingly serve the interests of themselves and the wealthy and powerful in society?	11

The questions relating to each aspect are then addressed in Chapters 6–10. Table 2.1 provides a summary.

THE PLACE OF CULTURAL PRODUCTION IN ECONOMIES AND SOCIETIES

The first task is to consider the changing place of commercial cultural production in economies and societies. This will enable us to establish a rough periodisation and some crucial terms. My concern here is with the longer-term history of cultural production. Understanding this will allow us to think about recent changes and continuities carefully and precisely.

A good starting point for thinking about long-term historical change in cultural production is provided by Raymond Williams in his book *Culture*. Adapting Williams (1981: 38–56), we can identify three **eras** in the development of cultural production in Europe (which have parallels elsewhere), each of them named after the main *form* of social relations between symbol creators and wider society prevailing at the time.

- *Patronage and artisanal*
  The term 'patronage' refers to a variety of systems prevalent in the West from the Middle Ages until the nineteenth century. Poets, painters, musicians and others would, for example, be 'retained' by aristocrats or the Church or protected and supported by them. Such systems were dominant until the early nineteenth century and can still be found today. An 'artisan' is a skilled worker or craftsperson who works largely under his or her own direction. Such workers, in their classic form, would sell goods directly to purchasers. These also still exist today (see Box 2.1).

- *Market professional*
  From the early nineteenth century onwards, however, 'artistic works' were increasingly offered for sale and bought in order to be owned. Symbolic creativity, in other words, increasingly came to be organised as a market. Under this system, more and more work was sold not directly to the public but indirectly, via intermediaries. These were either distributors, such as booksellers, or 'productive intermediaries' (Williams, 1981: 45), such as publishers. This made for a much more complex division of labour in cultural production than before, even if many symbol creators still worked as artisans – that is, largely under their own direction. By the late nineteenth century and throughout the early twentieth century, both distributive and productive intermediaries were becoming much more highly capitalised than before as leisure time and disposable income expanded in industrialised countries. Successful symbol creators achieved 'a form of professional independence' (Williams, 1981: 48) and, increasingly, were paid in the form of royalties.

- *Corporate professional*
  Finally, from the early twentieth century, but expanding enormously after 1950, there was a new phase that Williams calls 'corporate professional'. The commissioning of works became professionalised and more organised. Increasing numbers of people also became direct employees of cultural companies, on retainers and contracts. Alongside older activities, such as writing books, performing music and acting out plays, new media technologies appeared – most notably radio, film and television. Sometimes these new technologies included and altered the older types of cultural activity, other times they produced entirely new ones (such as the drama serial or the situation comedy). Alongside direct sales, advertising became an important new means of making money for creative work and an increasingly important cultural form in itself.

The term 'corporate professional' refers to social relations between symbol creators on the one hand, and patrons or businesses on the other, but the key point for the argument of this book is that it can be used to describe **an era of cultural production**. This involves a new social and economic significance for commercial cultural production in modern societies from the early twentieth century onwards, and in a moment I shall discuss this crucial point further. It also serves, though, as a term that can help us to periodise change across the other aspects addressed in this chapter and Part Three (those summarised in Table 2.1).

I wish Williams hadn't used the term 'corporate' in this context. To the modern ear, it sounds as though the chief issue is the rise of large private companies. Important as large companies are in cultural production from the early twentieth century onwards, Williams, in fact, intends the term in an older sense: 'a number of people in a unified group'. To avoid such confusion, I want to use a modified term – *complex professional* – to label this form (and stage or era) of cultural production. I prefer the word 'complex' because one of the most crucial features of this era was the increasing complexity of the division of labour involved in making texts.

Box 2.1   Understanding transitions

The complex professional form dominated cultural production from the 1950s onwards, but market professional and even patronage-based forms of cultural production continued to exist alongside the features of this dominant form, together with non-market or less marketised forms of cultural institution such as state and public service broadcasting companies. We can think of the cultural industries from the 1950s onwards as being composed of three different forms, each corresponding to terms developed by Williams (1977: 121–7) to refer to the historical variability of any period under examination in an 'epochal' analysis – that is, analysis of the characteristics of a particular time.

(Continued)

(Continued)

- The *complex professional form* was the *dominant* way in which production was organised, which is why it gives its name to the whole era.
- *Patronage and market professional forms*, dominant in previous eras, continued to exist in *residual* forms. Sponsorship of artists is one important and growing contemporary example. Importantly, though, artisanal relations also exist in residue. This situation is produced by, and in turn reinforces, the creative autonomy ceded to cultural workers, as discussed in the Introduction and later in this chapter.
- *State and public service broadcasting* had emerged in the 1920s and 1930s and continued to expand across the world with the spread of television in the 1960s. It can be seen as an *emergent* form within the early stages of the complex professional era.

I therefore use the term 'complex professional' as a heuristic device to describe the whole era of cultural production from the 1950s onwards, but, in fact, it refers to a mix of different forms.

So, we have established, using a periodisation based on Williams, that, beginning in the early twentieth century, but expanding and accelerating as the century progresses, cultural production gained a new economic and social significance. One of the questions we need to ask, then, in considering change and continuity in cultural production since the 1980s, is whether cultural production has become even more significant. One way to tackle this broader issue is to ask **to what extent have the cultural industries become increasingly important in national economies and global business?** In Chapter 6, I put forward the view that they have, slowly and steadily, become more important, but not to the extent that many commentators claim (see pages 216–221).

A QUESTION OF COMMODIFICATION

How might we *evaluate* the changing social significance of the cultural industries? This is a vast terrain, but one way of apprehending it is to step back and ask what major changes have taken place in cultural production over the last four or five centuries. Writers from a wide variety of perspectives – economists, Marxist political economists and some cultural studies writers – would want to emphasise *industrialisation* and *commodification*. As Lacroix and Tremblay (1997) note, these terms are used 'so often that authors often do not even bother to define them' (p. 68). *Industrialisation* involves significant capital investment, mechanised production and the division of labour, but *commodification* involves transforming objects and services into commodities. This commodification is 'a more encompassing process than industrialization' (p. 69) and does not necessarily entail the use of industrial production techniques. The two processes are intertwined but I emphasise commodification here. This is partly because, as Lacroix and Tremblay say, it is a more encompassing process than industrialisation, but also because such an emphasis can help to throw further light on the complexities and ambivalences of cultural production under capitalism, as discussed in the Introduction and my survey of approaches in Chapter 1.

What does it mean to transform something into a commodity? At its most basic level, it involves producing things not only for use but also for *exchange*.[1] With the development of capitalism, this involved exchange in markets increasingly extended over time and space, with money as the medium allowing for such extended exchange. This was crucially linked to systems of consumption and production. Production for extended exchange required the investment of capital and paying wages for labour. When commodities were bought, this involved private and exclusive ownership rather than collective access. When feudalism gave way to capitalism, many things became commodified – land and labour among them. John Frow (1997: 143–4) notes that even if we rightly resist the teleological notion of capitalism as necessarily involving endless commodification (for there has been some de-commodification, too, such as the sentimentalisation of love and the abolition of slavery), capitalism can nevertheless be understood as a system involving a continual, if uneven, extension of commodification.

The problem is how to judge commodification – and this is central to how we judge capitalism itself. This is a big question and one that some writers have, therefore, considered off-limits, but it still needs to be asked. Some Marxists, and other writers, too, in criticising capitalism, have made simplistic and sometimes romantic assumptions, opposing the commodities of capitalism to visions of a past or future society based on non-commodities. Other writers, including Marx himself, have provided a much more complex analysis,[2] seeing commodification as ambivalent, as enabling and productive, but also limiting and destructive. Various writers, including Frow (1997: 102–217), have engaged with anthropological perspectives that show how other principles for the exchange of goods, such as gift exchange (famously analysed by the French social theorist Marcel Mauss), might be compromised by hidden motives. Commodification produces massive proliferations

---

1 It can, of course, be used to mean basic goods, such as copper, oil and so on, but that is not the way in which I am using the term here.
2 It is a mistake to think that Marx was simply 'against' commodification. Marx was concerned with a number of aspects of modern commodities – most notably the way in which the immense collection of commodities that surround us conceal the labour that goes into them.

of goods, but there are many problems associated with this proliferation. To take just two here, on the consumption side, there is the problem that commodification spreads a notion of ownership and property as the right to exclude others, leading to huge inequalities, the promotion of private, individual interest and a threat to collective action for the common good; on the production side, there is the problem that labour goes unrecognised and is systematically under-rewarded. (Frow's orientation towards cultural studies is evident in his emphasis on the former rather than on the latter problem. I believe both are important.)

What of the commodification of *culture*? This has been a long and highly uneven process. It is entangled with industrialisation, but commodification preceded the large-scale industrialisation of culture that began in earnest in the twentieth century. To put this another way, industrialisation intensified and extended the commodification of culture. Again, we need to understand this not as a fall from grace from a non-commodified state of culture, but as fundamentally ambivalent, as enabling and constraining. This is, not least, because the commodification of culture is highly complex, happening in different stages and taking multiple forms.[3] To give an example adapting John Frow (1997: 139), we can distinguish three ways and stages in which printed texts have been commodified:

- The commodification of the material object ('the book') – taking place as early as the fifteenth century.
- The commodification of the information contained within the material object as 'the work' in copyright law – from the eighteenth century onwards.
- The commodification of access to printed text information via electronic databases and so on – in the late twentieth century.

Each of these forms and stages of commodification has different implications. There has been a massive profusion of books as a result of their commodification – a proliferation intensified by industrialisation. Copyright underpins the ownership of cultural commodities (and, therefore, the cultural industries as a whole: see Chapter 5) and the protection of works by copyright law has aided this proliferation, but at a cost of placing considerable restrictions on the use of such information. Arguably, such restrictions become more serious in the third stage identified here and inequalities of access become more marked also. As Frow stresses, there is serious conflict between commercial institutions that attempt to make cultural works their private property and common ownership of, or access to, cultural goods.

---

3 This is why a number of political economy writers have sought to distinguish between the different 'logics' involved in different forms of cultural commodity (Flichy, 1980; Lacroix and Tremblay, 1997; Miège, 1989). See also Dan Schiller (1994) for a useful discussion of the long-term history of commodification of information and culture.

This is a cultural version of the 'consumption-side' problem with commodification referred to above. Equally, however – and not so stressed by Frow – there is a cultural version of the production-side problem: the *cultural labour* that is necessary to produce the vast numbers of cultural commodities available to wealthier consumers goes unrecognised (and this cultural work is addressed below).

If the exchange of commodities over extended time and space leads to the problems identified above, then to draw attention to commodification raises questions about the line of demarcation between what can be sold and what cannot. All societies will attempt to withdraw certain domains from market relations: examples include religion, personal life, the political sphere and art. The penetration of market relations into culture and the increasing presence of commodification in the cultural sphere cannot be crudely dismissed as a problem in itself. It would be even more problematic, however, to neglect the negative implications for cultural production and consumption of further commodification. These issues are absolutely central to the current debates raging about the emancipatory possibilities of the internet. Digital networks make possible unprecedented sharing and collaboration, enabling new forms of commons, but they are also subject to a process of digital enclosure (Murdock, 2011).

Commodification, then, can be seen as a long-term and ambivalent process. We can understand the complex professional era as a new stage in the commodification and industrialisation of culture. If this is so, then the question we need to ask about the period since 1980 is as follows: **what are the implications of the further commodification of culture?** This question is addressed in Chapter 6 (see pages 221–225), but because copyright is so vital to the process of commodification of culture, the groundwork for addressing this question is laid in Chapter 5, where I consider changes in copyright law.

BUSINESS OWNERSHIP AND STRUCTURE

One of the most striking and significant features of the complex professional era was the increasing presence of large corporations in the business of cultural production. The biggest of these companies, such as RCA (Radio Corporation of America) in the USA, were huge *conglomerates*.[4] They dwarfed the publishing companies and newspaper empires that had formed the largest companies of the market professional era. In film, recording, radio and television, significant oligopolies had emerged before the middle of the century. The most famous oligopoly was made up of the eight **vertically integrated** Hollywood studios (see Box 2.2). Rather less famous was the oligopoly that dominated the recording industry – the British companies Decca

---

4 For example, including its non-media interests, RCA was the thirty-ninth biggest company in the USA in 1972 (Murdock and Golding, 1977: 27–8).

and EMI, plus Columbia and RCA in the USA, joined by Warner Brothers and Dutch consumer electronics giant Philips in the post-Second World War period. Many of these companies were vertically integrated, too, producing record players and developing new recording and playback technologies. In radio and television, the US networks, CBS and NBC, were dominant. There was also significant cross-media ownership in the early years of the complex professional era, with film studios such as MGM (Metro-Goldwyn-Mayer) having significant music industry interests and RCA running its own record company and its NBC network. One of the most notable oligopolies involved international news agencies (Boyd-Barratt, 1980), with an extraordinary domination of three Anglo-American agencies: Reuters, Associated Press and United Press/UPA, plus the French AFP.[5]

Beneath this layer of vertically integrated giants, most large companies were involved mainly in one form of cultural production. A key change came in the 1960s as *conglomeration* spread throughout the cultural industries. This was part of a more general trend in business as a whole. Neil Fligstein (1990: Chapter 8) provides evidence of the shared trend towards diversification in all industries from the 1940s onwards. Of the 100 biggest companies in the USA in 1939, 77 concentrated 70 per cent or more of their business in a single industry. By 1979, only 23 corporations concentrated in one industry in this way. Whereas none of the top 99 companies in 1939 produced across different industries that bore no relation to each other, by 1979 more than a quarter were following this strategy (these figures are from Fligstein, 1990: 261). What is more, Fligstein shows that this shift in strategy was adopted across all industries and driven by the need for senior managers to be seen to be achieving growth.

Conglomeration first hit the cultural industries in the 1960s, as part of this trend towards diversification. In some cases, it took the form of industrial and financial and business corporations buying up and investing in media interests. Box 2.2 summarises how conglomeration affected the film industry during the complex professional era. In the 1960s and 1970s, conglomeration mainly took the form of large, general conglomerates, with their businesses based on interests as diverse as oil, funerals and financial services, buying up film production studios and 'libraries' of old films. In other industries, conglomeration was based on projected 'convergences' and 'synergies', although these terms were not invented until later. For example, in the 1960s, big US consumer electronics and manufacturing companies, such as IBM (International Business Machines), RCA, Xerox, GE (General Electric) and GTE, bought up book publishers, anticipating convergence between book publishing and computers (Tunstall and Machin, 1999: 107–8).

However, ownership and structure in the complex professional period are not only about the rise of vertically integrated conglomerates, and this, to restate my earlier point, is one of the reasons for my preference for the term 'complex

---

5   The first two are still responsible for most of the world's news images (see Paterson, 2011).

professional' over Williams's 'corporate professional'. Small companies multiplied. The widespread existence of small companies in the cultural industries reflects some of the distinctive features of cultural production discussed in the Introduction. Even while the scale of reproduction and circulation of cultural goods grew during the complex professional period, the conception of cultural works could still take place on a relatively small scale.[6] As small companies proliferated, more and more importance was attached to them as sites of creative independence, reflecting anxieties about the negative effects of big, bureaucratic organisations on society and cultural production. Commentary about popular culture was booming in the mid-century as, for example, film and jazz, and even rock, criticism began to burgeon as notable cultural forms in their own right. By the late 1960s, many young pop and rock critics equated the corporations with commercial control and saw the independents as representative of a hucksterish entrepreneurialism (for example, Cohn, 1989[1969]) or more in touch with trends developed in local settings (such as, Gillett, 1971). We shall return to the issue of whether or not independents really *do* offer some kind of 'alternative' to the conglomerates in Chapters 7 and 10.

Box 2.2 The Hollywood oligopoly across the complex professional era

Eight companies dominated Hollywood during its 'classical' period (1925–1950). The major studios owned and controlled many parts of the value chain. They ran production facilities, made the films, had creative and technical personnel signed to contracts, owned distribution networks and owned the cinemas where the films were shown. A 'Big Five' both distributed films and owned their own cinemas, while the 'Little Three' had their own distribution arms, but no cinemas. A series of rulings by the US Supreme Court, aimed at breaking the Big Five's oligopoly, forced the studios to get rid of their cinemas from the late 1940s onwards, weakening their power. The studios increasingly subcontracted to independent film production companies from the 1950s onwards in an attempt to lower costs, control risk and outmanoeuvre television by producing new and spectacular genres. They also acted as national and international distributors and retained great power. All eventually became divisions of large conglomerates (see Chapter 6). As their names recur throughout this book, here is a brief guide to the later history of these important cultural industry corporations.

(Continued)

---

6 Making up stories and songs, for example, is an acitivity that can be carried out pretty much anywhere. Feature films might be impossible to make without access to considerable capital, but, in economic terms at least, anyone can write a script. Even inscription (putting a magazine design on to disk or making the master copy of a recording, for example) and reproduction (running off copies of magazines or CDs) can be relatively cheap, especially perhaps in the age of digitalisation.

(Continued)

The Big Five

- Paramount, bought by oil conglomerate Gulf & Western in 1967, now part of the Viacom media conglomerate.
- 20th Century Fox performed disastrously in the 1960s and 1970s, became part of a private corporation and was then sold (as Fox) to Rupert Murdoch's News Corporation in 1985.
- Warner Brothers was taken over by the general conglomerate Kinney National Services (a business based on funeral directors) in 1969 and merged with Time in 1990 to form what was for a while the world's largest media group, though it has been forced to shrink in the wake of Time Warner's disastrous merger with AOL in 2000–2001.
- Loew's/Metro-Goldwyn-Mayer – MGM – was just one subsidiary of the most successful film corporation of the classic Hollywood era. It changed hands countless times from the 1960s to the 2000s, merging with UA to become MGM/UA in 1981, but was not involved in the making of films. The libraries and names of MGM and UA were bought by Sony (with cable operator Comcast) in 2004.
- Radio-Keith-Orpheum (RKO) was broken up by Howard Hughes in 1954.

The Little Three

- Universal was taken over by MCA in the early 1950s (along with Paramount's film library and Decca Records) and MCA-Universal prospered in the television age to become the biggest film studio. It was taken over by Japanese consumer electronics company Matsushita in 1986, by Seagram in 1995 and Vivendi in 2000, remaining with them when NBC bought other assets associated with the name Universal in 2003.
- Columbia struggled in the 1950s and 1960s and was then acquired by Coca-Cola in 1981 and Sony in 1988. It continued to struggle under conglomerate control, but has revived as part of the Sony empire in the 2000s.
- United Artists was acquired by Transamerica Corporation, a 'multiservice' organisation involved in insurance and financial services, in 1967 and merged with MGM in 1981 (see MGM above).
- Disney was not part of the classic Hollywood oligopoly. It had no distribution wing, but had its pictures distributed by UA and, later, RKO. When RKO was broken up, Disney set up its own distribution wing, Buena Vista. On the back of its revitalisation as a creative and commercial force in the 1980s, it grew to become one of the largest cultural industry conglomerates in the world.

Sources: Mainly Gomery (1986), supplemented by Guback (1985) and Dale (1997), and later updates from various internet sources.

The above features of ownership and company structure in the complex pro-fessional period raise the following question: to what extent have changes in conglomeration and integration led to recognisably new and distinct forms of ownership and structure since 1980? We shall see in Chapter 6 (see pages 187–209) that the size and scope of cultural industry corporations expanded enormously from the 1980s onwards.

Once again, however, we need to ask how might we *evaluate* this expan-sion? The role of cultural industry corporations in society has been a key theme in political economy, especially in the Schiller-McChesney tradition. There are striking examples of the exercise of interests via cultural industry ownership by media moguls – that is, individuals with overall control of a company (see page 257) – but it can be argued convincingly that they are exceptions. Moguls are more prevalent in the cultural industries than in most other types of industry, but even there most companies are governed by a number of different shareholders. It could be argued, therefore, that control is spread over many owners and this prevents particular interests from being served. This, though, misses the point. It is not the interests of particular individuals that are at stake but the interests of the social class to which they tend to belong – wealthy and powerful owners of capi-tal with strong ties to other powerful and influential institutions and individuals.

This wider argument has been disputed. Many commentators on ownership and control in general (and not just of the cultural industries) have argued that, since the nineteenth century's 'managerial revolution', control has been delegated to managers, who represent a different social class and do not have such an interest in maintaining power relations (see Scott, 1995, for a survey of these debates). Companies thus become a mixture of fragmented class inter-ests. And yet once again the idea that owners and senior executives repre-sent different social classes is wide of the mark. Senior managers will often be drawn from backgrounds as wealthy and privileged as those of their owners. They might represent a different stratum of the dominant classes, but, given that they, too, are wealthy and privileged, they may well share the interests and political inclinations of the owners responsible for their appointments.

We should be in no doubt about the continued exertion of control by own-ers and executives. In a notable article, Graham Murdock drew on debates in the sociology of business enterprises to clarify a distinction between two types of control in organisations: 'allocative' and 'operational' (all quotations from Murdock, 1982: 122):

- *Allocative control* consists of the 'power to define the overall goals and scope' of the enterprise and to 'determine the general way it deploys its productive resources'. This includes decisions on whether or not and where to expand, the development of financial policy (including share issues) and the distribution of profits, but, crucially, it also includes 'the formulation of overall policy and strategy'.
- *Operational control* 'works at a lower level and is confined to decisions about the effective use of resources already allocated and the imple-mentation of policies already decided upon at the allocative level'.

Does this mean, however, that wealthy and powerful owners and senior executives of cultural industry companies are able to pursue their interests via the cultural industries? To answer this means considering what their interests are. We can speak of **three different types of potential interest for owners and executives**. These are interests in the success of:

- their own business;
- companies like their own;
- business as a whole.

The first interest is in maximising the profits, revenues, market share, share price, and so on of their own particular company (or companies – many directors will serve on the boards of a number of companies). In this first respect, companies obviously pursue their own interests. Aiming for profit maximisation, all businesses will try to ensure that expenditure on staff pay and other costs is well below the level of revenues generated. Within this system, some companies will offer higher levels of pay and provide better conditions than others. Some industries will also have better working conditions than others. As we have seen, there are specific conditions surrounding the business of cultural production, whereby workers have been given greater creative autonomy than is the case in other sectors. However, the system of capitalist accumulation depends on exploitation. As Miège (1989) pointed out, cultural industry companies subsidise costs by means of pools of reservoir labour and the use of casualised cultural work. Other strategies include moving work overseas to countries where levels of pay are much lower (as is the case for most animation productions – see Lent, 1998).

The second type of interest that owners and executives are likely to pursue is that of companies like their own. Obviously, such companies compete with each other, except when they are involved in cartel arrangements, usually forbidden by law. Even within a system of mutual competition, though, companies will affiliate to form trade bodies, lobbying groups and alliances. There is a deeply rooted tendency in advanced capitalism for oligopolies of large companies to form in nearly all industries. These oligopolies are particularly effective at forming lobbying groups, campaigning against what they see as obtrusive government legislation and regulation – much of it, in fact, intended to protect workers and consumers. Such corporate lobbying has been an important feature of cultural policymaking (see Chapters 4 and 5). Oligopolies also come to embody a set of conventions for understanding how best to organise business. Non-profit enterprises and smaller commercial companies, including those aiming at lower profit margins and innovative working practices, will tend to be excluded or marginalised. They may even come to appear naïve or incompetent because of the greater wealth and prominence of companies in the oligopoly.

That companies pursue the interests of owners and executives in these two ways seems to me to be undeniable. The controversies surrounding such a system of self-interested production are mainly ones regarding the wider system of capitalism as a whole – principally, whether or not the advantages (such as dynamic growth and the production of greater amounts of total wealth) of economic systems based on such actions outweigh the disadvantages (the systematic underpaying of most workers, oligopoly, massive inequality, social fragmentation).[7] Here, of course, questions about business ownership and structure overlap with the questions raised above about the role of the cultural industries in society. Examination of actual businesses can more clearly locate *agency* – that is, who makes things change and how.

There is, however, a third type of potential interest that owners and executives might pursue. Other things being equal, all businesses will tend to want conditions in which businesses as a whole can thrive: political and economic stability and lively demand. This means that businesses will, for example, make huge donations to political candidates they think are likely to achieve these general business environment goals. They will oppose reform and the struggle for greater equality if they perceive that such developments might threaten their business interests. Here, the question of whether or not and how they pursue such interests in the general conditions for profitmaking becomes extremely controversial. The ability of cultural industry corporations to give an account of such issues makes their role the subject of special debate. Do cultural industry companies produce texts that systematically support the interests of businesses? Do they hold back progressive reform and try to prevent the forms of social conflict that are often necessary to bring it about? These questions are addressed in Chapter 11 and previewed later in this chapter. For now, however, this discussion of interests will serve to inform a further evaluative question that I address directly in Chapter 6, when I survey the growth of cultural industry corporations since the 1980s. The question is this: **What are the effects of the growth in size and power of cultural industry corporations on cultural production and wider society?**

ORGANISATION, MANAGEMENT AND CREATIVE AUTONOMY

How did cultural labour come to be organised and managed during the complex professional era? Bill Ryan (1992), following the cultural industries approach outlined in the Introduction and Chapter 1, has provided a useful way of approaching this question. In the market professional era, the creative stage of making cultural products used to be carried out primarily by individuals, but in the era of the complex professional form of cultural production, it came to be carried out by a *'project team'* (Ryan, 1992: 124–34). Within

---

7   There are also problems concerning how to imagine and/or bring about alternative systems, but such problems need to be actively considered, rather than used to imply that criticism should not be mounted.

this team, various people will perform the functions listed below. Adapting from and building on Ryan's discussion, I will give examples from five particular cultural industries – books, film, magazines, recording and television.

- *Primary creative personnel* such as musicians, screenwriters and directors, magazine journalists and authors (symbol creators). This category also includes technical personnel who have come to be recognised as taking a creative role, such as sound mixers who, as record producers, have become increasingly important in the music industry (see Kealy, 1990 [1974]).
- *Technical workers* are expected to perform a technically orientated set of tasks efficiently, such as sound engineers, camera operators, copy editors, floor managers, typesetters, page designers. Some of these jobs are deemed to be crafts, as they require special skills and workers performing them identify collectively with each other in terms of the work they do. Creativity is involved here, but not the conception of ideas that will be the basis of the finished text – or, at least, that is something like the rationale for designating some workers as 'technical' rather than 'creative' (which is more prestigious).
- *Creative managers* act as brokers or mediators between, on the one hand, the interests of owners and executives, who have to be primarily interested in profit (or, at the very least, prestige), and those of creative personnel, who will want to achieve success and/or build their reputation by producing original, innovative and/or accomplished works. Key examples are artists and repertoire (A&R) personnel in the recording industry, commissioning editors in the books industry, editors of magazines, and producers in the film industry. I find Ryan's concept of the 'creative manager' much clearer than Miège's term 'editeur' or DiMaggio's 'broker' (1977) for more or less the same role. To add to the confusion, 'editeur' is translated as 'producer' in Miège (1987). The most confusing term of all is 'cultural intermediaries' (see Hesmondhalgh, 2006a; 2007: 66–7, for an explanation of problems in the way this term has been used and, therefore, of why I avoid it here).
- *Marketing personnel* in the cultural industries aim, along with creative managers, to match the work of primary creative personnel to audiences. They sometimes create symbols to publicise and promote cultural work. It seems right, then, to classify them separately – not just because their work is 'secondary', in that it relies on a separate act of creativity, but also because they act in the interests of owners and executives and often come into conflict with creative personnel. Creative managers often mediate between marketers and creative personnel – even if it is the executives' goal of profit maximisation that is ultimately behind the marketers' actions.[8]

---

8 The division of labour within the advertising and marketing industries involves all the categories here, including primary creative personnel (advertising 'creatives') and creative managers, but also marketers who will try to match marketing messages to the right audience.

- *Owners and executives* who have the power to hire and fire personnel and set the general direction of company policy, but who will have a limited role in the conception and development of particular texts, except in rare cases, such as in the film industry where 'executive producers' may be credited.
- *Unskilled and semi-skilled labour* is made up of a vast body of unskilled workers who are also involved in the creation, circulation and reproduction of products.[9] So it could likewise be said, then, to include assembly line workers involved in maintaining the machines that reproduce the countless millions of DVDs that are sold each year. Much of this work has been poorly paid and is contracted overseas.

Some notes on this breakdown of functions. First, I say 'functions' because these are roles as well as occupational groupings – one person may perform more than one of these roles in any project. For example, the same person might be both a creative manager and responsible for marketing. This is especially the case in small companies or temporary projects on the margins of a cultural industry. On the other hand, the breakdown also reflects occupational groupings as, in many cases, a person will carry out that function (as a publisher, for example) for an entire career.

Second, these functions are, more often than not, organised *hierarchically*, in terms of pay and status, in something like the following way: owners and executives, creative managers, marketers, then most primary creative personnel, craft technical workers and semi-skilled and unskilled labour (see Tunstall, 2001: 14). But this hierarchical ordering is by no means fixed. 'Star' creative personnel and even creative managers can earn more even than fat cat execs. Craft technical workers can earn more than creative personnel, depending on unionisation.

Third, this is a heuristic way of dividing up the functions in the cultural industries. However, the way in which work is conceived in particular industries and on particular projects can itself be a product of status inequalities. For example, the very designation of some staff as 'technical' and others as 'creative' is itself, in many cases, down to decisions about whose work really counts.

Box 2.3 adapts Ryan's (1992) analysis of the stages in making and circulating texts and the division of labour within each stage. The stages themselves are not unique to the cultural industries – many industries involve the conception of an idea, its execution and reproduction of an object, followed by its circulation – but what happens within each stage, and the relations between the stages, reflects the distinctiveness of the cultural industries. One key feature is that the project teams involved in creation and conception **are given a large degree of autonomy**. At the time that the cultural

---

9   Sharon Zukin quotes a story told by the eminent cultural commentator Daniel Bell about a circus employee whose job it was to follow the elephant and clear up after it. When asked, she said that her job was in 'the entertainment business' (Zukin, 1995: 12). Zukin also remarks that today the same woman might say that she works in the cultural industries.

industries were developing in the early- and mid-twentieth century, such creative autonomy was rare in other industries. So, one of the defining features of the complex professional era of cultural production is this unusual degree of autonomy, which has been carried over from preceding eras where artists, authors and composers were seen as working more independently of business imperatives than other workers. This autonomy is by no means a complete autonomy, however, as it is carried out under the supervision of creative managers. It is not unique to the cultural industries and it was not so even in earlier periods of strict Taylorist control over work, but such autonomy is of huge significance in cultural production.

Box 2.3   'Stages' of cultural production

Note: These stages do not necessarily follow on from one another, as in the popular image of a factory production line. Instead they overlap, interact, and sometimes conflict.

Creation

- *Conception* – design, realisation, interpretation; the writing of screenplays and treatments, composition and improvisation of songs and so on.
- *Execution* – performance in recording studios and television sets, as well as on film.
- *Transcription on to a final master* – involving editing (film, books and magazines) and mixing (music, film).[10]
- *Reproduction and duplication* – in the form of printing, copying CDs from a master recording, and making multiple copies of a film from a negative (there is no equivalent in television); or the dissemination of digital files. The text now takes the form that the audience will experience.

Circulation

- *Marketing* – including advertising and packaging (each of which has its own processes of conception and reproduction), but also aspects that might take place alongside conception or between the transcription and reproduction of the main text, such as market research.
- *Publicity* – involving trying to ensure that other organisations provide publicity for the commodity.
- *Distribution and wholesaling* (or the broadcasting of a television programme).
- *Retailing/exhibition/broadcast*

Source: Adapted from Ryan (1992).

---

10 Ryan includes this in the reproduction stage, but while these tasks might be undertaken by skilled, technical professionals, they will often be carried out under the supervision of creative personnel, as this is a vital part of the creative stage.

The notion of creative autonomy is absolutely crucial for an understanding of the cultural industries in the late twentieth century. It shows that the metaphor of the traditional factory production line – often used in critiques of industrial cultural production – entirely misses the point (see also Negus, 1992: 46). Because of the history of attitudes towards symbolic creativity discussed in the Introduction, factory-style production is widely felt to be inimical to the kinds of creativity necessary to make profits. Even in the Hollywood studio system, which developed at the beginning of the complex professional era and exerted very tight control over the conception and execution of films compared with the control over these stages in other cultural industries, there was still considerable autonomy for screenwriters and directors within certain formats and genres.

Crucially, companies in the business of cultural production exert much stricter control over the other stages of making texts after the creation stage (see Box 2.3) – that is, reproduction and circulation.[11] The reproduction stage was heavily industrial, often reliant on technically complex electronic systems and strictly controlled, especially in terms of when master copies of films, books, records and so on were *scheduled* to be copied and released or when a programme was scheduled to be broadcast. Now important elements of circulation have become digitalised. Increasingly, it is possible to download music and films online, or through mobile devices via radio waves. This still requires a massive technological infrastructure, however, and release schedules are still tightly controlled by senior management so that they can be co-ordinated with marketing and publicity.

This combination of loose control of creative input and tighter control of reproduction and circulation constitutes **the distinctive organisational form of cultural production during the complex professional era**. The form developed in the early twentieth century persisted and became much more widespread. I have referred to this organisational form in the present tense throughout the discussion above, but the key issue for the argument of this book is **to what extent have the dynamics of this distinctive organisational form changed since the late 1970s?**

Creativity and commerce relations

Once again, this question is tied to a more explicitly evaluative set of questions. If I am right in focusing attention on the role of the cultural industries as systems for the management of symbolic creativity (see Introduction), then a key issue here will be the relationship between symbol creators and cultural industry organisations. This focus is not intended to devalue the

---

11 This stage is often referred to as 'distribution' (see Garnham's seminal discussion, 1990: 161–2), but I prefer 'circulation'. 'Distribution' refers to getting products to audiences. 'Circulation' includes this distribution aspect, but also includes the equally problematic and important issue of marketing and publicity.

lives of those workers deemed to be 'technical' workers. As noted above, some such workers have considerable creative input, but are designated 'technical' for reasons of status. Nor is it intended to demean those workers who objectively have no creative input into final products. The decision to put the spotlight on creativity derives from the recognition that symbol creators are crucial to determining the final outcomes and they have a central place in fantasies and beliefs about what 'good work' might involve in modern capitalism (see Stahl, 2006, for a superb dissertation on this topic).

We saw in the Introduction that tensions between commerce and creativity are a fundamental feature of the cultural industries. The influences of the romantic movement and modernism have been profound and helped establish a widespread view in the West that symbolic creativity can only flourish if it is as far away from commerce as possible. This view is embodied in prevailing myths about great artists. We often think of the greatest symbol creators as either being unrecognised, having little or no commercial success in their lifetime (such as Van Gogh), or being driven to despair by the superficiality of the commercial world they came to inhabit (Kurt Cobain, for example). This polarisation of creativity and commerce can confuse and mystify our understanding of the media and popular culture. In everyday conversation, various texts, genres, performers, writers and so on are often judged on the basis of assumptions about whether or not the symbol creators had commercial intentions. Often, the assumption is that those creators who reject commercial imperatives most entirely are the best. This, though, is an overly polarised view of the relationship between creativity and commerce. All creators have to find an audience and, in the modern world, no one can do this without the help of technological mediation and/or the support of large organisations. Moreover, we can't assume that the input of creative managers (as mentioned earlier, the professionals who mediate between the interests of cultural industry companies and those of symbol creators) is negative in terms of textual outcomes. Take, for example, the tendency of creative managers to push symbol creators in the direction of genre formatting in order to facilitate marketing and publicity for a particular audience. This isn't necessarily a bad thing in and of itself. Genre can be a productive constraint, allowing for creativity and imagination within a certain set of boundaries and enhanced understanding between audiences and producers: think, for example, of the variety of ways in which the writers, musicians, arrangers and sound mixer/ producers of the Detroit record label Tamla Motown made creative use of the three minutes available for vinyl singles in the 1960s.

Yet it remains the case that the relationship between creativity and commerce is a matter of negotiation, conflict and struggle. However rewarding they find their work, nearly all symbol creators seem at some point to experience the constraints imposed on them in the name of profit accumulation as stressful and/or oppressive and/or disrespectful. Many are forced to do 'creative' work that they hardly experience as creative at all. What's more, the fate of the symbol creator's work is in the hands of various other workers, especially creative managers, marketers and senior executives. This can function well, of course, as marketing can ensure the widespread dissemination of creative work, to the satisfaction of all concerned. Alternatively, texts can sink without trace as these managers and marketers prioritise other projects.

Here we encounter a contradiction. However mystifying and confusing the polarised view of creativity versus commerce can be, it has some positive effects. It allows people who want to work creatively (this includes journalists) to argue for more time, space and resources than they might otherwise get from their commercial paymasters. Whether this results in better work or not can only be judged in particular cases, but the goal of producing work that is autonomous of the demands of profit accumulation helps to produce richer and more varied communication. This is not to celebrate or romanticise symbol creators but simply to grant them due recognition. So, a number of questions concerning the organization and management of cultural production follow from this:

- How have relationships between creativity and commerce changed?
- Linked to this, how have the distinctive organisational features of the cultural industries in the complex professional era of cultural production changed, or stayed the same?
- What changes have there been in the extent to which creative workers within the cultural industries determine how their work will be edited, promoted, circulated? (This is a question about the extent to which creative **autonomy** has been expanded or diminished).

These issues are addressed in Chapter 7.

THE QUALITY OF CULTURAL WORK

Clearly, the distinctive organisational form of the cultural industries has considerable implications for the conditions under which symbolic creativity is carried out. But how has such creative work been rewarded in the complex professional era? In order to address this question, we need to consider the cultural labour market.

All human beings are symbol creators at least some of the time. Billions of us sing, dance or write every day (and if you think I can't write, you should hear me play the piano). Professional creativity has been merely the tip of the iceberg, but, like many iceberg tips, it is the bit that is most visible. As the media came to dominate symbol-making in the twentieth century (see Hesmondhalgh, 2006b), more and more people have aspired to work in the supposed glamour of the cultural industries. One feature of cultural work in the complex professional era is that many more people seem to have wanted to work professionally in the cultural industries than have succeeded in doing so. Few make it and surprisingly little attention has been paid in research to how people do so, and what stops others from getting in.

Nevertheless, some do make it. As with most forms of work, it has tended to be older, whiter, able-bodied people who have done best and earned most. As elsewhere, men generally earn more than women (Tunstall, 2001). What may be most distinctive to the cultural industries, however, is a particular type of split between waged and unwaged work. In the 1945–1980 period, waged work became the norm in advanced industrial countries. Many in the cultural industries worked on this basis. This included:

- workers in *craft/technical occupations*, who increasingly formed themselves into relatively strong trade unions;
- symbol creators in what Tunstall (2001: 14) calls *the 'professionalising' occupations,* such as journalism and advertising;
- *creative managers*, who were also professionalising to some degree, so, for example, being an editor in a publishing company was increasingly understood to involve a particular set of procedures with a certain social prestige attached (see Coser et al., 1982).

Many symbol creators, however, worked on a casual or contract-by-contract basis – in many cases trying to get by on royalties from previous jobs.

We can turn to Bernard Miège for a picture of the labour market for creative personnel in the complex professional era of cultural production. Miège (1989: 82–3) argued that creative workers bear the costs of conception on behalf of cultural industry companies by being willing to forgo the benefits of secure working conditions and, in nearly all cases, earning relatively little when they do. Creative labour within the cultural industries, claimed Miège, is underpaid because of a permanent oversupply of artistic labour, which takes the form of 'vast reservoirs of under-employed artists' (1989: 72).[12] The biggest reservoir or pool is composed of non-professional cultural workers, who work occasionally and have to take other jobs to subsidise their artistic activities. Wages are also kept down by the ready availability and willingness of creative professionals in other cultural industries to transfer across into another field (such as journalists who might want to publish books or pop musicians who may wish to compose film scores).

The result, in the complex professional period, has been **a labour market in which most creative workers are either underemployed – at least in terms of the creative work they actually want to do – or underpaid**. This should not be seen as a natural phenomenon: it is a result of specific economic and cultural conditions. These conditions include the failure of creative workers to come together to defend their interests against such forms of low pay and exploitation: this is in part because symbol creators are permanently competing with each other for recognition and rewards (Miège, 1989: 87).[13] The main exceptions are difficult-to-enter professional guilds, such as actors' unions.

---

12 Elsewhere, Miège, or his translator, uses the term 'tank'.
13 Caves (2000), writing from a mainstream economics perspective, discusses differential success for creative workers by referring to the A list/B list property of the creative industries. B lists still comprise very successful creative personnel – stars who are not superstars. Miège's reservoirs or pools, referred to above, suggest the existence of C, D, and other lists right down to Z, involving levels of inequality that Caves fails to address.

For those relatively few creative workers who do succeed in having their works released on to the market, and for the cultural industry companies who undertake the circulation of such works, copyright law is vital, as we shall see in Chapter 7. Outside the few cultural workers who manage to gain salaried employment, many have to try to eke a living out of occasional work, and infrequent royalty payments.

All of this should make it clear, I hope, that the emphasis on the relative creative autonomy of symbol creators in the complex professional period should not be taken to mean that I think modern symbol creators have had a wonderful life, idling about in recording studios and on film sets while everyone else toils and/or watches the clock. On the contrary, I know that most creative workers make very little money. Great sacrifices have to be made to achieve even the limited and provisional autonomy that is available. The question we need to confront, then, when thinking about the extent of change and continuity in the cultural industries, is **to what extent have the cultural labour market and systems of reward for cultural workers changed since the late 1970s?** This question about the extent of change is, as will be witnessed throughout the book, tied to an evaluative question, which is **have the rewards and working conditions of creative workers – and indeed, other workers in the cultural industries – improved during this time?** Chapter 7 examines some of the evidence regarding these issues.

INTERNATIONALISATION AND DOMINATION BY THE USA

International movement of cultural texts and cultural workers goes back many centuries. The first global media corporations, however, date from the nineteenth century, in the form of the British and French imperial news agencies (Reuters and Havas) which 'in the 1870s established a world cartel in fast news by ocean cable' (Tunstall, 1994: 14). Tunstall also provides other examples of internationalisation, including:

- *cultural forms* – the spread of the daily entertainment newspaper from the USA, where it was introduced by moguls such as Hearst and Pulitzer, into Europe and across the world;
- *cultural technologies* – such as the sound film, which spread across the world in the 1930s;
- *cultural industries* – in particular, the 'speedy capture of the world movie market by the young Hollywood' from 1914 to the 1930s.

As Tunstall notes, these waves of internationalisation in the twentieth century mainly emanated from the USA.

Therefore the decades preceding the complex professional era of cultural production had already seen considerable amounts of international traffic in cultural goods. This grew in the post-Second World War period. Alongside developments in communication and transport, it led to much higher levels of transnational flows of texts, genres, technologies and capital. This can be seen, for example, in the phenomenal spread of Anglo-American rock music and pop music culture across much of the world in the 1960s and 1970s, including even the Stalinist states of Eastern Europe. The television industry in the USA developed ahead of that of most other countries and the USA's system was dominant internationally in the early years of television. In particular, most countries drew heavily on US programming during the television boom years of the 1960s (very few had developed television systems before the late 1950s). Television exports from the USA reached their peak in the late 1960s and then 'in the early 1970s remained at around US$100 million a year – meaning a real decline against inflation' (Tunstall, 1994: 144). In film, domination by the USA was even more impressive. In 1925, films from the USA accounted for over 90 per cent of film revenues in the UK, Canada, Australia, New Zealand and Argentina, and over 70 per cent in France, Brazil and Scandinavia (Jarvie, 1992: 315). This domination remained robust throughout the complex professional period.

Nevertheless, as Tunstall (1994: 62) notes, there were other international cultural flows, too. These included long-standing flows of texts within particular regions, often dominated by a regional 'media imperialist', such as Egypt in the Arab world or Sweden in Scandinavia, and Britain reaped the benefits of empire, even after its own went into decline. There were also cultural flows from Latin America and Africa into the USA and other advanced industrial countries, especially in music and dance. The 1980s and 1990s saw intensified global cultural trade and, indeed, economic, political and cultural contact across the globe – the phenomenon of globalisation. These issues are discussed in Chapter 8, where the following questions are addressed. **To what extent have international cultural flows changed sufficiently for us to speak of a new era in cultural production and circulation? To what extent has the USA retained its international dominance?**

We see in Chapter 8 that the last 30 years have encompassed a further intensification of the internationalisation of cultural industry businesses and texts, but how should we evaluate this internationalisation? The neo-liberal view is that 'free trade' in cultural goods will be beneficial for all. This is usually based on the neo-classical economic notion of the *theory of comparative advantage*. This holds that 'every nation is better off specialising in goods in which it has a comparative advantage and trading some of these goods for others in which it possesses no such advantage' (Hoskins et al., 2004: 328). Economists aim to show through their demand and supply curves that when protectionist measures such as tariffs and quotas are introduced, then there is a net economic loss for the country imposing those measures. Social and cultural losses in forgoing production in a particular area are seen as 'externalities' – that is, costs or benefits 'not taken into account by either of the parties' (Hoskins et al., 2004: 290) in an economic transaction. In the general economy, externalities might include environmental damage, unemployment and so on. These are often sidelined by economists because they are hard to measure, but these factors are often crucial. For example, cultural goods make a significant contribution to the diversity of a particular space, be it that of a nation or region. Not having an effective domestic film, television or recording industry is likely, other things being equal, to reduce that diversity.

We need to move beyond the narrow vision of neo-liberalism and focus on the social and cultural implications of international movements of cultural goods, especially power and identity. So Chapter 8 asks the following questions. **To what extent does the increasingly global reach of the largest firms mean an exclusion of voices from cultural markets? What opportunities are there for cultural producers from outside the 'core' areas of cultural production to gain access to new global networks of cultural production and consumption?**

DOMINANT TECHNOLOGIES

The dominant technology at the dawn of the complex professional era of cultural production was print publishing. But new media technologies in succession supplemented newspapers, periodicals, sheet music and books, all beginning in Europe and North American, and then fanning out to the rest of the world: cinema from the 1890s, the gramophone and records from the 1910s, radio from the 1920s, and television from the 1950s. All these technologies can be seen as contributing to a highly asymmetrical set of relations between relatively small numbers of producers, on the one hand, and audiences sometimes numbering millions on the other (Thompson, 1995).

The fervent debate that greeted each of these new technologies has been echoed in the introduction of the internet since the mid-1990s. We should not forget that earlier technologies, notably radio, were greeted as potentially democratizing. But the claims regarding the emancipatory possibilities of the internet and digital networks far outstrip those that accompanied earlier innovations. Such claims partly depended on utopian hopes for the *convergence* of telecommunications, computers and media. Chapter 9 provides the longer-term history of digitalisation, convergence and the internet, and Chapters 9 and 10 address questions concerning changes associated with these developments. One concerns the extent of change. **To what extent have digitalisation and the internet transformed cultural production and consumption?** The other, related, questions are more evaluative. Many proponents of the internet and other digital technologies claim that they are opening up access to the means of cultural production and circulation in a positive, democratising way, and that barriers between production and consumption are being eroded. Instead of the few-to-many quasi-mediated interaction of the analogue age, some foresee a flatter, peer-to-peer, many-to-many form of communication emerging in the age of digital networks. Chapter 9 evaluates such claims. **Is access really opening up? Are barriers between producers and consumers really breaking down?**

TEXTUAL CHANGE

The complex professional period saw the circulation of unprecedented numbers of mediated texts to unprecedented numbers of people. This was accompanied by great anxiety about these texts. We can identify a number of issues that emerged from debates in the twentieth century about the products of the cultural industries. There are three main ways in which the relationships between cultural industries and textual outputs have tended to be discussed, which are in terms of:

- diversity and choice;
- quality;
- social justice – in particular whether or not the interests of the wealthy and powerful are served (the question deferred from earlier).

Here, questions about the *extent* of change are especially entangled with questions of *evaluation*, so I shall treat them together.

Choice, diversity, multiplicity

The issue of diversity has been particularly important in discussions of oligopoly, concentration and conglomeration throughout the complex professional era. Mainstream economics has argued for many years that markets tend to oversupply products in 'the middle of the market' (Hotelling's Law – see Hotelling, 1929). Liberal-pluralist communication studies scholars and others have tried to show that concentration leads to homogenisation and standardisation, or at least reduced diversity, but with contradictory results (see Chapter 11). Even in the rare cases where decreasing diversity is clear, it is very difficult to show that concentration *causes* homogenisation. Indeed, it is possible to make the argument that concentration can – at least in particular cases at particular times – be beneficial for diversity. As Richard Collins and Christina Murroni (1996: 58) put it, 'risky new media markets require venture capital and market power in order to launch new products'. As they also point out, challenging, authoritative reporting needs lots of money to back it up.

In fact, there is evidence that the complex professional era has seen a marked increase in the range and diversity of cultural goods on offer. The high street record shops, newsagents and bookshops seem awash with products and nearly everyone in the developed world can receive more radio and television stations than ever before. How can we possibly speak of a lack of diversity? One political economy writer (Mosco, 1996: 258) has responded to this criticism by making a distinction between *multiplicity* – the sheer number of voices – and *diversity* – whether or not these voices are actually saying anything different from each other.[14] This is a crucial point. There are

---

14 A similar argument runs through Adorno and Horkheimer's analysis of '[the] Culture Industry'.

hundreds of magazines available in the USA and Europe catering for every kind of interest imaginable, from needlework to the mercenary soldier business, from gay porn to religious affairs. No doubt many of these magazines add pleasure and interest to their readers' lives, but is there real diversity when it comes to the expression of viewpoints about how we might understand the world? Similarly, are audiences exposed to a wide range of voices or are we increasingly encouraged to stay tuned only to those channels of communication that we have already decided we are interested in? These questions suggest the very real difficulties involved in providing any objective assessment of what constitutes diversity in the cultural industries. This is a great problem because much writing that is critical of the present formation of the cultural industries assumes the assent of readers regarding these questions. Nevertheless, one question remains on the agenda: **to what extent are the texts produced by the cultural industries growing more or less diverse?** I return to this issue in Chapter 11.

Quality

Since the industrialisation of culture, and probably long before, it has become common to hear claims that the quality of our culture is in decline. In the complex professional period, a huge amount of cultural commentary was devoted to such ideas (see, for example, Bloom, 1987; MacDonald, 1963; see also Ross, 1989, for a brilliant overview of this terrain). The most recent version of this approach has it that the faster, more frenetic way in which we read, watch and listen to texts has led to a decline in the quality of our cultural experiences and the actual texts themselves. According to such views, the cultural industries can 'get away with' investing less energy, time and resources in high standards because we are too distracted to appreciate quality anyway. Closely related to this is the view that overall quality is declining because of the drive to make a profit. As I will show in Chapter 11, such arguments are extremely difficult to prove. This is not simply because judgements of quality are subjective. The real problem is that many of those who argue for overall decline in a particular industry offer very little substantial argument (in the form of an explicit reference to aesthetic criteria) to back up their case. Nevertheless, the question remains an interesting one: **has the overall quality of texts declined?**

Texts, social justice and the serving of interests

Here we return to the question raised earlier in the discussion of the interests of cultural industry corporations. To what extent do companies serve the interests of their owners?

- *Companies promoting their own interests as companies via texts* In one obvious sense, cultural industry companies clearly serve their own interests via texts. Since the market professional period, whatever the mixture of motivations among individuals and across different roles, cultural industry companies produce and circulate texts primarily in order to make money.

- *Companies promoting the interests of cultural industry companies as a whole (or those of fellow members of an oligopoly of major corporations) via texts* There is a strong tendency for texts made by the largest corporations to refer to the products of other corporations. This is not always the result of conscious and deliberate attempts by large companies to reinforce each other's positions; it is sometimes simply because these corporate products tend to dominate in modern capitalist culture. The main way in which cultural industry companies act as joint interest groups is evidenced in their lobbying activities. Naturally, such lobbying can, at times, be supported by texts. An example of this would be attacks on the BBC in British newspapers with broadcasting and internet interests.

- *Companies promoting the interests of businesses in general and of the social class that owns them* The cultural industries have, for many decades, via advertising and marketing, served the interests of businesses as a whole by creating a context in which consumption is stimulated and satisfaction becomes associated with the buying of commodities, again, via advertising and marketing. It isn't nearly so clear that non-advertising messages systematically support the business environment, however. Numerous texts celebrate selfish consumerism as a means to happiness, but many also prioritise other values over acquisition. Promoting the interests of businesses above the interests of people as citizens and workers can lead to a deterioration in the quality of working life, the environment and personal relationships. The most difficult question of all is whether or not texts promote the interests of businesses and dominant social groups by encouraging political and economic stability and discouraging progressive social change. Any increasing tendency for the cultural industries to support these powerful interests would undoubtedly be negative.

Clearly, the textual products of the cultural industries do not come about purely as a result of conscious efforts by owners and executives to serve their own interests. There are many mediating and contingent factors at work. The complex systems of modern commercial production produce many unintended consequences. It is possible, for example, that the pursuit of market segments by cultural industry businesses, in the interests of profit, helps to bring about processes of social fragmentation, but such fragmentation is not necessarily in the interests of cultural industry companies.

In Chapter 11, I discuss these issues of social justice and the serving of interests under a number of headings:

- Advertising, promotion and commercialism.
- The politics of entertainment.

- Journalism.
- Social fragmentation and market segmentation.

The overall question guiding the discussion in that chapter, then, is do the cultural industries increasingly serve the interests of themselves and the wealthy and powerful in society?

* * *

My claim in this chapter has been that the complex professional form represented a new era in cultural production, beginning from the early twentieth century onwards and consolidating from the middle of the century. If this is right, then one way of differentiating fundamental transformations from superficial changes in the cultural industries since 1980 (so that continuity can be recognised) is to ask the following questions. **Has the period since 1980 seen the emergence of a completely new era of cultural production? Alternatively, do the changes represent shifts *within* the complex professional era?** These questions represent a refinement of the central question of the book, outlined in the Introduction. This chapter has broken down these broader questions into more manageable ones, summarised in Table 2.1. The next chapter examines how we might explain change, and how a number of changes began to take place in the cultural industries from the 1970s onwards.

RECOMMENDED AND FURTHER READING

There is a huge amount of media history, and there are many historical studies of periods and moments in cultural production – far too many to discuss here. I focus here on studies that place cultural production and the cultural industries in systematic long-term historical perspective, as I have tried to do in this chapter. As the above suggests, I find the approach in Raymond Williams's *Culture* (1981) and Bill Ryan's *Making Capital from Culture* (1992) particularly helpful. Janet Wolff's *The Social Production of Art* (1993[1981]) and *Aesthetics and the Sociology of Art* (1983) are brilliant works of historical sociology. Theodor Adorno (see Introduction) and a contemporary German writer Friedrich Kittler (*Optical Media*, 2011[2002]) provide problematic historical critical theories relevant to an understanding of cultural production. The emphasis in Jason Toynbee's *Making Popular Music* (2000) on the historical ambivalence of symbol making has been a major influence on my thinking in this book. Peter Burke and Asa Briggs' *A Social History of the Media* (third edition, 2009) is the best single-volume history relevant to the cultural industries. Michael Bailey's *Narrating Media History* (2008) collects research that follows James Curran's example in making historical understanding central to an understanding of the power of media institutions (see Curran,

2002, 2011). The work of Jeremy Tunstall is admirably informed by long-term history (see, for example, *The Media Are American*, 1994, originally published in 1977). Film history is a rich terrain. On Hollywood studios, see Thomas Schatz's *The Genius of the System* (1996) and Douglas Gomery's *The Hollywood Studio System* (2005 [1986]). Of researchers who are more directly associated with the term 'cultural industries', the work of Nicholas Garnham (2000) and Justin O'Connor (2010) is most informed by a serious consideration of the historical development of culture. Arnold Hauser's *The Social History of Art* (originally published in 1951) offers a long-term historical perspective that is all too often missing from analysis of cultural industries, as does the social theory perspective of John B. Thompson's *The Media and Modernity* (1995), one of the best books available on the media.

3

Why the Cultural Industries Began to Change in the 1980s

How not to explain change: three forms of reduction   93
Contexts for change and continuity in the cultural
     industries, 1945–1990   95
Political-economic change: the Long Downturn   97
Political and regulatory change: the rise of neo-liberalism   99
Changing business strategies   102
  Investment shifts towards service industries   102
  Internationalisation   105
  Organisational innovation and restructuring   107
Sociocultural and textual changes   109
Technological change: information technology
     and consumer electronics   112

HOW NOT TO EXPLAIN CHANGE: THREE FORMS OF REDUCTION

Why have the cultural industries changed so much since the 1980s? And what are the forces driving these changes?

There are no easy answers here. In complex societies, adequate explanations of social processes are rarely going to be simple. It would be wise, therefore, to avoid answers that *reduce* complicated, interwoven webs of causality to a single driving force. Of course everyone thinks that her or his account avoids such reduction, yet the need to achieve coherence and directness often drags such accounts into an overemphasis on one particular factor at the expense of others.

The term most widely used in sociological and historical writing to refer to such an overemphasis on one factor is **technological determinism**, which obviously suggests that the factor being given too much weight at the expense of others is the causal role of technology. I prefer the term 'reduction' or **reductionism** to determinism because the problem is not that technology is given a determining role but that this determining role is over-emphasised, thus reducing complexity to simplicity. The term 'technological determinism' was introduced to social and cultural studies by Raymond Williams in his (1974) book *Television: Technology and cultural form*, where he provided a critical account of such thinking as it applied to television and, indeed, technologies in general. However, it is often forgotten that Williams was also criticising what he called 'symptomatic technology' (1974: 13) – the view that technologies are merely by-products of wider social processes. What mattered for him was that technologies should never be seen in isolation, but always be understood *in relation to* other processes and factors.

Obviously, technologies have effects. The introduction of the telephone helped to transform the way that we communicate. The introduction of video recorders into homes in the 1980s played an important role in changing the experience of television. These are relatively uncontroversial statements, involving no reduction. Reduction would come in if we were, for example, to answer the question, 'What has caused the transformations in the way we experience television over the last 30 years?' with a broad response, such as 'New technologies, such as video, cable and satellite'. This begs a number of questions. What caused these technologies to be introduced in the way that they were? And how did they take the particular form they did? In accounts that are afflicted by the technological reductionism of their authors, the relationship of technologies to economic, political and cultural forces becomes obscured or even lost altogether.

It is also common to hear charges of **economic determinism**. Again, I think that reductionism is a more accurate term here too. Such charges tend to be levelled particularly against political-economic accounts, for their supposed reduction of social and cultural events and processes to ultimately economic driving forces, such as the imperative of companies to make a profit or the interests of the social class who control the means of production. Indeed, some cultural studies analysts and many pluralist communications studies scholars (such as Neuman, 1991: 16) make the claim that Marxism is more or less inherently reductionist. However, economic reductionism is by no means confined to Marxists – orthodox, mainstream economics often makes strong claims for the explanatory power of its economic models. As with technological reductionism, the issue here is not whether or not economic forces have any causal effect. It is clear, for example, that the behaviour of companies in the pursuit of profit does have significant social effects. The question is whether or not an overemphasis on economic explanation means that the analyst fails to provide an adequate account of the relationship of such economic factors to other processes.

Neuman (1991: 17) has drawn attention to the much less often heard charge of '**cultural determinism**', which he defines as the view that systems of values and beliefs have causal primacy.[1] Although it is not nearly so common to hear this phrase as it is to hear about technological and economic determinism, a belief in the causal primacy of culture is very widespread. A version of such cultural determinism underlies the commonly expressed, but mistaken, view that 'the media give people what they want' – that is, the shape of the media is determined by its audiences' culturally shaped desires and expectations. Few people are bold enough to go into print to attempt to justify such a view (an exception is Whale, 1977). However, this view can be heard with alarming regularity in cultural industry organisations and among public commentators and politicians. The main problem with it is that it ignores the huge role the media themselves play in shaping the desires and expectations of audiences.

The objection to cultural reductionism is not that it attributes causal properties to cultural processes. Clearly, for example, changes in leisure time and practices have an enormous influence on what cultural industry companies can do. The problem here, as with any reduction, is the begging of further questions about causality, such as, 'How did these cultural practices come to take the form that they did?' There are added difficulties in discussing the causal effects of cultural processes that are connected to the difficulties of definition surrounding the term 'culture', as discussed in the Introduction. 'Culture' has become such a widely used word in contemporary societies, whether in academic writing or journalism and popular publishing, that it has come to mean everything and nothing. Does it mean the prevalent attitudes, beliefs and values within a particular society or the ordinary, lived experiences of people or the general conditions of living within a particular place, organisation or institution? Everyone agrees that the term is difficult and contested, yet it is commonly invoked as a means of explanation superior to an approach centred on 'technology' or 'economics', without any recognition of these difficulties. As should be clear from the Introduction, I prefer Williams's definition of culture as 'the *signifying system* through which ... a social order is communicated, reproduced, experienced and explored' (1981: 13). This at least helps to avoid the clumsiest invocations of culture and draws our attention to the concept of the 'sociocultural' – an inherently non-reductionist concept, involving interactions between such cultural dimensions and more broadly *social* systems and behaviours (for a discussion of this difficult and neglected terrain, see Williams, 1981: Chapter 8).

CONTEXTS FOR CHANGE AND CONTINUITY IN THE CULTURAL INDUSTRIES, 1945–1990

In what follows, I develop an account that attempts to combine analysis of economic, technological and cultural processes with other key dimensions,

---

1 Neuman uses the concept of 'monism' – namely, accounts of determination based on single factors.

including politics, legal and regulatory frameworks and the internal dynamics of cultural industry organisations themselves. When I began thinking
about issues of determination and change in the cultural industries, I thought
that I would be able to summarise political economy work in order to provide a concise and coherent historical account as a lead-in to my assessment
of change and continuity. However, political economy approaches have, to
a remarkable degree, lacked an explanatory account of such changes. Even
writers such as Nicholas Garnham and Graham Murdock, whose writings
are scattered with insightful nuggets of explanation, have not provided any
systematic, overall view of the relationship between economic and cultural
change via a historical examination of the cultural industries. This chapter
takes some steps towards an overview of change, turning to a broader literature in social theory, politics and economics, to do so.

Having said that, social theory and social science have neglected the
cultural industries. Some major contributions have attempted to deal
with them, but nearly always in a very limited way. David Harvey's *The
Condition of Postmodernity* (1989: 284–307), for example, attributes considerable importance to the cultural industries in terms of mastering and
controlling sign systems in an era of new cultural volatility and unpredictability. Harvey, though, gives no space to their distinctive organisational forms (apart from one brief reference on page 290) or the conflicts
and contradictions within cultural production. Manuel Castells' chapter on
the media in *The Rise of the Network Society* (Castells, 1996) is the weakest
in his remarkable trilogy on *The Information Age* (of which *The Rise of the
Network Society* forms the first part) and he resorts to futurology and simplistic descriptions of a previous era of media (1996: 327–75). A significant
exception to such neglect of cultural production in social theory is Scott
Lash and John Urry's (1994) book *Economies of Signs and Space*. In it, an
entire chapter is devoted to the cultural industries and they have interesting things to say about the relationship between the cultural industries and
wider economic and social changes.

Where to begin? In my view, the most promising starting point for understanding changes in the cultural industries is the **Long Downturn**, which
affected much of the world from the late 1960s onwards. A number of
accounts (most notably, for my purposes, Castells, 1989, and Harvey, 1989)
have shown how corporations and governments responded to this economic
crisis in a number of ways in an attempt to fix the problem. In beginning my
narrative from an economic event, am I guilty of economic reductionism?
No, because I use the term 'starting point' advisedly here. This economic
crisis was itself produced in part by social, cultural, organisational and technological factors. There is no single point of origin for the chain of cause
and effect. The Long Downturn has served as a catalyst to accelerate and
consolidate certain processes that were already under way. So, while this is
an account that begins from the political-economic, it also recognises the fact
that these political-economic events were entangled with a large number of
other factors.

POLITICAL-ECONOMIC CHANGE: THE LONG DOWNTURN

It would be wrong to portray the era following the Second World War as one of global peace and prosperity. Disease and poverty were widespread and, outside Europe, there was unprecedented military conflict. There is no doubt, however, that, for the 'advanced', capitalist economies of Europe, North America and Australasia, the period from the 1950s to the early 1970s was one of steady economic growth, rising standards of living and a relatively stable system of liberal democratic government. The Stalinist economies of Eastern Europe and the Soviet Union also achieved significant growth. There was even evidence that the increasing inequality in wealth and social opportunity that had marked feudal and capitalist societies was beginning to be reversed (see Hobsbawm, 1995: 257–86, for an overview of this period). Because of the relatively strong macroeconomic performance of advanced capitalist economies, some economists have referred to this period as 'the golden age of capitalism' (Marglin and Schor, 1992). In the late 1960s, mainstream economists were predicting an end to the cycles of boom and bust that, in the views of all commentators, be they from left or right, had characterised industrial capitalism for 150 years.[2] However, in the early 1970s, after decades of these relatively favourable conditions, the advanced capitalist economies hit the beginning of the Long Downturn that continued into the 1990s, marked by particularly severe recessions in 1974–1975, 1979–1982 and 1991–1995. In the G7 countries between 1970 and 1990, profits fell significantly across all sectors, but especially in manufacturing. Other key economic indicators also showed a significant downturn, as can be seen in Table 3.1, which is drawn from Brenner (1998: 5).

There is some controversy over the causes of the Long Downturn. For David Harvey (1989), international financial movements began to undermine the stability of financial system from the early 1960s onwards. For other scholars (such as Armstrong et al., 1991), the primary cause was that the increasing power of working-class wage-earners disturbed the balance of capital and labour that had been sustained during the 'golden age'. As labour solidified its power, a 'wages explosion' squeezed profits, leading to crisis. For Robert Brenner (1998), the main cause of the decline in profits associated with the Long Downturn was not the increased pressure brought about by labour, but the tendency by capitalists to compete with each other without any regard for what happened to the system as a whole. As German and Japanese corporations increased their successful involvement in manufacturing, the world's key economy, the USA, experienced a crisis of overcapacity and production in manufacturing – which

---

2   See, among other examples quoted by Brenner (1998: 1), the remark by Paul Samuelson – one of the most eminent mainstream economists of the twentieth century – that the National Bureau of Economic Research had 'worked itself out of one of its jobs, the business cycle'.

Table 3.1 Comparing the post-war boom and the Long Downturn (average annual rates of change, except for net profit and unemployment rates, which are averages)

Manufacturing

	Net profit rate		Output		Net Capital Stock		Gross Capital Stock		Labour Productivity		Real Wage	
	1950–1973	1973–1993	1950–1973	1973–1993	1950–1973	1973–1993	1950–1973	1973–1993	1950–1973	1973–1993	1950–1973	1973–1993
US	24.35	14.5	4.3	1.9	3.8	2.25	–	–	3.0	2.4	2.6	0.5
Ger	23.1	10.9	5.1	0.9	5.7	0.9	6.4	1.7	4.8	1.7	5.7	2.4
Jap	40.4	20.4	14.1	5.0	14.5	5.0	14.7	5.0	10.2	5.1	6.1	2.7
G7	26.2	15.7	5.5	2.1	–	–	4.8	3.7	3.9	3.1	–	–

G7 net profit rate extends to 1990; German net capital stock covers 1955–1993; Japanese net profit rate and net capital stock cover in manufacturing 1955–1991.

Private Business

	Net Profit Rate		Output		Net Capital Stock		Gross Capital Stock		Labour Productivity		Real Wage		Unemployment Rate	
	1950–1973	1973–1993	1950–1973	1973–1993	1950–1973	1973–1993	1950–1973	1973–1993	1950–1973	1973–1993	1950–1973	1973–1993	1950–1973	1973–1993
US	12.9	9.9	4.2	2.6	3.8	3.0	–	–	2.7	1.1	2.7	0.2	4.2	6.7
Ger	23.2	13.8	4.5	2.2	6.0	2.6	5.1	3.0	4.6	2.2	5.7	1.9	2.3	5.7
Jap	21.6	17.2	9.1	4.1	–	–	9.35	7.1	5.6	3.1	6.3	2.7	1.6	2.1
G7	17.6	13.3	4.5	2.2	–	–	4.5	4.3	3.6	1.3	–	–	3.1	6.2

G7 net profit rate extends to 1990; German net capital stock covers 1955–1993.

Source: Brenner, 1998: 5

was, and remains, its key sector (see Brenner, 2000: 8) – and this triggered an international crisis, exacerbated by the OPEC oil price rise of 1973.

POLITICAL AND REGULATORY CHANGE: THE RISE OF NEO-LIBERALISM

Whatever the precise causes of the Long Downturn, there is widespread consensus that it had profound consequences. One set of consequences was political and these provide important contexts for understanding changes in the regulation of the cultural industries (discussed in detail in Part Two). The various advanced capitalist states responded to the crisis that hit capitalism in the 1970s by attacking the institutional strength of labour movements and moving away from the arrangements for state intervention in economic life that had prevailed in the post-war period, whereby government spending was used to supplement consumer spending whenever it was inadequate to sustain economic growth (see Harvey, 1989: Part II). Employers and governments ensured a long-term reduction in real levels of pay, but this was not sufficient to restore profits. From 1979, after some years of attempting to reflate Western economies, governments made permanent a set of anti-inflation strategies that had been tried in 1974–1975. Emergency cutbacks in public spending and the stripping away of regulation by democratically elected governments were promoted from emergency measures to permanent policy. The view that human needs are best served by an unregulated 'free market' – a view that had been popular with various nineteenth-century liberal economists, but had mostly been confined to cranks and nutcases for much of the late twentieth century – made a comeback, hence the terms '*neo*-liberal economics' and 'neo-liberalism'.[3]

Such neo-liberal free market thinking took particularly extreme forms in the UK and USA, where far-right conservative governments were elected (by a small minority of the eligible-to-vote population) in 1979 and 1980 respectively. These governments were re-elected with bigger majorities in 1983 and 1984 respectively, partly because an influential minority of people benefited from such policies, but also because the labour movements in the USA and the UK – traditionally the basis of leftist politics in both countries – were in complete disarray and this chaos on the left helped make the rightist governments look competent, in spite of record levels of unemployment and inequality. This was an era in which the cultural industries had an especially important role in legitimising political and economic strategies, as press and television news portrayed trade unions as regressive.

---

3 In the USA, 'liberal' has come to mean politically centrist (as opposed to conservative or radical), but that is not the sense of the term used when writers refer to nineteenth-century liberal economics or neo-liberalism. The primary meaning here is that these doctrines advocate minimal state intervention in societies, in the interests of individual freedom. See Crouch (2011).

From the late 1970s, most governments of whatever political persuasion attempted to weaken the bargaining power of labour in order to lower wage costs. Credit was restricted by the raising of interest rates, which forced unprofitable firms out of business and weakened labour still further as a result of the spread of unemployment (Brenner, 1998: 181). Following the second election victories of Margaret Thatcher and Ronald Reagan in 1983–1984, however, extreme neo-liberal dogma spread into elected social democratic, reformist governments, such as that of New Zealand from 1984 onwards (see Gray, 1998) and most governments of advanced capitalist countries in the late 1980s. When Stalinist communism collapsed in Eastern Europe, the Soviet Union and many of their client states in 1989–1991, it was neo-liberalism rather than social democracy that was adopted as a political model.

Within these general shifts towards neo-liberalism in government policy, there was a specific set of policy shifts that were to have a particularly profound impact on the cultural industries and their status within contemporary societies. In this book, I use the term **information society** to denote the thinking and rhetoric behind this specific set of policies. This refers to the view that information and knowledge are now central, as never before, to the way that modern societies operate. Box 3.1 explains why this idea is so vital. (Some writers use the term 'knowledge society', but they are usually referring to pretty much the same idea with slightly different emphases.[4])

Box 3.1   The Information Society

The idea of the information society is that we live in societies that are as different from those based on industry as industrial societies were different from agricultural societies. There is an implicit teleology – that information societies will succeed industrial ones, just as industry displaced agriculture as the main basis of global economic life. In the industrial era, work and prosperity were based on manufacture and manual labour, while in the information era they are supposedly based on information and knowledge. For information society discourse, in the words of one of its critics, the goal of production is much less to make and circulate things that can be touched – oil, steel, cars – and much more about producing changes in 'relationship, image and perception' (Webster, 1995: 1). In some formulations, this is a way of interpreting the shift in employment from manufacturing to services, discussed in the next section, but the idea of the information society also derives from the increasing importance of research and development and science and technology in modern economies.

---

4   Some writers and politicians use 'economy' interchangeably with 'society' in these debates and a great deal of information society thinking and rhetoric is indeed about the economy, but, as Webster (1995: 6–29) shows, 'information society' thinking incorporates other dimensions – technological, occupational, spatial and cultural – and this is a reason for preferring 'society' here. Another is simply that it is more widely used.

These were big issues as information society discourses took root in the 1960s and 1970s. Marc Porat's massive study published in 1977, *The Information Economy*, estimated that information accounted for 46 per cent of the USA's GDP. However, this figure could be arrived at only by separating the information and non-informational elements of massive industries such as oil and automobiles and assigning a value to each – an operation that rests on very difficult and always controversial value judgements, as Webster (1995: 12) points out. Moreover, such statistics say relatively little about how information is supposed to operate within supposed information societies. Even if we accept the value of quantifying information in this way, other studies have suggested that information accounts for much less economic activity than Porat estimated.

Nevertheless, such accounts laid the basis for the popularisation of the idea of the information society in Peter Drucker's notion of the 'knowledge economy' (1992[1968]) and Daniel Bell's (1974) notion of a 'post-industrial society, where theoretical knowledge, especially in science and technology, was seen as a new, emerging 'axial principle' of society. There was intense debate over these ideas, but, by the 1980s in government policymaking, the idea that information and knowledge were key to future prosperity and employment in industrial societies, faced by new competition from newly industrialising countries outside Europe and North America, had become absorbed as a kind of commonsense notion, backed up by dozens of reports and committees, many of them drawing on emerging neo-liberal forms of policy (a good example is the British Cabinet Office report of 1983, *Making a Business of Information*).

According to information society thinking, the cultural industries are based on information and knowledge and,therefore are part of the burgeoning 'knowledge economy'. Significantly, they are a highly visible part of this economy, which perhaps allows their role to seem greater than it is. In the 1990s, with the rise of the internet and the world wide web, discourses about the information society, and the role of communications and media within it, were proliferating ever more wildly and an array of quite different assumptions and claims fed into visions of the future. These have tended to be blurred when politicians, business executives, journalists and academics use the term. The idea of an information society is a confused one, but it has had real effects on policy and the role and status of the cultural industries in contemporary societies. It became widely accepted among policymakers and academics that the cultural industries were going to form very important parts of future economies and their growth needed to be supported in various ways – usually in order to give nations or regions a competitive advantage or avoid a disadvantage in relation to other nations or regions. This had a considerable role to play in spreading the view, which I discuss in Chapter 5, that intellectual property needed to be more rigorously policed and laws changed so that cultural industry businesses could make more money out of their copyrights. More indirectly, the general emphasis on the importance of information and communication technologies in the various types of information society discourse fuelled the 'deregulation' of telecommunications and government efforts to boost the growth of the IT industries (both hardware and software). This was to lead to a massive proliferation of the channels through which cultural content could be carried, as we shall see. These developments were certainly not without contradiction – in fact, some people argue that the increased policing of copyright, in ways that have favoured the oligopolistic corporations dominating cultural production, actually inhibits creativity rather than promotes it.

Neo-liberalism and the information society are the vital *political* contexts for understanding changes in communications and telecommunications law and policy since the 1980s. Neo-liberalism has framed the view underlying a great deal of policy that human needs are best served by the 'free' market. Such **marketisation** has been fundamental to bringing about a whole series of other changes in the cultural industries. I trace the paths of marketisation in a number of different contexts in Chapter 4 and analyse their effects in more detail there.

CHANGING BUSINESS STRATEGIES

A second major consequence of the decline in productivity and profits associated with the Long Downturn was that capitalist businesses across the developed world began a period of intense innovation. There were three main aspects to this:

- A shift towards service industries – that is, away from the extractive (for example, mining and agriculture) sector and, to some extent, the transformative (mainly manufacturing) sector and towards the various industrial sectors that deal primarily with services, such as distributive, producer, social and personal services, to use the terms adapted by Castells (1996: 311) from Singelmann (1978).
- Internationalisation.
- Organisational innovation and restructuring.

Investment shifts towards service industries

There was a significant overall move – on the part of businesses in advanced industrial countries – away from agriculture, raw material extraction, construction and manufacturing and towards service industries. This had been a longer-term trend, as Harvey (1989: 157) shows, but it became irreversible in the wake of the Long Downturn. Companies in advanced industrial countries faced rising wages and increased competition, not only from the newly industrialised countries of the Asia-Pacific region (most notably South Korea, Taiwan, Hong Kong and Singapore) but also from Latin America (principally Mexico and Brazil). However, this shift is often simplified or

Table 3.2   The shift to services

Industry	US 1970	US 1991	Japan 1970	Japan 1990	France 1968	France 1989	UK 1970	UK 1990
Extractive	4.6	3.5	19.8	7.2	15.6	6.4	3.6	3.3
Transformative	33.0	24.7	34.1	33.7	39.4	29.5	46.7	27.3
Distributive services	22.4	20.6	22.4	24.3	18.8	20.5	18.7	20.6
Producer services	8.2	14.0	4.8	9.6	5.0	10.0	5.0	12.0
Social services	22.0	25.5	10.3	14.3	15.1	19.5	17.7	27.2
Personal services	10.0	11.7	8.5	10.2	8.2	14.1	8.1	8.1

Figures refer to the percentage of total workforce.

Sector definitions

Extractive: agriculture and mining

Transformative construction, utilities and manufacturing

Distributive services: transport, communication and wholesale

Producer services: banking, insurance, estate agency, engineering, accounting, legal services, miscellaneous

Social services: medical, hospital, education, welfare, religious services, non-profit-making organizations, postal service, government, miscellaneous personal services: domestic service, hotels, eating and drinking places, repairs, laundry, barbers and beauticians, miscellaneous and unclassifiable services

Source: adapted from Castells, 1996: 282–93

exaggerated. The figures in Table 3.2, based on Castells' data (1996: 282–93) provide some indication of the overall patterns. These are useful in painting a much more sophisticated picture of industrial change than the old primary–secondary–tertiary model of agriculture, manufacturing and services. Castells, drawing on industrial historian Joachim Singelmann's work, instead uses the broader terms 'extractive' and 'transformative' to describe the primary and secondary sectors and breaks services up into four constituent sectors.

The decline of manufacturing tends also to be exaggerated. In Japan, for example, the transformative sector – including construction, utilities and manufacturing – showed only a very small decline in the proportion of employment during the post-1973 period. However, there were substantial declines in the USA, France and the UK. Even more significant was the decline in the extractive sector (agriculture and mining) in countries such as Japan and France with sizeable rural populations.

The 1980s and 1990s boom in the cultural industries needs to be seen in the context of this shift in investment strategies. Unfortunately, Singelmann and Castells' categories are not flexible enough to include figures specifically on the cultural industries. Chapter 5, however, takes the view that there is slow, steady growth in the relative size of the cultural industries. This growth can be understood as an aspect of a general shift towards investment in service industries in advanced industrial countries. Let us examine the forces driving that shift in more detail. Nicholas Garnham argues (1990: 117) that the demand for labour-saving domestic consumer electronic goods had helped fuel the 'golden age' of the 1950s and 1960s, but Western markets were fast becoming saturated by the beginning of the 1970s. Companies had the chance to use the vast amount of high-tech research generated by the US government in defence and space as a result of the Cold War.[5] By the early 1980s, as Europe and North America faced economic recession and newly industrialised countries in Asia continued to achieve high levels of economic growth, the perceived advantages for Euro-American corporations of moving into high-tech and cultural industries were even more overwhelming, in spite of high research and development costs.

The cultural industries were profoundly affected by these changes. As competition in the new consumer markets intensified, there was increasing demand for advertising and marketing opportunities. This proved crucial in fuelling the growth in media outlets that continued into the 2000s. Here are some relevant data.

- Table 3.3 shows how the proportion of gross domestic product (GDP) devoted to advertising in a wide range of countries increased significantly during the 1980s.
- Between 1984 and 1989, advertising expenditure in the European Union (EU) increased by more than 6 per cent every year. In 1988 alone it increased by 10 per cent (Howard, 1998).
- EU growth continued at a reduced rate in the early 1990s, but picked up again from 1993. Growth was 73 per cent in real terms between 1980 and 1996, reaching £58 billion, or US$74 billion, in the latter year (Howard, 1998: 117).
- The most striking growth figures were to be found in the developing markets of the Middle East and Latin America. Middle Eastern advertising expenditure increased by over 1000 per cent in real terms between 1987 and 1996 (IJOA, 1998a: 515). In Latin America, growth was 377 per cent in the same period (IJOA, 1998b).
- Growth in advertising expenditure in the USA in the 1980s and 1990s was slower, but the USA already had phenomenally high advertising expenditure in the early 1980s. In 1998, 42.9 per cent of all advertising investment was spent in North America and the USA accounted for roughly 95 per cent of this figure (IJOA, 2000).

Such figures indicate the increasing economic rewards afforded by the cultural industries during the period under examination. The cultural industries were

---

5 For example, although the internet cannot be explained entirely as a defence-driven phenomenon – the familiar story is that it developed as a means of maintaining computer systems in case of a nuclear strike – Brian Winston's account (1998: 321–36) makes it clear how the development of key research into switching protocols was primarily funded by defence spending.

more than just another investment opportunity, however. Increasingly, they came to be seen as a *prestigious* form of making profits as the entertainment industries came to be perceived as a key economic sector, at least in North America and Europe (see Wolf, 1999). Vast companies in other sectors, such as General Electric in the USA or Sony in Japan, made significant investments in cultural production during the 1980s. Such industrial conglomerates had intervened in the cultural industries before, especially in the 1960s, but in the 1980s they were entering the very core of the cultural industries: the television networks that dominated the cultural landscape in the USA (NBC and CBS). Meanwhile, companies already involved in the cultural industries grew and come to operate across different cultural industries. This meant that, more and more, the production of culture was the concern of ambitious and well-resourced sectors of economic activity. The implications of these changes for the cultural industries are discussed throughout this book, but especially in Chapter 6.

Internationalisation

A second major type of industrial and organisational restructuring in response to falling profits in advanced industrial countries was what Harvey (1989: 183) calls a 'spatial fix'. Owners and operators of capitalist enterprises attempted to restore higher profits by investing abroad in order to spread fixed costs and make the most of cheaper labour markets, as real levels of pay rose in advanced industrial countries. Such internationalisation has a long history, as David Held et al.'s (1999: 242–55) account shows admirably. There had been a massive expansion in foreign direct investment (FDI) – a significant marker of business internationalisation – during the Gold Standard period, from 1870 to 1914, but this was dominated by the UK, highly concentrated in certain areas and primarily concerned the extractive industries. Cartels focused on raw materials, such as oil, began to form during the inter-war period. Consumer goods were increasingly sold on an international basis, but production tended to be organised nationally. In the post-war period – particularly in the 1960s – there was huge expansion in the role of the multinational corporations, especially on the part of manufacturing corporations based in the USA. Internationalisation of production began to be expressed in the emergence of global production and distribution networks, marking a qualitatively new phase of internationalisation.[6]

The last three decades have seen an acceleration of such internationalisation in response to the Long Downturn. Internationalisation was slowed by the severe recession of the early 1980s, but the next decade saw very large increases in the annual growth rates of foreign direct investment. The annual

---

6   Held et al. (1999) use the popular, but, in this context, confusing term of 'globalisation'. I prefer internationalisation, for reasons that I explain in Chapter 8.

Table 3.3   Increases in advertising expenditure, 1980–1990 (This table shows the percentage of gross domestic product spent on advertising)

Country	1980	1990
Austria	0.47	0.63
Belgium	0.47	0.65
Canada	0.98	1.05
Switzerland	1.02	1.07
Germany	0.75	0.82
Denmark	0.76	0.84
Finland	0.71	0.94
France	0.48	0.78
UK	1.11	1.37
Greece	0.26	0.77
Ireland	0.65	0.82
Italy	0.37	0.62
Japan	0.95	1.12
Norway	0.77	0.74
Netherlands	0.87	0.87
Portugal	0.19	0.77
Sweden	0.64	0.80
Turkey	0.20	0.38
USA	1.32	1.51
Europe	0.70	0.91

Source: Sánchez-Tabernero et al., 1993: 125, drawing on Zenith Media Worldwide

growth rate in FDI flow was 7.3 per cent in the period 1980–1985 and 19.4 per cent between 1986 and 1994.[7] Meanwhile, the neo-liberal economic policies of the 1980s and 1990s led to the removal of protection measures for national industries. The GATT rounds – a series of negotiations between nations aimed at reduction and eventual elimination of tariffs and other barriers to 'free trade' – culminated in the Marrakesh agreement of 1993 and the formation of the World Trade Organisation (WTO) in 1995. The removal of trade restrictions helped to fuel the internationalisation of business activity by corporations of all kinds. A concurrent internationalisation of financial markets – beginning in the 1950s, but culminating in the deregulation of

---

7   These growth rates were considerably higher than the rates of growth of gross world product, indicating that growth in international activity was outstripping economic growth.

international financial flows in the 1990s – helped further to delegitimate the role of national governments in managing economies, as such governments became apparently helpless when faced with speculators on currency markets. Vast regional trading markets were formed in Europe (the European Union), North America/Mexico (NAFTA) and the Asia-Pacific (APEC), forcing a rush to locate in these regions. There was also a massive wave of mergers and acquisitions as transnational corporations bought up overseas companies to expand their production and distribution networks. By 1995, overseas affiliates accounted for 7.5 per cent of world GDP – in 1970, the figure had been 4.5 per cent (Held et al., 1999: 246).

The cultural industries internationalised their operations, too, and there were sound economic reasons for their doing so – most notably the low marginal costs of some of their key products (see Introduction). However, the general internationalisation of businesses as a whole affected the cultural industries in key ways. International communications became crucial for business in general and developments in the telecommunications industry came to have profound effects on the cultural industries.

International communications became vital for multinational corporations of all kinds as the different parts of these vast companies needed to communicate with each other, quickly and securely via public and, increasingly, private networks. Partly to provide for these needs, high-tech companies began a wave of technological innovation in communication technologies in league with the huge European public telecommunication operators (PTOs) and private corporations in the USA. This culminated in the development of digital 'intelligent networks' in the 1970s and 1980s. Besides servicing the needs of multinational corporations, the development of these networks was, in large part, aimed at protecting the positions of public and private monopolies as new entrants came into the telecommunications market (see Mansell, 1993).

Such innovations in telecommunications technologies have been vital in providing new distribution forms for the cultural industries, including, of course, not only the internet and world wide web, but also digital television and private information networks. In fact, a more accurate way to put this is that the cultural industries have had to expand to fill the huge capacity created by the telecommunications industries. Up until the 1970s, most telecommunications traffic was voice only; now images, text, graphics and music flow through the intelligent networks alongside phone conversations.

Internationalisation in another industry – consumer electronics – also had important knock-on effects on the cultural industries. Spreading fixed costs across many national markets funded expensive research and development for new hardware devices (see the section 'Technological change: information technology and consumer electronics', below).

Organisational innovation and restructuring

A third form of industrial and organisational change relevant for an account of the cultural industries was that new forms of organisational innovation were introduced in order to achieve higher profits, reduce labour costs and win market share over competing firms. Writers from a number of perspectives have examined the general restructuring of businesses that took place in the 1970s and 1980s and many of them attribute this to a response to the Long Downturn. Various phrases have been used to label this restructuring – most notably 'flexible specialisation' (Piore and Sabel, 1984), 'flexible accumulation' (Harvey, 1989) and 'post-Fordism' (Hall and Jacques, 1990). Castells (1996: 151–68) provided a valuable breakdown of some of the main elements of this restructuring.

- *The 'decline' of the large corporation and the rise of interfirm networking*
  Castells argued – following commentators such as Bennett Harrison, whose (1994) book *Lean and Mean* argued for the continuing importance and vitality of the large corporation – that the large corporation was not nearly so much in a state of crisis as some 'post-Fordist' commentators suggested in the 1980s. Rather, said Castells, the traditional, vertically integrated large corporation was in decline as a model for how to organise production, but it was still very much in existence. Corporations changed their organisational structures and, increasingly, subcontracted to small- and medium-sized firms. These smaller firms were potentially more dynamic and able to innovate than large ones, but they were often involved in close relationships with the corporations that subcontract to them.

- *Corporate strategic alliances*
  An important emergent pattern has been the formation of strategic alliances between corporations – not as in traditional cartel arrangements but, rather, for specific projects. This is especially relevant, said Castells, in high-tech sectors where research and development costs are enormously expensive. For Castells, the self-sufficient corporation was increasingly a thing of the past. What is more, small- and medium-sized firms are often drawn into such alliances as an extension of interfirm networking.

- *New methods of management, and corporate restructuring*
  Many discussions of organisational innovation concern forms of production developed in Japanese car production (thus sometimes labelled 'Toyotism'). Much of this involves using information sensibly to reduce inventories by delivering supplies just in time and improving quality control. Most significant for the management of labour, however, is the idea of involving workers in production by reducing hierarchies and creating autonomous working units. Castells also pointed to developments in the organisation of corporations – in particular, the tendency to move away from traditional, hierarchical forms of organisational structure and towards the setting up of decentralised, sometimes semi-autonomous working units – even to the point, at times, of having these units compete with each other. The corporation becomes a network.

The job of the corporate centre is to make sure that the network communicates adequately. Castells says that such arrangements, originally developed as cost-saving devices during the economic restructuring of the 1980s and the horizontal corporation of the 1990s, represented an extension of these arrangements. Closely related to such changes is the idea of flexibility. The idea was that, as markets became ever more volatile and unpredictable, firms would need to be able to switch production rapidly to conform to changing tastes. These changes are particularly interesting in the present context because, as we saw in Chapter 2, the cultural industries have had this network form for much of the complex professional era.

- *Changing work patterns*
  In a separate discussion, Castells (1996: 264–72) noted the new working conditions associated with new organisational forms. In particular, he noted the increasing disintegration of workforces, with substantial rises in temporary, part-time and self-employment. This may take the form of increased work options for the relatively privileged, but also of casualisation and insecurity for the less well-off and those with fewer skills and less education.

The discussion here of changes in businesses of all kinds paves the way for the discussion of industrial and organisational shifts in the cultural industries that I undertake in Chapter 6 and 7. An important theme there is the extent to which the cultural industries are becoming more or less distinct from other sectors. Are the cultural industries losing their distinctiveness as they become increasingly important in advanced industrial economies? Alternatively, are, as some writers (for example, Lash and Urry, 1994) argue, other industries becoming more like the cultural industries as, for example, companies increasingly organise themselves into semi-autonomous divisions?

SOCIOCULTURAL AND TEXTUAL CHANGES

Understanding changes in the cultural industries over the last two decades needs, then, to lay great emphasis on restructuring in response to the economic crisis of the 1970s. An adequate account needs to go beyond restructuring also. We should avoid a mode of thinking whereby economic change 'happens to' politics and production organisations and this then brings about changes in the cultural industries and thereafter in cultural life more generally, moving upwards from the economic foundations or 'base' to the building or superstructure. There are three main ways in which we need to go beyond such an account.

   First, an account of changes in the cultural industries since 1980 needs to acknowledge the complex interplay of, on the one hand, economic and political processes and, on the other, the social, cultural and institutional processes that are sometimes conceived as being by-products of events at the macro level. The cultural industries could hardly evade the effects of the accelerating sociocultural transformations taking place in advanced industrial societies from the 1960s onwards, including the dismantling of many forms of social authority in educational, religious and other institutions, changes in family life, sexuality, relationships between women, men and children, the very meaning of what it is to be a person and an increasing emphasis on, and reflexivity about, issues of personal identity. In order to gain audiences in time-rich and/or newly prosperous constituencies, such as the baby boom teenager and student in the 1960s or working women in the early 1980s, cultural firms had to appeal to changing values – at least in some market sectors. Not that cultural industry corporations were answering the pre-existing needs of consumers: they were simultaneously helping to shape these new needs. Obviously enough, citizens affected by these sociocultural changes, imbued with new ways of being and thinking, were allowed to enter the cultural industries and were able to transmit their values into the texts they created. One striking example is the development of new genres, forms and narrative modes in the New Hollywood cinema of the early 1970s. This was partly the result of organisational and institutional factors, in that the old studio system had broken down and film studios perceived that the core audience for cinema was young baby boomers. However, the shift was also sociocultural as film-makers of a new generation brought new ideas and values into film production (see Tasker, 1996).

Second, an adequate analysis of the cultural industries needs to take account of continuity and multiple and coexisting processes of change occurring at different rates. An overemphasis on restructuring exaggerates short-term transformation at the expense of these different temporalities. The increasing centrality of the cultural industries in economic life, for example, was certainly not caused *exclusively* by post-crisis restructuring. Culture was already becoming increasingly central to modern social life throughout the twentieth century as leisure time expanded and consumer culture began to pervade advanced industrial economies. When Stuart Hall (1997a: 209) refers to the increasing importance of culture as a long-term 'cultural revolution' – taking place throughout the twentieth century, whereby 'the domain constituted by the activities, institutions and practices we call "cultural" has expanded out of all recognition' – he is surely right to think that this process predates the restructuring processes under discussion earlier.[8] We might be wise, then, to think of the transformations since 1980 as *accelerating* processes that were already in train.

Third, all histories need to recognise the possibilities of contingency and chance. An account of the cultural industries that sees transformations

---

8   In his chapter Hall uses what I believe is far too broad a definition of 'culture', which he seems at times to equate with 'discourse' or even 'meaning' (Hall, 1997a: 225–6).

there as a seamless response to economic and political crisis may well fail to acknowledge such contingency. This is particularly significant in an account of industries that are based on irrational (or at least arational) aesthetic experiences. This brings us back to the unpredictable ways in which people make use of aesthetic and informational products (see Introduction). This dimension of the cultural industries makes it especially likely that certain changes in the cultural industries might come about as a result of sudden, unexpected cultural phenomena rather than be outcomes of structural economic patterns.

It would be impossible to do justice to the immense sociocultural changes taking place across the world in the late twentieth century, but we can point to those aspects of most direct relevance to the cultural industries. Two crucial issues are, first, working time versus leisure time and, second, disposable income. Harold Vogel (1998: 6) cites figures showing the huge decline in the USA in average weekly working hours between 1850 (70 hours a week) and 1940 (approximately 44 hours a week) – the years of growth during which the cultural industries made their transition from the market professional era to the complex professional era. Meanwhile, as disposable incomes have risen, the proportion of that income spent on essentials, such as food, has tended to fall (this phenomenon is often referred to as Engel's Law) and more money is spent on non-essentials, such as cultural products of the kind produced by the cultural industries.

US working hours worked per year stayed roughly even during the 1970s and 1980s. But in most countries, according to the Organisation for Economic Co-operation and Development (OECD) figures, the trend in working hours was markedly downwards during the 1970s and 1980s (see Vogel, 1998: 8). Even in the USA, though – with its relatively stable working time versus leisure time split – the amount of time spent on media consumption has increased enormously, from 50.7 hours to 65.5 hours per week (Vogel, 1998: 9). Leisure time was dominated, to a quite remarkable degree, by one activity: television. The amount of television watched by the average American increased considerably between 1970 and 1995, from 1226 hours per person per year to 1575 (Vogel, 1998: 9). Americans, on average, spent 30 hours a week watching television (Webster and Phalen, 1997: 108). This made television by far the most heavily consumed medium in the 1990s. It represented over 46 per cent of the 65.5 hours per week spent consuming media, which was about the same proportion as in 1970 (Vogel, 1998: 9).

What is more, expenditure on recreation increased out of proportion to the increase in non-working time. In the USA, the figure rose from $93.8 per person per year in 1970 to $395.5 per year in 1995, expressed in 1992 dollar terms and, therefore, adjusted for inflation. This represented a doubling of the percentage of total personal consumption spending made up by such recreation spending, from 4.3 per cent to 8.6 per cent. These are the factors that most directly helped to bring about growth in the cultural industries during the period under discussion, at least in the USA. It is likely that similar developments are under way elsewhere.

TECHNOLOGICAL CHANGE: INFORMATION TECHNOLOGY AND CONSUMER ELECTRONICS

Finally, we return to the factor of change most commonly invoked in journalism and popular publishing. Technological reductionism saturates everyday discourses about the cultural industries. This means that we need to be particularly cautious in addressing technology as a causal factor, for technologies are themselves the effects of choices, decisions, contingencies and coincidences in the realms of economics, politics and culture.

Technological innovation is nothing new. It is one of the main ways in which companies (and nations) try to outdo each other in competitive markets. Technologies are more than just economic opportunities, however. Some become the repositories of hopes for a better life or symbols for anxieties about the future. From the 1960s, information and communication technologies spawned huge amounts of commentary and debate – and much of it was mediated through the information society discourse introduced in Box 3.1. Two absolutely key developments were the increasing power and diminishing size of computers (Augarten, 1984); and research in telecommunications and computing that allowed for the developments of digital networks, including new possibilities for computers to be connected together in networks. By the 1970s, it was becoming apparent that digitalisation would make possible a degree of 'convergence' between computers and telecommunications. As we shall see in Chapter 4, this was to have significant effects on government policy, when, in the economic crisis of the 1980s, neo-liberal policymakers increasingly turned to the information and communication sectors to revive US prosperity. At the same time, however, in the 1980s, the internet was being developed by engineers and scientists with a strong sense of the value of open, informal co-operation – and this was to have a lasting impact on the form that digital networks took, once the internet unexpectedly became a global phenomenon in the 1990s.

These remarkable technological developments were possible because of vast research expenditure. So why were such huge amounts of research resources diverted to advances in computing?

- Initially, because there were many perceived military uses for computing, the high-tech computer and communications sectors benefited from vast defence spending on computer-mediated communication. This was especially the case in the USA, where the Department of Defense was, for many years, 'centrally concerned in the development strategies of the entire US computer software business' (Tunstall, 1986: 41).
- As we have already seen, transnational corporations were expanding rapidly during the post-war period and they needed faster, more efficient communication technologies to bind their operations.
- There was the later context of the downturn in Western economies from the late 1960s onwards and, in particular, the threat to manufacturing

industries in Europe and the USA from newly industrialising countries in Asia. Many Western governments and enterprises invested enormous amounts of money and resources in the development of high-tech sectors.

- The information society discourse discussed above (see Box 3.1) helped to feed the idea that the onward march of the computer was either beneficial or inevitable – or both. Importantly, the microcomputer was mythologised in early 1980s media coverage as both highly desirable and derived from small-scale garage entrepreneurialism (Streeter, 2011: 82–8). This allowed the idea of networked personal computers to be embraced both by left and right, by the business community, and by those who wanted to forge alternatives to Western consumerism.

Thinking about the causes of technological innovation in this way takes us away from technological reductionism. Technologies should not be thought of as the best answers to pre-existing needs, which is the way we are often encouraged to think about them by media coverage. Instead, their evolution is determined by many choices and decisions and the unintended consequences of dynamics that are external to the companies developing them. But of course they still have effects. The impact of the computer on the cultural industries has been profound. Computers became increasingly central to many people's working and leisure lives during the 1980s. The cost of personal computers fell sharply in the early 1980s, when Apple launched as a public company and IBM entered the market (using Microsoft software). According to Tom Forester (1987: 134), sales of personal computers went from none in 1975 to 7 million in 1983, 1.4 million of which were sold in the USA. In a single decade, the number of personal computers installed worldwide grew from 200,000 to over 50 million in 1987.[9] The explosion in discussion of 'new media' dates from this period, when ownership of computers became sufficiently widespread for industry analysts, policymakers and so on to envisage a future where digitalisation would become the basis of home-based information and entertainment.[10] By the early 1980s, commentators were increasingly discussing the idea of convergence between computers and telecommunications. We shall see the consequences of this on policymaking in Chapter 4. It helped give rise to the break-up of

---

9 The rise of the personal computer, mainly used for work, should not be confused with the rise of the home computer, which were fewer in number – 6 million in the USA by 1985 (Forester, 1987: 151) – and often underused.

10 Debates about new media took distinctive forms in continental Europe, where there was also great emphasis on public 'videotex' systems. Most notable was the French Minitel network. See Castells, 1996: 343–5, who as part of his celebration of American entrepreneurialism and individualism, denigrates Minitel in spite of his interesting and frank comments about his own involvement in the 'democratised sexual fantasy' of Minitel chat lines in the 1980s.

national telecommunications monopolies, and led to a massive investment in infrastructure, in ways that would have profound effects on the cultural industries.

There were other important technological developments besides those related to computers and information technology during the 1945 to 1990 period. Particularly significant were developments in consumer electronics, especially new technologies for the storage and retrieval of texts. The most notable were:

- various tape formats, of which the audio cassette and its players (Philips) triumphed;
- the video cassette recorder, where a battle was fought between Matsushita's VHS format and Sony's Betamax and Philips' V2000 formats;
- the personal stereo – most notably, Sony's Walkman;
- the various compact disc technologies (initially developed by Philips), especially music CDs, but also CD-ROMs, as personal computers developed, and, later, DVDs.

The 'best' technology did not always win. In a well-known case, the battle over video cassette formats in the early 1980s, Matsushita's VHS format, for example, triumphed over Sony's superior Betamax format because of Matsushita's more effective marketing and because they agreed to license the technology rather than manufacture it under their own name.

The interplay between consumer electronics and cultural industries has been crucial. Many of the key transitions in cultural industries in the twentieth century involved new storage-retrieval devices. Indeed there have been times when consumer electronics companies have entered into the cultural industries – for example, General Electric's ownership of RCA Records, or Sony's continuing involvement in the film and recording businesses. However, these ventures have often been problematic. (This suggests what might increasingly happen with the information technology companies who have partly taken their place.)

The replacement of old formats – such as vinyl records by CDs and video cassettes by DVDs – and the appearance of new ones helped to create new selling opportunities for the cultural industries from the 1980s through to the early 2000s. By then, however, the digitalisation unleashed by telecommunications and computing technologies and consequent policy developments (see Chapter 4) was to lead to significant problems by making the old problem of controlling scarcity in cultural markets considerably more pronounced.

In this chapter, I have been discussing the major contexts for understanding patterns of change/continuity in the cultural industries in the last 30 or so years. The emphasis has been on factors external to the cultural industries: the end of the supposed golden age of growth and the beginning of the Long Downturn; the neo-liberal political-economic response; general changes in the business environment, of which the cultural industries were a part; social and cultural transformations; and technological developments outside the cultural industries. I have been concentrating here on transformation, but we should note that there was also important economic, political, organisational, sociocultural and technological continuity alongside these changes. Economies continued, for the most part, to be run by national governments, even if there were increasing interconnections between different parts of the world; liberal democracy remained the model for government in the advanced industrial countries; the legal frameworks governing businesses remained fundamentally intact in these countries; people continued to work hard, worry about their children and seek pleasure in watching and participating in cultural events; radio and television remained dominant as cultural technologies throughout most of the world.

Much of this chapter has been concerned with what explains change, but what explains such continuity? Even in a time of remarkable transformation, certain structures are hard to shift. Powerful groups feel threatened by change and fight for the retention of the status quo. There is the force of habit – it often seems easier to just carry on doing things the same way. Then there are aspects of human life that are hard to change and may even be rooted in the long-standing characteristics of human beings across many different societies. One such is the pleasure of having a story told to us, which can be found, in many different contexts, even if the characteristic forms of stories vary. There are powerful forces for continuity in the internal dynamics of the cultural industries, too.

A key argument of this book, outlined in the Introduction (see pages 25–33) and expanded upon in Chapter 2, is that certain distinctive properties of the production and consumption of cultural goods, as opposed to other commodities, help explain why cultural production tends to be organised in particular, recurring ways. To recapitulate, the main dynamics are the high levels of risk to be found in the cultural industries; high production costs and low reproduction costs; the tensions between creativity and commerce; and the way that cultural products act as semi-public goods and various distinctive responses to these conditions, including offsetting misses against hits, concentration and integration, the creation of artificial scarcity, formatting and the loose/tight control of production and circulation. For all the changes of the last 30 years, including the massive expansion of the cultural industries and their increasing centrality in social and economic life, cultural businesses still have to manage these problems, which derive from the difficulties of managing creativity and information. Because the ways in which creativity and information are understood to have very deep historical roots, problems and complexities surrounding the task of managing them persist and are not going to be blown away by new technologies, new organisational strategies or new market conditions. The growth and huge profitability of the cultural industries suggest that owners and managers have been largely successful in their strategies for controlling cultural production and consumption. But the management of creativity remains a fraught business. And the problems faced by cultural industry corporations continue to push business strategies in certain directions rather than others.

Part Three attempts to distinguish fundamental changes from superficial changes in a number of key aspects, setting continuity against transformation and separating out different types and rates of alteration. Before then, though, Part Two outlines crucial policy changes that were to have a significant effect on cultural production from the 1980s onwards.

RECOMMENDED AND FURTHER READING

Raymond Williams's opening chapter in *Television: Technology and Cultural Form* (1974) is still a worthwhile discussion of communication technologies. An enjoyable and provocative book about technological change relevant to the cultural industries is Brian Winston's *Media Technology and Society* (1998), which even manages to be funny at times. A critical and historically-informed overview of major technological developments is provided by Stephen Lax, in his *Media and Communication Technologies* (2009). Thomas Streeter's *The Net Effect* (2011) is highly recommended as an analysis of technological change, and a piece of cultural history.

David Harvey's book, *The Condition of Postmodernity* (1989), remains a scintillating read about the relationship between economic, political and cultural change, even if it sometimes overemphasises the causal effects of economic dynamics and underplays cultural effects (see Meaghan Morris's brilliant 1992 cultural studies critique). Scott Lash and John Urry's *Economies of Signs and Space* (1994) has a similar breadth, although it drifts into social theory jargonese at times. I am critical of some of the work of Manuel Castells elsewhere in this book, but his trilogy *The Information Age* (1996) is, as this chapter suggests, helpful, and remains an extremely impressive intervention. David Held et al.'s *Global Transformations* (1999) is an important contribution to debates about globalisation and a treasure trove of information. An excellent book that is critical of information society theory is Frank Webster's *Theories of the Information Society* (3rd edition, 2006).

The continuing crisis afflicting North America, Europe and the global economy as a whole must surely have convinced even sceptics that it is vital to understand global financial and political-economic developments. I found Robert Brenner's work in *New Left Review* (1998, 2000) cogent and informative about economic change in the post-war era. His work is especially worth reading in the light of the incredible corruption and incompetence revealed when the global banking crisis went into meltdown in 2008, with the utter complicity of the Bush administration. Other good books on post-war changes in capitalism include Andrew Glyn's *Capitalism Unleashed* (2005) and David Harvey's *The Enigma of Capital* (2010). An entertaining and informative explanation of the financial meltdown is John Lanchester's *Whoops* (2010). The documentary *Inside Job* (2009) is devastating.

On socio-cultural changes, Luc Boltanski and Eve Chiapello's *The New Spirit of Capitalism* (2006) provides a remarkable analysis of how capitalism incorporated countercultural critiques following the 1970s. In the same spirit, but with a much more specific focus, Thomas Frank's *The Conquest of Cool* (1997) is a great book about post-war popular culture. Neo-liberalism is an indispensable concept for understanding transformations since the 1970s. See Nick Couldry's *Why Voice Matters* (2010), Colin Crouch's *The Strange Non-Death of Neo-Liberalism* (2011) and an excellent chapter by Daniel Hallin (2008)

PART TWO
POLICY CHANGE

4

Marketisation in Telecommunications and Broadcasting

Deregulation, re-regulation and cultural marketisation   126
Telecommunications and broadcasting – why was the
    state so involved?   128
  Telecommunications as a public utility   129
  Broadcasting as a national resource and a limited one   129
  The power of broadcasting   130
The 1980s: the rationales are dismantled and
    marketisation follows   131
  Challenge to the telecoms as utility rationale   131
  Challenge to the broadcasting as scarce, national
     resource rationale   131
  Challenge to the power of broadcasting rationale   132
Four waves of marketisation   132
The first wave: changes in communications policy in
    the USA, 1980–1990   134
The second wave: changes in broadcasting policy in
    other advanced industrial states, 1985–1995   137
  Defining characteristics of public service
     broadcasting systems   137
  Variations in public service systems   138
  The social and cultural role of PSB   140
PSB under attack: case studies of change   140
  The UK   142
  France   143
  Germany   144
  Australia   144

Japan   145
Summary of PSB under attack   146
The third wave: transitional and mixed societies,
    1989 onwards   146
India   147
Russia and Eastern Europe   149
China   149
Latin America   150
Summary of marketisation in transitional societies   150
The fourth wave: towards convergence and
    internationalisation, 1992 onwards   151
Convergence   151
International policy bodies   153

It is impossible to understand the cultural industries without understanding government policy. The changes in policy with the most far-reaching consequences for the cultural industries in the 1980s and 1990s were in the telecommunications, media (especially broadcasting), intellectual property and cultural policy domains, so this chapter and the next are devoted to them (see Box 4.1 for the definition of 'policy' being used here). In outlining these changes, I draw on the account in the previous chapter of contexts for change and continuity in the cultural industries. The most important of these contexts are the rise of neo-liberalism and the rise of information society thinking.

Box 4.1   Defining policy in communications, media and culture

In all areas of commercial life, governments intervene. The free market does not exist in modern, complex societies but is merely a goal aspired to by those who believe that the market, in its ideal state, is the best way to distribute resources and answer human needs. Even those national economic systems based most on private enterprise, such as the USA, are built on a huge foundation of laws concerning competition, tax, contracts, the obligations of companies and so on. They also rely on government funding of infrastructures (transport, energy, money and communications) and regulation of companies to ensure that market powers are not abused. As Thomas Streeter (1996: 197) suggests, however, the false opposition between government and markets often prevails, with the frequent result that 'political action of any kind is popularly assumed to be "government interference"', at least in the USA.

Governments intervene in communication, media and cultural markets in three main ways. They:

- *legislate*: that is, they create laws concerning the general issues mentioned above, such as competition and contracts, plus more specifically cultural issues, such as copyright, obscenity, privacy and so on, and these are subject to constitutions and to the decisions of courts;
- *regulate*: via these laws, governments create agencies that monitor a particular industry or group of industries and have powers to affect the behaviour of companies and other institutions and actors;
- *subsidise*: directly, via grants, in order to supplement the provision of texts provided by the private sector, in areas such as theatre, ballet, opera, fine art and so on, or indirectly, by allowing research and other knowledge created in the public sector (especially defence) into the private sector.

These constitute the three main elements of **government policy** in telecommunications, media and culture. Government policy operates at the international level (for example, the EU), national level (individual national governments), and sub-national regional level (for example, state government in the USA or Germany, or the North West region of England), as well as at the level of cities and towns.

Neo-liberalism and information society discourse had a huge impact on all these key areas of government policy relevant to the cultural industries in the 1980s and 1990s. One key impact was that the relationships between these different domains changed, particularly as the development of the internet, mobile communications, wireless and broadband began to blur areas of policy that had previously been more distinct. This is an issue that I return to later in this chapter, and later in the book, but in the 1980s and 1990s, it was still possible to make a fairly clear distinction between the three main areas of policy outlined above.

Telecommunications, like the other major economic infrastructures (transport, money, energy), have long been fundamental to the operation of businesses within modern societies. But as government economic, education and even social policy fields became increasingly affected by information society discourse from the 1970s onwards (see Chapter 3) telecommunications became even more central than before. Policymakers came to accept the information society view that nations with the most advanced telecommunications systems were likely to be the most competitive in a new global information-driven market. Telecommunications is not a cultural industry in the sense that I define it in this book, but developments in telecommunications policy have had a profound impact on cultural production.

At the beginning of the period of transformation under consideration here, an identifiably separate domain of **media policy** existed. In fact, in many countries, what is generally referred to as **media policy** has generally consisted of a number of distinct policy areas directed towards individual industries – broadcasting, the press, film, and so on. Many information society visions of the economic future placed considerable emphasis, from the 1970s onwards, on the multimedia convergence between telecommunications, computers and media – especially, in the latter case, broadcasting. Broadcasting has dominated people's leisure activities in advanced industrial countries and still does so, even in an era where the PC and the internet feature increasingly (see Chapter 9). For this and other reasons to be explained in what follows, governments have made fundamental changes to broadcasting policy and so I concentrate on these changes here. These changes have been closely intertwined with transformations in telecommunications policy and 'information policy'. **Cultural policy** and copyright law are addressed separately in Chapter 5.

Changes in all of these fields, but especially in telecommunications policy and in other fields of economic policy, such as competition law and regulation, have helped bring about the creation of a 'network of networks', consisting of the internet, mobile telephony, broadband, wireless and other elements (Noam, 2001). This has had profound consequences for the cultural industries so far in the twenty first century, and more consequences are yet to follow. It has also meant that many analysts now think of telecommunications policy as part of a broader domain often known as information policy, or information and communication policy. Media policy is sometimes merged into this broader domain, too, in an era of 'convergence'. I return to these issues after discussing the convergence and internationalisation policies that developed in and across many countries in the 1990s. But at the beginning of the period of transformation that we are examining, telecommunications, media, cultural policy and copyright were still recognisably distinct domains of government action.

Box 4.2 briefly outlines the assumptions guiding my analysis of policy in this and the next chapter, borrowing terms from David Marsh's (2002) critique of pluralist political theory and Robert Horwitz's impressive (1989) discussion of regulation in the USA.

Box 4.2   How policy works

I assume in what follows that policy is shaped by a number of factors that have complex relations with each other (see Marsh, 2002).

- Particularly important is the balance between social forces, which is in turn deeply affected by structured inequality (along class, gender, ethnic and other dimensions) within and between societies and by the different resources available to agents.
- But policy is not utterly at the mercy of the wealthy and powerful. Political institutions and processes have some autonomy. To some extent at least, democratic governments need to retain legitimacy with those classes and

groups (the working classes, peasants, ethnic minorities) that are excluded from the political 'mainstream'.

- Political problems and solutions are discursively constructed and this construction is an important site of contestation, but here, too, structured inequality is at play.
- An important, but not determining, feature of public policy formation is the strategic alliances made by political parties with other social institutions. Large corporations, with their enormous financial and communication resources, are particularly significant in this respect. Political parties in advanced industrial countries are unlikely to achieve power without the support of such businesses.
- However, there is no need to assume that businesses necessarily intervene directly in the policy process (although, of course, they often do) as policy on key matters is often formulated *in anticipation* of a corporate business reaction. Also, businesses often clash on what policies they prefer – and especially businesses in different industrial sectors.
- In general, policy bodies in modern capitalism work towards combining the accumulation of capital on the part of businesses with a certain degree of popular legitimation, as emphasised by neo-Marxian state theory. However, as Horwitz (1989) points out, an analysis of the origins of state policy agencies in particular balances of social forces does not always account for how they operate in practice.
- Policy needs to be understood as operating at both a national and international level (see Sinha, 2001).

Throughout this chapter and the next, in outlining the policy changes that were to have a significant effect on cultural industries,[1] I refer to relationships between the state, political parties and businesses at national and international levels. The story I tell is one of a general but not total victory of marketisation, especially in the form of an information society discourse. First, I discuss what I mean by the marketisation of telecommunications and broadcasting and why I prefer the term to 'deregulation'. I then examine the rationales for state intervention in telecommunications and broadcasting that had prevailed for much of the twentieth century (focusing here on advanced industrial countries) and explain the process by which neo-liberal discourse dismantled these rationales in the 1980s, clearing the way for the onset of marketisation. After this I go on in Chapter 5 to address the significance of the changes in copyright law and practice and how the neo-liberal information society discourse operated in arts and cultural policy.

The victory of information society marketisation involved struggle and negotiation. It was not a complete victory for all time. Marketisation, as we shall see, was to some degree counteracted by principles of openness and sharing

---

1 Effects that are explored in Chapters 6–11. Of course these changes had reciprocal effects on policy, but, because I believe that policy was such a key driver of initial dynamics of change, and because of the demands of clear exposition, I deal with policy first here.

that partly derived from the early development of the internet, and which also had deeper roots in enlightenment and romantic conceptions of the value of sharing knowledge and expressive, aesthetic works. The internet and the web became widely available during the 1990s and 2000s. These networks were built on principles of openness and sharing that can in no way be reduced to neo-liberalism, even if pro-market ideologies affected the form that the internet and the web have eventually taken. In time, the internet provided a challenge to the established players in the telecommunications and cultural industries, but digital networks also came to be dominated by a new generation of IT giants (Microsoft, Yahoo, Apple, Amazon, Google and others).

Not everyone involved in arguing for marketisation can be described as a neo-liberal. Many policymakers saw benefits to marketisation, and sought to balance it against new ways of protecting the interests of society, democracy and publics. These centrist, non neo-liberal policymakers and politicians were not always successful, however, and were to some extent carried along by a tide of neo-liberalism. As a result, marketisation principles became deeply embedded in telecommunications, media and cultural policy across much of the world, although they co-existed with other principles, and resolute action could lead to a challenge to market ideologies.

As I discuss at the end of Chapter 5, marketisation has interacted in complex ways with other changes to be discussed in later chapters. Nevertheless, in some key ways, it paved the way for the changes discussed in Chapters 6 to 11. There was something of a shift in the relations between culture and economics, symbol making and capitalism. Whether this is an epochal change, of the kind claimed by information society rhetoric, is more doubtful, but this can only be judged after considering those other changes.

DEREGULATION, RE-REGULATION AND CULTURAL MARKETISATION

We saw in Chapter 3 how the neo-liberal political doctrine spread across the world in response to the Long Downturn. During the 1945–1973 period, there had been some consensus among political parties across the political spectrum about the need to protect workers and consumers from actions undertaken by private companies in pursuit of profit. In some countries and sectors, this involved the nationalisation of private companies. Neo-liberalism, from the 1970s onwards, using the false government/market dichotomy discussed in Box 4.1, presented public ownership and close regulation as the causes of the economic downturn and undertook programmes of privatisation and regulatory change. The neo-liberal term for such programmes was often *deregulation,* but in some cases the term *liberalisation* was preferred.

The rhetoric of deregulation and liberalisation was particularly powerful in the cultural industries because the notion of freedom from government intervention fed on anxieties about government interference in personal and political expression. The right to a free expression of views is a fundamental aspect of democratic liberal thought and, superficially, government regulation might appear to undermine such 'speech rights' (Stein, 2006). However, terms such as 'deregulation' and 'liberalisation' can potentially confuse the removal of censorship with measures that are actually intended to increase the access of citizens to a wider variety of personal and political expression, such as restrictions on how many local stations a national network might own (in the USA) or what percentage of the national newspaper market one company's newspapers might reach (in the UK).

Some analysts of the cultural industries have argued, in response to this use of the term 'deregulation', that **re-regulation** is a more appropriate name for changes in media and communications policy in the 1980s and 1990s (such as Murdock, 1990: 12–13). The term 're-regulation' points to the fact that legislation and regulation were not removed by these changes and highlights the introduction of new legislation and regulation, much of which favoured, as we shall see, the interests of large, private corporations and their shareholders. As governments tried to negotiate competing interests during the deregulatory years of the 1980s and 1990s, in many cases they actually introduced new and more complex sets of regulations. The UK, as Peter J. Humphreys showed (1996: 191), introduced a number of new regulatory bodies, including the Broadcasting Complaints Commission (1982) and the Cable Authority (1984), during an era when it was supposedly beginning to deregulate. Equally France's deregulatory legislation of the mid-1980s created a complex network of rules.[2] For all its advantages, however, the term 're-regulation' also disguises a key issue, as Humphreys points out: this is that much new legislation and regulation did in fact legitimate 'a lighter touch' – the creation of a business environment in which commercial cultural industry companies could operate in a relatively unhindered way. Often, the interests of such companies are not necessarily conducive to a fair and equitable system of cultural production, in the terms developed in Chapter 2.

The terms 'loose' and 'tight' and 'light touch', as opposed to 'tight' regulation, may go some way towards avoiding the misleading implications of the terms 'deregulation', 'liberalisation' and 're-regulation', so I use them here, but these terms also have misleading positive connotations, as if governments should just lighten up, get loose and let businesses get on with what they do (with businesses as teenagers, and governments as oppressive parents). The term I prefer to describe the main thrust of policy changes of the period from 1980s onwards is **marketisation**. In general, this refers to 'the permeation of market exchange as a social principle' (Slater and Tonkiss, 2001: 25), a long-term process taking place over many centuries, involving commodification, a growing use of money as the basis of exchange and an

---

2 Digital television has involved very high levels of government intervention. Hernán Galperin (2004) calls this 'the digital paradox': why were such high levels of government regulation considered necessary in an era of 'deregulation'? I consider digital TV policy in Chapter 9.

increasing division of labour. Various theorists stress these and other elements to different degrees. In modern capitalist societies, market and non-market relations coexist, but market relations dominate in terms of how society is coordinated and organised. Here, however, I use the term more specifically to refer to the process by which market exchange increasingly came to permeate the cultural industries and related sectors. This involved a number of processes, but three stand out here:

- The *privatisation* of government-owned enterprises and institutions, many of which were once privately owned.
- The *lifting of restraints* on the activities of businesses so that they could pursue profit more easily, often at the expense of other considerations, such as serving and informing publics.
- The *expansion of private ownership* as a result, together with other changes in the law and regulation that allow this to occur.

There is nothing wrong with markets in themselves. They can potentially act, in certain cases and in certain social systems, as efficient and equitable allocators of resources. For many critics of neo-liberal marketisation, though, markets in modern complex capitalist societies need careful management by governments to ensure efficiency and equity. For a Marxian perspective, marketisation is closely linked to the steady commodification of more and more areas of social life – a commodification that, as we saw in Chapter 2, is viewed by Marxian analysts as an essential but highly problematic feature of capitalism. A different view prevailed among policymakers from the 1980s onwards: the neo-liberal view that the production and exchange of cultural goods and services for profit is the best way to achieve efficiency and fairness in the production and consumption of texts.

Let's now examine how such neo-liberal marketisation affected telecommunications and broadcasting policy. First, we need to establish the prevailing situation in a previous era of policy – that is, prior to the 1980s.

TELECOMMUNICATIONS AND BROADCASTING: WHY WAS THE STATE SO INVOLVED?

Until the 1980s, in liberal democracies as well as authoritarian states, most of the world's broadcasting and telecommunications organisations were owned and controlled directly by the state. Even in the USA, with its long tradition of preferring private enterprise to public ownership, broadcasting and telecommunications were, for many decades, subject to tight regulation by government bodies.

So why were broadcasting and telecommunications more subject to public ownership and tight regulation than cultural industries such as newspapers, film and music? We can divide the reasons for this into three, generalising broadly across very different political and cultural contexts:

- An understanding of telecommunications as a *public utility*.
- An understanding of broadcasting as a *limited, national resource*.
- An understanding of broadcasting as *powerful and therefore in need of control*.

Telecommunications as a public utility

In most nations in the early twentieth century, telecommunications (mainly telegraphs and telephones) were widely recognised as something that, in principle, the state would want to make available to their entire populations in order to foster national identity and encourage economic development. In most liberal democratic states and their colonies, the responsibility for organising telecommunications was passed to the authorities charged with dealing with the postal system. In some European countries, national post organisations expanded to become postal, telegraph and telephone authorities (PTTs): for example, the General Post Office in the UK, the Reichpost and, after the Second World War, the Bundespost, in Germany, the Direction Générale des Telecommunications in France, and so on.

In the USA, where businesses were especially fervent and successful in their resistance to the democratic regulation of markets, the private company AT&T (American Telephone and Telegraph Company) was allowed to act as a private monopoly covering nearly all of the USA. US policymakers used their own distinctive language, whereby telecommunications were treated, like the roads and railway lines, as a 'common carrier' – namely, a system or network that had to carry any messages, vehicles and so on, paid for by customers, within certain legal boundaries. The justification for AT&T's monopoly was that the high costs of installing telephone infrastructure meant it was a 'natural monopoly' and that such a monopoly, closely regulated by government, was the best way of achieving standardisation, high quality and, thus, 'universal service' in providing a common carrier.[3] In return for being granted such a monopoly, until its partial break-up in the 1980s, AT&T accepted a close regulation of its prices and a ban on its being involved in the production and distribution of programming.

Broadcasting as a national resource and a limited one

Radio was initially developed as a form of one-to-one communication, envisaged as something like a telephone or telegram of the airwaves, rather than as the broadcasting (one-to-many) form it became. It was widely used by the military and increasingly by amateurs for personal communication in the 1910s and

---

3 'Universal' did not mean that everyone had equal access. It took decades for poorer sections of the population to reach high rates of installation and then it was as a result of lowering costs rather than any commitment on the part of either government or company (see Aufderheide, 1999: 16; Garnham, 1996: 3.)

was essentially unregulated. In the early 1920s, private companies in a number of countries began to experiment with broadcasting music and other entertainment. In the USA, a radio craze developed, but the airwaves remained unregulated for years, causing chaos and bad reception more or less everywhere.

In many countries in Europe, however, the public ownership and regulation of national resources and utilities, such as gas, water, electricity and postal services, were considered desirable. The responsibility to provide a public service was an increasingly important part of many national cultures, even if, in many cases, such as that of the UK, this involved a 'paternalist definition of both service and responsibility' (Williams, 1974: 33). It seemed natural in many European states, therefore, that radio should be run, or at least overseen, by PTTs. This seemed particularly the case given *spectrum scarcity* – the fact that the airwave frequencies used to transmit radio messages were very limited. Even in the USA, with its already strong tradition of resistance to regulation, it became widely accepted that the state had to be closely involved in the allocation of spectrum space, so that broadcasters did not overlap on the same frequencies, thereby ruining the radio experience. As a result, a Federal Radio Commission was finally introduced in 1927.

Eventually, in most countries, new bodies were formed to govern broadcasting. Many were initially under the auspices of PTTs, but eventually developed their own autonomy, including the British Broadcasting Corporation (BBC) and various similar organisations (some of them modelled on the BBC), such as the CBC (Canadian Broadcasting Corporation). When television, which of course relied on radio waves for transmission, was introduced, its regulation was often passed on to these state organisations or, in some countries, a dual system of public service and commercial television was established, as in Australia and Japan in the 1950s.

The power of broadcasting

When radio became a broadcasting technology rather than one for point-to-point communication, its potential social power quickly became apparent, both commercially (in terms of its power to advertise and promote goods) and politically (in terms of its power to affect people's voting habits and attitudes towards democratic goals and procedures). In nearly all countries, it was accepted that the state, again via democratic accountability, should be the agency to ensure that these powers were not abused. In some countries, such as post-1945 France, this meant very strong and direct state control of the main broadcasting organisation. In the UK, the BBC was (from 1926) a public corporation, governed by a Royal Charter that laid out its mandate and by governmental appointees. Even in countries such as the USA or in post-war Luxembourg, which favoured private enterprise, high levels of government regulation were widely accepted compared with those in operation in other business sectors, largely because of radio's perceived power. When television became widely popular and available in the 1950s and 1960s, its obvious potential social power meant that it inherited legislative and regulatory frameworks from radio.

THE 1980S: THE RATIONALES ARE DISMANTLED AND MARKETISATION FOLLOWS

By the 1980s, the rationales behind such high degrees of government intervention in broadcasting and telecommunications were breaking down. We saw in Chapter 3 how the rise of neo-liberalism in the 1980s helped to de-legitimate public ownership and certain forms of regulation in nearly all forms of economic activity. We also saw how commercial companies in Europe and North America, observing diminishing margins in manufacturing, were becoming increasingly aware of the potentially greater profits to be made in the cultural, communication and leisure industries. They put increasing pressure on national governments to remove the restrictions on access to certain markets – and in particular telecommunications and broadcasting, which had previously been very closely regulated.

All of the major rationales for broadcasting and telecommunications policy came under ferocious attack in the 1980s and 1990s – especially from private corporations and from policymakers and commentators who supported their interests. These interest groups argued instead for marketisation. They attacked each of the rationales listed above in the following ways.

Challenge to the telecoms as utility rationale

Various agencies and interests (along with influential academic analysts, such as Pool, 1983) argued, especially from the 1970s onwards, that the need to provide telecommunications as a national utility (or common carrier, as in the USA) no longer applied because telecommunications services were now already widespread among the populations of the advanced industrial countries. They increasingly argued that telecommunications needed to be opened up for national and international competition. This would, claimed the proponents of marketisation, increase the efficiency of the sector by exposing it to the rigours of the market. This would then provide more advanced services that could help to drive the economies of these countries out of their Long Downturn. Large telecommunications companies and senior executives of PTTs (who stood to become enormously wealthy out of privatisation) were particularly keen to make such arguments. They nearly always claimed that they also needed protection from the rigours of the market in the form of limitations to the entry of new rivals, so that they could compete with other large companies in the international market. Such contradictions in the discourses of marketisation have been a consistent feature of the policy landscape in the past few decades.

Challenge to the broadcasting as scarce, national resource rationale

Instead of the limited part of the electromagnetic spectrum available for analogue broadcasting, new cable, satellite and digital technologies potentially offered an almost limitless capacity for the transmission of information and entertainment. The proponents of marketisation claimed that new communication technologies meant that spectrum scarcity was coming to an end and state intervention in broadcasting on the grounds of ensuring clear signal reception could therefore no longer be justified. These claims were often based on a highly strategic use of technological reductionism. Technology did not delegitimise existing policy in itself. Rather, these technologies should be seen as the result of investment decisions by businesses. Cultural industry corporations and their political allies were able to present such new technologies as inevitable motors of change, which required new forms of looser regulation that would allow companies to compete in national and global markets.

Challenge to the power of broadcasting rationale

It became increasingly difficult for the advocates of public service and/or the public interest to argue that public ownership or tight regulation of television was justified by the medium's power of influence and persuasion. By the 1980s, corporations were involved in a wide range of cultural enterprises. Why, they asked, were they excluded from entry into television – the most important (and lucrative) of all media forms? Television had become thoroughly absorbed into the fabric of everyday life. Although it was still authoritative and the cause of great concern over its social and behavioural effects, arguments that viewers needed to be protected from it were increasingly difficult to sustain. However, calls for the ending or relaxing of public ownership and regulation tied this sense of television's declining power to a different and much more problematic rhetoric – that existing systems of broadcasting provided insufficient choice for the viewer and the best way to increase this choice was to provide more (commercial) channels (the Peacock Report, 1986, was one important British formulation of such a view).

FOUR WAVES OF MARKETISATION

As a result of the successful de-legitimation of rationales for public ownership and regulation, the 1980s and 1990s saw extremely important historical changes in the policy landscape.

- Telecommunications authorities were privatised and national telecommunications markets were opened up to competition, in particular from cable and mobile operators.
- Some public broadcasting institutions were privatised.
- Even where public broadcasting institutions remained in place, television systems were opened up to other terrestrial, commercial broadcasters and, increasingly, to cable and satellite providers.
- Regulatory 'walls' between telecommunications, broadcasting and new media (such as cable and satellite) companies came down, so telecoms and cable companies were allowed to enter into television

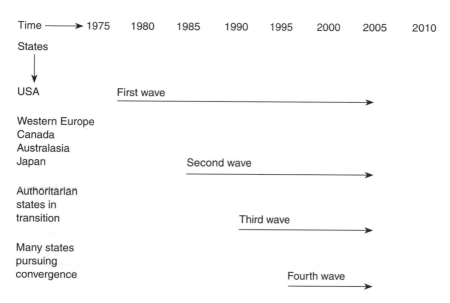

Figure 4.1 Four waves of marketisation

markets, cable television companies were allowed into telephony, and so on.

- Marketisation created new contexts for the understanding of cultural policy in an era of technological innovation, so, when new communication technologies were introduced or disseminated more widely, they were often assumed to need minimal legislation and regulation beyond competition laws and rules.
- Restrictions on content were significantly relaxed, such as on the amount of advertising allowed per hour, and how much educational programming broadcasters were required to transmit and at what times.
- Laws and regulations governing media ownership were removed or relaxed.
- Subsidies to non-profit and public-sector cultural institutions, such as libraries, museums, theatre, film and so on were reduced (see the discussion of cultural policy in Chapter 5), which made further space for private companies in cultural markets by opening up new market opportunities (for example, in providing private information databases) and reducing competition (for example, by reducing the number of films made in most European countries and, therefore, allowing Hollywood films even more access to European markets).

Specific examples of such changes in different countries are provided in the historical account that follows. These changes in cultural industry policy played a crucial role in initiating and accelerating many of the changes that are the subject of the rest of this book. It cannot be emphasised enough that these changes were consciously and deliberately brought about in order to support the interests of large, commercial, cultural industry companies.

Governments did this because they wanted their own cultural industry companies to be able to compete in a new global cultural industries sector. Any suggestion that they were made inevitable by, for example, technological change or some external process known as 'globalisation' disguises the willed and intentional nature of these changes (though they had many unintended and unanticipated consequences).

The next four sections discuss four waves of marketisation, as follows (see also Figure 4.1).

1   The policy changes with the most profound consequences in terms of marketisation initially took place in the USA from 1980 onwards.
2   Changes there had an important influence on changes in other advanced industrial states, in Western Europe, Canada, Australasia and Japan from the mid-1980s, but, of course, with significant national and regional variations.
3   Then, a number of countries with more authoritarian traditions of state control and ownership initiated policies of marketisation and 'liberalisation'.
4   Finally, a further round of policy changes involved paving the way for convergence between telecommunications, media and computers. Especially important here were trade agreements and policy bodies that had pursued marketisation at an international level.

THE FIRST WAVE: CHANGES IN COMMUNICATIONS POLICY IN THE USA, 1980–1990

The state had a significant role in the development of radio in the USA and the setting up of the Radio Corporation of America (RCA, who later owned the television network NBC and the record company that released Elvis Presley's records). However, in its 1934 Communications Act, the USA radically departed from the norm in other liberal-democratic countries, whereby governments would have a very pronounced role in media and telecommunications ownership and regulation.[4] The Act set up the Federal Communications Commission (FCC) to monitor 'public interest, convenience and/or necessity' (originally a phrase used in the 1927 Radio Act) and a dual system of media and telecommunications regulation was created. In radio, and later television, broadcasters were given access to the scarce spectrum in return for promising to serve this 'public interest, convenience and/or necessity'. There were restrictions on how many television stations these programme-making broadcasters could own nationally, but locally owned

---

4   Robert W. McChesney has shown how various commercial and right-wing interest groups played a crucial role in ensuring this outcome during debates in the period 1927–1935 over the best way to organise telecommunications (see McChesney, 1993, 1999: Chapter 5).

stations across the USA affiliated themselves to what eventually (from 1955 to 1985) became a trio of major networks: NBC, CBS and ABC.[5] These companies formed a *de facto* vertically integrated national oligopoly. Their revenues came mainly from advertising rather than a radio or television licence fee, which was the system favoured in Europe and elsewhere.

Meanwhile, in telecommunications, as we saw earlier, AT&T was granted monopoly control in the interests of efficiency. In return, they agreed not to have any involvement in content creation and circulation. The first big change in telecommunications regulation relevant to the main period covered by this book came in 1982, as a result of a Justice Department case against AT&T that was first brought in 1974 (which is typical of how slowly US regulation works – see Box 4.3). AT&T agreed out of court to be divested of their local business and opened up for competition in long-distance markets. In 1984, as a result of this divestiture, seven 'Baby Bell' local phone companies were formed. Some of these became key players in the 'converging' telecommunications, media and information technology markets of the late 1990s and early 2000s. In return for agreeing to this divestiture, AT&T were allowed access to information and computer markets that they had previously been forbidden from entering. Developments in the regulation of telecommunications took many years to have an effect, so I return to these in the chapters that follow.

Box 4.3 The peculiarities of broadcasting regulation in the USA

One notable feature of broadcasting policy in the USA is that very little legislation has ever been passed by Congress. Indeed, the Telecommunications Act of 1996 was the first major piece of legislation since the Communications Act of 1934. Many of the biggest decisions affecting communications have been 'made by Federal Judges adjudicating in merger and anti-monopoly cases' (Tunstall and Machin, 1999: 41). Such cases are often brought by the Federal Trade Commission or Justice Department rather than the Federal Communications Commission (FCC).

Chad Raphael (2005) added a new twist to the view that the role of the FCC is sometimes overstated. He argued that the 1990s and early 2000s history of regulation in the USA should be seen not as a move from stringent government oversight to a long process of deregulation, but as the gradual *privatisation* of regulation. He also showed that television journalism is now overseen less by the FCC, Congress and the executive branch of the government, than it is by tort law, public relations campaigns and market pressures.

---

5 A fourth network, Dumont, lasted until 1955. News Corporation's Fox network began in 1985, and had established itself by 1991. Time Warner and Viacom established new networks in the 1990s – WB and UPN respectively.

Changes in broadcasting were more immediate in their impact than those in telecommunications. The most significant changes in policy took place in regulation rather than legislation (with the exception of the 1984 Cable Act) and were brought about by a change of personnel at the FCC. During the period in which television developed into a national mass medium (1945–1970), the FCC clashed with broadcasters on a number of issues, most notably over 'the Fairness Doctrine' – the rules by which the FCC tried to ensure that broadcasters would not abuse their power by acting as biased advocates. By the 1970s the FCC had moved away from tight regulation of media content, but in general retained strong controls of structural issues, such as restrictions on concentration, cross-media ownership and convergence.

The far right administration of President Ronald Reagan (1981–1989) appointed a zealous neo-liberal conservative, Mark Fowler, as chair of the Commission. Fowler's FCC did away with numerous controls on concentration, leading to a surge in merger and takeover activity in broadcasting in the 1980s (Sterling and Kittross, 2002: 500, 575–7). It largely repealed the Fairness Doctrine in the late 1980s and, among other consequences for content, this helped to lead to the rise of right-wing talk show hosts on radio. Meanwhile, it took a harder line on issues of obscenity than ever before, leading to a series of conflicts with shock-jocks such as Howard Stern. Limits on the amount of advertising allowed per hour were relaxed and, in general, the FCC encouraged an atmosphere in which the public interest – never properly defined – was equated with the economic prosperity of US commercial enterprises.

The shift towards marketisation in the USA was the result of a struggle over how to regulate and organise cultural production at a time when capitalists were increasingly looking to invest in culture as a means of returning profit. Jeremy Tunstall (1986) showed in a contemporary study how this struggle was to a very large degree waged within specific areas of Washington DC by interest groups and their lobbyists. The pro-marketisation interests included, for example, the broadcasters, represented by their trade association, the National Association of Broadcasters and the various cable companies, who succeeded in gaining ground in the early 1980s. Against them were ranged various groups seeking to represent the 'public interest', such as civil rights, consumer groups and church activists (see Aufderheide, 1999: 18–19, for details on such public interest groups). Some of the pro-marketisation forces had, in certain respects, competing interests, and most were in favour of marketisation as it would serve their own interests above all else (see Chapter 2). However, they were united by a shared neo-liberal commitment to the free market – that is, unregulated private business, the notion of supposed consumer sovereignty and choice (as opposed to citizens' rights) and the goal of economic efficiency by means of competition. We have already seen the core arguments mobilised by these interest groups and their political allies on the radical right against traditional forms of communications policy – the need for competition to encourage efficiency, the supposed breakdown of spectrum scarcity as a rationale for regulation and the privileging of consumer choice over citizens' rights. They drew on, and provided a significant part of, the turn towards neo-liberalism.

Together, these changes made it clear that government policy was moving in a direction that would be highly favourable to corporations looking to expand their interests in the cultural industries. What is more, the success of companies and conservative politicians in dismantling special regulatory apparatuses in the USA, especially in broadcasting, gave great encouragement to companies and policymakers elsewhere with similar goals.

THE SECOND WAVE: CHANGES IN BROADCASTING POLICY IN OTHER ADVANCED INDUSTRIAL STATES, 1985–1995

Historically, the liberal democracies of Western Europe, Australasia, Canada, Japan and other countries have followed a very different route from that taken by the USA in telecommunications and broadcasting policy. In these countries, to different degrees, telecommunications have been run essentially as public utilities and, rather than a very loosely defined notion of public interest, as in the USA, the key concept in broadcasting policy has been *public service*. One of the most significant changes in the cultural industries in the 1980s and 1990s has been the dismantling of this public utility/public service mix. Marketisation in telecommunications is addressed in the section below on the fourth wave of marketisations, which was towards convergence and internationalisation, but here I focus on the challenge to non-commercial broadcasting in advanced industrial states.

In advanced industrial countries, television was the most important cultural industry of the late twentieth century, in terms of both the sheer amount of time people spent watching it (see Chapter 3) and its cultural significance. The marketisation of television in these countries has already had enormous effects on the cultural industries, not only in the states themselves but also in many other places as well. The pulling apart of public service television has important implications for the social relations of cultural production and for the texts produced by the cultural industries.

Defining characteristics of public service broadcasting systems

The key features of public service broadcasting (PSB) as outlined by its advocates (see Brants and Siune, 1992; Blumler, 1992: 102; Tracey, 1998: 26–9) include the following.

- *Accountability to the public* (via their political representatives) beyond that provided by market forces.
- *Some element of public finance* mainly carried out via a licence fee. In 2004–2005 this was about £10 (about US$16) per month in the UK, and about 17 euros per month (US$20.64) in Germany. Revenue for public broadcasters can include commercial income from advertising and the

sale and licensing of programmes and formats to other broadcasters. But significantly, all profits must generally be fed back into programming or administration, whereas in a private system a large chunk must be paid to shareholders. In the UK the annual TV licence fee pays for the BBC's public service radio and internet provision, as well as television.

- *Regulation of content* including not only restrictions on advertising, violence and pornography (a feature of regulation of private broadcasting), but also rules concerning balance, impartiality and the serving of minority interests, and the obligation to provide educational programming and programming for all regions of a country.
- *Universal service* across all the territory of a nation and a 'comprehensive remit' (Blumler, 1992: 8) requiring public service broadcasters to encourage and satisfy the tastes of the full range of people in a society.
- Perhaps the most crucial feature of all in this context is that *audiences are addressed primarily as citizens*, rather than as consumers – at least at some key moments. This is reflected in the provision of mixed and pluralistic schedules, whereas in a consumerist system schedules would be determined primarily by the imperative to maximise ratings and/or profits. In Blumler's terms, public broadcasters were charged with the responsibility of maintaining the cultural wealth and diversity of a nation. This concern with citizenship is also apparent in the way that, in Blumler's words (1992: 12), PSB 'assumed some responsibility for the health of the political process and for the quality of public discourse generated within it'. This meant, in general, a commitment to 'distance from vested interests', even if that was not always achieved, especially in times of war, conflict or crisis.

Variations in public service systems

Of course, there were many variations on this generalised system of PSB. As Humphreys (1996: 177–8) observes, many of these differences can be explained by the very different political cultures in the countries involved. There is insufficient space here to provide a full classification of national differences (details can be found in many comparative studies, including Goldberg et al., 1998; Hoffman-Reim, 1996; Humphreys, 1996; Kelly et al., 2004; Raboy, 1997), but the most important variations include the following.

- Funding of the television system and public service channels within it
- In most liberal democracies, television began as a public monopoly, funded only by a licence fee, and consisting of just one channel. Further channels were added in the 1960s and 1970s. By 1980, most of these had begun to mix advertising with the licence fee. By 1990, as part of the changes to be discussed in this chapter, many countries had shifted to a mixed revenue (licence fee/advertising) public monopoly, but a roughly

Table 4.1 Changes in television funding systems in the 1980s and 1990s

System	1980	1990	1997
Public monopoly/ licence fee only	Belgium, Denmark, Norway, Sweden		
Public monopoly/ mixed revenue	Austria, Finland, France, Germany, Greece, Iceland, Ireland, The Netherlands, Portugal, Switzerland, Spain	Austria, Denmark, Iceland, Ireland, The Netherlands, Portugal, Switzerland	Austria, Ireland, Switzerland
Private monopoly/ advertising only	Luxembourg	Luxembourg	Luxembourg
Dual system	Italy, UK	Belgium, Finland, France, Germany, Greece, Italy, Norway, Spain, Sweden, UK	Belgium, Denmark, Finland, France, Germany, Greece, Iceland, Italy, The Netherlands, Norway, Portugal, Spain, Sweden, UK

Source: Siune and Hultén, 1998: 27

equal number had moved to a dual system of public broadcasters alongside commercial channels (see Table 4.1). This represented a huge expansion of opportunities for cultural industry corporations in the television market, with important consequences for the cultural industries as a whole.

- State control of public service broadcasters
- In some liberal democracies, such as France (up to 1982) and Greece, there was direct state control of the broadcasting organisation. Much more commonly, public corporations – such as the UK's BBC, Australia's ABC, NHK in Japan and CBC in Canada – were set up in order to be generally autonomous of the state, though key appointments might be made by the government.
- Relationship to political institutions
- In some countries, such as Austria, the governors of public broadcasters were appointed in proportion to the strength of the political parties in the country. In many countries, there were places on boards for non-political appointees from other sectors, such as trade unions, church groups and universities.

- Programming styles
- It would be a mistake for readers from countries such as the USA – where public service broadcasting is positioned as a worthy supplement to an overwhelmingly commercial, weakly regulated system – to think that public service broadcasters served up a programming diet consisting purely of highly serious, educational programming. The whole point of PSB was that it should be mixed and diverse, though how this worked on a day-to-day level varied from country to country.

The social and cultural role of PSB

So to what extent did PSB systems promote social justice in the terms presented in the model in Chapter 2? From the 1950s right into the 1980s, PSB was subjected to considerable criticism from the political left. It was criticised for its pseudo-objective notion of balance and impartiality in current affairs coverage (Glasgow Media Group, 1976), for management policies and labour relations that reproduced class power (Garnham, 1990: 128–31) and for its failure to provide programming that appealed to working-class or non-elite audiences (Ang, 1991). In the 1950s and 1960s, in countries where advertising was not allowed but government support was low (such as the Scandinavian countries), the resulting lack of funds meant a heavy reliance on imported television programming and, often, low-quality domestic TV production.

Yet, the achievements of PSB should not be underestimated. One laudable result was near-universal service. Huge amounts of money were spent ensuring that remote regions were given access to national broadcasting systems, which would have been unthinkable in a commercial system. There was also a constant commitment to providing regions with access to the national system. Some public service broadcasters even achieved occasional flashes of high-quality broadcasting. The UK's BBC is an often-discussed example, with its sometimes high-quality drama, situation comedy and music radio in the 1960s and 1970s. However, the quality of broadcasting in other European countries prior to marketisation in the 1980s and 1990s is hard to ascertain. Work on PSB tends to have little to say on this topic. For advocates of PSB, however, there may be a good reason for this. The point is not necessarily to defend PSB as it was (often under-funded, paternalist in tone and substance), but as it could be.

PSB UNDER ATTACK: CASE STUDIES OF CHANGE

As with the shift towards marketisation in the USA, the pulling apart of the PSB system in liberal democracies was based on a struggle over how best to organise cultural production in an era when its perceived economic importance was on the rise. Peter J. Humphreys (1996) has provided a very useful

Table 4.2 Marketisation interest groups in Europe

The pro-market actors	Their interests
The electronics industry	To exploit markets for new TV sets, pay-TV decoders, satellite reception equipment, etc.
The cable and satellite television lobbies	Freedom to provide commercial services
PTTs	To develop and diffuse new media technologies and maintain monopoly or dominant market position in telecoms provision
Newspaper publishers	To diversify media operations and pre-empt further competition for advertising revenue (Not universally the case. In some countries the press remained a force resisting commercial broadcasting).
Advertisers	To gain outlets and strengthen market position
Governments	To promote the economy and attract media investors
Parties of the Right	Pursuit of neo-liberal agenda and promotion of business interests
European Commission	To liberalise European markets
Public service supporters	Their interests
Public service broadcasters	Self-defence, continuance of public resources, etc.
Unions	Protection of employment and conditions of employment
Parties of the Left	Promotion of public service ethos and communitarian values, promotion of labour interests

Source: Humphreys, 1996: 176

outline of the key actors in reformulating broadcasting policy in Western Europe in the 1980s and early 1990s (see Table 4.2).

The pro-market coalition worked via lobbying and public relations with policymakers and key opinion formers in the media. Again, this echoed developments in the USA, but in Europe the pro-market coalition's task was more substantial. In the USA, deregulation mainly comprised the breaking down of an unpopular private monopoly (AT&T) and important but obscure changes in concentration policy. In Europe, public ownership and programming was sometimes popular. Elsewhere, while public broadcasting was not loved, it was at least felt by some elite groups to represent a bulwark against dubious forms of commercialism.

In Western Europe, significant changes in broadcasting policy began in earnest in the mid-1980s, following an early and disastrous experiment in Italy in the late 1970s, where quality plummeted and hucksterism ruled the airwaves. These changes took different forms in different places, but there is only space for a brief survey of a few countries here.

The UK

Very much under the influence of communications 'deregulation' in the USA, the UK was exceedingly quick to privatise telecommunications and introduce a 'light touch' cable policy. Margaret Thatcher's far-right government, and newspapers belonging to her political ally Rupert Murdoch, launched an attack on British broadcasting in the early 1980s. Thatcher appointed a gifted conservative economist, Alan Peacock, to run a public enquiry into broadcasting (Peacock Report, 1986). However, the resulting legislation, the Broadcasting Act of 1990, was far less radical in its marketisation of British broadcasting than public service advocates had feared. The BBC was not privatised, and nor was Channel 4 – set up by the previous Labour administration (1974–1979) to serve minorities, and introduced early in the Thatcher years, in 1982. In addition the BBC was not, as many had feared, forced to take advertising. This was for economic, not cultural, reasons: the commercial companies did not want the BBC to have their market. The marketising thrust was weakened by strong support on the traditional, paternalist wing of the Conservative Party for the mix of licence fee and commercial television that had existed in the UK since the 1950s. Moreover, strong controls were retained on concentration and cross-media ownership (though these were eventually weakened by the 1996 Broadcasting Act). Nevertheless, the impact of Thatcherite legislation should not be underestimated, especially on ITV, the network of closely regulated commercial franchises established in 1955 operating under a public service remit. In the 1990s ITV moved quickly from 14 regional franchised stations, dominated by six companies, towards effective monopoly control by two companies, Granada Media Group and Carlton.[6] A lot of advertising money went not on making national programmes but, instead, to shareholders and the 12-yearly auction system for franchises set up by the Broadcasting Act of 1990 (Tunstall, 1997: 247). To fend off political hostility, the BBC was forced to introduce 'internal markets and a ruthless regime of cost-cutting dressed up in the rhetoric of Thatcherite management consultancy, allied to a play-safe news and current affairs policy' (Garnham, 1998: 216). The Labour government of 1997 onward was considerably more generous in its funding of the BBC, but continued to apply political pressure – most notoriously in the furore over a news report implying that a government adviser had interfered with documents purporting to outline the security threat posed by Iraq in the run-up to the Gulf War of 2003.

A key development in the 1980s was that cable and satellite were introduced to the UK on terms that allowed Rupert Murdoch's British Sky Broadcasting (BSkyB) to gain a virtual monopoly over new television technologies in the UK. The Cable Act of 1984 attempted to introduce cable

---

6 The process of consolidation was completed when these two companies merged in 2004 to form ITV PLC.

under a very 'light touch' regulatory regime, but cable failed abysmally because the Thatcher government of the 1980s gave none of the state support to the incipient cable sector that was provided by some other Northern European countries.[7] As a result of this failure, by the mid-1990s News Corporation's BSkyB satellite package was completely dominant in the UK pay-TV sector, helped by its purchase of key sports rights, which provided a powerful base from which to launch its bid to dominate digital television (see Chapter 9).

France

France had a long tradition of state intervention in the cultural industries – not only in broadcasting but also in the form of ambitious communications and audio-visual strategies and programmes. This included enormous investments in a very modern and efficient telecommunications infrastructure in the 1960s and 1970s, including the popular and widely used, state-run videotex system, Minitel.

In the 1980s and early 1990s, France was in some ways more radical in its marketisation of broadcasting than the UK, even though it was headed by a socialist president, François Mitterrand, from 1981 to 1995. Communications policy is very strongly influenced by presidents, but officially remains a matter for governments and, for crucial periods in 1986–1988 and 1993–1995, Mitterrand cohabited with right-wing governments under Chirac and Balladur respectively. In any case, the leftist governments of 1981–1986 and 1988–1993 were also involved in commercialisation. One reason for this was that the very direct nature of state intervention in broadcasting helped to discredit French public service TV. The state broadcasting system had been modified into a public service system in 1982 with an independent regulator (fierce battles were fought over the name, make-up and status of this body throughout the 1980s and early 1990s), but this was too little, too late to save the reputation of French PSB. Another was the general drift across Western Europe towards marketisation in all areas of public policy – even in France, with its long statist traditions. Commercial channels were launched in 1984[8] and 1986 to create a dual system, but then the right-wing Chirac government of 1986–1988 went much further and privatised a key public channel, TF1,

---

7   In 1995, only 6 per cent of UK TV homes were connected to cable (Collins and Murroni, 1996: 92, citing UK government figures). According to Zenith Media figures, 95 per cent of Netherlands TV homes were connected in the same year. Only Turkey and Portugal had lower connection figures than in the UK in Western Europe. From the mid-1990s, however, marketisation allowed cable companies to compete with British Telecom in the telephone market and cable penetration rates increased.

8   Canal Plus, privatised in 1986, originally seen as a challenge to US cultural imperialism and stuffy French public service programming, later a major player in the European subscription television market as part of the doomed Vivendi-Universal conglomerate and, for the last few years, in some trouble.

along with other publicly owned communications companies, including the TV and advertising company Havas.

An ambitious plan to cable France using public money was abandoned and cabling was turned over to the private sector. New commercial terrestrial and satellite channels appeared in the late 1980s and the socialist government of 1988–1993 did not reverse earlier privatisations. The result was that, from 1990 onwards, France 'had one of the most marketised broadcasting systems in Europe' (Humphreys, 1996: 181) with its public service channels comparatively marginalised.

Germany

The third major European media market, West Germany, launched a new commercial sector in 1984 – later than many other economically powerful countries – and its decentralised public service system remained intact, confirmed by a ruling of the Federal Constitutional Court in 1986. This ruling was partly a result of campaigning by the leftist Social Democratic Party (SPD). Nevertheless, the rapid growth of commercial channels had a huge impact on the German media landscape after unification in 1990. This growth was largely due to the central state funding of a massive cabling programme in the 1980s. Relatively weak ownership laws have meant strong and significant links between publishing and broadcasting. Two 'families' dominated both publishing and television for many years: Bertelsmann and Kirch (with the latter going bankrupt in 2002 after a disastrous attempt to dominate pay-TV).

The growth in commercial channels has made German television extremely reliant on English-language imports from the UK and, especially, from the USA (Tunstall and Machin, 1999: 198). However, Kevin Williams notes (2005: 58) that, after a crisis in the mid-1990s, public service broadcasters have consolidated their position 'without copying the formats of commercial channels'. Indeed, commercial channels showed the influence of the public service model in the relatively low amount of human interest news and current affairs programming. All major stations must allocate windows in their schedules to independent film-makers. While the commercial channels have relied on light entertainment, news and sports coverage has been innovative (Burns, 2004: 73). This relatively successful version of the mixed public service/commercial ethos is a result, says Williams (2005: 59), of the way that broadcasting in West Germany was shaped by 'efforts to use the media as instruments of democracy'.

Australia

Australia's television system was a dual one from its inception in the 1950s. It represented a distinctive mix of British public service and US commercialism – with the latter in the form of regulated, advertiser-supported city-based stations and networks. Consequently, events in the period 1985–1995 were concerned not so much with the introduction of commercial channels, as was the case in much of Western Europe, but with changes in ownership laws, which determined how much a particular company could control the television market and to what extent these interests could be combined with press ownership.

In 1987, strict limits on how many stations a particular company could own (two) were considerably loosened. This was partly in order to generate improved television facilities in the less-populated areas by allowing the wealthy stations of Southern Australia to expand. The new limit was 60 per cent of the national audience, but this was in any case breached (by Network Seven). To pacify anti-concentration campaigners, new rules forbade cross-media ownership across print and broadcasting – traditionally a strong feature of the media landscape. As magnates such as Kerry Packer and Rupert Murdoch chose to go with print, their stations were sold at huge prices to, as it turned out, corrupt and incompetent bosses (with the result that Packer bought back his Nine Network for a song in 1990).

However, the main deregulatory act came in 1992, with the Broadcasting Services Act, which weakened the restrictions on broadcasters, abolished radio ownership laws almost entirely, and introduced pay-TV in such a way as to favour satellite – which was dominated by Packer and Murdoch. The 1980s and 1990s, then, can be seen as a period in which commercialisation was intensified, PSB was weakened, and Australia added to its reputation as the (advanced industrial) country 'with perhaps the greatest degree of media concentration in the world' (Hoffman-Reim, 1996).

Japan

For decades, the Japanese public service broadcaster NHK, established on the BBC model, has been closely linked not just to the state but also a political party – the conservative Liberal Democratic Party that has ruled Japan for much of the post-war period (Sugimaya, 2000).

Commercial television came early to Japan. Numerous commercial TV stations operated in the country from the 1950s onwards, adopting the apolitical stance of NHK (Kato, 1998). 'Deregulation' has not been considered as significant in Japan as elsewhere. The poor standards of news journalism in Japan are related to other factors, such as loose professional codes, different assumptions about authority and personal privacy and the massive cultural presence of sensationalist weekly magazines. (There are parallels here with the way in which British broadcasting is often forgiven for some of its poor practices because of the tabloid press's much worse standards of news journalism.)

The most significant act of marketisation has been the entry of satellite channels, but this has had relatively little impact. Most academic surveys of broadcasting hardly mention deregulation. Since the early 1960s, Japan has imported very little television and has more recently exported a great deal, including television formats (Iwabuchi, 2003). This has been partly because the country has a large, prosperous audience and partly because Japan has an image in other countries in South East Asia as embodying a distinctive and desirable kind of Asian modernity. It is also because of the considerable economic and political power of the companies that have dominated the public service–commercial mix. This strength should not be celebrated as a counter to 'Western' cultural imperialism, however. It is based on strong control by an oligopoly of companies and the very close ties between the country's influential subscription-based newspapers and its main television stations. There have been frequent scandals about the quality of journalism, including some recent ones that have severely dented NHK's credibility. Japan is a further reminder that there was no golden age of PSB prior to marketisation – but neither has marketisation democratised Japanese broadcasting.

Summary of PSB under attack

In some countries, PSB remains relatively strong even in the second decade of the twenty first century, but often there is a strong drift towards a cosy consensus between businesses and governments that the best way to run a broadcasting system is to have a vigorous private sector with some kind of corrective provided by a public service broadcaster. The ethos of public service, as outlined above, can only become more marginal with such a consensus in operation. There can be little doubt that the new, more marketised system has produced greater choice and diversity for viewers, compared with the underfunded public service monopolies that prevailed in some countries in the 1950s and 1960s, and there is still programming of a high quality. Crucially, however, this has generally been the case where the notion of public service has retained its presence within mixed systems, such as happened in the UK. I return to these issues in Chapter 10, where I discuss the arrival of cable, satellite and digital television, and in Chapter 11, where I discuss notions of quality and diversity more fully. The key point here is that, as the public service ethos became increasingly marginalised and beleaguered and, for the most part, unable to gain the resources to reinvent itself, market-driven broadcasting began to look like an inevitable future. Marketisation was never inevitable, though – it was fought for by interested parties. The success of marketisation advocates in achieving this appearance of inevitability has led to huge growth in the commercial opportunities available for businesses in the key cultural market of television.

THE THIRD WAVE: TRANSITIONAL AND MIXED SOCIETIES, 1989 ONWARDS

Marketisation spread throughout the world's telecommunications and media systems in the 1990s. The 'success' of neo-liberal measures in advanced industrial countries helped bring this about, but it was by no means the only factor. In India, a bureaucratic democracy attempted to reinvent itself by means of market reforms. In the former Soviet Union and Eastern Europe, the fall of Stalinist regimes, where state intervention had become discredited, brought about an unfettered marketisation of economies, including communications, media and culture. In China, the Communist party bureaucracy held on to power by letting go of communism, producing a distinctive form of 'bureaucratic monopoly capitalism' (Zhao, 2003: 62) in which the cultural industries played a growing part. In Latin America (and also in other countries, such as South Korea), there were transitions of a different kind in the 1980s and 1990s – from military authoritarianism to liberal democracy – and cultural markets were opened up to global competition. Although not addressed here, many Arabic countries, while maintaining strict controls over content, opened up their media systems to penetration by transnational media corporations (see Sakr, 2005, and also Chapter 8 below for more discussion of Arabic media).

As Colin Sparks (2000) remarked with regard to Eastern Europe, these various mixes of private media ownership and political influence can actually be seen as the global norm, rather than an aberration from European models of a mix of public and commercial broadcasting under arm's length regulation. Of course, the idea that political influence is neatly separated from 'free enterprise' in advanced industrial countries is just as much a fiction in the realm of culture as it is in economies as a whole. We have already seen evidence of the huge influence that cultural industry corporations can have on national governments and policymakers in Europe and the USA. Nevertheless, it is fair to say that, because the end of the Cold War in the late 1980s, and the fall of the Soviet Union in 1991, accelerated the rise of neo-liberalism, a large number of the world's economies were brought under the aegis of a particular notion of marketisation, including their cultural sectors. As the brief survey of some major territories in this section suggests, vast new markets for cultural industries have opened up, but this has not been a process without conflict or contradiction. Concerns about national identity and cultural standards continued to clash with marketisation in complex ways. Whether marketisation in these countries has involved any significant shift in the global balance of cultural power is the main subject of Chapter 8.

India

I begin this brief survey with India because, for all its unique cultural and political features, it echoes the way that neo-liberalism was introduced in many advanced industrial countries. The post-war Indian state was a compromise between traditional Indian conceptions of state power and aspirations to model a secular nation state on the European model (I draw on the valuable account in Sinha, 2001, here).

A highly interventionist, quasi-socialist state presided over a market economy that favoured rich farmers, industrial capitalists and professionals. These different groups fully supported the state's protectionist measures, but via deficit financing the state was able to pursue some ameliorative populist measures and gain sufficient legitimacy among the vast numbers of urban and rural poor.

This tense settlement was falling apart by the 1980s and, when a serious economic recession hit in 1990–1991 and much of the rest of the world turned to marketisation as a supposed cure for economic ills, the Indian state accepted a neo-liberal package proposed by the International Monetary Fund (here we see how national and international forces can combine in shaping policy transformation) in return for a loan. There was opposition from the left and right, but the result was massive deregulation, privatisation and liberalisation, and the opening up of markets to global competition.

Telecommunications was 'liberalised' from 1994 onwards and broadcasting was included in the package. It had become perfectly clear in the spread of neo-liberalism in advanced industrial countries that telecommunications marketisation was a prerequisite for developing opportunities for the private sector in the cultural industries.

India is not only the largest democracy in the world, it also has the world's largest middle class, estimated to be 200–250 million in number even in the 1990s (Thussu, 1999: 125) – a potentially huge and lucrative market for multinational cultural industries conglomerates. The marketisation of Indian broadcasting from 1991 onwards has been extremely significant, then, for these conglomerates and Indian audiences. Up until that date, Indian television was essentially a single-channel state system, often criticised for its close relationships to the dominant Congress Party and its worthy dullness, but with important and sometimes effective commitments to public service ideals, including national spread and the provision of education (Thomas, 1998). Commercials were allowed on the Indian state channel, Doordarshan, from 1976 onwards, but – in a country dominated by cinema – the massive potential of television as a cultural industry only began to be realised with the transmission of two serials based on Hindi religious epics, *Ramayana* and *Mahabaratha* (1987–1990).

By 1991, transnational satellite transmissions, including CNN and the Hong Kong-based STAR TV before its takeover by Murdoch's News Corporation in 1993, were being received in India in large numbers (Sinha, 1997). The result was a huge explosion in television channels throughout the 1990s, and especially of pay-TV. By 1998, nearly 70 cable and satellite stations were operating in India (Thussu, 1999: 127). Many, including STAR, initially transmitted 'Western' programming, but were increasingly orientated towards local content by the late 1990s.

There were debates within India about whether or not this explosion represented a new diversity or the strangling at birth of an incipient public sphere. There is no space to assess those debates fully here, but India indicates how global marketisation has helped to trigger significant internationalisation. This can be seen not only in the investment by multinational conglomerates, such as News Corporation in India, but also in the increasing presence of Asian broadcasters, such as India's Zee TV, in Europe and the USA. The significance of such complex and new flows of culture – which, to a significant degree, are a result of marketisation – will be addressed in Chapter 8.

Russia and Eastern Europe

A vision of liberal democracy as the basis of a prosperous and stable global future spread across much of the world during the 1980s and 1990s. This, however, was a version of liberal democracy with a very strong emphasis on the neo-liberal goals of businesses being as unhindered as possible by government action. The cultural industries play an important part in such visions, for cultural production is closely linked to ideas of freedom and self-expression in many countries. The mistake, encouraged by neo-liberal thinking, is to confuse freedom (including freedom of speech or expression) with a lack of government regulation. Regulation can promote freedom.

With the collapse of post-Stalinist systems in the Soviet Union and Eastern Europe, a generally well-educated population of nearly 400 million people became potential consumers of cultural goods and services. However, events in Eastern Europe and other 'transitional' societies have not justified optimistic projections of benign globalisation and this is true of the cultural sector also.

In all Eastern European countries, the press moved from subsidy and state control to advertising and subscription, and telecommunications and broadcasting were soon privatised. Regulatory authorities had to be created from scratch and the regulatory vacuum created powerful local monopolies and relationships between government and businesses that often bordered on illegality and, in some cases, were thoroughly corrupt (see, for example, Goldberg et al., 1998, on Hungary).

Efforts to introduce a PSB ethos in these countries have floundered, as Jakubowicz (2004) usefully but depressingly shows. Political structures and traditions do not exist that could bring about a successful inculcation of these new systems. Governments give lip-service to freedom, but are keen to exert control, and this appears to be undermining popular legitimacy. PSB is under such threat in Western European countries where it has been long-established that success in the longer term looks unlikely.

China

Marketisation in the cultural and media sectors began in the 1980s, but accelerated after Deng Xiaoping's landmark 'Tour of the South' in 1992. State and market have become thoroughly intertwined. In Eric Kit-wai Ma's words, 'lively and commercially vibrant media are actually essential to the continued governance of the state' (2000: 28). Leisure is encouraged in order to stimulate consumption and the burgeoning Chinese cultural industries are essential to this.

The development of the cultural industries as a strategic economic and cultural objective was signalled in the Chinese Communist Party's proposals for its tenth Five Year Plan in 2001 – the year in which China joined the World Trade Organization. A principal aim of media policy, as with much else in Chinese government policy,is to build big Chinese corporations that can compete in the global economy.

The party state, which retains very close control over communication, is introducing various reforms. These are very much contested and there are real tensions within the Party and the state. The results of these reforms are clear though: a distinctive form of marketisation, on a vast scale, and a 'bureaucratic monopoly capitalism' (Zhao, 2003: 62) with huge numbers of new entrants, often in league with non-Chinese businesses, but under the control of the party state. Meanwhile, non-Chinese cultural industries eyed up massive new markets in the country – not for outright ownership just yet, but with the possibility of further vast opportunities after gaining toeholds in joint ventures.

Zhao (2003) convincingly argues against two dominant frameworks for understanding these changes. The first is the Chinese nationalist one, emphasising the need to build Chinese conglomerates, which fails to notice that the 'popular classes' (workers and peasants) are doubly marginalised by political control and economic inequality. The second is an understanding, especially strong in Hong Kong and beyond China, which assumes that the interests of global capitalism and Chinese bureaucratic capitalism are more in conflict than they actually are.

Latin America

Latin America, meanwhile, underwent transitions of a related but different kind in the 1980s and 1990s. The USA's Cold War propaganda often contrasted the Soviet bloc with the 'free world', but in the mid-1970s more people were living under military, authoritarian regimes in Latin America – the USA's 'back yard'– than was the case in the whole of the Soviet Union and Eastern Europe together. Most television systems were thoroughly commercial, after the USA's model, but they were also subject to authoritarian, rather than public service, monitoring, and private owners who were often in close alliance with military rulers (see Chapter 8 on the Brazilian company, Globo).

Under the influence of critiques of 'cultural imperialism', many democratic and authoritarian Latin American governments sought to protect their nascent television industries from US imports and direct investment in the 1960s and 1970s. However, by the arrival of the neo-liberal 1980s and 1990s, as television internationalisation intensified, experiments with state-funded alternatives were largely discredited due to their association with the military authoritarian regimes of the 1960s and 1970s (Waisbord, 1998).

The result has been a lack of substantial resistance to cultural marketisation in the region, even on the left. The introduction of satellite television is transforming the broadcasting environment in Latin America, but very much on terms that are favourable to partnerships between dominant Latin American companies and transnational cultural industry corporations (see Sinclair, 2004: 87–90).

Summary of marketisation in transitional societies

These changes either consolidated processes that were already under way or brought huge new swathes of the Earth's population into the ambit of companies that aimed to make a profit from the production and dissemination of culture. By the late 1990s these changes had greatly increased the importance of the cultural industries in the projections of financiers and business people.

THE FOURTH WAVE: TOWARDS CONVERGENCE AND INTERNATIONALISATION, 1992 ONWARDS

In the last two sections, I have concentrated on developments in broadcasting policy, but we should not forget the key role that telecommunications marketisation has played. The changes brought about have been longer-term ones and they happened in conjunction with the longer-term effects of changes in broadcasting and crucial changes in the computer and IT industries. A key issue here has been the convergence of the cultural industries with telecommunications and information technology. Crucial policy decisions were made in the late 1990s that effectively treated this notion of convergence as inevitable. These can be seen as part of a fourth wave of marketisation. Also apparent in this period was the increasing significance of *international* policy making institutions: by this I mean institutions operating above the level of the nation state, such as the European Union.

Convergence

Chapter 2 discussed a number of technological developments that provide vital contexts for understanding changes in the cultural industries. Two of these were the emergence of the microcomputer and the development of information and communications technologies that allowed for the digitalisation of telecommunications, as well as communication between computers. By the late 1970s it was becoming apparent that digitalisation would enable a certain amount of convergence between computers and telecommunications systems. The information society discourse that had sprung up in the 1960s (see Chapter 2) was taken up by analysts, think tanks and futurologists. They saw the developments taking place in US research labs and university departments as the shape of the information society future. The context in the 1980s was one where governments were seeking new ways to restore economic prosperity as the Long Downturn took a turn for the worse. In such a context, policymakers were receptive to visions of economies and socieities connected by new information infrastructures. What's more, the nascent microcomputer and software industries were being mythologised by the media as entrepreneurial and countercultural. This was a conducive environment for the interests of the information technology industry to be promoted. At the same time, neo-liberalism was in the ascendant. In Thomas Streeter's words, 'information society rhetoric and neoclassical economics intersected, with powerful effects' (Streeter, 2011: 76). Streeter notes that the very concept of information, increasingly popular from the 1970s onwards, allowed meaning to be treated as a manageable, ownable thing. Fuelled by the previously marginal ideas of the neo-liberal thinkers of the law and economics movement (based around Milton Friedman and others at the University of Chicago), the law courts in the early 1980s began to make legal decisions that radically extended the notion of intellectual property (such as the extension of patents to genes and software). Digital convergence and the construction of digital information as property came together. We shall explore some of the consequences in intellectual property in Chapter 5. A further crucial consequence, however, was that by the late 1980s and early 1990s governments began to invest enormous sums of money in providing an infrastructure for the trade in information that they foresaw as a potential means to economic growth.

It was at this point in the mid-1990s, with the extraordinary and completely unexpected hype which appeared in the USA, that the internet was suddenly presented as the future of commerce, and it was in this context that the 1996 US Telecommunications Act was passed.[9] This solidified perceptions of emergent convergence and paved the way for it in three main ways.

First, it freed the local Bell telephone companies created by the AT&T divestiture to enter long-distance markets, in return for allowing competition in their own regions. This allowed these enormous companies access to huge markets in new communications technologies. In the wake of the Act, these Baby Bell companies became major players, as a series of massive telecoms mergers 'seemed to presage a reduction from about 10 or 12 big telecoms companies to about four major survivors. The seven regional Baby Bells were melting down to only two or three big regional telecoms players' (Tunstall and Machin, 1999: 56).[10]

Second, it provided legislation that was enormously favourable to the cultural industry corporations that dominated broadcasting in the USA. Free spectrum was allocated to the main broadcasters for digital television, with only minor and difficult-to-enforce legislation preventing them from using this spectrum for non-media services. New rules made it easier to renew broadcasting licences, and the period for holding them was extended, thereby granting broadcasting companies control of a vital node in the new, converged cultural industries. These changes gave them the potential to be key partners in future convergence mergers and alliances.

Third, the Act favoured existing cable companies by relaxing the regulation of charges and it allowed phone companies to enter the cable market to provide content. The 1984 Cable Act had removed cable price regulation and reduced the powers of local government to demand public interest facilities from cable operators. By 1992 cable had to be re-regulated, as its prices had

---

9 Patricia Aufderheide (1999) provides a valuable overview and insightful context.
10 This is what has happened in a series of complex mergers, in which the Bell name has all but disappeared. One of the Baby Bells took over its old parent, AT&T, in 2006.

soared and the cable industry had become deeply unpopular with the pub-lic and policymakers. The 1996 Act took away these regulations once again, with effect from 1999, leading to big increases in rates in that year.[11]

The Act was immediately followed by massive consolidation and frenetic trading. It helped pave the way for a wave of mega-mergers in the cultural industries in the late 1990s (see Chapter 6), as it drastically reduced the barriers to consolidation, cross ownership and vertical integration. It represented a cul-mination of the trend towards marketisation in media policy in the USA – now enshrined in legislation rather than just embodied in changes in regulation.

Meanwhile, in the USA and other countries as well, the ending of the state monopolies and technological developments in digitalisation (see Chapter 3) had led to big changes in telecommunications regulation, as dozens of new players entered the telecommunications market, including mobile teleph-ony providers, cable companies, internet service providers, local area net-works and so on. The role of regulators increasingly involved balancing the needs of these different players, ensuring reasonable efficiency and costs, and crucially, working with government, to invest in broadband infra-structure. The main challenge was to ensure an effective interconnection of networks (Noam, 2001), not only at the national but also the international level (Cowhey and Aronson, 2009). The primary goal was to ensure an effec-tive communications infrastructure for businesses rather than for consum-ers. As Nicholas Garnham (2011: 54–5) shows, investment poured in from businesses and governments, but with the latter scrambling to outstrip each other in providing the best infrastructure to serve the information economy that analysts confidently predicted lay ahead, there was a massive over-provision of capacity. This led to a search for increased traffic in order to cover the considerable investment costs. Particularly attractive in this con-text was 'value-added services' – services that could gain enhanced reve-nues, such as video on demand. This made huge new distribution capacity available to cultural-industry firms. But this capacity was also available to new players offering new 'platforms' and applications such as video-shar-ing sites and social networking sites. At the same time, this massive new infrastructure was extremely 'leaky' because it was digitalised, and because significant portions of it were provided over the internet and web. The only weapon that the cultural industries had was to argue for greater enforcement of copyright – as we shall see in Chapter 5.

International policy bodies

Another key component of the fourth wave of marketisation in cultural industries policy has been the growing importance of international policy bodies. These bodies have increasingly tended towards pro-convergence

---

11 On this and numerous other important points of detail in this chapter, I owe thanks to Chad Raphael.

policies in the name of marketisation. They have also been involved in reconfiguring intellectual property rights (see the next chapter). The most significant ones are outlined in Box 4.4.

Box 4.4　Main international policy agencies

EU European Union, comprising 27 countries as of 2012.

NAFTA North American Free Trade Association, comprising the USA, Canada and Mexico.

MERCOSUR Southern Cone Common Market, comprising Argentina, Brazil, Uruguay and Paraguay, established in 1991.

ASEAN Association of South East Asian Nations and its organisation for developing free trade in the area, Asia Pacific Economic Cooperation (APEC).

GATT General Agreement on Tariffs and Trade, originally signed in 1947 and developed and expanded over a series of rounds, most recently the Uruguay Round (1986–1993), culminating in the Marrakesh Agreement of 1993. This last round set up the much more powerful and formalised WTO.

WTO World Trade Organisation, which consists of 149 members, as of 2006, and can make binding judgements on cases where trade rules are subject to dispute. China joined in 2001.

GATS General Agreement on Trade in Services, which, together with the agreement on Trade-Related Aspects of Intellectual Property Rights (TRIPS), form the most important elements within GATT/WTO's operations related to the cultural industries. TRIPS integrates intellectual property into a world trade regime governed by free trade principles (see the next chapter for further discussion).

These bodies have fuelled business internationalisation of all kinds by encouraging trade between countries, but they have also, in some cases, provided regulation to protect industries by setting quotas on how much content can be exported to limit concentration and so on. All of them work in the direction of enabling free trade between member countries. Because such marketisation tends to favour the wealthier and more powerful companies and nations, some of these organisations have been opposed by activist groups – most famously in the form of the actions against the WTO in Seattle in November and December 1999. The cultural industries have been exempted from some of these free trade agreements in order to protect cultural diversity by insulating national cultural industries from the effects of cultural exports from the USA. The most notable instances were the exemption of Canadian cultural industries protection measures in NAFTA and the provision in GATS for cultural industries (argued for by the EU under French pressure). However, the general drift of policy in these bodies has leaned heavily towards marketisation.

This can be illustrated by the case of the EU, which, of all the international bodies named, is the organisation most informed by social democratic notions of public interest. Advocates of the public interest have put constant pressure on proponents of deregulation and achieved occasional victories, but there has been a relentless drift towards marketisation. EU policy bodies have moved away from sector-by-sector legislation regarding the social impacts of the media and towards regulation whereby telecommunications, computers and the media are governed by general competition legislation and regulators ensure compliance (Østergaard, 1998).

The *Television Without Frontiers* initiative of the 1980s (Commission of the European Communities, 1984) aimed to develop European audio-visual industries that could form a power bloc to match those of the USA in the global market, while respecting national diversity. It may be that this was always going to be an impossible goal to achieve, given the national diversity within Europe (Galperin, 1999), but after years of discussion a directive based on the policy (Council of the European Communities, 1989) finally came into effect in 1991 to try to make it happen. It was widely condemned as an ineffective and confused failure. It set quotas for the proliferating television channels of Europe, in terms of how much they could import from outside the EU, but rendered the policy useless by including the qualifying phrase 'if practicable', and its fudged attempts to combine economic growth and cultural diversity contrasted with the supposed 'success' of EU telecommunications policy. Here, because the implications for content were not fully understood, there was consensus over policy – and the consensus was pro-marketisation. Ten years of EU telecommunications marketisation culminated in an agreement by all EU member states to open up their telecommunications markets to privatisation and free competition from 1 January 1998.

Meanwhile, public service advocates continue to do battle with the marketisers over 'information society' policy and this often takes the form of battles between different sections of the EU's bureaucracy.[12] This was particularly apparent in debates over the EU's evolving information society policy. The Bangemann Report of 1994 (Commission of the European Communities, 1994) advocated an extreme pro-marketisation approach, but a High Level Group of Experts (including Manuel Castells) appointed by the Commission focused on issues of access and exclusion to this information society in their response. Nevertheless, the Green Paper on Convergence issued by the Commission of the EU in September 1997 (European Commission, 1997) was heavily pro-marketisation and, while public interest advocates succeeded in having it revised more in the direction of public interest, it remains the thrust of EU information society policy.

---

12 Such as the battles between the Directorate General (DG) X for Communication, Culture and Audiovisual Media, and the DG XIII on Telecommunications.

Underpinning EU policy is the assumption that convergence on corporate terms is inevitable and therefore the EU's role should be to allow European corporations to compete on equal terms with other companies in the global economy. As a result, convergence functions as a self-fulfilling prophecy: policy change is both brought about by perceived convergence and, at the same time, is likely to accelerate it. The drive to marketise telecommunications across Europe in the 1990s was very much propelled by such convergence talk, although advocates of public interest and PSB continued to fight hard to resist such notions (see Downey, 1998; Murdock and Golding, 1999). The consequences for the cultural industries are profound, as we shall see in Chapter 8.

The EU illustrates the pressures towards marketisation that exist in even those policy bodies that are most amenable to being influenced by social democratic notions of the public interest. It suggests that the pressures towards globalisation and convergence are proving extremely difficult for policymakers to resist. International policy bodies are pushing the global cultural industry landscape in the direction of conglomeration and commodification, with convergence increasingly accepted as some kind of technologically-driven fact rather than a product of policy in itself. Whether such convergence of telecommunications, computers and media is inevitable and/or desirable will be discussed in Chapter 9.

* * *

The push towards marketisation has not gone unresisted. Activist groups and national governments have put many obstacles in its way at different times. PSB has been surprisingly resilient in the face of barrages from its commercial rivals. Nevertheless, the four waves of marketisation suggest that, across very diverse national and regional contexts, neo-liberalism and the neoclassical conception of the market have made huge advances in the cultural sphere. Much of the world seems to have looked increasingly towards the USA as a model for how to regulate culture. Policy changes have had massive consequences for the cultural industries as a whole. Policies are responses to, and products of, sociocultural, economic and technological conditions, but they are also fundamental in triggering and/or inhibiting transformations in the cultural industries. This is particularly the case with broadcasting and telecommunications policy, where there have been strong traditions of public ownership and regulation, but where such traditions were abandoned or severely limited during the neo-liberal turn of the 1980s and 1990s. The changes described above have played a vital role – in conjunction with the changes and continuities described in the next six chapters – in determining the new landscape of the cultural industries at the beginning of the twenty first century.

RECOMMENDED AND FURTHER READING

The study of communications policy, law and regulation in the USA has been well served. I have found the following books very valuable: Patricia Aufderheide's *Communications Policy and the Public Interest* (1999); Robert Horwitz's *The Irony of Regulatory Reform* (1989); Sterling and Kittross' textbook history of broadcasting in the USA, *Stay Tuned* (3rd edition, 2002); Thomas Streeter's *Selling the Air* (1996); and Jennifer Holt's *Empires of Entertainment* (2011). Philip Napoli's *Foundations of Communications Policy* (2001) provides a helpful introduction to some of the key concepts in US policy, while John Durham Peters' *Courting the Abyss* (2005) and Laura Stein's *Speech Rights in America* (2006) are excellent on freedom of expression. Eli Noam's *Interconnecting the Network of Networks* (2001) is terrifically lucid on telecommunications regulation. Useful statements of the principles underlying PSB include chapters by Jay Blumler (1992) and by Kees Brants and Karen Siune (1992). Of the many useful comparative accounts of national media policy published in the 1990s, the most valuable (and readable) was by Peter J. Humphreys (1996). Jonathan Hardy's *Western Media Systems* (2008) admirably updates and synthesises information on developments in 20 different countries. *European Media* (2011), by Stylianos Papathanosassopoulos and Ralph Negrine, is also valuable on policy and industry, including at the EU level. The major contribution to comparative media research of the last few decades is Daniel Hallin and Paolo Mancini's *Comparing Media Systems* (2004). More recommendations on other aspects of policy can be found at the end of Chapter 5.

ONLINE READING

All the online material referenced below can be accessed free of charge at: **http://www.sagepub.co.uk/hesmondhalgh**
   Simply click on the 'Sample Materials' tab to find the links to each article.
   Among many useful articles about the effects of convergence on communication policy and public broadcasting are the following.

- Bar, François and Sandvig, Christian (2008) 'US communication policy after convergence', *Media, Culture & Society*, 30: 531–550.
- Raboy, Marc (2008) 'Dreaming in technicolor: the future of PSB in a world beyond broadcasting', *Convergence*, 14(3): 361–365.
- Syvertsen, Trine (2003) 'Challenges to public television in the era of convergence and commercialization', *Television & New Media*, 4(2): 155–175.

Further Changes in Policy:
Copyright and the Cult of Creativity

Copyright   159
    Longer, bigger, stronger copyrights   160
Cultural policy: the creative industries moment   165
    The Greater London Council and leftist cultural
            industries policy   166
    Local and urban cultural industries policy   167
    The creativity cult: cities, clusters and classes   170
    Contradictions of national creative industries policy   174
    Creative industries policy goes global   177

This chapter concerns two further types of policy change that irrevocably transformed the place of the cultural industries in modern societies. The first is copyright law and practice. Changes here are closely linked to the dynamics of internationalisation and 'convergence' that were discussed in the final section of the previous chapter. The international trade agreements and policy bodies introduced there – most notably the WTO and the EU – have played a key part in bringing about key changes in copyright. Copyright has been fundamental to the cultural industries throughout the complex professional era (i.e., from the early twentieth century), but the 1980s and 1990s saw an intensification of policy interest in intellectual property, including copyright. What's more, copyright increasingly became a focus for debates about cultural production in modern societies. By the 2000s, as digitalisation and convergence began to affect the cultural industries, copyright emerged as a battleground between three forces: established cultural-industry interests, new entrants into digital distribution from the information technology industries, and audiences and users. This brought to the surface old and newer contradictions regarding the ownership of cultural products, and about the very nature of property itself.

The second set of changes discussed in the chapter concern cultural policy. As the cultural industries grew in the mid-twentieth century, cultural policy was initially formulated as a defence of art against commercialisation, industrialisation and commodification. In the 1970s and 1980s, some progressive policymakers and academics began to question this type of cultural policy, on the grounds that it privileged elite, high culture. At the same time, there was a rising interest in what forms of employment might replace manufacturing industries in 'post-industrial' and de-industrialising cities and nations. But by the 1980s and 1990s, the policy ground began to shift, partly under the influence of neo-liberalism and information society discourse. The commercial cultural industries increasingly came to be grouped together with a variety of other arts-based activities and renamed 'the creative industries'. The reasons behind this move are discussed, and so are some of the consequences for policy and for cultural production. The increasing importance of intellectual property and copyright played a role here too.

COPYRIGHT

Copyright is one of the three main areas of modern *intellectual property*, each of which protects a particular type of 'knowledge' or idea:

- *Patents* protect ideas that are new, non-obvious and useful or applicable to industry.
- *Trademarks* protect symbols intended to distinguish the products of companies from one another.
- *Copyright* protects those expressions defined in law as 'literary and artistic works' (the principle is that it protects the expressions, not the ideas; patents supposedly protect ideas).

All three of these areas affect the cultural industries in different ways, but it is undoubtedly copyright which is the most significant here.

Mainstream economists and policymakers usually conceptualise the function of copyright as providing an incentive for authors to create. If authors wrote books and they could simply be copied without paying the author, then there would be less incentive to produce books. For some political economy approaches (see, for example, Bettig, 1996; Garnham, 1990: 38–40), copyright law is better understood as an attempt to regulate one of the distinctive problems facing the cultural industries, which is that cultural commodities often tend to act like public goods, in that the act of consuming them does not diminish their value (see Introduction). Copyright law responds by limiting the right to copy, thus making cultural goods scarcer than they might otherwise be. Other, more recent, political economy approaches stress copyright as just one part of the expanding role of intellectual property in modern societies. According to this view, new markets are opened up for commodification as capitalists search for new areas of life to gain a return on investment (see May, 2000).[1] Copyright is the main means by which culture becomes commodified.

---

1 I discuss this view in some detail in Hesmondhalgh and Baker (2008), using David Harvey's (2005) concept of 'accumulation by dispossession'.

Since the eighteenth century, copyright laws have underpinned the own-ership of cultural commodities and, therefore, to some extent, the cultural industries as a whole. Trade in books, films, music and other cultural prod-ucts was governed by a series of international agreements, most notably the Berne Convention of 1886, which was then extended to cover new forms such as films, in a series of further conventions. The Universal Copyright Convention of 1952, signed in Geneva, brought other countries, including the USA, into an international system of copyright recognition. Nevertheless, enforcement of copyright was extremely varied, even within and between those countries that were signatories to these treaties.

By the 1980s, however, as Thomas Streeter (2011: 146) points out, '[u]nder the sway of neoliberal habits of thought', property relations in gen-eral were being extended ever more widely: 'to water, to genes, and, in the realm of intellectual property, to software patents, to business models, to the "look and feel" of software'. As we saw in Chapter 3, a potent mix of neo-liberalism and information society rhetoric prepared the ground for 'information', including cultural expression, to be understood as ownable. As well as patent and trademark, and newer ways of owning culture (such as the idea that celebrities and stars might have rights in their own images), copyright became increasingly interesting to policymakers. In the USA, in particular, cultural-industry lobbyists were able to point to the considerable contribution that copyright revenues made to the US economy. Other coun-tries quickly followed suit. The cultural industries were expanding in the 1980s and 1990s, and this gave the broadcasting, music and film industries greater lobbying power, in many countries. At the same time, the concurrent development of digital networks meant these industries were beginning to present themselves as under threat from 'copyright theft' (a completely new concept), both at home and abroad.

Longer, bigger, stronger copyrights

In this new environment, in the 1990s, there was a flurry of international treaties and national legislation aiming at the 'harmonisation' of copyright law and practice. The supposed threat offered by digital technologies – in particular the internet –brought about a legislative response that has 'vastly increased the scope of copyright but also has done so in a way which benefits corporate interests at the expense of those of both artists and consumers' (Frith and Marshall, 2004: 4).

A major event was the signing in Marrakesh, Morocco, of the agreement on Trade-Related Aspects of Intellectual Property Rights (TRIPS) at the end of the 'Uruguay round' of world trade negotiations in 1994. The agreements signed in Marrakesh in 1994 also included the creation of the World Trade Organisation. This was a key development in economic 'globalisation', occurring at the peak of neo-liberalism's grip on policy-making, and it had a significant impact on intellectual property and copyright (see Box 5.1).

Box 5.1   The WTO enters the field

As one book on international media policy has commented, the World Trade Organisation (WTO) is 'the most powerful global trade institution ever created' (Ó Siochrú and Girard, 2002: 51). It grew out of the General Agreement on Tariffs and Trade (GATT) – a temporary body formed in 1947 to administer and negotiate the treaty of the same name. The WTO was formed in 1993 by treaty and has considerably more powers than GATT. It covers three main areas:

- *Goods* covered by the ongoing GATT.
- *Services* covered by a new agreement called the General Agreement on Trade in Services (GATS).
- *Intellectual property* covered by the agreement on Trade-Related Aspects of Intellectual Property Rights (TRIPS).

The fact that there is an agreement specifically devoted to intellectual property is in itself a sign of the importance governments and big business place on the role of intellectual property in the modern global economic system.

Prior to 1995, the multilateral treaties covering intellectual property rights (such as the 1883 Paris Convention on Intellectual Property, the 1886 Berne Convention and their revisions) were overseen by the World Intellectual Property Organisation (WIPO). This organisation continues to exist and remains significant (see May 2007), but intellectual property was brought under the much more powerful WTO because the USA wanted to avoid revisions to treaties on industrial (patent and trademark) properties that might hinder its advantages and also wanted much a more rigorous international enforcement of the control of piracy and settlement of disputes. GATT had shown that this was possible and the WTO has come to embody this kind of policing (Ó Siochrú and Girard, 2002: 90). Corporations in the USA played a major role in these developments and, as Dave Laing (2004) has outlined, the changes to national legislation regimes around the world that have been brought about by TRIPS are complemented by the actions of the United States Trade Representative (USTR), who, under Special Provision 301 in the 1988 Omnibus Trade and Competitiveness Act, can blacklist countries that have intellectual property practices that are harmful to copyright industries in the USA. This list is announced each year and the USTR draws heavily on information provided by the International Intellectual Property Alliance (IIPA), which, effectively, is a lobbying arm for the major cultural industries in the USA (Laing, 2004). This is cultural neo-liberalism, buttressed by the trading power of the USA.

Compliance with TRIPS and the Special 301 list means huge adjustments have to be made in countries that have no notion of intellectual property in the sense in which it is enshrined in 'Western' copyright law. Christopher May (2004)

(Continued)

(Continued)

has shown how developing countries are receiving extensive technical support in training legislators and administrators from a variety of international, government and non-governmental organisations. This however is double-edged because it means that developing countries will have more expertise that they can use to take advantage of flexibilities in TRIPS. Many symbol creators and policymakers in developing countries welcome copyright because they believe it will protect their work from exploitation by others within their own society and Western corporations, but the spread of TRIPS means that a neo-liberal vision of culture is becoming normalised and legitimated across the world. This vision sees copyright as a necessary incentive for symbolic creativity. It portrays individual compensation as the main driving force of human activity.

The first major response to the rise of the internet came with the WIPO conference in Geneva in 1996. Signatories agreed to update their national laws to allow rights holders to extend their rights to cover the internet and other computer networks. The result was the Digital Millennium Copyright Act in the USA in 1998 and the EU Copyright Directive of 2001, with various European countries making this law in their respective countries in 2002 and 2003. Such an extension of copyright law into digital terrain was to be expected, but these acts also contained clauses making it illegal to develop software that could counter the digital rights management (DRM) systems then being used by cultural industry corporations to protect their content (see Chapter 10 for a further discussion of this in the context of controversies over the digitalisation of music). This was a sign that the copyright industries, such as the music industry, were becoming adept at presenting the digital environment as a threat and arguing that they needed legislation to protect them from this danger.

The extension of copyright terms has been a key part of efforts by the cultural industries. An EU directive of 1993 aimed to 'harmonise' the copyright terms of all its member states, but it chose as its template the law in Germany, which had been extended to take account of the 'interruption' to copyright caused by Nazism. Once the various nations had changed their laws, this meant that copyright ran until 70 years after the date of the author's death. This meant that if an author were to write a book at the age of 25, which became a part of many people's lives, and if that author lived until she was 100, it would be 145 years before the book was out of copyright (the 75 remaining years of the author's life, plus 70 years).

When the US Congress passed the Sonny Bono Copyright Term Extension Act in 1998, cultural- industry lobbyists argued that it was only fair to match the EU figure. The British Statute of Anne of 1710 – the first to grant copyright to authors – provided a term of 14 years, renewable for another 14 years. Under the Sonny Bono Copyright Term Extension Act (named after a writer and performer of 1960s pop hits such as 'I got you babe', who, as a Republican congressman, strongly supported the bill), protection for works was extended from 75 years to 95 years and the 'neighbouring rights' protections granted to works made by corporations, including films and most popular music recordings, were also extended.[2] The Act was the result of significant lobbying of Congress by agencies briefed by corporate copyright holders, such as Disney.

Copyright extension continues. In the 2000s, there were campaigns by copyright holders in the EU (fronted in the UK by another purveyor of mediocre pop hits, Sir Cliff Richard) for it to lengthen the copyright in recordings from 50 years from the date of recording to 95 years. In 2011, the Council of Ministers ratified a European bill to extend the term to 70 years. Cultural industry corporations are busy lobbying for similar changes to copyright legislation in other territories.

It is not just the duration of rights that has expanded over time and with lobbying but also their scope. When copyright was introduced to the USA in the eighteenth century, it was necessary to register. With compulsory registration removed, 'every creative act reduced to a tangible medium is now subject to copyright protection' (Lessig, 2001: 107). As Lawrence Lessig shows (2001: 4), this has created a system whereby, for example, film-makers have to seek permission and often pay a fee to include any piece of artwork, furniture, sculpture, architecture, music in their works. Copyright, intended to foster creativity, has become an almost insane restriction on it in many cases.

Not all creative works that have been fixed in a tangible medium are subject to copyright. Some works are in *the public domain* – a body of works that can be used by anyone because no one can claim exclusive rights to their use. National copyright laws determine when a work passes out of copyright and into this public domain. Cultural creativity is dependent on the public domain because acts of creation work by (sometimes unconscious) borrowing from and referring to other works. The result of extensions to the scope of copyright is that this public domain shrinks, other things being equal, with detrimental effects on creativity. While the industrialisation of culture has undoubtedly expanded the amount of cultural work in circulation in modern societies, the move towards lengthening copyright terms potentially shrinks the number of works that are available for creative recontextualisation. This is particularly important given that corporations routinely monitor any use of their copyrighted materials, even those that seem trivial or incidental. This

---

2 Neighbouring rights are not, strictly speaking, copyrights. In music, for example, they are the rights of ownership in the performance of a composition, rather than the composition itself. It is the recording that is owned rather than the composition underlying it. Nearly all recordings are owned by the companies that produce them, rather than by individual performers. In spite of this key difference, I follow the convention of treating all the various rights in cultural works under the heading 'copyright'.

has implications that reach considerably beyond the cultural industries them-selves – in education, for instance. To give one example of this, a number of years ago, I was involved in producing a new media studies course for the Open University, a British distance-learning higher education institution. We wanted to use a British daytime chat show, *Trisha*, as an example of how working-class families were being represented in such programmes. We wrote an analysis and wanted to provide the students with a clip from the show to make things clearer. The Open University's rights department wrote to the rights holder (ITV) to ask for permission. Permission was denied and no explanation given. Rights holders can have significant influence on what is taught in public education systems and they do not even have to provide an account of their reasons.

Copyright law and practice also limits copyright holders' power by allow-ing exceptions to the requirement that copyright holders authorise use of 'their' materials. In some countries, notably the USA, this is known as *fair use*.[3] Exceptions are stipulated in statutes or judged in the context of cases. Examples include parody, copying a certain restricted portion of a work (per-haps you're reading a photocopy now?) and educational use. As copying technologies (such as photocopiers, video recorders and digital samplers in music) have proliferated, this has become a big issue. Holders have become increasingly keen to protect their copyright and so fair use is also increasingly under threat. And even where fair use might be claimed, many institutions advise creators against using material in such a way in marginal cases – which are legion – because they fear action by rights holders: this might for example involve the withdrawal of a product or even litigation. Remember that the purpose of copyright is supposedly to provide an incentive to create works within a society. Ruth Towse (2002: xvii) summarises the economic perspec-tive on balancing fair use with the incentives provided by copyright:

- A too strong copyright regime that tolerated little fair use would favour holders over users, but would also increase the costs for holders of cre-ating more works.
- A too weak regime would not provide sufficient incentive.

'Fair use' in this broad sense also includes public domain material. It is hard to believe that the hugely increasing scope of copyright is necessary to protect creativity. Indeed, many analysts, from a wide variety of fields and perspec-tives, are now arguing for a weakening of copyright.[4] Most of these writers

---

3   The equivalent term in the UK is 'fair dealing', but it covers a much narrower set of exceptions than does 'fair use'. 'Fair use' is increasingly used as a generic term to cover the principle of such exceptions in debating the scope of rights.

4   Many of these voices come from the left (such as Toynbee, 2004) and the political centre (Lessig, 2001), but they also come from the right as well. For example, *The Economist* has favoured shorter copyright terms.

favour the existence of some kind of rights system, but popular perception has often been more militant in its opposition to copyright. One remarkable manifestation of this opposition has been the success of fringe political parties in support of 'piracy' in Europe, notably in Sweden and Germany.

Perhaps an even greater price to be paid for the spread of copyright, both within advanced industrial countries and other societies, is that in more and more places the prevailing conceptions of what constitutes creative or cultural work begin to shift towards the individual property model and away from a notion of social or collective creativity. While Western copyright law in theory protects the individual creator in the interests of creators and users, in practice, copyright tends to be owned by corporations (which, in another of the bizarre contortions of modern law, are defined as individuals for the purposes of contracts). This then feeds into a vicious spiral in which cultural corporations become more powerful and more effective in lobbying governments and this in turn increases their power – a dynamic that will be investigated further in Chapter 6.

CULTURAL POLICY: THE CREATIVE INDUSTRIES MOMENT

Relations between the cultural industries and cultural policy (see Box 5.2 for a definition of this term) need to be understood in their long-term historical context. In many countries, government subsidy has tended to go to the 'classical', legitimated arts.[5] Throughout the post-Second World War era, in many countries, there were various struggles to include more groups in the ambit of funding for the sake of democratisation (see Looseley, 2004, on the French version of this). In the UK, for example, funding for the 'fine arts' was gradually expanded to the arts more generally, and then beyond these to include traditional crafts, such as pottery and 'folk' arts. In the 1970s, there were 'community arts' movements, and in the 1980s, an increasing emphasis on multiculturalism. The content of subsidised 'legitimated' culture has shifted over time – arts cinemas came to be funded and subsidised alongside the opera and regional theatres, for example. One of the reasons that Jack Lang became an internationally famous Minister of Culture in the 1980s and 1990s was that he attempted to extend French cultural policy to forms that had previously been excluded, such as rock, hip hop and rai (Looseley, 2004: 19).

---

5   The two principal exceptions were public broadcasting systems, as discussed in the previous chapter, and film.

Box 5.2　What is cultural policy?

To start with, it's a term used to refer to two overlapping but different fields. As with definitions of the cultural industries, much depends on how you define 'culture' and culture is notoriously difficult to define. In its broadest use, it can designate all those forms of policy that might directly have an impact on the forms of cultural identity within a particular space, be it international, national, regional or urban, but if we start to include too much (food and drink as well as films) then the word 'culture', as in so many other instances, starts to lose its usefulness. The term has tended to be used for policy that has an impact on the primarily symbolic domain. In a similar way, my definition of the cultural industries in the Introduction emphasised the relationship of symbolic to functional elements in their products. Broadcasting and telecommunications policy, as discussed in the previous chapter, might be seen as forms of cultural policy in this broader sense, in that they can have a vital impact on culture (as can film policy). Cultural policy in this broad sense could include public broadcasting, the use of quotas and scheduling limitations to protect 'national' culture, national ownership rules, subsidies and so on (see Grant and Wood, 2004, for one breakdown of elements).

The term 'cultural policy' is often used, in the anglophone world at least, in a second and somewhat narrower sense, to refer to the subsidy, regulation and management of 'the arts', which I define here as those inventive, creative, non-scientific forms of knowledge activity and institution that have come to be deemed worthy of this elevated title – the visual arts, 'literature', music and dance, theatre and drama and so on. My focus in this chapter is primarily on this domain – though the issue of how governments use cultural policy to promote and protect industries is also a vital one.

The Greater London Council and leftist cultural industries policy

The seminal introduction of the concept of the cultural industries to cultural policy represented a more radical revision of cultural policy than the democratic spreading of arts funding described above. This took place at the left-wing Greater London Council (GLC) from 1983 until the Council's abolition by the British Conservative government in 1986.[6] This policy thinking was directed against elitist and idealist notions of art, but was also a challenge to those activists and policymakers who had concentrated on expanding the field of arts subsidy to include new groups. Instead, it was argued by some

---

6　There were significant precedents at the international level, in discussions of the cultural industries as part of UNESCO (see UNESCO, 1982), but these had no direct impact on national and urban policy in the advanced industrial countries.

at the GLC, cultural policy should take full account of the fact that most people's cultural tastes and practices were shaped by *commercial* forms of culture and by PSB. The aim was not to celebrate commercial production, but simply to recognise its centrality in modern culture. One key position paper (written by Nicholas Garnham and reprinted in Garnham, 1990) argued that, rather than concentrating on an artist-centred strategy that subsidised 'creators', policy should focus on distribution and the reaching of audiences. This argument reflected the emphasis on the centrality of circulation in the cultural industries tradition of political economy and the importance of thinking about the distinctive characteristics of primarily symbolic production and consumption, as opposed to other forms (see the Introduction). The practical implications of such thinking, according to Garnham's paper, were that 'debates, organisational energy and finance' ought to be redirected towards the following cultural practices:

- Broadcasting – which Garnham described as the 'heartland of contemporary cultural practice'.
- Libraries – which were the recipients of over 50 per cent of all public expenditure on culture at the time in the UK.
- Providing loans and services to small- and medium-sized cultural businesses in London for the marketing and dissemination of their products (Garnham, 1990: 166).

There was a second major element to the GLC strategy, which was the use of investment in cultural industries as a means of economic regeneration. As Garnham pointed out in a later retrospective (2001), this had no necessary connection to the quite separate argument about shifting the focus of policy from the artist to the audience. It was also less novel, in that the use of cultural initiatives to boost the image of cities was under way elsewhere (Bianchini and Parkinson, 1993). Such policies were often directed towards the boosting of tourism and/or retail in an area or making an area attractive as a location for businesses, rather than the democratisation of cultural provision. In the late 1980s and 1990s, such strategies boomed and spread across the world. Notable cases included Glasgow's remarkable success in becoming the European City of Culture for the year 1990 and reinventing its image. Super-expensive flagship projects, often based on adventurous architecture, proliferated. The best-known example is probably the Guggenheim Museum in Bilbao, opened in 1997, which succeeded in making post-industrial Bilbao a tourist attraction. Such projects have been controversial locally, but criticisms are rarely heard internationally.

Local and urban cultural industries policy

Because the GLC was abolished, its cultural industry policies were never implemented in London. All the same, the idea of local cultural policy based on the cultural industries had a big impact during the next decade. In many cities, cultural industries policies became bound up with broader strategies to use culture for urban regeneration. However, the rise of local cultural industries policy, initially in the form of 'cultural quarters' in post-industrial cities, was not entirely a result of the appeal of GLC's pragmatic anti-idealist egalitarianism. In fact, in many cases, the idea of cultural industries policy chimed with a fast-growing desire in the 1980s and 1990s to think about all areas of public policy, including culture and media, in terms of *a return on public investment*. This was fuelled by increasing doubts, as a result of the sociocultural changes discussed in Chapter 3, about the legitimacy of 'high cultural' forms. In this context, the use of money to promote 'ordinary' culture was seen as anti-elitist – and this contributed to the popularity of cultural industries policies with many left-wing councils in Europe. So it was that in the late 1980s, shaped by economic neo-liberalism and a breaking down of long-standing forms of cultural hierarchy (though by no means the end of cultural hierarchies themselves), the notion of the cultural industries or the cultural sector became increasingly attached, in a new era of local and regional development policy, to the goals of regeneration and employment creation. It was this second element of GLC policy that was often emphasised, not the first, but now bound up not only with culture-led urban regeneration strategies but also with an increasing emphasis on entrepreneurialism in the private and public sectors. In a pamphlet written for the think tank Demos, for example, Charles Leadbeater (a figure associated with the GLC, who, by the late 1990s, was closely linked to Tony Blair's 'New Labour' project) outlined the way that entrepreneurs in the cultural industries provided a new model of work and a key basis for local economic growth in that their local, tacit know-how – 'a style, a look, a sound'– showed 'how cities can negotiate a new accommodation with the global market' (Leadbeater and Oakley, 1999: 14). The view that independent cultural production might be connected to wider movements for progressive social change, implicit in at least some of the GLC work, was by now being steadily erased.

A crucial further connection was with new developments in arts policy, whereby institutions increasingly sought to legitimise their funding on the basis of its contribution to a somewhat uncomfortable and potentially contradictory mixture of economic and social goals. An influential, though not uncontroversial, report by economist John Myerscough (1988), for example, put the cultural industries together with the arts and analysed how they contributed to job creation, tourism promotion, invisible earnings and urban regeneration.[7] Alongside such developments, many arts policymakers also

---

7   See Belfiore (2002) for a survey of arts policy developments in this domain in the UK. Myerscough's study used the economic concept of multiplier effects to understand the contribution that policy might make. However, as Garnham (2001: 451) points out, if this is taken to be the main basis of the efficacy of funding given scarce resources, then the question of whether or not other investment – for example, in public transport – might be a more effective option is unavoidable.

sought to justify arts subsidy on the basis that the arts – and the cultural industries increasingly linked to them in policy discourse – could contribute to combating *social exclusion* – a new term that spread like wildfire through European social policy in the 1990s and 2000s. Some analysts see social exclusion as a term that allows those who use it to avoid a consideration of deep-seated structural inequalities, including class (see, for example, Levitas, 1998). These developments were to have an important effect at the national policy level, as we shall see.

This is not to say that all such local cultural industries policies were ineffective and represented an accommodation with neo-liberalism or with new centrist forms of policy. In some cases policymakers, with a genuine desire to promote new and interesting forms of cultural activity within an area and provide support for struggling entrepreneurs and practitioners, could persuade local government to provide funding by talking about the regenerative possibilities of cultural industries' development.

Elsewhere (for example, in Sheffield, in the north of England), such policies were able to support local infrastructures, to the lasting benefit of symbol creators who wanted to work in the city (see Frith, 1993). However, the economic and social effectiveness of local cultural policies orientated towards the cultural industries remains controversial. It surely made sense to emphasise the importance of the cultural industries to a news and entertainment hub city, such as London, and it may make some sense even in some smaller but substantial cities where the cultural industries have some growing presence, but in other places the idea that investment in the cultural industries might boost local wealth and employment has proven more problematic.

Mark Jayne (2004), for example, analysed the difficulties a local council had in developing an effective cultural industries development policy in Stoke-on-Trent, in the English Midlands – a city with an overwhelmingly working-class population. The issue of class is significant here. Much of the burgeoning policy discourse (and associated academic literature) seems implicitly to portray working-class populations as regressive, holding back cities from entering into competition with the thriving metropolises of the West. So what are the dangers of foisting inappropriately metropolitan policies on predominantly working-class or rural places? This question was considered all too rarely as some rather hasty investment decisions were made.

Nevertheless, cultural industries policies can, it seems, make a contribution to people's lives in 'unlikely' areas. Chris Gibson and Daniel Robinson (2004) considered a small entertainment industry association on the far north coast of New South Wales, Australia, hundreds of miles from Sydney and other urban areas further south. They acknowledged that the effects of such an association on employment and economic activity were very hard to ascertain because of the perennial data problems in this area (see Chapter 6). However, Gibson and Robinson felt that the association's campaigns (keeping venues open, putting on events, getting better remuneration for musicians, publicising activity by means of awards and so on) helped to encourage young, aspiring creative workers to stay and thereby also encouraged a sense that there might be an interesting and rewarding cultural life in the region. In other words, funding such grassroots cultural industries institutions may have other, less directly economic but nevertheless positive benefits.

The creativity cult: creative cities, clusters and classes

By the mid-1990s, two related concepts had grown out of cultural quarter policies, each of which has been the subject of a great deal of policy interest: *creative cities* and *creative clusters*. These terms represented a key shift in the policy vocabulary surrounding the cultural industries. A sense of what was at stake in the former idea can be gained from booklets and policy documents associated with the Comedia consultancy group. In some of these publications (see, for example, Landry, 2000) creativity was presented as the key to urban regeneration and the main reason given was that 'the industries of the twenty-first century will depend increasingly on the generation of knowledge through creativity and innovation matched with rigorous systems of control' (Landry and Bianchini, 1995: 12). Television, software and theatre were examples of such industries, but so was dealing in stocks and shares, and the claim was that they all needed creative cities to help them thrive. A number of examples of creativity in local planning and policy were offered by Landry and Bianchini, including the culture-led urban regeneration strategies referred to above. How these were to induce creativity in a city's inhabitants was not made clear, but by the turn of the century the cultural industries were being thoroughly incorporated into a more general notion of creativity as a boon to a city's ills (see Box 5.3).

Box 5.3   Creativity: business with feeling

The adoption of the term 'creative' in creative industries policy in the late 1990s and 2000s was no accident. There had been a keen interest in the concept among management analysts and economists for many years (see Hesmondhalgh and Baker, 2011: 3), some of it deriving from the new fashion in economics of endogenous growth theory which, drawing on information society discourse, assigned a central role to idea generation, creativity and knowledge (see Menger, 2006: 801). Crucially, the term 'creativity' had a set of benign connotations, derived from the high status attached to creativity and knowledge in many societies and civilisations. Humanist psychology (see, for example, Abraham Maslow, 1987[1954]) had stressed the widespread presence of creativity in human behaviour, making the concept adaptable for a demotic age. Even in 1961, Raymond Williams (1965[1961]: 19) could write that '[n]o word carries a more consistently positive reference than "creative"'. It was these connotations that the British Labour government drew upon in using the term 'creative' to replace the 'cultural' in cultural industries (see below) as they developed new cultural and arts policies in the mid-1990s. So too did many other governments and consultants, presumably finding close equivalents in their own languages. The result was that by the 2000s, in the words of Philip Schlesinger (2007: 378), creativity had become not merely a discourse but a doctrine for policymakers, 'an object of unceasing advocacy by its proponents'. Some critics responded by impatiently attacking the concept (Osborne, 2004). As Sarah Baker and I stress in our analysis of work in the cultural industries, however (Hesmondhalgh and Baker, 2011), we should not and cannot abandon the term, in spite of its motherhood-and-apple-pie associations (by this I mean that it blandly invokes things to which people are unlikely to object) and its dubious uses in cultural policy. As Williams noted, we should be glad of the positive connotations of creativity, 'when we think of the values it seeks to express and the activities it offers to describe' (1965[1961]: 19). The danger though is that those values might be distorted or diminished by appropriations of the term.

The idea of creative clusters was even more significant. The concept of the business cluster was derived from the writings of economist Michael Porter (1990), which attempted to explain how nations and regions would gain a competitive advantage over others. An important element, which distinguished it from older theories, such as that of the nineteenth-century economist Alfred Marshall, was Porter's explanation of why firms from the same industry would tend to gather in the same places. This emphasised notions of innovative entrepreneurialism and competitiveness that were coming to be fetishised in neo-liberal discourses of the 'new economy' (Martin and Sunley, 2003) and made 'business clusters' a hugely influential concept across the world. Unsurprisingly, in the late 1990s, policymakers concerned with the development of the cultural industries adapted the term 'business clusters' by linking it to the rising cult of creativity in management, business and government and using the term 'creative clusters'.[8]

For Hans Mommaas (2004: 508) 'cultural clustering strategies represent a next stage in the ongoing use of culture and the arts as urban regeneration resources'. Once all major cities had developed their festivals, major museums and theatre complexes in the culture-led urban regeneration boom of the 1990s, the action moved on to creating milieux for cultural production. However, like 'business clusters', creative clusters was an idea built on a shaky conceptual foundation. Mommaas distinguished between a number of discourses, which tended to be merged together in policy discussions of

---

8   This continued into the 2000s as, for example, the British Labour government put its national creative industries strategy (see below) into operation in 'the regions' via the increasingly important Regional Development Associations – see below. Clusters remained a key concept in this new phase.

the benefits of creative clusters and which, in his view, were in danger of undermining and contradicting each other:

- Promoting cultural diversity and democracy.
- Strategies of place marketing, in the interests of tourism and employment.
- Stimulating a more entrepreneurial approach to the arts and culture.
- Generally encouraging innovation and creativity.
- Finding new uses for old buildings and derelict sites.

Mommaas noted that, while some clustering strategies were limited to artistic cultural activities, most of them incorporated many other leisure and entertainment elements – bars, health and fitness complexes and the like. In another critical study, Ivan Turok (2003) showed that the concept of cluster is highly problematic in cases such as Scotland's film and television industries. The term 'cluster' implies networks of small knowledge-intensive firms generating regional growth by means of an endogenous process. But Scotland's television and film industries were in fact largely dependent on the UK television channels based mainly in London.[9]

Development strategies based on notions of creativity and culture proliferated across the world in the late 1990s and early 2000s. Perhaps the most ardent treatment of the role of creativity in modern economies (see also Box 5.3) came from the US academic and policy consultant Richard Florida. In a widely-read book, Florida (2002: 4) made the cheering assertion that, while most transition theories tended to see transformation as something that was happening to people, in fact, society was mostly changing because we wanted it to and the driving force of these desired changes was 'the rise of human creativity as the key factor in our economy and society'. This, he claimed, had led to a change in the class system itself, with the rise of 'a new creative class', comprising an astounding 30 per cent of all employed citizens in the USA – a creative core of people in science and engineering, architecture and design, education, the arts, music and entertainment, and then an outer group of creative professionals in business and finance, the law, healthcare and related fields. As will be clear from this, Florida's claims about creativity, like many other such claims, derived from lumping together a very diverse set of activities, but they allowed him to address himself to political leaders seeking new strategies of urban regeneration in a globalised marketplace for business relocation and tourism. In a version of the Comedia argument about creative cities, Florida claimed that creative people wanted to live in creative cities and, if cities wanted to attract these often wealthy and influential creative people to live and spend their hard- and creatively-earned money on local taxes and local services, then

---

9 Pratt (2004) also notes that claims for the effectiveness of cluster strategies often rely on dubious forms of statistical evidence.

governments would need to foster 'a creative community' in their cities. He also offered his services as a consultant to advise city governments on how to create such communities.

Box 5.4   The role of creativity in the new economy

Kieran Healy (2002) identified a number of questions that might be asked about the role of creativity in the new economy as identified by writers such as Howkins and Florida. In particular, he separated out four claims concerning why the relationships between the so-called creative sector and the new economy might matter to policymakers.

- The 'creative sector' will continue to grow, justifying more policy research in this area. This is the easiest claim to defend, wrote Healy, but it establishes little in itself. What kinds of policies? And can there be any shared policy agenda among the very varied interests involved?
- The creative sector is a miner's canary for the wider economy because of its uncertain labour markets, flexible collaboration and project-based work (see also the reasons for interest in the cultural industries outlined in the Introduction). However, is the project work of a project-based stage actor really relevant to those of a project-based systems administrator? And is the cultural labour force a good model, given the problems of labour markets there (see Chapter 7)?
- Creativity in general is becoming increasingly important to competitiveness. This, Healy pointed out, is not established and the demand for different kinds of creative people will be very unequal across different industries and sectors.
- The so-called 'creative class' is intensely interested in cultural goods of many kinds, so cities should invest in culture. As Healy observed, this is unlikely to be uniform (especially, we might add, given how absurdly broad-ranging this category of culture is).

By this point, the democratising intent behind 'cultural industries' urban policy, manifest in the original GLC strategy, had become deeply submerged. Cultural policy analyst Justin O'Connor later reflected on these developments and sought to correct a number of misconceptions in what he saw as an overly celebratory literature concerning the insertion of local – especially urban – sites of cultural production into the global circulation of cultural products. One was the view that clusters of local cultural producers deriving their success from creativity depended on local, tacit knowledge (including the *genius loci* of the city where the cultural production takes place). According to such views, which can be found in the work of the consultancy Comedia but also in other policy discourse, cities and regions could gain a competitive advantage because such knowledge could not easily be codified and therefore transferred. In fact, wrote O'Connor, successful clusters were increasingly predicated not so much on tacit 'creativity' but on access to a range of *formal* knowledge about global markets, larger companies and distribution networks. To miss this was to ignore the reality of local cultural production and local policy: few of the agencies set up to help nascent cultural industries had the kinds of formal knowledge that were actually needed (O'Connor, 2004: 139). O'Connor was making a broader point, too. The emphasis on using 'creativity' and urbanity for the competitive advantage of cities risked going beyond a reconciliation of economics and culture to being an annexation of the latter by the former (p. 146).

As we shall now see, it is not just at the 'sub-national', regional or urban level that this issue of the relationship between economics and culture is relevant. It is also raised by creative industries policies at the national level and the adoption of certain assumptions about the role of creativity in the 'new economy'.

Contradictions of national creative industries policy

We saw above that the terms 'creative' and 'creativity' were becoming increasingly popular in local cultural policy in the 1990s. By the late 1990s, they had spread to the national policy level. 'Creative industries' is a concept that has been widely adopted in the spheres of cultural policy and higher education. Its first major use in policy appears to have been by the British Labour government elected in 1997, though there were significant precedents in other countries, notably the Australian Labour government's *Creative Nation* initiative of 1994. The adoption of the term 'creative industries' was, in part, a way for cultural policymakers (whether concerned with arts, crafts or film production) to legitimise their concerns at the national level. Local policy had shown that, by linking arts to the cultural industries, even these most refined of activities could be made to seem part of economic development – the *sine qua non* of most government policy in the era of neo-liberalism. At last, cultural policy makers might have found a way to be taken seriously by those who held real political power, in departments of business and trade, and most crucially of all, in the treasuries that determined which departments got how much money.

Nicholas Garnham (2001: 25; see also Garnham, 2005) identified two major claims implicitly made by the mobilisation of the term 'creative industries':

- The creative industries are the key new growth sector of the economy, both nationally and globally.
- They are therefore the key source of future employment growth and export earnings.

For Garnham, the use of the term 'creative' achieved a number of goals with regard to these claims in the British context. In the first instance, it allowed for a very broad definition. Various documents issued by the UK Department for Culture, Media and Sport (for example, DCMS, 1998, 2001) included not only the industries that I call the 'cultural industries' in this book (see Introduction), but also dance, the visual arts and the more craft-based activities of making jewellery, fashion, and furniture design. This made it possible to link these subsidised sectors to the supposedly booming commercial creative industries of music and broadcasting. It also, crucially, included computer software, which allowed the creative industries sector to be presented as a much larger and more significant part of the economy than would otherwise have been possible.[10]

According to Garnham, this broad definition, in turn, had two valuable policy consequences for the interest groups involved. First, it enabled software producers and the major cultural industry conglomerates to construct an alliance with smaller businesses and cultural workers concerned with strengthening intellectual property protection. Crucial here was the way that the defence of intellectual property became associated with 'the moral prestige of the "creative artist"' (Garnham, 2005: 26). Second, it enabled the cultural sector to use arguments for the public support of the training of creative workers originally developed for the ICT industry. This argument, in turn, had much wider implications, in that it pushed education policy much more strongly in the direction of an often dubious discourse of skills, on the basis that future national prosperity depended on making up for a supposed lack of creative, innovative workers. The result was that UK creative industries policy is based on an 'artist'-centred notion of subsidy, rather than an audience-orientated policy of infrastructural support – the very opposite, in other words, of the original GLC vision.

British creative industries cultural policy at the national level (as outlined, for example, by government culture minister Chris Smith in his 1998 book *Creative Britain*) claimed to resolve a long-standing dilemma facing social democratic cultural policy in the post-war era: that, given limited resources, there were hard choices to be made between *raising* (promoting excellence by, for example, attracting the best orchestral conductors, museum curators and theatre directors to national cultural institutions) or *spreading* (touring productions, supporting local groups). The British Labour government's creative industries policy claimed to resolve this contradiction by eliminating the high/low distinction by supporting the whole sector, thus combining access (spreading) with excellence (raising). For Garnham, however, this was to miss the entrenched nature of contradictions in structurally unequal societies. Excellence smuggles the high/low distinction back, but in the form of a celebration of the highly skilled creative artist as a model worker in the new 'creative economy'. This went against access and inclusion because, as Garnham (2001: 457) puts it, it is likely to be the case that 'a key element in

---

10 This of course relates to the broader question of how to measure the changing role of culture, or the cultural industries in modern economies. I address this question in the next chapter.

social exclusion is the existing hierarchy of cultural forms and experiences and the very definition of excellence itself' and this problem can be thought of, at least in part, as being a product of the creative industries now deemed worthy of support under the new regime. For example, it could be argued that the working classes and other excluded groups consume mainly commercially produced culture and this reinforces their position in cultural hierarchies. If this is the case, then supporting the growth of the creative industries on the grounds of economic growth may not in fact solve the problem of access to excellence and instead exacerbate it. The contradictions of class society will not be easily resolved.

At the same time, as we saw above, policymakers and politicians had already begun, from the 1970s onwards, to link arts and cultural policy to the pursuit of social goals, or, in the term increasingly adopted by governments and consultancies, *regeneration*. A UK report on the impact of culture on regeneration summarised some of the principal elements regarding regeneration: 'reduced levels of crime, increased health and well-being, increased educational attainment, reduced unemployment, greater community cohesion, greater environmental quality and quality of life (or liveability)' (Evans and Shaw, 2004: 2). But creative industries were also presented as a sector that was informed by meritocratic principles, so that, for example, ethnic communities might achieve greater levels of participation than in other areas of employment, because talent and skills might shine through.

In the age of neo-liberalism, such goals were in themselves strongly linked to economic principles: less crime, better education, and better health were considered good not in themselves, but because they could contribute to economic growth. It would be wrong to ascribe the pursuit of such goals entirely to an economically-driven neo-liberalism. Some analysts of public policy (see, for example, Craig and Cotterell, 2007) have sought to differentiate the very broad concept of neo-liberalism by referring to the way that the 'after neo liberal state' purports to repair the social damage of earlier neo-liberal reform. According to this view, in the 1990s, national and local governments increasingly aimed to enable businesses while also seeking to ensure some social amelioration, to provide a check on the most damaging outcomes of market forms of governance.[11]

Whether or not this is the correct way to understand government policy in the 2000s, there is no doubt that creative industries policies were part of a more general trend in cultural policy: culture was increasingly connected to goals of social amelioration (Yúdice, 2003). This led, in some cases, to critics raising questions about an increasing 'instrumentalisation' of cultural policy, whereby 'intrinsic' values of culture – the way in which culture might be valued for its own sake – were being subsumed (Belfiore, 2002; Holden, 2004). This could result, for example, in symbol creators and arts organisations

---

11 See Scott (2009) for an excellent application of this concept to cultural policy, using New Zealand music as a case study.

distorting the nature of what they did in order to conform to government measures of how to combat social exclusion.[12] Other critics of creative industries policy took a different tack and questioned whether the creative industries might in fact be a basis for pursuing regeneration and other social goals at all. Kate Oakley (2006), for example, outlined some ways in which hopes attached to creative industries were not grounded in a realistic appraisal of continuing inequalities and other problems in the sector.[13]

- First, hopes that investing in the creative industries at a 'local' level, in cities and regions, would provide regional growth opportunities ignored the massive centralisation of cultural employment and infrastructure in London and the South East of England.
- Second, aspirations that providing jobs in the creative industries might balance out inequalities in job markets in general, on the grounds that the creative industries are dependent on diverse talent, ignored the strength of social networks in the creative industries, and the continuing marginalisation, for example, of black and ethnic minority people from the cultural workforce. (These issues concerning inequalities in cultural labour markets are taken up in Chapter 7).
- Third, attempts to use creative industries investment as a way of attracting the 'creative class' to cities suffering from a lack of skilled, professional labour led to investment in facilities that were not aimed at the populations of particular cities, but at outsiders. It ran the danger of fuelling processes of gentrification which, as many studies show, have inflicted considerable harm on cities and communities (Zukin, 1995).

Creative industries policy goes global

Creative industries policy, in the UK New Labour mode, involved protecting and promoting cultural policy by linking the arts to the economic and social benefits of a wider sector that included growing commercial industries. The idea was a hotchpotch of already existing ideas. It mixed marketization – including a stronger reinforcement of intellectual property – with progressive aspirations. But the packaging of this fusion drew enormous attention in the international policy world. In parallel, the 'creative cities' idea was

---

12 There are considerable conceptual problems surrounding the debate about 'instrumentalisation' – see Throsby (2010) and Gibson (2008) – though we should not ignore the dangers of subsuming cultural value to economic goals, or to confused notions of the relations between social benefits and cultural activities.

13 The context, as with Garnham's critique, is the UK, but the lessons are applicable to a much wider range of contexts. Oakley (2006) explains that very few actual policies were produced by the UK national government under the 'creative industries' rubric. Most relevant developments were undertaken at the regional level by bodies such as the Regional Development Agencies – later abolished by the Conservative-Liberal Democrat Coalition government elected in 2010.

adopted by city governments as a means of achieving urban regeneration by attracting creative class professionals. Without a doubt, this was enabled by the murky sense of a link between these hazily-defined creative industries and workers, on the one hand, and the burgeoning software and new media sector, on the other.

In a classic piece of 'policy transfer', these ideas went viral across national and city governments throughout the world in the late 1990s and 2000s. British and American policy entrepreneurs spread the word (in the case of the former with help from the British Council). Dozens of reports and statistical surveys were produced (see Chapter 6). Building on its Lisbon strategy, aimed at regenerating European economies through a Schumpeterian version of information society ideas, the European Union developed myriad initiatives, such as its 2007–2013 Culture Programme and its 2010 Green Paper on *Unlocking the Potential of Cultural and Creative Industries*, which declared that '[f]actory floors are progressively being replaced by creative communities whose raw material is their ability to imagine, create and innovate' (p.1). Throughout the 2000s, museum quarters sprang up all over Europe, industrial sites were converted into arts districts, and mayors across the USA unveiled regeneration plans built on creativity (Ross, 2009: 38). The results of these international developments were mixed. Some initiatives were more based on sensitivities to local culture and social divisions than others, for example. All this seemed to make sense as property prices soared in the 2000s economic bubble. Questions, however, continued to be raised by community activist groups and others about the effects of gentrification and whether sustainable jobs were being created by all this expenditure (see some of the contributions gathered in Lovink and Rossiter, 2007).

One of the most significant manifestations of the international trend towards creative industries policies was in China. In 2001, the National People's Congress ratified the concept of cultural industries (*wenhua chanye*). At this stage, according to Justin O'Connor and Xin Gu (2012), the concept embodied the Chinese leadership's aspiration not only to develop its big companies in the area of film, television, publishing, crafts and tourism, but also to maintain control. Chinese president Hu Jintao told the Communist Party's national congress in 2007 that 'culture has become a … factor of growing significance in the competition in overall strength' (quoted by Ross, 2009: 53). A term closer to the meanings of the English phrase 'creative industries' (*wenhua chuangye*) was increasingly used in some Chinese cities from about 2005, to refer to design, fashion, animation, advertising, marketing and so on (see Hui, 2006, for an account), a sector based more around small-scale producers and entrepreneurs. Policies aimed at the growth of the creative and cultural industries were also introduced into the five-year plans of various cities, including Beijing, Shanghai, Chongqai, Nanjing, Shentzen, Quindao, and Tianjin in 2006.

Commentators have identified in China a moment of fascinating transition. While some see true economic development in China as impossible without greater political freedom, others view the growth of the cultural and creative industries as part of a broader set of changes that will create a demand for democratic freedoms and a thriving entrepreneurial sector.

O'Connor and Gu (2012) critique the first position for its ethnocentrism, but against the second position argue that the development of the cultural and creative industries in China may not bring with it values that will challenge the power of the state, or provide a set of ethical values that will act as a check against unbridled (state) capitalist development. Small entrepreneurial businesses have to operate within a framework that is set by the local state and by the larger state-owned enterprises. In line with this, Andrew Ross observes that the Chinese state sees considerable economic potential in the translation of Chinese heritage, stories and myths into nationalist narratives on a grand scale, especially if intellectual property is secured. This would also serve Chinese nationalism. But he doubts whether policymakers will tolerate 'the kinds of idiosyncratic and unpredictable initiatives characteristic of the Western creative paradigm of originality' (Ross, 2009: 58)

Faced by these difficulties, the new Chinese creative start-ups may not achieve the threshold for market entry – or they may fail to get the licences necessary to operate legally. If so, Ross points out, they may have to take their chances in the 'gray economy'. 'No doubt', he comments, 'this underground economy is where the more interesting, unpredictable energies will thrive, but it is also a crucible for the worst kind of exploitation' (2009: 59). All this suggests that the consequences of the adoption of creative industries policies are difficult to predict, but they involve difficult dilemmas and problems, including the challenge of creating sustainable creative jobs of reasonable quality.

Other policy concepts associated with creativity have also been exported around the world, some of which more closely tie the concept of creativity to the developments in intellectual property discussed in the first part of this chapter. One increasingly popular notion has been that of the **creative economy** (see UNCTAD, 2008). Policy consultant and journalist John Howkins (2001: vii) claimed in his book of that title that 'the creative economy will be the dominant economic form in the twenty-first century'. He sustained this claim by defining the creative economy and the creative industries as those involved in intellectual property. This allowed him to include not only those industries based on copyright, which is the form of intellectual property that is the basis of the cultural industries as they are defined in this book, but also those industries that produce or deal in patents. This justified the inclusion of massive sectors, such as pharmaceuticals, electronics, engineering and chemicals. Even the impossibly nebulous categories of trademark and design industries were incorporated. Howkins was right to stress the importance of intellectual property in modern economies, across both symbolic and scientific domains, but he extrapolated from this importance to make dubious claims about a transition to a new economy based on creativity. This was typical of the way information society discourse was repackaged around creativity and innovation in the 2000s.

* * *

These various developments concerning creativity and the cultural or creative industries, often built on conflicting and imprecise notions of creativity, raise significant questions about how we see culture in relation to economy and society and how we understand relations between creativity and commerce. So, too, do the changes in copyright law surveyed in the first part of the chapter. Together with developments in telecommunications, information technology and broadcasting, these developments provide an important basis (but not, as Chapter 3 stressed, the *only* basis) for the various changes discussed in the next six chapters. In different ways, **they have paved the way for a considerable expansion of commercial activities based around symbol making, but on terms that potentially transform the significance of symbol making in modern societies.** The next six chapters will now assess and evaluate some of the changes that have followed on from these policy developments, and which have been partially (though not entirely) caused by them. It is only after a careful consideration of these consequences that we can evaluate the policy changes that helped bring them about.

RECOMMENDED AND FURTHER READING

There is a massive, and often difficult, body of legal studies literature on copyright, but the best way in for many readers interested in the cultural industries is probably still the polemical literature on intellectual property produced by US academics. A number of these books, including Lawrence Lessig's *The Future of Ideas*, Kembrew McLeod's *Owning Culture* and Siva Vaidhyanathan's *Copyrights and Copywrongs*, were first published in 2001, reflecting how rights had become a political battleground at that time. Those earlier books are obviously now somewhat outdated, but all these authors have produced further works since then, which essentially reiterate and update their earlier contributions. Even better than these compelling books however is James Boyle's groundbreaking treatment of intellectual property in relation to the idea of the information society, *Shamans, Software and Spleens* (1996), which is still well worth reading. At about the same time, John Frow (1997) also made an impressive though less-noticed contribution to our understandings of intellectual property and copyright.

In my view, the best combination of historical analysis and information is Simon Frith and Lee Marshall's edited collection *Music and Copyright* (2004). Marshall's book *Bootlegging* (2006) explores the romantic legacies involved in copyright in the context of a study of 'illegal' recordings. Frith and a fellow popular music studies scholar, Dave Laing, have been arguing for the vital importance of copyright since the 1980s.

The neglect of copyright in the political economy of culture literature remains a disgrace. An honourable exception was Ronald Bettig's *Copyrighting Culture* (1996), while a new contribution is Trajce Cvetkovski's *Copyright and Popular Media* (2012). I have also recommended Thomas Streeter's *The Net Effect* (2011) elsewhere in this book. His Chapter 6 brilliantly places copyright developments in the context of debates over the meaning of information and culture in the 1990s, including the open source software movement.

On cultural policy, the terms of the academic debate on the left in the late 1990s and early 2000s were set by Jim McGuigan (*Culture and the Public Sphere*, 1996) and Tony Bennett (*Culture: A reformer's science*, 1998) – the former from a Habermasian and political economy perspective, the latter from a Foucauldian cultural studies one. The work of Terry Flew provides the most thorough and intelligent rationale for a Foucauldian cultural studies approach to cultural policy in relation to the 'creative industries'. His book on *The Creative Industries* (2011) was published as I was revising this book and is likely to be an important contribution. Stuart Cunningham has also made a number of significant interventions (see, for example, Cunningham and Higgs, 2008). I haven't had space to explore the spread of 'creative industries' policy around the world in sufficient detail here. On this, I strongly recommend the chapter on creative industries in Andrew Ross's *Nice Work If You Can Get It* (2009). Justin O'Connor has also provided a series of articles and book chapters on cultural and creative industries policy and local manifestations of it, from Manchester to St Petersburg to Shanghai. His literature review on cultural and creative industries (2nd edition, 2010) is well worth reading too. David Throsby's *The Economics of Cultural Policy* (2010) examines cultural industries as part of an intelligent and comprehensive analysis of cultural policy as a whole. Reading *The International Journal of Cultural Policy* is a good way to follow developments from around the world.

I have not had space enough to do justice to the key contributions that geographers and others have made to understanding the spatial dynamics of cultural production that are highly relevant to the issues discussed in this chapter as well as throughout the book. Examples include the work of Susan Christopherson (2011), Andy Pratt (2004), and Allen Scott (see, or example, *The Cultural Economy of Cities*, 2000). Excellent studies of relevant urban dynamics have also been provided by Sharon Zukin (*The Culture of Cities*, 1995), Richard Lloyd (*Neo-Bohemia*, 2006) and, again, Justin O'Connor.

ONLINE READING

All the online material referenced below can be accessed free of charge at: **http://www.sagepub.co.uk/hesmondhalgh**

Simply click on the 'Sample Materials' tab to find the links to each article.

Here are two articles which, in different ways, illuminate the way in which 'creative industries' and 'creativity' were taken up in policy and activist debates in the early twenty first century.

- Ross, Andrew (2008) 'The new geography of work: power to the precarious?', *Theory, Culture & Society*, 25(7–8): 31–49.
- Schlesinger, Philip (2009) 'Creativity and the experts: New Labour, think tanks, and the policy process', *The International Journal of Press/Politics*, 14(1): 3–20.

PART THREE

CHANGE AND CONTINUITY IN THE CULTURAL INDUSTRIES, 1980 TO 2012

Ownership, Structure and Size

1990s merger mania – and early twenty-first
   century reverses   187
A new generation of mega-corporations: the big get
   very big indeed   192
Conglomeration: from synergy to convergence   195
Vertical integration   200
Is ownership becoming more concentrated? And does it matter?   204
The continuing presence of small companies   209
Interdependence, inter-firm networks and alliances   212
Are the cultural industries getting bigger?   216
   Cultural industries in modern economies   216
   Cultural industries in global business   219
Continuing commodification   221

The changes in government policy discussed in Part Two created a new business environment for the cultural industries from the late 1980s onwards. Marketisation meant that the cultural industries became an increasingly important sector for business investment. Underlying this was a more general economic context. As Chapter 3 showed, in response to the Long Downturn of the 1970s and 1980s, private corporations began to shift investment towards service industries, including the cultural industries.

Part Three now considers the changes that followed from these shifts. The present chapter looks at changes in the ownership, structure and size of the cultural industries in this new environment. It is guided by the following questions, introduced in Chapter 2 (see Table 2.1). The first two primarily concern the *extent* of change; the second two focus on how to *evaluate* developments.

- To what extent have changes in conglomeration and integration led to recognisably new and distinct forms of ownership and structure?
- To what extent have the cultural industries become increasingly important in national economies and global business?

- What are the effects of the growth in size and power of cultural industry corporations on cultural production and wider society?
- What are the implications of a further commodification of culture?

I begin by discussing the considerable growth in size and scope of large cultural industry corporations. An oligopoly of vast multinational corporations now dominates cultural production and circulation in North America and Europe, and to a lesser extent in Asia. Sometimes less noticed in business analysis, a second tier of big corporations dominates the cultural landscape of many individual nations.

The next four sections examine trends in how these large corporations pursue market domination via conglomeration and vertical integration. There is no doubt about the increasing presence of very large companies in cultural markets, but these behemoths are surprisingly varied in how they approach the business of making money out of culture. Some of these complexities are explored in these sections, including the new webs of ownership and alliance emerging from the entry of IT and telecoms corporations into cultural-industry territory.

The consequences of the presence of these vertically-integrated conglomerates in cultural markets are the subject of some controversy. Many of the debates centre on the issue of whether the ownership of media is becoming concentrated in fewer hands. In the fifth main section of this chapter I assess some of the evidence concerning recent trends in ownership. Although the measurement of ownership concentration is a fraught issue, it is clear that there are reasons to be concerned about the role of large media and cultural-industry corporations in modern societies. The problem of concentration can never be separated from broader questions concerning power and the nature of cultural markets.

The undeniable presence of bigger and more integrated companies in the cultural landscape does not mean that small companies are less important, and the following sections consider the continuing presence of such companies and new forms of relationship between them and large corporations (not only in the cultural industries, but also in 'neighbouring' industries such as information technology and consumer electronics). Naturally, the question of how to evaluate this change is tied in with establishing the facts about it. The picture regarding changing patterns of ownership and structure is, I think, more nuanced and complex than some critics of developments in the sector seem to believe. Nevertheless, corporate growth is an issue of great importance and should concern everyone interested in the role of cultural production in contemporary society, culture and democracy.

I then go on to examine the question of whether or not the cultural industries are becoming more central to global business and national economies. I discuss the flood of reports discussing the size of the creative and cultural industries that have appeared in recent years. It does appear that, in general, there have been increases in cultural industry activity slightly above rates of increase in Gross Domestic Product, even as some cultural industries struggled in the 2000s. Nevertheless, the cultural industries remain relatively marginal in global business (and this suggests that claims that the economy is becoming 'culturalised' need to be treated with scepticism). The final section takes a step back to locate the above trends in the broader historical context. It therefore considers the growth of the cultural industries as a manifestation of the continuing commodification of culture, and examines the implications of understanding growth in this way.

1990s MERGER MANIA – AND EARLY TWENTY-FIRST CENTURY REVERSES

One of the most crucial transitions from the market professional era of cultural production to the complex professional era involved the increasing presence of large corporations in cultural markets (see Chapter 2). This long-term trend intensified in the 1980s and 1990s, following marketisation and internationalisation. There was massive growth in the size and scope of cultural industry corporations. A small number of transnational corporations came to have enormous power, not quite globally, but across much of the developed world.

The increasing size and conglomeration of cultural industry companies were part of a trend towards more and larger mergers and acquisitions in all industries, which quickened during the 1980s in response to the Long Downturn, but then exploded in the late 1990s and again in the mid-2000s. Figure 6.1 shows this by tracking the value of worldwide mergers and acquisitions for all industries, as well as for the media, IT and telecoms sectors.

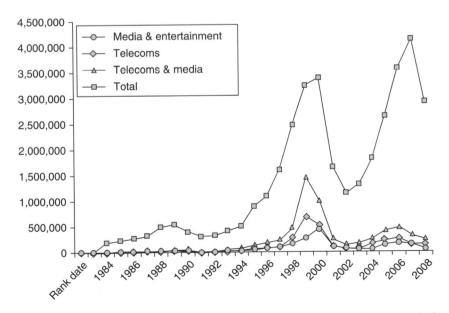

Figure 6.1 Worldwide mergers and acquisitions in the media and telecoms industries, 1984–2008 (millions, US$)

Source: Thomson Reuters (2009).

The 1980s represented a key period. There were 4900 mergers in the USA between 1968 and 1973, but there were over 3300 corporate acquisitions in 1986 alone (Greco, 1995: 229–30). This was the period of marketisation in broadcasting policy in the USA and two of the three great broadcasting networks (CBS and NBC) changed hands via huge deals in 1985–1986. Following the Wall Street Crash of October 1987, the House of Representatives eliminated certain tax breaks that encouraged acquisitions. As a result mergers of all kinds substantially decreased in the USA in the following years (Greco, 1995: 230). But this did not prevent a series of spectacular international mergers affecting the cultural industries at the turn of the 1980s/1990s:

- Consumer electronics company Sony purchased CBS Records in 1988 (US$2 billion) and Columbia Pictures Entertainment (US$3.4 billion) in 1989.
- Time-Life and Warner Communications merged in 1989, in the form of a 'friendly' US$14.9 billion buyout by Time-Life.
- In 1990, following the Sony/CBS deal, another consumer electronics giant, Matsushita (which later changed its name to Panasonic), purchased MCA, a music talent agency that had become a media conglomerate, for US$6.8 billion.

The 1990s then saw an eruption of mergers in industry as a whole, as relatively low-interest credit poured into the global economy. For example, 1997 saw the highest ever figures for mergers and acquisitions in the USA up to that point – US$912 billion worth of deals (*Business Week*, 30 March 1998: 47). This partly reflected a growing sense on the part of executives, consultants, academics and gurus that the best way to deliver profits to shareholders was by combining business interests that might mutually reinforce each other.

Sectors that were most relevant to the cultural industries were particularly prone to merger activity, as capital recognised the immense profit potential in telecommunications, information technology and media. Greco (1996: 5) reported that there were 557 media business acquisitions between 1990 and 1995 – an amount that was only just short of the entire total of such deals between 1960 and 1989. Particularly significant were two waves of mega-acquisition in 1994–1995 and in 1999–2000. According to one source (Sánchez-Tabernero and Carvajal, 2002: 7), in 2000, 40 per cent of the mergers and takeovers of companies on a global scale (worth US$3.5 trillion) took place in these sectors.

There was another reason for the growth of cultural industry corporations in the late 1990s, besides the general trend towards more and larger mergers and acquisitions and the growing interest of business in communications and related sectors. This was the beginning of a boom in the US economy, and to a lesser extent in European economies too, from 1995 onwards. This is sometimes described as the 'dot.com' bubble, but it went much further than the nascent IT companies that eventually went belly up at the end of the millennium. Finally, the Long Downturn seemed to be in reverse. There was rapid growth in gross domestic product, labour productivity and investment. Even real wages went up – though inequality continued to increase. This boom led to what Robert Brenner (2000: 5) called 'the greatest financial bubble in American history', as equity prices lost touch with reality and household, corporate and financial debt all reached record levels, leading to an explosion in consumption. Importantly, all this helped to fuel increases in the advertising spending that was central to profitability in many cultural industry businesses. This encouraged mergers and acquisitions in the cultural industries, but so did the general sense that the world – or at least the most developed parts of it – was becoming a global information society.

Between 1992 and 2000, the biggest media corporations were involved in hundreds of mergers and acquisitions. Bertelsmann, for example, took part in 249 as an acquirer and 137 as a seller or target (Chan-Olmsted and Chang, 2003: 223). Following the interruption of the crash that followed the dot. com boom, merger activity resumed in the 2000s. But then came the massive financial crash of 2008 and the subsequent economic crisis. This quickly eroded the advertising base that the cultural industries depended upon, and it combined with increasing competition from the IT and telecommunications industries. The cultural industries were increasingly seen by business analysts and investors (including some 'institutional' investors, such as pension funds, who can be particularly influential) as vulnerable in a period of technological and, in many respects, cultural transition.

Table 6.1 provides details of some of the most important mergers and acquisitions in the 1990s and 2000s relevant to the cultural industries. As the table shows, very significant deals directly involving cultural-industry businesses continue to take place even in the wake of the economic crisis. Examples include Vivendi's acquisition of the games publisher Activision in 2008 and Comcast's purchase of NBC Universal in 2010. Two other trends are striking however. The first is the increasing activity of the IT giants in making media/cultural-industry purchases: Google and Microsoft, for example, both made significant acquisitions of companies that have enabled them to gain information about users for advertisers – Double-Click and aQuantive respectively. This reflects competition over advertising between established players in the cultural industries and new entrants from the IT world. A second key trend has been the massive deals taking place in wireless communications and broadband. The AT&T takeover of BellSouth in 2006 dwarfs the IT and cultural-industry related deals, and this is a reminder of the size, scope and centrality of telecoms as an industry (an issue that has been largely neglected in media and communication studies).

These two trends are milestones in the long-predicted convergence between telecoms, IT and cultural industries (a convergence though that will always be partial). The IT giants have to some extent replaced consumer electronics companies as deal-makers. Whereas Sony and Matsushita's takeover of American media giants grabbed business headlines in the 1980s, it is the

Table 6.1   Some major cultural industry mergers and acquisitions

Date	Acquiring firm	Acquired firm (new name in brackets)	Price (US$ billions)	Strategic motivation
1994	Viacom	Paramount Communications	8.0	Conglomeration across publishing, film, broadcasting, cable, theme parks
1994	Viacom	Blockbuster	8.5	Distribution control
1995	Disney	Capital Cities/ABC	19	Vertical integration and control of content creation
1995	Time Warner	Turner Broadcasting	7.4	Vertical integration and conglomeration/synergy
1995	Seagram	MCA (Universal)	5.7	General conglomerate moves into diversified media
1995	Westinghouse	CBS	5.4	General conglomerate moves into broadcasting
1998	Seagram	PolyGram	10.6	Recording market share plus European film interests
1998	AT&T*	TCI (including Liberty Media)*	48**	Telecoms and media convergence
1999	Viacom	CBS	22	Media conglomerate consolidates broadcasting power
2000	Vivendi	Seagram/ Universal	35	Very diversified European leisure conglomerate diversifies further
2000	AOL*	Time Warner* (AOL Time Warner)	128**	Internet service provider merges with media conglomerate
2002	Comcast	AT&T Broadband	47.5	Cable company expands via acquisition
2003	General Electric/NBC	Vivendi Universal (NBC Universal)	5.5	'Merger' between two media giants, but with NBC by far the dominant partner
2003	Sony*	BMG (Sony-BMG)	??	Music arms of two majors merge; Sony eventually bought out Bertelsmann's stake
2004–5	Sony	MGM	4.9	Massive acquisition of back catalogue; cable company
2006	Disney	Pixar	7.4	Studio buys production company with strong affiliations to it
2006	AT & T Inc.	BellSouth Corp	67	This deal followed SBC's acquisition of AT&T in 2005 (the latter's name was adopted). The later deal allowed for increased bundling of wireless and fixed-line telephony with television and broadband services.

Table 6.1   (Continued)

Date	Acquiring firm	Acquired firm	Price USD billions	Strategic motivation
2006	Google	YouTube	1.6	A relatively small acquisition, but of great symbolic import, signalling Google's entry into the cultural industries
2006	Comcast	Adelphia Cable	17.6	Significant consolidation of the US cable broadcasting industry, also involving subscriber swap with Time Warner Cable
2007	News Corporation Inc.	Dow Jones & Company Inc.	5.6	Murdoch's controversial purchase of the *Wall Street Journal*
2007	Google	Double-Click	3.1	Google purchased internet advertising services company
2007	Microsoft Corporation	aQuantive	5.7	Microsoft purchased a Seattle advertising company as it sought to compete with Google's acquisition of DoubleClick
2008	Vivendi*	Activision	18.8**	A merger of Vivendi's games division with top US games publisher
2010	Comcast	NBC Universal	13.75	Cable broadcasting giant purchases media conglomerate
2010	Walt Disney	Marvel	4.24	Disney buys comics division, acquiring various brands, characters etc

Key

* a merger

** evaluation of new merged company rather than price

Note: Prices and values are based on reports at the time that the merger or acquisition was announced, except for AOL Time Warner, which was evaluated at US$350 billion in January 2000 when the merger was first reported but US$128 billion when the merger was approved by the US regulatory body the Federal Communications Commission. The fall in value reflected the fall in share values over the year, as internet and new media hype subsided.

IT giants that now dominate coverage. Meanwhile, the telecommunications companies continue to be the biggest operators of all, providing the infrastructure upon which the cultural and IT industries depend. These trends are discussed in greater detail in the sections below on conglomeration and vertical integration.

Yet a third trend is just as vital, but is not apparent in these reports of vast deals. This is that, alongside the continuing merger deals, which often reflect the strategies of conglomeration and vertical integration that I shall discuss later, there is also evidence of a great deal of de-merger and de-conglomeration activity (Fitzgerald, 2012; Jin, 2011). This reflects the problems that were facing some sectors of the cultural industries in the early twenty first century, even as cultural markets grew. As Dwayne Winseck (2011a) points out, these problems should not simply be attributed to the arrival of the internet, or to the migration of advertising expenditure from 'old' to 'new' media – a shift that in any case, as we shall see in Chapter 10, has been slower and more complex than much of the business journalism suggests. Instead, according to Winseck, these problems reflect a short-term, cyclical decline in advertising caused by the economic downturn, and by the two waves of mergers discussed above. He sees the crisis of the 2000s as the accumulated results of two waves of consolidation and the *financialisation* of the media, for merger mania was itself partly a product of 'the extraordinary growth in the size of the financial sector and financial assets relative to the industrial and other sectors of the economy' over the past 25 years, especially since the mid-1990s (Winseck, 2011b: 143).

Cultural-industry troubles were evident early in the century in the form of some prominent closures and failures, such as the bankruptcy of the German media giant Kirch in 2002. They were also made clear by the rapid changes in strategy that were sometimes a legacy of the heavy debt burdens bequeathed by the very deals that created some of the giants in the first place – Time Warner's misfortunes in the 2000s were a prime example of this. The economic crisis that followed the crash of 2008 has not greatly inhibited conglomeration and integration through mergers and acquisitions, as companies make the most of low interest rates for borrowing and the low stock prices of potential purchases. But there have been further significant failures (such as Canadian cable conglomerate Canwest in 2009, or the Tribune Company (of Chicago) in 2008) and a significant trend towards de-conglomeration and divestment. This does not mean that the cultural industries can be thought of as diminishing in importance or power. Rather, it reaffirms that their status in the complex professional period of cultural production is both powerful and vulnerable to risk. There is evidence, as we shall see below, that the size of the economic pie available to cultural industries has grown, and continues to grow. As we shall see in the next section, in spite of the increasing problems some of them have faced, particularly in the late 2000s, the creation of a group of massive cultural-industry corporations over the last 30 years has significant implications for culture and society.

A NEW GENERATION OF MEGA-CORPORATIONS: THE BIG GET VERY BIG INDEED

Partly as a result of mergers and acquisitions of the kind discussed in the last section, a new generation of global multimedia mega-corporations had come to dominate the revenues gained from global cultural industry markets by the late 1990s. These were very much bigger companies than those that had previously dominated particular cultural industries, such as film or television or newspapers. Their reach across different industries gave them considerable potential influence on government policy and on the very nature of cultural production itself. The biggest companies were also increasingly international and this too enhanced their lobbying clout.

The names and structures of the mega-corporations change regularly, as further mergers, acquisitions and sell-offs take place. Nevertheless, because of their potential importance for culture, communication and business, it is worth knowing their names and something about their operations. Table 6.2 lists the seven biggest cultural industry businesses, as they stood in late 2011, based on figures for fiscal years ending in 2011. Manuel Castells (2008: 74) has dubbed these companies 'the Magnificent Seven'.[1] These seven corporations have a significant presence in both North America and Europe, the world's two largest continental cultural industry markets. Only Rupert Murdoch's News Corporation has a significant market share across cultural industries in more than two continents (North America, Europe and Asia/Australasia). So the 'global' scope of the biggest corporations is often exaggerated. Nevertheless, they are involved in cultural products that reach hundreds of millions of people across dozens of countries.

But below these seven vast corporations, each with annual revenues of over US$20 billion from their cultural industry activities, sits a 'second tier' (Herman and McChesney, 1997: 53) of regional or national giants, consisting of dozens of companies with revenues in excess of US$1 billion per year from cultural industry operations, which have an enormous impact within their own national bases, and sometimes across a particular region. Apart from a small number of Latin American and Australian concerns, most are based in North America, Europe, China or Japan, but Asian companies are increasingly becoming present – a fact discussed further in Chapter 8. Even below these two tiers of global giants, there are many other companies exerting a sizeable influence on particular markets. A report by Zenith consultants (cited by Sánchez-Tabernero et al., 1993: 100) usefully classified the biggest cultural industry companies using the following categories:

- Companies dominant in one cultural industry in one country.
- Companies influencing one cultural industry across several countries.
- Companies having interests across more than one cultural industry in one country.
- Companies with interests in more than one cultural industry internationally.

---

1 Named, of course, after the classic western released in 1960. I wish I'd thought of that name in the previous edition of this book, instead of the leaden term 'Big Seven' that I used there. Castells' book shows that he is fully aware that the magnificence of this oligopoly is one of size and scope rather than its contribution to culture or human life. The identity of the actual seven corporations has changed a little since Castells' book was published, but seven companies still stand out as particularly dominant.

Nearly all the biggest 50 or so cultural industry corporations are in one or more of the first three categories. With the growth of cultural-industry markets, combined with conglomeration and internationalisation, more and more companies are entering, or moving into, the final category.

From time to time, one of the second-tier corporations joins the elite of global cultural industry mega-corporations. One example of this is what the company then known as Viacom achieved in the 1990s, but by the end of the first decade of the twenty first century it had sold off some of its assets and slipped back into the second rank. Likewise Comcast, a US-based company primarily involved in cable television, made a number of attempts to expand in the 2000s, but only became part of the Magnificent Seven with its acquisition of NBC Universal (itself a previous member of the mega-corporate oligopoly) in 2010.

Collectively, the first and second tiers of companies have an enormous impact on the cultural industry landscape in terms of policy lobbying and the standards they set for what constitutes standard practice in the cultural industries. Concentrating only on the internationally famous Magnificent Seven can distract attention from the huge importance, in particular nations and regions, of this wider range of large corporations. Take, as one example, Grupo Clarín, an Argentinian corporation. Its annual revenues of US$1.8 billion in 2010 look relatively small compared with those of the Magnificent Seven and their IT allies and rivals. It did not even make *Screen Digest*'s list of the 50 biggest audio-visual corporations in August 2011. But it runs Argentina's leading newspaper and newsprint supplier. It also has significant holdings in broadcasting, internet access and cable (it owns not just one, but two of the country's cable operators) and wields an extraordinary amount of power in Argentina, where it has been involved in a series of disputes with the centre-left governments of Presidents Nestor and Cristina Kirchner. And because of the country's economic and cultural position in the Southern Cone of the Americas, it has considerable power and influence in Uruguay and Paraguay as well. Alternatively, consider the USA's Clear Channel Communications, which earned over US$2.8 billion in 2010. Again, this looks small compared with the first tier of multinationals, but the company has a massive portfolio of radio companies, including a presence in just about every major urban space in the USA, since the massive wave of takeovers that followed the 1996 Telecommunications Act. This in turn links up with significant investments in advertising and in live music. It is both the first *and* second tiers of companies that we should focus on to get a real sense of the expanded role of large cultural industry corporations within nation states and regions, not just the Magnificent Seven and the IT giants.

What are the implications of these massive mergers and the formation of large cultural companies with international reach? That is a question that is best addressed as part of a consideration of the more general problem of concentrated ownership of the media. First, however, we need to consider the dynamics of conglomeration and vertical integration.

Table 6.2   The 'Magnificent Seven' cultural industry corporations

This list ranks the biggest companies by revenue gained from cultural-industry activities, as defined in this book. Revenue is in US$ billions for fiscal years ending in 2011. The figure for Sony is for its games, music and films divisions; most of its revenues come from its much larger consumer electronics sales. See Table 6.6 for further details of the companies involved.

Company	Revenue
Vivendi	38.5
Walt Disney	38.1
Comcast	37.9
News Corporation	32.8
Time Warner	26.9
Sony	23.1
Bertelsmann	22.3

Source: company reports.

CONGLOMERATION: FROM SYNERGY TO CONVERGENCE

A key feature of the complex professional era of cultural production, especially from the 1960s onwards, has been conglomeration (see Chapter 2). This has continued into the 2000s, and it takes very tangled forms in the cultural industries as well as in other sectors. Chan-Olmsted and Chang have compared the remarkable number of sub-divisions in the Magnificent Seven oligopoly in the early twenty first century (see Table 6.3). They have also demonstrated that companies can vary considerably in the degree to which they diversify across different sectors and in the number of entities under their control (see also Fitzgerald, 2012).

Corporate strategy with regard to conglomeration in the cultural industries has altered in significant ways. In the early years of the complex professional period, most cultural businesses were privately owned entities. Newspapers and film studios, for example, often principally belonged to and were operated by moguls, and mainly confined themselves to that one industry. In the 1960s and 1970s, as we saw in Chapter 2, non-cultural industry conglomerates began to buy into the cultural industries as a form of diversification: for example, the purchase of book publishers and record companies by manufacturing giants (such as electrical engineering company Thorn's purchase of EMI in 1979) or the buying of film studios by oil, insurance and even funeral services companies in the late 1960s (see Gomery, 2005).

The late 1980s and early 1990s saw a shift. A fashionable business concept of the time was *synergy*. This was originally a medical term, referring to how two elements (such as two drugs or two muscles) might work together to produce a result greater than the sum of the two parts. The idea behind the metaphor

Table 6.3   Conglomeration in the Magnificent Seven, c 2003

Diversification	Vivendi			AOL Time			News
Measures	Universal	Bertelsmann*	Sony	Warner	Disney	Viacom	Corporation
Extent of diversification							
Number of business units** (ranking)	316(2)	531(1)	150(4)	190(3)	113(5)	30(7)	71(6)
Number of SIC sectors involved (ranking)	80(1)	29(4)	32(3)	28(5)	15(7)	17(6)	
Directions of diversification							
BSD (ranking)	30(1)	na	13(4)	18(2)	16(3)	8(6)	9(5)
MNSD (ranking)	2.67(1)	na	2.46(2)	1.83(5)	1.75(6)	1.88(4)	1.89(3)
Overall ranking***	1	2	4	3	5	7	6

Note: SIC = Standard Industrial Classification; BSD = Broad Spectrum Diversity; MNSD = Mean Narrow Spectrum Diversity. * Because of the lack of specific SIC codes for the German based Bertelsmann, a proxy system was used to measure its product diversity that is consistent with the SIC measure used for other conglomerates. Drawing on Bertelsmann's annual reports, its list of divisions (e.g., television group) was treated as the 2-digit SIC group and its subdivided sets of businesses under each division (e.g., pay-TV) as unique SIC codes. Over 500 business units were reviewed to derive the proxy measures. Because of the proxy system, it was not possible to calculate the BSD and MNSD for Bertelsmann. However, because of the extensiveness of Bertelsmann's business units and its sectors were comparable to those of other conglomerates, except for Vivendi, it is still considered number two in the overall ranking assessment.

** A business unit is a subsidiary business entity of a parent company (e.g., MTV as a business unit of Viacom).

*** The overall rankings are based on the averages of BSD, MNSD and business unit/sector rankings.

Source: Chan-Olmsted and Chang (2003: 221)

was that the different parts of a corporation should relate to each other in such a manner as to provide cross-promotion and cross-selling opportunities, so that sales would exceed what was possible when divisions acted separately. As the popularity of such ideas spread from business schools and management gurus and into corporations, conglomerates began to specialise again, rather than spreading themselves across a range of often unrelated activities (though some more general companies continued to do this, especially those involving financial investment). This time, however, the specialisation tended to be not just in one activity, such as film or radio – as in the pre-diversification era of the early twentieth century – but in a set of related ones.[2]

The form of conglomeration that received the most publicity in the late 1980s was the purchase of media producers by consumer electronics companies (so-called hardware/software synergy).[3] Sony's purchases of CBS Records and Columbia Pictures Entertainment in 1988 and 1989 respectively were widely assumed to represent the future shape of cultural industry corporate strategy. The idea was that Sony would be able to use prestigious US rock music and cinema to help persuade consumers to buy new consumer technologies, such as the CD, and then utilise their dominance in hardware to sell more cultural products.

Other significant purchases in the 1980s were based on very different strategies. For example, general conglomerate General Electric's purchase of NBC in 1985 was about spreading investment across a range of sectors. This strategy was deemed somewhat outmoded in an age where the fashion in business was for synergy, so this purchase gained relatively little attention compared with acquisitions by Japanese corporations of US cultural industry businesses in the USA. Acquisitions such as that of MCA Records by Matsushita in 1990 not only fed recession-fuelled fears on the part of US businesses in the USA about a loss of global economic domination, but also exacerbated cultural anxieties about the loss of supposedly distinctive US cultural production.

By the mid-1990s, however, such hardware/software synergies were widely viewed as failures. Certain commentators have explained this apparent lack of success by referring to the different production cultures needed to produce consumer electronics on the one hand and music/films/TV programmes on the other. A proportion of these accounts were convincing (Negus, 1997), but some press versions of this view bordered on racism: the

---

2 Very diverse general conglomerates continue to be a feature of the South East Asian business landscape. Some North American general conglomerates, such as General Electric, thrived in the late 1990s and early 2000s.

3 Such hardware/software synergies were not unprecedented by any means. The Dutch consumer electronics group Philips had its own record division (PolyGram) for decades until it sold it to Seagram in 1995. The networks in the USA were also founded on such synergies as NBC, for example, was part of the communications conglomerate RCA, which made radio equipment.

implication was that the Japanese were incapable of producing entertainment and could only produce efficient machines. When hardware/software mergers were deemed to to have failed, the electronics companies began to sell off their media properties and form alliances and joint ventures with media producers on particular projects.

The late 1990s and 2000s saw somewhat different developments in conglomeration. In the merger mania of this period (see Table 6.1), telecommunications companies made some efforts to enter into cultural industries, mainly via the purchase of cable subscription companies which were an important part of the vast US broadcasting market. AT&T's 1998 takeover of cable group TCI, including the Liberty Media Group, was a prime example of this. More significant still, as indicated above, was the entry of a new generation of IT giants. The merger of AOL with Time Warner in 1999 was greeted as the harbinger of this type of 'convergent' conglomeration, but proved to be something of a disaster, saddling the new company with enormous levels of debt. More notable in the longer term have been purchases by Google and Microsoft of games divisions, and most significant of all, companies providing advertising and market information such as Double-Click and aQuantive. But what these purchased companies are really involved in is the gathering of data about users, which can then be sold on; they are not really cultural-industry businesses, in the sense of being involved in the production and/or circulation of content (see the discussion of definitions in the Introduction to this book). Microsoft's main cultural-industry interest is in the production of games for its X-Box. In this sense, its ownership of a whole series of 'first-party' games developers recalls how electronics manufacturers owned record companies.[4] The idea was to provide content to play on their hardware.

By far the most significant intervention by IT companies into the cultural industries so far has been the purchase of YouTube by Google in 2006. As Ken Auletta points out, like the television networks, 'YouTube publishes content produced by others and sells advertising. The more consumers linger on YouTube, the more pages they view, and the more page views, the more YouTube's ads rise' (Auletta, 2010: 154). In their provision of search, Google do not have any particular interest in the destinations of users, but with YouTube they do. This was to result in a massive battle between Google and cultural industries, especially broadcasters, over copyright. This was not as novel as many claimed in the heat of new millenium IT hype. Conflicts between video cassette recorder (VCR) manufacturers and film studios raged for a decade from the mid-1970s onwards. And what Google recognised in its purchase of YouTube was a longstanding reality: that power in culture and communication inheres in the control of distribution or circulation. The

---

4   For example, Dutch consumer electronic giant Philips' ownership of PolyGram Records
    in the 1970s (and, before that Phonogram Records), or Microsoft's licensing agreements
    with 'third party' games developers.

most crucial fact about Google's takeover of YouTube was that corporations were now operating across the IT and cultural sectors, and this was especially significant given Google's massive eminence in the vital search market.

These changing trends in conglomeration remind us that cultural-industry corporations are both powerful and yet also operate in a highly uncertain environment. As Christopher Anderson (2007: 280) has elegantly pointed out, both the business press and critical media analysts are sometimes guilty of overestimating the seamlessness of the process of concentration and conglomeration:

> In the publicity that surrounds high-profile mergers and acquisitions – not to mention the fears of media critics – conglomerates perform with orchestral grace, each distinct business blended in concert under the baton of a charismatic chief executive. The reality is quite different: companies brought together by investment capital are frequently torn asunder; mergers that make sense on paper dissolve once people from different professional backgrounds lock horns over strategic decisions.

In line with this realistic appraisal, a number of analysts (for example, Jin, 2011). have pointed out that many notable companies have recently turned to 'de-convergence' as a strategy, focusing on a few core business areas and selling off other areas of their operations This is because media conglomeration, especially forms associated with 'convergence', has met with a number of problems.

Using data on the communication and media sectors, Jin reports that mergers and acquisitions involving a minimum of 5 per cent of stock declined significantly from its all-time high of 858 deals in the year 2000 to 444 in 2005, and only recovered to 569 by 2009. Shares in one prominent merged corporation, Viacom-CBS, halved in value in the two years from 2003 to 2005. Sumner Redstone, principal owner of Viacom and CBS via his National Amusements corporation, and a master deal-maker, proclaimed in 2005 that synergy was in its death throes. But Viacom/CBS and other struggling giants such as Time Warner were not alone in de-converging. Drawing on a comprehensive trawl of industry reports, Jin claims that, alongside continuing merger activity, there was a huge number of spin-offs and split-offs in the media industries. The peak actually preceded the 2008 Financial Crisis, with 442 such spin-off and split-off deals in 2005, but there were strikingly high numbers in the late 2000s too. Fitzgerald (2012) attributes some of the trend towards spinning off in the biggest conglomerates to financialisation. Increasing pressures from institutional investors to produce high returns for shareholders resulted in a shift away from big, transformative deals aimed at dominating a sector and towards producing higher profits in the shorter term. Time Warner sold Warner Music Group in 2003, its book publishing operations in 2006, and AOL in 2008, and is now no longer the world's biggest cultural-industry corporation by revenue, a position it had occupied for some years.

Nevertheless, conglomeration remains a feature of the cultural-industry landscape. And crucially, it continues to be linked to a potential increase in the scope and power of individual cultural industry corporations, in that the same corporation can have stakes in many different forms of communication. Fewer companies will come to dominate the cultural industries as a whole, other things being equal.[5] So there are undoubtedly are reasons to be concerned about the rise of cultural-industry conglomerates. Some of these are linked to questions concerning the concentration of media power in general and we will return to this issue below. But at least two issues specific to conglomeration, to the spreading of corporate activity across different areas of cultural production, can be mentioned here. One is that the lobbying power of the corporations grows as they increasingly operate in a number of different sectors. A second is that conglomeration allows the corporations to cross-promote their products. One notorious case was the way in which News International's newspapers in the UK promoted the services operated by a satellite broadcaster in which it owned a significant stake, BSkyB, in the late 1990s. This case has been analysed in impressive detail by Jonathan Hardy (2010) who shows that much of this cross-promotion took place in sections of newspapers that would normally fall outside the attention of critical analysis – supplements, reviews and listings of 'critics' choices'. Such cross-selling reinforces the power of the oligopolies dominating the cultural industries and promotes commercial imperatives at the expense of artistic values (in fiction and entertainment) and objectivity, independence and professionalism (in journalism).[6]

VERTICAL INTEGRATION

Another key element of how businesses in the cultural industries seek to make a profit and control risk is vertical integration. The imperative towards vertical integration is strong in the cultural industries because of the centrality of circulation. To recap from the Introduction, circulation is vital because of the need to control relationships with fickle audiences and create artificial scarcity for cultural products with 'public good' characteristics. That is why so many of the core cultural industries have been dominated by an oligopoly of vertically integrated companies.

However, it would be wrong to portray developments in the cultural industries as a relentless march towards vertical integration. As with conglomeration,

---

5 Though other things are rarely equal: new industries tend to appear alongside old ones, redistributing power to some degree. Whether the rise of the internet has meant that we should no longer be concerned with conglomeration, or with concentrations of corporate power, as some analysts suggest, is an issue we return to in Chapters 9 and 10.

6 Chapter 11 addresses effects of various changes, including ownership, on the quality and diversity of content.

vertical integration strategies are subject to change and there are signs of partial disintegration in some industries and new forms of integration. Whereas in the late 1980s commentators thought that Sony would be the archetypal cultural industry corporation, in the 1990s the future seemed to be represented by Disney. The latter's success in that decade was based on an understanding of the importance of intellectual property – that the cultural industries increasingly operated according to the ownership of rights to films, TV programmes, songs, brands (see Wasko, 2001). By circulating these symbols across many different media, Disney characters, icons and narratives became increasingly present in the public consciousness. New characters and icons were launched by means of intensive cross-promotion. Crucial to this strategy, though, was vertical integration. Disney not only owns a remarkable back catalogue of films and recordings, as well as its theme parks, hotels and so on, it also has its own television network and cable channel, and in addition to this it has had its own international film distribution company, Buena Vista, for decades. With its purchase of Capital Cities/ABC in 1995, Disney became one of the largest cultural industry companies in the world. But it was not just the size of the corporation that made this a significant event. The perception was that Disney had understood the nature of the new cultural industries – that combining ownership of content and distribution (or circulation, to use the term favoured here) was the way forward. In its list of the biggest media companies in 1998–1999, *Screen Digest* (July 1999: 176) noted that 'the top companies are all highly diversified – vertically and horizontally integrated'. Yet by 2001 analysts were speculating that Disney's fortunes were in reverse after the poor performance of their blockbuster film *Pearl Harbor*. Vertical integration based on the marriage of content creation and distribution was suddenly out of favour.

There has been plenty of movement *away* from vertical integration since the 1980s. One of the major organisational forms of the early complex professional era – public service broadcasting – represented a striking example of vertical integration in the public interest, justified on the grounds that it ensured a coherent schedule of entertainment and information for national citizens. Many of the PSB monopolies had programme-makers of all kinds, technical and creative, on permanent contracts, made programmes, controlled broadcasting distribution and, in some cases, even made television sets. In the 1990s, however, there was a boom in independent television production across much of the world, driven mainly by two processes. First, PSB organisations dealt with budget cuts by subcontracting production out to independent producers, and second, policymakers wanted to encourage growth in the independent sector by measures such as setting quotas for how much production had to be outsourced. This gave rise to a boom in independent production and led many commentators to talk about a new era of post-Fordist television, involving flexible working arrangements and networks of interdependent firms rather than monolithic organisations (Lash and Urry, 1994: Chapter 5; see also Robins and Cornford, 1992, for a more sceptical account). Whether this resulted in greater creative autonomy for programme-makers or not is another matter. Added to this the independent producers became highly conventional and routinised, with many having links to finance capitalism through venture capital and private equity funding.

But while trends can change, according to business fashions and changes in the regulatory environment, vertical integration remains a recurring feature of most cultural industries. In the USA of the 1990s, for example, there was a strong shift towards vertical integration in the television industry. While classical European PSB organisations had been vertically integrated right through to the 1990s, it is striking that the system in the USA, which tends to be associated with a more market-orientated approach to cultural production, aimed to discourage such integration, at least in the 1970s and 1980s. With the trend towards marketisation in US government policy, however, the disintegration taking place among European broadcasters was reversed in the USA and vertical reintegration combined with conglomeration to create a newly powerful oligopoly – at least temporarily (see Box 6.1).

Box 6.1   Vertical integration in US television

The US television system represents a remarkable case of the power of vertical integration. Government attempts to combat network power did not last long and soon gave way to an era of integration combined with conglomeration.

A relatively stable system of television production had come to prevail by the 1960s. Dozens of independent producers made programmes for the TV networks (NBC, CBS, ABC). These programmes were made mainly in Hollywood studios owned by the major film companies. The 'independents', which actually included film majors such as Warner Bros, could make huge profits from their later 'syndication' of successful programmes – re-runs on local television stations affiliated to the networks – and from overseas sales. But the networks were extremely dominant in this system. They financed most but not all of the programme costs, determined what was shown and what was not, directly influenced programme content, decided how shows would be scheduled and promoted, and 'participated' in the profits generated through syndication and sales.

By the late 1960s a political consensus had emerged that network power needed to be curbed. The Federal Communications Commission introduced Financial Interest and Syndication Rules ('the Fin-Syn Rules') in 1970. Television networks could not own shares in their primetime programming (except news and sport). This led to what many regarded as a golden era of independent production (Lotz, 2007: 86). But by the 1980s, faced with competition from cable and new networks such as Fox, the big networks argued that such rules should be removed: these were eventually relaxed in 1991 and eliminated by 1995. This action was followed by further 'deregulation' in the Telecommunications Act of 1996, which eliminated the previously existing controls on ownership of local television and radio stations.

The elimination of fin-syn destroyed independent producers (Curtin and Shattuc, 2009; Lotz, 2007). The networks regained ownership of 40 per cent of their primetime schedules by 1995, and 75 per cent of them by 2000 (Holt, 2003). Crucially, vertical integration was integrally connected to the conglomeration that, as we have already seen elsewhere in this chapter, had swept through the cultural industries in the 1980s and 1990s. Building on affiliations created in the 1960s and 1970s (such as NBC's links with Universal Studios, and Disney with ABC), networks in the USA were increasingly part of the same media and leisure corporations as the major Hollywood studios. Consequently, they turned to these sibling companies for most of their productions. According to a report cited by McChesney (1999: 21), the six major Hollywood studios produced 37 out of 46 new prime-time shows scheduled for autumn 1998. Such integration was apparent further 'downstream' too. Not only were companies such as Columbia (today belonging to Sony) buying up cinemas, the film and television studios were also now owned by the same companies that had purchased the other major outlets for films – broadcast and cable television, and video and DVD rental networks. Disney owned ABC, plus numerous cable networks; News Corporation owned Fox and had launched a new television network of the same name in the mid-1980s; Viacom owned Paramount Studios and the fledgling network UPN and, in 1999, bought the CBS network that had created it as a spin-off in the early 1970s; Time-Warner dominated cable networks and, as a result of its purchase of Ted Turner's company TNT in 1997, also owned the key cable channels. The late 1990s were boom times for these vertically integrated conglomerates.

However, longer-term developments were quite complex. Station ownership deregulation gave rise to new radio conglomerates, notably the notorious Clear Channel, with some significant impacts on quality and diversity (Klinenberg, 2007).The networks faced increasing competition from cable and the internet. Audience share and eventually advertising revenues plummeted. Increasingly powerful stars and their agents demanded ever-higher fees. Chasing younger audiences and cheaper costs, the networks turned to low-cost reality television programming in the 2000s, often made by independent producers. For some this would indicate a decline in quality, but as Michael Curtin and Jane Shattuc (2009) show, the success of 'quality' cable shows aimed at wealthier more educated demographic groups also spawned some adventurous developments in the scripted fiction that had been the mainstay of US network television from the mid-1950s to the early 2000s (we examine this boom in quality television in Chapter 11).

The recording industry provides a further illustration of some of the complexities regarding integration and disintegration in the digital age. For decades, the major companies were vertically integrated. They owned pressing and distribution facilities and contracted musicians to record for them. However, the big record companies ('the majors') rarely attempted to own retail outlets – in part because of the complexity and multiplicity of the markets for music. In addition, the relationship with independent production is more complex in the music industry than in any other industry (see the section on small companies below). In the 2000s, however, the pressing and distribution of hard copies diminished in importance, with the rise of digital technologies, and the majors largely lost control of circulation, mainly to new entrants from the IT industries– notably Apple's iTunes and Amazon. Eventually, the record companies made some belated attempts to re-establish control of circulation – for example, by setting up a music video site, Vevo. This demonstrates how tenuous control can be even for large corporations in the cultural industries. Whether this has really led to any kind of democratisation, or enhancement of musical experience, is another matter. Digital purchases might be quicker, and more convenient, but the pleasures of record and CD shopping have largely disappeared and many people are astounded by the prices charged for individual tracks on iTunes. On the other hand, the prices of CDs in the 1990s were even more outrageous. (See Chapter 10 for a further discussion of changes in the recording industry).

Vertical integration is best seen, then, not as a constant process – whereby companies become more and more vertically integrated over time – but something that is historically variable for different industries. Changes in government policy, the arrival of new technologies and new business fashions can all bring about shifts either towards or away from vertical integration. Nevertheless, it remains a significant factor in the market and media power of the major cultural industry corporations.

IS OWNERSHIP BECOMING MORE CONCENTRATED? AND DOES IT MATTER?

Strategies of conglomeration and vertical integration in the cultural industries tend to be treated as sub-sets of a larger question concerning concentration of ownership. The issue of market concentration has been central not only for work on the cultural industries in political economy approaches to culture, but also in some pluralist communications scholarship and certain mainstream economics approaches. Chapter 2 noted high levels of market concentration in the cultural industries, but pointed out as well that, in some cases, the arrival of corporations in new markets actually reduced the level of market concentration. Good, historically and nationally comparative statistics on market concentration are hard to find. Instead, we often have to rely on snapshots of particular times and these need to be treated with caution. In recent years there have been efforts to find a more consistent research methodology in order to make assessments that might inform activism and policy (Noam, 2009).

So what have been the effects of conglomeration on corporate domination of cultural markets? Ben Bagdikian (2004) has provided something of an indication of the effects of such conglomeration in terms of a general cultural market concentration. For the first edition of his book *The Media Monopoly*, Bagdikian compiled an apparently unpublished list of the dominant media firms in the market in the USA in 1983 in the following industries: newspapers, magazines, television, book publishing, motion pictures. For each of these he worked his way down the lists of dominant companies, counting how many it took to account for more than 50 per cent of market share (measured in different ways for different media). He then added the figures together and calculated a total of 50 dominant corporations across the media as a whole. He has since repeated the exercise for subsequent editions of his book and the count eventually came out as follows.

- 1983 – 50
- 1987 – 29
- 1990 – 23
- 1997 – 10
- 2000 – 6
- 2004 – 5

This drew attention to the increasing size and scope of the biggest corporations and their growing tendency to work across all the various cultural industries. But it is a very crude method for measuring overall cultural industry concentration and conglomeration and in itself should not be treated as a reliable indicator of increased concentration.

Also writing about the USA, McChesney (2004: 178–9) provided a number of examples of concentration, with some historical comparisons:

- Following the 2003 merger of Sony and Bertelsmann's music divisions, four firms sold almost 90 per cent of US recorded music by revenue.
- The six largest film companies accounted for over 90 per cent of box office revenues.
- The two largest firms in radio broadcasting did more business than the firms ranked 3–25 combined.
- In 1990, the three largest publishers of college textbooks had 35 per cent of the market in the USA and they had almost doubled their share by 2002.
- In cable, which was once a market without significant oligopoly control, according to McChesney, six cable companies had effective monopoly control over local markets across 80 per cent of the USA by 1998.

The accumulation of evidence presented by McChesney suggests an irresistible tide sweeping the cultural industries towards ever-greater levels of market concentration, but much depends on the historical framework we decide to examine. In the USA, radio became more concentrated in light of the 1996 Telecommunications Act, but it was still less concentrated than in the days of network control (in 1945, 95 per cent of all radio stations were affiliated with one or more of the four national networks; see Sterling and Kittross, 2002: 283). Concentration levels in cinema exhibition were relatively low compared with other industries and certainly compared with the days when the major studios owned them – namely, prior to 1948, when government antitrust action resulted in the studios selling off their cinema interests. As for new industries, such as cable, there is bound to be a process of oligopolisation as such industries mature and smaller firms are snaffled up by those aiming to increase their market share.[7] This is not to be complacent about existing levels of market concentration, but such statistics as those quoted above do not prove, in themselves, the existence of long-term processes of *increased* concentration in US markets.[8]

Recently, Eli M. Noam (2009) has made an invaluable contribution to analysis of ownership concentration. He painstakingly examined trends in ownership concentration between the 1980s and the late 2000s. In order to analyse ownership concentration in the media, he rightly looks across the information ecology as a whole and claims that trends in media ownership can be understood only in relation to developments in telecommunications, information technology and the internet (a claim that also underlies the present book). He therefore analysed over 100 industries across what he calls the information sector as a whole, compiling data from many different sources, including Securities and Exchange Commission and Federal Communications Commission filings, studies by constultants and financial analysts and so on. Among Noam's conclusions are the following:

- The concentration of the information sector as a whole declined after 1984, partly as a result of the break-up of the AT&T monopoly in telecommunications, but increased after 1992.
- Concentration of ownership in the media sector (the cultural industries) increased markedly, especially during the period following the US Telecommunications Act of 1996.
- However, the average concentration of the media sector was at a much lower level than the rest of the information sector, and was 'unconcentrated' by the legal standards of the US government's Antitrust Merger

---

7   There might be very real grounds for being concerned about the possibility of increasing integration between telecommunications and cable companies, however, as Cooper (2002) shows. This, though, is a problem of integration and the removal of entry barriers between sectors rather than concentration per se.

8   Christianen (1995: 89–91) argues that concentration in the music industry should take account of different record company divisions as separate entities, so that all the various labels under each conglomerate's control would be counted separately because they are in internal competition with each other. This would make the concentration figures much lower and help account for the greater diversity of product that followed from some periods of apparent market concentration (see Chapter 11).

Guidelines. (Noam recognises controversies over whether the same standards should be applied to the media/cultural industries as to other forms of industry – see below).

- The internet is highly concentrated.
- The cultural (media) industries are mainly owned by institutional investors – rising from 40 per cent in 1984 to 57 per cent in 2008. Each institutional investor owns only a small amount of any one firm, but the largest investors have stakes in many firms.

At the time of this writing a project is under way, led by Noam, to collect similar data internationally. It is likely to be of major interest to analysts of the cultural and media industries. Until then, we must make use of some now rather outdated figures. For example, in their study of media concentration in Europe, Meier and Trappel (1998: 51) provided some figures on concentration based on EU sources (see Table 6.4). They suggested very high levels of concentration in book publishing, newspapers and television. However, once again these were non-historical and, given that in many countries television was entirely dominated by one or two channels until the 1980s, some of these figures may indicate reductions of concentration. What the figures do suggest, however, is enormous variation between different countries, even within Europe.

Even following the advances made by Noam, we should not underestimate the problems involved in agreeing on reliable measures of market concentration for the same period (see Iosifides, 1997). For example, one issue, among many others, is whether or not different divisions of the same corporation – which, at least in principle, compete with each other – should be counted as competitors.[9]

These problems and ambiguities mean that the way in which ownership concentration has been criticised by some 'political economy' leftists has been vulnerable to attack from the right and the political centre. Compaine and Gomery (2000), for example, were able to amass a vast body of statistics, questioning polemical portrayals of never-ending concentration. Their approach was sometimes more nuanced than the simplistic analysis to be found on some media activist websites.

Even some political economists would consider that too much attention has been paid to market concentration and that other issues should now be prioritised. Nicholas Garnham (2004: 100) has observed that 'the critique of concentration per se is more of a liberal than a left critique'. The 'per se' is significant here: market concentration is important as a fact, but only because it leads us on to other connected questions. Garnham (2004: 100) continues,

---

9 Even more difficult to prove via reliable statistics is that increased levels of market concentration lead to reduced levels of diversity of output (see Horwitz, 2005; Noam, 2009; and Chapter 11, below).

Table 6.4   Media concentration in Western Europe in the 1990s

Country	Circulation share of top five publishing companies	Circulation share of top five newspaper titles	Audience market share of top two TV channels
Austria	45	69	68
Belgium (fr)	77	55	47
Belgium (fl)	–	–	58
Denmark	50	49	78
Finland	42	39	71
France	–	–	60
Germany	–	23	31
Ireland	–	–	60
Italy	–	–	47
Luxembourg	100	–	–
The Netherlands	95	–	39
Norway	53	38	80
Portugal	55	91	88
Spain	–	–	51
Sweden	49	33	55
Switzerland (d)	–	–	45
Switzerland (fr)	–	–	49
UK	95	–	68

Source: Meier and Trappel, 1998: 51, based on EU statistical sources

urging pragmatism, 'the mass media are by their very nature, for better or worse, the products of economies of scale and scope and thus are by their very nature concentrated'. Baker (2007: 205) points out that a 'partial dissent' from the critique of concentration commonly to be found in versions of political economy that I have labelled the Schiller-McChesney tradition 'might describe the central problem of a democratic media as not the specifics of ownership but the market forces that are the main determinant of media content'. Consistent with this broader view, Horwitz (2005: 181) notes that curbs on ownership are not likely to be effective in themselves – though they have their place as part of aspirations to a 'mixed media system' governed by principles of social justice, equality and complex democracy (see Curran, 2002: 217–47, for one outline of what such a system might look like). Policies to limit certain forms of concentration can act as curbs on the worst abuses of corporate power in certain situations. However, in arguing for such policies, critics of the cultural industries need to be clear about what the problems are that they are trying to correct, and what system of media and democracy is being advocated. In this respect contributions by writers such as Horwitz (2005) and Baker (2007) are helpful, because they locate discussions of the problem of ownership concentration within a sophisticated understanding of the problems of media, especially problems derived from commercial imperatives. Baker provides three reasons for opposing ownership concentration:

- in order to achieve a more democratic distribution of communication power;
- in order to provide a set of democratic safeguards against abuses of economic, political and cultural power;
- and in order to get the media into the hands of people who are likely to provide high-quality products.

THE CONTINUING PRESENCE OF SMALL COMPANIES

We saw in Chapter 2 that independent producers proliferated – and became important to debates about cultural production – even as large corporations became dominant in the cultural industries in the middle of the twentieth century. As cultural corporations have become bigger and more dominant, small companies have continued to boom in number. According to one analyst, 80 per cent of the Hollywood film industry is made up of companies with four employees or fewer (Jack Kyser, cited by Magder and Burston, 2002). Even during the period when the book industry was involved in successive waves of mergers and acquisitions, the number of book companies active in the USA increased from 993 in 1960 to 2298 in 1987, according to Department of Commerce figures (Greco, 1996: 234).

The continued importance of small companies can partly be explained by the factors analysed in Chapter 2 – that is, the conception stage of texts remains small scale and relatively inexpensive and still takes place in relatively autonomous conditions. However, there are other factors more specific to the period since 1980 that may account for the still prevalent role of small companies.

- *The onset of new media technologies brought about by the combined factors of government marketisation policy and intensified business interest in leisure and culture*   This has created new types of cultural industry and, before industries 'mature', there is often more room for manoeuvre for independents than is possible in established industries. Key examples of such independent-friendly new cultural industries over the last 30 years are computer games (see Chapter 10), what was once called 'multimedia' production (for example, educational CD-ROMs and DVD-ROMs), and website design. However, the introduction of new technologies is also a product – and, in turn, a cause – of a proliferation of new subsectors within longer-established industries. For example, as live performance by successful rock acts has become more and more important, from the 1970s onwards, a host of new companies have sprung up providing technical and other forms of support, including not only amplification specialists, but also lighting and set designers and so on.
- *The rise of a discourse of entrepreneurialism in the economy as a whole* (Keat and Abercrombie, 1991) There has been increasing emphasis since the

1970s on the value of 'going it alone' – namely, working separately from large bureaucratic organisations. This has not only made people willing to set up their own businesses but has also made large businesses more willing to interact with them.

- *Venture capital has become much more available to small- and medium-sized cultural businesses* as culture has become recognised as a valid form of profitmaking.
- *Dominant vertically integrated companies have seen some disintegration* As we have seen, these have been industries such as television. This has not only brought about an independent production sector but also created many ancillary and technical support companies, from film and television catering specialists to companies that rent out editing suites and personnel.
- *There has been an increasing emphasis in cultural industry companies on marketing* As a result, there are also scores of design studios, independent advertising agencies, public relations businesses and the like aimed at servicing companies that are increasingly willing to pay more to market their goods and services in innovative ways. What is more, in this way, actors, performers and other symbol creators can subsidise their other work, which they may feel is their 'real' work. This has happened for a long time, but now more than ever.

Perspectives that focus on conglomeration, integration and the increasing size of the cultural industry corporations (such as many accounts from the Schiller-McChesney tradition of political economy) often understate the significance of small companies. Such companies may account for small levels of market share, but they are vital in terms of the numbers of people they employ and their potential to foster – or at least act as a conduit for – innovation. This, along with other factors, has meant that a strong ethical and aesthetic premium has been placed on institutional independence.

This is particularly apparent in the film and recording industry. (Indie cinema is discussed in Chapter 11.) A key factor within many music genres has been a discourse of independence among musicians, fans and journalists that has allowed independent record companies, in some exceptional cases, to serve as the centres of commercial networks that together form something of an alternative to prevailing systems of cultural production and consumption.

For Jason Toynbee (2000: 19–25), the particular importance attached to independent production in popular music derives from a long-standing history of 'institutional autonomy' that cuts against the efforts of large companies to make profits out of music. This autonomy is based on the dispersed, decentralised nature of music-making. It means that not only do companies cede control of production to symbol makers (as in all cultural industries) but there is also a tendency towards 'spatially dispersed production in small units' (rock groups, swing bands) and 'a strong continuity between production and consumption' in musical subcultures (Toynbee, 2000: 1). Audiences and performers come together in 'proto-markets', which are only partially commodified, and where there is a great deal of resentment towards the industry and 'selling out'. The possibility of institutional autonomy and the high value attached to it in musical subcultures means that spaces have been created where alternative arrangements for the management and marketing of creativity can be tried out. I discuss an important example of such an 'alternative' dynamic in the next chapter (see Box 7.4).

However, this does not mean that small companies are not vulnerable to the power of large corporations, especially at certain moments of regulatory and technological change. Take, for example, the case of a Syracuse, New York, radio station, WRDS, which catered mainly to that industrial city's African-American population (Klinenberg, 2007: 58–60). Following the introduction of the US Telecommunications Act in 1996, in the words of station owner Robert Short Jnr, '[t]he playing field changed right beneath our feet. I was competing against some big companies before, but it was a relatively fair battle because they couldn't monopolize the whole advertising pie. Clear Channel moved in and took over seven stations' – a result of the withdrawal of FCC rules limiting the number of stations that one company could own in any particular market. Clear Channel's operating costs were extremely low, because they combined the stations together, and by using standardised 'voice-tracking' DJ links, spread their costs across different stations. This allowed them to offer special advertising packages to big customers, and to pay for bigger and better sales teams. But Clear Channel also benefited from conglomeration and vertical integration.

> They also owned the billboards, which you need for radio promotions. They owned the theaters [where the acts played on music radio might play concerts] so it was hard to promote your own concerts. And they owned SFX Entertainment, which books the talent, which means they basically owned the artists. They would squeeze you out, and the little guys couldn't compete.

Short and his partners sold the station in 2000, and it was converted away from the 'urban music' format (namely, music appealing to African-Americans). Music, then, is certainly not immune to the centralising tendencies of cultural industries, especially when government favours deregulation over intervention to protect smaller companies and non-profits.[10]

---

10 Klinenberg (2007) also discusses the effects of marketising government policy on the US radio industry – including how the homogenisation of content resulted in a massive increase in National Public Radio's audience in the decade following the US Telecommunications Act of 1996. See Ahlkvist and Fisher (2000) for a discussion of the standardisation of music radio formats in the face of technological change and ownership changes.

INTERDEPENDENCE, INTER-FIRM NETWORKS AND ALLIANCES

Smaller companies, then, are vulnerable to the strategies of larger corporations. They also increasingly exist in relations of **interdependence** with larger companies, linked to them in complex networks of licensing, financing and distribution.

One of the most important ways in which corporations have changed their organisational structures, in nearly all major areas of business, is that they increasingly subcontract to small- and medium-sized firms (see Chapter 3 on organisational innovation in the wake of the Long Downturn). These smaller firms are potentially more dynamic and able to innovate than the large conglomerates, but they are becoming more and more involved in close relationships with the corporations that subcontract to them. This is also true of the cultural industries.

Such webs of interdependence are not entirely new in the cultural industries. In film, as the Hollywood corporations lost their control over production in the 1950s, new, independent production companies entered the market to cater for specialist products, but the Hollywood studios still acted as distributors and financiers of independently produced films (see Aksoy and Robins, 1992). Even in an era in the recording industry when 'majors' and 'independents' were seen by fans, musicians and critics as polar opposites, in truth they were often linked in licensing, financing and distribution deals. Such arrangements, whereby small and large companies form interdependent webs, became increasingly prevalent in the 1980s and extended into new areas of the cultural industries, most significantly in European broadcasting, where traditionally production had been handled 'in-house' by large state and public service broadcasters (Robins and Cornford, 1992).

There are rewards for both corporations and small companies in such systems of interfirm networking. For the corporations, acting as distributors and financiers of independent producers is an extension of what they already do – acting as distributors and financiers of their own semi-autonomous divisions. A large multidivisional corporation might get a lower cut of revenues from a text produced by an independent company than from the sales of a text created within one of their own divisions, but the arrangement means that they can get independent companies to bear some of the risks associated with the difficult business of managing symbolic creativity. What is more, symbol creators might well *feel* as though they are more autonomous of commercial pressures, especially in those cultural industries and genres where there is a mistrust of corporate bureaucracies, such as rock or indie film-making or certain kinds of games.

This makes interdependence sound very rosy. However, in the eyes of many, increasing levels of interdependence in the cultural industries mean the end of an era when independents could provide an alternative to the majors – another sign of corporate takeover. (This is an issue raised in the discussion of indie cinema in Chapter 11.) Many forms of interfirm networking involve links between very large companies in different industries and, increasingly, in different sectors. These give rise to strategic alliances between corporations not as happens in traditional cartel arrangements but on the basis of specific projects. Such 'alliance capitalism' has been a feature of a very wide range of businesses over the last 30 years. It is especially relevant, noted Manuel Castells (1996: 162–4), in high-tech sectors, where research and development costs are enormously expensive. For Castells, the self-sufficient corporation is, more and more, a thing of the past.

While cultural industry companies compete with each other, at the same time, they operate complex webs of joint ventures and ownership. Auletta (1997: 225) lists a number of reasons for such alliances with potential rivals:

- To avoid competition.
- To save money and share risks.
- To buy a seat on a rival's board.
- To create a safety net, as technological innovation makes for increasing uncertainty.
- To make links with foreign companies to avoid 'arousing the ire of local governments'.

The interconnections between the Magnificent Seven conglomerates and the 'second tier' of corporations are almost impossible to encapsulate neatly. One of the best attempts at doing so was printed in *The New Yorker* in 1997 (see Figure 6.2). It shows the 'web of collaboration' between six of the most powerful cultural industry corporations in the world at the time, plus Microsoft, and lists some of the many joint ventures between them. In the rapidly changing world of the cultural industries this diagram is now a historical document, but it gives a good sense of how closely intermeshed the major companies are in terms of joint ventures and ownership. Auletta (1997) described such links as an American version of *keiretsu* – the 'ancient Japanese custom of co-opting the competition' by creating structures of collaboration with rivals – a system of 'co-opetition' (Murdock, 2000: 48, quoting the *Financial Times*) rather than competition. As Auletta (1997: 226) suggests, such alliances have implications for texts. As more and more companies become tied to one another, will their journalists cover controversial stories about other companies in the web? Without question, it helps to reinforce the economic power of the biggest corporations and entrench the way that they do business.

In the 2000s, a new set of interdependent alliances arose, between cultural industries and internet-related IT companies. Arsenault and Castells (2008: 713) captured the state of this 'dense web of partnerships, cross-investments, board members, and managers' in 2008. Their illustration is reproduced as Figure 6.3. They focus on some examples, such as the way in which NBC

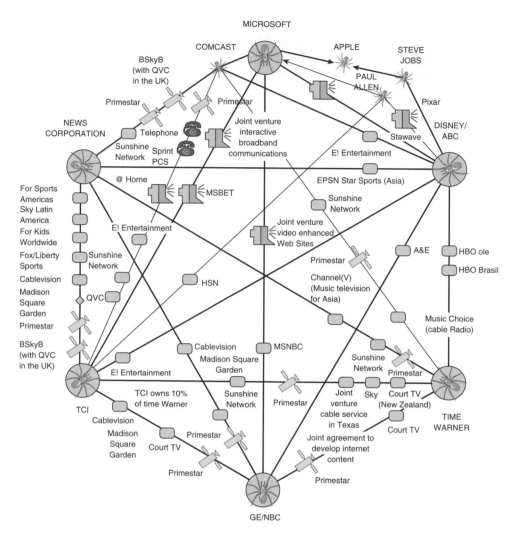

Figure 6.2   A web of collaboration between corporations. This diagram, reproduced from a 1997 edition of *The New Yorker*, illustrates the many complex connections existing at the time between a number of companies in the cultural industry and IT businesses (Auletta, 1997: 227)

Universal and News Corporation came together in 2007 to form Hulu as a rival to YouTube, with AOL, MSN, MySpace (owned by News Corp) and Yahoo also providing distribution. But its backers, note Arsenault and Castells, also formed strategic partnerships with Google, the very company whose hold on the digital video market they were trying to break – notably Google's provision of advertising delivery for News Corp's MySpace social networking site.

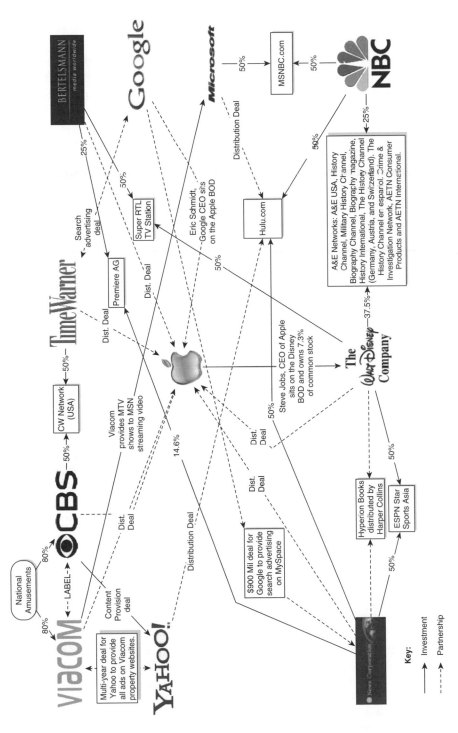

Figure 6.3 Key interlockings between multi-national media & diversified internet corporations

*Please note that this diagram represents key partnerships and cross-investments. It is not exhaustive. The relationships were current as of February 2008.

ARE THE CULTURAL INDUSTRIES GETTING BIGGER?

The figures involved in mergers and acquisitions, and the now massive size of revenues accruing to the biggest cultural industry companies, suggest that the cultural industries are an increasingly significant component of global business and, therefore, of national economies. If this is so, it has potentially important consequences for understanding relationships between economics and culture, as well as between creativity and commerce. Potentially, for example, this new centrality might threaten the relative autonomy, or creative freedom, that has been traditionally ceded to workers involved in making cultural products. It may also quicken commodification, with all its complex consequences. So just how significant are the cultural industries in national, regional and urban economies?

Cultural industries in modern economies

There is no shortage of government-commissioned reports 'mapping' the size of the cultural and creative industries, the rate at which they are growing, and their contribution to national employment and growth. The main ways in which size, growth and significance have been measured are by employment, firm activity (such as revenues), gross value added to the economy, and exports (Cunningham and Higgs, 2008). Many of these 'mapping studies' are a product of the policy developments discussed in Chapter 5, whereby governments, often consumed by information society fever, have seen the cultural industries as new potential sources of employment and national or regional competitive advantage. Some use the term 'creative industries', others stick with 'cultural industries'. As most of these reports are commissioned by government and policy agencies with an interest in presenting the sector as one of great significance and/or growth, there has been a tendency over time for broader definitions to be adopted, for example the increasing use of the concept of a 'creative economy' (Howkins, 2001) or even a 'creative class' (Florida, 2002) rather than creative or cultural industries. A shift to such broader definitions allowed, for example, designers in industries outside the cultural industries to be counted as part of the relevant economic activity.

Here is a sample of the conclusions from some of these reports. (Note the range of terms used here and recall the discussion in Chapter 5 on the motivations behind the shift to the term 'creative' industries.)

- The proportion of employment in Hong Kong in the creative sector grew from 5.0 per cent in 1996 to 5.3 per cent in 2002 (CCPR, 2003).
- Between 1998 and 2002, cultural employment grew in Austria by 6 per cent (Kulturdokumentation et al., 2004) and, from 1995 to 2000, there was a 49 per cent rise in revenue from cultural industries (KMU Forschung, 2003).

- Employment in creative industries made up 20 per cent of Iceland's labour market in 1991 and 23.4 per cent in 2002 (Einarsson, 2005).
- Between 1996 and 2001, employment in the cultural industries in Australia increased from 167,000 to 190,000 – an average growth rate of 2.62 per cent (Queensland Government, 2005).
- The proportion of Singapore's GDP accounted for by 'copyright industries' rose from 2.0 per cent in 1986 to 2.8 per cent in 2000 (ERC Services Subcommittee, 2002).
- In 2003, creative industries in the UK accounted for 8 per cent of gross value added (GVA) in the economy as a whole – equivalent to £56.5 billion. These industries grew by an average of 6 per cent per annum between 1997 and 2002, compared to growth rates of 3 per cent per annum for the UK economy (DCMS, 2005).

Fascinating stuff. Are you still awake? Dozens of such reports appeared in the 2000s, as the fashion for the concept of creative industries spread across national, regional and urban governments. For the reasons suggested above – that the point of such reports was to show to Ministries of Finance, central government and so on that the creative industries were key areas of economic activity – nearly all of them suggested that the creative industries were, indeed, important and growing. The problem is, of course, how to define the industries and occupations concerned.

The categories used by the British Department of Culture, Media and Sport in its initial 'mapping documents' (DCMS, 1998, 2001) were limited by the lack of fine-grained statistical data concerning industry segments and occupations. Nevertheless, their definitions and methods were, initially, adopted widely. As we saw in the previous chapter (see page 175), the 'UK definition' included peripheral (in the terms I used in Chapter 1) but nevertheless significant industries, such as dance and the visual arts, and also industries as diverse as jewellery, fashion and furniture design. Most significantly of all, it included software (not just 'leisure software', or computer games, but also software for business applications). This was done in order to bolster the figures and provide a more powerful alliance around the 'creative industries' banner. Developing such software is a very different activity from the artistic-expressive (or journalistic-informational) pursuits evoked by the use of the term 'creative'. This concept inevitably connotes a strong artistic-expressive element – the aura of the 'artist', which allowed it to be presented as 'sexy' for politicians and other policymakers, and yet also attractive for its financial clout (Garnham, 2005).

Other definitions are even broader than the UK model. The one used in the People's Republic of China included gambling, education, sports, tourism and consultancy services (CCPR, 2003), while in Taiwan, the term 'cultural creative industries' was used and included such things as tea houses and wedding photography (CCPR, 2003). Finland's categorisation included amusement parks, games and recreational services. In each case, definitions were shaped by local political and business interests. A widely-cited report on Hong Kong employment, put together by the Centre for Cultural Policy Research at the University of Hong Kong (CCPR, 2003), developed a framework that included statistics by occupations as well as by industry, as other agencies had done. It also counted non-creative employment in the creative industries, and creative employment in industries that fell outside the definition of these industries. So car designers could now be included, for example.

As I made clear in the Introduction (pp. 15–22), I prefer a more restricted definition of the cultural industries, centred on those industries that are chiefly concerned with the social production and dissemination of meaning. This is because, as I explained there, my view is that one of the main reasons the cultural industries matter is that they make and circulate texts. Other definitions may have other motivations, but the point is that when we read figures purporting to show that an entity called 'the cultural industries' or 'the creative industries' has grown, we need to think carefully about what that entity is. It may sound as though a nation or a city has a high proportion of its population employed as musicians, writers, games designers and their ilk, but, in fact, such activities are likely to be dwarfed by activities such as computer software, gambling and education, which may well have sneaked into the definition because of political pressures and tensions. (This is not to say that all efforts to 'expand' definitions are aimed simply at legitimating narrow interests; see Box 6.2 for a discussion of 'depth' models of defining cultural industries).

Box 6.2   Depth versus breadth in defining cultural industries

Cultural geographer Andy Pratt has argued that, when it comes to defining cultural industries, 'depth' is as significant as breadth. This means including those activities that are necessary for cultural outputs to take place, including back- and front-of-house staff in theatres, cinemas and music venues, and those involved in the manufacture of items, archiving and education and training. Pratt (2005: 34) argues that such an approach brings into view a range of institutional structures that has been invisible in much policy.[11]

This is reasonable when considering how interlinked systems of employment are necessary to get cultural products to audiences. However, when such an expanded depth definition is used, we need to bear in mind that most of the work included in this expanded definition has little effect on the form and content of the texts and it is the potential of such texts to have a particular type of influence on society through their symbol-laden content that distinguishes

---

11 The British DCMS has adopted something like this idea for its definition of 'the cultural sector' in more recent documents. The 'creative industries' are considered a subset of this broader sector.

the cultural industries from all others. We should not lose sight of the fact that the making of DVD players is a very different kind of industrial activity from the making of the films and television programmes that we might use these players to watch.

One possible partial solution to this problem is to try and distinguish in figures between those having *direct* creative input and other workers *associated* with cultural products. However, the data in many countries scarcely support the most general of definitions, let alone these more specific breakdowns.

The diversity of concepts and measures that have been used at national and local levels makes comparisons between the presence of the cultural (or creative) industries in different countries, regions and cities very difficult. Even if everyone agreed a single definition of those industries, the fact that each national census body has a different system for classifying industries and occupations would still make meaningful comparison very challenging. So, in order to compare two cities in different countries, account needs to be taken of these different classification methods as well as different definitions of the cultural industries. For this and for other reasons indicated above, reports of facts and figures for the cultural industries should always be 'viewed as indicative rather [than] as categorical' (Power, 2003).

Nevertheless, for all these problems of definition and measurement, one broad trend seems clear from the various, often mind-numbingly tedious, reports. In many places there is evidence, over a number of years (allowing for cycles, recessions and setbacks), of **increases in cultural industry activity slightly above the rate of increase in gross domestic product**. However, we still need to dispel the idea that such increases reflect a growing presence of glamorous creativity in modern societies. One report estimated that, from 1977 to 2002, the 'communications industry' grew at a compound annual rate of 8.4 per cent, thereby exceeding nominal (that is to say, not adjusted for inflation) GDP growth by 1.6 percentage points (VSS, 2003). The segmentation of the communications industry in this report is revealing, however, and more useful in the present context than many reports on the cultural industries, for it suggests just how little of the money spent on communications comes from consumer end-users. When we think of the cultural industries, we might think of, say, the kind of production involved when we watch a drama series on television or download a new song from the internet. But at least measured by spending, such activities are dwarfed by advertising, marketing and 'institutional end-user' spending on such things as business information services, professional and training media, trade shows and the like (see Figure 6.4).

Cultural industries in global business

The conclusion to be drawn from the preceding section is that the cultural industries – even defined in the relatively narrow way preferred in this

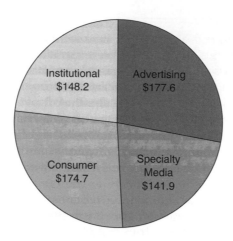

Figure 6.4   Sectors of US communications

Source: VSS, 2003: 38

book – are becoming more important as a part of national economies than they were in the past. Yet we should not make the leap made by some commentators and suggest that the cultural industries are now at the centre of global business (Lash and Urry, 1994).

One way to approach this is to look at the size of the biggest cultural industry corporations in relation to the size of the biggest corporations in general. Table 6.5 shows the biggest corporations with significant cultural industry interests, along with their rank in the *Fortune* magazine list of the biggest 500 companies in the world by revenue in the year 2004. Historical comparison of the relative sizes of the largest cultural industry corporations is difficult. Companies based on 'services' were only included in the Fortune 500 and Global 500 lists from 1995 onwards. However, we can discern one or two interesting trends. When an equivalent table was compiled for the second edition of this book, based on the Fortune Global 500 list for 2006, the key cultural industry corporations all improved their positions from the table compiled for the 2002 edition, based on the 2001 Fortune Global 500. Walt Disney moved up from 174th to 159th, Viacom from 245th to 196th, and Bertelsmann from 299th to 271st. The major cultural-industry corporations have slipped considerably since 2007, reflecting not only the declining fortunes of the sector, but also business analysts' gloomy prognostications about the future of the cultural industries, compared with IT and other sectors, as advertising declines in a global recession. Vivendi, the world's biggest cultural-industry conglomerate by revenue, is merely 225th in the *Fortune* rankings, while Time Warner, which squeaked into the global top 100 in the 2006 rankings, has dropped to 363rd in the wake of its policy of divestment, as it seeks to clear the enormous debts accumulated in the mega-merger era.

Even in 2007, with the Magnificent Seven riding higher than ever before in the global corporate league table of revenues, the very biggest cultural industry corporations were dwarfed by the biggest corporations in the world, and this continues to be the case. The giants of automobile production and oil for example still dominate, all capped by US retail monster Wal-Mart: it would take more than ten Vivendis to match its revenue. Likewise Sony's cultural industry activities alone would leave it languishing at the lower end of the Global 500: consumer electronics are the basis of that firm's massive global presence.

The big cultural industry corporations are not the same thing as the cultural industries, but these figures should put into perspective the idea that these cultural industries are now part of a global business core. That is a long way from happening. And it is worth noting that even the big IT companies, such as Google, Microsoft and Apple, are dwarfed by the oil, automobile and retail companies, not to mention by IBM, by the biggest telecommunications companies, and even by the corporate group formed around the Japanese Post Office, Japan Post Holdings (the 9th biggest company in the world, with revenues of over 200 billion US dollars in 2010).

CONTINUING COMMODIFICATION

I have spent some time in this chapter discussing questions concerning conglomeration and concentration and the size of the cultural industries relative to other industries in modern societies. These are vital issues covering the power of cultural producers in modern societies, and they generate a great deal of public debate and numerous policy dilemmas. But we now need to take a step back from these developments and examine them together with the policy changes discussed in the previous two chapters in order to take in a longer-term historical perspective, and look at the growth of the cultural industries. Central to this growth is the commodification of culture.

In Chapter 2, I outlined why I think that commodification matters. I explained that the most useful analyses of commodification in general see it as an ambivalent process – enabling and constraining, productive and destructive. Negative aspects of the extension of commodification include an emphasis on private, exclusive ownership and a tendency to produce systems of unrecognised and under-rewarded paid labour.

This is as much the case for cultural production as it is for other sectors. The complex professional era saw a pronounced industrialisation of culture, which accelerated and intensified the slow, uneven process of commodification of culture that had begun many centuries previously. The commodification achieved in the era of growth of the cultural industires, and the formation of huge corporations, remains partial and incomplete (Garnham, 2011). The question we now need to consider is the one raised in Chapter 2: what are the implications of the *further* commodification of culture that has taken place over the years since the 1980s?

To address this question, we must, in turn, consider various issues discussed in Chapters 3 to 5 concerning the marketisation of telecommunications

Table 6.5   The largest corporations with cultural industry interests

Numbers indicate ranking in the Fortune Global 500 List for 2011 (based on company reports for fiscal years ending in 2011). Figures are in US$ millions and refer to revenue.
Italics indicate those companies that generate most of their revenues from cultural industry interests.

1 Wal-Mart Stores 421, 849 (no cultural industry interests – included for sake of comparison)

2 Royal Dutch Shell 378, 152 (ditto)

31 AT&T 124,629
The biggest telecommunications corporation in the world by revenue, included for the sake of comparison. A number of telecommunications giants dwarf the biggest cultural industry companies. Others include Nippon Telegraph and Telephone Company and Verizon.

73 Sony 83,845
Sony has six main divisions at time of writing: consumer electronics, games, music (Sony Music Entertainment, now merged with Bertelsmann's music interests) films (Columbia TriStar), mobile phone manufacture and financial services. Consumer electronics accounts for the vast majority of its income.

111 Apple 65,225
Apple designs and markets computers, software and consumer electronics goods. Since the launch of the iPod in 2001 and the iTunes Store in 2003 it has become a major player in the cultural industries, especially the recorded music industry. But the iTunes Store accounts for a small proportion of its revenues. It has only been involved in content production briefly, when it owned the animated film company Pixar. This was sold to Walt Disney in 2006.

120 Microsoft 62,484
The world's most important software company has only one significant cultural-industry interest: producing games for the X-Box.

225 Vivendi SA 38,248
Vivendi is the biggest cultural industry corporation in the world (defined as corporations that gain most of their revenue from cultural-industry activities). It was an engineering and water company that, under the control of a megalomaniacal CEO, tried to refashion itself as a global cultural industries leader in the dot.com boom. It came close to collapse, sold many of its cultural industry interests, but is still a media company whose divisions are dominant or significant players in television, games and recorded music.

226 The Walt Disney Company 38,063
Still the most famous cultural-industry business in the world: films, theme parks, theatre.

228 Comcast Corporation 37,937
A US cable and broadband internet provider that bought NBC Universal from Vivendi in 2010, giving it control of one of USA's major television networks.

284 News Corp. 32,778
This ranking underestimates the influence of News Corp and its mogul Rupert Murdoch. For example, News Corp owns a substantial share of BSkyB, which is a major player in European digital and satellite television. Murdoch is its Chairman, but BSkyB reports its figures separately (it had over US$8 billion in revenue for 2010–11). News Corp made moves to take full control in 2011, but this was interrupted by the *News of the World* phone-hacking scandal in the UK. See Chapter 7 for more on Murdoch.

325 Google 29,321
Google is not a cultural-industry corporation, in spite of its ownership of YouTube and its Google Books project. Nor is it really a media company: it does not 'produce' content in any

Table 6.5   (Continued)

previously understood sense of production. It's an IT company, run by software engineers. However its domination of search makes it by far the most important IT company for the cultural industries, because of the relationship of search to circulation and, in particular, to advertising revenue.

363 Time Warner 26,888
Time Warner's 2000–2001 merger with AOL led to huge financial losses and massive debts. It has lost its place as the world's largest media company as it has sold off many assets.

444 Bertelsmann 21,791
Unusually for a very large cultural-industry corporation, Bertelsmann is privately owned, by the Mohr family. It controls RTL, the biggest European television and radio entity, and significant publishing interests.

and broadcasting and shifts in copyright and cultural policy. These policy shifts can be seen as complex responses to the perceived need on the part of businesses and states to restore growth and political order in the wake of the economic downturn and political and cultural crisis facing advanced industrial societies in the 1960s and 1970s (outlined in Chapter 3). They were not concerted responses in that they were based on meetings of some committee of the ruling class. But they were fought for in order to meet particular sets of interests – especially economic ones. Culture was seen as a crucial opportunity for investment growth. The set of assumptions I called 'information society discourse' in Chapter 3 – the assumption that modern economies and societies (at least previously dominant post-indus-trial ones) need to develop towards a greater concentration on knowledge assets – was an essential basis for this. Such discourse, on the part of policy-makers, journalists and business analysts legitimated an acceleration of cap-ital investment in the production of culture, information and knowledge. Culture had been growing steadily as a sector of capitalism throughout the complex professional era, but opportunities for growth were restrained by public ownership and oversight of telecommunications channels and broadcasting. Cultural policy (such as arts policy) was more marginal. But the introduction of information society discourse into this area of public policy from the 1980s onwards, often justified as an attempt to democratise 'paternalist' or 'elitist' practices, added fuel to the accelerating commodi-fication of culture. The strengthening of copyright law and enforcement across the world – in the form of the TRIPS elements of the WTO agreement of 1995, and various other agreements – has been particularly important. This was an essential prerequisite of growth in cultural businesses, which rely fundamentally on ownership, licensing and the exploitation of rights. In the shrinking of the public domain and of fair use-style provisions, we can see the way in which commodification can encroach on public, collec-tive access to resources.

To recap Chapter 2, all societies – by virtue of law and conventions – will draw lines between elements of the world that can be bought and sold and those that should not (see Frow, 1997). These boundaries are subject to technological change, driven in part by a desire on the part of businesses to accumulate capital. At times, entirely new domains will become available for commodification: Frow, for example, discusses the rise in the trade in human organs. At other times, there will be an increasing encroachment on domains already open to commodification, but relatively protected. This is what has happened with culture over the last 30 years.

So how should we interpret this? There is no need to offer a romantic vision of the superiority of primitive society over capitalist society or imagine that we can return to a state where we simply make culture together, free of commodity exchange. In fact, such visions and fantasies are themselves a product of modern commodified culture. My view is that we need to recognise the ambivalences involved in capitalist development, resist the more negative aspects of commodification, and seek to develop alternatives.

On what I have called the consumption side (though this involves production, too, in that we draw on our consumption of existing resources to make new things), the extension of the scope and duration of copyright, a necessary underpinning of commodification, has placed undue restrictions on freedom. While some restrictions on freedom are desirable as they are in the interests of the common good, the exclusive ownership of cultural goods has become excessive. Moreover, commodification leads to a situation where cultural experience is increasingly privatised and individualised. Many libertarians and liberals would agree with the view that copyright is now excessively hindering access to culture and offer phenomena such as the Open Source software movement and various web-based initiatives as alternatives. However, there are other problems associated with commodification in the realm of culture.

Another negative aspect of commodification concerns labour. Commodification can lead to greater innovation, and the reduction of costs, but in a world where labour sources can often be moved to cheaper locations, such a cost reduction is often achieved through making workers redundant and then employing them in other industries. We shall see how this has begun increasingly to happen in the realm of culture in Chapter 7. When combined with uneven development, as workers are paid different wages in different places, commodification also gives rise to a situation where consumers are cut off from the work that goes into making their products. This is as true of culture as it is of other goods. Just as we might pay scant attention to the labour that goes into the shoes that we wear, we will rarely consider the labour that goes into our cultural products. A complex and globally-distributed division of labour means that we are unaware of the work involved in bringing a DVD or a downloaded movie into our homes. Many less well-paid creative and technical workers will be responsible for such products besides the stars whose name appears on the product. Non-commodified or partly-commodified cultural labour is likely to be less distant in space and time than the products of the cultural industries. It could even be argued that because so few people are aware of cultural labour, believing it to be cushy and even glamorous, it is a particularly potent example of the way in which work is not recognised under capitalist commodity production.

There are further implications of the extension of commodification raised by the analysis of corporate growth in this chapter. As the scope for investment in culture grows, corporations grow bigger and come to undertake more and more of the cultural production that people see and hear. They have much greater resources for the vital work of marketing and publicity necessary to make us aware of their products, amidst the tens of thousands of others available. Corporate forms of cultural production thus become the model for creativity in societies. It is not true to say that alternative and independent forms of production are suppressed. The rise of collaborative forms of peer-to-peer production suggests that there is still a great deal of cultural production in modern societies that does not neatly fall into the category of commodities, to be bought and sold; based on principles of giving and sharing. But, as we shall see in Chapters 9 and 10, these innovations are often drawn into corporate systems of cultural production, in indirect ways.

* * *

This chapter has provided evidence of considerable change in the role of the cultural industries in modern economies and societies. Bigger-than-ever corporations towered over the new terrain of cultural production in the 1990s and 2000s. Their growth was encouraged by the policy changes outlined in the previous chapters, along with a related perception among business investors that the cultural industries represented a good opportunity for high returns (though this began to change in the second half of the first decade of the twenty first century). Various waves of mergers and acquisitions enabled this growth and new types of relationships between companies have emerged. There were also increasing numbers of strategic alliances between cultural industry companies and large corporations in other industries, while small companies increasingly formed complex licensing, financing and distribution deals with the major corporations.

However, there is considerable continuity in addition to this. Small companies continue to play a key part in the cultural industries. The dynamics identified in the Introduction continue to drive company strategy, even if the exact form vertical integration and conglomeration take will vary according to the general business fashion. As for market concentration much depends on how this is defined, but there is no doubt that the cultural industries are, in general, highly concentrated.

My argument is that the significance of changes in the cultural industries is broader than it would appear. Along with increasing leisure time and disposable income, the developments traced in this chapter mean that the cultural industries have become slowly and steadily more important in advanced industrial economies than they have been in the past. Claims about the cultural industries need to be treated with real caution because of the statistical and definitional problems outlined above. It is clearly the case that the big corporations are not in the league of Big Oil, the car industry, and the banks. Nevertheless, the growth of the cultural industries has significant implications because the oligopolistic corporations that inevitably come to dominate capi-talist forms of production can mobilise huge resources to campaign on behalf of their interests and put together the kinds of promotional budgets that will allow their texts to gain more attention than any others. This often works against the public interest – for example, when campaigning for changes that will extend the scope of copyright which will in turn diminish public access to culture. The growth of large corporations also affects prevailing concep-tions of how to carry out the management of creativity. The biggest firms often tend to be the most prestigious and will set the standards other busi-nesses will follow as they carry out their work.

In the final part of this chapter, I tied these various developments to the longer-term historical picture. The policy developments analysed in the last two chapters and the associated corporate growth discussed in this one can be seen as aspects of an ongoing, but accelerating, commodification of cul-ture. This has significant implications for the organisation and experience of cultural work, which are discussed in the next chapter.

RECOMMENDED AND FURTHER READING

As discussed above, Eli M. Noam has made a major advance in debates about the media with this *Media Ownership and Concentration in America* (2009), which actually covers the whole 'information sector'.

The most sophisticated critical treatment of conceptual issues related to democracy and justice in relation to the issues discussed in this chapter is C. Edwin Baker's *Media Concentration and Democracy* (2007). Also helpful are the contributions in Ronald Rice, *Media Ownership: Research and Regulation* (2008). An older treatment of ownership is provided by Benjamin Compaine and Douglas Gomery's *Who Owns the Media?* (2000). Compaine's website makes it clear that he takes a strongly neo-liberal perspective.

Dwayne Winseck's introductory essay to the collection edited by himself and Dal Yong Jin, *The Political Economies of Media* (2011), explores changes in owner-ship concentration and in relations between cultural industries and neighbour-ing industries (telecommunications, internet and information technology). Jin's chapter in the same volume analyses evidence of some de-conglomeration.

Scott Fitzgerald's *Corporations and Cultural Industries* (2012) is an overdue and highly accomplished application of political economy theory and business analysis to three major corporations. Jonathan Hardy's *Cross-Media Promotion* (2010) is a valuable study of some of the consequences of conglomeration.

On developments in specific industries, the US television industry has been well served, with books by Amanda Lotz (*The Television Will Be Revolutionized*, 2007) and Michael Curtin and Jane Shattuc (*The American Television Industry*, 2009). As with much of the research on television, these works do not systematically relate the television industry to other media industries. Jennifer Holt's *Empires of Entertainment* (2011) provides a lucid and informative account of the growth in corporate power in the US film and television industries in the 1980s and 1990s.

On questions of commodification of culture, see Harvey's *The Condition of Postmodernity* (1989), Mosco's *The Political Economy of Communication* (1996, 2nd edition 2009), and Frow's brilliant essay entitled 'Gift and commodity' (1997). Nicholas Garnham's recent essay in Wasko, Murdock and Sousa's *The Handbook of Political Economy of Communications* (2011) discusses the troubled and incomplete nature of commodification. A fine essay by Graham Murdock in the same collection updates debates about cultural commodities for the digital era, and is highly recommended.

The best way to keep in touch with developments in the ever-changing cultural industries is by reading business publications and their associated websites, such as the *Financial Times*, the entertainment trade paper *Variety* and, if you can tolerate the conservative political perspectives they take, *The Wall Street Journal* and *The Economist*. *Screen Digest*, available in those university libraries willing to pay its eye-watering subscription fees, is an excellent source of data.

ONLINE READING

All the online material referenced below can be accessed free of charge at: **http://www.sagepub.co.uk/hesmondhalgh**

Simply click on the 'Sample Materials' tab to find the links to each article.

The international media concentration mentioned above, lead by Eli Noam, which aims to track international ownership concentration in the media, has a website at http://internationalmedia.pbworks.com.

Several websites are devoted to questions of media ownership. Even websites, however, seem to struggle to keep up with the pace of change here, as corporations buy or sell off divisions. Knowing the details of who owns what this year, this month, this week, is perhaps less important, though, than understanding the significant overall trends and what they say about issues of *power* in the cultural industries.

A bracing introduction to the heated debates about media ownership can be found in the web journal *openDemocracy*, initiated by articles by Robert McChesney and Benjamin Compaine in 2001–2002. All the contributions can be accessed via the website at www.opendemocracy.net.

Arsenault and Castells (2008) provide an excellent analysis of the state of cultural-industry business networks just before the financial crisis. Tremblay (2011) critiques the statistics produced by creative industries policy-making.

- Arsenault, Amelia H. and Castells, Manuel (2008) 'The structure and dynamics of global multi-media business networks', *International Journal of Communication*, 2: 707–48.
- Tremblay, Gaëtan (2011) 'Creative statistics to support creative economy politics', *Media, Culture & Society*, 33(2): 289–298.

Creativity and Commerce, Organisation and Labour

Managing cultural production: loose control of
   creativity, tight control of circulation   229
The increasing importance of marketing and
   market research   233
   Audience research and autonomy in film,
      advertising and television   236
   A note on audience research in the digital age   242
Control of creativity: tighter or looser?   243
   Journalistic autonomy   243
   Creativity, commerce and control in popular
      music and theatre   248
Division of labour and working conditions   253
   Characteristics of cultural labour   253
Terms and conditions of cultural work in different roles   258
   'Unskilled' and semi-skilled workers   259
   Technical workers   260
   Creative managers   260
   Symbol creators   261

The changes in ownership, structure and corporate strategy discussed in the previous chapter tell us only a limited amount about what actually happens in cultural-industry organisations, and in the more general world of cultural production upon which such organisations must draw. Seeing things from the point of view of ownership says little, for example, about the ways in which cultural industry owners and executives attempt the difficult business of producing, managing and marketing cultural products, and about how the hundreds of thousands of people who seek to make a living from making culture experience their worlds. These are the central concerns of this chapter.

At the heart of cultural production is the question of the relationships between commerce and creativity, or between the drive to make profits, and those other values which also motivate production: the quest to make inter-esting, intriguing, pleasurable, beautiful, informative, enlightening products. As Chapter 2 showed, even in the complex professional era (which, follow-ing Williams 1981, I am dating from the 1920s, but which markedly intensi-fies in the post-Second World War period), as large corporations began to dominate cultural production, much cultural work was nevertheless based on a certain amount of operational autonomy for creative workers and man-agers. In the 1970s and 1980s, businesses of all kinds were going through a long phase of organisational innovation and restructuring. So how did these changes affect the cultural industries?

In this chapter, I address a number of issues outlined in Chapter 2 (pp. 77–83). First, I consider the following linked questions.

- In what ways have relationships between creativity and commerce changed?
- Linked to this, how have the distinctive organisational features of the cultural industries in the complex professional era of cultural production changed?
- What changes have there been in the extent to which creative workers within the cultural industries determine how their work will be edited, promoted, circulated? (This is a question about the extent to which crea-tive **autonomy** has been expanded or diminished.)

I begin by examining competing ways of understanding changes in the manage-ment of creative work in the cultural industries. I argue against accounts that see a move towards greater operational autonomy in commercial enterprises. I then show this by examining the significance of the increasing role of marketing and market research in cultural production, including at the creative stage. I confront directly the issue of whether creative control is getting looser or tighter, using evi-dence drawn from studies of journalism, popular music and live theatre. In these domains, we can see further evidence of shifting relationships between creativity and commerce, and a potential erosion of autonomy. Autonomy continues to be a feature of cultural production, but it also continues to involve considerable sacrifices on the part of cultural workers. The issue of the changing conditions of cultural work is then addressed in greater detail in the final section of the chapter.

MANAGING CULTURAL PRODUCTION: LOOSE CONTROL OF CREATIVITY, TIGHT CONTROL OF CIRCULATION

Management in the cultural industries fundamentally involves negotiating tensions between commercial imperatives, on the one hand, and creative or informational goals, on the other.[1] Management analysts Howard Davis

---

1   Amongst those who recognise and explore this fact are the following: Banks (2007); Hes-mondhalgh and Baker (2011: Chapter 4); Lampel, Shamsie and Lant (2006); Ryan (1992).

and Richard Scase (2000: 104–27) have provided one account of changes in the management of symbolic creativity. They argue that there has been a shift in the way that the cultural industries are organised. Using a Weberian approach that focuses on bureaucracy and charisma, they posit four ideal types of cultural industry organisation, based on how companies control and coordinate work (see Davis and Scase, 2000: 99, and Figure 7.1).

- *Commercial bureaucracies* where control and coordination are highly explicit and formalised, emphasising hierarchical reporting mechanisms and the close measuring and monitoring of employees for performance. There is a very strong emphasis on making a profit built into the functioning of the organisation.
- *Traditional/charismatic organisations* in which a high level of coordination is achieved by means of shared values, but 'mechanisms of formal control are relatively less developed'. These tend to be small businesses. There is less emphasis in working life on profit than in other organisations. Charismatic leaders – often owner-managers – tend to provide direction.
- *Cultural bureaucracies* usually operating under a public service remit, where there is a high degree of formalised control and hierarchically structured authority relations, but coordination is achieved by means of relatively autonomous departments. There are strong clashes over commercial pressures. Davis and Scase seem to have the BBC in mind here.
- *Network organisations* which tend to be micro-companies and are essentially too small to have formalised control or coordination. They operate in networks with other companies.

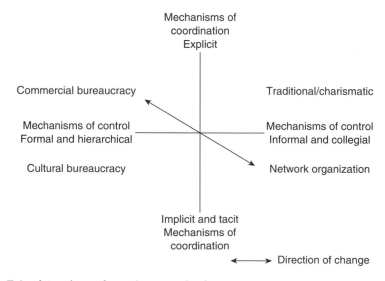

Figure 7.1   A typology of creative organisations

Source: Davis and Scase, 2000: 99

Davis and Scase believe that a major shift in cultural industry organisations took place during the 1990s: the decline of the traditional/charismatic organisation and of the cultural bureaucracy and the corresponding rise of the commercial bureaucracy and network organisations (2000: 102).

Traditional/charismatic firms, such as the small publishing houses that were the centre of the book industry until the 1950s, were bought up by corporations and put within commercial bureaucracies. Cultural bureaucracies (such as the BBC) came under threat from commercial pressures. Network organisations have proliferated as more and more work is outsourced from cultural and commercial bureaucracies.

For Davis and Scase, changes *within* commercial bureaucracies have been just as important as the increasing presence of such companies in the cultural industries. They claim that as large conglomerates entered into the cultural industries in the 1960s and 1970s, they attempted to bureaucratise creative work in a number of ways: by rationalising and specialising work tasks, curtailing the autonomy of employees by stipulating duties, and establishing strict line management. However, according to Davis and Scase, such practices soon fell out of favour and were replaced by new organisational structures.

In order to move beyond mere compliance on the part of employees and foster the kinds of commitment found in smaller companies, commercial bureaucracies began to break up the larger organisation into smaller autonomous operating units. Instead of strict, hierarchical line management, workers were given autonomy for operational decision-making. In Davis and Scase's account, this resulted in 'highly decentralised organisational structures operating units functioning as subsidiary companies' (p. 139). Under this new system, control was exercised by means of tight financial budgets, the setting of deadlines, and measuring outputs (pp. 140–1). These changes took place 'in the 1990s, and sometimes earlier' (p. 130). Management-worker relations become more like those between purchasers and providers and, because work could therefore either be done in-house or out-of-house, this led to the growth of network firms outside the company (and, presumably, 'downsizing' within the commercial bureaucracy).

This is an interesting attempt to understand change, but it is a flawed one. Davis and Scase overemphasise organisational change, especially in commercial bureaucracies.[2] In particular, they misrepresent the 1950–1980 period, drawing on assumptions derived from other industries. Substantial operational autonomy for creative personnel has been a feature of large cultural industry companies *throughout* the complex professional era, not only in the 1990s (Ryan, 1992; Toynbee, 2000). Davis and Scase recognise that creative personnel are given relative autonomy and it may be that they are referring primarily to the operational autonomy of creative managers, but even here their

---

2 It would have been helpful if Davis and Scase had given concrete examples of pre-1990s commercial bureaucracies of the 'old' kind.

historical assumptions are not supported by the evidence. In the large publishing companies established in the post-war era, for example, commissioning editors were given considerable independence (Coser et al., 1982), as indeed were A&R personnel in record companies. The film industry made the kind of move from 'bureaucracy' to 'networks' that Davis and Scase describe from the early 1940s onwards and producers (the key creative managers in that industry) increasingly came to operate as independent companies during the 1950s and 1960s. It is also true that some companies did try to control production more closely during the period 1950–1980 (the period Davis and Scase are discussing as the era of the 'old' commercial bureaucratic model). One example would be formatted popular fiction, such as Mills & Boon's romance novels, but such formatted production with tight control over budgets and outcomes long preceded the 1950–1980 period and, besides, often took place in smaller companies that Davis and Scase might categorise as 'traditional/charismatic' rather than in the commercial bureaucracies.

There *have* been organisational innovations during what I am calling the complex professional era (from the 1920s on, but especially the 1950s onwards), but Davis and Scase are wrong to assume that the 1990s can be seen as the crucial period for change. Many shifts preceded that decade. For example, a key move towards divisional structures in the major record companies took place in the 1970s and was based on generic divisions that were already in place when record companies were smaller (see Christianen, 1995: 89–91; Negus, 1999: 47–50).[3]

Ryan's (1992) research on cultural industry organisations provides a better basis for assessing change and continuity in the management of creativity than does Davis and Scase's model. Chapter 2, drawing on Ryan, outlined the division of cultural labour and organisational form that was characteristic of the complex professional era. As we saw there, a number of cultural work functions had emerged by the middle of the twentieth century – namely, primary creative personnel/symbol creators, technical craftworkers, creative managers, unskilled and semi-skilled labour and owners and executives. The organisational form common across nearly all cultural industry companies was one in which creative personnel were loosely controlled by creative managers acting on behalf of the interests of owners and executives, but where circulation and reproduction were much more tightly coordinated. In smaller companies, owner-managers acted like creative managers when dealing with creative personnel, but like executives when negotiating relationships with outside distribution, reproduction, marketing and publicity organisations.

So to what extent is the distinctive division of labour and organisational form – involving loose control of creativity by creative managers but tight control of

---

3   There are strong echoes in Davis and Scase's model of the faulty historical assumptions in research on 'post-Fordism' and 'flexible specialisation' in the cultural industries. See Christopherson and Storper (1986; 1989) and Lash and Urry (1994: Chapter 5) for the most sophisticated versions of cultural industry post-Fordism, and Aksoy and Robins (1992) and Hesmondhalgh (1996) for critiques of their positions.

circulation by executives – a stable one? And what might this tell us about chang-ing relationships between creativity and commerce in the cultural industries? One way to examine these inter-related questions is by examining the role of market-ing and market research. For it is through marketing in particular, as Ryan (1992: 30) pointed out, that cultural organisations will most intensively seek to impose some control over the unpredictability and arationality of cultural production.

THE INCREASING IMPORTANCE OF MARKETING AND MARKET RESEARCH

The most important change in the organisational structure of cultural indus-tries in recent decades has been that the variety of activities gathered under the title 'marketing', including market research, have become professional-ised and more important to the coordination of activities in the cultural indus-tries. This represents a further tightening of control over circulation strategies.

The other major relevant aspects of marketing besides research – design, packaging, advertising and publicity management – have been present in the cultural industries for many decades, but have also increased their impor-tance and visibility. Budgets for advertising in films produced by the major Hollywood studios soared in the 1980s, 1990s and 2000s:

- Even though the average cost of producing the negative/first copy of a major-produced film more than doubled between 1980 and 1995 to US$39 million, during the same period advertising budgets greatly increased their proportion of total costs, to nearly 45 per cent (based on Dale, 1997: 31).
- Grant and Wood (2004: 65) report that, by 2002, production budgets had risen to US$58.8 million, with print and advertising (P&A, in industry parlance) costs taking average costs to nearly US$90 million.
- According to Edward Jay Epstein (2005a), P&A costs for a studio film in 2003 averaged US$39 million, which is US$18.4 million more per film than studios actually recovered from box office receipts (though other sources complement these).
- The marketing costs for the *Matrix* sequels of 2003 exceeded US$100 million dollars (Menand, 2005: 85).

Advertising has long had a key role to play in the film industry, but there was a move in the 1990s towards 'blitzkrieg marketing' (Dale, 1997: 32), which is when blockbusters open simultaneously across a particular coun-try, rather than being 'rolled out' in different regions.[4] *Jaws* was considered to have 'opened wide' (geddit?) in 1975, when it was released on 460 screens in

---

4   Justin Wyatt (1998) tells the story of how such a strategy of saturation releasing devel-oped in the 1970s as a result of marketing and distribution innovations in independent companies in the art, adult and family film genres.

its first day. By 1995, say Grant and Wood (2004: 77), virtually all of the 150 or so movies released by the majors opened on more than 800 screens, while by 2001, openings on 2000 or 3000 screens were commonplace. *Harry Potter and the Sorcerer's Stone* opened in that year, on 8200 screens – a quarter of all the cinemas in the USA at the time. Such figures greatly reinforce **the block-buster syndrome** – whereby fewer big hits dominate the cultural industries and popular culture in general.[5] In fact, domestic box office has for some time been diminishing as a proportion of total revenue for films, as international sales and 'ancillary' forms of revenue such as DVD and download sales have grown, but a good opening had become an important part of the publicity for films, with its knock-on implications for overseas distribution, for purchases of DVDs by rental chains and consumers, and increasingly today, for downloads via online film subscription retailers or digital television one-off purchases.

Marketing is often thought of as something that happens after the other stages of cultural production have occurred, as something that is carried out on a completed project. But this downplays the increasingly important role of marketing, and the way it is used to inform the conception and creation of cultural products. It has also become much more significant in industries where it has traditionally played a minor role. This matters because it potentially undermines the traditional division between the loose control of creative work and tight control of reproduction and circulation, which, as we saw in Chapter 2, constitutes the distinctive organisational form of cultural production in the complex professional era. Marketing departments have been consulted for decades on the likely success of cultural products that will require significant investment, whether in the form of production costs or on the basis of large payments to the creators. As Sarah Baker and I ascertained in our (2011a) empirical examination of creative work in three cultural industries, what is new is the increasing prestige of marketing departments and their greater clout in settings where decisions are negotiated concerning the selection of prospective acts or products and how they might be modified to achieve 'success'. Here is how one music PR company director answered our question about whether marketing and PR people now have greater influence than before.

> In terms of presentation of creation, how something is viewed, yes, definitely…. [I]n terms of artistic creation, yes, sometimes we do have input. More often we're in the background but it is starting to become more and more frequent. People are willing to listen to us a lot more. (Hesmondhalgh and Baker, 2011a: 54)

---

5 See, among other treatments, Stringer (2003). See also Chapter 9 of this book, where the 'long tail' thesis, which implicitly predicts that the internet will lead to the end of this syndrome, is also discussed.

A magazine editor described how a magazine company he had worked for shifted from a system of having a marketing person or two assigned to individual publications, to one where an overall marketing department covered all music publications in the company:

> So instead of having a marketing person as well as an advertising person for each magazine, attached to that magazine you had a self-directing marketing department which has its own priorities ... It was a situation where the marketing department turned up with [a magazine] and plonked it down on the editor's table. 'There's your new logo, we've designed your new logo' ... The editor was so furious that he left the room and subsequently moved to another job within [the company]. (Hesmondhalgh and Baker, 2011a: 104–5)

The shifts indicated by these workers may derive from a partial erosion, in the era of neo-liberalism and conglomeration, of the principle that creative work, at its best, is as autonomous of commerce as possible. This has not just been a feature of independent or alternative production (or what translators of the French sociologist Pierre Bourdieu's work on sociology of culture call 'restricted production'). It has also been apparent in mass or large-scale cultural production, though with a greater acceptance of a necessary role for commerce. It seems as though people working in cultural industry organisations across both 'mainstream' and 'alternative' forms of cultural production are finding it harder to argue against short-term commercial imperatives in the name of prestige or providing creative innovation. Greater levels of oligopolistic competition may put more pressure on firms to deliver higher profit margins, but just as important is the erosion of faith among cultural producers themselves in notions of autonomy and creative freedom, in the name of an often 'postmodernist' critique of supposed romanticism (Hesmondhalgh and Baker, 2011a). Box 7.1 explores the implications of this for the actual quality of cultural products.

Box 7.1   Effects of marketing on creativity: the high concept movie

So how does the increasing role of marketing affect the actual products made by the cultural industries? Chapter 11 of this book will examine a number of textual developments in the light of the changes and continuities outlined in this book, but for now, the Hollywood film industry provides an interesting example of potential dynamics. Justin Wyatt argues that, in the conglomerating film industry of the 1980s, the increased role of marketers in making decisions over what

(Continued)

(Continued)

film – and which types of films – get made led to the rise of the 'high concept movie' in Hollywood. This is, in essence, a film, the central idea of which can be conveyed in a single sentence – both in its initial 'pitch' (a metaphor from baseball) to financiers and so on, and to audiences in the marketing of the product. The film *The Player* (1992) dramatised this beautifully in the form of numerous fictional pitches, 'in 25 words or less', such as 'It's *Pretty Woman* meets *Out of Africa*'.[6] At the core of high concept, then, is the reduction of narrative to a simple, underlying idea. Wyatt considers that the rise of the high concept film was a major factor in bringing about a decline in the quality of Hollywood cinema during the 1980s and 1990s following its embracing of cultural prestige in the 1970s (see Biskind, 1998). It is not impossible for qualities of complexity, richness and ambivalence to survive the domination of high concept – and Wyatt pays insufficient attention to this possibility – but it almost certainly makes such qualities more difficult to achieve, other things being equal. Although there are many countervailing tendencies against formula and repetition in cultural production, and although marketers are quite happy to promote original products as distinctive and unique, there is a strong tendency in marketing to embrace the familiar. As Bill Ryan puts it (1992: 220), 'Marketers need predictable commodities to work their magic on'. Equally, in the words of one veteran market researcher, Hy Hollinger, quoted by Wyatt (1994: 59), 'Anything that is innovative is hard for market research to clue in on'.

Audience research and autonomy in film, advertising and television

Central to contemporary marketing is market research, or audience research as it is usually known in the cultural industries. A major component of the growing influence of marketing in cultural production has been the rising intensity of efforts to use audience research as a means of controlling risk. Here, too, there are potential implications for relationships between creativity and commerce.

The problem with market research in the cultural industries is that every product is different (see Coser et al., 1982: 203–5) and this makes it extremely time-consuming and onerous to track potential audience reactions to the myriad products on offer. It might be possible to use market research to test a new chocolate bar before it is launched, but it would be a monumental task

---

6   The fact that this great satire on Hollywood was produced within that very place is one of thousands of examples of how cultural industries are capable of critical reflexivity, at least within certain types of production.

for a television channel to test all the programmes it puts on. As a result most audience research has traditionally measured sales or exposure (Napoli, 2011) through quantitative measures that can track how many people watch television programmes ('ratings'), go to see films ('box office'), or buy recordings (charts, or in the strangely attractive parlance of the mid-twentieth century, 'the hit parade', and so on). The use of such data in cultural industries has enormous implications for the creative freedom of symbol creators. The degree to which an organisation monitors exposure and/or sales, and uses such exposure/sales to monitor performance, is an indicator of the degree to which that organisation is seeking to control creativity. Changes in measurement techniques and technologies can have notable impacts on production. For example, when the audience research group, Neilsen, introduced the much more accurate 'people meter' to measure US television audiences in 1987, it was discovered that cable television was far more popular than had been assumed, because the previously used diary methods tended to privilege the more easily remembered well known programmes shown on the major networks (Napoli, 2003: 88–9; Toynbee, 2006: 102). This gave rise to more advertising on cable channels, and the launch of more cable channels, with a significant effect on the ecology of US broadcasting. This has been exacerbated by the fact that these measurements are made public in the form of bestseller lists and so on. When the popular music trade publication *Billboard* introduced new, more accurate sales measurement techniques for its charts in 1991, the change showed that country music had been much more popular than had been recognised by the previous panel survey methods (see Anand and Peterson, 2000). It also suggested that the domination of the charts by the majors had been underplayed, and so the change hurt independent record labels, as their recordings made the charts much less frequently.[7]

With the growth of marketing in general, and more specifically within the cultural industries, there has been a marked increase in the use not only of such quantitative data, but also of other forms of qualitative data, that are intended to track how audiences interpret and emotionally respond to cultural products. The main instrument has been the focus group, where a small group of potential audience members are asked to reflect on a product, but there has also been increasing use of ethnographic methods where industry researchers 'hang out' with potential audience members.

The utilisation of both kinds of audience research, statistical and qualitative, has notably increased in the cultural industries. Justin Wyatt (1994: 155) affirms that, although market research was used occasionally in the classic Hollywood era, it was only in the late 1970s that the studios engaged systematically with it. This claim is supported by earlier studies, such as Hortense Powdermaker's classic anthropological study of Hollywood, where she

---

7 Success in music sales charts and 'hit parades' has always been a spur to further success, as other media such as radio, magazines and television look to such lists for indications of what music and trends they ought to be covering.

remarked that a typical studio 'research department, situated in New York, is small, operates on a meager budget, and is not equipped to undertake extensive work' (1951: 33). Instead, creative managers and film-makers relied on intuition and tacit knowledge. Wyatt attributes the shift towards market research in part to the purchase by general conglomerates of film companies in the 1960s. Films were now part of a culture that was used to market research for packaged goods. As releases fell and costs rose, executives wanted more accountability (Wyatt, 1994: 156).

Similar changes happened in the recording industry. Keith Negus (1999: 53) has described a shift in record company strategy away from 'inspired guesswork, hunches and intuition' and towards the widespread use of various research methods, including the electronic monitoring of sales, large-scale interview panels provided on subscription by a separate company and various broadcast data systems. Again, the shift seems to have taken place in the 1970s and, although Negus does not attribute the change to this, it was during this period that the recording industry was increasingly integrated into larger, general conglomerates. As for television, here is one television executive discussing the importance of research:

> Research is the key instrument in the selling of airtime because if I'm selling a minute or half a minute of airtime in *Coronation Street*, *Coronation Street* will have a number of categories, demographic categories, of viewers watching. It will have young ABC1 men or whatever. Now, unless you know precisely which demographic groups in which proportions are watching these programmes very scientifically you can't sell that audience at the optimum value to the advertiser. So, for example, an advertiser can buy adults in *Coronation Street* for eight pounds a thousand, but if he wants to buy ABC1 adults it might be forty-eight pounds a thousand. And if he wants to buy 16 to 24-year-old adults it might be seventy-eight pounds a thousand and that's a hell of a different yield. So it's a bit like an aeroplane or a hotel. You're maximising the yields of your rooms or your airtime seconds by optimising who buys what audiences ...[8]

This way of talking about research would have been impossible 30 years ago in Europe. Only since the 1980s has market research become such a priority that software packages of sufficient sophistication have been developed to undertake such exact calculations. It is not technology that has driven the change, however. Such technology came into being largely because of a desire on the part of executives to exert more careful control over broadcasting production and scheduling, partly because of the erosion of public

---

8 From an interview I conducted with the Chief Executive of a British media group in February 2001. ABC1 refers to professional and skilled occupational groups – the most desirable target consumers.

service imperatives, but also because of an enormous increase in competition in the television market.

A particularly notorious use of market research in what is effectively still the creative stage of cultural production is the screening of movies to test audiences, with a view to amending the film in response to the result of audience questionnaires. The most quoted example is *Fatal Attraction* (1987). Glenn Close's character originally committed suicide to an aria from *Madame Butterfly*, but, after poor test responses, the ending to the film was changed and her character was killed. A *Los Angeles Times* report from 1999 stated that most major Hollywood films were tested and nearly all of this was done by the National Research Group based in Los Angeles (Lerner, 1999). Many successful films can test poorly, but go on to achieve success. They include innovative movies such as *The Blair Witch Project* (1999) and *Reservoir Dogs* (1992) (Lerner, 1999). Lerner outlined how such market research operated in the late 1990s. The National Research Group would recruit an audience, the demographic characteristics of which supposedly matched those of the film's target audience. They filled in response cards and some may have taken part in a focus group discussion. Some directors, especially those of comedies, will apparently embrace the process, while many will resist and find that executives can use tests as ammunition. Such tests are a means of attempting to find objectivity in order to deal with the perennial unpredictability of the film business, but directors opposed to the process think that testing favours a restrictive control of creativity. As one director puts it, 'If the test is bad, the studio panics. If it goes well, they say, "It doesn't mean anything"' (Andrew Bergman, quoted by Willens, 2000: 11).

Not all changes in the cultural industries, and in the use of audience research, can be uniformly understood as an increase in commercially orientated aspects of cultural industry work at the expense of creative autonomy. Take, for example, the effects of the 'creative revolution' in advertising. According to Thomas Frank (1997), substantial sections of American business in the 1960s developed a critique of their own industries, and he focuses in particular on advertising and menswear. The new style of advertising was not based on countercultural ideas forged by hippies, rather it was founded on longstanding ideas of a resistance to conformity, particularly those developed in widely-read and debated books and articles of the 1950s, such as Whyte's *Organization Man* (1956) The result was a shift in advertising, with a much greater stress on suggestion, humour and style. But there was also a shift in advertising practice, and greater emphasis on advertising as an art, rather than a science based on careful analysis of research.[9] Discussing the

---

9   This shift provides some of the drama in the great US TV series *Mad Men* (2007-). The alliteration of its hero's name Don Draper seemingly echoes that of Bill Bernbach, the key figure in Madison Avenue's creative revolution (see Frank 1997: 55ff), but Draper's agency is a more typical, conservative organisation and Draper only slowly makes the transition to a new era.

British version of this 'creative revolution' in the late 1970s and 1980s, Sean Nixon (1997: 195) wrote that new practices were 'established in opposition to what was represented as the boring and unimaginative advertising produced by the large multinational agencies'. The old advertising practices were reliant on the written or spoken word and attempted to convey the 'unique selling point' of the product. The new, more creative advertisements worked at the levels of desire and identity rather than adopting the 'hard sell'.[10] The shift towards 'creative' advertising involved creative personnel working in relatively autonomous groups that were separate from the buyers, planners and researchers. Copywriters and art directors became the crucial creative pairing at the heart of the modern agency, and were accorded a much greater level of prestige than before, one that was akin to that of artists. Whereas Frank focused on the cultural legacy of mid-century anti-conformism, Nixon forefronted new forms of market research in advertising agencies, which meant that advertisers were much more concerned with targeting specific market segments than entire social classes or 'the mass audience'. So, here, according to Nixon, a greater use of market research seemingly gave rise to higher levels of operational autonomy for creative personnel in the most commercially orientated of all the cultural industries. In this respect, however, the changes that Nixon discussed may be the result of a particularly strong emphasis on creativity and autonomy in the third quarter of the twentieth century. Similar moves towards greater levels of creative autonomy can also be seen in the rise of the 'Movie Brats' era of film-makers in American cinema and in rock music. However, a later set of organisational changes in advertising companies was based on somewhat different notions of creativity, mediated through contemporary notions of entrepreneurship, whereby all workers were expected to be flexible innovators (Nixon, 2011). In some companies this led to a tighter integration of creatives into wider project teams, alongside account planners, buyers and researchers. But some firms, such as BBH (Bartle Bogle Hegarty), who continued to define themselves as particularly creative, retained a sense that 'creatives' (copywriters, art directors, etc.) were a special case, and a privileged source of creativity (Nixon, 2011: 206).

Television provides a further case study of the impact of marketing and market research in cultural industries. In her (2005) ethnographic study of the BBC, Georgina Born describes how, in the 1990s, using the model of US broadcasting where 'marketing plays an integral part both in the conception of channels and in determining their outputs', British television was transformed (and many other European public service broadcasters followed suit). The notion of branding – both of the BBC itself and of individual channels such as its pop music station, BBC Radio 1 – became particularly prevalent. As one executive told Born, 'It all comes from defining the brand:

---

10 Grabher (2002) suggests that by the late 1990s, Soho, the heart of the UK advertising industry, had become the new centre of global creative advertising.

once you've done that you can create your world with those values in mind; it makes decisions on content easy'. For Born, this led to a situation where the values of the BBC and each of its services 'now had to be consciously formulated and *performed* by branding, where before they had been part of the collective subconscious' (2005: 268). A major problem for BBC staff was *artificiality*, that the surface changes hid a deeper reality. How to make the new relationship to BBC values authentic? The BBC felt it had to market itself to gain trust, but 'BBC professionals were haunted by an awareness that the more trust is marketed, the less substantial it seems' (ibid).

One way in which executives sought to make contemporary BBC public service values more authentic and lived was via an increasing use of audience research. The BBC had established a Listener Research department in the late 1930s. According to historian Asa Briggs, by 1961 BBC Audience Research was 'probably the largest department of its type maintained by any broadcasting organisation in the world' (quoted by Born, 2005: 270). However, when organisational sociologist Tom Burns carried out his fine study of the BBC in the 1960s and early 1970s (Burns, 1977) he found that managers made rather limited use of such research, and programme-makers demonstrated an 'apparent imperviousness to outside criticism' (quoted by Born, 2005: 269). Burns was adamant that this was not the result of complacency. Rather, BBC officials were perpetually concerned with quality and many were 'self-critical to the point of hypersensitivity ... The pressure on those responsible for programmes is such that deeper analysis of audience reactions would amount to an intolerable strain'(ibid.).

In the 1990s, as the BBC marketised under pressure from the neo-liberal Conservative UK government, audience research at the BBC became less independent. Much of it was conducted in order to serve the needs of senior managers, and in close consultation with them. There was also more of it – the steady flow of information about audiences became a flood of statistical and qualitative data – and much greater use of focus groups together with audience ethnography performed by market research groups. The aim, Born writes, was to provide a 'subtler, more humanising knowledge of audiences than ratings, and to throw light on the meanings and emotions attached to broadcasting'. The proponents of such research at the BBC genuinely saw it as a responsible attempt to understand the publics that the corporation sought to serve, and in a way that was more accurate to lived experience than ratings. Yet much of the research was banal or contradictory. Programme makers felt that the research failed to address the complexity of what they did, and of what they were trying to achieve.

Born provides a balanced appraisal. There was no question, she writes, that 'qualitative research does generate more humanising representations of audiences than ratings'(286), and this helped to boost reflection and stimulate debate at the BBC about the audiences they were trying to serve. But the move to using greater audience research also brought delusions. One was that focus groups could come closer than ratings to providing a transparent window on to the audience. For Born, in the context of the BBC and other cultural institutions, focus groups in reality offer a substitution in which a social part represents the social whole. 'But what is this whole?' asks Born. 'Nothing more than a sociality which the research conjures up as a fantasy and keeps at bay' (287). A second delusion was that focus group research can help to foster creativity and invention in production. Born points out a number of problems with this: the quality of audience insights delivered was often 'achingly banal' (287); research examines existing tastes for past programmes; this can frame 'spaces for attention' but does not generate new ideas. In Born's view, the deterministic use of research undermined creative responsibility and eroded the BBC's capacity to carry out its central obligation of delivering high-quality programmes.[11]

A note on audience research in the digital age

In recent years, digitalisation has changed audience behaviour, but has also led to the development of new forms of audience research – or audience surveillance. So what might the implications of these changes be for relations between creativity and commerce, and for the organisation and management of cultural production? Napoli (2011) claims that technological developments have produced two key changes in media audiences – greater fragmentation and greater (inter)activity – and that these have major implications for how the cultural industries conduct audience research. Napoli argues that the fragmentation of audiences has resulted in problems of accuracy and 'unpredictable fluctuations' in the data, making it harder to say what audiences are doing, as well as how they might behave and respond to future products. At the same time, a more interactive media environment makes it harder for audience researchers to capture the more active behaviour of audiences as they skip between sites, block content, fast forward, etc. But technological developments have also meant that new streams of data can be gathered and analysed about audiences, including their habits, preferences, degrees of engagement, and appreciation, mainly because audiences now carry out 'online chatter' in public forums that are much more open to scrutiny from researchers than before. For some researchers, this represents a worrying opportunity for cultural industries to carry out surveillance of audiences – or 'users', as we are now often known in more digital parts of the new cultural-industry universe. We shall return to this issue in Chapter 10, in discussing how phenomena such as search engines and social networking sites affect relationships between producers and audiences, and in particular, whether digitalisation has led to a democratisation of such relationships. For now, however, the main issue to be considered is

---

11 The use of audience research in relation to programme production at the BBC declined after the 1990s heyday, notes Born, but instead came to be applied to BBC networks (television channels and radio stations) and schedules, rather than programmes.

the changing relationships between creativity and commerce, and in this respect, we can note Napoli's view, which is that the new audience research technologies and their uses by cultural industries reflect a continuing rationalisation of audience understanding. By this, Napoli explains, he means that 'the days of movie studio executives, or television or radio station programmes, or magazine or newspaper editors making decisions based on their own subjective assessments of what will succeed and what will fail have largely been replaced' by a decision-making environment that is increasingly scientific and data-driven driven, 'with more impressionistic or instinctive approaches to audience understanding increasingly falling by the wayside' (Napoli, 2011: 11). If it is true, as the research discussed in this section suggests, that the increasing use of audience research is a factor that gives more weight to commercial rather than creative considerations in cultural production, then Napoli's perspective should prepare us to expect further moves in this direction, given the intensification of audience research that new digital technologies potentially afford.

CONTROL OF CREATIVITY: TIGHTER OR LOOSER?

The increasing presence and status of marketing, then, represents a shift in the relations between creativity and commerce, and also in the organisational structure of cultural production, whereby the relative autonomy of symbol creators is threatened. But we need to examine these changes in somewhat greater detail by further examining what has happened to the freedom (or otherwise) of symbol makers. Marketing and market research are not the only threats to creative autonomy and to the ways in which symbol makers might enrich contemporary societies.[12] An examination of developments in journalism will allow us to explore such threats more, because questions regarding autonomy from commercial, ideological and state pressure have been particularly debated in studies of journalism. I then turn to somewhat more difficult terrain, to examine notions of autonomy and control in the realm of entertainment and other forms of cultural production that are not so based on the sharing of knowledge and information.

Journalistic autonomy

Journalists have generally placed considerable value on their autonomy from owners and from other powerful influences in society. A series of

---

12 My perspective is that high degrees of autonomy for symbol makers in modern societies are likely, other things being equal, to serve the interests of democratisation and well-being for greater numbers of people. (See the Introduction.)

important sociological studies in the 1970s suggested that journalists worked relatively autonomous from the demands of newspaper owners and senior executives (Gans, 1979; Tuchman, 1978; Tunstall, 1971). The notion of professionalism – in the sense of an ethos of serving the public via the pursuit of objectivity (see Hallin, 2000: 220) – was central to this notion of relative independence. In his study of the big US TV news networks, and the two main US news periodicals *Time* and *Newsweek*, Herbert Gans, for example, saw the control of owners and shareholders as having been delegated to managers who in turn delegated decision-making to journalist professionals who insisted on individual autonomy.

Autonomy has been central to the notion of journalistic professionalism, and vice versa,[13] but any consideration of independence should not be confined to the question of freedom or otherwise from the influence of owners and shareholders. Autonomy and independence are also about freedom from the influence from commercial goals (achieving profits for the employing organisation), from powerful sources, and from dominant discourses and values, especially those relating to nation, class and gender. Some analysts – particularly those writing from political economy approaches – have argued that the independence of journalists has been overstated, both in relation to owners, and to other factors such as commerce, sources and dominant values. James Curran (1990: 120), for example, preferred the term 'licensed autonomy' to 'relative autonomy' in considering news and remarked that 'journalists are allowed to be independent only as long as their independence is exercised in a form that conforms to the requirements of their employing organisations'. Curran also argued that, in the 1970s and 1980s, the British press adopted a more partisan stance than had been the case for many decades, under the influence of a new generation of interventionist owners (see Box 7.2). He provided evidence of how, on the one hand, under this new regime, British press journalists were pushed by their senior executives to write stories presenting the left-wing Greater London Council of the 1980s in a negative light. Broadcasting organisations, on the other hand, portrayed the Council and their policies more favourably, partly because of the way public service obligations were internalised, even in commercial news organisations.

---

13 Others have questioned the role of professionalism in maintaining autonomy and independence in journalism. Philip Elliott (1977: 150) characterised post-war journalistic professionalism much more negatively as a form of self-legitimation, where skill in routine tasks (keeping to deadlines and so on) was elevated to the occupational ideal, although he was expressing this view before the onslaught of commercialism unleashed by the changes discussed in this book. Hallin's more upbeat assessment is perhaps a product of the fact that, in an era of marketisation, the faults of journalistic professionalism's inward-looking complacency and clubbiness seem outweighed by its outward orientation towards objectivity and serving publics.

Box 7.2   Media moguls and control of news

In the market professional era (the late nineteenth and early twentieth centuries), strong-minded individuals dominated the family firms that ran the newspapers and publishing companies which were at the heart of the cultural industries. In other industries, family firms with dominant figures have given way to complex systems of control, under boards of directors, where most directors represent other companies and there are many interlocking directorships. This new pattern of ownership has come to the cultural industries as well (and, as in other industries, it has been further complicated by the increasing involvement of financial institutions such as pension funds), but the figure of the *media mogul*, who owns a dominant interest and has an overwhelming control over his own company, has been remarkably persistent in the complex professional era. Even as cultural industry corporations grow in size and complexity, a large number remain under the control of such individuals.

Many of these moguls are prepared to push their own political views extremely hard via their cultural industry interests. Perhaps the most spectacular example of the pursuit of political ambition via media ownership in advanced industrial countries in recent years has been that of Silvio Berlusconi, who, by promoting his political party 'Forza Italia' across his various television, publishing and sports interests, managed to make himself prime minister of Italy in 1994–1995 (see Mazzoleni, 1995) and again from 2001–2006, and 2008–11.[14] The most internationally prominent of all media moguls, however, is Rupert Murdoch. He represents an extraordinary case of the use of media interests to promote a political agenda. Curran (1990) showed how *The Sunday Times*, once it had been taken over by Rupert Murdoch's News International, moved from being a centre right, even liberal, newspaper to become a Thatcherite one (1990: 132–3). Murdoch revived the strategies of direct control associated with the press barons of the early twentieth century, such as Northcliffe, Beaverbrook and Hearst (the man on whom Orson Welles based *Citizen Kane*). Murdoch would apparently rewrite leaders that were insufficiently supportive of the hard-right Prime Minister at the time, Margaret Thatcher, and remove left-leaning or moderate conservative editors. He also exerted pressure on his centrist editor at *The Times* by refusing to fix an editorial budget and thereby grasped the chance to approve any editorial decision that needed significant spending. Likewise the centrist editor at *The Sunday Times* was forced out to make way for the Thatcher-supporting Andrew Neil. Overt and abrasive pressure was applied to journalists to reorientate the editorial direction

(Continued)

14 See Downey (2006) for further discussion of Berlusconi and media power. Mancini and Hallin (2001) argue that Berlusconi's 2001 success was not achieved by using his television stations for propaganda, but by using his television empire as a resource for negotiation and bargaining with other political, economic and social institutions.

(Continued)

of the paper: more than 100 left the paper between 1981 and 1986 (the staff was 170-strong in 1981). *The Sunday Times* has pursued a very conservative editorial policy ever since, as has *The Times*.

But surely, given that Murdoch owns a vast global media empire, operational autonomy is left to editors? In the words of a later *Sunday Times* editor, Andrew Neil,

> Rupert has an uncanny knack of being there even when he is not. When I did not hear from him and I knew his attention was elsewhere, he was still uppermost in my mind ... Rupert expects his papers to stand broadly for what he believes: a combination of right-wing republicanism from America with undiluted Thatcherism from Britain. (Quoted in Curran, 1998)

In 2003, this knack was confirmed in the most striking way, when a survey by media commentator Roy Greenslade found that the biggest-selling and most influential newspapers of the 175 owned by News Corporation across the world unanimously supported the invasion of Iraq, which the USA, UK and their allies were about to embark on at the time. Just as significantly, opponents of the war, whether political leaders or ordinary citizens, were routinely derided. Greenslade commented, 'You have got to admit that Rupert Murdoch is one canny press tycoon because he has an unerring ability to choose editors across the world who think just like him. How else can we explain the extraordinary unity of thought in his newspaper empire about the need to make war on Iraq?' (*The Guardian*, 17 February 2003).

Moguls receive massive amounts of attention – partly because the media thrive on reporting the actions of charismatic individuals. Such interventions are extremely important but they are also, in the context of the cultural industries, relatively rare. They illustrate that autonomy is never irrevocable, but focusing to an excessive degree on media moguls can distract attention from the more systemic features of these industries. It can obscure the centrality – and ambivalence – of the operational autonomy granted to journalists and other creative personnel in cultural industry companies. Direct intervention by owners and senior executives of the kind analysed by Curran must not be ignored, but neither should the very indirect coercion exercised in everyday professional routines. The notion of journalistic autonomy still holds strong as a means of gaining legitimacy and credibility for cultural industry organisations. Gitlin (1997: 8) suggested that, since its takeover by General Electric in 1990, NBC had routinely covered scandals involving its parent company General Electric, and ABC News's Peter Jennings had 'gone out of his way to cover criticisms of Disney' (who owned ABC). In Gitlin's view, the greater danger was self-censorship – that is, journalists deciding not to pursue certain interests that might clash with a corporate culture – and that news media would be used to promote entertainment aspects of the conglomerate's business. (I return to these issues in Chapter 11.)

Even in the last century, Curran's point was supported by evidence of conglomerates using news organs to promote their business interests. The previous chapter discussed News International's cross-promotion of their satellite broadcasting interests through their UK newspapers (Hardy, 2010). Conglomeration in the US TV networks and local press encouraged greater commercialism in the 1980s and 1990s. The rise of the Fox News Channel heralded a new form of partisanship, previously alien to American journalistic traditions. And yet, as family-owned newspapers were purchased by conglomerates expected to provide a return to shareholders, there were more and more examples of increasing damage to 'the Wall of Separation between Church and State' (Bagdikian, 2000: xxv–xxvii), with the Church in this metaphor being editorial independence and the State being the business interests of the newspaper. For instance, in the late 1990s, a new CEO of Time-Mirror Company, one Mark Willes, reorganised the company's flagship paper, *The Los Angeles Times*, so that news stories would be allocated by a staff that included someone from the business department of the newspaper. News staff were, it seems, increasingly involved in special corporate advertisements.

In addition to this, in many countries, not just the USA, the notion of journalistic autonomy was already being qualified by the increasing efforts on the part of other organisations and institutions to position themselves as key sources – and in this they were greatly aided by a rapidly growing public relations industry (Ewen, 1996). In the UK in 1963 there were an estimated 3000 public relations professionals, but by 1995 the top 150 consultancies alone employed a total of nearly 5000 staff (Miller, 1998: 67). While journalists in general retained an attitude of professional scepticism towards efforts to attract their interest and sympathy, in practice this often involved forming hierarchies of sources, from 'most trusted' down to 'unknown' and, therefore, 'untrustworthy'. Naturally, the most powerful organisations will often have the most credibility. Studies have shown that access to journalists does not depend entirely on resources – sometimes weaker and oppositional sources are given great prestige (Schlesinger and Tumber, 1994). Nevertheless the pressures on journalists exerted by the more powerful and wealthy organisations can be tremendous. Journalists, then, even if they act in relative autonomy from the requirements of owners and executives on a daily basis, are not independent of other pressures to pursue particular interests and their everyday autonomy is shaped and formed by the overall interests of the organisation they work for.[9]

There are reasons to question the real autonomy of even the very best examples of professional journalism from the interests of state and nation, and the ability of even the most reputed publications and programmes adequately to give coverage to structural problems in the societies in which they are based. This is true even in the heartland of American professional journalism: as James Curran puts it, 'the underlying conservatism of American society left a gelatinous imprint on American journalism' (Curran, 2011: 10). This was especially true of coverage of overseas interventions by the USA.

American media have generally supported American invasions of foreign countries, and critical perspectives have been given tiny amounts of space.[15] This, claims Curran (2011: 35), is largely a result of a 'strongly embedded though variegated imperial culture that conditions both politicians and journalists', but is also explained by the way in which American journalists turned to powerful sources in the White House, Pentagon and Department of State rather than to civil-society groups and independent intellectuals. The American news media have also contributed to a political acceptance of the extraordinary inequality of American society, where millions of people still live in poverty.

Nevertheless, with the accelerating decline of newspaper sales and advertising revenues in the 2000s, even the highly compromised 'high modernist' (Hallin, 1994) period of relatively autonomous professional journalism of the 1950s and 1960s starts to look like a golden age. Journalism, it is almost universally agreed, is in crisis, and particularly so in the USA, where newspapers have been devastated by a loss of readers and advertising income to the internet, made worse by the economic recession of the late 2000s (see McChesney and Nichols, 2010). The first domino to fall was the classified advertising that helped to sustain the local and regional press. Once display advertising went into a precipitous decline as well, bankruptcies at even some of the most prestigious regional newspapers soon followed. High-quality professional newspaper journalism in the complex professional era depended on high levels of advertising and newspaper sales. In the era of conglomeration, when returns and profits were still high, profit-seeking newspaper owners and executives were already laying off large numbers of journalists. This accelerated as the recession hit, fuelled by the internet's impact on sales. Far fewer reporters became available to cover major areas of news coverage, such as local city desks, and entire areas of coverage disappeared. Inevitably, the commercial pressures on journalists have further eroded autonomy during this period. The degree to which new forms of online journalism, notably 'citizen journalism', have helped to redeem this situation, is an issue that is addressed in Chapter 11.

Creativity, commerce and control in popular music and theatre

It is of course challenging to assess questions of truthfulness, accuracy and objectivity in relation to commercial goals in news. But in other industries oriented towards the production of entertainment and other pleasures, such questions of quality can prove even more difficult, because of the difficulties in arriving at shared notions of quality and performance. It might be feared,

---

15 Only in cases where there is dissent among elites was there any critical coverage of overseas intervention, most notably in the largely exceptional case of the Vietnam War (see Hallin, 1986).

for example, that a judgement on the quality of entertainment products is likely to be overly subjective. These issues cannot be dodged, but they should still be approached cautiously. I now examine changing relations between creativity and commerce in two other industries that are less concerned with 'information' than the press and broadcast news examined above. These add to the case studies of film, advertising and television discussed in the section on marketing above. The case of popular music allows us to examine how tensions between creativity and commerce were renegotiated in an age where less value has been placed on creative autonomy. The case of live theatre points to how different sections of the same industry might emphasise either commerce or creativity, but creative autonomy tends always to carry a cost – though its pursuit may still be worthwhile.

Popular music

Popular music has been a site for some of the most intriguing attempts to reconcile creative and financial goals in the context of a commercially-driven system. The 1960s and 1970s saw a remarkable marriage of commerce and creativity, as faced with demands for high levels of originality and meaningfulness on the part of youth audiences across much of the developed world, the recorded-music corporations granted considerable autonomy to talented musicians, in return for access to a newly empowered mass of young consumers. This built on earlier demands for autonomy in jazz and folk, and on a romantic and modernist disdain for commerce. For some time a substantial degree of artistic innovation and experimentation became possible, as record companies sought emergent sounds in a chaotic and unpredictable market. This was the tactic of throwing mud, etc. against the wall to see what might stick (see the discussion of recurring features of the cultural industries in the Introduction). But it produced an enormous quantity of strange and interesting music.[16] For Simon Frith, writing in 1981, rock was 'a mass-produced music that carries a critique of its own means of production' (Frith,1981: 11). Yet this contradiction was productive, and the demand for autonomy was shared in other forms besides rock. Fuelled by a new sense of anger and cultural empowerment, African-American, Asian, Latin-American, Caribbean and African musicians constantly broke new barriers of self-expression and sonic innovation during this period.

Much of the discourse about music relied on dubious romantic notions of authenticity and individuality. The critique of commerce was often self-contradictory and naïve. This made some anti-commercial thinking easy prey for postmodern and neo-liberal attacks in the backlash of the 1980s and 1990s.

---

16 Of course vast amounts of music continued to be made by musicians and consumed by audiences that were unaware of or uninterested in critiques of commerce (the many Northern and Eastern European variants of what in German is called *schlager* music for example). This too had its own charms, but that is a different issue. The point here is about the high levels of autonomy in rock and related genres.

By the 1990s and 2000s, some of the rigid opposition to commerce at the heart of the most anti-commercial sub-fields of rock music had begun to loosen. Or, to put it another way, the entire field had started to move towards a greater embracing of commerce. At the corporate end of production, in the 1980s, many of the most successful rock groups no longer made any pretension to question the commercial system that had helped to produce them. Examples would be successful soft metal acts such as Bon Jovi and Aerosmith. In the middle were massive rock acts that made gestures of anti-corporate politics, and indulged in charity exercises to save the planet, while accepting huge sponsorship deals with barely a second thought. At the 'independent' pole was the indie rock and pop that grew out of punk and post-punk, and the electronic music that echoed some of indie's ethics and aesthetics, which were caught between a furious critique of alienation, and a postmodern critique of the pretentiousness of hippies and other romantics who rejected capitalism.

Rock-related popular music's changing relationships with commerce can be illustrated by examining views of advertising and sponsorship. Bethany Klein (2009) has discussed how changing uses of rock in advertising have reflected and constituted changes in the relationship between commerce and creativity. She provides a series of quotations from the advertising trade press and from journalists claiming that the relationship between rock and advertising has irrevocably changed. For example, referring back to Nike's controversial use of the Beatles' song 'Revolution' in 1987 – a key moment which Klein analyses in some detail – the trade magazine *Creativity* was able to proclaim in 2003: 'At the time some purists screamed "Heresy!" Now it's no big deal'. Music licensing by advertisers was described by the same magazine as 'what used to be called selling out'. *The New York Times* reckoned in 1999 that 'the stigma of selling out has begun to wane', while *The New York Daily News* decided that 'suddenly serenading clothes and cars has become the hallmark of cool' (all quotations from Klein, 2009: 20). Klein relates these discursive shifts to some of the developments analysed in this book, including the marketisation of broadcasting, the consequent concentration of ownership in radio, and the vagaries of copyright law (the surviving Beatles were powerless to prevent 'Revolution' being used by Nike because American copyright law had no 'moral right' allowing creators to determine the uses of their work). Analysing a wide range of attitudes and practices, Klein questions the way in which the use of certain songs in advertising can affect people's experiences of music that has played an enriching role in their lives. She examines cases such as the use of Iggy Pop's song 'Lust for Life', which is about the experience of addiction and its consequences, in an advert for Caribbean cruises, and a jeans company's adoption of an anti-patriotism song by Creedence Clearwater Revival, with the anti-patriotism message suppressed. Nevertheless, as Klein shows, opposition to such use of adverts has by no means died out in popular music, and in popular culture. The satirical magazine *The Onion*, for example, took up the use of 'Lust for Life' in a piece on a fictional advertisement for a bank (at time of writing, this is easily findable via a search engine).

Continuing tensions between creativity and commerce in popular music were also evident when, in 2009–2011, after the publication of Klein's book, Iggy Pop himself, an icon of punk rebellion, appeared in a series of UK television and billboard adverts for car insurance aimed at the elderly. The later adverts were witty and Pop played his role with a wry recognition of the absurdity of his situation. However, that did not stem the widespread disappointment and even fury of his former admirers. Continuing resistance to commerce is also evident in cases such as the lasting reverence in Anglophone countries for the comedian Bill Hicks, who died in 1994, but whose inspired rants against commercialism in popular music (and in modern culture) are still widely consumed on DVD and YouTube.[17]

Live theatre

For a very different case of tensions between creativity and commerce, and for a transition to the discussions of labour conditions in the cultural industries, we can turn to theatre, an industry that in the 1990s and 2000s became a global multimillion dollar industry, with much investment from some of the largest transnational cultural industry corporations, such as Disney. Based on an ethnographic study of such shows, Jonathan Burston (1999) argued that, as the profit-making potential of live entertainment became more apparent and as the sector has therefore become increasingly integrated into entertainment conglomerates, assembly line production methods were increasingly seen in the theatre. Burston examined the mega-musicals that have dominated live theatre economics since the 1980s – shows such as *Cats*, *The Phantom of the Opera*, *Miss Saigon* and *Disney's Beauty and the Beast*. These are all large-scale musical works with very big casts and a strong emphasis on special effects. The huge amounts of money invested in, and made from, these shows, have meant that production companies very carefully control what can be done with their intellectual property after the original production of the show. Shows are 'franchised' by their owners and can only be put on if very specific conditions are met. The consequence for those involved in such productions is, in Burston's view, increasing alienation. One of his interviewees, a director, described his deep dislike of 'having to be the person who stands there and says, "[male principal], you're six inches too far to the left" and who trains endless [male principals and female principals] to go through the mechanics again' (Burston, 1999: 75).

The German case suggests that plenty of live theatre still aspires to autonomy from commerce, but that autonomy may come at a cost. Doris Eikhof

---

17 Eithne Quinn (2004) has provided a fascinating analysis of the relationships between creativity and commerce in gangsta rap. In this genre a frank acknowledgement of the individual's pursuit of commerce is a badge of authenticity, in an age where ruthless entrepreneurial individualism had been accepted by significant numbers of the 'post-soul' generation of black Americans. As Quinn makes clear, this does not make gangsta rap 'inferior' to other genres – it makes it extremely interesting.

and Axel Haunschild (2007) have described how public funding and the principle of *kunstfreiheit* ('freedom of art') have created a situation in which German theatres can perform a rich repertory of plays, including not only avant-garde productions but also very popular shows that will book up weeks in advance. This is cultural production at the opposite end of the creative-commercial spectrum from the highly commercial mega-musicals. Creative innovation, originality, depth, and a lack of predictability are valued above spectacle. In the terms that Eikhof and Haunschild adopt from the French sociologist Pierre Bourdieu, artistic logics are placed ahead of economic logics, because of the protection from market imperatives provided by state funding – and by the commitment of audiences and theatre workers to the autonomy of art.

Yet Eikhof and Haunschild also show that constraints still operate even in this relatively protected space. Autonomy, it seems, is only possible because of a highly skewed labour market, in which the supply of actors constantly outstrips demand, even in such a highly-subsidised sector. There is ferocious competition for work, partly because of the (in many respects) desirable nature of the work itself, and actors must constantly be involved in interactions that are poised uncertainly between genuine, friendly interaction and strategically building up contacts. Theatre work must also be constantly supplemented by other work, leading to problems in balancing a commitment to the theatre with other projects, including teaching. And the requirement on actors to be flexible and geographically mobile puts a great deal of stress on many of them.

Autonomy, then, is achieved at the cost of a great deal of time and effort on the part of actors, who must negotiate between their own commitment to artistic practices and the need to make a living, for example by undertaking work beyond their contract. Actors and managers will regularly clash over what is the right way to balance artistic and economic goals. In the words of one theatre manager, recognising the contradictions in the creative freedom of actors,

> The basic schizophrenia in theatre is that you ask your actors to understand themselves as independently acting, creative and critical partners, while at the same time you expect them to dispose of their independence on the spot and at your discretion, whenever decisions simply have to be accepted as orders and have to be carried out. (Eikhof and Haunschild, 2007: 534)

But none of the 'human resource management' mechanisms associated with many contemporary workplaces are used to resolve these issues. Instead, an enormous amount of time is spent in individual meetings, trying to sort out the conflicts resulting from staffing decisions or artistic disagreements. Eikhof and Haunschild suggest that human resources management techniques might help prevent the waste of time involved in such discussions, and this may or may not be the case. But this interesting example illustrates how freedom is not 'free' (as in 'without cost'), and how commercial imperatives are displaced from the production system to the labour market. Cultural labour markets are the topic of the next section.

DIVISION OF LABOUR AND WORKING CONDITIONS

The final sections of this chapter examine the extent to which the cultural labour market and systems of reward for cultural workers have changed in recent decades. We have already seen evidence in Chapter 6 that the number of workers employed by cultural industries has grown substantially. But what kinds of working lives can these workers expect? Chapter 2 outlined the division of labour in cultural industries, and placed this within a historical context. This division developed during the period that I call the *complex professional period of cultural production*, and represents a central feature of production during that time. It is based upon a relative autonomy for the creative work discussed above. But here I concentrate on broader questions concerning the labour market, and pay, satisfactions and rewards for cultural workers. **So in what ways, if any, have the cultural labour market and systems of reward for cultural workers been changing? And have the rewards and working conditions of creative workers – and indeed, other workers in the cultural industries – improved or deteriorated during this time?**

Characteristics of cultural labour

A significant strand of management studies has addressed the changing nature of work and careers in modern societies. The notion of the 'boundaryless career' (Arthur and Rousseau, 1996) refers to a range of supposedly newer forms of employment, which involve moving between various employers to work on different projects, and drawing validation from networks outside the organisation in which people work. Careers in the cultural industries have always taken this form, and so there has been considerable interest in management studies and elsewhere in the working patterns associated with these industries. Candace Jones (1996), for example, reports on how – following the break-up of the Hollywood studio system in the 1950s – film production increasingly came to be organised as a series of one-off projects, with each one of these separately financed. It is hard not to get a sense in some of the management studies literature that the new mobile career represents a better, brighter future than the supposedly dour world of traditional organisations (see Anand et al., 2002, and the concept of the 'creative career'). But studies of labour markets and income patterns for artists by economists and sociologists suggest that the world of cultural work can be a difficult one for those who choose to work there. Adapting Ruth Towse's valuable (1992) summary of the findings from studies of the characteristics of 'artistic' labour forces,[18] we can list a number of things that we now know about workers in the cultural industries:

- They tend to hold multiple jobs.
- There is a predominance of self-employed or freelance workers.
- Work is irregular, contracts are short-term, and there is little job protection.
- Career prospects are uncertain.
- The distribution of earnings is highly skewed (that is, unequal).
- Workers in the cultural industries tend to be younger than in other sectors.
- The workforce appears to be growing.

A sense of what 'highly skewed' earnings might mean is provided by Montgomery and Robinson (1993, cited by Caves, 2000: 79). Their figures are drawn mainly from the world of artists and professional classical musicians, but they indicate some of the dynamics to be found in other cultural industries. A 1989 survey of 2000 visual artists found that median earnings from art were only about US$3000 per year. The same study showed that the costs of pursuing such a career were about US$9625 per year, so the median net income was minus US$6000! Median total earnings, including other work, for the various artists in this group came to between US$10,000 and US$20,000 per year. Family and other jobs had to provide the support to get creative workers through. This particularly seems to be the case for those attempting to gain entry into sustained professional work – those, in other words, who are trying to 'make it'.

We saw in Chapter 2 how, according to Bernard Miège's analysis, creative labour within the cultural industries is underpaid because of a permanent oversupply of artistic labour, which takes the form of 'vast reservoirs' of non-professional cultural workers and the mobility of creative professionals between different fields. This over-supply of labour remains a central fact about working conditions in the cultural industries, even in an era where cultural employment has grown (see Chapter 6). Given the factors above, especially the irregular, uncertain and unequally compensated nature of work, it is striking that there is no shortage of workers aiming to fulfil the growing demand for them in the cultural industries. So why do more and more people, many of them very young, appear to want to work in the cultural industries? Menger (1999: 554) usefully distinguished three different explanations for this phenomenon

---

18 Many studies take 'artists' to mean actors, musicians, dancers, writers, etc., working in the subsidised arts sector, but in fact many such performers work primarily in the commercial cultural industries, and the characteristics identified by Towse very much apply to that larger sector.

(in the context of 'artistic labour markets' – but his insights apply to the cultural industries in general).

- The first is the labour-of-love explanation (Freidson, 1990) – that artists, or symbol creators, have a strong sense of a 'calling', of potential fulfilment, and because of this they are prepared to accept the risk of failure.
- A second set of explanations claims that artists might be risk-lovers, or like lottery players, simply haven't considered properly how likely it is that they will fail (though success and failure aren't quite as arbitrary as in a lottery).
- A third explanation is that cultural work brings non-monetary, psychological rewards: that it is attractive because of some of the features noted earlier. The high levels of personal autonomy achieved by some workers are particularly significant here. There are other factors at work too – a sense of sociality and community, the possibility of self-realisation, and potentially high degrees of recognition, perhaps even celebrity. Some would argue that contemporary labour markets function by balancing differences, so that work which has these non-monetary rewards is compensated less. But as Menger points out, these non-monetary benefits apply very unevenly in artistic and cultural work. And there are non-monetary downsides as well that are associated with job insecurity and maintaining networks.

Other, more recent research has analysed how representations of cultural labour in film and television encourage the acceptance of these poor conditions in the cultural industries by providing a picture of authenticity and authorship that seems rebellious, but also conforms with the requirements of contemporary capitalism (Stahl, 2006).

In the years since Towse and Menger's accounts, the creative industries policies that we discussed in Chapter 5 have sought to expand the number of jobs devoted to symbol making in modern societies. They have advocated such an expansion not only on the grounds that this will provide new sources of economic growth, but also because these are jobs and occupations that supposedly allow for a better quality of working life. So to what extent is this the case? Kate Oakley reports empirical evidence suggesting that the British cultural labour market, after many years of creative industries policies that paid little attention to labour (Banks and Hesmondhalgh, 2009), 'remains polarised by gender, ethnicity and class' (Oakley, 2011: 281). Despite the presence of many graduates in the workforce, wages remain low. The UK's Creative and Cultural Skills Council released figures in 2009 showing that 62 per cent of those in the cultural industries (by the Council's own definition) earned less than £20,000 per year, and 31 per cent earned less than £10,000 per year. These are very low wages, especially in an expensive city like London, where UK cultural-industry jobs are concentrated. The reliance on internships to gain entry to highly competitive industries greatly disadvantages young people from less privileged backgrounds, and reinforces the domination of symbol making by people born into highly educated families. In an earlier piece, Oakley (2006: 263) cited figures showing that about 4.6 per cent of the creative and cultural industry workforce in the UK came from an ethnic minority background at that time, compared with 7 per cent of the UK labour force as a whole, and with figures of over 25 per cent in London where cultural labour is concentrated (and up to 35 per cent in inner London).

Other studies reinforce such worrying profiles of cultural labour. Susan Christopherson (2011) has analysed a number of related developments that have had negative repercussions for the US cultural labour force in film and television over the last few decades:

- *The downsizing of broadcasting networks in the wake of marketisation and conglomeration* This was accompanied by significant attempts to de-unionise labour. There has been a shift in the previously stable conditions of television production towards something resembling the more uncertain, project-based nature of film production.
- *Increasing use of freelance independent contractors and growth in jobs in the low-cost environment of cable television* Even in unionised jobs working hours have become longer and the work has become more arduous.
- Christopherson also recounts how, *in association with the conglomerates, both creative and technical workers have supported the use of production incentives by state governments, which attempt to attract productions away from Los Angeles to other states.* Such production incentives are superficially attractive to labour as well as business because they seem to offer a subsidy that might allow for greater amounts of production. But these subsidies have had the unintended consequence of undermining the 'industrial commons' of film and television workers in Los Angeles. Basing production in states where there has previously been no history of cultural work requires a great deal of mobility on the part of workers.

More generally, many analysts have offered in recent years analysis of a highly casualised, risky and precarious set of labour conditions in the cultural industries and in related industries such as IT and fashion, while others have stressed how the attractions of relatively exciting jobs can lead to processes of 'self-exploitation' whereby workers will push themselves to the limit in an attempt to establish reputations that will gain them sufficient autonomy to pursue high-quality production (Banks, 2007; Hesmondhalgh and Baker, 2011a; McRobbie, 2002; Neff, 2012). While endorsing such pessimism, some later contributions also qualify it, by drawing attention to some aspects of life in the contemporary cultural industries that may offer some hope. Mark Banks argues, for example, that there are widespread signs that 'social creativity and independent artistic production are actually on the increase' (Banks, 2007: 102) and that many cultural producers continue to seek intrinsic rewards from their work, rather than fame, fortune, or an easy buck. Moral systems of trust, honesty, obligation and fairness have not become completely lost in modern workplaces, Banks claims. And what's more, many cultural workers still seek to intervene in social relations as well as pursuing aesthetic goals. Cultural production has not entirely dispensed with its connections to struggles for human emancipation. Sarah Baker and I conducted interviews with and observation of a range of cultural workers, across different industries, genres and positions. We found evidence of a low quality of working life: short-term jobs constrained their ability to make their work the basis of meaningful self-realisation; autonomy was often highly constrained; many workers left the cultural industries at an early age, burnt out by excessive demands and uncertainty about the future. But we also saw and heard of many positive experiences, and not just from workers who had had the mixture of luck and talent to 'make it', but also from relatively junior workers, who gained genuine satisfaction from doing work that attempted to communicate with and please audiences. A key issue, it seemed to us, also noted by other writers such as Andrew Ross (2009), is how societies might ensure that the cultural industries might provide a better quality of working life for their workers, and sustainable jobs, rather than ones that vanish as capital moves on from one entrepreneurial venture to another. Unions, we argue in our book, are likely to be a significant part of struggles to spread 'good work' in the cultural industries (Hesmondhalgh and Baker, 2011a: 222–6; see also Mosco and McKercher, 2008). But so too are social movements and developments that emphasise the need for people to make choices not to put success in their working lives above other aspects of life, such as contributing to the communities in which they live, providing love and support for family members and friends, and showing solidarity with others, including distant strangers (Hesmondhalgh and Baker, 2011a: 226–8).

Box 7.3   Contracts, copyright and cultural work

In the complex professional era, copyright law and practice has been the arena in which the rewards for cultural labour have been determined. Contracts between cultural workers and businesses specify rewards from rights in cultural works. Overseen by national copyright and national or sub-national (for example, state) labour laws, which are often determined by forms of collective bargaining by symbol makers and corporations (see Stahl, 2009), these contracts determine which creative workers get what percentages of revenues or profits, how long for, and who has the right to say what happens to the cultural work produced under the terms of the contract. These contracts, except in very rare cases (superstars), strongly favour the companies rather than the artists.

(Continued)

(Continued)

As we saw in Chapter 5, copyright law developed in the seventeenth and eighteenth centuries in book publishing and took its modern form in the nineteenth century. In the twentieth century, this already contradictory and complex legal framework became vastly more complex as new media forms developed, such as film and recorded music, requiring their own modifications to the national copyright laws and international conventions originally developed for publishing. Nearly all the new media forms by this point involved a much more complex division of labour than before, creating further problems concerning the authorship of cultural works.

Copyright law adjudicates between the interests of three groups: *creators*, *users* and *owners*. *Creators'* expressions of ideas are protected from plagiarism under copyright, but the *owner*ship of copyrights is assigned to companies for a fixed term. Different legal systems have provisions that are more or less protective of authors' rights, in terms of their 'moral rights' to say how the work might be further modified or reproduced, but the tendency in all modern copyright systems is for cultural industry companies to become the owners of rights. By the late twentieth century, this was creating important contradictions as corporate owners were increasingly successful in broadening the scope of their ownership in various ways, including the extension of the periods for which they could own works under national laws (see Chapter 5). Many commentators believe that this situation has now developed to the extent where the interests of both *users* and 'primary' symbol *creators* are threatened.

Addressing recent debates about these issues, Philip Schlesinger and Charlotte Waelde (2012) show, on the basis of their interviews with dancers and musicians, that cultural workers are motivated primarily by a commitment to an art form, and/or desires for self-realisation. This contradicts the way that cultural policy tends to conceive of the relations between copyright and cultural work, where cultural workers are 'incentivised' by rewards from rights.

I now explore these issues further by examining cultural work across different types of role or function in the cultural industries.

TERMS AND CONDITIONS OF CULTURAL WORK IN DIFFERENT ROLES

Chapter 2 explained the division of labour in the cultural industries by identifying a number of roles or functions performed in these industries:

- Owners and executives.
- Creative managers.
- Marketers.
- Primary creative personnel.

- Technical and craft workers.
- Unskilled workers.

These still represent distinct categories. There has been no significant blurring of these functions, even if they interact in different ways, as the discussion of marketing earlier in this chapter suggested. However, there have been some shifts within the categories, in terms of conditions of work and the internal divisions within them. I pay more attention to creative personnel here because of their role – if only their perceived role in some quarters – as primary workers in the production of symbols, information, entertainment and meaning – the core products of the cultural industries.

'Unskilled' and semi-skilled workers

As with any industry, the cultural industries would simply not function without the work of a large number of people performing relatively humdrum (though often essential) tasks. This extends to cleaners and other ancillary workers in places where cultural production is carried out, such as recording studios or live venues (see Hesmondhalgh and Baker, 2011a: 233), or where films are exhibited. We know little about the conditions of such workers and this could be a significant topic for future research, if theorised well.

Even as digital circulation becomes more widespread, the cultural industries still arrange for the manufacturing and circulation of products, such as CDs, DVDs and Blu-Ray discs, video games and celluloid films. These products are nearly always made by second-party companies, usually using cheaper overseas labour, and often they are distributed by wholesaling companies on contracts. Again, insufficient attention has been paid to the working conditions of those involved in such production and circulation.

In addition, and as I have stressed repeatedly in this book, the cultural industries are integrally related to a set of neighbouring industries, most notably the consumer electronics, IT (including internet) and telecommunications industries. The cultural industries simply would not function without the efforts of workers in these other industries. A striking example of this is the manufacture of television sets in the consumer electronics sector. Based on her participant observation, Vicki Mayer (2011) has written about the lives of television set assemblers in the 'international industrial zone' of Manaus, Brazil. She powerfully describes the working conditions of these assemblers, with high levels of physical and emotional stress, and their attempts to cope with the demands of their working lives. She also analyses the factory's attempts to encourage and discourage certain forms of 'creativity'.[19] I fully endorse Mayer's concern with the total division of labour behind the cultural

---

19 This is tied to criticism of a very diverse body of research, including Florida's (2002) work on the creative class, my and Sarah Baker's study of television industry personnel (Hesmondhalgh and Baker, 2011a) and others, all of which are accused of adopting 'exclusive definitions of the producer as a creative professional' (Mayer, 2011: 16).

industries, and with the working conditions of those who are rendered 'invisible' by other forms of analysis. And it is certainly the case that all workers (people) exercise creativity in their work. I believe it it is still vital, however, to distinguish between the different kinds of creativity that might be involved in different kinds of work, and the various political implications of these diverse forms of creativity and how they are managed. Mayer's analysis, impressive though it is at uncovering the conditions of such 'invisible labour', does not, in my view, achieve such a theorisation of creativity, which is ultimately necessary for her overall argument to work.

Technical workers

While some unionised technical workers are still paid relatively well (for example, camera operators in the film and television industries), their conditions are increasingly under attack (see the discussion of Christopherson's work above). In the advanced industrial countries, there has been large-scale de-unionisation. Internationalisation has meant that many tasks have been shifted abroad to countries where labour laws are even weaker. This has been the case in animation, as John A. Lent (1998) shows. The creative elements are carried out in the USA, while the more humdrum technical aspects of execution are contracted out. These working practices may not be quite so exploitative as offshore production in the clothing/fashion industries (see Ross, 1998), but they still represent part of what Miller et al. (2005) have called the New International Division of Cultural Labour (or NICL – and no, I don't know where the 'D' went either). This concept is centred on the fact that, as the cultural industries have become big business, it is not just manufacturing that is increasingly moved to cheaper locations, it is cultural production, too. Animation companies in the USA, such as Hanna-Barbera, achieved huge economies by opening major offshore studios in Australia (1974) and Taiwan (1978). Most of the animation for US and European companies continues to be carried out in Asia (Yoon and Malecki, 2009). Disney contracted for many years to a set of Japanese subsidiaries and, in turn, by the 1990s, Disney Japan was subcontracting most of its work to South Korea or China. As both the television and the film markets for animation have boomed in the 2000s, some studios outside the USA have achieved success on television, and even in film. But big-budget features have moved to CGI animation, which is highly specialised in a few locations (Yoon and Malecki, 2009).

Creative managers

Ryan (1992: Section 4.3.2) argued that creative management had become much more professionalised in the decades immediately preceding his study, in that its roles and duties are established and even, in some cases, formally taught on courses. This tendency has become even more marked. The creative management function has become completely established in all 'mature' cultural industries and is frequently carried out in teams. This has spawned internal divisions of labour and hierarchies. For example, the A&R department in a record company will include a senior manager who might have responsibility for dealing with more established artists or pushing through the signing of an expensive act, while younger, new members of the team will take on more of the work of making contacts and sampling new acts, whether in the form of recordings or live shows. Some creative managers achieve a kind of stardom within their own area and, because such managers are now increasingly mobile, can command higher financial rewards than ever before. After the conglomerates entered book publishing in the 1960s and introduced strict accounting and bureaucratic managerial practices, it became common for successful commissioning editors (the main form of creative management in that industry) to leave the conglomerates in order to set up their own smaller companies – often taken over by a conglomerate years later. In the last 30 years, there has been a trend towards the same thing in the recording industry, as A&R personnel leave to set up their own independent companies. Once again, we can see the 'networked' nature of much cultural work– creative managers moving back and forth between independent production and corporate cultures.

Symbol creators

The poor working conditions and rewards for many cultural workers, referred to in the previous main section, have often been obscured by the fact that, in the complex professional era, very generous rewards are available for symbol creators who achieve name recognition in the minds of audience members. This over-rewarding of stars derives in part from the way that cultural businesses counter risk by formatting their products with 'author' names (see the Introduction). However, the situation for the majority of people attempting to make a living out of cultural production in the complex professional era has contrasted strongly with the small number of highly rewarded superstars. [20]

Creative workers frequently work tremendously long hours under difficult conditions. They trade in financial reward and security for creative autonomy. But a model of power as coercion is insufficient to explain this. There is rarely an authority figure present to tell symbol creators to work so hard for so little reward. In fact, many cultural workers, including symbol makers, and to some extent, creative managers and technical personnel, seem to accept poor working conditions (for example, long, difficult hours) for the benefits of being involved in creative projects and the glamour surrounding these worlds.

---

20 This is one of the reasons why it is wrong to treat a focus on symbol creators as a concentration on a group of pampered professionals, and to see them as privileged 'above the line' workers whose conditions are better than those involved in 'below the line' labour. As noted in the Introduction, 'below the line' technical workers, because they are more unionised, often enjoy better pay and conditions than creative personnel.

What about symbol creators who *do* manage to achieve access to the cultural industries? Their rewards are, of course, dependent on the contracts they sign, but they are also dependent on the work done by the cultural industry companies they work for. Deals in the recording industry will serve as an example.

Publishing and recording deals for musicians have generally taken the following form during the complex professional era. Musicians agree to render their services exclusively to a company, usually for a specified number of recordings and in certain specified territories. In return, the company will normally make commitments to promote the work of the artists. The musicians are paid an advance and then, if and when this advance has been recouped via sales, they are paid a royalty.

The long history of dubious contracts and career-breaking rip-offs cannot be recounted here,[21] but there are two main areas of controversy surrounding the 'standard' advance-royalty/exclusivity contract between musicians and companies. The first area concerns the financial rewards available for artists. The advance is essentially a loan against money that the musicians' recordings will make in the future. Repayment is 'cross-collateralised' against costs such as recording and touring (and often against royalties on different contracts with the same company, such as publishing ones – see Passman, 1998). The effect is that musicians will pay towards such expenses out of their loan. In many cases, the advance will never be recouped and musicians can be in debt to their record company for many years. Many young bands enter into this system unaware of the difficulties of recouping the substantial advances that they initially welcome.

There have been significant changes since the 1970s. Musicians are much more aware of the dangers of rip-offs and the need to take legal advice when signing contracts. Royalty rates have also risen considerably since the 1970s, when 7 to 9 per cent was common (Caves, 2000: 62). The level of royalty rate is set in the initial contract as a certain percentage of retail sales. Big stars will gain much higher royalty rates (16 to 20 per cent, according to Caves, 2000: 62), whereas middle-range acts will get 14 to 16 per cent and new acts something like 11 to 13 per cent. Generally, the level of the royalty will rise as musicians make more records: the justification for this is that the company has to invest more resources initially, in order to establish the musicians' careers. In most contracts, however, costs are still recoupable against royalties – in other words, musicians will pay for their recording and many promotional expenses out of their earnings. Yet the company will retain the lion's share of the money and retain control of copyright – increasingly, the source of much of the wealth in the cultural industries.

---

21 Some key developments in contractual law in the cultural industries are surveyed by Greenfield and Osborn (1994) and a journalistic account by Garfield (1986). My thanks to Matt Stahl for corrections to this section; any remaining faults are my responsibility alone.

The second area of controversy relates to the creative autonomy of musicians and the level of commitment shown by a company to a symbol creator's output. (Clearly, this relates to the earlier discussion of creative autonomy, but I deal with it here as a key facet of the experience of cultural work.) A particularly important issue in the music business in recent years has been the restraints on symbol creators brought about by the long-term nature of the recording and/or publishing contract. Although established star names are able to negotiate relatively high royalty rates, many contracts remain very long term in nature and this is actually a disadvantage for the artist. Normally, the company has a right to exercise an option or a series of options to retain a musician's services. Nearly all contracts are asymmetrical, however, in that the musician must fulfill certain criteria if he or she wants to be retained by the company, but cannot choose to leave. These criteria will usually include sales, which are dependent on the efforts of the record company. A danger for musicians in being held to a long-term contract is that the sympathetic staff who signed them may leave the label, to be replaced by creative managers with little interest in the band. Another is that any change of direction by a musician may receive an unsympathetic reception from the record company.[22] Both these dangers remain current in the recording industry. In this particular respect little has changed since the 1970s, except that record company staff are even more prone to moving between companies and that record companies can claim, more than ever, that they have limited resources to support artists. Box 7.4 discusses an interesting attempt to change these arrangements in the 1980s.

Box 7.4   The post-punk intervention

At various independent record companies associated with punk in the late 1970s and 1980s, new ways of dealing with artists were developed that challenged the standard arrangements in the music industry. Deals with musicians were often on a 50–50 basis, rather than the single-figure percentage royalty rates usual at the time. Also, long-term contracts were rejected in favour of deals based on personal trust. The aim of such deals was to be as 'musician-centred' as possible. Contracts were avoided on the grounds that the standard contracts were loaded in favour of companies and if the personal trust between musicians and companies broke down, there was no point in pursuing the relationship anyway.

(Continued)

---

22 This was a central issue in Panayioutou versus Sony Music Entertainment (UK) Limited – the George Michael case, resolved in 1994. Michael tried, unsuccessfully, to argue in this important dispute with his record company that his long-term contract with Sony was a 'restraint of trade' under European law. Star symbol creators are increasingly challenging these contracts, reflecting the rise of star power, but this is unlikely to improve contracts for the majority of creative personnel.

(Continued)

These companies generally favoured record-by-record deals, which gave artists the freedom to move to other companies, should they wish to do so. The 50–50 deals meant that payment rates for musicians were enormously higher than the single-figure percentage royalty rates common even for established bands on major labels. If a band could achieve high sales on such a deal, they would make quite a bit of money.

Recognising the vital strategic importance of circulation, British punk independents formed distribution and retailing networks. What is more, many extremely talented musicians came to work with the punk independents because they wanted to work with people whom they felt had a closer understanding of their music than the creative managers in the transnational corporation divisions. Their records achieved considerable success and brought very different voices into the mainstream of British cultural life (see Hesmondhalgh, 1997, 1999, for more details on this).

The post-punk intervention illustrates the potential that many musicians and audiences have attached to independence, not only in terms of musical innovation but also of the politics surrounding the conditions of symbolic creativity. It serves as an example, too, of attempts to transform the apparatus of *commercial* cultural production. All too often the literature on alternative media is confined to very small, marginal interventions, operating so far outside most people's experience of popular culture that they are known only to small groups of activists and intellectuals.[23] Here, however, activism took place actually in the field of commercial entertainment production itself.

In the end, the post-punk rebellion was unsuccessful. The key companies went bankrupt, many musicians became disenchanted with the limited promotional budgets available in small record companies and, gradually, more and more independents forged distribution and/or financing deals with transnationals (Hesmondhalgh, 1999). However, new genres continue to develop in what Toynbee (2000) calls proto-markets and independent record companies still act as vital conduits for the more widespread dissemination of the music produced within them.

A further change in the organisation of cultural labour can be noted. As the cultural industries have grown, they have become more complex and there has been a further growth in the number and significance of functions involving mediation between cultural industry organisations and the pool of creative workers. The two most notable occupations are *agents* and *artist managers*. Caves (2000) suggests that agents were once shunned by companies, but are now welcomed

---

23 John Downing recognises this in his outstanding book *Radical Media* (2001).

as a means of reducing recruitment costs in book publishing, film and television, and the various performing arts. He explains why by quoting figures from Coser et al. (1982: 130–2) that show only three or four out of 10,000 books submitted for publication are accepted. Agents do some of the publishing companies' filtering work for them. Artist managers perform a similar function in the recording industry. A key change in recent years has been the increasingly entrepreneurial role played by managers or management teams in recruiting and training bands, often using finance capital that they have raised themselves. In this respect, the recording industry in the 2000s has become more like the film industry, with artist managers acting as independent producers who will attempt to 'develop' a particular project. Such mediators are likely to become more important still in the years to come, not least because star creative personnel are so well rewarded and artist managers and agents tend to work by taking a commission on payments to stars. It is highly unlikely that this will lead to any more sympathetic treatment of aspiring creators, but it will represent a new form of challenge to the major corporations, which they will seek to absorb via partnership.

* * *

The case studies discussed in this chapter provide evidence of some tightening of control in various industries and genres, and some loosening elsewhere. It is not possible to conclude that the increasing levels of conglomeration and capitalisation in the cultural industries, discussed in Chapter 6, have resulted uniformly in a loss of autonomy, as suggested by some political economy work. Equally, however, there does not appear to have been a widespread loosening of control, as suggested by analysts such as Davis and Scase. Yet there can be little doubt of the continuing pressures on autonomy, from practices and discourses that emphasise marketing and market research, from the pursuit of commercial gains over public service, and so on.

Since Davis and Scase's work, a new generation of digital technologies has occasioned even stronger claims regarding loosening of control. According to these claims, digital production technologies have enabled a democratisation of cultural production, especially regarding the possibilities for amateur symbol makers to reach audiences via the web. These issues will be addressed in Chapter 9, but it is worth making clear in advance my view that digitalisation does not render the discussion of autonomy (and its limits) void. For the 'digitalised' cultural industries are only just emerging and have not been created out of thin air. They are likely to retain many of the dynamics and features of the pre-digital industries discussed in this chapter.

This chapter has surveyed changes and continuities in the organisation of cultural production and the terms and conditions of cultural work. Sadly, there is little reason to believe, on the basis of the preceding survey, that the terms and conditions of cultural labour have improved, in spite of the expanding economic importance of the cultural industries outlined in the previous chapter. There might be signs of restrictions of creative autonomy in production in some industries and genres, but cultural work can hardly be thought of in general as subject to oppressive levels of supervision and surveillance. It could be argued though that the appeal of the autonomy that persists in the cultural industries continues to attract many young people to often underpaid and insecure cultural work. In this respect, the idea of creative autonomy as something that needs defending requires some qualification. Meanwhile, businesses ensure that they have tight control over circulation. The organisational form of the cultural industries – loose control of creativity, tight control of circulation – established in the twentieth century still persists in the twenty first.

RECOMMENDED AND FURTHER READING

Because the focus of this book is a historical examination of change in the cultural industries, this chapter has not been able to 'go inside' cultural-industry organisations in detail. But there is a wealth of sociological and cultural studies work that aims to do so. In my view, the best of it is alert to the tensions between creativity and commerce that I emphasise in this chapter.

Keith Negus's studies of the recording industry, *Producing Pop* (1992) and *Music Genres and Corporate Cultures* (1999), suggested how fruitful a cultural studies approach to organisations and organisational sociology could be for understanding the entertainment-based cultural industries, although his focus was primarily on creative managers; symbol creators were relatively sidelined. His insights are still highly relevant for the very different recording industry that exists now. The same is true of Simon Frith's wonderful book on *The Sociology of Rock* (1978), later revised as *Sound Effects* (1981).

The television industry has been a rich terrain for analysis of struggles over creativity and commerce as well as working conditions. The UK independent television production sector has been the subject of doctoral research by David Lee (2009) and Anna Zoellner (2010), both of whom have also written journal articles and book chapters based on their analysis. Jeanette Steemers (2010) has analysed the commercialisation of pre-school television.

The recent growth in cultural studies of media industries, discussed in Chapter 1, has seen much greater attention being given to the rituals, values and practices of workers, especially in television and film. See John Thornton Caldwell's empirically rich *Production Culture* (2008) and the essays collected in Mayer, Banks and Caldwell's *Production Studies* (2009).

Tensions between creativity and commerce are at the heart of French sociologist Pierre Bourdieu's work on cultural production (most notably, *The Rules of Art*, 1996). An understanding of Bourdieu is indispensable for analysis of the cultural industries, but he remains a tough read. (Perhaps his translators do him no favours.) Editor Randal Johnson's introduction to the essays collected in English as *The Field of Cultural Production* is extremely helpful, while Richard Jenkins (1992) provided a clear but critical introduction to Bourdieu in general. I have also assessed elsewhere Bourdieu's potential contribution to understanding the cultural industries (Hesmondhalgh, 2006a). Rod Benson and Erik Neveu's collection, *Bourdieu and the Journalistic Field* (2005), examines news in the light of Bourdieu's work.

Some of the richest treatments of autonomy have come from studies of journalism, such as work by Philip Schlesinger (*Putting 'Reality' Together*, 1978), Gaye Tuchman (*Making News*, 1978), Herbert Gans (*Deciding What's News*, 1979) and James Curran (see his 1990 book chapter entitled 'Culturalist perspectives on news organizations'). Curran's recent *Media and Democracy* (2011) includes a superb discussion of questions concerning journalistic autonomy. Also valuable are the overviews of journalism provided by Lance Bennett (*News: The Politics of Illusion*; see the most recent edition from 2011) and Michael Schudson (*The Sociology of News*, most recent edition 2012).

For other treatments of developments regarding marketing and publicity in the film industry, besides those discussed in the chapter above, see Paul Grainge's *Brand Hollywood* (2008), and *Global Hollywood 2* (2005), co-written by Toby Miller, Nitin Govil, John McMurria, Richard Maxwell and Ting Wang. The latter includes a critique of Hollywood branding and marketing practices, which bears Maxwell's distinctive stamp. Chapters by Philip Drake (2008) and Alisa Perren (2011) in other collections provide valuable background and information on marketing and publicity. I have had little space to deal with branding here, but John Sinclair (2011) has recently provided a valuable survey of the literature.

On market research or 'audience research' see James S. Ettema and D. Charles Whitney's collection, *Audiencemaking* (1994), and Philip Napoli's *Audience Economics* (2003). Amanda Lotz's chapter on television audience research in *The Television Will Be Revolutionized* (2007) is helpful. Napoli's more recent *Audience Evolution* updates these issues for the era of the web. Jason Toynbee has also provided an excellent overview of a number of debates about how cultural industries seek to know their audiences (2006).

I have neglected public relations in this book. See Stuart Ewen's social history *PR!* (1996) and a very good collection edited by Lee Edwards and Caroline Hodges, *Public Relations, Society and Culture* (2011).

The last decade has seen a boom in studies of cultural labour, and there have been some outstanding contributions. Much of the best analysis puts creativity/commerce relations at its heart, including Mark Banks's *The Politics of Cultural Work* (2007).

A number of important contributions have addressed issues of labour in information technology industries, including web design companies, in ways that have a bearing on understanding work in the cultural industries. This includes Andrew Ross's ethnographic study of a web design company, *No-Collar* (2003), and more recently, Gina Neff's *Venture Labor* (2012), which examines the question of risk, and Helen Kennedy's *Net Work* (2011).

Ross made an early vital intervention with his piece on 'The mental labour problem' (2000), and built on this in his book *Nice Work If You Can Get It* (2009) which addresses a number of important topics regarding contemporary labour in general, including cultural industries. A collection edited by Alan McKinlay and Chris Smith, *Creative Labour* (2009), collects some useful essays on work in the cultural industries. Vincent Mosco and Catherine McKercher's *The Laboring of Communication* (2008) is a valuable study of labour in the media, telecommunications and information technology industries, which rightly seeks to build solidarity between workers in these different sectors. Vicki Mayer's *Below the Line* (2011) is an illuminating study of the kinds of cultural labour which are not usually considered in research. Matt Stahl's research is the most sophisticated analysis of legal, historical and ideological issues surrounding cultural labour (see Stahl, 2006, 2009). Sarah Baker and I have also made our own intervention with *Creative Labour* (2011a).

ONLINE READING

All the online material referenced below can be accessed free of charge at: **http://www.sagepub.co.uk/hesmondhalgh**

Simply click on the 'Sample Materials' tab to find the links to each article.

A special section of the journal *Theory, Culture and Society* in 2008 (volume 25, numbers 7-8) was devoted to the issue of 'precarity and cultural work'. It contains valuable pieces by Rosalind Gill, Andy Pratt, Andrew Ross, Brett Neilson, Ned Rossiter and Susan Christopherson, and an article on 'emotional labour' in television by myself and Sarah Baker. Ros Gill and Andy Pratt's introductory article sets the scene.

For an illuminating article on creativity/commerce relations in popular music, see Klein (2008).

- Gill, Rosalind and Pratt, Andy (2008) 'In the social factory? Immaterial labour, precariousness and cultural work', *Theory, Culture & Society*, 25(7–8): 1–30.
- Klein, Bethany (2008) '"The new radio": music licensing as a response to industry woe', *Media, Culture & Society*, 30(4): 463–478.

Internationalisation: Neither Globalisation nor Cultural Imperialism

Factors behind cultural domination by the USA   270

    Size and nature of the domestic market for leisure
       in the USA   270

    Active role of the US state in promoting its
       industries abroad   271

Neither cultural imperialism nor globalisation   272

Television and geo-cultural markets   277

    Reversing cultural flows? The case of Latin
       American drama   280

    Transnational TV transmission and reception:
       post-national broadcasting?   284

The rise of East Asian television   287

The international film industry: Hollywood power   293

Other film industries, other texts: India and Hong Kong   295

Cultural imperialism and popular music   301

    Authenticity versus hybridity   302

    Western cultural products can be interpreted
       in different ways   302

    Spread of ownership   304

An important feature of the cultural industries over the last hundred years has been the domination of much international cultural trade by the USA and, to a lesser extent, Europe. This chapter examines the degree to which this domination has come under threat. It also examines some of the complexities of this domination, including counter-currents, and the existence of other centres of production.

We have already seen (in Chapter 2) that there were significant instances of internationalisation of technologies, texts and genres in the late nineteenth and early twentieth centuries and that one of the features of the complex professional era of cultural production was the intensification of such internationalisation. The last 30 years have seen the further and accelerated intensification of international cultural flows, including, as we shall see, much greater internationalisation on the part of cultural industry businesses. This took place, in part, as a response to the need to generate higher levels of profit that businesses of all kinds experienced during the Long Downturn. Also significant here was the increasing ease of doing business across national borders as communications and transport improved. As leisure time and disposable income increased in some parts of the world, such as Asia and Latin America, cultural industry multinational corporations based in Europe and North America expanded their operations there. But Asian and Latin American companies expanded too, and some benefited from increasing demand for cultural products in the larger markets. Internationalisation, then, took place in different directions. The successive waves of marketisation discussed in Chapter 4, and the further policy developments in Chapter 5 (especially the changes in copyright), were crucial in paving the way for such internationalisation by removing the many policy barriers to cultural trade. This chapter seeks to analyse and evaluate these developments, using the terms established in Chapter 2. Before doing so, however, we need to examine more carefully the question of how and why the USA came to dominate international television flows and, indeed, cultural trade in general, during the complex professional era.

FACTORS BEHIND CULTURAL DOMINATION BY THE USA

So how did the USA come to dominate international cultural trade? This question raises fundamental issues concerning the relative roles of economics, political power and symbolic content in determining developments in the cultural industries. This domination was never total, of course, and I examine ways in which it has been contested and qualified in later sections, but it remains a remarkable degree of domination nevertheless. We can identify two major factors:

- The size and nature of the domestic market for leisure and entertainment in the USA.
- The active role of the state.

Size and nature of the domestic market for leisure in the USA

This market was, from an early stage, larger and wealthier than any other in the world, and this allowed production companies in the USA, across all cultural industries, to cover their costs at home and treat overseas markets as sources of further profit. In the early years of television these companies built up greater repertoires of programming, giving overseas importers or international partners a bigger range of products to choose from than was available in their own countries. In a period when many economies were rebuilding, in the aftermath of the Second World War, the television market in the USA established itself much earlier than elsewhere in the world. Television exporters were able to draw on an already established global success in film and, to some extent, in popular music, both in terms of the prestige and reputation of American entertainment and the recognisability and perceived desirability of its stars and styles. Genres, stars, and other creative personnel – including technicians – could be moved across from these industries. Furthermore, the American TV industry could invest in the expensive process of putting its products on to film at a time when many countries were still transmitting programmes live, allowing it to export its products earlier than anyone else.

Two other related factors have been emphasised by some commentators. One was that the USA had a more developed production system, and one based more on competition than in other countries – though of course this was between large, oligopolistic companies (Hoskins et al., 1997). Another was the positive effects of having to appeal to a diverse audience at home. This, arguably, enabled US cultural exports to appeal to a variety of different audiences abroad. But this contrast between the USA's 'melting pot' of different migrant cultures and a supposed cultural homogeneity in other nations may be too crude and too celebratory of American diversity. More seriously, Hoskins et al. complacently dismissed accounts that stressed the role of the US state in promoting the interests of their cultural industries as 'conspiracy theory' (1997: 45). However, this role should not be dismissed so lightly, as we shall see.

Active role of the US state in promoting its cultural industries abroad

US government organisations have played a central role in promoting its cultural industries abroad, in alliance with US corporations and trade associations. There were two explicit motivations for such government intervention. One was to secure greater import revenue. The other was to export beliefs and values compatible with US global hegemony, including – crucially – the place of consumption in American life.

In international forums, such as UNESCO in the post-Second World War years, representatives from the USA 'pressed relentlessly' for the notion of a free flow of information and entertainment across the world, which would allow multinational cultural corporations to operate abroad and limit national governments' regulation of their activities (Schiller, 1998: 19). Foreign aid from the USA in the post-war period was tied to stipulations that its cultural exports would be permitted. In addition, the US state contributed enormously to the development of communications infrastructures, such as satellites. Its cultural exports boomed during the post-Second World War period (see Herman and McChesney, 1997: 18–21) and interventions by the state on behalf of the copyright interests of cultural industry corporations, as we saw in Chapter 5, led to the TRIPS agreement, which regulates the way in which the WTO deals with intellectual property.

However, we must qualify this account in two ways. First, US interests and businesses did not work in perfect harmony in pursuing these goals: some elements of the US state were more keen to use cultural products as prop-aganda than others. Second, as I've stressed throughout this book, cultural products are complex and ambivalent in their meanings: not all American exports showed American culture in a good light. The principles of creative autonomy meant that some of these products revealed deep and creaking tensions in American society, for example regarding whether life should revolve around hedonistic pleasure or duty. The thrilling shriek of rock and roll singer Little Richard told a very different story from the westerns and war films that filled many cinemas across the world.

NEITHER CULTURAL IMPERIALISM NOR GLOBALISATION

While some media economists have tended to downplay the role of the state in the USA in international cultural flows, this has been strongly emphasised by radical writers who, especially in the 1970s and early 1980s, used the concept of *cultural imperialism* to refer to the way that the cultures of less developed coun-tries have been affected by flows of cultural texts, forms and technologies associ-ated with 'the West'. However, this approach also has its problems when it is used as a way of understanding internationalisation in the cultural industries.

The 'cultural imperialism thesis' held that, as the age of direct political and economic domination by colonial powers drew to an end, a new, more indirect form of international domination was beginning. This involved, in Herbert Schiller's words (1976: 9), the adoption in economically peripheral countries of 'the values and structures of the dominating center of the [modern world] system'. As Annabelle Sreberny (1997: 49) has pointed out, the concept of cul-tural imperialism is an 'evocative metaphor' rather than a 'precise construct', but the term draws attention to a number of key issues, such as:

- the imposition of Western cultural products on the non-West;[1]
- the potentially homogenising effects of Western culture as it spread across the world;
- the destruction of indigenous traditions by such cultural flows.

---

1   Terms such as 'Western' and 'non-Western' are very problematic. Western societies are not only extremely different from each other, they are also internally heterogeneous too. The same is true of non-Western societies. Nevertheless, the adjectives do have real political resonance in certain parts of the world as a means of resisting some of the worst aspects of modernisation and commodification.

The term 'cultural imperialism' was at its most popular during the 1970s and early 1980s when concerns about such developments found expression in a series of UNESCO reports, seminars and declarations (most notably the MacBride Report: see UNESCO, 1980). From the early 1980s onwards, however, a paradigm shift occurred in the way that radical writers understood international mass communications (see, for example, Fejes, 1981). Many writers began to react against the cultural imperialism thesis and some began to prefer the term *globalisation* to cultural imperialism.

Globalisation was a term developed by social theorists (such as Giddens, 1990; Robertson, 1990) working in very different contexts from the international policy forums and activist circles where the cultural imperialism thesis initially became widespread. The concept of globalisation developed by these theorists was also quite distinct from the understanding of international cultural flows advocated by many neo-liberal policymakers and economists. Globalisation was intended to capture the increasing interconnectedness of different parts of the world. Partly because it referred to a wide variety of economic, political and cultural practices, it spread quickly to become the most widely discussed social science concept of the 1990s, going beyond academia to reach many other circles. Most notably, in the late 1990s and early 2000s, the term came to be used to denote a certain aspect of economic globalisation: the removal of barriers to trade across national borders. The view of many radical writers and activists is that such 'free trade' in fact favours the wealthiest countries in the global system of nation states. This was why tens of thousands of people participated in protests against globalisation in this sense in various cities around the world, most famously perhaps in Seattle in 1999. As a result of the dissemination of the term 'globalisation' across many different contexts, confusion has surrounded the idea (see Box 8.1 for clarification of a significant use of the term in media analysis).

Box 8.1   Herman and McChesney: globalisation as cultural imperialism

One of the most thorough analyses of internationalisation in the cultural industries– Herman and McChesney's *The Global Media* (1997) – used the term 'globalisation' in a way that strongly echoed the concept of cultural imperialism. This was a very different use of the term from that adopted by social theorists such as Anthony Giddens, which stressed the notion of a complex and ambivalent global interconnectedness (see Tomlinson, 1991). This is partly because Herman and McChesney derived the term from its uses in activist circles, where it was primarily used to refer to economic globalisation, the removal of state measures to protect national economies from unequal distributions of economic power, and the role of multinational corporations. Herman and McChesney did not address conceptual debates regarding cultural imperialism: rather, they indicated some recognition of the contradictory effects of global cultural exchange

(Continued)

(Continued)

and pointed briefly to some positive effects of cultural industry internationalisation associated with the dissemination of commercial popular culture, such as 'a greater connectedness and linkage between peoples' and the export of certain positive values, such as a scepticism of authority and the questioning of repressive traditions (1997: 8). However, Herman and McChesney were clear that, for them, the primary effects of internationalisation (or globalisation in their terms) of cultural products were systematically and almost uniformly *negative* – the implantation, extension and intensification of 'the commercial model of communication' (1997: 9). Indeed, the rest of their book was devoted to a catalogue of the activities of media companies in spreading this model and creating an entertainment-based culture that, in their view, was incompatible with real democracy. They are therefore best understood, in terms of my argument here, as using the term 'globalisation' to mean cultural imperialism, and they are among the foremost critics of cultural imperialism.

There are fierce debates about the extent to which globalisation – in the sense of significantly new global interconnectedness – has actually taken place over the last decades and whether it is a long-term or more recent development. David Held, Anthony McGrew, David Goldblatt and Jonathan Perraton (1999: 425) argued that 'contemporary [that is, post-1980] patterns of globalisation have ... surpassed those of earlier epochs', and that the

> contemporary era represents a historically unique confluence or clustering of patterns of globalisation in the domains of politics, law and governance, military affairs, cultural linkages and human migrations, in all dimensions of economic activity and in shared global environmental threats.

Held et al. usefully described the increasing and quickening interconnectedness of the world, examining how this affected various economic, political and cultural phenomena in very different ways. However, such empirical work on globalisation tends to be concerned only very marginally with *cultural* aspects of global interconnectedness. For example, Held et al.'s treatment of cultural globalisation is confined almost entirely to (important) issues of cultural trade, without any reference to debates about cultural identity.

Much more common in research on cultural aspects of globalisation is a reaction against the cultural imperialism thesis and related Marxian approaches. Such research attempts to develop a more sophisticated way of understanding the complexity and contradictions of global cultural flows. Globalisation theory helped to bring about the rapid fall from favour of the cultural imperialism thesis in the 1990s and early 2000s. A number of factors explained this.

First, some writers argued that it was no longer possible to portray the global cultural system as one in which the countries of the West (or, in a slightly more sophisticated version, the 'core', to include powerful 'eastern' countries such as Japan) imposed their cultures on the non-West. The rise of newly industrialised countries, according to such writers, made such a perspective outdated, if it was ever valid (see Tomlinson, 1997: 140–2).

Second, whereas some cultural imperialism writers assumed that the spread of Western cultural goods and technologies involved a flattening out of cultural difference, using terms such as 'homogenisation' or 'cultural synchronisation' (Hamelink, 1983), critics of the concept of cultural imperialism pointed out the very strong processes of cultural differentiation taking place throughout the world. As Stuart Hall (1997: 211) put it, 'there are many countervailing tendencies which prevent the world from becoming a culturally uniform and homogenous space'. And it did indeed seem to many observers that diversity may actually have increased as new syncretic cultural texts and genres circulated within societies exposed to Western cultural influence, such as global hip hop (Mitchell, 2001). Even phenomena such as formatted performance contests (the *Idol* shows), often considered a symbol of global cultural homogenisation, took quite different forms in different countries (see Kraidy and Sender, 2010). Whereas a previous generation of writers was deeply concerned that Western cultural exports might inhibit or destroy indigenous cultural traditions, cultural studies approaches tended to see cultures as 'hybrids' of older forms (Canclini, 1995; Chambers, 1994) and the idea of a pure, uncontaminated tradition as problematic – even dangerous – because it might serve to support racism and reactionary versions of nationalism (see Chapter 1 on cultural studies). Culture, these critics argued, could no longer be equated with place in any simple way. Globalisation, by contrast, involved 'deterritorialisation' (Canclini, 1995) – that (nearly?) all places were full of influences from elsewhere. Again, this suggested that modern international cultural flows brought about heterogeneity rather than a universal sameness.

Third, whereas the cultural imperialism thesis tended to assume the negative impact of Western cultural exports, many writers stressed the creative and active uses made by audiences of internationally distributed cultural goods – most famously in a study by Tamar Liebes and Elihu Katz (1993) of the reception in different countries of the TV series *Dallas*, a classic of 'active audience' theory in communication studies.

Globalisation theory exposed some of the conceptual limitations of cultural imperialism theory. But many of the critics of cultural imperialism theory had their own limitations. For a start, there was a lack of empirical evidence in the work of commentators such as John Tomlinson, Stuart Hall, and others associated with globalisation theory. It could be argued that cultural imperialism writers such as Herman and McChesney (1997) provided empirical evidence but no adequate theory. Active audience theory usefully problematised unstated assumptions in some cultural imperialism writing about non-Western populations, for example the lingering idea that they unquestioningly accepted the values associated with Western cultural products. The problem was that a number of urgent political questions were sidelined in many of the critiques. What, for example, are the relationships, if any, between flows of texts and continuing international and intra-national inequalities of wealth and opportunities? Active audience theory did not really address this question in any detail at all. It merely suggested that such relationships were more complex than had been thought by a previous generation – which is a correct but rather limited insight.

No doubt globalisation theorists were on to something when they wrote about the *ambivalence* of international cultural flows. John Tomlinson, for example, argued that globalisation was 'double-edged: as it dissolves the securities of locality, it offers new understandings of experience in wider – ultimately global – terms' (1997: 30). But Tomlinson usefully forefronted a problematic assumption underlying the concept of globalisation when he portrayed it as an essentially *undirected* process (1991: 175):

> The idea of imperialism contains, at least, the notion of a purposeful project: the intended spread of a social system from one centre of power across the globe. The idea of 'globalisation' suggests interconnection and interdependency of all global areas which happens in a far less purposeful way.

Tomlinson's stress on ambivalence and undirectedness is intended to counter the functionalism and lack of recognition of complexity in cultural imperialism writing, but again, this leaves certain questions – though admittedly these are issues raised by him in the course of his thoughtful analysis – unanswered. So how do we assess global economic and cultural inequality? And which actors are involved in the creation and maintenance of such lasting economic and cultural inequalities?

In this book, I attempt to deal with these questions more adequately by putting the interests of the companies that dominate the international production and circulation of culture at the centre of the story, but I also do so in a way that recognises the complexity and ambivalence of their motives and outcomes. With the treatment of questions of assessment and explanation outlined in Chapters 2 and 3 behind me, my aim in this chapter is to ground the abstractions of globalisation theory by asking 'middle level' questions about internationalisation. To recap, as asked in Chapter 2, the guiding 'measurement' questions are as follows:

- To what extent has the USA retained its international cultural dominance?
- To what extent have international cultural flows changed sufficiently for us to speak of a new era in cultural production and circulation?

The evaluative questions are the following:

- To what extent does the increasingly global reach of the largest firms mean an exclusion of voices from cultural markets?

- What opportunities are there for cultural producers from outside the 'core' areas of cultural production to gain access to new global networks of cultural production and consumption?

I investigate these questions across three cultural industries – television, film and recorded music – in each of the following three sections.

My use of the term 'internationalisation' is intended to avoid the problems surrounding the term 'globalisation'. To clarify further, however, there are three main aspects of cultural internationalisation that I am concerned with here:

- *Internationalisation of cultural businesses* Many cultural industry companies will invest in more than one country. This might mean producing in many countries, but more usually it will mean distributing texts made in one place across many others. Some would claim that the transnational corporation has no identity, and even though the head office of the corporation might be based in one country, the company itself has no nationality. However, much of the money made from the operations of the transnational corporation will (at least in an electronic form) be 'returned' to the base country.
- *Internationalisation of cultural texts* Texts originated in one country are increasingly seen, heard, and so on in other countries. Because of this increasing flow of cultural products, audiences and symbol creators can, in many places, draw on texts from many other different places. Texts, genres, and even technologies (such as musical instruments) will often be reinterpreted and adapted by symbol creators in other contexts.
- *The local is increasingly affected by the global* Partly as a result of this increasing movement of texts, but also because of other, wider factors, cultural identities are becoming increasingly complex. It was probably never wise to think of culture as being linked to territory in a simple, one-to-one way, but more and more the culture of a particular place is comprised of inputs from many other places. Many texts are now based not on the interests, concerns and culture of particular nations, but on those of a variety of nations or groups of people who share a transnational culture across different national spaces – for example, diasporic groups, or groups that share a taste for a particular feel and type of cultural expression (such as global extreme metal fans – see Kahn-Harris, 2007).

My main concern here, given this book's focus on cultural industries, and cultural production, is the first of these aspects of internationalisation, but this can never be fully separated in analysis from the other two.

TELEVISION AND GEO-CULTURAL MARKETS

By the 1960s, the USA completely dominated international flows of television programming (see Chapter 2) and television became closely linked to concerns about American popular culture more generally. For some (for example Schiller, 1969) television was the latest and most significant development in the USA's cultural domination. This view was based not only on programme exports, but also on US companies' direct investment in overseas broadcasters, especially in Latin America (see Wells, 1972). Other commentators were concerned about the *quality* of the USA's television products, culminating in 1980s debates about whether or not the dominance of its programmes and formats would lead to 'wall-to-wall *Dallas*'.[2]

Ironically, in the 1970s and early 1980s, when the cultural imperialism thesis was at its peak, US television's international domination was in decline. Already, even before Jeremy Tunstall's ground-breaking analysis of media and cultural imperialism (*The Media Are American*) was first published in 1977 (Tunstall, 1994), most prime-time programming, including the most popular programmes, was local in origin. In other words, the most popular programmes in Brazil were made in Brazil, and so on. The only major exceptions were very small countries with few media resources (such as Jamaica, for example, which is culturally close to the United States, and which shares a first language). Consequently, as Tunstall (1994[1977]: 14) pointed out, prime-time television tended to be produced either within the home nation or by a larger neighbouring nation with similar linguistic and cultural traditions – this was the USA in some countries, but Egypt for many Arabic countries, or Mexico for Central America. Programming from the USA was primarily used to fill less popular times more cheaply than could be done using home-grown programmes. Direct investment by US television companies in Latin America was short-lived and these firms had withdrawn from such ventures by the mid-1970s – in many cases as a result of protectionist measures introduced by national governments, such as was the case with Brazil. These measures should not be thought of as an enlightened resistance to US cultural imperialism, however – they were often introduced by military, authoritarian governments (see below).

The 1970s and early 1980s saw further declines in television imports. According to Tapio Varis and Kaarle Nordenstreng (1985), in the television stations of the 'Third World' (as developing countries were known at the time) the proportion of foreign programmes broadcast declined on average by over 15 per cent between 1973 and 1983. In the six largest Latin American countries, imports fell by 29 per cent between 1972 and 1986 (Berwanger, 1998: 192).

In spite of *The Media Are American*'s striking title, Tunstall's book suggested that it was too simplistic to see the international cultural industries as dominated by the USA (or the USA plus the UK). A later attempt to move beyond this 'concentric perspective', with its vision of '"the West" at the centre dominating the peripheral "third world" with an outward flow of

---

2 This term was widely used in Britain in the 1980s, especially in the wake of *Financial Times* journalist Christopher Dunkley's (1985) book which had this as its subtitle. See also Collins (1986).

cultural products' was made by the Australian writers, John Sinclair, Elizabeth Jacka and Stuart Cunningham (1996: 5). Sinclair et al. introduced the useful concept of 'geolinguistic regions' (1996: 11–14) to capture the increasing complexity of international television flows. Geolinguistic regions are groups of countries defined by common cultural, linguistic and historical connections. They might be actual geographical areas, where countries with these kinds of connections are actually next to each other, but in many cases these relationships will rely on cultural rather than physical proximity. This is because they are forged out of long histories of transnational contact, including especially the legacy of colonial empires. It is possible, for example, to see the USA, Canada, the UK, Ireland, Australia and New Zealand as forming one such geolinguistic region, based on the use of English as a first language, and primarily white, Christian cultural traditions, once indigenous populations were suppressed or annihilated. Another potential region comprises Spain, Spanish-speaking Latin America, plus Spanish-speaking parts of the former Spanish empire and the massive Spanish-speaking population of the USA. Some might also include Portugal, Brazil and the former Portuguese colonies in Africa and Asia in the same 'region' within a broader set of countries influenced by Hispanic languages and cultures.

I prefer the modification *geocultural markets*. 'Geocultural' is better than 'geolinguistic' because language is only one of a number of potential cultural connections between places and peoples. The countries of Eastern Europe and the European nations of the former USSR, for example, form a particular geocultural region, with shared histories of Soviet oppression and longer Christian traditions, but there is no shared language. 'Markets' is a better term than 'regions' because such cultural connections can work across enormous distances that transcend geographical proximity. A particular country can belong to more than one geocultural market because nearly all countries contain different groups of people with varying cultural identifications. More significantly still – and this is an insight of cultural studies approaches – the same people can have multiple cultural identifications. A woman of Indian origin living in the UK might feel part of an anglophone geocultural market, familiar with a wide range of TV programming from the UK, the USA and Australia. She may well also feel affiliated to a different geocultural market, comprising India itself, plus substantial Indian migrant communities in the Arabian Gulf and elsewhere. Her affiliations may also shift according to her different experiences in life, who she is with, and even her personal mood.

These different geocultural markets have other centres of production besides Hollywood. Sinclair et al. (1996: 8) drew attention to some of these: 'Mexico and Brazil for Latin America, Hong Kong and Taiwan for the Chinese-speaking populations of Asia, Egypt for the Arab world, and India for the Indian populations of Africa and Asia'. They noted that these regional television production centres were built on previously existing centres of film production and I discuss some of these later in this chapter.

The new complexity of global television culture, however, is more than a matter of recognising that trade takes place *within* these geocultural markets.

Sinclair et al. (1996: 5) are certain that these regions are not bounded, discrete spaces. In the new era of television culture, 'global, regional, national and even local circuits of programme exchange, overlap and interact in a multi-faceted way'. To make this more concrete and delineate further this complex, polycentric picture of global television, I will deal with two important but also ambivalent examples of recent developments and the questions these provoke.

- **The circulation of non-USA programming in Europe, the USA itself, and other geocultural markets**. For many years, a widely discussed example of this was the export of Latin American television fiction. So to what extent did this really presage the rest of the world exporting its culture back to the West, as was claimed in some of the research on this topic? And can this be understood as a breakdown of the cultural imperialism model and a move towards a more equitable model of transnational cultural flows?
- **The breakdown of the system whereby programmes were transmitted nationally and schedules were comprised of a mixture of domestically produced programming, plus foreign imports** (often mainly from the USA), and the associated rise of systems of satellite transmission where channels are received across national borders. So to what extent can this be seen as a move away from a system of national broadcasting and towards a truly international audiovisual system? And crucially, to what extent can such shifts be understood as progress towards systems of greater choice and diversity?

Reversing cultural flows? The case of Latin American drama

Latin American television was often invoked from the 1980s to the 2000s in order to question the simplistic notion that non-Euro-American television is dominated by Hollywood television and US conglomerates. It was also frequently used to suggest a model for how non-core television-producing countries might gain more presence in the international television market.[3] Strangely, these celebrations of reverse cultural flows often ignored the concentrated and undemocratic nature of the systems producing the programmes.

There has been a developed television industry across most of Latin America, particularly in Mexico and Brazil, since the late 1960s. In the 1980s and 1990s both these countries, and other Latin American countries such as Venezuela, became exporters of considerable amounts of programming to other countries, not just within the Hispanic geocultural market, but also beyond this, to many other countries, such as the USA and the

---

3 See, for example, Mattelart and Mattelart (1990: 2), citing Italian policy research of the 1980s.

UK – countries usually considered to be at the geographical core of the cultural industries.

The international presence of the Mexican and Brazilian television industries is founded on the domestic strength of two mighty corporations – Televisa and Globo. In Mexico in the mid-1990s, Televisa was taking about 80 per cent of the domestic television market share, which increased at peak times. In Brazil during the same period, Globo had a market share of about 76 per cent, in a huge market of 160 million people where television dominated advertising spending (Sinclair, 1996: 35). Televisa has also drawn on a formidable overseas market in Spanish-speaking Latin America, Hispanic USA and Spain. Globo has been able to rely less on linguistic ties overseas, but it founded its export success on initial success in Portugal in the late 1970s.

Telenovelas have been central to debates about Latin American television. The term 'telenovela' is sometimes translated to mean 'Latin soap', but the term 'soap', which is complex enough in anglophone contexts, is misleading.[4] Whereas British prime-time soaps and day-time soaps in the USA run, in principle, forever, and have no overall narrative resolution, telenovelas will move towards closure over a large number of episodes. The prime-time soaps in the UK and USA also take the form of a series of about 20 programmes, transmitted in 'seasons' over a number of years. By contrast telenovelas do not run in series, instead they will form one continuous serial, often of about 100 episodes. And unlike prime-time soaps in the USA they are shown five to six times a week. As many as 15 telenovelas might be shown by different channels on the same day, often in blocks, in the afternoon and evening. They share with soaps in the UK and USA a concern with family relationships and invite strong emotional responses. There is often much more emphasis on polarised moral forces than in UK soaps,[5] but there is a strong 'quality aesthetic' apparent in some telenovelas, especially those from Brazil (Sinclair, 1996: 50). Some of the most important telenovelas have been literary adaptations. Whereas soaps have traditionally been thought of as debased, trivial entertainment in the anglophone world, telenovelas are often more prestigious in Latin America. However, as in the UK and USA, the fact that the programmes are primarily enjoyed by women and less educated audiences (Vink, 1988: 221–2) is often implicitly, and sometimes explicitly, interpreted as a sign of their supposed lack of worth.[5] Nevertheless, telenovelas are the central television genre in Latin America, in a way that has no parallel in Australia, Canada, the UK or USA. Although introduced to

---

4   One interesting similarity between soaps and telenovelas, in spite of their differences, is that early radio *novelas* were sponsored by UK and US detergent companies, just as many early drama serials were in the USA. Such sponsorship in the USA was the source of the term 'soap opera'.

5   This emphasis is sometimes called 'melodramatic'. Jostein Gripsrud (1995: 242–8) showed, in his brilliant study of the prime-time soap *Dynasty*, how complex this notion of melodrama is and how the term is sometimes misapplied in the study of soap opera.

television in the early 1960s, they draw on a much longer history of melodramatic serials in Latin America, in popular fiction, film and radio (Mattelart and Mattelart, 1990). Telenovelas, then, must be understood as being culturally specific.

It follows from this that the success of Latin American television outside Latin America in the 1980s and 1990s represented, at least to some degree, a new international presence for Latin American culture. One of the reasons for the international spread of the telenovela was economic. Mattelart and Mattelart (1990: 2) showed, for example, that the cost to Italian television of importing a telenovela in the late 1980s was between US$3000 and US$6000 per 40-minute episode, whereas dramas from the USA would cost Italian TV buyers between US$6000 and US$48000 per half hour. As the desire for more content boomed with television marketisation and channel proliferation in the 1980s and 1990s, Globo's exports increased in a healthy fashion. Various novelas became television events in the countries to which they were exported, such as Globo's *A Escrava Isaura* in China, Czechoslovakia and Cuba, *Gabriela* in Angola, and *The Rich Also Cry* in Russia (Paterson, 1998: 62).

So how can the widespread success of telenovelas be explained? Cost cannot be the only reason because many other programmes would be as cheap, so there must be cultural factors at work as well. Mattelart and Mattelart (1990: 144) speculated that such non-Western programmes were increasingly popular in the West because their exoticism provided an alternative to 'the tired logos of Western modernity' (1990: 152). They also claimed that melodrama in the late twentieth century increasingly revealed its 'potential for universality' and that it therefore served as a kind of supergenre, which can be all things to all people, at least some of the time, incorporating suspense, comedy, grief, action and so on.[6]

However, it is necessary here not to exaggerate the significance of telenovelas. Telenovelas formed only 8 per cent of television hours produced by Televisa in the early 1990s (Sinclair, 1996: 49) and a significant and often overlooked fact is that the news was a more popular form of programming in Brazil than telenovelas during the period when the latter were being widely discussed in academic and policy circles (see Vink, 1988: 11). Whereas 50 per cent of television sales in the USA come from overseas, in the mid-1990s Globo was gaining only 3 per cent of its revenues from abroad, even including Latin America. The figure for Televisa was 10 per cent, much of it from the sale of telenovelas and other genres to the USA market, with its large and increasing Spanish-speaking population (Sinclair, 1996: 49, 52).

The attention paid to telenovelas might help to correct the picture of a homogeneous world market dominated by the USA, though, and it suggests the

---

6   The international melodrama super-genre seems to have faded, to be replaced by pop contests and quiz show formats – though this does not mean that Mattelart and Mattelart's argument had no credibility. See Liebes and Katz (1993) for a somewhat similar approach to the international success of the US TV serial *Dallas* (1978-1991).

possibility of more cultural exports from periphery to centre, or to other peripheries, *in the future*. All the same, economically speaking, telenovela exports are relatively insignificant and, culturally, they still form a small part of the television landscape, even in countries such as Russia where they have been very popular. In most countries, domestic programmes continue to attract higher ratings than do imports from the USA (Hoskins et al., 1997: 29). Most non-domestic programming that is aired, however, is still that produced in the USA – it accounts for at least 75 per cent of all television programme exports (Hoskins et al., 1997: 29). Therefore, it may be premature to speak of a new era of transnational television on the basis of the sporadic success of a few telenovelas.

In any case, we should be cautious about celebrating the existence of such Latin American corporations as a means of countering cultural imperialism. As Mattelart and Mattelart (1990) show, companies such as Globo and Televisa monopolise their domestic markets in a way that the CEOs of conglomerates in the USA can only dream of. Both companies rely on significant horizontal integration. Globo was built up by the Marinho family from its ownership of a leading daily newspaper and Televisa has significant press and radio interests. Globo has, at various points, owned record and video manufacturing and distribution, an electronics firm, an advertising company, and major art galleries. Mattelart and Mattelart (1990: 42) cite *Variety* estimates from 1987 that an average telenovela helped to sell an average of 200,000 records in Brazil and up to 1 million records internationally. Both companies were strongly vertically integrated, too. Each produced 78 to 80 per cent of the programmes it aired and virtually all Brazilian actors who were known names were under contract to Globo.

Often portrayed in the West as examples of Latin American commercial media vigour, Televisa and Globo were both founded on close links with repressive, authoritarian states. The military government paid for the satellite infrastructure that united the huge territories of Brazil into one television market and it was this unification of the television market that allowed Globo its dominance. In Mexico, private companies benefited from government expenditure on developing television infrastructure. Here, the relationship with the state was especially contradictory. Televisa was formed out of two commercial channels, in opposition to the Mexican government's newly established Channel 13. Yet, Televisa had close relationships with the party that ruled Mexico (PRI) from the 1910s to the year 2000. In both Mexico and Brazil there was extremely weak government regulation, allowing significant cross-media ownership and massive commercialisation – in the 1980s and 1990s, Brazilian broadcasters were allowed to transmit 15 minutes of advertising per hour. This government support of media industries contrasted with a lack of commitment to the well-being of their populations in other, more fundamental ways. Tunstall (2008: 20) cites a claim from *The Economist* that in 1990 more Brazilians had a TV set in their household than had either clean water or a primary school education.

While Latin American telenovelas are still of great cultural interest, and continue to be exported across the world, it would be wrong to see Latin

American television fiction as having offered a significant counter to the forms of cultural inequality towards which the cultural imperialism thesis, however simplistically at times, tried to direct attention. Telenovelas could hardly be considered a democratising form. They represented a relatively small transfer of programming from South to North, as opposed to the long-standing flows from North to South. The corporations that dominate Latin American television certainly do not provide a model of emancipatory cultural production. While globalisation theory might be better than the cultural imperialism thesis at registering the complexity of international cultural flows, issues concerning the interrelation of economic, political and cultural power remain pressing.

Later developments have reinforced this view but democratisation in the region makes it a particularly interesting area for cultural industries research. Marketisation has developed apace – and this in a region where PSB was already extremely weak. Structures of control based on family ownership have more recently been supplemented by a new generation of media conglomerates (Fox and Waisbord, 2002). In countries such as Mexico, a television monopoly gave way only to duopoly (Sinclair, 2004). The domination of Globo, meanwhile, was challenged by a new force – the rise of religious channels in Brazil, both Protestant evangelical and Roman Catholic.[7] However, Mastrini and Becerra (2011: 73) suggest some encouraging developments, following the election of various governments that were more committed than previous regimes to social justice: increased regulatory intervention, some modest limits to ownership concentration, and the increasing participation of civil society actors in debates about the role of the media. Others have claimed that this partial democratisation has been accompanied and abetted by the development of journalistic professionalism, at least in Brazil (Matos, 2008).

Transnational TV transmission and reception: post-national broadcasting?

The second major aspect of television internationalisation I want to examine here is the increasing transmission of television channels across and beyond national borders. Transnational satellite television has been interpreted as a form of cultural imperialism. It is true that new technologies meant that Western – in particular, USA-based – channels, such as MTV, developed initially to cater for the USA's domestic market, were increasingly available for consumption overseas via satellite cable and direct broadcast satellite. However, this was not a simple imposition of 'Western' programming on the rest. As Kevin Robins (1997) showed, channels such as MTV and CNN

---

7   The erosion of its audience share led Globo to support deregulation of rules on foreign ownership as it began to search for suitable business partners (Straubhaar, 2004).

found in the 1990s that they had to adapt their programming to local audiences. New hybrids were produced, often US-owned or jointly owned with local businesses or states, transmitting a mixture of locally sourced news or popular culture.

The period since the 1980s has seen increasingly complex cross-cultural flows in television that cannot be reduced to the notion of cultural imperialism. The global spread of the video cassette recorder during the 1980s meant that diasporic populations could import films and television programmes from their countries of origin. Cable and satellite technologies, available in many countries from the early 1980s onwards, have made this practice of cross-border programme consumption even more widespread. Hamid Naficy (1993: 62), for example, wrote about an independent station, Channel 18 (KSCI TV), which, at the time of his research, provided 'round-the-clock programming in some 16 languages, produced by various diasporas in the United States or imported from their home countries', including Arabic, Armenian, Cambodian, Mandarin, French, Tagalog/English, German, Hungarian, Hindi/English, Italian, Japanese, Hebrew, Korean, Russian and Vietnamese. Across many of the advanced industrial countries, such 'diasporic television' has boomed in recent years. It must not be assumed that these stations are necessarily addressing and fulfilling the cultural needs of the communities they address and there are many places outside the major metropolitan cities where such services are unavailable. Also, few people would watch these programmes if they were not from the specific diasporic population being addressed. Nevertheless, the availability of such 'peripheral' programming at the 'core' defies the simplifications of some versions of the cultural imperialism thesis.[8]

A number of studies have cast important light on these new forms of cross-border reception and some have argued that there are potentially progressive cultural consequences. Researching the Indian Punjabi community in London, Marie Gillespie (1995: 76), for example, argued that 'the juxtaposition of culturally diverse television programmes and films in Punjabi homes stimulates cross-cultural, contrastive analyses of media texts' within those homes. This, she claimed, heightened awareness of cultural difference, intensified the negotiation of cultural identities, and led to aspirations for cultural change.

The implications for international television of the development of cable and satellite go beyond such diasporic channels however. There is simply much greater transnational broadcasting transmission than there has ever been before. Using early 2000s data, Amezaga (2007) identified 13,750

---

8 One of the most interesting aspects of Naficy's account was that he showed how Iranians, because they were an exile culture rather than a transnational one, were forced to produce their own programming rather than import it from their homeland.

satellite 'broadcasts' or sources.[9] Such profusion of satellite transmission has often been understood as a key example of increasing flows of culture across national borders – a major theme of social theory in the 1990s and 2000s. Concepts such as 'ethnoscapes' and 'mediascapes', intended to theorise such flows of people and culture, were among the most (over) cited concepts of the era. But as Amezaga (2007: 40) points out, such processes are contradictory. They involve the expansion of geolinguistic and geocultural markets, as diasporic populations have increasingly consumed television produced from their country of origin. But satellite services also strengthen the hegemony of a few dominant languages and cultures on a planetary scale, notably English. Indeed English accounted for over 40 per cent of the broadcasts identified by Amezaga. What's more, only 80 of the thousands of languages spoken throughout the world were employed. Languages not used in such broadcasting included some with millions of speakers. And in addition to this, practically all the languages with the most significant global presence were the official languages of at least one state.

This suggests that we should be cautious about interpreting the proliferation of cross-border satellite broadcasting as representing the rise of 'post-national' television systems (Sinclair, 2009), at least in the sense of television that can evade the political control and regulation of individual nation states. Colin Sparks makes the important point that while satellite broadcasting allows us to uplink from one country and down to another, 'there is no point on the surface of the earth that is outside the legal remit of one jurisdiction or another' (Sparks, 2008: 164). The state where the uplinking takes place 'retains effective control over the service in question'. Sparks illustrates this using the dramatic example of how British regulators closed down the Kurdish satellite station Med-TV in response to pressure from the Turkish state in 1999, but he also discusses other issues, such as how differing notions of obscenity operate across different borders. Here too government policy and state politics matter enormously. Sparks points out that satellite services can only make money through either advertising and subscription, and both require the existence of offices, staff and bank accounts that mean that any satellite service is 'every bit as much subject to the legal environment of the country within which its audience is located as is a terrestrial broadcaster'. He also discusses the well-known examples of how News Corporation made a series of concessions to the leadership of the Chinese Communist Party in order to build up its Star-TV service there. Rupert Murdoch's News Corporation purchased the struggling Asian satellite service STAR TV in 1993 and, within a few years, it had made significant inroads into television

---

9   Amezaga and his colleagues were counting 'only those broadcasts that are either directed to the end user (in either open or encrypted form, analogue or digital), or to cable suppliers, inasmuch as the latter multiply the broadcast of the signal received from a satellite. Due to the fact that many channels are broadcast on different satellites, we would point out that we have counted the number of *broadcasts*, not *channels*' (241).

markets in a number of countries, including China (PRC), India and Taiwan. By the mid-2000s, it reached 300 million people with a variety of country-specific packages. All the mega-corporations were keen to gain access to the huge markets of Asia, but News Corporation has been particularly assiduous in courting the Chinese state, suspending the BBC's World Service from STAR in 1994 and making sure that his publishing company, HarperCollins, did not publish the memoirs of former Hong Kong governor Chris Patten – one of the PRC's main international political bogeymen.

Even if talk of 'post-national broadcasting' is premature, it would be a serious mistake to dismiss the cultural significance of the growth of television industries across the world and their increasing interpenetration (a phenomenon of which satellite broadcasting represents only a part). Nor should alliances between states and businesses lead us to end the analysis there. Even Star-TV does not represent a simple case of cultural imperialism, in the modern form of an alliance between global cultural capitalism and a repressive state. STAR TV is a distribution network for entertainment. Rather than a vehicle for the thoughts of Chairman Rupert, it transmits programmes that offer a similar mix to that familiar in the West. Individualist and consumerist values are emphasised, and these can have serious consequences for the societies in which such programmes are transmitted. But even programmes transmitted by STAR TV make available values that do not straightforwardly support capitalist accumulation, including stories emphasising the virtues of family and community loyalty (see the discussion of Ong, 1999, later in this chapter).

THE RISE OF EAST ASIAN TELEVISION

As Table 8.1 illustrates, the television industries of many countries formerly considered to be outside the Euro-American heartland of global television production grew rapidly in the 2000s. In the light of this growth, a number of analysts showed a particular interest in East Asian television. In fact the television industries of North America and Europe grew more rapidly in the late 2000s than those of the Asia-Pacific region, and still generate considerably higher revenues, as the Table also shows. But there are more reasons than revenue and growth to be interested in East Asian television as it is imbricated with profound economic and socio-cultural changes in the region.

A particular focus has been on the increasing flow of programming and formats between the different East Asian countries (Keane et al., 2007). But to what extent is such growth –bringing a new degree of diversity to the media ecology of non-western countries – an opening up of television systems to a more varied diet of television flavours, and a freeing-up of information and entertainment? (Box 8.2 more briefly examines another case, the growth of Arabic television, particularly in relation to satellite news).

The case of Chinese-language television is especially interesting because, to quote the title of a book by Michael Curtin (2007), it has the capacity to

Table 8.1   Change in worldwide TV revenue, 2006 onwards

By region	2006	2007	2008	2009 (estimate)	2013(forecast)
North America	92.9	101.1	106.1	104.1	120.4
Europe	75.5	80.8	84.1	82	98.5
Asia-Pacific	51.2	53.3	55.8	56	68
Latin America	20.4	23.7	29	30.7	42.3
Middle East and Africa	4.4	5.6	6	5.7	8.8
Total	238.3	257.9	272.1	268.9	322.9

	2006	2007	2008	2009 (estimate)	2013 (forecast)
China	6.9	7.7	8.7	9.2	11.3
India	3.6	4	4.7	5.2	6.9
Brazil	6.1	7	8.8	9.6	14.1

Figures refer to millions of Euros

Source: IDATE (2010)

communicate with 'the world's biggest audience'. This suggests its potential to unsettle the existing patterns of international television power, dominated for decades by the Euro-American industries. There has been considerable growth in the various television industries of Hong Kong, Taiwan and Singapore in the twenty-first century, and a transformation of the broadcasting landscape across the Chinese geo-cultural market. Yet Curtin (2007: 276–7) shows that these industries have faced considerable problems. A new generation of entrepreneurs was drawn to the potential glamour and influence of media ownership, as governments gradually relinquished their direct control of media content. These entrepreneurs however lacked capital and creative expertise and have tended somewhat opportunistically to target niche cable audiences in low-cost genres such as talk shows, studio dramas, variety shows and news. But such genres, when produced cheaply, are unlikely to be able to expand into the Greater Chinese market, and beyond – which is the only way in which these industries are likely to achieve significant profit and growth. What's more, as Curtin points out, to become a regional media powerhouse requires the ability to attract the creative talent that is essential to success in cultural industries. Hong Kong cinema succeeded in this, but the Taiwanese and Hong Kong television industries had largely failed at the time of Curtin's research.

Meanwhile, the biggest television industry of all, in terms of audience, that of the People's Republic of China, demonstrates other contradictions. Whereas news and informational content are dominated by the party-state, the provision of non-news content has been opened to the private sector, though on terms controlled by a complex bureaucratic apparatus, particularly since China's entry to the World Trade Organisation in 2001. Yuezhi Zhao (2008: 211–16) discusses how a vast and dynamic television production sector has sprung up, devoted to the production of the serial dramas that dominate television consumption, especially in rural areas, among less educated and well-off audiences. Between 2000 and 2005, the number of domestically produced drama episodes ranged from 9,000 to 11,000 per year. These were mainly handled by more than 700 production companies and funded mostly by private capital. A complex system of control operated, including a drama permit system, approval of proposed series by regulators, the issuing of distribution permits, and a 'topic planning' system. In 2004, for example, there was a crackdown on crime dramas and police-related reality shows, changing the face of prime-time television overnight. The aim was to reduce portrayals of violence and police corruption. Nevertheless, the result has been a 'dynamic and multifaceted televisual popular culture' (Zhao, 2008: 216). Drawing on production techniques and styles from Hong Kong, Taiwan and beyond, television drama serves as a 'controlled forum' for the discussion of a range of issues, from extramarital affairs to class and corruption (ibid). Elsewhere, Zhao, with Wanning Sun, has emphasised the relationship of television programming to the paradoxical process by which China simultaneously pursues neoliberal marketisation and an intensified rearticulation of China's communist legacies (Sun and Zhao, 2009). Television delivers spectacular and powerful telethon-style events celebrating the love and compassion unleashed by the party state. *Ji shi* programmes (roughly equivalent to the post-documentary genre known in Europe and North America as 'factual') provide emotionally compelling narratives of difficulties faced by ordinary people, offering 'education' in the moral, legal, medical and organisational ways in which problems can be fixed – but always keeping the social, political and structural causes of suffering firmly in the background. Marketisation in China has therefore given rise to a massive, dynamic and fascinating television system. But it is too full of contradictions to be celebrated as an alternative to American hegemony.

Just as crucial as the growth of individual nations' television industries (in Japan and Korea, as well as the Chinese-language markets discussed so far) is the increasing cultural exchange and hybridisation between many East Asian countries (Keane et al., 2007). Such transnational cultural flows make it clear that to use the terms 'Westernisation' or 'Americanisation' to describe television in the twenty first century is at the very least problematic – and quite possibly redundant. There is a proliferation of inter-Asian cultural production, circulation and consumption. Again, however, how ought we to assess this in terms of the degree to which it enriches the lives of those exposed to these cultural flows? For Koichi Iwabuchi, consumption of media culture between different East Asian countries, especially television drama, can serve to deepen audiences' understanding of their own societies and cultures and those of the other countries, especially in terms of gender relations and the lives of young people. For example, the consumption of Hong Kong and Korean media in Japan destabilised 'a historically-constituted belief in Japan's superiority over the rest of Asia; thinking which, while accepting that the country belongs geographically and culturally to Asia, makes a distinction between Japan and Asia' (Iwabuchi, 2010: 200). Yet this is not a naïve celebration of Asian cultural capitalism. For Iwabuchi, the rise of East Asian media culture needs to be considered in the context of the power of cultural industries. For example, successful exports from Japan often rely on Hollywood distribution networks, which require the removal of Japaneseness 'to make them more acceptable to global audiences from the perspective of American producers'. Iwabuchi also recognises problems associated with the control of copyright and labour, discussed in earlier chapters in this book (5 and 8 respectively).

Some research has considered the development and exchange of *formats* in the growth of inter-Asian television production and consumption to be of particular importance and significance in a new, decentred, more equal global television system (Jensen, 2007; Keane et al., 2007). Havens (2006: 36) identifies three advantages of formatting over the co-production and importing of actual programmes.

- *Lower risk*: the format has already proved its popularity in another market (though of course the programme can still fail, and there have been examples of spectacular failures).
- *Formats may outperform imports*: because, as we have already explained, television viewers nearly always prefer local programming, especially programming in their own language, to imported programmes.
- *Potentially cheaper*: format licence fees cost much less than programmes – though of course the programme still needs to be produced.

International television format trading has a long history, but intensified in the 1990s and 2000s as industries grew and trade fairs proliferated (Havens, 2006). The format market is very much dominated by European and North American exports (Tunstall, 2008) but there is considerable trade between non-Euro-American countries, and it is this that has made format trade the basis of claims about a new, more equal system of global television. For Michael Keane, 'formats are instrumental in promoting industry development, particularly in marginal systems and … in the process they extend the stock of televisual ideas' (Keane, 2004: 11). Formats supposedly defy political economy critics of cultural imperialism, who, presumably unconsciously, depict 'Asian media as unsophisticated compared with the gloss and glitter of Hollywood' (p. 14).[10] Instead, formats demonstrate a dynamic new cultural infrastructure in Asia, 'a reinvigoration of local content within

---

10 Such travesties of political economy of culture are, sadly, not uncommon. Political economy has its problems (see Chapter 1), but some writers treat it as a straw figure, and do little to identify better and worse versions.

the wider region' (p. 12), as Asian television systems creatively redevelop Western-originated formats and develop their own.

It certainly seems to be the case that format development and exchange in Asia has produced some fascinating cultural phenomena. Iwabuchi (2010: 199–200) discusses the example of how a Japanese *manga* comic series about high-school students, *Hana yori danga*, was adapted as a TV drama series, not in Japan, but in Taiwan. The resulting series, *Liuxing Huayuan* ('Meteor Garden', 2001–2002) was also used to launch a Taiwanese boy band, F4. Both the band and the series became enormously popular across East Asia, within the Chinese geo-cultural market, and beyond. A Japanese TV station then produced a Japanese version of the drama, which was also a successful export, before Korea brought out its own version in 2008. At first sight, this is an example of the vitality of inter-Asian cultural production. But such inter-Asian communication is marked by conflict and power struggles just as much as is the case within the cultural industries of Europe and North America – and sometimes intellectual property law and practice is even more uncertain. The aforementioned boy band, F4, had to change their name to JVKV in 2007, when the owners of the copyright on the original Japanese comic withdrew their permission for the band to use the name, just as a Japanese version of the series and the band were launched. Furthermore, even if such format trade highlights the proliferation of cultural exchange within Asia, we surely still need to consider the question raised at the beginning of this sub-section, addressed by Iwabuchi, but somewhat sidelined in many discussions of formatting, including format trades in Asia: to what extent are local adaptations of programme formats adding to the richness and diversity of public life and personal identity in Asia and elsewhere? Most of the trade takes place in three genres (Jensen, 2007): quiz and game shows, reality television, and lifestyle programming (makeover programmes and the like). Are these enriching the televisual worlds of audiences? This is an issue that we return to in Chapter 11.

Graeme Turner (2010: 55–66) has considered the adaptation of reality TV formats in Asia and Arabic countries. Rather than celebrating the commercial growth made possible by such formats, he registers the complexity and ambivalence involved. He recognises, for example, that the famous Chinese idol contest, *Supergirl*, may have unsettled Chinese popular culture in an interesting and refreshing way by producing an androgynous tomboy winner who was out of line with the traditional features of a Chinese heroine. He also, however, takes the example of an adaptation of the Western television format, *Fame Academy*, which became a massive phenomenon in Malaysia under the title *Akademi Fantasia*. At first sight, the enormous success of such a programme facilitates, through the portrayal of sexual co-habitation and the focus on individualism, celebrity and material consumption, a challenge to the entrenched traditionalism of an authoritarian Malaysian state that carefully polices the values of its citizens. Turner suggests that, in spite of the many debates and conflicts caused by the programme in Malaysia, many Western media scholars would regard the effects of the programme as progress: 'as unlikely in the long term to do any harm to the society concerned other than to nudge it gently towards the globalizing norms framing the modernity of the twenty-first century' (2010: 61). But what Turner draws attention to is the 'striking disproportion between the relatively short-term objectives of the entertainment product on the one hand and the long-term significance of the projected cultural effect on the other' (p. 63). And for Turner, what this in turn points to is 'how single-mindedly commercial on the one hand, and how ideologically casual on the other, is the trade in cultural identities through global television formats such as *Fame Academy*' (p. 63). Here he usefully challenges an empty populism that uncritically celebrates hybridity in the name of globalisation.

Box 8.2 Arabic television and Al-Jazeera: the export of journalistic professionalism?

Like their European counterparts, Arab governments hoped that satellite broadcasting would contribute to fostering a regional identity. The first major developments in the transformation of Arabic television from a national system to a transnational one took place in the early 1990s.[11] Egypt, though not the first Arabic country to introduce television, had dominated programme production and trade from the early 1960s onwards, partly because of its highly developed film industry and large numbers of trained technical and creative personnel. Egypt introduced its own satellite channel – SpaceNet – in 1991 and this had a huge impact, providing alternative coverage of the Gulf War during that year.

SpaceNet was closely followed by MBC, a privately owned Saudi station, and the Kuwaiti Space Channel. Soon after, national terrestrial channels were made available on satellite and many of the wealthier countries of the Arab world vied to put their own national satellite stations into operation as a means of gaining national prestige. These channels were also aimed at reaching the 5 million people of Arabic origin living in Europe and the 2 million living in the USA.

Again, such developments should not be portrayed as evidence of a brave new world of diverse and imaginative television. Arab-sourced television remained under very strict state controls and later private stations, such as MBC and Orbit, were often run by the wealthy elite, including the Saudi royal family or businessmen close to them (Boyd, 1998). (Cultural imperialism accounts tended to neglect such *intra*-national power dynamics.)

It may be that the Arabic channel Al-Jazeera (which means 'the island', referring to its location in the tiny gulf state of Qatar) represents a positive move in this respect. Certainly, it brought a new visibility to Arabic media in the rest of the world, though often the reception has been hostile. Al-Jazeera is funded by

---

11 In fact, Arab countries had teamed up to fund their own satellite in 1976 (Amin, 1996: 106–8). Although this made satellite programming possible, the satellite remained massively underused for 15 years.

the Emir of Qatar, but it has been granted an unusual and, in the Arabic context, impressive degree of independence. Terry Flew (2007: 182–3) has helpfully summarised some key developments. There was a demand in the Arab world for uncensored satellite news, much of it encouraged by the prominence of CNN coverage during the Gulf War of 1991. A joint BBC venture with a Saudi channel based in Rome, set up to establish a regional news service, was terminated in 1996 because of Saudi unease with its content. Al-Jazeera hired the staff formerly employed by the Arabic News Service. This meant a workforce of journalists trained in public service notions of objectivity and professionalism. But also crucial was the commitment of the modernising Emir's willingness to allow it to operate independent of government control (although with members of the Qatari Royal Family on the board) partly as a means to differentiate Qatar from an ultra-conservative Saudi Arabia. Its critical coverage of 'the Saudi-led Arab status quo' (Kraidy and Khalil, 2009: 84) gave it considerable credibility among many Arabs. In response, Saudi moguls financed Al-Aribiya, a new Arabic language satellite channel that aimed to provide coverage that would be more amenable to the Saudi-led Arab consensus. It is more oriented towards soft news, and is perceived to avoid the alienation of American state and business interests. Nevertheless, it has seen some controversy, for example offending the 'transitional' Iraqi government by broadcasting a speech by Saddam Hussein in 2003.

Al-Jazeera's channels, including its news channel, are relayed via cable and satellite TV in many Arabic countries and to diasporic audiences. It began English-language service programming in 2006. Its willingness to air videos made by Osama Bin Laden made it an enemy of the US state, and Al-Jazeera offices in Kabul and Baghdad were hit by US missiles in 2001 and 2003. From 2007, as relations between Qatar and Saudi Arabia thawed, the channel's coverage of Saudi affairs became less critical. Lately, there have been signs that the state has re-exerted control over its management and journalistic practice (Sakr, 2005). Hafez (2007: 78) claims that discussion of the limitations of Arab governments has increasingly given way to attacks on American and Israeli policy. For some, Al-Jazeera merely reflects a pan-Arabist consensus, and fails to uphold principles of professional objectivity. Others, however, defend this as 'contextual objectivity': the channel 'has to be pro-Arab to make up for the pro-American and pro-Israeli tenor of Western media' (Hafez, 2007: 79). Nevertheless, there can be no doubt that Al-Jazeera and Al-Aribiya have together formed a significant development in non-Western informational programming.

THE INTERNATIONAL FILM INDUSTRY: HOLLYWOOD POWER

The film industry offers a parallel but different perspective on these issues. Here, the domination of the USA over international production and distribution has been much greater than in television (for reasons discussed at the beginning of this chapter).

So to what extent has Hollywood dominated the international market in recent decades?[12]

- Garnham (1990: 176) estimated that the USA's majors and mini-majors accounted for over 70 per cent of non-socialist world gross film rentals from the cinema in 1979.
- Across the EU, Hollywood's share of box office receipts rose from 60.2 per cent in 1984 to 71.7 per cent in 1991 (Held et al., 1999: 356).
- Figures for US films' market share vary significantly from country to country. In the UK, they took 93 per cent of the 1991 market, while in France the figure was 58 per cent – the lowest in any major European economy (Wasko, 1994: 222).
- Even in France, though, indigenous productions' share of box office receipts had plummeted to 26 per cent by 1998 (*Variety*, 25 January 1999).
- In 2010, Hollywood still dominated global cinema. Of the 31 territories claiming more than 20 million cinema sales tickets per year, US films accounted for more than 50 per cent of admissions in 24 of them, including 90 per cent in Singapore and Mexico, 88.5 per cent in Canada, and 65 per cent in Spain and the Netherlands (figures from European Audiovisual Observatory Report, *World Film Market Trends*, 2010).[13]

The wave of internationalisation on the part of Hollywood in the 1980s and 1990s can be linked to the spiralling production and marketing costs discussed in Chapter 7 (this, for example, is the view taken by the various executives quoted by Wasko, 1994: 223). Even as the EU and national governments established programmes to support film production, Europe slipped further and further behind Hollywood. European films were particularly bad at making money outside their own territories: at the end of the 1990s, for example, German and Spanish films made less than 0.5 per cent of total box office receipts in any major European country other than their own (*Screen Digest*, June 2000: 189). Such failures are often attributed to language differences, but more significant is a lack of marketing and distribution clout – after all, countries such as India and the USA perform well in overseas markets where different languages are primarily used.

---

12 Reliable data are difficult to come by because of, among other reasons, the reluctance of the USA's trade association, the Motion Picture Association of America, to release full figures (see Garnham, 1990: 171, 174; Wasko, 1994: 293). However, as national governments have become more concerned about the cultural industries, figures have become more widely available, particularly for Europe.

13 An Australian website, Green Ash, provided a helpful summary of relevant data about Hollywood dominance, based on the European Audiovisual Observatory Report in 2011. If the site is still up, it is worth consulting.

Table 8.2 Domestic films' share of box office receipts, 2004

Country	Percentage of box office receipts*
USA	93.9
India	92.5
China	55.0
South Korea	54.1
Hong Kong	40.2
France	38.4
Japan	31.8

*The figures refer to the percentage share of box office receipts in the country named attributable to domestic films

Source: Screen Digest. April 2005. p. 108

Some figures on the share of box office receipts taken by local films in the mid-2000s are provided in Table 8.2. It is true that box office receipts are less and less important as other ways of making money from films (DVD rentals and sales, rights sales, and so on) become more significant. But the figures show what a weak domestic base a number of film industries have – and this was in a relatively good one for local films relative to previous years.

Nevertheless, such long-term inequalities should not obscure the fact that many feature films are made outside the USA. There have been significant film industries in many non-Western countries since at least the 1920s. The vast majority of the films made around the world are not North American. As can be seen from Table 8.3, eight other countries besides the USA produced more than 100 films per year on average over the period 1989–1998. But note the massive disparity in investment available.

By 2010, India was producing 1274 feature films per year to the USA's 754, and the People's Republic of China had emerged as a third major world centre, with 526 films in 2010 (*Screen Digest*, November 2011). Hollywood takes a high proportion of the world's box office receipts but many national cinema industries have significant markets and some have significant international ones. The Indian and Hong Kong film industries are sometimes cited as examples of a challenge to cultural imperialism. So do they represent a viable alternative to Hollywood?

OTHER FILM INDUSTRIES, OTHER TEXTS: INDIA AND HONG KONG

Hollywood has had surprisingly little impact on the Indian domestic film market. Up until the 1990s, this was for reasons of national protectionism:

Table 8.3   Most prolific feature film-producing nations in the 1990s

Country	Average number of feature films produced per year, 1989–1998	Average investment per production in US$ million in 1998
India	787	0.08
USA	591	14.00
Japan	255	3.57
Hong Kong	169	0.58
Philippines	160	figure not provided
France	148	5.26
China (PRC)	127	0.42
Russian Fed	124	figure not provided
Italy	105	3.93
Thailand	73	0.15
South Korea	73	0.72
UK	67	8.25

Source: Screen Digest, June 1999: 130

India did not allow foreign films to be dubbed into Hindi. However, even when this ban was lifted during the cultural marketisation of the early 1990s (see Chapter 4), Hollywood films were only sporadically successful in India. This was partly because Indian films have been markedly different from Hollywood films in their aesthetic. Their plots and narrative forms owe much to long traditions of theatre and religious epic (Thomas, 1985). They are generally about three hours in length, rather than the 90–100 minutes average length characteristic of Hollywood films. The classic Hollywood narrative works according to realist conventions, even where it deals with fantasy, whereas the emphasis in Indian films is on emotion and spectacle rather than tight narrative (Thomas, 1985). A certain kind of verisimilitude is expected, concerning ideal family behaviour, but, particularly in the song sequences, which are a fundamental feature of Indian cinema, continuities of time and place, nearly always respected in the Hollywood musical, can be subordinated to mood and spectacle. Whether or not the distinctive textual features of Indian cinema can maintain a cultural barrier around the Indian film industry remains to be seen.

Since independence India has always produced more films than the USA, though the gap has closed since the 1970s as the USA's film production has greatly increased. India still produces more feature films per year than any other country in the world, as we saw above. The term 'Bollywood' is often used to describe the Indian film industry as a whole and the 'B' in Bollywood comes from Bombay, renamed Mumbai in 1995, where the best-known, Hindi-language, 'all-India' films are made, many of which are distributed internationally.[14] The name is sometimes criticised as patronising, but it is widely used by Indians around the world, and I'll use it here for brevity's sake.

India's exports of film are important economically and culturally. In 1988, the main markets were the Arabian Gulf, Indonesia and, intriguingly, the USSR.[15] But significant importers also included the UK, Morocco and Latin American countries (Pendakur, 1990). Via video and new television technologies, the demand for Hindi-language films among the millions of Indian subjects living abroad has boomed. Indian film exports were worth about US$10 million in 1989, but this figure had climbed to more than US$100 million by 1999. This was a significant source of foreign income for a developing country and the Indian film industry was valued at US$5.5 billion globally by the end of the 1990s.

In the early 2000s, the Indian film industry boomed. In 2001, the Indian government recognised Bollywood as an official industry, 'opening the floodgates of tax concessions and investments from banks, foreign production houses and other legal financial institutions' (Jones et al, 2008: 10). The actual revenues generated are still small compared with that of Hollywood, but Bollywood is expanding its reach beyond India by attempting to distribute and market its products to the global Indian diaspora. The Bombay/Mumbai industry is still based around alliances between hundreds of small producers and regional distributors, rather than an oligopoly of vertically-integrated companies. But according to Lorenzen and Taübe (2008: 290–1) there are conspicuous signs of professionalisation among some production companies. These developments have been accompanied by some innovations in products. Alongside the traditional *masala* films (long, epic romances, with music), there has been the rise of a new generation of 'multiplex' films, catering to a young, urban population familiar with a great deal of Western media and entertainment, and a growing number of international co-productions, perhaps most famously *Bend It Like Beckham* (2002) and *Bride and Prejudice* (2004), both directed by the British Asian director Gurinder Chadha. There have also been changes in the traditional *masala* film (epic romances with songs), for example, in how urban youth are represented (Jones et al., 2008). There are signs, in other words, of an increasing diversity of representation as Bollywood expands.

---

14 Most films produced in India are not exported, but are made for local markets. This is partly because of generous support for film production on the part of regional state governments. Pendakur noted in 1990 that only about 20 per cent of Indian films at the time were made in Bombay. The same was still true in the 2000s. Bollywood dominates production in the Indian national language, Hindi. Hyderabad and Chennai produce more films, but Bollywood has the greatest market penetration in India (Lorenzen and Taübe, 2008: 287).

15 Transnational exchange of cultural products among Communist countries between 1945 and the 1990s is a neglected and potentially interesting topic in discussions of cultural 'globalisation'.

Another major film production centre has been Hong Kong. Hong Kong is often associated with the kung fu films that were popular throughout much of the world in the 1970s[16] and violent action films, but as Stephen Teo (2000: 166) points out it had been a significant film centre throughout the 1950s and much of the 1960s. Film production peaked at 311 per year in 1956–1957, when musical melodramas and swordplay-based historical epics were dominant (Lent, 1990). In the late 1960s, Cantonese cinema fell from fashion and Mandarin-language production became dominant, serving the Mandarin Chinese diaspora throughout East Asia. In the 1970s, there was a huge growth in domestic audiences as Hong Kong's economy boomed. Venture capitalists moved into the industry, recognising the potential for profit. Cantonese cinema became central to the colony's cultural industries. Local Cantonese-language television provided a new source of Cantonese-speaking stars, as did the Hong Kong-based Canto-pop music industry. Local television also provided a new wave of 'technically proficient, socially conscious, and aesthetically polycultural' directors (Stokes and Hoover, 1999: 24).[17]

Aihwa Ong (1999: 161–7) wrote of how the massive expansion in the numbers of middle-class consumers throughout Asia had vastly increased the market for Chinese cultural products. Ong stressed the fact that this Chinese diasporic public, spread over the USA, South China, Hong Kong, Taiwan, Malaysia, Singapore and elsewhere in South East Asia, was connected not only by news media but also,and just as importantly, by TV, films, magazines and so on. New forms of transnational Chinese identity were, she claimed, being forged by media products, including popular kung fu novels and satellite television, but in particular the kung fu and gangster movies that formed the main output of the Hong Kong industry. This was because these films, Ong (p. 162) argued, were 'a medium for exploring reified Chinese values … in conditions of displacement and upheaval under capitalism'. They were 'all about brotherhoods, hierarchised allegiances and kinship loyalty' and demonstrated the vulnerability and importance of these values in a way that Ong believed resonated with audiences.

Nevertheless, Ong was also careful to draw attention to the lingering influence of the USA's cultural industry corporations and cultural forms, including most notably STAR TV, which was beaming programmes to 38 countries at the time of Ong's study (1999: 167). India and Hong Kong may be examples of significant regional production powerhouses, with their own distinctive modes of address, but European and especially North American corporations and cultural products remain enormously powerful. This is apparent in the fact that, although Hollywood films and some of the USA's

---

16 The kung fu genre was not of specifically Hong Kong origin, although films made there were the most successful internationally. Japan, South Korea, Thailand, Indonesia, Taiwan and the Philippines all produced kung fu films as well (Lent, 1990: 5).

17 Like Hollywood, Hong Kong is as much a place for TV production as for film. See Curtin (2003a) for a discussion of Hong Kong, Hollywood and Chicago as 'media capitals'.

television programmes nearly always have some presence in overseas markets, there has been very little presence of Indian and Hong Kong films and TV in the USA and practically none outside the Indian and Chinese-language diaspora. (See Box 8.3 for a discussion of some recent exceptions that prove the rule.)

Box 8.3   Opening up world cinema?

At various times over the last few decades, the films of particular national industries have achieved international recognition. Examples include the success of Iranian cinema in the 1990s and South Korean cinema in the 2000s (see Box 8.4 on the latter). To what extent do these events represent an opening up of international audiences to new sources? Some good films have come from these places, but their impact in Europe and North America has largely been confined to the art house circuit and the 'foreign' or 'world cinema' sections of rental outlets.

For some, a more significant development has been the much wider success of films such as *Crouching Tiger, Hidden Dragon* (2000) and *Hero* (2002), which have reached mainstream cinemas and DVD racks (see Rawnsley and Rawnsley, 2010). These films represent a new strategy on the part of Hollywood studios – co-production with non-USA production companies, especially in growing and lucrative Asian markets. Some critical commentators, however (for example, Zhao and Schiller, 2001), have viewed such ventures as parasitical on cultural difference rather than representing a genuine engagement with it (see below for similar debates in relation to world music).

The Hollywood studios continue to dominate the USA's vast domestic market. Foreign films took less than 3 per cent of the USA's box office receipts in the late 1990s ('Culture Wars', *The Economist*, 12 September 1998). In 2010, the figure was still only 8.5 per cent, and 7.2 per cent of this came from the European Union, primarily the UK. This supposed aversion to foreign films is not something natural to audiences in the USA but a product of particular sociocultural and economic circumstances, including deeply held cultural beliefs about the superiority of the USA's popular culture over other forms (see Chapter 11). It goes without saying that Hollywood has an interest in cultivating such beliefs.

The USA has maintained its hegemony throughout the 1990s and 2000s. While some indigenous film industries in Europe, Latin America and Asia expanded, others collapsed. This was the case in Hong Kong, for example, where film production declined drastically in the mid-1990s and market share was rapidly lost to blockbusters from the USA (notably *Titanic*). By the early 2000s Hong Kong cinema was in crisis, and this was only partly offset by the international success of a small number of films (such as *Infernal Affairs*,

2002) and a new generation of crime films based around triads (Marchetti and Kam, 2007). We need to hold on to the complexity of cultural production and circulation here, however. Curtin (2003b) shows that this collapse was not entirely due to the intervention of the Hollywood studios. Rather, they exploited local developments, including overproduction of poor-quality films in Hong Kong, the arrival of new technologies (especially cable and DVD) and, in particular, the collapse of the release window system in the vital market of Taiwan: Chinese films were being shown on television so rapidly after their release that the cinema attendance for them declined. It could be argued that Hollywood had a role to play in bringing about these conditions, but it was a highly indirect one.

In most countries, local films – namely those involving some domestic financial or production input – experienced a decline in market share during the 1990s (*Screen Digest*, September 1999: 122). In part, this was because of an increasingly globalised film market, where films from more countries circulated to other countries, including regional production 'capitals' such as Bombay and Hong Kong, but it was also because of the even greater dominance of the USA's product. Only in 1997 did Hollywood overtake the market share of local films in Hong Kong. In 1998, Hong Kong movies took more than 45 per cent of Hong Kong domestic box office receipts – one of the highest local shares in the world – but this represented a decline of more than 30 per cent since 1990 (*Screen Digest*, July 1999: 173). In India, early predictions of a Hollywood invasion, after the USA's films entered the market in 1992, turned out to be wrong or at least premature. However, with growing promotional budgets and the introduction of multiplex cinemas to India, the USA increased its share of Indian box office receipts steadily in the 1990s and early 2000s. Sony/Columbia's *Spiderman* films were particularly popular, as of course was Fox's *Titanic*. By 2004, the USA's market share was 8 per cent, but this had slipped back to 6 per cent by 2010 (Audiovisual Observatory Report, *World Film Market Trends*, 2010).

But what does all this mean for cultural creativity and experience? We should be cautious about portraying the Indian and Hong Kong film industries as resistant alternatives to Hollywood hegemony. It is worth remembering that, in spite of the quick dismissals of some political economy writers, there is no simple equation between Hollywood and cultural homogeneity. Hollywood distributes a range of genres and texts – partly because of the vast and diverse audience it serves in its domestic market. Hollywood budgets may represent an appalling squandering of resources, and they may reflect disturbing inequalities of income. But the tiny budgets of, for example, some Hong Kong films mean that quality is sometimes elusive. There is significant textual repetition within the products of other film industries, including those of India and Hong Kong. Stokes and Hoover (1999) write, for example, about the very short production times and lack of adequate postproduction that characterised Hong Kong cinema at the time. There were often unacceptable working conditions for actors and a poor technical finish to films. Organised crime was also apparently closely involved in the industry – and the same was said of the Indian film industry (Jones et al., 2008: 10). So, as with Latin American television, we should be circumspect about portraying national cinema industries in Asia as an *enrichment* of film culture.

Nevertheless, such local film industries should not be dismissed on aesthetic grounds either. Although Stokes and Hoover were generally writing in praise of Hong Kong cinema, it may be that they were bringing 'Western' aesthetic criteria to bear on the film industry they analysed. One leading film scholar, David Bordwell, used the Hong Kong industry to argue that mass-produced films could achieve great aesthetic merit.[18] His book (2000: 2) amounts to something of a celebration of Hong Kong cinema:

> Hong Kong films can be sentimental, joyous, rip-roaring, silly, bloody and bizarre. Their audacity, their slickness and their unabashed appeal to emotion have won them audiences throughout the world … These outrageous entertainments harbour remarkable inventiveness and careful craftsmanship. They are Hong Kong's most important contribution to global culture. The best of them are not only crowd-pleasing but also richly and delightfully artful.

If Bordwell is right, this suggests that the survival and development of non-USA film industries can contribute in important ways to international aesthetic diversity and quality. Nevertheless, it should not be forgotten that the reduction of US domination itself would not solve all problems of diversity. As of 2009, just 12 countries accounted for over 75 per cent of the global production of feature films (*Screen Digest*, July 2010) and the USA remained able to invest far more money into production and marketing per film than any other industry (*Screen Digest*, November 2011).

CULTURAL IMPERIALISM AND POPULAR MUSIC

Debates about the cultural and aesthetic consequences of internationalisation and globalisation can be pursued further by examining the international recording industry. Popular music is a particularly testing arena for the cultural imperialism thesis and some of the most effective critiques of the cultural imperialism thesis have emerged from popular music studies (see, for example, Garofalo, 1993; Goodwin and Gore, 1990; Laing, 1986). The cultural imperialism thesis was felt to be inadequate to understanding international musical flows in the late twentieth century for a number of reasons.

---

18 Ironically, North American and European scholars began to celebrate Hong Kong cinema as it started to enter into something of a creative and commercial decline. In this context, some described Korean cinema as 'the new Hong Kong' – see Box 8.4.

Authenticity versus hybridity

Some ethnomusicologists (such as Lomax, 1978 [1968]) echoed the cultural imperialism thesis in warning of a 'cultural grey-out' as Western popular music affected indigenous cultures. Later writers, many influenced by cultural studies, stressed the value of mixing, syncretism and 'hybridity' in popular music. A number of studies have shown how various local popular musics are the result of complex reinterpretations of imported styles and technologies (see Hatch, 1989, on Indonesia; and Waterman, 1990, on Nigeria). Often, the imported music is itself the product of other groups marginalised within the world economy, such as the Hawaiian guitar-playing that influenced the Nigerian palmwine musicians in Waterman's account. Indeed, much of the popular music that traverses the globe is the result of the creativity of the African diaspora and very often of African-Americans. Transnational corporations may control the circulation of this music, but it would be wrong to identify it culturally as simply the product of a dominant Western culture.

Western cultural products can be interpreted in different ways

The internationalisation of rock and roll in the 1960s has often been given as an example of how some 'Western' popular music has encouraged people to question dominant forms of power in the societies in which they live. Laing (1986: 338), for example, stressed how rock and roll was 'an instance of the use of foreign music by a generation as a means to distance themselves from a parental "national" culture', and Wicke (1990) wrote about the positive dimensions of this use in post-war Stalinist Eastern Europe.

Against this, proponents of the cultural imperialism thesis stress that much of the most prestigious popular music of the world is sung in English. While local musicians might eventually synthesise distinctive versions of imported music such as rap (see Mitchell, 2001), these local variants are sometimes denigrated by local audiences, as well as by consumers in the more lucrative anglophone markets. Arguably, too, the emphasis on English in many genres excludes non-English-speaking audiences from a full identification and engagement with the global popular music on offer. On the other hand, critics of the cultural imperialism thesis have pointed out that lyrics are relatively unimportant in many key pop genres (see, for example, Frith, 1991), and that this means that, at least in principle, the domination of English-speaking audiences can eventually give way to a more even spread of global success. Chinese- and Spanish-language shares of global sales have now been increasing for many years. We should also note, as with film and television, the existence of geocultural markets with their own centres of production. Japanese pop music's domination of East Asian markets is a key example here (but see Box 8.4 for an interesting development in East Asia).

Box 8.4   K-pop and the Korean Wave: a counter to cultural imperialism?

Since the late 1990s, pop music from The Republic of Korea/South Korea (often abbreviated to K-pop) has achieved significant success in East Asia, where Japanese acts and organisations have traditionally been dominant. This market was worth some $US 30 million in 2009, and the South Korean government estimated it would be worth double that in 2010 (Williamson, 2011). K-pop is the latest example of the extraordinary success and vitality of Korean popular culture since the 1990s, in film and television, and across a range of popular music genres. This is sometimes known as 'the Korean wave' (Shim, 2006). A key factor has been the South Korean government's drive to expand its cultural industries in the 1990s. This involved cultural protectionism, notably Korea's screen quota policy, which allowed Korean films access to a specified minimum number of film screens. It also involved considerable amounts of government funding, in the wake of the Basic Law for Cultural Industry Promotion. Korean film-making flourished, across a number of different genres, and in terms of both commercial and critical success. Film exports boomed and Korean film-makers won prizes at prestigious film festivals overseas. Korean cinema was acclaimed as 'the new Hong Kong' (Leong, 2002).

There is no doubt that Korean media policies achieved significant economic and artistic results, but it is not always clear to what degree the success has created alternatives to Hollywood practices, both in business and creative terms. Some films rely on Hollywood blockbuster aesthetics. The explicit goal of government policy was 'learning from Hollywood', and this involved imitating the high expenditures on marketing and research characteristic of the US film industries (see Chapter 7 of this book).

Similarly, the success of K-pop is ambivalent. It builds on an earlier 'innovative hybridisation' of rap, soul, rock, techno, punk, hardcore and older Korean forms by acts such as Seo Taiji and Boys in the 1990s (Shim, 2006: 37). But later waves of K-pop relied for their success on singing in Japanese – arguably a kind of linguistic sub-domination. K-pop's march across East Asia has also been built on some rather dubious commercial practices, such as highly asymmetrical contracts, where performers have received extremely low royalties (Williamson, 2011).

In spite of the existence of regional power centres, some of them new, it is still the case that British and American acts achieve more globally widespread success than acts from any other country. Some sense of this can be gained from Table 8.4, which lists the top-selling albums in the world in 2008. Nearly all are produced by acts that are American or British. The only exceptions are AC/DC, an Australian band whose lead singer (since 1980) is English; and Il Divo, made up of singers from four different countries (including the USA) but managed by British impresario Simon Cowell. British and American acts particularly dominate anglophone countries and, to some extent, Europe. Japan has continued to import styles and records from the UK, USA, Brazil, and elsewhere. The only country producing albums that reach the list of the top 50 world's highest-selling albums outside the Anglo-American centre is usually Japan.

Taiwan dominates production for the Mandarin markets of South East Asia. What is striking about music, compared with film and television, however, is how many centres there are, overlapping and competing with Anglo-American domination. For example, Congolese musicians and companies are a strong presence in Central and West Africa and Tiny Cape Verde's recording studios are used by musicians from across much of West Africa. More recently Ivorian music has become a major presence in West Africa, in part due to digital technologies that have made possible the development of 'home studios'.[19] Brazilian music has been influential and widely sold throughout much of Latin America, but Cuba, Puerto Rico, Argentina and Colombia have also exerted strong influences throughout the continent at different times and in different ways. This multicentric aspect of popular music production and circulation may derive from its significantly lower costs of production when compared with film and television.

Spread of ownership

In the 1970s, the dominant transnational companies were mainly from the USA, apart from Philips/PolyGram. In the 1980s, Japanese companies such as Sony and Matsushita entered the fray, along with the German publishing giant Bertelsmann. In studies of the music industry from this time, some claimed that the spread of ownership of the dominant corporations meant that it was no longer possible to talk of an imperial centre imposing its popular music on the 'periphery' (see, for example, Frith, 1991: 267, and Garofalo, 1993: 22, 27). But this was a reconfiguration of the notion of the centre, rather than its eclipse. Again, cultural imperialism theory was at fault in placing too much emphasis on the geographical location of the major corporations rather than on the practices associated with these corporations. However, there are still nodal points in the musical world from where it is much easier to gain access to international distribution than it is from other places: Los Angeles, New York, London, Paris and Hong Kong are among them. Musicians shift cities and even continents in order to gain access to the gigging circuits, recording studios and informal knowledge networks that allow them to achieve success.

Meanwhile, the international music industry looks set to become an oligopoly of just three corporations, following the break-up of EMI Music that was announced in November 2011 (though still subject to regulatory approval at time of writing): Universal Music Group (owned by the French conglomerate

19 Thank you to Anne Schumann for bringing this to my attention.

Table 8.4   The world's best-selling albums, 2009

	Artist	Title	Company
1	Coldplay	Viva La Vida Or Death And All His Friends	EMI Music
2	AC/DC	Black Ice	Sony Music
3	Various Artists	Mamma Mia! The Movie Soundtrack	Universal Music
4	Duffy	Rockferry	Universal Music
5	Metallica	Death Magnetic	Universal Music/Warner Music
6	Leona Lewis	Spirit	Sony Music
7	Amy Winehouse	Back to Black	Universal Music
8	Various Artists	High School Musical 3: Senior Year	Walt Disney Records/Universal Music
9	Lil Wayne	Tha Carter III	Universal Music
10	Rihanna	Good Girl Gone Bad	Universal Music
11	Madonna	Hard Candy	Warner Music
12	Beyonce	I Am… Sasha Fierce	Sony Music
13	Pick	Funhouse	Sony Music
14	Guns N' Roses	Chinese Democracy	Universal Music
15	Britney Spears	Circus	Sony Music
16	Jack Johnson	Sleep Through The Static	Universal Music
17	Il Divo	The Promise	Sony Music
18	Taylor Swift	Fearless	Big Machine/Universal Music
19	Jonas Brothers	A Little Bit Longer	Hollywood Records/Universal Music
20	Various Artists	Camp Rock OST	Walt Disney Records/Universal Music
21	Kings of Leon	Only By The Night	Sony Music
22	Nickelback	Dark Horse	Warner Music/EMI Music
23	Miley Cyrus	Breakout	Walt Disney Records/Universal Music
24	Kid Rock	Rock n Roll Jesus	Warner Music
25	Enya	And Winter Came	Warner Music
26	Mariah Carey	E=MC2	Universal Music
27	Take That	The Circus	Universal Music
28	The Killers	Day & Age	Universal Music

Source: IFPI

Vivendi), Sony Music Entertainment, and Warner Music Group (owned by a private American company, Access Holdings). This ownership is spread across three continents, but operations are directed primarily from Los Angeles, New York, and to a lesser extent London.

Popular music, then, provides some evidence against the cultural imperialism thesis. Even if we should not talk in functionalist terms of the conscious imposition of one culture on another, the logic of the global market means that access to audiences and committed publicity and promotion still seems to be extremely unequal for musicians and this inequality is geographical and nationally differentiated. There are also, of course, significant inequalities in what is available to different sets of audiences. This may mean that it is possible to hold on to a modified version of the cultural imperialism thesis. The continuing currency of issues that the term 'globalisation' does not always seem adequate to address can be indicated by referring to the debates surrounding two controversial categories: 'Euro-pop' and 'world music'.

With rare exceptions, continental European popular musicians have often been held in contempt by British and American audiences. 'Euro-pop' was a scathing term for the pidgin English and perceived lack of authentic musicianship among a generation of 1970s and 1980s European acts. Laing (1992: 139) concluded a survey of national and transnational trends in European popular music by speculating that the next U2 might come from Wroclaw or Bratislava. There have been few signs of the emergence of such acts, however. In the history of European acts on the global scene, only Abba has even come close to being at the centre of pop myth, and even their significance has, since the 1970s, been primarily based on a kitsch aesthetic. Indeed, the mid-1990s saw the re-establishment of London as the European centre for the most fashionable pop sounds, whether in dance music or indie/alternative pop/rock. European pop of many kinds remained an object of haughty derision for many music fans. By the 2000s, however, British (and, to a lesser extent, American) snobbery towards European music was finally diminishing, as a number of artists gained significant critical acclaim and credibility, including a notable number of French and Swedish acts, such as Phoenix, Peter, Bjorn and John, Fever Ray and Lykke Li. Even in the world of global pop, acts such as Robyn (from Sweden) have achieved significant success in recent years. Nevertheless, it is striking that a performer such as the French-Spanish musician Manu Chao, widely revered by music-lovers across much of Southern Europe, remains almost unknown in the Anglophone world.

The term 'world music' was adopted in the 1980s by a number of recording and music press entrepreneurs to allow non-Western popular musics to be promoted more adequately in the UK (Frith, 2000). Without doubt, some musicians from outside the Anglo-American global core have achieved international success and recognition in Europe and North America as a result of a set of institutions associated with this problematic genre term (record labels, festivals, circuits of concert promotion). Notable examples include Nusrat Fateh Ali Khan (from Pakistan) and Amadou and Mariam (from Mali). The Buena Vista Social Club phenomenon brought mid-century Cuban big-band *son* to a huge international audience in the 1990s. However, it could be argued that the impact of such musicians has been limited. They are enjoyed by a rather older, middle-class audience. They hardly register as popular, either in terms of total sales or in terms of their centrality for global popular culture. In addition, such musicians are often the subject of discourses that see their music as valuable only to the extent that it conforms to certain Western notions of authenticity and tradition (see Feld, 1994, for a superb examination of such discourses). As a result the notion of world music sometimes serves as an all-embracing category for that which is not perceived as Western pop and this can work to exclude non-Western musicians from global pop markets by defining them as exotic.[20] Goodwin and Gore (1990) once argued that the existence of world music as a genre can be seen as the product of the effects of cultural imperialism rather than a significant counter to them. This may be too polarised a view. But world music is inevitably linked to international cultural inequality. If it provides some sort of corrective to that inequality – which is much more significant than the issue of whether the term 'imperialism' is the correct one or not – it is a limited and problematic one.

* * *

The situation of continental European and non-Western musicians in the international recording industry suggests, then, that even if the cultural imperialism model has conceptual flaws, as indicated throughout this chapter, it draws attention to problems that continue to exist in the world of popular music – in particular, systematic global inequalities in cultural prestige and economic profit. Much the same can be said of the television and film industries (international internet access is discussed in the next chapter). Producers from outside the 'core' countries still have only limited access to global networks of cultural production and consumption. The USA's cultural industries remain remarkably dominant. Countries outside a small core represent only a tiny proportion of global cultural trade. Oceania and Africa have a combined share of less than 1 per cent (UNESCO, 2005 – though note that this report relies on custom statistics). Africa remains highly marginalised, with only rare exceptions, 'bottom of the media pecking order' (Tunstall, 2008: 285–326) – which of course does not make its cultural products any less interesting or culturally valuable, or the lives of its people necessarily of a lesser quality than those in the West, whose cultural industries thrive.

In many respects, then, there has been significant continuity. Nevertheless, we should not underestimate the very real changes in the extent and complexity of international cultural flows. The internationalisation of the cultural industries over the last 30 years has, as suggested in Chapter 3, been driven by the need, on the part of 'Western' companies of all kinds, to find new markets for labour and for their products. Intensified internationalisation was in some respects an attempt to counteract the effects of the Long Downturn. However, the big US/European/Japanese corporations do not entirely dominate global production. There are other important flows, too. We can see a growing complexity in the social relations of cultural production on an international scale – as new industries emerge, old industries grow and new

---

20 The term is also used sometimes to refer to the work of Western musicians who draw on non-Western sources – most notably Paul Simon's 1986 *Graceland* album.

technologies are introduced on terms that allow for new relations between distant places. Globalisation theory has attempted to register this, but has failed to capture the agency of large, profit-making corporations in shaping, but not completely determining, the new cultural world order. This theory downplays the economic and cultural dimensions of international inequality and is often evasive about policy priorities. Neither cultural imperialism nor globalisation theory is adequate to assess spatial and geographical changes in the cultural industries across the world. Grounding analysis by examining particular industries and texts, as I have sought to do here, may provide a way out of the impasse between the two sets of theory.

RECOMMENDED AND FURTHER READING

Michael Curtin (2003a and b, 2007) has analysed the complex geography of international cultural flows, especially in relation to television, without losing sight of issues concerning power and identity. So too has Joseph Straubhaar, whose *Global Television* (2007) is highly recommended. John Sinclair with Graeme Turner's *Contemporary World Television* (2004) is a mine of useful information on transformations across the world, while Sinclair's work on Latin American media is always insightful and informative. See especially his book *Latin American Television* (1999), but also the more recent chapter in Graeme Turner and Jinna Tay's *Television Studies After TV* (2009). That collection also includes other helpful chapters on television.

In recent years there has been a welcome flood of English-language analysis of 'non-western' media and cultural industries, especially in Chinese geocultural markets. The leading writer on Chinese media and society from a political economy perspective is Yuezhi Zhao, especially her *Communication in China* (2008), but also the excellent chapter in James Curran's *Media and Society* (5th edition, 2010). Michael Curtin's *Playing to the World's Biggest Audience* (2007) is a fine study. Koichi Iwabuchi has provided valuable reflections on inter-Asian cultural communication in a number of sources, including his book, *Recentering Globalization* (2002).Also good is Marwan Kraidy and Joe Khalil's book on *Arab Television Industries* (2009). *China With A Cut* (2010), by Jeroen de Kloet, is a fascinating analysis of youth and popular music in that country.

Jeremy Tunstall's *The Media Are American* (1994, originally published in 1977) remains an informative source about the long-term history of cultural industry internationalisation. His later book, *The Media Were American* (2008), updates the earlier book, and provides a rich mine of historical information about media industries across the world.

Global Hollywood 2 (2005) by Miller et al. is a furious polemic against the US film industry's international dominance and operations. Paul McDonald and Janet Wasko's collection, *The Contemporary Hollywood Film Industry* (2008), contains noteworthy research on relations between Hollywood and other societies and industries, including by Nitin Govil on India, Tamara Falicov on Latin America, and John Lent on East Asia.

The work of Herbert Schiller frequently addressed internationalisation (*Mass Communication and American Empire*, 1969; *Communication and Cultural Domination*, 1976; *Culture, Inc.*, 1989). Schiller was apparently an inspiring teacher, and was certainly a writer of engaging polemics, but in my view his work often failed to provide a coherent theoretical underpinning for critique. Richard Maxwell's thoughtful study, *Herbert Schiller* (2003), gives a much more favourable assessment. So too does Colin Sparks, as part of a significant and scholarly study of international communication: see his (2008) book, *Globalization, Development and the Mass Media*.

An excellent book on contemporary issues in internationalisation, including cultural policy responses that I have neglected here, is Peter S. Grant and Chris Wood's *Blockbusters and Trade Wars* (2004). This is a thoughtful critique of global domination by the USA, and a helpful outline of potential policy responses. It particularly addresses the problems that Canada faces as a small neighbour of the world's major cultural power. Brett Christophers applies geography to media studies, and provides a comparision of the television industries of the UK and New Zealand in his *Envisioning Media Power* (2009).

A good overview of a wide range of issues regarding international media is supplied by Terry Flew's *Understanding Global Media* (2007). Also helpful but more polemical is Kai Hafez's *The Myth of Media Globalization* (2007). A fine PhD thesis by the Finnish scholar Marko Ampuja (2010) demolishes some major theories of media and cultural globalisation.

Many of the writers I have cited above are based in Australia, which, given its population size, has made a disproportionate contribution to our understanding of international cultural industries and media culture. As well as *Screen Digest*, *Variety* is also very useful.

ONLINE READING

All the online material referenced below can be accessed free of charge at: **http://www.sagepub.co.uk/hesmondhalgh**

Simply click on the 'Sample Materials' tab to find the links to each article.

See Amezaga Albizu (2007) for a study of geo-linguistic/geo-cultural regions. An article by Oliver Boyd-Barrett relates questions of internationalisation to the production of news.

- Amezaga Albizu, Josu (2007) 'Geolinguistic regions and diasporas in the age of satellite television', *International Communication Gazette*, 69(3): 239–261.
- Boyd-Barrett, Oliver (2010) 'Assessing the prospects for an Asian re-configuration of the global news order', *Global Media and Communication*, 6: 346–356.

Digitalisation and the Internet

'New media' and digitalisation: beyond the hype 310

The digital optimists and their key claims 313

    A more sophisticated digital optimism? Benkler,

        Jenkins and Castells 317

Criticisms of digital optimism – and three dilemmas 321

    1. Digital divides: inequalities in access, skills and activity 323

    2. Control of circulation and concentrations of attention 327

    3. Commercialisation, surveillance and 'free labour' 330

'NEW MEDIA' AND DIGITALISATION: BEYOND THE HYPE

Digitalisation and the internet could never be a minor part of any book about change and continuity in the cultural industries. No other area of debate about cultural production has seen such remarkable claims for transformation. This makes it all the more important that such claims are assessed carefully and soberly. After all, many parties have an interest in overstating the impact of new communication technologies. For journalists and academics, sensational reports of a transformed future can draw attention from readers, editors and funding bodies. For companies, the introduction and dissemination of new technologies could provide new market opportunities. For politicians and policymakers, predicting and supporting transformation may appear progressive.

The term 'new media' illustrates how much confusion the hype about technological transformation can cause. The phrase is very often used to refer to technologies that are really quite old, such as the use of coaxial cable and satellite broadcasting in television. Both of these 'new' technologies have been around since the 1960s. Technologies such as e-mail, third-generation mobile telephony and internet telephony are sometimes referred to as 'new media'. But they are primarily based on person-to-person or person-to-group communication, so can hardly be thought of in any meaningful way as media at all – at least in the sense in which the term is usually employed, to mean 'few to many', 'mass' media communication. 'New media' is applied to pretty much anything that happens on the internet and the web, with confusing consequences.

At the core of the issue, when all the conflicting definitions are put to one side, is **digitalisation**.[1] The 'old' electronic media that grew up alongside print media in the period from 1850 to 1950 – photography, phonography (sound recording), cinema, radio, television – relied mainly on *analogue* systems, rather than digital ones. In analogue broadcasting, to take one example, the main components of communication and cultural expression – words, images, music and other sounds and so on – were translated into a continuous body of information, radio waves, that would in some way reproduce the form or appearance of the original performance, image, or whatever. The radio waves would then be decoded by radio or television receivers (television was broadcast by radio waves). In other words, the radio waves were *analogous* to the original act of communication – they resembled or corresponded to it: 'Loud sounds produce big signals from a microphone and quiet sounds produce small signals', as Stephen Lax (2008: 105) puts it. In media such as photography, cinema and video, an analogy of the image to be captured would be imprinted in negative form on film and then be 'decoded' in the developing process. In phonography, the sound waves produced by musical instruments or the voice were converted into a signal, which was coded into the grooves of a record or on to magnetic tape, to be decoded at some later point by a record or tape player.

The vital innovation associated with the development of *digital* electronic storage and transmission was that the major components of cultural expression – words, images, music and so on – became convertible into binary code (elaborate sequences of zeros and ones) that could then be read and stored by computers. This was vital, because it made communication more transportable and manipulable than before. Perhaps most importantly of all, it also made different media potentially interconnectable. Box 9.1 discusses some of the early ways in which computerisation and digitalisation affected the cultural industries.

Box 9.1   Early forms of digitalisation in cultural production

Digitalisation had begun to have effects on the ways businesses were run from the 1960s onwards, but this happened principally as a result of the effects of mainframe or minicomputers. People in advanced industrial countries had growing contact with airline reservation systems, electronic databases and so on during this period. These were systems in which remote terminals would be linked by phone lines to central mainframe computers. The effects of such systems on the cultural industries were first felt in news gathering, as news agencies such as Reuters began to provide electronic financial data and news services to news organisations (see Tunstall and Machin, 1999: 80).

It was only in the late 1970s and early 1980s, however, that digitalisation started to have a more substantial impact on the cultural industries as a whole.

(Continued)

---

1   See Lister et al. (2003: 13–35) for a fuller definition involving the following elements: digitality, interactivity, hypertextuality, dispersal and virtuality.

(Continued)

In many cases, the most immediate impact of digitalisation was on technologies of cultural production. With the development of the personal computer in the 1980s (see Chapter 3) this digitalisation of production spread through all of the major cultural industries, with significant effects on the working practices of photographers, film animators, radio producers, television editors and so on. This dissemination of digital technologies was often accompanied by claims that they enabled a democratisation of production, by making the means of production more accessible to less powerful and well-resourced institutions, such as independents and alternative organisations, and even amateurs, by reducing costs and by making it possible to produce on personal computers.

As with later developments, music was in the forefront of such developments because of its low cost and low 'bandwidth' (it takes up less computer space than visual formats). In the music industries, musical instruments and, in some cases, recording studios were increasingly moving over to digital methods in the early 1980s, because they had the advantages of less interference, more accurate reproduction, and greater manipulability. There were intense controversies and debates over whether or not these new technologies made music-making less creative and less collaborative than traditional methods by making it possible for individuals to mix sounds themselves, drawing on the sounds stored and/or generated by computers (Théberge, 1997). As prices fell, digital technologies such as samplers, sequencers and MIDI (a standard digital interface) were then offered to the consumer market and marketed on the basis of their convenience and quality. These technologies made it possible to produce recordings without having to hire expensive recording studios. Especially in genres that placed less emphasis on sound quality, and that in some cases celebrated 'lo-fi' sound on the basis of its emotional power, authenticity or accessibility, the 'bedroom studio' became a real possibility. The electronic dance music boom of the late 1980s and early 1990s, for instance, was partly fuelled by this development. (The drug ecstasy or MDMA also helped.)

In addition, digitalisation and miniaturisation had profound effects on publishing, and especially magazine publishing, as desktop publishing software (software that could be used to produce and design documents, magazines and other publications on a personal computer) and other digital technologies became cheaper and more widely available from the early 1980s onwards.[2]

Digital music technologies, desktop publishing and other forms of digital cultural technology had substantial impacts on existing cultural industries, but the availability of relatively cheap and compact microprocessors from the late 1970s onwards also began to spawn new cultural forms. The earliest new form of any substance was the video game. This was initially a part of the amusement arcade and pub/bar entertainment business in most countries, but as

---

2   There is no space to address these developments in detail here, but see the first edition of this book, pp. 202–12, for a discussion.

ownership of personal computers spread in the 1980s the computer game increasingly became a domestic cultural artefact – albeit a very sophisticated, profitable and controversial one. In the section on digital games (the collective name for what used to be called video and computer games, plus other games, such as online games) in Chapter 10, I look at how such games developed into a cultural industry in their own right. As we shall see, although it was based on digital technologies, this industry obeyed many of the principles associated with older forms of cultural business.

The arrival of the internet and world wide web as technologies available to significant numbers of people in the 1990s and 2000s obviously intensified the digitalisation of cultural production. It also intensified claims about the benefits that digitalisation might bring. Some of these claims concerned *efficiency*. While digitalisation and the internet represent remarkable human achievements and make certain processes easier and more convenient, we should not read the development of digital technologies as unambivalent progress towards a more efficient communications world. It takes an enormous amount of resources and energy for organisations to make computers and microprocessors and for consumers to learn software programs. If such systems ultimately save time and money, it is only because enormous and often unnoticed amounts of money are spent elsewhere, such as on research and development, and in building up the banks of computers in schools, colleges and workplaces where computer use is still concentrated.

In any case, the primary concern of this book is not with such issues of efficiency and profit. In line with the discussion in Part One, my concern in this and the next chapter is with whether or not digitalisation and the internet have brought about a fundamental shift in the cultural industries, both in terms of power and in terms of the contribution of cultural production and consumption to culture, society and democracy.

THE DIGITAL OPTIMISTS AND THEIR KEY CLAIMS

In order to assess these developments, it is necessary to understand that the internet and web inherited an association of information technology with individual freedom, autonomy and decentralisation (see Flichy, 1999; Streeter, 2011; Turner, 2006). The academic and countercultural computing cultures that developed the internet and web involved many people who were sufficiently reflective to want to produce an account of the exciting developments of which they felt themselves to be a part. Drawing on a longstanding association of knowledge with human emancipation, they saw the computer as a means of liberation. In the 1960s and 1970s, it became increasingly clear that computers could soon be combined with telecommunications networks (this is the most basic sense of the term *convergence*). For some of those excited by the potential of the computer to enhance human life, knowledge and commerce, these emergent digital networks represented new utopian possibilities. From the 1980s onwards, a set of intellectuals associated with these computing cultures began to produce accounts of these cultures that were extremely influential in disseminating a utopian notion of digital networks as liberating.[3]

The fact that this took off in the 1980s, and especially in the 1990s, is highly significant. For it meant that the internet and world wide web developed at a time when neo-liberalism and marketisation were sweeping the world and affecting prevailing understandings of cultural production and consumption (see Chapters 4 and 5). At the same time, information society and knowledge economy discourse helped drive the growth of the cultural industries. Proponents of information society views welcomed these new developments wholeheartedly. Governments and businesses embraced the idea that the internet would combine prosperity with participation, business savvy with bottom-up control.

This meant that the internet and world wide web were framed as democratising, life-enhancing forces in culture and communication, but at a time when neo-liberalism, marketisation and commodification inhibited the realisation of their emancipatory potential. We should not underestimate the complexity of this contradiction. Previous chapters in this book have outlined the ambivalences surrounding the further commodification of culture that has taken place over the last few decades. Without doubt, markets under capitalism tend to combine forces involving competition and co-operation, centralisation and decentralisation (Fuchs, 2008). Over time, many technologies, from carpentry to medical testing, become cheaper and more available for greater numbers of people. But at the same time, there are also powerful tendencies in capitalism and in capitalist markets towards inequality. In general, there is a tendency for structural inequalities of class, gender, ethnicity and so on to be exacerbated unless resolute political and governmental action is taken to counter them. Even then, this may prove fruitless in the face of powerful business interests. In cultural markets more specifically, as I stressed in Part One of this book, certain recurring features of the cultural industries will give rise to concentrations of power, based particularly on the central importance of circulation (the process of getting cultural products to audiences) and the drive to capture human creativity for the needs of commerce.

So, because utopian understandings of the internet and web are buried deep in the culture, and are often reproduced unconsciously by journalists, academics, entrepreneurs, enthusiasts, and millions of ordinary users influenced by these prevailing discourses, we need to be especially on our

---

3 Examples include the work of Howard Rheingold (1992), Nicholas Negroponte (1995), and *Wired* magazine. The values shaping the development and understanding of the internet have been superbly analysed and critiqued in historically-informed accounts by Vincent Mosco (2004), Fred Turner (2006) and Thomas Streeter (2011).

guard when assessing claims that the internet and the world wide web have democratised culture.

Research on digitalisation and the internet has thrown up many issues. In this chapter I focus on those with special relevance for an evaluative analysis of change and continuity in the cultural industries. At the heart of the issue are two sets of claims, and the second is derived from the first:

- Digitalisation and the internet allow for substantially greater levels of control and/or creativity and/or participation on the part of non-professional 'users' and/or audiences.
- Because of this, the power of industrial, professional and institutionalised cultural production is eroding, and a more democratic and vigorous system of communication has either arrived, or is just over the horizon.

Many other claims have been made concerning the effects of digitalisation and the internet on the cultural industries, such as the idea that the boundary between producers and consumers is breaking down, and that amateur media and 'user-generated content' are now integral to cultural production. But I think that for now these claims are best treated as subordinate to the two key claims listed above.

These fundamental claims are the product of a potent mix of the information society and knowledge economy discourse of the 1960s and 1970s, and views of information technology as empowering and liberating. As the communicative possibilities of computers connected by long-distance telephony became increasingly apparent in the late 1980s and early 1990s, a new wave of techno-prophets began to write of a new era of media, based on interactivity rather than passivity. One extremely widely-read and influential commentator wrote in 1995 that 'the monolithic empires of mass media are dissolving into an array of cottage industries' (Negroponte, 1995: 58). This claim was made bang in the middle of the greatest wave of media consolidation and conglomeration in history, but the author was widely hailed as a digital sage.

Such prophecies, often based on the assumption that predicted changes were already happening, allowed many writers to fudge crucial political questions. For example, the vital issue of how to regulate the media and cultural industries for the good of culture, society and democracy rarely arose for the digital ultra-optimists: the decentralising forces of information and the personal computer would take care of everything (see Streeter, 2011: 69–92). Here the influence of neo-liberalism, which in the USA had begun to pervade liberal Democrats and the highly fragmented left, was abundantly apparent. This digital ultra-optimism was often based on extraordinarily simplistic dualisms – and this continues to be the case.[4]

---

4 Distinctions can be helpful and are often vital, dualisms can overly simplify complexity.

There has been a notable tendency, for example, to draw a strong line between 'old media' and 'new media', portraying the former as based on passivity, and the latter as based on (inter)activity. Negroponte's work is a classic and influential case. Later instances abound: Axel Bruns (2008: 13–14), for example, divides the history of culture into 'the industrial age' and 'the information age'. In the latter, access to the means of producing and distributing information is 'widely available', and consumers become cultural producers and distributors, bypassing 'traditional' organisations via peer-to-peer and 'many to many' (rather than 'one to many') communication systems, leading to a new form or model known as 'produsage', a mixture of production and use.

Realising that such claims are rooted in older discourses helps to show that analysts may well be projecting a set of desires and dreams on to technologies, rather than analysing what is actually happening. Those older discourses, like the more recent versions, blur the boundaries between prophecy and analysis. To take one example, Alvin Toffler, a former journalist who in the 1970s and 1980s was one of the most influential and widely read analysts of corporate and cultural change in the English language, many years ago coined the term 'prosumer' (Toffler, 1980). The idea was strikingly similar to some of the more recent rhetoric: production and consumption had been separated in the era of mass production, but with a transition to a new information-based, 'post-Fordist' economy, businesses would bring about the increasing integration of consumers into the process of production in order to achieve customisation and individualisation. There are many echoes of this kind of claim about the erosion of boundaries between production and consumption in recent discussions of digital communication technologies. Concepts such as 'user-generated content', 'co-creation' and 'pro-ams' abounded in the 2000s. Web 2.0 continues to be taken seriously as an idea (see Box 9.2). But it remains impossible to conceive coherently of economic life without a distinction between production and consumption, though the two should obviously be seen as interconnected, overlapping circuits, and the relations between them can change over time.

Capitalism generates, and depends upon, waves of technological innovation. So inevitably we see innovations that allow claims of transformation to be repackaged every so often, especially in fields such as information technology where innovations have been linked to rhetorics of liberation. The arrival of the internet as a consumer technology in the 1990s was greeted by a particularly striking surge in such rhetoric. It helped fuel the late 1990s dot.com boom – which, like so many other booms, turned out to be a bubble. This one spectacularly popped as the century ended. As the IT sector recovered in the financial/property/technology/marketing boom of the 2000s, the gurus claimed that technological development was only now realising the dreams of the information society techno-prophets. Hence, for example, the 2000s claim that 'Web 2.0' would achieve democratisation where the ancient and rusty old versions of the 1990s web had failed (see Box 9.2).

Box 9.2   Web 2.0

In the now-famous words of a figure closely associated with the term:

> Web 2.0 is the network as platform, spanning all connected devices; Web 2.0 applications are those that make the most of the intrinsic advantages of that platform: delivering software as a continually updated service that gets better the more people use it, consuming and remixing data from multiple sources, including individual users, while providing their own data and services in a form that allows remixing by others, creating network effects through an 'architecture of participation', and going beyond the page metaphor of Web 1.0 to deliver rich user experiences (O'Reilly, 2005).

The concept was developed as an attempt to describe the evolving world wide web in the early 2000s. It was applied to open-source software such as Linux, but was more usually exemplified by phenomena such as blogging, the video file-sharing site YouTube, and the online encyclopedia Wikipedia. For advocates of the term, Web 2.0 had many attractions: it 'manages a freeing of data … permits the building of virtual applications … is about sharing code, content, ideas … is about communication and facilitating community … is built upon trust' (Miller, 2005). It challenged 'outdated attitudes towards the rights of the user, customer choice and empowerment' (Miller, 2005). Web 2.0 quickly became a marketing buzzword with many companies, and the hype soon spread to certain academics. Ritzer and Jurgenson (2010), for example, argue that Web 2.0 facilitates a much more intensified version of Toffler's 'prosumption' (see above), one which generally empowers consumers and is characterised by the end of scarcity and an economy of abundance. As we shall see, there are reasons to be sceptical about the degree to which technologies lumped together under the heading 'Web 2.0' can be universally seen as empowering – and this includes the realm of cultural production.

A more sophisticated digital optimism?
Benkler, Jenkins and Castells

There has undoubtedly been a real shift towards a greater degree of interactivity in information technology and there are significant emancipatory potentials in these technologies. Coleman and Blumler (2009: Chapter 5), for example, discuss a number of ways in which the internet provides 'particular opportunities for citizens to interact beyond, around and across institutionally-controlled communication channels', examples of what they call 'e-democracy from below' (p. 117). These include the BBC's iCan e-democracy project; netmums, a grassroots information network; and the use of the internet to build the Stop the War coalition in the UK. The techno-prophetic rhetoric is not completely empty. This suggests that, for our specific task here, which is to assess the impacts of digitalisation and the internet on the cultural industries (rather than Coleman and Blumler's aim of examining its effects on democratic participation), we need to look at the more sophisticated and careful versions of digital optimism.

A now classic version of the optimistic view that digital technologies were transforming culture and communication for the better is Yochai Benkler's book *The Wealth of Networks*, published in 2006. In Benkler's words,

> A series of changes in the technologies, economic organization, and social practices of production … has created new opportunities for how we make and exchange information, knowledge, and culture. . . . [N]ewly emerging practices have seen remarkable success in areas as diverse as software development and investigative reporting, avant-garde video and multiplayer online games. Together, they hint at the emergence of a new information environment, one in which individuals are free to take a more active role than was possible in the industrial information economy of the twentieth century. (Benkler, 2006: 2)

Benkler delineates the emancipatory possibilities of this new autonomy for individuals:

> This new freedom holds great practical promise: as a dimension of individual freedom; as a platform for better democratic participation; as a medium to foster a more critical and self-reflective culture; and, in an increasingly information-dependent global economy, as a mechanism to achieve improvements in human development everywhere (Benkler, 2006: 2).

Benkler offers a serious and scholarly analysis of the possibility that we are moving to a new 'information network economy' and he is clear that there are serious impediments to the emancipatory possibilities of such a transition. However, these impediments mainly consist in business interests trying to hold on to their privileges by restricting flows of information and culture through intellectual property. From Benkler's perspective, ultimately we can all be winners in the new era of what he calls 'the networked public sphere', if businesses and governments realise that the new networked information economy needs to be based on free flows of information and a greater role for 'nonproprietary production'. But advanced versions of the political economy of culture suggest that contradictions may be too deeply rooted in capitalist forms of cultural production for such win-win scenarios to be truly realisable.

Another relatively sophisticated but problematic version of digital optimism vis-à-vis communication has been provided by Henry Jenkins in his book *Convergence Culture* (2006). We saw in Chapter 4 that 'convergence' became part of policy discourse in the 1980s and 1990s. At its heart was the notion that the lines between different forms of media and communication were blurring, so that wires, cables and airwaves might carry many different kinds of messages, and cultural forms (such as television, radio or the written word) might be conveyed in many different physical ways (Pool, 1983). Some were pessimistic about such convergence and envisaged that this process would allow a consolidation of corporate power. Jenkins is a fervent optimist and emphasises the way that such convergence enables participation and collaboration.

There is something very compelling about the way in which Jenkins marvels at people's abilities to share knowledge in playful and mischievous ways. He provides enlightening and entertaining case studies of the ways in which audiences use digital technologies – for example, the charming *Daily Prophet*, a web-based, imaginary school newspaper for Hogwarts.[5] He is also concerned with the creative experiences that people might have of media and this makes his book much richer than the dreary doom-mongering of some radical critics.

What's more, Jenkins is quite careful to acknowledge some of the potential limitations of his position. There is the sense of a dialogue with sceptical opponents. The problem is that he does not really address the potential objections and limitations he raises. He frequently refers to the entrenched power of media corporations (p. 11) – but throughout his book he strongly implies that such power is seriously challenged by new developments. He acknowledges that small numbers of rather privileged people are involved in the activities he describes (p. 23) – but in a move typical of digital optimists he claims that the early adapters provide the best guide to how media will be transformed in the future.[6] He says that he is not trying to predict the future (p. 257) – but his book is full of predictions. He recognises that participation and collaboration can be 'bad news' as well as creative (p. 17) – but then provides case studies that are overwhelmingly positive. The following passage nicely encapsulates some of the evasiveness in Jenkins' account:

> If old consumers were assumed to be passive, the new consumers are active. If old consumers were predictable and stayed where you told them to stay, then new consumers are migratory, showing a declining loyalty to networks or media. If old consumers were isolated individuals, the new consumers are more socially connected. If the work of media consumers was once silent and invisible, the new consumers are now noisy and public. (2006: 18–19)

---

5   In case you're one of the three people in the world who have never heard of it, Hogwarts is the school in the *Harry Potter* books and films.

6   The fact that many early adopters are young is a significant context for such claims. The bizarre idea that young people will carry on behaving in the same way as they grow older is a common assumption in studies of the media; see for example some of the claims in the 'digital natives' debates (see Bennett et al 2007). It's not unusual to hear ideas such as 'TV is dying - my students don't watch it'.

The conditional ifs here allow Jenkins to distance himself from these claims, as though he himself may or may not be making them. But he *is* making them, really: the old consumers are portrayed as passive, obedient, isolated and silent, and users of the new convergent technologies are represented as active, rebellious, communal and admirably noisy. All Jenkins's case studies emphasise creativity and control on the part of audiences and users. Ultimately, his analysis strongly implies that the uses of new (mainly digital) communication technologies enhance human life, without positioning the discussion within an adequate account of human needs, of which communication is only one.

A third and final version of sophisticated digital optimism is provided by Manuel Castells. In 1996 Castells published a remarkable trilogy of books that carefully delineated important ways in which economies and societies were evolving. I drew on his valuable account in Part One of this book. However, Castells – based at the time at University of California Berkeley, within a short drive of Silicon Valley, world centre of post-countercultural digital optimism – overstated the degree to which the industrial age had given way to the 'information age'. His analysis of the media was criticised for overstating the degree to which the supposedly liberating capacities of digital networks had already been realised in the media. In particular, he showed little engagement with the continuing importance of television and radio broadcasting. Perhaps in response to some of the criticisms of that earlier work, Castells has more recently offered an account of the network society that places networks of communication at the very centre of analysis and also provides a very detailed analysis of the contemporary communications environment. In the network society, this consists of both the 'mass media' and a new set of 'interactive, horizontal networks … built around the Internet and wireless communication' (2008: 4). These make possible what Castells calls 'mass self-communication'. It is mass communication, says Castells, because it can potentially reach a global audience. The odd example he gives is posting a video on YouTube. But only a tiny fraction of YouTube postings achieve anything remotely approaching a global audience. It is self-communication because 'the production of the message is self-generated, the definition of the potential receiver(s) is self-directed and the retrieval of specific messages or content is self-selected' (2008: 55). All this, Castells states, in a formulation that somewhat echoes Benkler, decisively increases 'the autonomy of communicating subjects vis-à-vis communication corporations, as the users become senders and receivers of messages' (p. 4). Here again, then, there is a rigid division into an old media based on passivity, obedience and concentrations of power, and new, emancipatory digital communication possibilities based on new possibilities of control. But while Castells recognises that some forms of 'self-generated production' are problematic – he uses the term 'electronic autism' to describe blogging at one point (p. 66) – he seems remarkably unwilling to consider how such individualistic forms of communication might be constrained by problematic forms of modern selfhood: how these forms of communication might, for example, both draw on and in turn feed a frenzy of narcissistic self-realisation (Hearn, 2008). Self-generation and self-selection seem to be equated with freedom.

CRITICISMS OF DIGITAL OPTIMISM – AND THREE DILEMMAS

A number of writers have challenged such optimistic accounts of digitalisation, and the impact of the internet and web (along with mobile communication technologies), and the central claims associated with them from a wide range of perspectives. Here I focus on three major sets of criticism that are most closely related to the primary focus of this book on questions of cultural production:

1   Critics have claimed that the ability of greater levels of participation and interactivity to contribute beneficially to culture, democracy and society are limited by **unequal access** to the internet and web. Some have said that we need to consider different types of inequality that might hinder the beneficial aspects of the internet and web, besides access, such as the very different **levels of skill** that people might have. Access to the internet has undoubtedly grown, and this has allowed some internet optimists to claim that such problems are outdated, or that they will be soon. (Other internet optimists seem not to believe that questions of unequal access matter, but I won't address that position here.)

2   Rather than the democratisation, interactivity and decentralisation claimed by digital utopians, critics have argued that there are **new dynamics of centralisation of power** associated with the internet, alongside the **continuing existence of concentrations of power in 'old media'** which the internet has not actually done much to shift.

3   Critics believe that the internet has spawned an intensification of commercialism in the sphere of culture and communication, partly because, in their view, it has been slow to develop a set of conventions for the separation of the realms of information and knowledge from commerce, and partly because the interactive properties of digital networks enable **an unprecedented degree of information to be captured** about users, which opens up **new forms of commerce**, which in turn raise questions about **power and surveillance**. Some critics say that the participation and interactivity in web-based activities (such as open-source software, blogging, putting clips on YouTube, and even posting messages on social networking sites) in reality constitute a form of **unpaid labour**. This is linked to the point about surveillance, in that such activity often generates value for businesses, because information about users' preferences and activities can be easily stored and sold on to other parties.

These criticisms give rise to three sets of questions or issues concerning the internet's impact on communication and culture. This section takes each of these criticisms in turn, and examines the degree to which the processes identified by critics might validly be seen as undermining the central claims of the digital utopians, looking across a range of practices of cultural production.

In the following chapter, I then go on to examine the effects of digitalisation and the internet on four separate industries: music, television, newspapers and book publishing. The final section of that chapter examines digital games as a cultural industry founded on digital technologies.

Box 9.3   The internet: different uses, varied elements

We need to differentiate the ways in which the internet has come to be used. It can be seen as all of the following (and more):

- A means by which commercial transactions take place; in this respect it is an extension of private networked computer systems.
- A medium for individual and small-group communication, especially via e-mail and **social networking sites**. As these social networking sites have grown, we have arguably seen the rise of a new kind of communication, which Castells (2008) problematically calls 'mass self-communication' (see page 320).
- A means for storing and finding information; in this respect, it extends the capacities of newspapers, networked electronic databases, libraries, and even museums, to archive and disseminate knowledge
- A means for providing and experiencing entertainment (like radio or television, but 'always on', and like print, but always there).

It is the extraordinary variety of purposes that they can be put to that makes the internet and web so important and yet so difficult to comprehend. All these aspects impinge on the cultural industries as defined in this book. The last two and the 'mass self-communication' enabled by social networking technologies are especially significant. Yet in assessing how effectively the internet allows these functions to be performed, compared with pre-internet cultural industries, we also need to differentiate between the different **elements** involved in enabling all these different uses and purposes:

- Computer hardware – PC microprocessors and routers – and infrastructure: telephone systems and the 'backbones' of wires and connections that carry information.[7]

---

7   See Starosielski (2011) for an illuminating analysis of how a great deal of global internet information is actually carried through a surprisingly small number of underwater cables.

(Continued)

- Computer software – microprocessors, operating systems.
- Service providers – connecting the above to consumers.
- Portals, search engines and principal sites – providing the gateways to the *content* of the world wide web for internet users.

Lessig (2001) sees these elements in terms of three *layers*: hardware, software, and content.

Because of this variety of uses and elements, it's not really possible to talk of an 'internet industry', rather a set of industries, which are integrally related to other industries (information technology and telecommunications – see Noam, 2009, and the discussion in the Introduction to the present volume). We can see a wide range of different companies, with specialisms at different levels, and in different uses.

Each of these elements also represents a different level at which state and market control may or may not be exerted, providing new challenges for policy. It is with the final level, namely content and access to it, that we are most concerned here, given our interests in the relations between culture and industry, creativity and commerce – but the hardware and software levels or layers cannot be ignored. As Matthew Hindman (2009) points out, all these elements work together in an integrated whole, and so while some may have features of considerable openness, the system is only as open as its widest point. For Hindman, the 'link structure' of the internet is particularly significant in shaping its democratising possibilities. Hyperlinks, fundamental to the web, create 'another, higher layer of Internet architecture, what we might call the search layer, which encompasses the various means by which users find and sort online content' (Hindman, 2009: 40). The implications of this are explored in the discussion of control of circulation and concentration of internet attention, below.

1. Digital divides: inequalities in access, skills and activity

First, the question of the degree to which the emancipatory potential of the internet in relation to cultural production and consumption is limited by inequalities in access. A term that has been widely used in policy circles to describe such inequalities is 'the digital divide'. Some conservatives claim that there is no problem and those not connected to the internet generally don't want to be. This is to ignore the centrality of communication and knowledge to democracy. As Graham Murdock and Peter Golding (2004: 245) put it, in the era of the internet, 'to be disconnected is to be disenfranchised'.

There has been massive inequality in access to the internet. Of course the most striking inequality is between advanced industrial countries and 'developing' countries (see below). But there are also massive inequalities within the 'developed' countries themselves. At the height of the first round of digital utopian hype, Raphael (2001: 203) quoted figures showing that levels of internet connection for black and Latino households in the USA in 1999–2000 were, in each case, about 18 per cent less than for 'all homes' and this gap had widened, not diminished, over the previous two years (these statistics were drawn from the USA's National Telecommunications and Information Administration data).

Proponents of cultural (and digital) markets claimed in response that, as technology spread and markets grew, costs would come down, encouraging even those with the lowest incomes to gain access to the technology. Access to the internet has indeed broadened, but huge inequalities in access by class remained. For example, between 1999 and 2003, home access to the internet increased in the UK from 10 per cent of all households to 46 per cent. Yet among the wealthiest 10 per cent, 85 per cent had access, but among the poorest 10 per cent, the figure was 12 per cent (Office of National Statistics data, reported by Golding and Murdock, 2005: 78). Furthermore, as Golding and Murdock point out, these figures should be read in the context of continuing increasing wealth and income inequality generally in the 2000s.

As home internet access has spread, at least in some countries, research has increasingly drawn attention to the importance of *skills* as a persisting feature of digital inequality. Digital technologies have a tendency to be in a constant state of flux and so distinctions are maintained, as skilled users move on to new uses. There is a great deal of difference between, on the one hand, using broadband to access information, post messages and creating blogs, and, on the other, checking an email account and a weather website every few days. Many computers with internet access are bought (or even provided by policymakers in an effort to narrow the digital divide), but soon need to be replaced as systems move on. Also, owners may lack the skills, confidence or motivation to make use of them (Murdock and Golding, 2004). It is easy for people who work with computers or who have grown up with them to underestimate how much needs to be learnt in order to carry out even basic functions. The digital divide, then, is a much more complex matter than just whether or not it is possible to get access to the internet. Inequalities go much deeper than this suggests. Class, gender and age continue to be factors which strongly determine which kinds of people gain which advantages from the possibilities of internet communication, and sometimes in surprising ways. Although it is sometimes assumed that younger people have good internet skills, and therefore may benefit more than older generations, this is by no means always the case. Andrea Press and Bruce Williams, reporting on earlier longtitudinal research by Press, recount the story of Rebecca, a young working-class woman who became a 'computer addict' during long periods of absence on the part of her mother, a lone parent. This did not lead to the development of skills that substantially helped Rebecca in her life. Instead, disillusioned with school, she used her time on the computer to communicate with friends – a potentially valuable activity in itself of course – and to avoid reading required books by 'relying on the book notes readily available online' (Press and Williams, 2010: 174).

Such inequalities in motivation and skill have significant repercussions for the claims made by digital optimists, that digitalisation and the internet allow for substantially greater levels of control and/or creativity and/or participation on the part of non-professional 'users'. Hargittai and Walejko (2008) conducted research on the extent to which young adults create video, music, writing and artistic photography, and share their creations on-line. Their findings suggest that far fewer people are engaging in the distribution of content than the 'here comes everybody' rhetoric of the digital optimists suggests. What's more, education and gender continue to play a key role in shaping who is involved in such 'participatory culture':

> Consistent with existing literature, creative activity is related to a person's socioeconomic status as measured by parental schooling. The novel act of sharing online, however, is considerably different by gender with men much more likely to engage in it. (2008: 239)

There is of course a further digital divide beyond that existing within individual countries: an international divide between industrialised and so-called developing countries. Hafez (2007: 106–9) summarises a series of reports that suggest the international digital divide at the beginning of the twenty-first century was not only deeply entrenched, but was also becoming worse. More recent statistics suggest that the situation is not improving. Table 9.1 demonstrates the massive inequalities in access to the internet, between countries classified as developed and developing, and illustrates how little the gap has narrowed. Note how the gap between 'developed' and 'developing' countries has not significantly reduced, even though the number of internet users in both countries has of course increased. Observe also how the 'world average' remains much closer to that of 'developing countries' – because most of the world's population lives in such countries.

Table 9.2 gives some indication of how such inequalities work spatially and regionally. These figures relate to household use, which is fundamental to claims that users can become active participants in cultural production outside work.

The internet, based as it is on principles of open access, undoubtedly offers hope for many countries where there is a dearth of accessible information, either through authoritarian control or a lack of resources or both (Hafez,

Table 9.1   Internet use in developed and developing countries, 2000–2010

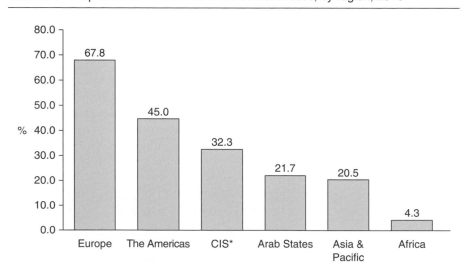

The developed/developing country classifications are based on the UN M49, see: http://www.itu.int/ITU-D/ict/definitions/regions/index.html

Source: ITU World Telecommunication/ICT Indicators database

Table 9.2   Proportion of households with internet access, by region, 2010

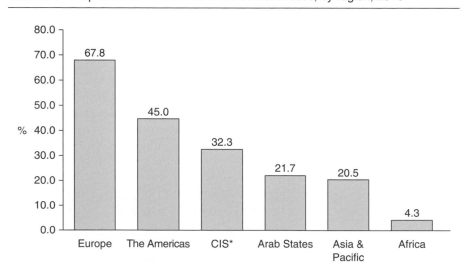

*Commonwealth of Independent States
Regions are based on the ITU BDT Regions, see: http://www.itu.int/ITU-D/ict/definitions/regions/index.html

Source: ITU World Telecommunication/ICT Indicators database

2007: 115). And digital networks have played some role, even if it is often exaggerated in media coverage, in bringing together movements aimed at progressive reform in 'developing' countries. Philip Howard (2010), for example, outlines the exciting developments in Iran in 2009, when tens of thousands of people used mobile phones and digital networks to bypass the government's information stranglehold, as they protested against President Ahminejad's election victory, which many felt was rigged. The internet allowed an alliance of local activists with international cyber-activists, who assisted Iranians by setting up proxy servers to aid anonymity, and by offering advice on how to launch 'denial of service' attacks on government servers. Yet Howard notes that 'it is not clear that the international cyber-activists had more than a symbolic effect on the infrastructure of the Iranian government' (2010: 9). He points out that the role of blogs, Facebook and Twitter was 'an easy peg for coverage by Western news agencies' when international media had few reporters on the ground. Twitter was 'an important communications tool during the heated days of protest', but actual numbers of users remains highly uncertain: 'an unknown number of the new accounts created in those days belonged to external supporters who identified themselves as being in Tehran' (p. 9). Use was overwhelmingly concentrated in the capital, Tehran.

Far more significant in the protests in Iran, and later protests in Tunisia, Egypt and Syria in 2011 ('The Arab Spring'), was another piece of technology: the mobile phone or cell phone – in most cases unconnected to the internet, but used simply for SMS and calling. For some reason this has been the object of considerably less wonder than the internet and social networking sites, even though it has had a somewhat greater impact than the internet on communication around the world, at least so far. Ling and Donner (2009: 8) estimate, using international survey data, that about two billion people acquired their first telephone during the first decade of the twenty first century. Most of them were in the developing world: 58 per cent of the world's mobile phones are in these countries. A key factor behind this growth is simply that building cellular towers is cheaper than laying cables, especially across long distances between communities. This is not a solution to the international digital divide, however, as only a small proportion of mobile phones are reliably and effectively connected to the internet in developing countries, and in any case concentration of access is much higher in developed countries.

2. Control of circulation and concentrations of attention

The idea that the internet (or the web, or Web 2.0) evades or seriously diminishes control because of its decentralised nature is a key feature of optimistic writing about the phenomenon. In the words of Manuel Castells (1996: 352), 'the architecture of this network technology is such that it is very difficult to censor or control it'. For Clay Shirky, the collective action enabled by digitalisation and the internet 'challenges existing institutions, by eroding the institutional monopoly on large-scale co-ordination' (2008: 143).

There is no unified 'internet industry' or 'web industry' (see the discussion of Noam, 2009, in the Introduction). Nevertheless, the web can be thought of as having separate elements of creation, reproduction and circulation (including marketing and promotion) in the same way that 'old' cultural industries like television and film do. There are plenty of symbol creators and enormous amounts of information and entertainment in cyberspace, but which sites get visited and which don't? This depends on the equivalent of circulation in the online world.

Supposedly, we can go anywhere we choose on the web by clicking on whichever icons and sections of text we choose. For some conservative proponents of the internet (Gilder, 1994), this supposed interactivity was what distinguished the online experience from offline cultural forms such as television – the individual consumer could rule in cyberspace. The problem is that where we go will, to a significant degree, be determined by our existing knowledge and inclinations. So how do we know where to go?

Early users – the amateur enthusiasts – got over this problem by spending enormous amounts of time on the internet. As the internet became more widespread, and uses of it became more routinised, a number of new cultural forms appeared that aim to guide users through the web. In the 1990s, it was assumed that the main gateways to the web would be portal sites, many of them associated with internet service providers (ISPs). This was partly what gave the company American Online (AOL) such great power in the late 1990s: it was valued very highly on the stock markets because such portals and ISPs seemed to represent the future of communication in a digital age. But by the early 2000s, it was becoming apparent that the main gateway to the web would in fact be constituted by *search engines*. It is impossible to assess claims about the decentralised nature of the web without reference to search engines.

Lucas Introna and Helen Nissenbaum (2000) provided a valuable early explanation of some major problems with search engines. They showed that the backlink method (so called because it uses a count of backlinks – that is, how many links to the web page appear over the entire web) used by many search engines meant that less well-known autonomous sites were much less likely to be visited and, hence, indexed by the search engine than the ones with greater numbers of hits. The PageRank method – the main means used by Google to form its pages – was, they said, even worse, because it weighed very highly links from pages that themselves had lots of backlinks. Search engines are reluctant to reveal their ranking criteria and one of the reasons they give for this is that such openness would encourage further 'cheating' by search engine optimisers, paid to achieve crucial high rankings for businesses and other institutions. But at least this would help to make people more realistic about the limitations of the notion of the web as infinitely open and decentred.

Table 9.3   Market share of the 4 main search engine companies

	Global	Europe	North America	Asia
Google	82.35%	94.81%	79.18%	73.20%
Yahoo	6.69%	1.57%	9.01%	9.84%
Bing	3.79%	2.33%	9.09%	2.16%
Baidu	5.12%	0.00%	0.00%	12.23%

Source: Netmarketshare. 2011. Search engine market share October 2011. http://www.netmarketshare.com/search-engine-market-share.aspx?qprid=4&qpcustomd=0

Introna and Nissenbaum's analysis preceded the rise of paid search (or 'sponsored search'), whereby content providers would pay to have their pages included or ranked highly in search engine listings. A later commentator noted that Introna and Nissenbaum 'could not have anticipated the prominence that paid search has in today's search engine marketplace' (Zimmer, 2005–2006). However, given the dominance of Google (which lists its sponsored links separately), a more pressing issue is the way in which Google's PageRank includes some sites and excludes others (anything listed lower than 20 is of course effectively excluded). Many claim that PageRank is the most effective system available because of its largely, though not entirely, automated nature. The keywords in the anchor text of external links are a key determinant of rankings.

It is certainly the case that search engines have become most people's first ports of call for finding out information about many different things and this represents a remarkable centralisation of information. What's more, search is dominated globally by just three companies.

The rankings of the leading engines, it has been argued, have a strong self-reinforcing effect – highly ranked sites increase their popularity because they are ranked highly. This leads to what Matthew Hindman (2009: 55) calls 'googlearchy: the rule of the most heavily linked'. Numbers of links determine site visibility, leading to a self-perpetuating domination of niches. Hindman (2009) analyses the consequences of this by providing a statistical analysis of US political blogs and websites, which shows the remarkable domination of the most popular sites in each of a number of key categories of political debate: abortion, the death penalty, gun control, the president, Congress, and general politics. These communities, Hindman shows, function as 'winner-take-all networks'.[8] The same dynamics are apparent in the various political spaces he examined: in overall web traffic, visits to news and media sites, political web traffic, and even sub-communities taking a particular side in a

---

8   See the Introduction for a discussion of how recurring features of the cultural industries produce winner-take-all markets in cultural production.

debate.[9] However, there is a difference here from the hit-driven dynamics of some industries. Hindman also shows that a host of tiny websites gain most of the remaining visitors, and between the big hitters and the microsites there lies a 'missing middle'. Nevertheless, audiences for political websites are, he concludes, more concentrated on the top 10 or 20 outlets than 'old media' outlets such as newspapers and magazines. Yet, as Introna and Nissenbaum noted, few web users are aware of the issues involved in search rankings and many treat search engines as near-objective sources of information, much like a library catalogue.

Hindman's argument has potentially serious implications for the *'long tail'* thesis developed by journalist Chris Anderson: the idea that media and the cultural industries are moving away from a model, where the hits generate most of the attention and profit, towards one where millions of niche markets add up to a market that matches or exceeds that of the hits. This is a typical piece of digital ultra-optimism, as one would expect from the editor-in-chief of *Wired*, the house magazine of Silicon Valley digital utopianism: the little guy wins as a result of digital networks (see Orlowski, 2009). But Hindman's research shows that 'for news and media sites as well as political sites, it is simply not true that the smallest outlets, taken together, get most of the traffic. Not even close' (p. 135). Similarly, economist Will Page and digital analyst Eric Garland (2009) have shown, in a rigorous analysis of music sales across a number of 'platforms', that most music that is available digitally gets no purchases at all. It is true that there is a huge amount of choice available, but consumers are simply not buying it. This is true not only of physical albums and singles, but also of digital tracks. Even in 'illegal' peer-to-peer consumption, most music remains untouched. In Page and Garland's terms there is a long tail of available tracks, but it is extremely skinny. If anything, the reliance on hits is becoming more entrenched. The same is true of the live music sector – relatively thriving compared with purchases of recordings at the time of their research. Page and Garland don't speculate on explanations of why the long tail of available digital recordings is not being purchased, but I shall: consumers probably don't know that the tracks are there. Page and Garland refer to other studies that show a similar focus on a small number of big hits in other emerging forms of digital distribution, such as Netflix. Circulation remains the central locus of power in the cultural industries.

3. Commercialisation, surveillance and 'free labour'

The emphasis on participation is rooted in countercultural notions that rejected commerce in favour of human flourishing. There was a strong emphasis in many internet and web user communities on the 'free circulation

---

9 Political websites also follow a power law distribution, where 'the size of an observation is inversely and exponentially proportional to its frequency' (p. 41). Such distributions result in 'starkly inegalitarian outcomes'. A series of studies by computer scientists has shown that such power law distributions characterise both inbound and outbound hyperlinks.

of information' (Flichy, 1999: 36) and 'the rejection of ... undeclared commercial interests' (Castells, 1996: 354).

So how have such interesting and positive aspects of digital networks among the relatively privileged social groups with access to the internet fared during the 2000s? Since 1994, when 'business "discovered" the Net' (Sassen, 1998: 177), the way in which the internet has developed has damaged its potential as a challenge to the forms of communication prevalent in other cultural industries. In particular, the internet and world wide web have become commercialised. Advertising encroaches on nearly all aspects of web communication, appearing as banner headings and pop-up advertisements, the automatic start-up pages on web browsers, portals and search engines (including concealed forms, such as the paid search discussed in the previous section) and, of course, websites themselves. Signing on to services and buying products can still bring about a flood of unwanted e-mail messages. Spam remains a huge irritant. Much web content is permeated by advertising to the extent that it is sometimes difficult to tell where advertisements end and the content begins. As Sparks (2004) points out, there are few conventions for the separation of commercial and non-commercial content on the web.

Online advertising expenditure boomed in the 2000s. This happened in the 1990s, but was interrupted by the dot.com crash. From 2003 onwards, online advertising in the USA resumed its inexorable climb, often growing at double-digit rates. Evans (2009) cites figures indicating that US online advertising increased from $8.1 billion in 2000 to $21.2 billion in 2007, and from 3.2 percent of all advertising to 8.8 per cent over the same time period. In Western Europe, as advertising expenditure recovered from calamitous falls in 2009, online advertising grew by 16 per cent, against 7 per cent for all other media (*Screen Digest*, November 2011). Search advertising (as opposed to 'display' advertising on other websites) has been an area of particular growth in the late 2000s.

It is still too early to be sure what mix of advertising and other mechanisms will fund the cultural industries in the digitalising environment. Purchasing and subscribing bring problems for business and for culture, but so does advertising. Forms of communication that come to rely on advertising as their main source of income tend to become beholden to their advertisers (see Curran, 2011: 153–67, on the history of advertising in newspapers). As C. Edwin Baker (2002: see especially 24–30) argues, this can have various deleterious effects on content. These are difficult to predict in advance and need to be assessed case by case, but in general, says Baker, advertising favours content that is increasingly connected to marketable products and services and tends to militate against that which is useful to, or valued by, the poorer elements in society.[10]

The fact is, however, that the internet and web under capitalism are headed inexorably in the direction of commerce. Influential commentators

---

10 Advertising on other companies' websites is just part of web commercialism. As Dan Schiller (1999: 132) points out, corporate websites must also be seen as a category of web advertising and billions of dollars have been spent on them.

on the internet, such as Manuel Castells, have taken the view that the liberatory nature of the medium will survive its commercialisation because of the inherent properties of the technology. Castells (1996: 354) was certain that commercialisation was changing the medium, but he believed that 'while its most heroic tones and its countercultural ideology fade away ... the technological features and social codes that developed from the original free use of the network have framed its utilisation'. In such passages, Castells edges close to technological reductionism. Technologies do have lasting features, based on the social codes and discourses surrounding their development, it is true, but these features can be reshaped by powerful users and interpreters. Patrice Flichy provided a corrective to Castells' assumptions. Asking whether or not the democratic features of the internet were a product of the technical characteristics of networks (1999: 39), Flichy replied 'It seems not, for other models of data processing networks do exist. IBM and other manufacturers have developed centralised networks for businesses, where the role of each actor is clearly defined: some input data, others consult it'. At around the same time, Saskia Sassen (1998, 2000: 19) drew attention to the 'enormous growth of private digital networks'. She claimed that:

> the leading Internet software design focus in the last few years has been on firewalled [that is, protected from access by outsiders] intranets for firms and firewalled tunnels for firm-to-firm transactions. Both of these represent, in some sense, private appropriations of a 'public' space. (2000: 20)

The social uses of the technology, in other words, outweigh what might appear to be fixed features of the 'technical architecture'

There is another dimension to commercialism in the digital era, which derives from how the interactive properties of digital networks enable an unprecedented degree of information to be captured about users. The capture of information is essential to the economics of the new hybrid cultural products created by the information technology industries, from search engines to social networking sites.[11] This has intensified with the development of third-generation mobile phones, which allow for the even more efficient capture of a much wider range of data. As we have already seen, many of these new forms of interactive technology, often classified as 'Web 2.0', have been interpreted by digital optimists as empowering ordinary people. But the profound reliance of such technologies on capturing and

---

11 Fuchs (2011: 8-9) provides a list of some of the technologies that extend and intensify consumer surveillance with the help of the internet: 'cookies, data mining, collaborative filtering, ambient intelligence, clickstream analysis, spyware, web crawlers, log file analysis'.

selling information about users raises important and difficult questions about power and surveillance. Is allowing companies to capture information about us a worthwhile price for the conveniences and pleasures afforded by search engines and social networking sites? Or does such information capture represent a worrying step in the way that societies conceive of people's behaviour, habits and values? This goes beyond the question of privacy, and the way in which people might defend themselves from intrusion, to touch on questions about social and cultural power.

Take the example of Google. Google, as I explained in the Introduction to this book, is not a cultural industry company, or a media company in anything remotely approaching the sense in which those terms have traditionally been used – though it is already having a vast impact on the cultural industries. It is a search engine company, run by software engineers, which has expanded into some other areas (see Auletta, 2010: 16). It does not *produce* content, it *distributes* and *circulates* content through YouTube and GoogleBooks, which make little or no money in themselves. The vast majority of its revenues have come from advertising: for example, 97 per cent of its $21 billion revenues in 2008 (Auletta, 2010: 15). There are two main planks to Google's advertising business (I draw here on the helpful explanation provided by Auletta, 2010: 6–8):

- AdWords – this allows potential advertisers to bid to place small text ads next to the results for key search words. Google achieves price discrimination by setting a minimum bid per keyword (see Lee, 2011, for a detailed discussion of how this works).
- AdSense – this automated programme matches advertisers to the right web destinations. Advertisers are charged only when the user clicks on an ad, based on a defined 'cost per click'.

These technologies would be impossible without Google's use of cookies (software files left on users' browsers). Cookies allow Google to track the search questions users ask, which web pages they visit and for how long, and what they buy. When Google purchased DoubleClick in 2007 (see Chapter 6), this gave them control over the digital platform that allows sites to sell online ads, and advertisers and ad agencies to buy them. DoubleClick's database of information about users allowed them to do this. Combining DoubleClick and Google's resources provides unprecedented power. Other things being equal, the information gets better and richer the more activity that Google tracks. Market dominance thus reinforces itself through what economists call 'network effects': in telecommunications and information technology networks, the advantages accrue exponentially to nodes that achieve market dominance. In addition, information provided by a dominant search engine is more likely to be accurate than that of a less dominant partner, because of the greater amount of data reaped by the dominant company, so advertisers are likely to turn to Google.

Similarly, Facebook gains most of its revenue by providing information it can glean about its users to third parties. Because people produce a great deal of information about themselves on Facebook, including indications of their habits, tastes and practices, Facebook (in association with its advertising partner, Microsoft, who in 2008 outbid Google for the right to become Facebook's main marketing collaborator), offers advertisers the potential to target advertising closely to customers.

Such targeting, with its promise to advertisers that there will be minimal waste, is the basis of massive transformations in advertising – and in the marketing industry of which advertising is just a part. Joseph Turow (2012) has written about these transformations, and some of their potentially damaging social and cultural consequences:

> Every day most if not all Americans who use the internet, along with hundreds of millions of other users from all over the planet, are being quietly peeked at, poked, analyzed and tagged as they move through the online world. Governments undoubtedly conduct a good deal of snooping, more in some parts of the world than in others. But in North America, Europe, and many other places companies that work for marketers have taken the lead in secretly slicing and dicing the actions and backgrounds of huge populations on a virtually minute-by-minute basis. Their goal is to find out how to activate individuals' buying impulses so they can sell us stuff more efficiently than ever before. But their work has broader social and cultural consequences as well. It is destroying traditional publishing ethics by forcing media outlets to adapt their editorial content to advertisers' public-relations needs and slice-and-dice demands. And it is performing a highly controversial form of social profiling and discrimination by customizing our media content on the basis of marketing reputations we don't even know we have. (Turow, 2012: 2)

Turow sees the activities of marketers as fundamentally damaging to cultural production and founded upon an unethical way of understanding the behaviour and values of ordinary people. He also shows how measures to protect consumers from the worst aspects of this system through regulation are not currently adequate. The protocols by which we sign up to have our data used are lacking in transparency. The wording of agreements is incomprehensible to many users.

For some researchers, working in Marxian traditions, the way in which digital businesses draw upon the activities of ordinary internet and social network site users is best understood as a kind of exploitation. In a seminal essay, Tiziana Terranova wrote about the phenomenon of 'free labour', which she described as 'an important, yet unacknowledged, source of value in advanced capitalist societies' (Terranova, 2004: 73).[12] Free labour was, she wrote, 'simultaneously voluntarily given and unwanted, enjoyed and exploited' and on the internet included 'building web sites, modifying software packages, reading and participating in mailing lists and building virtual spaces' (p. 74). Others have applied similar perspectives to other forms such as television and games. Greig De Peuter and Nick Dyer-Witheford (2005) have explained how, from the 1990s onwards, 'authoring tools' have been increasingly packaged with computer games, helping to foster a vibrant participatory culture of game 'modding', or modification. They argue that the work of such modders is a kind of free labour, a 'space-defying' process of exploitation of 'collective intelligence' which also serves as a kind of informal training for the future game development workforce. Mark Andrejevic, reacting against celebratory accounts of 'active audiences' in media studies, has written powerfully about 'the ways in which creative activity and exploitation coexist and interpenetrate one another within the context of the emerging online economy' (2008: 25). Andrejevic (2008) argued that online viewer activity serves television producers in two ways: by providing feedback, which saves the producers from having to undertake expensive market research, and by, in effect, publicising television programmes, which saves marketing costs. Andrejevic critiques the equation of participation and activity with real democratisation and shared control, and claims that regimes of surveillance and imperatives of profit-making hugely compromise the pleasures and progressive elements of online participation. Andrejevic has also applied these perspectives to YouTube. He sees the work of users as exploited by Web 2.0 businesses. Web 2.0 style technologies, says Andrejevic (2009), gain their popularity by offering users an escape from alienation by offering 'a modicum of control over the product of their creative activity in return for the work they do in building up online community and sociality upon privately controlled network infrastructures' (p. 419) and allowing themselves to be monitored. For Andrejevic, there is an important distinction to be made between 'user-created content' and 'user-generated data' (p. 418). It is the latter and not the former that is extracted under conditions of private ownership and turned into a commodity. All this suggests to Andrejevic a generalisation of the forms of subjection traditionally associated with women. Time spent building social relations in affective labour is both autonomous and subject to exploitation, he writes; so is the kind of immaterial labour involved in social networking sites such as YouTube. There are echoes here of older debates concerning the way in which media industries turn audiences into commodities by selling their attention to advertisers (see Box 9.4).

---

12 Terranova's essay was originally published in 2000, but was reprinted in only a slightly revised form as part of her book *Network Cultures* in 2004.

Box 9.4   Do (digital) audiences work for the cultural industries?

In 1977, the influential Marxist political economy analyst Dallas Smythe wrote an essay about how other Marxists, including political economists of communication, had failed to analyse the functions that the media and related industries such as marketing and PR served for capitalism and capitalists. This, he said, was a 'blindspot' in Western traditions of Marxism (though he had surprisingly little to say about what non-Western Marxism would offer). Political economists such as Graham Murdock (1978) responded by criticising Smythe's perspective for its economic reductionism. One aspect of Smythe's piece was, however, widely taken up in later debates by other researchers, and has recently been revived as the nature of advertising has been changed by the onset of digital networks. Smythe, followed by other writers (such as Jhally and Livant, 1986), argued that, when they paid for advertising from cultural industries, advertisers were buying 'the services of audiences with predictable specifications who will pay attention in predictable numbers and at particular times to particular means of communication' (Smythe 1977: 5). People, then, had been turned into audiences and commodities. Moreover – and this is where the link to more recent debates on 'free labour' is particularly apparent – these services were, Smythe claimed, a kind of work: 'The work which audience members perform for the advertiser to whom they have been sold is to learn to buy particular "brands" of consumer goods, and to spend their income accordingly. In short, they work to create demand for advertised goods, which is the purpose of the monopoly capitalist advertisers' (1977: 6). Media audiences, in other words, work on behalf of advertisers, thereby serving capitalism as a whole. This (somehow) leads to a situation in which, for all but the very rich and the very poor (the latter have no disposable income), there is not really any such thing as 'free time' or 'leisure'. All our non-working time, except for sleeping, must be spent trying to figure out what we are going to consume (1977: 14). Media products were just a 'free lunch', a cheap way of buying people off for the services they rendered. Smythe also stated that, if European readers felt sceptical about such claims, it was because they had been relatively protected from the version of 'monopoly capitalism' that was by then in operation in North America.

A number of later writers have discussed Smythe's contribution, which was generally seen as potentially productive, but also extremely problematic and limited in the way that it was originally presented. This has become known as the 'audience commodity' debate, and sometimes called the 'blindspot debate' (see Lee, 2011) – though this risks confusing the specific idea of the audience commodity with the broader claims that Smythe was making about Marxism. In recent years, because search engines and social networking sites seem particularly to be based on the tracking of audiences, and on free or unpaid labour, various writers have sought to clarify some of the confusions surrounding the concept of the audience commodity in order to assess its potential relevance to cultural production and consumption in the age of digitalisation and the internet. Rather than seeing audiences as working for media industries, Goran Bolin, drawing on Meehan (2000), suggests that it is more fruitful to see statistical representations of audiences as raw material that is shaped into a commodity by market research agencies and departments and sold as a commodity: 'It is not the viewers who work, but the rather the statisticians' (Bolin, 2009: 357).[13]

Micky Lee (2011) builds on the earlier response of Richard Maxwell (1991) to debates about the audience commodity. Lee argues that Google's vertically-integrated, non-competitive structure has created a peculiar market in information, rooted in a strange commodity fetishism where advertisers bid blindly for keywords, without really understanding Google's system. For Lee, the audience commodity debate, if not Smythe's original formulation, provides a potentially valuable way in which to understand and critique the changing nature of advertising in the online world. Finally, Brett Caraway (2011) has provided a critique of Smythe's contribution, and its echoes in later formulations such as those of Andrejevic. Caraway writes from a Marxist perspective, but one concerned with agency, contradiction and struggle. He points out the problems of assuming that audiences are providing services, and performing work, without their knowing that they are doing so. He suggests that Smythe overestimates the accuracy of audience measurement techniques and that later contributors who analyse the use of surveillance to ensure audience work underestimate the ways in which people question or bypass surveillance techniques. Portrayals of the media, search engines and social networking sites as merely a 'free lunch' need to pay much greater attention to the 'use values' that people gain from these products. Rather than labour, the economic transaction involved in advertising is better understood as rent. It's possible that, in creating the content for sites based on user-generated content, that people are involved in a form of work, but we should be careful not to assume that this work is completely controlled, as is implied in many analyses.

Smythe's account is crude, reductionist and functionalist, totally underestimating the contradiction and struggle in contemporary societies. The underlying but underdeveloped normative position is that all the time we spend under capitalism contributes to a vast negative machine called capitalism, that nothing escapes this system. Much of the discussion his intervention has generated has barely transcended these origins. Yet it has somehow also spawned a potentially helpful and stimulating debate about how to understand the changing relationships between cultural industries, technology companies and audiences in a critical way.

---

13 It would be an empirical mistake, Bolin argues, to see these statistics as representative of reality. They are notoriously slippery and inaccurate. He believes that Smythe, Jhally and Livant, and Andrejevic all make this mistake.

In a recent essay on user-generated content (Hesmondhalgh, 2010b) I tried to show that Andrejevic's analysis seems actually to be dependent on questions of **freedom and ideology** rather than on a coherent notion of **exploitation** per se. I also tried to emphasise the importance of finding a critique of activities covered by the term 'free labour' that would continue to highly value various forms of activity that are carried out without payment in modern societies. Otherwise, I argue in that essay, there is a danger that a critique of commodification of social activity might end up implying that all unpaid social activity that contributes to the profits of an industry is exploited labour. An example I gave was of volunteer football/soccer coaches, who unwittingly contribute to the profits of the football/soccer industry by providing a pool of football talent that the clubs can then draw on. At the very least we need to balance the social gains made by the provision of such 'free labour' against the harms it causes. Part of the problem here is the way that ideas such as 'free labour' are taken up in casual academic discourse. I have frequently heard in recent years at conferences and in academic conversations a crude version of the 'free labour' thesis – and it is usually only a matter of time before such ideas pass into the public sphere.[14] Terranova and Andrejevic do not offer such a crude critique, and it is not their fault if their ideas have been simplified by others. But even their critiques of digital optimism need to be grounded in a more careful conceptualisation of the problems surrounding the use of information by Web 2.0 companies. In this respect, Jakobsson and Stiernstedt (2010) provide a valuable contribution. They connect such activity to the idea that, in social networking sites, the very quality of social relations as such – the sense of community and social trust necessary for social interaction – is commodified. This is because they show how such sociality is incorporated into the legal structures determining cultural property. Google and Facebook are involved in the appropriation of cultural material, in ways which are every bit as open to legal challenge as the activities of so-called pirate sites, but the juridical frameworks of the USA and the EU have, in a series of rulings, protected these large corporations as they make use of the activities of users. This suggests that in at least one vital respect users are not 'empowered' in quite the way that the digital optimists suggest. Through the extremely opaque and confusing ways in which terms and conditions are presented, they have no intellectual property rights whatsoever. Instead, the problems of user data capture are presented in terms of privacy, an extremely amorphous concept that allows companies to claim that users can be protected via self-regulation on the part of the IT industry, rather than

14 The most common version of this crude version of the free labour thesis concerns Facebook use - the implication is that such unpaid labour is exploitative, and we should consider not using Facebook. For sophisticated critiques of Facebook along 'free labour' lines, but one which may still be vulnerable to the criticisms of the 'free labour' thesis I make elsewhere (Hesmondhalgh, 2010b), see Cohen (2008) and Hearn (2008) – the latter is discussed in more detail in Chapter 11 below.

more robust government regulation. However, it is commodification that is the basis of this critique, not 'free' or unpaid labour.

* * *

The claims of the digital optimists about the impact of digitalisation and the internet on cultural production and consumption need to be treated with great caution. They are founded on a particular discourse about the emancipatory effects of computers, which the IT and consumer electronics industries have a great deal of interest in promoting. Digitalisation and the internet have of course brought various benefits and I have tried to register some of these – in part by critiquing some of the excessively pessimistic accounts offered in response to the digital optimists. However, claims that they have resulted in entirely new arrangements for cultural production, heard with remarkable regularity over recent years, need to be rejected. Recurring features of cultural production under capitalist modernity continue to be present in the cultural industries, even as they interact with telecommunications, IT and consumer electronics in new ways. Inequality, concentrations of power, and the negative effects of unregulated commercialism still remain in the cultural industries of the twenty-first century, even if privileged individuals feel empowered by their access to new and exciting creative possibilities.

RECOMMENDED AND FURTHER READING

The best critique of excessive claims for the emancipatory effects of digitalisation and the internet that I have yet encountered is Matthew Hindman's *The Myth of Digital Democracy* (2009). Against this should be set an excellent expression of the vulnerable potential of the internet for encouraging democratic participation: Stephen Coleman and Jay Blumler's *The Internet and Democratic Citizenship* (2009). In spite of my critical remarks about digital optimists, the texts by Benkler, Castells and Jenkins discussed here are illuminating and intelligent. *Blogistan* (2010), by Annabelle Sreberny and Gholam Khiabany, is a fine study of the internet and politics in Iran. On search engines, Hindman's chapter on Google is good, and so are Siva Vaidhyanathan's *The Google-ization of Everything* (2011), Alexander Halavais's *Search Engine Society* (2008), and Elisabeth van Couvering's (2011) political economy account of the development of search engines. *Internet and Society* (2008), by Christian Fuchs, provides a critical perspective on digitalisation, using a very wide range of social theory. Ken Auletta's *Googled* (2010) is lively and informative, though its message that Google has led to 'the end of the world as we [knew] it' can be a little wearing. Joseph Turow's *The Daily You* (2012) is a highly readable account of how the internet has transformed the advertising industry in worrying ways. The next chapter ends with recommendations of books and other sources that deal with the effect of the internet on other individual cultural industries.

ONLINE READING

All the online material referenced below can be accessed free of charge at: **http://www.sagepub.co.uk/hesmondhalgh**

Simply click on the 'Sample Materials' tab to find the links to each article.

A series of excellent articles by José van Dijck (see for example 2009 and 2012) on social networking, user-generated content and other issues suggest that her forthcoming book on social networks will be well worth reading. Brett Caraway's article on the audience commodity (Caraway, 2011) is a hugely welcome intervention in an often confusing debate. Micky Lee's article on Google advertising is also insightful (Lee, 2011). As indicated above, I find Jakobsson and Stiernstedt's (2010) article a helpful contribution to debates about piracy.

- Caraway, Brett (2011) 'Audience labor in the new media environment: A Marxian revisiting of the audience commodity', *Media, Culture & Society*, 33(5): 69–708.
- Jakobsson, Peter and Stiernstedt, Fredrik (2010) 'Pirates of Silicon Valley: state of exception and dispossession in Web 2.0', *First Monday*, 15(7), available at http://www.firstmonday.org/htbin/cgiwrap/bin/ojs/index.php/fm/article/view/2799/2577
- Lee, Micky (2011) 'Google ads and the blindspot debate', *Media, Culture & Society*, 33(3): 433–447.
- van Dijck, José (2009) 'Users like you? Theorizing agency in user-generated content', *Media, Culture & Society*, 31(1): 41–58.
- van Dijck, José (2012) 'Facebook as a tool for producing sociality and connectivity', *Television & New Media*, 13(2): 160–176.

10

The Impact of the Internet
and Digitalisation on Existing
Cultural Industries

The music industry in crisis: distinguishing hype
    from reality   341

File-sharing   343

Legitimate digital distribution   343

Television: meaningful consumer control?   348

Newspapers, periodicals and books   356

The digital games industry   358

This chapter builds on the previous one by examining further the question of whether the claims of the digital optimists regarding increasing control by users and audiences has helped to bring about a de-concentration of power in the cultural industries. It does so by examining the impact of the internet and web across four industries: music, television, newspapers and book publishing. The final section of the chapter examines digital games as a cultural industry that has emerged from digital technologies over the last 20 years.

THE MUSIC INDUSTRY IN CRISIS: DISTINGUISHING HYPE FROM REALITY

The major challenge that digitalisation presented to the recording industry was the relative accuracy and ease with which digital recordings could be copied. As we saw in the Introduction, making a profit in the cultural industries depends on, among other factors, the production of **artificial scarcity**. Digitalisation makes the copying of any information easy, and so it radically threatens that scarcity. Furthermore, music takes up less disk space and bandwidth than other non-print media and can be experienced via computer without too much discomfort (unlike print); this is why the recording industry was the first cultural industry to face head-on the threat posed by digitalisation. In the first decade of the twenty first century, revenues from sales of recorded music dropped substantially.[1]

In all cultural industries, the spread of the personal computer and the internet has made digitalisation a major issue. A number of inter-related technological innovations made digitalisation a pressing issue for the recording industry, before other cultural industries (see Bakker, 2005):

- The development of the MP3 compression standard in the early 1990s, and then the later development of other, related compression standards which allowed vast amounts of digital audio information to be compressed into manageable files.
- The spread of flat rate, high bandwidth connections, such as ISDN, ASDL and cable, and the fact that even where such connections were not available domestically in the late 1990s and early 2000s, they were available at workplaces, places of study and so on.
- The introduction of multimedia computers with increased storage capacity, soundcards, CD players and speakers.
- The development of usually free and relatively easy-to-use software that could 'rip' CDs into MP3 files and also find and download MP3 files from distant networked computers.

These technologies were driven by the telecommunications and computer software sectors. The conflict between the cultural industries and these other industries echoes earlier battles with the consumer electronics sector – for example, over video cassette recorders (VCRs) and audio cassette recorders, and whether they represented a threat to the intellectual property of cultural industry corporations. While the cultural industries would have liked serious restrictions to be placed on the facilitation of copying on computers, the might of the USA's software and telecommunications industries was always going to make such measures unlikely. The main weapon that the recording industry exerted in response was lobbying power.

So, as a result, in the 2000s, the record companies that dominated the music business faced two major issues. The first of these concerned *file-sharing* over *peer-to-peer (P2P) networks*, centrally involving issues of property and so-called piracy. The second was how to find a way not only to distribute recordings digitally rather than in the form of hard copies (vinyl records, audio cassettes, compact discs), but also to make money out of doing so.

---

1   Global recorded music sales peaked in 1999 at 26.9 billion US dollars, and had fallen to 17 billion US dollars in 2009, according to IFPI (International Federation of the Phonographic Industry).

File-sharing

By 2000, users were sharing music files over peer-to-peer networks – the most famous and widely used of which was Napster. Napster was soon closed down by a lawsuit brought by various record companies in the USA, but was supplanted by other peer-to-peer file-sharing networks (e.g., Grokster and Kazaa) that, in effect, merely provided software that allowed networks of users to search each other's computers for musical files and therefore made prosecution more difficult.

The major record companies and the trade associations that represented them were quick to take action against the file-sharing threat. After successfully closing down Napster (though this name was later taken by a legal downloading site), they pursued litigation against the second-generation file-sharing companies operating such services and began lawsuits against downloaders of music. The Recording Industry Association of America (RIAA) prosecuted many thousands of individuals and other trade associations followed suit across much of the world. 'Illegal' file-sharing however continued to grow and the file-sharing software companies and websites continued to defend themselves successfully against the considerable resources of the cultural industries. But the joint strategy of pursuing individual users and software distributors deterred many and illegal file-sharing sites generally remained the preserve of a committed niche of users (see Bakker, 2005).

'Legitimate' digital distribution

For most ordinary users in the new millenium, the main way of purchasing music was still by buying CDs in record shops. Gradually more and more people shifted to buying CDs online, often avoiding purchasing tax by buying from off-shore providers. Following the introduction of Apple's i-Tunes in 2003, and other digital retailers, a larger and larger minority of consumers bought digital files either online or via mobile phones. During this period of transition, record companies and established retailers (in most countries, these were separate from the recording industry) struggled to adjust to digital distribution and purchase. A major sticking point was that the record companies wanted to find a way to prevent customers from simply reproducing infinite copies of digital files of music. An enormous amount of time and effort was spent on the development of *digital rights management* (*DRM*) systems. This posed major challenges, partly as a result of rivalries among the various hardware, software and telecommunications companies involved, and also generated enormous bad publicity for the record companies, because they were made to look slow and unresponsive and as though they were restricting the flow of culture. By the end of the decade, however, more moderate forms of protection (for example, limiting the number of devices that a file could be played on) were commonplace. 'Legitimate' music downloading services had proliferated, and many consumers were becoming used to on-line purchasing or streaming via sites such as Spotify (which used a mixture of subscription and advertising revenue, some of which was then passed on to record companies and artists).

Consumers who were sufficiently energetic and/or technically competent could bypass protection systems easily enough. Revenues plunged in markets where there was widespread publicity about on-line music, as most consumers went through a period of uncertainty and bewilderment about the consumption of music, especially in the largest, most 'developed' markets (though there was significant growth in some markets as economies grew). This led investors, and the analysts who advised them, to turn away from the recording industry, leading to falling share prices. The decline in sales and revenues was relatively slow. But this didn't matter, because the perception was that the recording industry was doomed, and perception matters a great deal in the world of financial speculation. Apple's I-Tunes sold only a relatively small amount of music compared with other retailers, but its growth seemed phenomenal – growth from zero will often seem remarkable. What really mattered was that it seemed to represent the future.

These developments led to a huge amount of coverage of the decline – or even death – of the music industry (see Barfe, 2003; Mann, 2000). A widely read book on the impact of digitalisation on music was typical in its portrayal of the music majors as flat-footed bureaucratic behemoths, 'an industry struggling to maintain control and remain relevant', while celebrating the nimble entrepreneurs of web-based music (Alderman, 2001: 1–2). Many commentators, often drawing on the countercultural discourses discussed in the previous chapter, hoped that a more democratic set of production relations would emerge from the mess, where artists might be able to market and sell their products directly to audiences via the web without the need for multinational entertainment corporations. **So to what extent has the introduction of digital technologies led to such democratisation? And to what extent have these developments empowered consumers, creators and small companies at the expense of the big companies? To what extent did the oligopoly of international conglomerates buckle as digitalisation was introduced?** Certainly, there was vertical disintegration, as manufacturing and distribution operations were sold off to third parties, but this should not be read as a sign of a democratising 'disintermediation' – the removal of intermediaries between creators and consumers. The major corporations still retained crucial control over the marketing and promotion that will largely determine what music most consumers get to hear and know about. Indeed, such marketing became increasingly centralised in order to produce blockbuster hits. A parallel here is with the increasing emphasis in the film industry on massive publicity to generate big revenues on opening weekends, as discussed in Chapter 7. Meanwhile, as the crisis hit the recording industry in the early 2000s, the sizes of record company rosters were drastically cut – especially non-English rosters in the overseas divisions of the multinational corporations (*Music and Copyright*, 23 June 2004), and there was further consolidation of an already highly concentrated business, as struggling majors created alliances, or were allowed by regulators to merge. The record companies sought to redefine themselves 'as creators and exploiters of intellectual property rights' (*Music and Copyright*, 1 September 2004). The high returns and low costs of music publishing, and the constantly expanding opportunities for rights exploitation, made copyright more and more central to the music business. This led to intensive and often successful efforts by record companies and their trade associations to lobby governments in favour of extended copyright terms and stronger copyright enforcement, as we saw in Chapter 5. These measures diminished the public domain and favoured private, corporate interests, even if a substantial minority of consumers were able to bypass such restrictions by using digital networks to share files.

The music business never consisted entirely of the sale of commodities such as CDs to consumers by record companies. It always involved other ways of exploiting its copyrights, such as charging to allow recordings to be played, or songs to be performed, in public places, or on the world's proliferating radio and television channels. These 'secondary' uses of music have expanded consistently over the last few decades. The multinational record companies also benefited from growth in emerging markets. The 2000s were undoubtedly an extremely challenging time for the major record companies. But we know that the cultural industries are a high-risk business, where market domination is often tenuous. The history of the recording industry has seen a number of crises, notably in the 1930s and late 1970s (see Hesmondhalgh, 2009b).

So did popular music culture benefit from the introduction of digital distribution technologies in the 2000s? There are various ways to consider this question:

- The quality of the texts on offer.
- At the level of media consumption: for example, the choice, control, diversity and quality of experiences for audiences.
- At the level of production: whether, as many claimed, or at least strongly implied, digitalisation and the internet enabled a democratisation of the music industry.

The first of these is the most difficult to address. Debates about texts are the subject of Chapter 11 of this book, but a few words are in order here. Many decry the lack of creativity and innovation in contemporary popular music, and some have related this to the crisis in the recording industry. For example, the rise of a particular kind of pop music associated with TV talent shows was often attributed in the 2000s to a desperate quest for multi-media 'synergy' on the part of record companies. But the idea of a previous golden age of music has been a familiar lament down the decades. Nostalgia seems strongly bound up with people's perceptions of musical history. The 1970s are now considered a golden period for rock and pop by many in Europe and North America, but at the time, many audiences bemoaned the sterility and self-indulgence of these genres.

It seems clear, though, that at the level of consumption relatively privileged audiences with a moderate interest in popular music, and with access to the internet and other digital technologies, benefited from the digital revolution. By the end of the first decade of the twenty-first century, it had become possible, at a relatively low cost:

- to gain access to vast repertoires via streaming websites such as Spotify;
- to purchase tracks quickly and conveniently via Amazon, Apple's i-Tunes website, or other sites;
- to purchase a massive range of CDs, easily and conveniently via the web (and at a fraction of what these CDs had cost 10 years previously); vinyl remained readily available via specialist retailers.

In addition, there was also an explosion of helpful and enjoyable ancillary information about music and musicians.

- It became possible to find, easily and quickly, the lyrics for a huge range of songs via internet lyrics sites (admittedly marred by the worst kind of pop-up ads).
- It also became easier to find fairly reliable and insightful discussion of a very wide range of musicians via sites such as AllMusic and Wikipedia, and an increasingly digitalised and diverse music press.
- Many mourned the passing of the old music press, but the internet saw a proliferation of sites, and their coverage was much better archived than the print versions. This new internet music press was also increasingly international. While obviously under pressure from public relations and marketing departments, and dependent upon unpaid labour, the standard of music commentary was impressively high across a wide range of genres (see Lobato and Fletcher, 2012). As with many internet forms, however, it relied on unpaid professional labour.
- MySpace,Facebook and Twitter made it easy to find out about musicians' activities (tours, new recordings, media appearances, side projects).

These features suggest a greater degree of choice and control for consumers, including a greater degree of ability to have experiences across different 'platforms' or technologies, as media fragmented or multiplied (Napoli, 2011). Yet there were negative dimensions to such consumption as well, involving the problems discussed in the previous chapter: the way in which these activities were tracked and monitored; concentrations of power that still determined the flow of information to consumers; and inequalities of access to this potentially rich diet of sounds and secondary texts.

This meant that claims about a democratisation of production and circulation often went too far. For example, it was tediously common in the 2000s to hear that musicians were now able to become successful 'via the web', without any assistance from 'the music industry'. Press and broadcast journalists gave considerable coverage to breakthroughs by acts who used web technologies such as webcams to publicise their work. The Sheffield band Arctic Monkeys became hugely successful in 2005–2006, selling hundreds of thousands of copies of their debut album in the week of its release in the UK. Their success was widely attributed to the internet, and in particular to MySpace, the social networking site that was widely predicted at the time to represent the future of Web 2.0 activities. But while the band had a website where their tracks could be downloaded, they pointed out in interviews that they had never even heard of MySpace at the time of the success of their first single. Their success owed much more to their repeated exposure on traditional media, notably radio.

A few months later, *The Sunday Times* (5 March, 2006) reported on another case of how the music industry was being transformed by the web:

> After the runaway success of the Arctic Monkeys, who built up their international following on the internet from their base in Sheffield, Sandi Thom, a 24-year-old Scot, is using the web to entertain nightly audiences put at more than 60,000 … Seating at the venue underneath her home in a Victorian terraced house in Tooting, south London, consists of six stools bought from Ikea for about £3 each. Thom uses a webcam to record a nightly performance before broadcasting it on the net later in the evening. In the past eight days she has entertained more than 250,000 fans worldwide. By contrast, her live audiences usually total about 200 when she plays in clubs around Britain. The blossoming success of Thom's web tour illustrates how a new generation of unknown singers and bands are connecting with fans directly through the internet before achieving conventional chart success.

Or, as the *Times* put it (22 May, 2006):

> Thom is a bona fide example of how people power is changing pop … Before the webcasts, Thom had recorded an album, but only a small Scottish label funded by a fisherman was willing to release it. Now her debut single, *I Wish I Was a Punk Rocker*, out next week, is a radio staple and her face is plastered on billboards.

The truth was rather more complex. Following initial interest via the web, Thom's success in fact came from widespread coverage in the mainstream media, enabled by the use of a public relations company. Tens of thousands of musicians would also use the same technologies, and remain in utter obscurity. The problem, as ever, remained one of circulation: how to let people know of the existence and desirability of the product? And how, in the business school jargon, to achieve 'product differentiation'? Most people still became aware of musical recordings via radio, television, and other 'old' media. And the surest way to gain access to such old media was via a contract with a vertically integrated major record company, which had the resources, and occasionally the expertise, to target appropriate consumers. To achieve such contracts, musicians still need to work with artist managers to establish skills and a nascent reputation. Digital technologies allow this to happen more readily, but they must be used skilfully – and only a limited number of acts will have access to such skills. And only certain artist managers and musicians will also have the requisite knowledge to go about building up a reputation by playing live, in the right venues. There have been many claims about the positive effects of digitalisation and the internet in producing a much greater degree of demand for 'niche' products, notably the 'long tail' thesis (Anderson, 2006; Napoli, 2011) discussed in the previous chapter. But as we saw in Chapter 7, such demand, if it really exists, does not seem to have significantly enhanced the ability of would-be creative workers – the tens of thousands of talented musicians who aspire to make a living out of music, for example – to gain a good quality of working life.

In summary, at least in North America and Europe, it was undoubtedly true that the recording industry, and the music publishing industry to which it is closely linked, went through a major period of crisis and transition in the first decade of the twenty-first century. Recording companies were lambasted for their lack of innovation, while new entrants from the high-technology sector, notably Apple, were lauded for offering new means of distribution – even while charging remarkably high prices for downloads to be played on devices that had vast mark-ups. The recording industry still revolved around the search for talent, and new forms of technology helped change how that talent developed, and could be made known to audiences. Various technologies had been involved in such transformations since the development of a recognisably modern music industry in the nineteenth century. The power remained in the hands of a few institutional entities, but the identity of those institutions had changed, to include more high-tech companies such as Amazon and Apple alongside a dwindling set of multinational entertainment conglomerates.

TELEVISION: MEANINGFUL CONSUMER CONTROL?

The world's most significant cultural industry, in terms of time spent and revenue earned, is still television. Even in the early 1990s, futurologists were declaring the death of television (Gilder, 1994), and such prophecies have continued ever since. This has failed to happen. In 1970, at a time when television was generally considered to be at its peak of influence and reach, Americans spent an average of 1,226 hours per week watching TV. By 2009, this figure had increased to 1,774 hours, an increase of some 42 per cent. Even as a proportion of major leisure time activities (which have greatly increased in number) time spent watching television has hardly declined at all. The

Table 10.1   Average hours of television viewing per day in the UK, 2001–2010

2010	2009	2008	2007	2006	2005	2004	2003	2002	2001
4.03	3.75	3.74	3.63	3.60	3.65	3.71	3.73	3.54	3.62

Source: Broadcasters' Audience Research Bureau, 2011

1970 figure represented 46.5 per cent of such time, the 2009 figure represents 42.1 per cent. In 2009, some 15 years after commercial internet service providers made the internet widely available, Americans on average spent 755 hours per year on the internet (17.9 per cent of the total for major leisure activities), massively less than they did on television. This may be likely to change, but the point is that it has not happened yet and the only thing we can be sure of is what has happened, and not what will happen in the future, interesting though it may be to speculate on that.[2]

Figures claiming that the internet has replaced television should be treated with scepticism. For example, in March 2006, a number of newspapers reported that Britons were spending more time on the internet than watching television. *The Guardian*'s Media Section (8 March, 2006) reported that 'the average Briton' was spending 164 minutes online every day, compared with 148 minutes watching television. But these figures were based on interviews in which people are asked to report their own estimates. People nearly always under-report their television viewing. Figures based on the more reliable (but still by no means infallible) method of using electronic technology to detect watching show that viewing figures for television have actually increased over the last few years. Table 10.1, for example, gives figures collected by the Broadcasters' Audience Research Bureau in the UK (the increase in 2010 may reflect a more accurate measuring system).

There have been many references to 'post-network' or 'post-broadcast' television (Lotz, 2007; Turner and Tay, 2009). While the audience share of the major networks has fallen significantly in the United States, elsewhere the picture is different. Even in the UK, where News International poured huge amounts of money into challenging the four 'terrestrial' channels through its BSkyB operations, and where the government devoted a massive regulatory project to ensuring that all television was digital by 2012, the audience share of the four main channels has not changed hugely. In 2010, over 70 per cent of television watching is of channels run by the four main broadcasters.

Crucially, the revenues of television industries grew rapidly during the 2000s, even as internet hype predicted the imminent demise of television as a medium. We saw this demonstrated in Table 8.1 when discussing the growth of television across the world. This growth was interrupted by the decline of advertising revenue in the wake of global recession from 2008 onwards,

---

2   All the figures in this paragraph are from Vogel (2011: 10).

Table 10.2   Audience share by terrestrial channel, 2001–2010

	2010	2009	2008	2007	2006	2005	2004	2003	2002	2001
BBC	32.90	32.62	33.54	34.01	34.46	35.21	36.65	38.28	38.50	38.13
ITV	22.86	23.13	23.23	23.21	23.12	24.13	24.14	24.66	24.87	26.96
C4	11.18	11.24	11.57	11.71	12.09	11.00	10.48	10.36	10.81	10.34
Five	5.91	6.12	6.08	5.99	5.87	6.43	6.57	6.46	6.29	5.75

Source: Broadcasters' Audience Research Bureau, 2011

but the continuing growth of paid-for television across much of the world is predicted to lead to further increases in revenue.

The internet, then, is not *replacing* television and other cultural forms; it is *supplementing* them, as often happens when new media technologies are introduced and disseminated. Nor is the internet *swallowing up* television. Instead, the internet and television are *hybridising* in complicated ways. Again, this is familiar from past technological developments: for example, the rise of television in the 1950s and 1960s and its effects on cinema. Television may decline in the longer term, but this is not happening just yet, and it is too early to predict what forms its mutations are going to take. In fact, because of the huge increase in television consumption in less developed countries, the 1990s saw a considerable increase in the ownership of televisions (see UNESCO, 1999) and this continued into the twenty-first century (CIA World Factbook, 2003).

There is no doubt that television changed significantly in the first decade of the twenty-first century. Some changes were primarily internet-driven, such as the rise of new ways of viewing television content via the computer. The most notable case here is of course YouTube (see Box 10.1). Some changes relate to developments in digital television that are separate from the impact of the internet, notably the continuing proliferation of channels in many countries, and the further erosion of the audience share of major networks in some countries – which has been much more significant in some countries than in others. One emergent phenomenon is the rise of 'non-linear television watching', where time-shifting is made possible by TV on demand services such as the BBC's i-Player and its equivalents. These are available via digital TV, on computers via the internet, by mobile phone, or on tablets such as the i-Pad. Some proclamations of the 'death of television' or the 'end of television' rely on a perception that younger viewers are particularly prone to watching television through computers and mobile devices and using timeshifting techologies. Here too though there are reasons to be cautious. The Neilsen figures in Table 10.3 suggest that in fact the heaviest watchers of video on the internet are in the 25–34 age group. Younger viewers watch more video on mobile phones than other users but they still watch very little. The other means of watching video are, as yet, very small compared with watching on traditional television for all age groups. Even in the USA, where non-linear TV viewing is most apparent, the proportion of such viewing rose above 10 per cent only in 2010. The figures for other major markets such as those of Germany, France,

Table 10.3   Hours per week spent watching television by 'platform', USA 2010

age	2 to 11	12 to 17	18 to 24	25 to 34	35 to 49	50 to 65	65+
On Traditional TV	24:52	22:24	24:17	28:08	32:58	41:04	46:16
Watching Timeshifted TV	01:50	01:29	01:30	02:57	03:07	02:42	01:42
Using the Internet on a Computer	00:30	01:25	04:02	06:03	05:50	04:58	02:38
Watching Video on Internet	00:07	00:21	00:45	00:50	00:35	00:23	00:12
Mobile Subscribers Watching Video on a Mobile Phone	NA	00:20	00:17	00:12	00:05	00:01	<0:01

Source: Nielsen, *The Cross Platform Report*: 5.

Italy and Spain are much lower, and are not expected to rise above 10 per cent for many years to come (*Screen Digest*, July 2011).

Box 10.1   YouTube: a new hybrid cultural form

YouTube has enabled a new type of screen viewing and an unprecedented mixture of content. Its remarkable rise in the 2000s was greeted as a prime example of Web 2.0 participatory culture. Even more sophisticated analysts echoed YouTube's own rhetoric in strongly emphasising its reliance on 'community' elements. For example, legal scholar and intellectual property activist Lawrence Lessig (2008: 194–6) saw it as an example of a new hybrid economy, based on a community where people interact on terms 'which are commerce free, though the motivations for interacting may or may not tie into commerce' (p. 186).

As William Urrichio (2009) notes, interactivity on YouTube is limited in Web 2.0 terms: you can upload, but not download. As in other sites based on so-called user-generated content, the vast majority of users do not produce video (van Dijck, 2009). What's more, as Siva Vaidhyanathan notes, in discussing some troubling removals of content from its site by YouTube, the site has no mechanism to establish community norms regarding its content. The lack of such standards, writes Vaidhyanathan (2011: 36–9), encourages flame wars and 'flag wars' whereby 'competing political activists flag the other sides' videos as inappropriate'.

A huge amount of material is created by amateurs, much of it watched by very small numbers of people. Much of it is also produced by a variety of small-scale producers, often with aspirations to become professional cultural producers or to break through to wider audiences. Such production is often mistaken for 'amateur' production. Much of the most-watched content is produced by major cultural-industry institutions. Of YouTube's list of its ten most-watched videos of all time in November 2011, only two were 'user-generated': 'Charlie bit my finger' and 'Parto in un letto', a clip of friends jokily enacting a live birth. The others were

(Continued)

(Continued)

mainly music videos – two were by Eminem and three by Justin Bieber. The sharing of clips from television shows, especially comedy, is extremely popular. In the 2000s, this fundamental reliance on video produced by the cultural industries resulted in battles between Google (owners of YouTube from late 2006 onwards) and copyright holders, notably Viacom. This famously led to videos of toddlers dancing to copyright recordings being removed from YouTube until the courts had done their business. But the resulting settlement is good for the cultural industries. YouTube makes little money for Google, and provides a massive grassroots promotional forum for the products of the cultural industries.

YouTube is not only a promotional forum for the cultural industries. It is also a crucial part of new ways in which people use email, mobile telephony and social networking sites to share content. It is a wonderful resource and a remarkable feat of software engineering. It has changed the way people share and recommend culture. But it does not represent a democratisation of cultural production based on community in anything like the way that some commentators have claimed.

As with the consumption of music, such phenomena involve a proliferation of the ways in which television can be experienced. They have also given rise, superficially at least, to a greater degree of audience control over the consumption of television. Viewers can choose much more readily where and when to watch television. There is no doubt that these changes are, collectively, threatening to the advertising revenue which sustains commercial broadcasting. This is partly because the viewing of individual television programmes has declined, owing to the sheer amount of leisure competition faced by television in most countries. Television programmes are now only rarely watched by a high proportion of a particular national population; the main exceptions are TV talent shows and major sporting events. The biggest hit shows generate fewer viewers. Interactive digital television technologies, such as TV on demand services, allow viewers to skip adverts. But as we saw in Chapter 8 (Table 8.1), television revenues have actually been increasing. This has been because of the rise of pay television – people are prepared to pay much more for content than they ever did before.

The extent and nature of audience control in the new television environment are often overstated. In his intelligent overview of changes in how media industries (primarily television and radio) understand audiences, Philip Napoli claims that there have been two major evolutions in the nature of media audiences in recent years: **audience fragmentation** and **audience autonomy**. By the latter term, Napoli is referring to his view that a range of features of the new media environment (interactivity, mobility, 'on-demand functionality' and 'increased capacity for user-generated content') all 'enhance the extent to which audiences have control over the process of media consumption' (Napoli, 2011: 8). The degree to which such facets constitute meaningful control and autonomy for consumers is another matter. Many of these features are pleasurable or convenient. But terms such as 'autonomy' have significant political connotations far beyond relatively trivial consumer features, such as being able to use a remote control device so that you can watch a particular player during a football game, or choose from three or four acts performing on different stages at a televised music festival. To what extent do these really involve the exertion of control over the circulation of experiences, ideas and knowledge in modern societies? Only in cases where people are actually producing and circulating their own content could such a claim validly be made. And yet, as we saw in the case of YouTube, and as Jose van Dijk (2009) discusses in an important contribution, user-generated content that is genuinely produced by amateurs receives very little exposure.

Nor should we underestimate the amount of work that has had to be done to persuade people that interactive gadgets and the like are meaningfully desirable. James Curran (2011: 99–110) has tracked how the British media treated a number of different 'new media' technologies in the 1980s and 1990s, including cable television, local community television, the internet, and interactive digital television. On the latter, Curran provides a number of quotations from British broadsheets in the 1990s, including, among many other examples, the now-familiar rhetoric that it would lead to a 'fundamental shift in power from the TV director to the consumer in the home' (*Sunday Times*, 30 April 1995, quoted by Curran, 2011: 101). Yet he also provides evidence showing just how reluctant viewers have been to take up this offer, and how slow the long-predicted interactive technology has been to arrive (101–2). The exaggerated claims of journalists, according to his analysis, were the result of misinformation on the part of the business interests proposing these new technologies: principally developers of interactive TV such as BSkyB, British Telecom, but also politicians supporting the idea of the 'information society', finance industry consultants and experts whose reputations depend on seeming ahead of the game, and publicity-hungry academics (105–6). Box 10.2 outlines some of the factors behind the rise of digital television.

Box 10.2   The rise of digital television

Hernán Galperin (2004: 25–52) identified three main factors behind the rise of digital television:

- The perceived need on the part of regulators in the USA to **salvage the ailing consumer electronics industry** during the downturn of the 1980s – High definition television (HDTV) was perceived at the time as the new frontier in consumer electronics and a consortium led by the Japanese public service broadcaster was leading the way. Digital was seen as a way for firms in the USA and Europe to counter this, but spillover effects into related industries (telecommunications and computers) were also hoped for.

(Continued)

(Continued)

- **Information society policy** – The Clinton administration's notion of a National Information Infrastructure (NII) was a key development in information society thinking. This saw 'digital video' as a major driver of access to this NII. While the USA feared Japan, the EU feared domination by the USA and imitated its initiatives, most notably in the Bangemann Report of 1994 (Commission of the European Communities, 1994).
- **Spectrum shortage** – As we saw in Chapter 4, the notion that spectrum shortage was no longer such an issue as it had been provided legitimation for marketisation, but with the rise of mobile telephony in the 1990s (with third-generation systems seen as a key basis for expansion in high-tech industries) spectrum shortage was becoming a key issue. Analogue broadcasting was seen as a 'spectrum hog' and digital as the solution. Unexpectedly, spectrum auctions for mobile telephony generated billions of dollars for governments, accelerating the international push towards digital.

The result of these various developments was that, by the end of the 1990s, the transition to digital television was a top priority for policymakers in the USA and the EU. The motivations were fundamentally economic. There is no doubt that the results have been beneficial for businesses in the consumer electronics, telecommunications and cultural industries. Sales of televisions boomed in the 2000s, as flat-box sets and high-definition television went mainstream. But the social and cultural consequences are much more uncertain, as discussed elsewhere in this section.

So what have been, and are likely to be, the main effects of digital television on the cultural industries in terms of production and circulation?

First, the introduction of digital television has involved – to a degree unprecedented in any other medium – the kinds of strategic alliance discussed in Chapter 6. Complex networks of companies have worked together because a number of difficult and expensive technologies need to be combined to produce a workable system. The most crucial of these are conditional access systems, which involve encrypting the transmitted programmes and then developing decoding software for set-top black boxes. This technology also involves systems for installing boxes and (if necessary) satellite dishes and others for sending out decoding cards, subscription bills and advance information about programming. Add in the cost of subsidising installation in order to gain a critical mass of subscribers capable of attracting advertisers and the huge resources necessary for research, development, expertise and infrastructure make it clear why alliances of enormous telecoms, cable, computer and cultural industry corporations dominate the television industry today in many countries more than ever before.

Second, huge amounts of content are needed to fill the hundreds of new channels. This has favoured a number of groups:

- Those who hold the rights to existing catalogues of audiovisual material. This confirms the increasing importance of ownership of copyright, apparent over many years (see Chapter 5 of this book).
- Hollywood film companies, the USA's TV networks, and those at the centre of the all-powerful content creation business in the USA.
- New independent producers - the largest of which have become significant industry players and lobbyists in some countries, notably the UK. Some of these make vast amounts of money from the international sales of programming ideas and formats. This has made them attractive to venture capitalists and other investors. The larger 'independents' are now thoroughly linked to financial capital.
- The 'creative talent' at the top of the celebrity scale, including sports people, and the talent agencies and managers who represent them. This widens still further the enormous inequalities, noted by Miège (1989) and others, between the underused pool of creative talent and a vastly overpaid few (see Chapter 7). By the 1990s, such stars were increasingly operating as businesses in their own right, with significant independent production companies based around them.

Third, in spite of the increasing importance of content and the increasing rewards for it, circulation remains central to the industrial dynamics of television in the digital age. Those who run the distribution systems for digital television have a large say in which channels are adopted. Although regulators have attempted to ensure that producers and 'publishers' (that is, the television channels that make the programmes or commission them from other producers) are not discriminated against, there is no doubt that distributors use their competitive advantage to favour their own programming, for example in the design of electronic programme guides.

All this means that the commercialisation of television has taken an important step forward. Public service broadcasters are more beleaguered than ever, fighting to maintain their legitimacy as they are attacked by newspapers that are often owned by companies with a strong interest in the television market. Conditional access systems have led to charging mechanisms that provide new avenues for commodification. Those sections of the public with relatively high levels of disposable income seem to have accepted that it is worth paying a lot more for something that is not that much better - if at all - than what existed before. For all the rhetoric about choice and interactivity, much of it derived from digital utopianism, digital television ultimately remains the centralised, top-down medium that developed in the era of analogue broadcasting.

NEWSPAPERS, PERIODICALS AND BOOKS

Meanwhile, alongside recorded music and television, other industries are being affected by related but somewhat different transformations. I shall address three 'print-based' cultural industries here. As with the recording industry my focus will be on what happened between 2000 and 2012, rather than on speculating about what might occur in the future.

In newspapers, and to a lesser extent periodicals (such as magazines), plunging advertising revenues have had a profound impact. Local newspapers have been highly reliant on classified advertising (low-cost ads usually placed by individuals). In the 2000s, websites such as eBay and Craigslist became increasingly popular alternatives to newspaper classifieds. At the same time, the increasing availability of news via the web, easily accessible and frequently updated, began to erode the readership of newspapers. Another factor was changing lifestyles. Younger professionals – a highly desirable demographic group for advertisers – were less predisposed to the daily ritual of reading a newspaper than their older peers. As Colin Sparks (2004: 311) pointed out, the internet erodes advantages based on physical place. Newspapers (and broadcasting organisations too) could achieve dominance within a particular city, region or nation, but all online newspapers, radio stations and so on are, in principle, available everywhere, at any time. The economic problems in Europe and North America from 2008 onwards compounded the difficulties caused by internet technologies to newspapers.

The closure of large numbers of American newspapers in the light of such decline gave impetus to discussions about a crisis in journalism (McChesney and Nichols, 2010 – see Chapter 11). Most newspapers and periodicals in the 2000s made their content freely available on the web, subsidising their web operations through hard-copy advertising and sales, some on-line advertising, and an increasing use of add-on operations (selling goods and services such as holidays, games, music and books). The costs were written off as an uncertain future investment, and/or as a way of building the publication's brand. The only major exceptions for most of the 2000s were business publications (*The Financial Times, The Wall Street Journal*) and product review publications (such as *Which?* in the UK and *Consumer Reports* in the USA) which were able to charge subscriptions for their potentially valuable information. This began to change at the end of the decade. In 2010, News International started to put up 'walls' around the content of a wider range of its newspapers, beyond *The Wall Street Journal. The New York Times* introduced a 'soft paywall' in 2011, based on voluntary registration, and with some considerable initial success. The success of the i-Pad led some commentators to hope that the transition to digital editions might be eased. Slovakia introduced an innovative scheme where citizens would pay a small fee for access to a consortium of nine major news producers. It is, however, still too soon to be clear about the future of newspapers and magazines in the era of digitalisation.

As with television and newspapers, there have been many predictions about the death of the printed book. Ebooks have existed since the early

1990s. In the late 1990s and early 2000s, a number of consultants predicted a massive market share for ebooks in very little time. But this did not transpire; sales of ebooks remained tiny, defying the projections of the analysts. The far bigger transformation at that time in many countries was the decline of the independent bookshop, already threatened by the rise of giant retail chains and supermarket book retailing in the 1980s and 1990s (see Rønning and Slaata, 2011) and the rise of Amazon as an IT retail giant.[3]

The real digital revolution in the book industry, in John B. Thompson's (2005, 2010) view, has been in the production *process*, with operating systems, content management , sales and marketing, and content delivery all radically reconfigured. But the digital prophets have been saying that a new generation of ebook readers will now bring about the delayed digital revolution in *product*. In 2006 and 2007, respectively, Sony launched its ebook reader and Amazon launched its Kindle. These used non-reflective screens and 'ink' that better approximated actual print. The Kindle had dropped substantially in price by 2010, and this led to a surge in the purchasing and free downloading of ebooks, as new owners splurged to provide content for their devices. So does this mark the beginning of the end of printed books? Thompson (2010: 331-3) puts forward a number of reasons for the very slow and erratic progress of the ebook revolution:

- The reading devices have tended to be clunky. (Even with the new era of improved ebook readers, polls continue to show that a vast majority of readers prefer the printed book; see, for example, *The Guardian*, 21 July 2010: 'Better read than dead'.)
- There has been a bewildering array of formats and as a result consumers have feared obsolescence and a lack of usability across different devices.
- There exists great uncertainty on the part of publishers about rights ownership.
- Ebooks still cost a great deal to produce, but consumers have reacted badly to being charged a price only just below that of the physical object, the book – which is still cherished by hundreds of millions of people.

Many commentators asserted or assumed that events in the music industry would provide a model for what was going to happen in other digitalising cultural industries. According to this view, the decline of sales of CDs presaged declines for books. But Thompson summarises some of the reasons why some sceptics in the book publishing industry feel that 'music is a poor analogy for the book' (p. 319):

---

3   Amazon used its increasing domination of book retailing to diversify into a wide range of products, thereby becoming the 'Walmart of the web' (*The Economist*, 1 October 2011). However, its profit margins have remained low as it has sought to enter into competition with Apple to provide 'cloud computing' for users.

- Many consumers want to listen to songs rather than albums, and are happy to skip tracks – this is not true of the book.
- Even with e-ink technology, reading a book on screen remains a substantially worse experience for most readers than reading a printed book.
- Carrying lots of music on a mobile device such as an i-pod is clearly an advantage. Other than academics and some professionals who travel a lot, most people don't need to carry around lots of books and publications – 'one book will do' (p. 319).

Thompson (2010: 318) wisely remarks that although digitalisation is in the process of transforming the book industry, it is too soon yet to be certain about what form these transformations will take. If only more commentators were so circumspect.

THE DIGITAL GAMES INDUSTRY

Finally, I now turn to digital games, which are interesting because, among other reasons, they represent a new cultural industry that emerged from digitalisation, rather than a cultural industry that digitalisation affected. They therefore raise interesting questions about the newness of new media. Are they substantially different from 'pre-digital' industries? How distinctive is this new cultural industry, based on digital technology? What might it tell us about digitalisation as a technological development in the cultural industries?

As it developed in the 1990s and 2000s, the games industry came to be based on a number of sectors: the producers of games machines or consoles; games developers; the companies that publicised and distributed those games (namely, controlling their circulation); and retailers. The console games industry, unlike all other cultural industries, was dominated by three Japanese corporations – Nintendo, Sony, and Sega. This domination derived from the fact that the games industry had been centred on hardware/software synergies to a greater degree than any other cultural industry in recent times. The small companies commissioned to develop games have been very much reliant on events in the console/hardware sector. The hardware companies, in turn, were reliant on games development for their profits as the hardware (consoles) sold at relatively small profit margins, whereas games had a very high mark-up (Caves, 2000: 215).[4]

In its 'software' (that is, games) development and publishing sectors, the digital games industry conformed to patterns established in the cultural industries more generally. In its organisational form, the industry has

---

4 When Sega's Dreamcast console failed to match sales of Sony's PlayStation 2 in 1999-2000, Sega withdrew from console production. Microsoft were already set to enter the market in 2001, with their X-box. They soon established themselves as a new third power in console production and games commissioning.

followed the *publishing logic* (or 'editorial model') of commodity production identified by Miège (1987) as characteristic of the production of books, records and films. In this model of cultural production:

- texts are sold on an individual basis to be owned;
- a publisher/producer organises production;
- many small- or medium-sized companies cluster around oligopolistic firms;
- creative personnel are remunerated in the form of copyright payments.

Miège contrasts this 'publishing logic' with a number of other 'logics' of production – mainly, the *flow logic* associated with broadcasting, where, instead of individual commodities for sale, the emphasis is on the provision of an uninterrupted flow of entertainment (an idea Miège borrows from Flichy, 1980) and the production of written information – that is, principally the press, including magazine publishing.

The 'software' part of the computer games industry, then, according to this analysis, is organised like books, music and films. Since 2001, Sony, Nintendo and Microsoft have been the oligopoly controlling the console and hand-held devices sectors at the core of the industry, but with significant interests in publishing; US-based Electronic Arts is a fourth powerful publisher, but with no stake in hardware. Some of these companies have designed games in-house, but these are mainly commissioned by the large corporations from specialist companies. There is a premium on inside knowledge of what fan subcultures are looking for and large corporations gain access to this knowledge by entering into transactions with small companies made up of enthusiasts. In this respect also there are important parallels with other industries, notably music (see Chapter 7 on this aspect of the music industry).

For many years, games were condemned or worried over as simple, violent fare for the young. In this respect too games conform to a familiar pattern – many other new cultural forms have been treated in the same way. It was apparent by the 1990s, though, that the digital games industry was going to last. Although the competition for market share between the various formats has been fierce, the corporations and their software associates have competed for an ever-expanding cake as games devotees have continued to buy games in their twenties and thirties and the next generation of boys and girls has joined the audience. This has also led to formidable creativity and innovation. *Screen Digest* (October 1999) attributed the success of the games industry in the 1990s to 'a far greater depth of quality product than the filmed entertainment market'. A number of writers have noted the increasing sophistication and quality of games. There is also a considerable variety of genres. Poole (2000: 35–58) listed the following:

- Shoot-em-ups
- Racing
- Platform

- Fighting
- Strategy
- Sports
- Role play
- Puzzles

Henry Jenkins (2000) noted the possibility that a new generation of games would legitimate digital games as a new popular art form, just as the films of the late 1910s and 1920s legitimated the then infant cinema. There is certainly now a wide range of intelligent critical commentary available.

Some misinterpreted the growth of the games industry as meaning that games were replacing music, film, books or television (or any other industry as it experienced any sort of period of crisis, especially if youth audiences are diminishing). It is certainly true that the digital games industry achieved high rates of growth in the early twenty-first century (see Kerr, 2006: 50) whereas, as we saw above, revenues from recorded music stagnated or declined. However, Aphra Kerr (2006: 51–2) showed the claims that games were outstripping other industries were often based on dubious data. For example, the sales of hardware (consoles, hand-held devices) were included alongside games software. This would be like including the figures for sales of DVD players and recorders in the figures for film. These figures were then compared to the box office figures for film alone, thus ignoring 'secondary' film markets such as DVD sales and rental. When sales of *games* (as opposed to devices such as consoles) were compared with revenues from cinema box offices *and* DVD sales and rentals, it was apparent that the games industry was very big and fast-growing, but not yet in the same league as television or even film. This remains the case in 2012.

By the time of the launch of 'seventh generation' consoles in 2006–2007 (Nintendo's Wii, Microsoft's X-Box 360, and Sony's PlayStation 3) the video games industry had achieved a significant degree of business maturity. Randy Nichols (forthcoming) provides an account of the state of the global games industry in the late 2000s. By this stage, debates about the effects on young people of playing games had receded, as video games became integrated into everyday life in developed countries. Audiences had become older; the average player age in the USA had risen from 29 in 2004 to 35 in 2010. Women and girls were players and purchasers to an increasing extent – estimates cited by Nichols vary between 20 per cent and 40 per cent depending on territory, player age, and games genre. The oligopoly of Microsoft, Nintendo, Sony and Electronic Arts dominated software publishing. Development and marketing budgets soared, as the industry increasingly relied on hits that were launched with a huge fanfare, such as *Call of Duty: Modern Warfare 3*, which was published across all three major consoles in November 2011.

At the beginning of the second decade of the twenty-first century, the games industry looks set to be marked by significant changes. The increasing popularity of games played on digital and mobile devices (such as iphones) had given power to new entrants such as the Finnish company Rovio and the Californian company Zynga, who make products for (mainly) Apple devices and Facebook, respectively. Meanwhile, Nintendo and Sony have struggled. But will games such as Angry Birds, developed by Rovio, just be temporary fads?

As long as leisure time and expenditure on it expand, new cultural industries and forms such as digital games can be accommodated without necessarily destroying or even substantially eroding previously existing industries. And synergies can be found as well – games based on films, films based on games, music publicised via games, games publicised via music, and so on. The digital games industry, then, is a significant new entrant in the cultural industries sector and digital games are an interesting and significant cultural form. But they do not represent a major shift in the prevailing structures and organisational forms of the cultural industries generally.

*   *   *

The introduction of digital technologies into the cultural industries was ultimately the product of post-war developments in the computer and consumer electronics industries. No development in the period since 1980 has been accompanied by such wild claims as has digitalisation (see Feldman, 1998, for an example of a Panglossian treatment of digital media). The last two chapters have shown that the term 'digitalisation' makes little sense unless it is discussed in the context of *specific* applications, *particular* digital technologies. Computer games are treated as dangerous, but have produced exciting innovations. The internet has been hailed as the most democratic communications technology in history, but its exciting and progressive uses are in danger of being submerged by commercialism and recentralisation. Digital television has been introduced on the grounds of choice and interactivity, but offers little real progress for consumers, given the massive costs involved, and the huge benefits for businesses in a range of industries. It also involves a much more thorough commodification of broadcasting.

The internet and the web, combined with mobile communication and digital forms of broadcasting, have, to a limited extent, altered existing social relations of production and consumption. They have produced huge amounts of small-scale cultural activity. They have enabled new ways for people to communicate with each other, and to find information easily and quickly. They have provided mechanisms to enhance political activism. The internet is full of material that is arcane, bizarre, witty and profane, as well as inept, mundane and banal. These many minor forms of subversion, insubordination and scepticism don't cancel out the enormous concentrations of power in the cultural industries, but they might be thought of as representing a *disturbance*. The problem is that this disturbance of existing relations of cultural production and consumption has happened mainly within a very specific section of the world's population. The radical potential of the internet has been largely, but by no means entirely, contained by its partial incorporation into a large, profit-orientated set of cultural industries. Surveillance remains a significant concern.

The technologies discussed in the last two chapters have all had significant effects on cultural industries, but not even the internet and digital television have yet had *such* an impact that we can speak of a new era in cultural production. New industries, such as digital television, ISPs and computer games, all carry very strong inheritances from previous ways of organising cultural production. The characteristics of the complex professional era are still intact in the era of digitalisation – even down to the continuing domination of television.

RECOMMENDED AND FURTHER READING

Music
A more detailed version of my analysis of music digitalisation in this chapter can be found in Hesmondhalgh (2009b). Simon Frith and Lee Marshall's collection *Music and Copyright* (2004) is excellent on the rights issues. Musicologist Joanna Demers's *Steal This Music* (2006) is a good study of how intellectual property affects musical creativity. Patrick Burkart and Tom McCourt's *Digital Music Wars* (2006) provides a forceful political economy account. Burkart's more recent *Music and Cyberliberties* (2010) discusses activist opposition to the actions of copyright holders. Greg Kot's *Ripped: How the Wired Generation Transformed Music* (2009) is a readable journalistic history of what happened to the music industry, heavily focused on rock and rap. It is critical of the recording industry, but is implicitly uncritical of the IT industries.

Television
Hernán Galperin's *New Television, Old Politics* (2004) is the definitive study of the transition to digital television in the UK and USA. The introduction to Toby Miller's *Television Studies: The Basics* (2010) passionately argues that television is not dead, and not even dying. *Television After TV* (edited by Lynn Spigel and Jan Olsson, 2004) was a good collection of essays on television in transition. The title of Graeme Turner and Jinna Tay's *Television Studies After TV* (2009) deliberately recalls it, and analyses recent changes across a range of international contexts. Jean Burgess and Joshua Green's short book *YouTube* (2009) is an intelligent and balanced piece of digital optimism; *The YouTube Reader* (2009), edited by Pelle Snickars and Patrick Vonderau, is a useful collection. It includes an essay by Mark Andrejevic, who has made a major contribution to critical analysis of television as it goes increasingly digital.

Newspapers
Robert W. McChesney and Victor Pickard's collection, *Will the Last Reporter Please Turn Out the Lights* (2011), provides a really valuable range of perspectives, from journalists, academics and commentators, on the crisis in American journalism and what might be done about it. Another good collection, *New Media, Old News*, edited by Natalie Fenton (2011), addresses the effects of digitalisation on news and democracy – an issue discussed in Chapter 11.

Books

Albert Greco's *The Book Publishing Industry* (2nd edition, 2005) and his book with Clara E. Rodriguez and Robert M. Wharton on *The Culture and Commerce of Publishing in the 21st Century* (2007) are rich in information. John B. Thompson's *Merchants of Culture: The Publishing Business in the Twenty-First Century* (2010) is one of the best books on an individual cultural industry to be published in recent years. His preceding book, *Books in the Digital Age* (2005), which focuses on academic publishing, is also very good. A classic still worth reading is Coser, Kadushin and Powell's *Books* (1982).

Games

Steven Poole's *Trigger Happy* (2000) provides an entertaining and informative journalistic treatment of digital games. Kline, Dyer-Witheford and de Peuter's *Digital Play* (2003) is a sophisticated and readable Marxist study of the games industry. Aphra Kerr's *Digital Games* (2006) has a useful chapter on the games industry.

A collection that examines the impact of the internet on the cultural industries is *The Internet and the Mass Media*, edited by Lucy Küng, Robert Picard and Ruth Towse (2008).

ONLINE READING

All the online material referenced below can be accessed free of charge at: **http://www.sagepub.co.uk/hesmondhalgh**

Simply click on the 'Sample Materials' tab to find the links to each article.

Various contributors to a special issue of the *Annals of the American Academy of Political and Social Science* (volume 625, September 2009), edited by Elihu Katz and Paddy Scannell, discuss 'the end of television as we know it: its impact on the world (so far)'. A good article by Rønning and Slaatta (2011) analyses changes in the book industry.

- Katz, Elihu and Scannell, Paddy (eds.) (2009), *Annals of the American Academy of Political and Social Science*, 625(1).
- Rønning, Helge and Slaatta, Tore (2011) 'Marketers, publishers, editors: Trends in international publishing', *Media, Culture & Society*, 33(7): 1109–1120.

Texts: Diversity, Quality and Social Justice

Choice, diversity and multiplicity   365
   How might we measure diversity? The case of
      popular music   367
   It's all the same: assertions of homogeneity   369
   Is television offering a greater diversity of experiences
      and perspectives in the 'post-network' era?   371
   Diversity or otherwise in the powerful UK press   373
Social justice and changes in texts   375
   Advertising, promotion, commercialism   375
   The politics of entertainment   381
   Has news journalism become less questioning
      of power?   385
   Social fragmentation and market segmentation   388
Has quality declined?   392
   Short attention spans, shock and cultural authority:
      reality televsion   392
   Comparing quality: book publishing   395
   Quality, independence and niche markets: indie cinema
      in the 1990s   398

In this chapter, I address the moment at which the cultural industries arguably have had their most profound effects on culture, society and democracy: their products, the texts that circulate in modern societies, consumed by audiences in a wide variety of ways, from the absorbed to the distracted. So how might we think about the ways in which the changes and continuities discussed in this book have affected texts? In what significant ways have texts changed since the early 1980s? And in what ways has textual change/continuity then had reciprocal effects on the institutions, organisation and economics of the cultural industries? This is obviously a vast terrain, one that incorporates the question of the place of the media in contemporary life. Only a few themes can be addressed in the space allowed by a chapter in a book of this kind.

I have divided my discussion of these areas roughly according to the issues raised when I dealt with textual issues in the evaluative framework offered in Chapter 2: choice, diversity and multiplicity; questions of social justice in relation to texts; and the issue of aesthetic and informational 'quality'. Running through these are two main strands of discussion. First, against the reductive claims or assumptions of mass culture critics and some leftist commentators (including certain political economy writers), I aim to show that the products of the cultural industries remain complex and ambivalent. Indeed, these qualities are becoming more apparent rather than less so amid the industrial and institutional changes since the 1980s that have been discussed in previous chapters. However, I also consider some of the significant problems concerning the nature of the texts produced by the cultural industries in modern societies, against the complacent assumptions and claims of many media economists and other analysts. I recognise throughout the difficulty of providing definitive answers to questions concerning such textual issues. But these do need to be asked.

CHOICE, DIVERSITY AND MULTIPLICITY

One outstanding feature of the texts produced by the cultural industries in the complex professional era has been their proliferation.

- The number of new book titles published in the USA grew from 15,012 in 1960 to 53,446 in 1989, and to 68,175 in 1996 (Greco, Rodríguez and Wharton, 2007: 17–18). These figures were an underestimate, it transpired. When Bowker Annual changed its methodology for tracking book publications, the figures soared to 141,703 in 2001 and 195,000 in 2004 (ibid).
- The theatrical release of motion pictures in the USA went up from 233 in 1980 to 454 in 2001, and to 560 in 2010, following a historical peak of 634 releases in 2008 (Motion Picture Association of America figures).
- Interestingly, the number of albums released in the USA also peaked in 2008, at an extraordinary figure of 106,000, before falling back to more or less 2006 levels of about 75,000 new releases per year (Nielsen figures, reported by Peoples, 2011). This represented a massive proliferation from previous times.
- In 1990, there were 104 cable and satellite channels across Europe. By 1994, this figure had almost doubled to 198. By 1998, this larger figure had more than tripled to 659 channels, including digital terrestrial ones (*Screen Digest*, May 1999).
- One research source claims that about 10,000 magazines were being published in the USA in 2005 (*Industry Profile: Magazine Publishers*,

http://www.researchandmarkets.com). *Magazine Week* stated there were 3,300 magazines available in the UK in 2008.

- There is proliferation in news, too. In advanced industrial countries, more news is available to us than ever before, in the shape of specialist rolling news radio and television channels, on the internet and in newspapers and magazines, even though print newspapers have been closing down, as a combination of economic recession and digitalisation has hit the industry.

Add to this increased output across the different cultural industries the growing number of media technologies that most of us make use of in our everyday lives and it is clear that we are being exposed to an unprecedented potential amount of entertainment and information. However, recalling the discussion in Chapter 2, does this proliferation under conditions of increasing conglomeration, integration and corporate growth represent 'real' diversity or just 'meaningless' multiplicity (Mosco, 1996: 258)? In Chapter 10, I argued that the case of multichannelling in television suggests that, even as the number of channels increases enormously, there is not necessarily any real increase in diversity as these various new channels have tended, in the main, to provide only slightly modified versions of what was already available on the core channels that existed before. Most significant of all is evidence that the availability somewhere in the market of many channels or albums or magazines or films does not equate with knowledge or awareness on the part of audiences about a wider range of forms. Here again we return to the centrality of circulation in the cultural industries. Shops in any reasonably sized city in any advanced industrial country are still bursting with cultural products (books, DVDs, CDs, games) even as the era of digital distribution dawns. Many contain more than most of us could consume in a lifetime of leisure. The internet now provides us with access to millions more, either by virtue of online shopping or in digital form. How to select from among them? As consumers, we rely on information provided in the form of promotion and publicity, often filtered for us by friends. Most of those products remain so unknown to us that they may as well not exist. We should not assume that proliferation equals diversity.

Take the example of film consumption. Most of us mainly consume films made either in the USA or in the country in which we live. Films from other countries are available in rental and other shops and via online rental sites, but most of us will 'choose' not to watch them. This might be because of laziness – 'Why would I want to watch a film with subtitles?' – or it could be the result of a defensive parochialism on the part of some people, who might feel that they couldn't possibly be interested in anything foreign (unless it was from the USA). It could even be because films from the USA are great and everyone else's films aren't very good. This, however, seems unlikely as, even with their greater resources, why would film-makers based in the USA be more creative than people based anywhere else? (I am discounting the specious assumption made by some economists that quality can be equated with production budgets.) The most likely explanation is that audiences are given too small an idea of the pleasures that foreign films not from the USA might contain as they aren't promoted. Thus narrowness of consumption remains a problem, even in an era of proliferation, because of problems concerning the information audiences receive about which products are available.

Proliferation does not necessarily equate with diversity, then, but is there any way of providing harder statistical evidence concerning trends in diversity? In surveys of the cultural industries as a whole, even those commentators who are concerned about concentration, conglomeration and integration have found it difficult to provide firm evidence of diminished diversity. Sánchez-Tabernero et al. (1993: 151–60) for example, in their chapter on the consequences of media concentration, were reduced to offering observations on *potential* links that they recognised were unproven. In addition Neuman (1991:141–2), whose book demonstrated a remarkable grasp of empirical work in the pluralist communication studies tradition, could cite only a single 1970s survey that was of dubious relevance.

Some of the most developed debates regarding trends in textual diversity have been in popular music studies. I address debates about the relationship between concentration and diversity in music in the next section, because the failure of scholars in that field to find adequate measurements, in spite of their best efforts, is instructive. It is also enlightening to observe the difficulties researchers have faced in attempting to pin down the causes of any perceived trends in diversity.

How might we measure diversity? The case of popular music

A seminal but flawed article by Peterson and Berger (1990[1975]) attempted to quantify musical diversity and innovation. Just as importantly, it sought to examine the relationship between diversity and innovation in music, on the one hand, and concentration of ownership, on the other. So did increased concentration reduce diversity? Focusing on the period 1948 to 1973, they claimed to find evidence for two hypotheses:

- That there was a weak but inverse relationship between concentration and diversity/innovation – namely, the more concentrated the ownership of firms, the less diversity there was.
- That this inverse relationship formed a series of cycles, whereby long periods of gradually increasing concentration and homogeneity were followed by brief bursts of competition and creativity.

Peterson and Berger's study had serious methodological limitations. They used Top Ten hit singles as the basis of their samples, even though by the late 1960s and early 1970s *albums* were a more significant format and the charts were inaccurate measures of sales. Added to this, they measured diversity by reference to lyrics rather than musical form. However, aside from these problems concerning how to define diversity, their study also suggests that there are simply too many other, unquantifiable variables around to 'prove' any kind of link between concentration and diversity. For example, their figures for 1964 to 1969 show increasing concentration *and* increasing diversity – seemingly against their hypothesis of a weak but inverse relationship between concentration and diversity. They explain this problem by reference to sociocultural and organisational factors, such as a new lyrical diversity brought about by the civil rights movement in the USA and the Vietnam war and increasing creative autonomy brought about by the increased competition for talent among the oligopolistic firms. Similarly, burgeoning diversity in a period of reconcentration in 1970–1973 was brought about, in their view, by the conglomerates forming separate divisions that competed with each other. These suggestions are fruitful – so much so, in fact, that it is hard not to see such sociocultural and organisational factors as more important than ownership concentration.

Burnett (1992) applied Peterson and Berger's analysis to the 1980s and found historically high levels of concentration *and* diversity – which was a troubling conclusion for critics of oligopoly. Lopes (1992) then reinforced these conclusions. Burnett (1995: 107–10) felt that the main factors behind such an apparently surprising conclusion were organisational. His explanation was that the maturing recording industry had found a way to deal with the problem of innovation in risky musical markets, by co-opting independent record companies and working with them in interdependent networks (see Chapter 6).

Christianen (1995) went much further than these previous studies by gaining access to a database of all albums released in the Netherlands between 1975 and 1992. He analysed diversity according to the amount of music available within 27 different popular music genres and found that, during a period of generally decreasing concentration, diversity and innovation generally increased, in that there was more of each and every genre in the Dutch market. This supported Peterson and Berger's argument, but he found that total demand was more significant than concentration in determining diversity and innovation. Yet even Christianen's thorough analysis raises questions about definitions of diversity. His attempt to use genre as a means of thinking through diversity is admirable, but it flounders. This is because his genre classification is based on an old industry model that was unusable in the 1980s and 1990s, where a huge undifferentiated super-genre called pop coexisted with dozens of regional folk musics and a few fringe genres (military music and the like). Genres mutate, hybridise, disappear and appear so rapidly that no genre classification would work over any historical period greater than three or four years.[1]

---

1   See Einstein (2004) for one attempt to get round these problems, in the context of a measurement of programme diversity in television in the USA, where, arguably, generic mutation is less rapid than in music.

In a historical survey of music charts in the USA from 1940 to 1990, Timothy Dowd (2004) has offered the latest chapter in the story of these debates. Like Burnett and Lopes, he emphasises the importance of interdependent networks or decentralised production and affirms their conclusions by showing that this led to greater diversity in performers and firms. Dowd says that new performers and independent firms do not create more musically diverse recordings than the majors. Instead, musical diversity rises because the majors co-opt emergent styles (2004: 1445). Musical diversity is understood here by Dowd as the number of new performers and new recording firms in the mainstream market, but this is also linked, he claims, to greater diversity in musical content, which he sought to demonstrate in an earlier study (Dowd, 2000). There, diversity of musical content was measured by exhaustively tracking 29 features associated with melodic, rhythmic, chordal, key and verse structure, in a random, unbiased sample of 110 of the 781 records that made number 1 in the *Billboard* charts in the period 1955–1990. Dowd's studies are without doubt the most thorough and impressive of the contributions to these debates so far. The problem here is whether a sample of number 1 records is really an adequate measure of diversity. Certainly, it is a good choice of sample, given the influence number 1 records can have on other performers, but it may be that the very concept of musical diversity within a particular nation over an extended time is simply not measurable quantifiably, without using up impossible resources of time and energy. Even a well-chosen sample fails to do justice to the concept being measured.

It's all the same: assertions of homogeneity

The debates about the relationship between concentration and diversity in popular music illustrate the problems of applying quantitative empirical methods to resolve these difficult issues. Cultural commentary sometimes involves a very different kind of problem: assertions and assumptions about homogeneity or the standardisation of texts are sometimes made without adequate evidence or analysis. It is quite common, in the era of digital hype, to read or hear people dismissing the products of a previous age – such as 'the industrial age', now supposedly being superseded by a digital or information age (see Chapter 9). This is a simplifying critique often based on an optimistic belief that things are getting better. This is a reversal of the way that much cultural analysis used to work. In the twentieth century it was common for cultural pessimists, of various political persuasions, to bewail the standardisation of genres or the output of entire cultural industries. The most sophisticated version of such an approach was Theodor Adorno's critique of the standardisation of 1930s and 1940s pop songs.[2] A curious mixture of both approaches was offered by Manuel Castells in *The Rise of the*

---

2 See Adorno (2002: section 3), and the excellent commentary provided by musicologist Richard Leppert.

Network Society (1996: 364) where he wrote about how 'in the second half of the 1990s a new electronic communication system started to be formed out of the merger of globalised, customised mass media and computer-mediated communication'. The past tense was odd, given the publication date. Castells acknowledged that 'the newness of multimedia' made it difficult to assess their cultural implications (p. 369). Nevertheless, he then proceeded to develop a theory of cultural change around the emergence of the grand multimedia fusion (pp. 369–75), even though, by his own account, this started happening only after his book was completed. Some of the changes he discussed, such as audience differentiation and stratification, had been debated for decades and are discussed below, but the key changes he discussed were textual. First, there was the integration (or convergence) of messages in what Castells called 'a common cognitive pattern' (p. 371) where news, education and entertainment had become blurred together. To illustrate this, he drew on changes in television, where different genres of programming would borrow from one another. But the intermingling of information and entertainment is more complex and ambivalent than he suggests (see Curran, 2010). Second, Castells claimed that multimedia 'capture within their domain most cultural expressions, in all their diversity' (p. 372). The distinctions between audiovisual and printed media, popular and learned culture, entertainment and information were eroded. The result for Castells (though he was actually predicting change rather than describing it) was a 'culture of real virtuality … in which reality itself is entirely captured, fully immersed in a virtual image setting, in the world of make believe' (p. 373). In other words, if you're not in the system, you effectively don't exist. This culture of real virtuality was crucial in Castells' overall account of social change, because it was supposed to produce profound transformations in the experience of space (pp. 376–428) and time (pp. 429–68). Yet, the only evidence he provided for such a transition was this reference to genre-blurring in television.

The homogenisation-through-convergence that Castells described/predicted seems unlikely even now. In predicting it, he showed the influence of mass culture criticism. The complex professional era has seen a pattern whereby new technologies would tend to supplement existing ones rather than replace or merge them, leading to an accretion of separate devices, though, of course, with television still dominant. In fact, what Castells seems to have been describing is television as it actually existed during much of the complex professional era.

It feels harsh to focus on this aspect of Castells' work, when his intellectual achievements are in many respects so impressive. His discussion of convergence perhaps illustrates that even the most accomplished analysts can be swayed into generalisations. The main point here though is that diversity need not be conceptualised in terms of output diversity (which is what economists and policymakers sometimes crave); equally, we need to be careful about asserting homogenisation when we assess the products of the cultural industries. We have to look beyond empiricism or speculation for conceptualisations of diversity. For the real reason to be interested in diversity, from the point of view of the approach of this book (concerned as it is with the relations between culture, power, equality and social justice), is its effects on the distribution of communicative power (see Baker, 2007: 12–16). We need to reflect, then, on whether the cultural industries are providing diversity in ways that might enhance culture, society and democracy.

Is television offering a greater diversity of experiences and perspectives in the 'post-network' era?

Given television's centrality in modern culture and communication, it seems an appropriate example to consider in reflecting on whether the range of forms, narratives and experiences offered by cultural industries might be expanding or diminishing. As television began to transform in the 1990s (see Chapter 7), Michael Curtin (1999) provided a useful understanding of textual change. Curtin outlined a transition from the 'high network era' in which television was a mass medium, offering widely shared political and cultural experiences, premised on 'an interlocking system of mass production, mass marketing, mass consumption, and national regulation' (p. 59). In what he called the neo-network era of cable and satellite television, from the 1980s onwards, the cultural industries pursued new strategies not only of trans-nationalisation (discussed in Chapter 8 above) but also of fragmentation and an increasing focus on niche marketing. As a result, according to Curtin, there was a shift towards the production of texts using 'multiple circuits of information and expression. They ... seek less to homogenise popular culture than to organise and exploit diverse forms of creativity toward profitable ends' (p. 60). Whether the previous era of television was quite as homogenised as this implies is open to question. But Curtin's analysis – which focuses on changing representations of femininity from a broadly feminist perspective – gives us a way of thinking about new circuits of textual meaning in the wake of indus-trial change.

According to him, that dual strategy of transnationalisation and fragmen-tation involved dual textual strategies – one focused on mass cultural forms aimed at national or global markets and demanding low involvement, and the other targeted at niche audiences and aimed at producing/circulating texts with an 'edge' that would produce very intense responses in their audiences. As an example of the type of text that results from the first strategy, Curtin discusses the huge global success of the song 'Macarena' by Los del Rio, which began as a hit in Spain on a small label in 1993, but was distributed globally, in a remixed form, by Bertelsmann's BMG record company, and became a huge hit in the USA for the duo in 1996. The video for this single, shown across the world, provided complex representations, says Curtin: Macarena is portrayed as powerful, in charge of her life, but ultimately the video contains her feminine desire via the appreciative gaze of the two, middle-aged male singers who approve her, and this turns Macarena's active pursuit of pleasure into a mirror image of masculine fantasy (p. 62). Curtin discussed two texts as examples of the second strategy. First, *Absolutely Fabulous*, a BBC sitcom, first shown in 1992, which was a big hit on the USA's cable/satellite niche station The Comedy Channel. This was a show in which feminine desire was represented as 'voracious and uncontrollable' (p. 62). Unlike 'Macarena' (song and video), it made little apparent effort to broaden its appeal. (The challenging nature of the programme is permitted by the nature of its audience – that is, middle-class women in advanced industrial countries.) The second example is Alisha Chinai's 1995 indo-pop music video 'Made in India', which Curtin felt inverted dominant representations of desire 'by transforming the male body into the sight of spectacle', thus raising suppressed questions, such as 'What does an Indian woman want, need and deserve?' (p. 64).

Such textual diversification is also apparent within national television systems. Amanda Lotz (2007) offers some indication of this in her discussion of how, in the USA, 'audiences now choose among a broader array of televised storytelling than at any previous moment in the medium's history' (p. 239). Lotz (2007: Chapter 5) provides five different case studies of programmes made in the 2000s to demonstrate this range, and I extrapolate key points from her much more detailed discussion here:

- *Sex and the City* (1998 to 2004): an example of how new cable networks target a series of niches in order to provide a spread of subscribers. In this case, the niche was young, professional women.
- *Survivor* (2000 to the present): an example of the unpredictable mass (including international) success of some 'unscripted' shows in an environment increasingly concerned with targeting niches.
- *The Shield* (2002 to 2008): an example of how cable networks (News Corp's FX, which bought the series from its conglomerate partner Fox), seeking to provide a brand identity for themselves, may support significant innovation: the series reinvigorated the police drama genre through its focus on a rogue detective.
- *Arrested Development* (2003 to 2006): an example of an innovative show, shown on a network (Fox) rather than on a cable channel, which challenged the main conventions of mainstream situation comedy (and the representations of family life usually to be found there), and was supported by the network in spite of low ratings.
- *Off to War* (2004 to 2006): a documentary shown on an 'ultra-niche' cable channel (Discovery Times – a joint venture of Discovery and *The New York Times*) about the effects of war on part-time soldiers which, to an unusual degree, represented the experiences of working-class, rural, southern Americans.

Lotz does not focus much on the textual richness (or otherwise) of these programmes or their ideological meanings. Nor does she undertake a historical comparison with a previous era. Instead she helpfully indicates the range of forms and stories available. Curtin's perspective suggests that diversity might have more international and cross-class dimensions.

Two qualifications need to be made regarding these perspectives on diversity. First, we might ask: **to whom is diversity actually available**?[3] Is diversity mainly available to the well-off and educated who consume innovative shows on niche cable channels? Second, it may be the case that television – or particular national systems such as the American 'post-network' television systems – may exhibit some ideological homogeneity beneath its diverse exterior. Certainly key genres may demonstrate a certain kind of political homogeneity (see the discussion of 'The Politics of Entertainment' below). But that is different from a critique that claims **a lack of diversity**. Such a critique would surely only be effective if it engaged properly with this undoubted multiplicity of forms and stories.

Diversity or otherwise in the powerful UK press

Analysing homogenisation and diversity in cultural industries dealing in information, rather than entertainment, may lead to somewhat different conclusions. One example, discussed among others by Peter Humphreys (1996: 77), is the UK's national press, which enjoys very high levels of readership and great political influence. The post-war period saw a growing concentration of ownership, and a marked homogenisation of the political views represented by the press.

In 1945 there were four Conservative national daily newspapers, two Liberal ones, and two Labour ones. At the 1987 General Election, seven out of eleven national daily papers supported the Conservative Party, two supported the Labour Party, and two did not commit. What is more the two Labour papers represented only 20 per cent of the total readership, even though Labour received between 30 and 42 per cent of votes in general elections. Liberals were even more under-represented. Yet in 1992, in Humphreys' words (1996: 77), '70 per cent of the national daily readers and 62 per cent of Sunday readers were advised to vote Conservative'.

Yet such figures tell only part of the story of political homogenisation. For the UK national press have, almost without exception, supported the drift towards conservatism and neo-liberalism in public policy since the 1980s, and sometimes with fervent partisanship. During the 1980s, in James Curran and Jean Seaton's words, 'A large section of the national press ... *went into coalition with the government*' (Curran and Seaton, 2010: 73, original emphasis). This coalition broke down in the 1990s, and a number of traditionally Conservative newspapers, such as the Murdoch-owned *Sun*, supported the Labour Party (or, rather, the Labour Party's leader, Tony Blair – and this perhaps reflected the increasing 'presidentialisation' of British politics) in the successive general elections of 1997, 2001 and 2005.

---

3   There is a surprising neglect of this question of access and availability in the new cultural studies of media industries.

This change of political allegiance reflected a broader kind of political homogeneity (Curran and Seaton, 2010: 76ff). For most of the newspapers that backed Labour did so on the basis that the Labour Party would more competently deliver economic growth than the Conservative Party, rather than because of the Labour Party's stated though muted commitment to equality and social justice. This was made possible by the very high degree of ownership concentration in UK newspapers; the three biggest groups commanded 62 per cent of daily circulation in 2008, and 79 per cent of Sunday circulation. The swing in support on the part of the national press was really brought about by New Labour's ability to court just two men: Rupert Murdoch and Richard Desmond, the latter the owner of various television soft-porn channels and publications, and of what must surely be Britain's worst national daily newspaper, *The Daily Express*.

The result was that by the early 2000s, in a reverse of the situation in the 1980s and 1990s, Labour's support in the UK national press greatly exceeded its support in the country: 70 per cent of readers at the 2001 general election were advised to vote Labour. The pendulum had swung in a different direction, but in effect the press were still supporting economic conservatism. Of course, the fact that only 43.2 per cent of the voters chose Labour reflects that direct statements of support during elections will usually have only a limited effect. The more significant issue is the constant drip feed of support over many years for conservative and neo-liberal policies, no matter which party is in power. And in case this is not clear to non-UK readers, such support is not confined to leader columns and op-ed pieces. Front-page headlines, taking up more or less half of the front page, will make political statements that might, without exaggeration, be described as propaganda. On 30 November 2011, nearly three million British workers went on strike for one day to protest against considerable cuts in their retirement pensions on the part of the government. *The Daily Mail*'s front-page headline, accompanying a story entirely based on the government's perspective on the strike, was 'Still think striking is a good idea?'

The political profile of newspapers can, however, be more complex than the views expressed in news coverage of political and social issues. For example, *The Daily Mail*, now the UK's most prominent newspaper in terms of its influence on political agendas, takes right-wing stances on most issues and yet its television and entertainment pages may sometimes feature sympathetic coverage of soap storylines with progressive implications. This may derive from the greater autonomy allowed to writers in these sections of newspapers. However, this should also be understood in the context of a marked decline of coverage of public affairs in the UK national press (Curran and Seaton, 2010: 88–9), which seriously limits the potential contribution of this enormously powerful cultural industry to the functioning of democracy in the UK – a gap that is only partly filled by Britain's tradition of public service broadcasting and its small number of relatively high-quality 'broadsheet' newspapers. These are increasingly editorialising in their news pages and their front page headlines as well.

The proliferation of texts since the 1980s, in the wake of the expansion of the cultural industries, does not automatically mean diversity. Nor can we assume, however, that the increasing size and scope of cultural industry corporations have led to homogenisation or standardisation. The jury remains out. The task must be to find better ways of discussing diversity, including questions concerning *diversity for whom*. Quantitative studies of the kind discussed above, in the section on concentration and diversity in popular music, may be able to contribute to this, but they are unlikely to be sufficient in themselves.

SOCIAL JUSTICE AND CHANGES IN TEXTS

Chapter 6 showed that there has been a huge increase in the size and scope of cultural industry corporations. These corporations are owned and operated by people with a significant interest in maintaining existing power relations. Has the period since 1980 seen any changes in the nature of the texts produced by the cultural industries, in terms of the **interests** they support and their potential role in, for example, promoting or inhibiting the pursuit of social justice? (See also the discussion of these interests in Chapter 2.)

Advertising, promotion, commercialism

In one respect, I think, a clear answer is available. In the period of their accelerated expansion, since the 1970s, the cultural industries have helped to bring about an unprecedented **commercialisation** of the everyday cultural lives of billions of people. In doing so, cultural industry companies have expanded their role, already emergent in the early years of the complex professional era, as the promoters of their own interests as companies – always their primary interest – and those of businesses in general. Here we return to some of the questions regarding relations between art, creativity and knowledge on the one hand, and commercial imperatives on the other, discussed in Chapter 7; and the discussion of commercialisation in relation to the internet discussed in Chapter 9.

There are various reasons to be concerned about an increasing presence of advertising in the media and in societies. In Michael Schudson's words, advertising

> glorifies the pleasures and freedom of consumer choice. It defends the virtues of private life and freedom of consumer choice. It idealizes the consumer and consuming. It holds implicitly or explicitly that freedom, fulfilment, and personal transformation lie in the world of goods. (Schudson, 1993[1984]: xix).

Schudson quotes the great writer and critic, John Berger, who wrote that advertising 'proposes to each of us that we transform ourselves, or our lives by buying something more' (ibid). Schudson argued that advertising is an equivalent in capitalist countries of socialist realism: the official art of the Soviet Union, charged with providing representations that would advance the Stalinist form of socialism. Like socialist realism, the **capitalist realism** of advertising is required to picture reality in simplified and typified ways; it pictures life not as it is but as it should be lived; it should carry an air of optimism and represent struggle positively; and should focus on creating pleasing images of contemporary life (Schudson, 1993 [1984]: 216).

Advertising is a cultural industry in itself, but nearly all the other cultural industries act as important vehicles for advertising, too. In fact, most advertising comes to us inserted in other media, except for billboards and other forms of publicly displayed advertising (which, in a sense, is inserted into our living environments). Examining newspapers in a significant and sophisticated analysis of the effects of advertising, C. Edwin Baker argued that while advertising clearly subsidises media consumption it also caused a decline in content diversity in US newspapers and helped to establish a particular and ideologically-laden style of journalism centred on the notion of professional objectivity (see Baker, 1994: Chapter 1). As well as this indirect, structural effect on journalism, Baker points out that advertising can be shown to affect media content in a number of other ways. Advertising encourages the media to tailor their content:

- to treat advertisers' products and their broader interests kindly in news reports;
- to create a buying mood that will incline readers or viewers to act favourably to advertisements;
- to reduce partisanship and controversy to avoid offending advertisers' potential customers;
- to favour middle and higher income audiences whose greater purchasing power advertisers value most (all from Baker, 1994: 44).

There is considerable evidence that the growth of the cultural industries has been integrally related to an increase in the amount of advertising in the media and in modern societies. As well as the advertising expenditure figures discussed in Chapter 3, there are various other pieces of evidence. In the 1990s, for example, all the major television networks in the USA increased the average time per hour they devoted to product advertising. Robin Andersen (2000) quoted the following figures for each of the Big Four, comparing minutes per hour in 1991 to minutes per hour in 1996:

- ABC went from 9 minutes to 11.26.
- CBS from 9.10 to 10.29.
- Fox from 11.03 to 11.40.
- NBC from 9.57 to 10.33.

By the early 2000s, according to figures cited by Matthew McAllister (2005: 219), in the USA roughly a quarter of all the time on advertising-supported broadcast and cable television was devoted to commercial and promotional messages and this figure was rising. The average child viewer was exposed to 40,000 television commercials a year at that time, nearly double the figure from 20 years earlier (ibid).

Just as significant as the increasing space devoted to advertising is a huge increase in the amount of promotional material carried by the cultural industries in texts that we do not consider to be advertising. Andersen (2000: 3) claimed that placing brands in films really took off after the time when in *ET* (directed by Steven Spielberg, 1982) the title alien ate a certain brand of sweets and sales increased by 300 per cent. She provided many examples of more recent product placements and cited evidence showing that audience recall of such products is two and a half times greater when products are submerged in TV programmes than when they are advertised separately. Andersen also raised ethical questions surrounding a situation where clothes are being promoted not in a section marked as an advertisement, but hidden away in what purports to be 'just a story'. One agency believed that the greater effectiveness of product placement was because 'products shown in motion pictures or in television are perceived by the audience to be chosen by the star thus receiving an implied endorsement' (Andersen, 2000: 2). Product placement also often masquerades as 'hip cynicism' (p. 4). Andersen (2000: 4) gave an example from *The Wedding Singer* (1998), starring Adam Sandler:

> Sandler, playing the wedding singer, is lying in bed depressed after his fiancée has left him. A friend comes to visit, lies down on the bed [fully clothed] and says, 'Hey, these sheets are soft. Do you use Downy?' Sandler replies, 'No, All-Tempa-Cheer. You can wash your clothes at any temperature and the colours don't run together'.

The 'humour' here is not at the *expense* of product placement, as in, say, the film *Repo Man* (directed by Alex Cox, 1985). The aim is to evoke laughter at the sheer cheek of the film-makers for getting away with such blatant placement. Perhaps this is less offensive or irritating than the submerged quality of much product placement, but it is a close call.

However, advertising is only part of a much larger apparatus of marketing and 'promotional culture' (Wernick, 1991) and the general spread of commercialisation through culture (Ruskin and Schor, 2009), including the built environment of cities and towns (Gendelman and Aiello, 2010). Another important change in texts over the last 30 years is that they often promote other texts produced by the same cultural industry company. We can consider this on two levels. First, a particular channel or product will promote itself. In 1999, the USA's TV network ABC aired 7000 promotions for its own programmes – nearly twice what it had aired ten years before (McAllister, 2000: 111). However, as a result of conglomeration and the strategies of corporate synergy (see Chapter 6), companies will increasingly plan and design texts in order to encourage subsidiary, spin-off texts, often of low quality. At the most prestigious, high budget end of the market, there is the example of *Batman* (Meehan, 1991). The rights to the character were purchased by Warner Communications when it bought DC Comics. Besides reviving the comic, Warner (Time Warner from 1990 onwards) produced three films, plus soundtracks, novelisations and huge amounts of merchandising. The films and comics had their merits, but the spin-offs were blatant and imposing in their promotional quality. See Box 11.1 for another example of such synergy strategies, but one which adds less compelling textual results than the *Batman* series.[4]

Box 11.1   Cross-media promotion and dubious secondary texts

The release and marketing of the film *The Chronicles of Narnia: The Lion, the Witch and the Wardrobe* in 2005 illustrates how vast numbers of texts can proliferate around a core text in the era of corporate synergy. The project of adapting C.S. Lewis's Narnia series of children's books was begun by Paramount Pictures but dropped after five years. It was then picked up by the Anschutz Film Group (AFG). AFG negotiated a long-term franchise plan with C.S. Lewis's stepson and now owns the rights to make films based on all seven books in the Narnia series. AFG teamed up with the Walt Disney Co. to cover distribution, with Disney paying for half the production costs. Unlike its rivals Time Warner and Sony Pictures Entertainment, which had long-term franchises with Harry Potter and Spiderman respectively, Disney was without a 'signature movie' and saw a series based on the Narnia series as a means to rectify this.

The film has spawned a number of 'secondary' texts – by which I mean texts that are reliant on a pre-existing 'primary' text (which is not necessarily superior or inferior). The book preceded the film, of course, but a massive re-release programme of C.S. Lewis's novel was initiated. Walden Media, an AFG and Walt Disney company, worked closely with the book's publisher HarperCollins (owned by News Corporation) on the release of 19 new versions of the book to coincide with the film's opening. Walden Media provided complimentary copies of the book to libraries in over 200 locations in the USA to replace worn copies. Over 100,000 teachers in the USA were also provided with copies of the book, as well as educational guides that included lesson plans relating to issues raised in the book. HarperCollins' imprint Zondervan released products into Christian bookshops and gift shops. Disney Interactive has published Nintendo and PlayStation Narnia games.

Many albums were also released that were officially associated with the film. The first was *Music Inspired by The Chronicles of Narnia*, distributed between EMI and released on Sparrow Records in September 2005. This was a collaboration by Christian artists. In December, a traditional movie soundtrack was also released (produced by Walt Disney Records) and a CD+DVD special edition movie soundtrack featuring an extended score and behind the scenes footage.

---

4 Advertising and commercialism can of course also have effects on journalism, which I address in greater detail under 'quality' below.

Besides these various secondary texts, we can identify a huge number of what we might call 'tertiary' texts and activities that were more explicitly aimed at promoting and publicising the film. Prior to the release of the first film in the planned series, *The Chronicles of Narnia: The Lion, the Witch and the Wardrobe*, Disney placed the Narnia trailer on approximately 20 million DVDs, including those being released by Disney's ABC network, such as series 1 of its hit TV show *Lost*. Promotions of the film also appeared on screen during ABC network programmes such as *Commander in Chief*.

The marketing of *Narnia* drew on the strategies used for Disney's 1994 film *The Lion King*. Over 60 Narnia products were licensed. Marketing partners included Unilever, General Mills, Georgia-Pacific and McDonald's. Promotions appeared on Oral B toothbrushes, Quilted Northern toilet paper (as well as paper towels and napkins from the Georgia Pacific company), McDonald's Happy Meals (which had eight different pop-up story books with Narnia figurines), Verizon mobile phone packages, Energizer batteries, and 21 brands of General Mills cereal. There were also Christmas displays in shopping malls where children could visit Santa Claus surrounded by props from the movie.

Disney also drew on the strategy used for the promotion of the immensely successful *The Passion of the Christ* (2004) and hired the Christian firm Movie Marketing to hold screenings of the movie in churches and promote Narnia-themed Bible study classes. Finally, as with *The Lord of the Rings,* tour companies began to offer Narnia tours to places where the movie was filmed in New Zealand.

So how good was this film, given that it was specifically designed to generate synergies and sequels? Film critic Anthony Lane (2005) commented in *The New Yorker* that the plodding allegory of the book meant that the film 'seizes up with a kind of enforced pageantry ... [E]ven the climactic fight between Peter's army of truth and the Witch's bevy of demons has an air of heraldic artifice, as if we were witnessing not a brawl to the death, red in tooth and claw, but an enamelled clash of ideas'. But the film and its sequels (*Prince Caspian*, 2008; *The Voyage of the Dawn Treader*, 2010) gained some good reviews as well. The directors of the three films, Andrew Adamson (the first two) and Michael Apted (*Voyage*), are talented; they were responsible for *Shrek* and the wonderful *7 Up* documentaries respectively. There have been diminishing but nevertheless significant box-office returns. Yet there seems little affection for the films among young people or adults. And it seems highly unlikely that many people have had their lives enhanced by *Music Inspired by The Chronicles of Narnia*. Might this 'franchise' – the vile marketing term for a series of films based on such synergies – be an example of how commercialism and the pursuit of profit might result in vastly expensive but rather mediocre cultural production?

Sources: Albright (2005); Grover (2005); Marr (2005); Prichard (2005); Rowan (2005); Toynbee (2005); Wasserman (2005).

The increased emphasis on promotion, marketing and branding in contemporary culture (which was also discussed in Chapter 7, in the context of changing relations of creativity and commerce in cultural production) extends even to how we think of ourselves as persons, as individuals. Self-promotion is not new, as Alison Hearn (2008: 197) points out. But as flexible neo-liberal capitalism became entrenched in the 1980s, contemporary culture emphasised the importance of branding the self, rather than a commitment to public service or an institution. In a key piece, Hearn (2008) describes how reality television and social networking sites have extended this notion of the branded self, first articulated by management gurus such as Tom Peters, in new directions. As she points out, shows such as the *Idol* and *Top Model* formats 'have the story of self-branding as the central theme of their narratives and include explicit instruction on how to manage the demands of fame and effectively perform one's own celebrity brand' (2008: 202). These developments are clearly related to general socio-cultural developments (see Giddens, 1991), but they can also be seen as indirect effects of the intensified competition for audiences and revenues in late 1990s and early 2000s television. Reality television cheaply created hundreds of lesser-grade celebrities, who could operate across a range of media sites, and who were more accessible than the increasingly powerful 'A' list film and music stars who now, more than ever, sought to protect themselves from media intrusion.

Social networking sites take these dynamics of self-promotion a stage further by providing a mediated forum for self-branding for billions of people. Of course, a phenomenon such as Facebook is more than this. In his rich (2011) anthropological study of Facebook, Daniel Miller points to the way in which Facebook revives and expands our complicated sense of what it means to exist in a community – including the downsides of communing. For some who live in quite intense community situations, where it feels as though everyone knows what everyone else is doing (this was the case in some of the Trinidadian settings studied by Miller), Facebook provides something of a refuge. Nevertheless, as Hearn points out, the logic of sites such as Facebook 'encourages users to see themselves and others as commodity signs, to be collected and consumed in the social market place' (2008: 205). Combined with the developments in monitoring and surveillance of users discussed in Chapter 9, Facebook and other social networking sites become central aspects of how the cultural industries work on the self (and how we ourselves 'work' in unexpected ways as part of the cultural industries).

These developments are surely significant if we are concerned about the quality and integrity of the culture we consume. Perhaps the most noteworthy feature of the commercialisation of texts is that it may reinforce a continuing shift in the conception of political subjects in contemporary capitalism. We are less and less encouraged to think of ourselves as citizens; more and more we are treated as consumers. The cultural industries did not initiate such a shift; it was primarily brought about by the actions of businesses seeking profit and governments seeking economic growth. And it would be quite wrong to say that the entire function of the cultural industries is to support the interests of businesses and governments, or some abstract system called capitalism. At the same time, there are striking ways in which the capitalist production and circulation of culture at times demonstrates a striking degree of complicity with state and corporate power. Once again we need to recognise **contradiction** as part of a critical analysis of cultural production under capitalism. This issue can be investigated further by stepping back to take a broader view of the changes and continuities in entertainment texts over the last 40 years.

The politics of entertainment

Is there any tendency, during the various changes (and continuities) of the last four decades, for entertainment texts to have become more or less compliant, more or less likely to favour dominant and powerful interests in society, and to work against the pursuit of social justice and greater equality?

Here it is particularly vital to consider the intermeshed dynamics of socio-cultural change, and the industrial and economic changes that are the main focus of this book. For the explosion of the cultural industries and the proliferation of texts, from the 1970s onwards, coincided with crucial political developments. Perhaps the most notable of these involved attempts by people previously marginalised or excluded from power on the grounds of their identities to achieve greater levels of respect, recognition or voice for the groups with which they identified. Some women challenged the marginalisation and oppression of women through various kinds of feminism; some people of colour challenged racism through a variety of anti-racist and multiculturalist programmes and activisms; some lesbians, gay men and transgendered people fought homophobia and prejudice based on sexuality. As these and other related political perspectives developed, and were picked up by symbol makers, many of them were articulated in entertainment texts in new ways. To make a strong woman the centre of a series of science-fiction films, as Sigourney Weaver's character Ellen Ripley was in the first four *Alien* films, would have been unthinkable in earlier decades. Some activists focused on the cultural industries themselves, arguing for greater levels of representation of these groups in key positions. The result has been a more complex relationship between the texts produced by the cultural industries, and the key dimensions of inequality in contemporary societies.

Nevertheless, in spite of an increasing consciousness of the problems of racism, sexism and other forms of social difference, at least in some sections of modern societies, many of the entertainment texts produced by the cultural industries continue to contribute to these problems. We might differentiate a number of ways in which this happens, though all three problems might co-exist in the same genres, or even in the same texts:

1 A continuing lack of visibility or audibility, in certain genres at least – a lack of interesting, rounded disabled characters in contemporary Hollywood and Indian films for example.

2   A continuing use of negative stereotypes and problematic representa-
    tions of relatively powerless groups – in some cases, this might be the
    result of a determined 'backlash' against feminism, multiculturalism
    or socialism. In other cases, the cause might be a lack of interest in or
    knowledge of stereotypes and representations. An example of this could
    be the sexism of the men's magazines that became popular in Europe
    and North America in the 1990s and 2000s (Jackson et al., 2001). Anoth-
    er might be the way that certain 'makeover' programmes unconsciously
    encode a profound disrespect for working-class ways of life. The only
    way to achieve popularity, or love, or respect, such programmes seem
    to suggest, is to dress and act more like a middle-class person.

3   A more complex 'post-feminism' and 'post civil rights' set of repre-
    sentations that seemingly value the (partial) freedoms and equalities
    achieved by political projects such as feminism, anti-racism and social-
    ism, but which also distance themselves from them. As Sarah Banet-
    Weiser (2007) shows, texts involving such representations might, for
    example, seek to portray such movements as extreme, or overly dour,
    and because of this will set the sensibility, or sense of life, encapsulated
    in the text against these political programmes in a way that potentially
    undermines those freedoms for others.

4   Well-meaning and explicitly politically motivated producers, aiming to
    challenging existing power relations, can find themselves reproducing
    problematic stereotypes, representations and viewpoints, partly as a
    result of industrial dynamics – Anamik Saha (2011) illustrates this in
    his work on British-Asian independent record companies. He shows
    how a desire not to be placed on the margins leads some producers,
    who are otherwise critical of recurring representations of British-
    Asian, to embrace deals with major corporations that will potentially
    lead them to be marketed or branded in such a way that reproduc-
    es the very representations that they sought to move beyond in the
    first place.

It would be wrong, then, to imagine that the widespread permeation of
feminism, anti-racism and even a demotic questioning of upper middle-class
authority (for example in *Wife Swap*-style programmes) throughout contemporary entertainment texts has democratised entertainment – I return to this
question in considering debates about the 'quality' or otherwise of reality
television below. But it may well be the case that entertainment programmes
are even less critical in orientation when it comes to matters beyond identity
politics, such as questions of national security, or of consumerism and economic prosperity. For example, there is evidence that popular drama that
relates to the role of the American military and security services, such as *24*
(2001–2010) 'has celebrated and justified America's national security state',
with support and subsidy from that state (Curran, 2010: 45).

Yet alongside these undoubtedly worrying tendencies the media and
popular culture are full of emotions and sentiments that do not simply

coincide with the interests of business, or capitalism, racism, imperialism, or patriarchal power. Rupert Murdoch, for example, has consistently supported the most socially and politically conservative causes as an individual and through his newspapers, as the discussion in Chapter 7 showed, but his Fox Television network commissions and broadcasts *The Simpsons*, which has provided a powerful and sometimes politically charged commentary on the traumas and limitations of life in the USA (see Downey, 2006) and a rich mine of parody of contemporary culture, including television adverts, sitcoms and news (Gray, 2006). Or take the HBO TV series *Sex and the City*, discussed above in the context of Lotz's claims about diversity on contemporary US television: Jane Arthurs (2003) has shown how the programme allowed a sexually explicit and critical feminist discourse into television comedy, which established a space for educated women to interrogate their own complicity in processes of commodification and narcissism that ultimately threaten women's well-being.[5]

These are only a couple of examples from tens of thousands of texts that can be construed as *not* supporting existing social relations, at least not in any simple sense of 'support'. Here are some more examples of the values, emotions and experiences to be found not just on the margins of the cultural industries but also often right at their very centre, at peak time, in prime time, and with huge audiences.

- Popular culture is full of cynicism, anger, sarcasm, the celebration of lazy hedonism. Irony and pastiche are to be found everywhere – even in advertising, which was an irony-free zone until the rise of 'creative advertising' in the 1980s. In this sense, media texts have become generally more reflexive about their own operations. If a cliché develops, there is often – though by no means always – a team of comedy writers waiting somewhere to develop a sketch about it for a programme.[6]
- Alongside the many texts that fawn on power and wealth, in the shape of glamorous portrayals of the rich and influential, there is also evidence

---

5 Others, however, have seen the programme as an example of the worst traits of a post-feminist media culture (Gill, 2007: 242). Even if Arthurs is correct, her sympathetic assessment can surely not be applied to the egregious 2010 film *Sex and the City 2*, which was almost universally panned by critics, and which lacked any of the complexity and reflexivity detected by Arthurs in the original series (see also Curran, 2010, for an excellent and generally sympathetic discussion of the television series). This would make an interesting case study of how different production conditions can affect textual outcomes – and how the study of such production can explain different levels of quality and of critique. What was it about the production of the film that made it so bad, so unfunny, and so uncritical?

6 'Rwanda Revisited ... a harrowing report from *Big Brother* 2 winner Brian Dowling'. An episode of the comedy series *Extras* broadcast in September 2006 featured this parody of TV's misguided efforts to draw attention to poverty through the use of celebrities.

of radical scepticism about the claims of the powerful and a questioning of authority. The powerful and the prestigious are regularly satirised. Members of the British Royal Family are treated, in some sections of the media, with reverence and respect, but elsewhere they are also the object of ridicule and scandal-mongering (though less so during the royalist upswing of recent times).

- There is plenty of evidence of anger and rage in the media and popular culture. This is often undirected or else directed against those with no real power in society (such as hip hop lyrics directed implicitly at an imaginary peer group enemy). Cultural forms such as hip hop and thrash metal, however, draw attention to the widespread existence of social suffering and counter the sentimental and optimistic implicit claims of other kinds of popular culture.
- A utopian belief in the hope of a better world and better society has also been present in popular culture throughout the twentieth century (see Dyer, 1981), but continues to be expressed in many musical cultures (such as rave in the UK in the late 1980s and 1990s) and much popular film.

These modes of thought and feeling are hardly ever directly subversive of oppressive economic and political power. They do not cancel out inequality, instead they reflect and reinforce the fact that the naturalisation of existing power relations is never complete.

Associated with these changes has been a reconfiguration and partial questioning of cultural authority (an issue raised by debates about postmodernism, but rarely addressed with adequate sociological imagination). There are new relationships between 'high' and 'low' culture. These have not been fully democratised – the rich continue to have extremely different cultural habits and tastes from the poor. As Richard Peterson and Roger Kern (1996) suggested, the educated may have become more omnivorous in their tastes, indulging in low culture while also maintaining an interest in high culture. This is easily mistaken for a postmodern blurring of high and low, but the less educated continue to be excluded from, and/or are uninterested in, high culture.

The entertainment culture produced by the contemporary cultural industries surely cannot be seen as liberating or emancipatory. Some researchers surely overstate the ability of audiences to knowingly or playfully subvert some of the more dubious ways in which, for example, men's magazines represent gender. But contemporary entertainment is certainly contradictory. As I pointed out in the Introduction to this book, such contradictions derive, in part, from the fact that cultural industry companies are happy enough to disseminate cynical or even angrily political works as long as they produce a profit (or else prestige that can be turned indirectly into profit). However, they are perhaps less happy to allow for the provision of information that provides an analysis of overall power relations. So are things any different in the world of news and factual reporting?

Has news journalism become less questioning of power?

News journalism can play a vital role in providing citizens with the informational resources to counter social injustice. We saw in Chapter 7 that there is more commercial pressure on news organisations than ever before and I noted evidence above that this has had some impact on some aspects of news reporting. As a result, has journalism's capacity and willingness to challenge power, and to promote social justice as well as inform readers about issues of public concern, been diminished in the period under discussion?

For some, the answer is unequivocally yes. Robert McChesney, writing in the late 1990s, saw recent trends in journalism as representing a collapse of the standards of professional reporting founded on the goals of objectivity and public service. McChesney (1999) was careful to point out the limitations of professional journalism as it developed in the USA in the twentieth century: that journalists were never as objective as they claimed and were always prone to falling into line with commercial and government forces. He highlighted long-standing silences and absences in news media coverage concerning the incredible size of US military budgets and the activities of the CIA. Nevertheless, compared with the state of journalism in the 1990s, McChesney (1999: 51) saw the period after the Second World War as one where 'the calibre of professional journalism prospered and developed a certain amount of autonomy from the dictates of owners and advertisers, and from the corporate sector as a whole'. The subsequent decline was manifest in staff cuts and an increasing tendency towards soft news, such as celebrity lifestyle pieces, court cases, plane crashes, crime stories and shootouts, which were uncontroversial and cheap to cover. McChesney cited figures that show international news was cut back from 45 per cent of the network TV news total in the early 1970s to 13.5 per cent in 1995. Meanwhile, the annual number of crime stories on network TV news programmes tripled between 1990 and 1992 and 1993 and 1996 (1999: 54). As we saw in Chapter 7 (on the effects of increasing commercial pressures on journalistic autonomy) and Chapter 10 (in discussing the impact of the internet on newspapers), more recent developments – especially the declines in newspaper circulation, revenue and staffing – have led some commentators, including McChesney and his co-author John Nichols, to talk of a fully-fledged crisis in journalism (McChesney and Nichols, 2010).

Numerous other analysts have echoed McChesney's points, including many professional journalists. In crucial ways during the 2000s, journalism in a number of societies seemed to fail its citizens, further undermining their confidence and trust in the news. W. Lance Bennett, Regina G. Lawrence and Steven Livingston (2007) have analysed journalism's failure to question the Bush administration's arguments for going to war against Iraq, and its ultimately uncritical treatment of the appalling treatment of prisoners at the USA's prison facility at Abu Ghraib in Iraq. They attributed this to a consensus shared between Washington DC-based journalists, politicians and

government officials, that was 'heavily shaped by government communications officers and their public relations agents' (2007: 169).

Others, however, have taken the view that new technological developments, such as in camcorders and mobile phones, and the internet and world
wide web, are leading to a democratisation of news reporting that will ultimately redeem journalism. In 2006 Jay Rosen, one of the prime advocates
of citizen journalism, posted a blog that was a pretend letter to Big Media,
laying out what he saw as changes in the media and journalism landscape:

> You were once (exclusively) the editors of the news, choosing what
> ran on the front page. Now we can edit our news, and our choices
> send items to our own front pages ... Now the horizontal flow,
> citizen-to-citizen, is as real and consequential as the vertical one.

One notable and frequently cited case is the South Korean website Ohmynews,
which supplements professional reporters and editors with freelance contributors
who are 'ordinary citizens'. The resulting news is often interesting and certainly
different from that of the established news organisations. James Curran (2011:
117) summarises some ways in which the internet has valuably contributed to
journalism, such as making available for global scrutiny footage of the killings of
Nada Soltan and Ian Tomlinson during demonstrations in Tehran and London
in 2009. Genuinely admirable and exciting though some of these developments
are, however, they rely on the interaction of continuing institutions of good journalism with other technologies – most notably the mobile phone. Discussions
of successful citizen journalism often seem reliant on a rather limited number
of examples (though see Allan and Thorsen, 2009, for an unusually wide range
of international cases). As Curran points out, new web ventures have mostly
failed to be able to attract sufficient advertising to support themselves.

Here we are back in the territory surveyed in Chapters 9 and 10. We
saw there some of the factors limiting the internet's ability to democratise
and decentralise cultural production: these included inequalities in access
and skills, continuing and sometimes growing concentrations of attention and
of power, and rampant commercialisation and surveillance. Others have
pointed out that the celebration of amateur or citizen reporting risks underestimating the importance and integrity of professionalism at its best. Good
journalism needs an infrastructure of training and financial support (see
Keen, 2007: 46–50). Much internet journalism is in fact heavily reliant on
old media sources. As McChesney and Nichols (2010: 16–17) point out

> [T]o a significant extent, Internet news sites are aggregators of
> the news gathered by old media rather than producers of news
> content. The information discussed online is still gathered
> by newspaper and broadcast reporters, and while a few high-
> profile journalists have begun to migrate from old-fashioned
> newsrooms to the blogosphere, they tend to arrive as commentators
> rather than collectors of news. The leading news Web sites are

almost all affiliated with the 'old media', and much of what the
bloggers blog about comes from the old media in digital form.

Although his piece preceded claims about the effects of blogging and 'citizen
journalism', Daniel Hallin (2000) provided a useful overview of a number of
issues that continue to be highly relevant to any discussion of how news may
or may not enhance contemporary society, culture and democracy as journalism migrates to the internet. He pointed to a number of changes marking
a new era in US journalism from the 1980s onwards:

- The fragmentation of the news media, with more and more outlets
  claiming to be journalism.
- A blurring of the line between news and entertainment.
- A growing uncertainty on the part of journalists about their role –
  should they be objective informers or take partisan stances, showing
  empathy with the people they deal with? (Hallin, 2000: 221)

Hallin outlined a number of reasons for these shifts. Some were commercial,
such as increased competition from local news, the rise of news magazine
programmes and the greater concern of the conglomerates with 'the bottom
line'. Others were political and cultural, including a decline in the high prestige of public affairs in the decades after the Second World War, the increasing presence of women and ethnic minorities in newsrooms (which made the
former model of professional objectivity harder to sustain, as female, Latino
and African-American news workers detected a bias in such supposed objectivity), and the increasing challenge to the separation of private and public
realms from feminism and media texts themselves. (Hallin thus allowed for
feedback from texts to the cultural industries.)

Hallin refused to portray changes in journalism as either an out-and-out
decline or a steady improvement. He found that new formats for representing political debate had a certain inclusiveness that was not present in the
golden age. Against those who would mourn the rise of 'infotainment',
he pointed out that news and entertainment have never been absolutely
separate and good journalists have always been good storytellers. Tabloid
television does at times, Hallin claimed, give a voice to individuals who
would not have gained access to the old journalism. Some of the stories
bemoaned as 'soft' by professional journalists, such as when the character
and actress Ellen DeGeneres came out as a lesbian on her sitcom *Ellen* in
1998, could, said Hallin, be seen just as important in public life as the inside-
the-beltway Washington stories that passed for hard news in the golden
age of professional journalism. Nor was Hallin sure that the move towards
interpretative reporting, whereby journalists will bring their own subjective responses to bear on a story, necessarily represents a fall in standards.

Nevertheless, Hallin was absolutely clear about the negative aspects of
developments in journalism. There was a tremendous amount of sensational
coverage of ultimately trivial matters. Tabloidised news, on television and in

newspapers, depended 'heavily on the exploitation and amplification of fear' (p. 231). The ethos of professional neutrality helped to resist the imperatives of owners, but was increasingly eroded in the 1980s and 1990s. And while there had not yet been a return to the era of newspapers acting as vehicles for the views of their owners, he also (p. 233) pointed out that the 'new Fox news division ... reflects the politics of owner Rupert Murdoch in a way we have not seen at a major news organisation since the death of *Time* founder Henry Luce'.

In Europe, the decline of news journalism's potential to promote social justice has also been the subject of much debate. The decline of PSB has brought about debates very similar to those in the USA regarding the decline of journalism. However, the press in some European countries has always been much more partisan than in the USA and this has been true of both tabloid and broadsheet newspapers. In the UK, the tabloid press was already heavily reliant on sensationalism and scandal even before the new era of conglomeration. These tendencies were reaffirmed in 2011, when the media themselves finally began to acknowledge what critical journalism researchers had been writing for many years: that the ethical practices of many UK newspapers were simply abysmal. What made this story so powerful was, however, a piece of good investigative journalism. It had been known for some time that journalists at *The News of the World* (part of News Corporation, and the UK's biggest-selling Sunday newspaper) had used illegal methods for obtaining stories. *The Guardian* newspaper made a series of revelations: that the 'hacking' of phones was not confined to celebrities (though this itself was unjustifiable) but had also been used to access the phones of murder victims and many other people; and that use and knowledge of such methods at the newspaper were far more widespread than had previously been acknowledged. While such stories might seem to confirm the digital optimists' view that 'big media' are doomed, it should be noted that the story broke via a very old newspaper, operating forms of investigative journalism that are difficult for low-cost, internet-based operations to sustain. The story also helped to reveal the importance of good government action in relation to the cultural industries because it demonstrated the utter failure of the complacent system of 'self-regulation' that was operated in the UK by the Press Complaints Commission, which was in effect run by the newspapers themselves. In other European countries, as Rodney Benson (2011) shows, public funding has helped to maintain a considerable degree of journalistic independence.

SOCIAL FRAGMENTATION AND MARKET SEGMENTATION

Another significant and much discussed change since 1980 has been that more and more texts are produced for particular segments of the audience rather than a 'mass', undifferentiated audience. This is partly a result of more products entering cultural markets as leisure time and disposable income have increased in advanced industrial countries. It is probably also a result of social fragmentation, as people have diverged more and more in the ways that they spend their leisure time.

What have been the main causes of this social fragmentation? For Russell Neuman (1991: 116–17) the key factors were increasing levels of education (the strongest demographic predictor of breadth of cultural pursuits), a 'rebirth of pride in social differentation', plus the increasing numbers of unmarried (Neuman probably means 'childless') young adults with energy and income to spare. We can assume that social fragmentation has been accelerated by the growing number of cultural options available for people as a result of developments in the cultural industries.

For Joseph Turow, advertisers and advertising have had a crucial role to play. Since the rise of large-scale advertising in the late nineteenth century, mass and target marketing had always coexisted, but the 1980s saw 'the emergence of target marketing as a hot, hip, even central, strategy after decades of being considered a relatively marginal part of the national ad industry's thinking' (Turow, 1997: 19). The increasing sophistication of demographic information and the market research discussed in Chapter 7 began to guide the way in which the advertising industry and TV networks talked about programming in the late 1960s and early 1970s, but it was only in the 1980s that target marketing really began to take hold. This, wrote Turow (p. 36), was not so much a product of technological change as arising from a belief on the part of advertising practitioners that technological changes 'were themselves symptoms of a more profound change in America'. Segmentation was also a result of changes in the way that executives and creative managers conceived of their relationship with audiences. Jane Feuer (1984: 3–4), for example, describes the shift in the USA's network television at the beginning of the 1970s away from 'total audiences' and towards 'demographics'. It was discovered that young, urban adults (especially women) aged 18–49 were the main consumers of the types of goods advertised on television. The result was that, from the early 1970s, the networks competed to offer programmes aimed at this demographic group alongside the 'mass' programming that had formed the staple of prime-time programming since television became widespread in the late 1950s. Stephen Driver and Andrew Gillespie (1993: 186) recounted how, as the circulation of mass market magazines in the UK declined from the 1960s to the 1980s, magazine publishers sought refuge in targeted readerships and niche markets. This has helped to drive the proliferation of magazines, as advertisers will use specialist publications to target consumers more specifically.

Some commentators have been concerned that audience segmentation means the end of television's role in producing a 'public sphere' in which issues of common concern for a society can be highlighted (see Stevenson, 1999, for a sophisticated discussion of a number of related issues) and here we can see the relevance of the issue of segmentation for questions of social justice. This is a particular concern for writers (such as Keane, 1991) impressed by PSB's ability to introduce people to new subjects and ways of thinking. However, we should not rush to make hasty prognostications about segmentation without a further examination of the evidence.

Are we *really* seeing a transition – brought about by the changes in the cultural industries in the 1980s and 1990s and moving from an era of mass audiences to an era of segmentation and specialisation – as many commentators (such as Castells, 1996: 340–1) claim? Audiences have always been very much segmented, particularly along gender lines: entire genres of feature films, magazines, radio serials and so on have often been explicitly aimed at women. Mass markets also continue to be central to the cultural industries. Magazines are perhaps the most niche-orientated of all the cultural industries and there were over 18,000 consumer and business titles being published in the USA alone in 1997, according to the Magazine Publishers of America (MPA). Yet at the end of the 1990s, according to *Advertising Age*, the advertising and circulation revenue brought in by the 10 largest consumer magazines represented over 26 per cent of the US$25.8 billion achieved by the top 300 titles (Standard & Poor's *Publishing Industry Survey*, 13 May 1999: 10). *TV Guide* alone earned US$1.1 billion. As we saw in Chapters 7 and 9, the film industry revolves more than ever around the production of mass market blockbusters and the recording industry is still centred on the big hits that will cancel out the misses and global superstars who are able to provide 'brands' across a series of releases.

It is, above all, the rise of multichannel television and the internet that has resulted in increasing claims and anxieties about market segmentation and social fragmentation. The Big Three networks' share of the prime-time viewing audience fell from around 90 per cent in the 1970s to below 50 per cent by 1996–1997 (Caves, 2005: 30). Cable was in under 18 million homes in the USA in 1980, but had reached 73 million by 2002, and the average number of channels per household had also increased to over 60 by 1999 (2005: 127).

Even these figures should not be over-interpreted, however. Surveying an impressive range of audience research in the mid-1990s, James Webster and Patricia Phalen (1997: 114) concluded that 'mass appeal network television still dominates media consumption in the United States. That is not likely to change any time soon'. Segmentation, then, is best thought of as a gradual and uneven process linked to social fragmentation, but with the shared consumption of hit texts likely to remain a feature of consumption.

How should we view market segmentation in terms of its effects on society (see Box 11.2)? It certainly cannot be dismissed as a bad thing, in and of itself. It is hard to object to the provision of television channels catering to specific minority audiences. Nevertheless, we can point to some unfortunate ways in which segmented viewing practices reflect and reinforce more negative aspects of social fragmentation in ways that are consistent with the concerns of writers working in the Habermasian tradition of 'public sphere' thinking.

An interesting example is the long-standing, and perhaps increasing, tendency for black and white audiences in the USA to consume different media products. Oscar Gandy (2000) cites some statistics on this. Only *Monday Night Football* occurs in the top ten most-watched television programmes of both black and white audiences. This suggests that the super-commercialised world of sport in the USA at least provides some kind of common culture for black and white people. However, more strikingly, the figures also suggest that, in general, there is a vast gulf between the tastes of these different ethnic groups. Of course we can value difference and recognise the fact that different peoples may have different tastes, but with disparities this pronounced, it is hard to imagine any kind of national public sphere that would bring together black and white citizens in the USA over issues of common public concern. As Todd Gitlin has pointed out, the question here is whether democracy requires *a* public or a *set* of publics, a public *sphere* or 'separate public sphericules' (Gitlin, 1999: 173). While the internet may enrich the possibility of a plurality of publics, says Gitlin (ibid), such an arrangement can only be welcome if we assume 'a rough equivalence of resources' and a situation where 'society is not riven by deep-going fissures which are subject to being deepened and exacerbated in the absence of ongoing negotiation among members of different groups'.

Box 11.2   The HBO model: high-quality television in the USA, but not for everyone

In the words of journalist Joy Press (2004), the early 2000s were 'a great time to be a couch potato – if you have cable, that is'.

A worrying aspect of segmentation is that programming requiring effort, skill and creativity (all of which cost money) might increasingly come to be provided for wealthier, more educated audiences, while working-class ones will be left with cheaper, less prestigious programming.

In the old network television system, the urban upper middle class might have been more inclined to watch *Hill Street Blues* – the most acclaimed US drama series of the early 1980s – than the working class, but the programme was still available for the working class to watch on network television in the USA and various television systems in countries where it was imported. As the series developed, it gained a mass audience (see Feuer et al., 1984).

By the late 1990s and early 2000s, television companies in the USA were producing a large number of high-quality programmes. This led some commentators (for example, Steven Johnson, 2005) to argue that television – along with other cultural forms, including games and films – was becoming richer and more complex. As journalist Dana Stevens pointed out in a dialogue with Johnson in *Slate* (10–13 May 2005, available at http://slate.msn.com), his praise for the cognitive complexity of an hour-long episode of the TV programme *24* failed to mention that, when shown on television in the USA, a full third of that hour was made up of one-minute advertisements.

Many of the new generation of high-quality TV dramas were produced by cable channels. This was because, by the late 1990s and early 2000s, the USA's cable television had expanded to the point where it was able to pump considerable

(Continued)

(Continued)

resources into original programming, rather than merely show old network shows or cheaper imitations of the genres and formats developed there (see Caves, 2005: 127–54). (Cable and satellite television channels in Europe are still at this stage and produce little original programming of any worthwhile quality.)

A related factor in the rise of the quality of television in the USA is that cable channels have attempted to 'brand' themselves by means of expensive and carefully crafted series, such as Showtime's *The L Word*, FX's *The Shield,* or AMC's *Mad Men* and *Breaking Bad.* The most prominent producer of high-quality television in the USA's market has been the premium channel HBO, renowned for *The Sopranos, Six Feet Under* and *Deadwood.* In principle, this channel is available to working-class viewers, if they can afford it, but its programming is targeted at the concerns and lifestyles of upper middle-class people. (This can be contrasted with, for example, the BBC's equally good drama serial, *The Street.*) The same might become true of news – that the wealthy and educated, who feel they have a stake in national policy, get hard news, while the working class get tabloid television. Debates about the erosion of national public spheres have helped draw attention to such potentially negative aspects of segmentation.

HAS QUALITY DECLINED?

I now turn to a consideration of various aspects of debates about the decline – or rise – in quality in contemporary culture in the era of expansion of the cultural industries. Because of this book's interest in the relations of the cultural industries to society as a whole, this inevitably involves some consideration of the questions of power, authority and democracy discussed above.

Short attention spans, shock and cultural authority: reality television

Does the proliferation of texts produced by the cultural industries in fact represent an abundance of rubbish?

A key issue here is the increasing volatility and ephemerality of culture referred to by David Harvey[7] and explained by him as a product of time-space compression, in turn brought about by the need of capitalist businesses to accumulate profit. Speeding up is manifested in audience behaviour. Audience research suggests that cultural consumers increasingly want their products in bite-sized and portable chunks, as people monitor their daily

---

7　See the discussion of his book, *The Condition of Postmodernity* (1989), in Chapter 3 above.

time much more carefully than they used to and form it into grids (see Wolf, 1999: 38–40). There is a growing tendency here to skip from text to text – not only channel-surfing or skipping between tracks in a CD selector or MP3 player, but also moving between the various media on offer. There are pleasures to be had in such skipping, but does this have negative effects on the quality of cultural texts, as many cultural commentators have argued?

The proliferation of texts means that cultural industry corporations are faced with the task of finding new ways to capture and retain attention, with potentially negative consequences for the human experience of narrative and argument. Ratings-hungry producers increasingly resort to shock tactics in order to keep the attention of their audiences. This has meant much greater sexual explicitness, which might help to challenge prudery and puritanism and, in some cases, encourage people to experiment with different forms of sexual behaviour and identity. In many cases, however, it means an explosion of un-subversive titillation and unimaginative, un-erotic pornography. The impulse to shock has also led to much greater levels of violence on television, too, as study after study has shown. Whether or not this makes people more violent has never been proven conclusively.

Textual proliferation should not necessarily be thought of as a welcome abundance, then. In order to generate a feeling of specialness amidst the mass of product, conglomerates will spend more and more money on promotion. The concept of the 'media event' – developed by Daniel Dayan and Elihu Katz (1992) to describe important moments arranged outside the television institution but covered by television – needs to be supplemented more and more by the television-generated event, even if as yet they are rarely as significant as major sports events, coronations, royal weddings and funerals. The last episode of *Seinfeld* and the release of *Star Wars: The Phantom Menace* in 1999 were just two successful examples of massive promotional efforts by cultural industry companies that helped to create a special level of publicity for a text. As the rhythms of consuming television change and people become less accustomed to watching scheduled programmes on a weekly basis, broadcasters are turning to 'event television', involving long-running competitions and major sporting events, to generate ratings.

This has had unexpected and complex consequences. There has, for instance, been a surprising revival of liveness, which was a pervasive feature of early television, but because of the high risks involved, this gave way to playing prerecorded shows from the 1960s onwards, as video and film became cheaper and easier. For Nick Couldry (2003: 99), taking an unusual and thoughtful critical Durkheimian perspective from within cultural studies, this leads to a reaffirmation of the status of the media – especially television – as 'a privileged connection to a social centre'.

The competitive drive to create events – 'water cooler television' is now one of the most hackneyed phrases in UK cultural journalism – is one of the forces behind the growth of reality television. This phrase covers a wide range of texts, but has most often been applied in recent years to two related genres:

- Game shows, which claim to show us the reality of people's lives or personalities, whether these are 'ordinary' people or celebrities.
- 'Factual' shows, in which 'ordinary' people (which usually means working-class people, or at least people with working-class backgrounds) are observed facing some kind of challenge or situation.

Big Brother and *Wife Swap* are perhaps the paradigmatic cases of each genre respectively, at least in the UK. Such programmes have been lambasted for their voyeurism, but this seems to me to be an uninteresting criticism. They have also been dismissed as cheap, but many are not. In fact, they involve massive amounts of investment, planning and research. Their politics also need to be taken seriously – and here we return to questions raised in the sections on commercialism and on the politics of entertainment, above. As Graeme Turner (2010) points out, the politics of reality television programmes are complex. They display forms of behaviour that invite audience disapproval, but at the same time they suggest that such behaviour should be 'enjoyed as entertaining performances of demotic excess' (p. 51) which ultimately challenge authority. Whether the nature of this challenge of authority is emancipatory in any meaningful sense is another matter, as Turner recognises. Helen Wood and Bev Skeggs (2008) have investigated how a number of television genres, perhaps especially makeover shows, provide spectacles which are ultimately 'morality tales'. The lessons they teach concern the importance of people being able to manage themselves, to fend for themselves. What's more, on reality television and makeover shows, people –namely, working-class people and in particular working-class women – are put in situations 'in which they can be only out of control, making them appear as completely incapable and inadequate' (p. 190). Similarly, Anita Biressi and Heather Nunn (2005) contrast the representation of working-class experience on reality television with that of a number of other realist genres. They find reality TV is often 'overwhelmingly conservative' (p. 155), closing down the potential for progressive change. From a perspective influenced by the French historian Michel Foucault, Laurie Ouellette and James Hay (2008) argue that recent changes in how societies are governed explain the proliferation of television programmes that emphasise the merits and benefits of self-management and personal responsibility. These critics reject elitist dismissals of reality television and other genres. Their work suggests that pompous debates about 'quality' can distract from debates about the effects of texts on culture and society.

This raises broader questions about the authority of cultural production to influence people. I do not intend here to enter into the complex debates about influence as a whole. But it is important to note that developments in the cultural and related industries mean that cultural production is not as 'special' as it once was. Television has lost the massive cultural authority it had in the 1960s and 1970s as low-budget variations have proliferated. If the press representations of audiences' views of television are anything to go by, controversies in the UK and elsewhere (notably Japan) in the early 2000s about 'docusoaps' and talk shows were the sign of a growing disenchantment and scepticism regarding television. Such doubts about the aura of television and other media represent a positive development. The problem is that such scepticism can coexist alongside an underlying *trust* in television, as Couldry emphasises.

For some, innovation is to be found in forms of cultural production that most actively seem to resist commerce: alternative or underground production. Here we come back to the creativity–commerce dialectic, which, as I have stressed throughout, can sometimes take naïvely expressed forms, but can nevertheless serve as a basis for questioning the way the cultural industries operate.

However, these underground worlds of cultural production are increasingly subject to co-optation. Texts are introduced to other audiences, which may be perceived as 'mainstream', by the original audience for them. A burgeoning set of specialist journalists gain money and credibility from being able to spot such forms of underground activity and bring them to the attention of some wider audience, whether in the form of comics, fanzines, music genres, or movements of film-makers. And yet the sense of the underground as a sacred cultural sphere, away from profane commerciality, remains undiminished, and is perhaps even enhanced by the institutionalisation of such cycles. Such undergrounds are rarely a real 'resistance' to the large corporations that dominate the cultural industries, but they often represent a partial questioning of them.[8] They help to maintain an independent sector in many cultural industries – at least until the conglomerates become aware of these new styles or genres.

Comparing quality: book publishing

Proliferation and speeding up have ambivalent results, then. But let me now turn more directly to the issue of whether or not the overall quality of cultural texts has declined. Many people assert that this is the case, but providing substantial evidence is a different matter altogether. One way to examine the difficulties surrounding such questions is to examine an account that forthrightly argues that quality in a particular industry has radically deteriorated. A rare and brave example of such an account has been provided by Mark Crispin Miller (1997) on the decline of book publishing in the era of conglomeration.

Miller argues that, in spite of the seeming proliferation of books in the dominant chains (Borders and Barnes and Noble in the USA, Waterstones in the UK), things are very bad in book publishing. He contrasts book

---

8   The work of Bourdieu on 'restricted production' is important and useful in this context (see Bourdieu, 1996, and Hesmondhalgh, 2006a, for discussion), but, ultimately, I find his approach towards small-scale production to be too haughty and cynical.

publishing in the mid-1990s with a previous era, before conglomeration, when publishing was not 'a profit-centered venture but a true labour of love' (1997: 113). The new focus on profits has, says Miller, resulted in a serious decline in quality. The common run of literature, he admits, has always been 'lousy' (p. 114): 'Revisit any seeming "golden age" and read it all, and what you'll find is mostly dreck', he says, and he goes on to survey some of the golden ages. However, 'there's been no golden age – and yet books have gotten worse: worse in every way'.

What evidence does Miller provide of this diminished quality? He tells the story of the decline in standards in three publishing companies (Little, Brown, Random House and Bantam Books) once they were taken over by conglomerates. Whereas once they published great novels and serious commentary, these corporations now sell various other books that Miller objects to in a variety of different ways. These other books include novels that may become films made by major studios (p. 108), romans-à-clef about famous people (p. 111) and books concerning stars and entertainment products distributed by other conglomerates (p. 108). Miller seems to have a particularly violent objection to books about cooking, gardening and interior design (p. 111). He also claims that standards of proofreading have slippped genrally (just kidding) and that many books lack indices and notes. Poor commissioning practice has resulted in many that are poorly edited, overlong and badly argued, and he quotes reviews from *The New York Times Book Review* to prove this.

In comparing the eras before and after conglomeration, Miller says that the previous lists of the major publishing houses contained nothing as 'half-baked, ill-informed, and crudely written as Newt Gingrich's *To Renew America*, or as prolix, muddled and me-me-me-me as Nancy Friday's *The Power of Beauty*' (p. 116). Meanwhile, the Duchess of York's memoirs are 'empty and self-serving', and children's books contain nothing about 'boogers, farts, or puking' (p. 116).

Miller seems to be making two arguments here: that the overall quality of books is declining and this is associated with an unethical, excessive concern with making money on the part of conglomerates. The main evidence for the latter claim seems to be the first – that they publish bad books. Miller moves back and forth between an ethical condemnation of the overly commercial practices of the companies and a denunciation of poor aesthetic standards. For example, his objections to lifestyle books appear to be primarily based on the fact that they allow 'synergies' with other wings of the same conglomerate, such as cooking, gardening and interior design magazines. The old publishers, he writes (p. 117)

> ... did their share of the eternal dreck, but for them it was a necessary evil – and that, finally, is the crucial difference between then and now. As book lovers and businessmen, they did the high-yield trash in order to be able to afford the gems they loved (although the gems might also sell).

Today, says Miller, 'crap is not a means but (as it were) the ends'. However, his main evidence for this is that the companies which formerly fostered good writing now publish crap alongside the good stuff. So the bottom line of his argument is aesthetic – that the resulting texts are poorer than they used to be.

The problem is that the argument for overall decline is impossible to substantiate in this way. To compare two different eras fully would be impossible – more books were published in 1950 than could be read in an individual's lifetime and more books were published in the year 2000 than a 12-strong research team could read in three decades. Thus, any statistically significant sample would be too vast to handle in a realistic period. Miller is perhaps therefore entitled to engage in cultural criticism. Nevertheless, he might at least have made reference to the possibility that others might find the books published by the major companies pleasing or useful or beautiful. Instead, his argument rests on his own particular tastes in books.

The nature of Miller's tastes is quite clear: he likes highbrow literary fiction and serious political and cultural commentary. Therefore, his argument about declining quality (as opposed to the ethics of preferring commerce over creativity) ultimately rests on his claim that highbrow literary fiction and other serious works, such as political commentary, are undersupplied by the book publishing industry. However, his evidence for this amounts simply to showing that three companies which used to specialise in such books now publish other, more commercial books, too. Miller hardly mentions the dozens of small publishing companies and university presses in the USA catering to the tastes of educated readers.

Having said this, I am sure that his concern is not about whether or not his own tastes are being satisfied. Rather, he is worried that the most powerful companies in the market are encouraging people to read substandard books. This is a valid point. The problem is that he cannot prove that this is happening using evidence drawn principally from such brief references to his own personal tastes and changes in three companies as they have passed from independence to conglomerate divisions. He hints at important points about the lack of concern with the quality of the finished work within conglomerate organisations, but beyond his suggestions that there are more typos in corporate books than there used to be, can only prove this by reference to the fact that he, and a few reviewers, find the books overblown, superficial, or lacking in various other ways.

My close reading of Miller's analysis is intended to show the problems surrounding a critique of the cultural industries on the grounds of aesthetic quality. I have scrutinised this piece carefully not because it is an example of bad writing – I suspect that it was intended as a polemic, rather than as a fully argued piece – but because it illustrates a problem that is typical of much work in the field of political economy. Arguments are often made that rest on an unacknowledged assumption that readers will share the aesthetic tastes of the writer. Of course, it is not always possible to forefront and examine problems concerning differences in taste. Nevertheless, the limits to Miller's approach suggest that arguments based almost entirely on insufficiently scrutinised aesthetic criteria need to be treated with caution.

Quality, independence and niche markets: indie cinema in the 1990s

We can address such issues of quality further by discussing another signifi-cant cultural industry – cinema. As I hope is apparent, I am not saying that we should be complacent about the quality of products disseminated by the cultural industries, but merely that bold statements about such quality tend to conceal important issues. The case of independent cinema in the USA over the last 30 years offers a useful case study of the relations between the cul-tural industries and their resulting texts.

Many commentators feel that there has been a decline in the standards of mainstream films from the USA since the 1970s with the rise of special effects blockbusters (see, for example, Biskind, 1998). On the other hand, many young, urban, educated cinephiles would point to a richness in its film-making, especially its independent cinema, during the 1980s and 1990s.

Particularly in cinema it is often felt that institutional 'independence' (as we shall see, this term is weighed down by problems of definition) can help foster better texts. There are echoes of this view in popular music also (see Chapter 5). Independent cinema received huge coverage in the 1990s, as films such as *Reservoir Dogs* (1992) achieved cult status and huge admiration, while others like *Pulp Fiction* (1994) and *The Blair Witch Project* (1999) were box office hits. Independent film production boomed. In 1999, for example, 1716 films were sub-mitted to the Sundance Festival – the main showcase for independent cinema.

There was a strong tendency among audiences and film critics to associate independence with aesthetic adventurousness. In the words of one history of independent cinema in the USA, independents were seen as 'celluloid mavericks' (Merritt, 2000). As Emanuel Levy (1999: 21) puts it, independent film-makers 'cre-ate alternative films that are different, challenging the status quo with visions that have been suppressed or ignored by the more conservative mainstream'.

In the 1960s the Hollywood studios hit a crisis, based on declining audiences and profits. In 1967, however, the huge success of *Bonnie and Clyde* (directed by Arthur Penn) among youth audiences around the world led them to believe that innovative films aimed at the youth audience might be their saviour, rather than the big-budget family spectaculars that they had relied on since the 1950s. This trend intensified following the unexpected success of *Easy Rider* (directed by Peter Fonda, 1969). Hollywood entered a period where young directors, pro-ducers and scriptwriters were given considerable creative autonomy within the studio system, via package deals with independent producers. With the success of *Jaws* (directed by Steven Spielberg, 1975) and *Star Wars* (directed by George Lucas, 1977), however – both made by young directors brought in to revitalise Hollywood – the studios began to turn back to big-budget special effects mov-ies, aimed at the burgeoning teenage market. Fewer and fewer films aimed at older viewers were made in the late 1970s and early 1980s. With the mid-1980s success of films such as *Blue Velvet* (directed by David Lynch, 1987) and *She's Gotta Have It* (directed by Spike Lee, 1986), this began to change. *Sex, Lies and Videotape* (directed by Steven Soderbergh, 1989) is often cited as an important transition, because it crossed over from the independent and art cinema circuit in the USA into the multiplexes, showing a very high return on its low costs. Production costs were US$1 million, while profits were US$25 million. It became apparent that there was significant money to be made from off-beat, small-scale films dealing with personal relationships and appealing to an older audience. Levy describes 1992 as an *annus mirabilis* for indies, with films such as *Howard's End*, *The Crying Game*, *The Player* and *Bob Roberts* achieving critical plaudits *and* considerable financial success. In 1994, the hip nihilism of *Pulp Fiction* (directed by Quentin Tarantino) made the crossover into the teen market that was drawn to horror films and 'sick' comedy.

Levy outlines a number of conditions that facilitated the emergence of the new US independent cinema as an alternative system:

- The need for self-expression on the part of young film-makers drawn to films that expressed personal visions rather than operating primarily within Hollywood genre conventions.
- Hollywood's increasing tendency to make big-budget blockbusters rather than lower-budget, personal films left a gap in the market for the indies to fill.
- There were increasing opportunities and capital for financing indies – partly because of internationalisation, which has meant the availability of foreign capital, but also because of a greater demand for visual material as channels proliferated.
- 'Supportive audiences' – that is, older, more highly educated audiences who were looking for 'more mature themes'.
- The decline of foreign-language films and the European art cinema.
- A proliferation of film schools in the USA, producing 'a large number of ambitious film-makers eager to take advantage' of the new opportunities for making independent films.
- The Sundance Film Festival, now the second most important film festival in the world according to Levy, serves as an important showcase for independents and there are numerous other festivals and associations, such as the Independent Feature Project and the Black Film-makers Foundation, which support independent film-making.
- The growing commercial success of indies and their increasing success at the Oscars.

Examining the issue of 'supportive audiences' for independent cinema will allow us to explore further the issue of quality. Levy, without citing sources, describes the 'typical indie public' as being composed of:

- college students and college graduates;
- singles and childless couples;
- discriminating viewers seeking provocative entertainment;
- informed viewers with a sharper sensibility and greater awareness of new film releases and new directors than average;
- frequent moviegoers who go to the cinemas at least once a month.

All this pretty much translates into urban, highly educated and relatively prosperous audiences. Levy clearly thinks that independent films are better than studio pictures. In his view, the major Hollywood studios redeem themselves with a few interesting pictures each year (1999: 500). And for Levy 1999 was an exceptionally good year for Hollywood, in that it produced five 'great or near-great films' – *Saving Private Ryan*, *The Truman Show*, *Bulworth*, *He Got Game*, and *Rushmore*. He doesn't stop to give a definition of greatness, but he clearly shares the aesthetic tastes of the higher-income, more highly educated audience for indies. There is a danger, then, that praise for the products of independent cinema is merely praise for films that correspond with the tastes of other highly educated people. These tastes will change with time, but in recent years such audiences have tended to favour thoughtful, sensitive pictures about human relationships, hip, energetic satire and films full of reference to the codes of popular and high culture, reflecting the cultural omnivorousness of this kind of audience.

Perhaps it is too cynical to think of such high-quality indie films as merely representing a kind of niche marketing to a wealthy, urban elite. And perhaps it is also too pessimistic to think of the tastes for such films as being confined to wealthier, more educated audiences. People are more able to enjoy different kinds of cultural experience than sociologists and market researchers sometimes give them credit for. It could be that the film industry assumes in advance that certain audiences will not be interested in certain kinds of films. The increasing use of market research, discussed in Chapter 7, would reinforce this tendency.

* * *

In this chapter, I have attempted to assess changes in the texts produced by the cultural industries since the early 1980s, but the discussion has continually returned to the difficulties of providing an evaluation on the kind of historical scale that I am dealing with here.

Diversity is an elusive concept. Writers identify trends towards homogenisation, but provide little substantiation. Adequate transhistorical comparisons of quality may well be impossible. Also, the sociological problems surrounding taste haunt textual evaluation – texts claimed as innovative and adventurous could just be aimed at the niche market to which the intellectual belongs.

Clearly, my own analysis favours thinking about texts in terms of their role in promoting or inhibiting social justice. I have identified commercialisation as a key development in texts since 1980 (though not one of sufficient breadth and depth to merit the view that we have entered a new era of production of texts). However, this focus on issues of social justice marginalises the experiences that people are looking for in texts, which are various forms of aesthetic pleasure.

Some people's solution is to reduce aesthetic experience to ethical questions concerning the stance of a particular film, but this will not do either. The solution may be to build bridges between the two and recognise how tenuous, indirect and contradictory some of the connections may be. However, in researching this book, one of the main conclusions I have come to is that the project of a sociologically informed reflexive aesthetics is still in its infancy and the spectre of mass culture criticism haunts much political economy work that takes an aesthetic perspective.

One of the reasons that the cultural industries are important is that they make texts, yet the critique of texts in historical terms is so difficult that I might seem to be suggesting we abandon textual analysis altogether. I am not advocating this. Engagement with content remains the most difficult terrain in analysis of media and popular culture, but that does not mean that the task can be abandoned. Students and researchers of the cultural industries need to engage with issues of pleasure, interpretation and meaning.

RECOMMENDED AND FURTHER READING

On links between industrial/institutional change and textual change in entertainment, see Jostein Gripsrud's *The Dynasty Years* (1995), Jason Toynbee's *Making Popular Music* (2000), and Georgina Born's book on the BBC, *Uncertain Vision* (2005). On questions of diversity and quality in journalism, see Daniel Hallin's *We Keep America On Top of the World* (1994), James Curran's *Media and Democracy* (2011), Michael Schudson's *Why Democracies Need an Unlovable Press* (2008), and *The Sociology of News* (2nd edition, 2012); W. Lance Bennett's *News: the Politics of Illusion* (7th edition, 2012); and McChesney and Nichols' *The Death and Life of American Journalism* (2010). Natalie Fenton's edited collection, *New Media, Old News* (2010), provides a number of fine contributions regarding ways in which developments associated with the internet might actually constrain good journalism. For a balanced account of book publishing, see John B. Thompson's *Merchants of Culture* (2010). An excellent collection relevant to the discussion of commercialisation above is *The Advertising and Consumer Culture Reader* (2009), edited by Joseph Turow and Matthew P. McAllister. Graeme Turner's *Ordinary People and the Media* (2010) provides a superb discussion of debates about the celebration of 'ordinariness' in a number of aspects of contemporary popular culture, including celebrity culture, reality television and journalism.

ONLINE READING

All the online material referenced below can be accessed free of charge at: **http://www.sagepub.co.uk/hesmondhalgh**
Simply click on the 'Sample Materials' tab to find the links to each article.
Saha (2012) interestingly explores the relationship between production processes and textual representation. Jaramillo (2002) addresses the production context of 'quality television'.

- Jaramillo, Deborah L. (2002) 'The family racket: AOL Time Warner, HBO, *The Sopranos*, and the construction of a quality brand', *Journal of Communication Inquiry*, 26(1): 59–75.
- Saha, Anamik (2012) '"Beards, scarves, halal meat, terrorists, forced marriage": television industries and the production of "race"', *Media, Culture & Society*, 34(4): 424–438.

Conclusions:
A New Era in Cultural Production?

The extent of change   402
Evaluating change/continuity   407
Explaining change/continuity   410
Implications for future study   411

I had three main aims in this book: to assess the extent of change in the cultural industries since 1980, to evaluate it, and to explain it.

THE EXTENT OF CHANGE

My treatment of change has gone beyond the historical timeframe employed in most studies of the cultural industries. I borrowed from Raymond Williams's work on changing social relations of cultural production across different periods of history in order to put recent changes into their long-term historical context.

Williams described how social relations based on patronage gave way in the nineteenth century to a system he dubbed 'market professional' and how this system in turn gave way in the twentieth century to the dominance of 'corporate professional' market relations. I modified Williams's term 'corporate professional' to 'complex professional' and used it to refer to a whole matrix of conditions of cultural production and consumption, which emerged in the early part of the twentieth century and which were thoroughly ensconced by the 1950s.

These conditions centred on a particular set of relationships between primary creative personnel (symbol creators), other workers, and the companies that commissioned and employed them. A crucial feature of these relations was a combination of loose control of creative input with much tighter control of the reproduction and circulation stages. The complex professional era, as I described it in Chapter 2, was also marked by other key features:

- A labour market in which some creative workers are vastly rewarded but most are underemployed and underpaid.
- The increasing presence of large corporations, often in the form of vertically integrated conglomerates.
- Significant internationalisation, dominated by the USA's cultural industries.
- Associated regimes of technology, consumption and policy.

Much of the rest of the book has been concerned with assessing the degree to which these characteristics of cultural production, which developed in the mid-twentieth century, were still apparent in the 1980s, 1990s and 2000s. This allows us now to confront more directly this question: did the period since 1980 see a new era of cultural production, a new phase as markedly different from the complex professional era as the complex professional was from the market professional era?

Chapters 4 and 5 assessed changes in government policy. Here there were considerable transformations, in that governments all across the world altered their policies in the direction of marketisation – that is, the view that the production and exchange of cultural goods and services for profit is the best way to achieve efficiency and fairness in the production and consumption of texts. Various rationales for high degrees of state intervention were systematically attacked by a number of parties, including cultural industry companies. The result was:

- the privatisation of public telecommunications organisations and some PSB institutions;
- the opening up of television systems to other terrestrial, commercial broadcasters and cable and satellite companies;
- the tearing down of regulatory walls between different industries;
- significant changes in laws and rules on content, media ownership and subsidies.

In Europe, PSB was attacked but was surprisingly successful in resisting the onslaught in some countries. In many societies, authoritarian-statist governments gave way to 'democratic' governments pursuing neo-liberal economic policies.

By the 1990s, neo-liberalism was being further pursued by a number of important international bodies. Particularly important were increases in the scope and duration of copyright, including a much greater international enforcement of the ownership of rights. Also significant were changes in cultural policy, which, in the name of democratisation, became increasingly bound up with efforts on the part of government to boost culture as a new opportunity for investment for businesses in their domain. All this added up to a real transformation in the policy landscape and many of the changes were major drivers of other processes of upheaval and realignment.

So was this a new era in policy? Within the advanced industrial countries, there was a shift of emphasis within a fairly stable policy system, in that many policy initiatives happened within states, regulating on the basis of tensions between the interests of citizens/voters and dominant business interests. Nevertheless, the move towards neo-liberalism was remarkable and the fact that it was adopted in so many advanced industrial countries reflected the global interconnectedness of the late twentieth century. The impact on other places was perhaps even more marked. Nations such as India were making a transition from national protectionism to globalisation, from delinked national cultural-economic systems to participation in a new international system of cultural trade. This was part of a wider political-economic and sociocultural set of shifts, which may, in retrospect, be seen as the beginning of a new phase within these specific national societies. This in turn might help to bring about epochal changes in the advanced industrial countries, but we do not yet live in a 'global professional era' of cultural production. The nation state continues to be the main forum for cultural industry activity.

These policy shifts helped to create a context in which the cultural industries were seen as a good business investment. Chapter 6 showed the expansion of large cultural industry corporations – a growth that might have reached its fastest rate in the boom-bubble years of the late 1990s. These cultural industry corporations achieved an unprecedented international reach and level of revenue generation. Conglomeration fed into the growth of the corporations, but it is not a new thing in the cultural industries – it is a distinctive feature of the complex professional period as a whole. It coexists with strategies of de-conglomeration at times, as we saw in Chapter 6. Conglomeration strategies vary over time and we should be wary of analyses that present any particular strategy (such as hardware/software synergy) as representing the future. Vertical integration also supported the growth of large corporations, but again, from the 1980s to the 2000s, it was not of a qualitatively different kind from that which was present in earlier generations. Indeed there has been some movement, in some industries, towards disintegration. This is not only because of the actions of regulators but also because some companies have found it profitable to disintegrate. As with conglomeration, we should cast a sceptical eye on claims that see movements towards or away from integration as marking epochal shifts. Business fashions and strategies come, go, and come again. Meanwhile, small companies continue to play a vital role in the cultural industries. Again, their proliferation represents an extension of processes already observable in the mid-twentieth century. However, a key change is that large and small companies are increasingly interdependent and mutually entangled in complex networks of licensing, financing and distribution, not only with each other, but also with companies in the IT and telecommunications industries.

All these phenomena are signs of the steadily growing significance of the cultural industries in modern economies. However, this growth is not nearly as pronounced as is often claimed by commentators (especially those who want to appropriate the cultural industries for information society discourse). We saw in Chapter 6 that cultural industry companies are nowhere near the size in revenue of the world's very largest corporations. Corporate growth in the cultural industries is an extension of a process that was already under way in the early part of the twentieth century and is not sufficient to merit claims that the cultural industries are, or even look set to become, a new core in global business. Underlying all these changes and continuities has beeen an extension and gentle acceleration of the long-term process of a commodification of culture. This commodification is an important way in which to understand some of the positive and negative changes that I examined later in the book.

Chapter 7 went on to examine changes and continuities in the distinctive organisational form of the cultural industries in the 1980s, 1990s and 2000s, in relations between creativity and commerce, and in the terms and conditions of cultural work. Given my emphasis on the social relations of cultural production, this is clearly a key area for assessing change. Across the cultural industries as a whole there are significant levels of continuity, in that symbol creators continue to exercise relatively high levels of operational autonomy but very low levels of power when it comes to the circulation of texts. Journalistic autonomy continues to be important, in spite of some significant attacks on it. Although there were signs of a superficial loosening of control of creative work in some cultural industries, I argued that the prevailing trend was in the opposite direction, towards a tighter control of creative work (though this was still loose relative to other industries). This was manifested in the increasing importance of marketing and market research in the creative stages of cultural production. Even here, however, there has been a mixture of trends, with some parts of certain industries allowing for greater creative autonomy than before (such as advertisers), others turning towards more rigid, bureaucratic forms of control (live theatre, for example), and trends elsewhere appearing highly ambivalent.

Internationalisation of cultural industry businesses and their texts is not new, but this process greatly accelerated in the 1980s and 1990s. The complex professional period saw a complicated mixture of geocultural markets develop across the world, with the USA generally but unevenly dominant and local or regional cultural products that are often just as popular as ones from the USA, if not more so. This arrangement largely continued into the 1990s and 2000s, as I showed in Chapter 8. There I assessed the growth of Latin American cultural industry companies that based their operations on television. I also examined the huge growth in cross-border transmissions (including 'diasporic television'). Both of these are significant and interesting developments, but they do not as yet even threaten the domination of the transnational corporations based mainly in North America, Europe and Asia, so the power geometry of international television remains largely intact. I showed the rise to further dominance of Hollywood film in the 1980s and 1990s, but also examined the important film industries of Hong Kong and India. Although these represent very different types of cinema from the Hollywood system, the presence of such domestic industries in global audio-visual markets is not a new phenomenon. The erosion of Hong Kong's industry should not be interpreted as signalling a greater level of domination by Hollywood, the hegemony of which rises and falls in cycles. Finally, in spite of some claims to the contrary, new genres such as world music and Euro-pop did not represent significant disturbances to the geographical distribution of musical power that has been prevalent since the Second World War. The international distribution of cultural power was always more complex than the core/ periphery models so effectively questioned by Sinclair, Jacka and Cunningham (1996). Nevertheless, there was significant inequality in access to global markets, international prestige and influence. That inequality remains.

Are the changes associated with digitalisation sufficient for us to speak of a new digital era in cultural production? Our consideration of this question began in Chapter 9. Every era brings with it technological innovations, but perhaps the last 30 years have seen a greater intensity of innovation in cultural technologies than ever before. This is surely not unrelated to the growing opportunities for profit available in the cultural domain. Whether this is the case or not, the production relations and business strategies and asymmetrical relations between production and consumption, all characteristic of the complex professional era, remain largely intact. A significant change is that IT companies now vie for control of circulation – the locus of power in culture – with cultural-industry companies. This is particularly evident in Google's domination of search.

Chapter 9 traced the impacts of digitalisation and the internet on a number of cultural industries. The recorded music industry went through a major period of crisis, and was held up as a cultural industry that was unwilling or unable to adopt to change. The nature of music retailing was transformed and IT companies such as Apple and Amazon became significant players. A few corporations still dominated the recording industry, however, and the search for talent and control of rights remained central. Even the entry of IT companies echoed the way in which the cultural industries have always engaged in a dance of alliance and competition with neighbouring industries such as consumer electronics companies. Digital television has transformed the experience of television, and has also helped to erode public service broadcasting, but television remains a dominant cultural form. Digitalisation has helped to create a massive demand for cheap content. Intensified competition has fuelled commercialisation. In some countries, notably the USA, digitalisation has led to the closure of print newspapers and a crisis in journalism. But books demonstrate how slowly some prophecies of the death of print have come to be realised – and may not be realised at all. Finally, the rise of the games industry suggests that new cultural industries continue to obey the same principles and dynamics as have governed older ones.

Digitalisation, then, should be seen as differentiated in its impacts, according to its various manifestations. In fact, it hardly makes sense to speak of 'digital media' as one category at all. Digitalisation does what designers ask of it and that depends on so many other factors that the actual zeros-and-ones nature of its technological apparatus matters very little in terms of the social uses of the technology, other than allowing devices to be marketed as efficient and convenient. This suggests that terms such as the 'digital era' or 'being digital' (Negroponte, 1995) risk technological reductionism. However, even if it were feasible to speak of all these different technologies as part of one larger systemic change, the changes have not yet been sufficient to merit the idea that we have moved into a new era of production beyond the complex professional era: a 'digital era', for example.

The overall conclusion, in terms of considering the extent of change, has to be that there is sufficient continuity to undermine the suggestion that we have entered a new era of cultural production. Rather, we should think of the period since 1980 as representing a new phase *within* the complex professional era, marked by greater competition and a greater centrality for the cultural industries within advanced industrial economies as a whole, but latterly with those cultural industries under serious pressure from developments in the telecommunications and IT sectors (namely, digitalisation and the internet). The fundamental features of the cultural industries established in the mid-twentieth century remain.

Some writers have suggested that other industries are becoming more like the cultural industries, in that there seems to have been a new emphasis on issues of aesthetics, design, information, planning and knowledge in all industries, most notably Lash and Urry (1994). Others (see, for example, Padioleau, 1987) have suggested that the cultural industries are 'normalising', becoming less distinctive and more like other industries. In fact, there have always been tensions between differentiation from and imitation of strategies in other industries throughout the complex professional era. The cultural industries continue to be driven by the problems of making money from cultural production, and a number of distinctive attempts to resolve those problems (see the Introduction to this book, and Box 0.2). But the view that they are forming a new core to advanced industrial economies is premature, as can be seen from the figure presented in Chapter 6 on the relative sizes of cultural industry companies compared to other large corporations. There may have been a partial shift towards economies based on culture, information and symbols, but none of us yet lives in a 'knowledge economy' or an 'information age'.

EVALUATING CHANGE/CONTINUITY

Chapter 2 (see Table 2.1) set up the main questions guiding my evaluation of change in the cultural industries. The continued and accelerated growth of the largest corporations is an obvious fact, while their increased scope and power (via means discussed in Chapter 6 such as consolidation, various types of conglomeration, and either the vertical integration or co-optation of contracting companies) carry significant implications.

These corporations have the resources and expertise to pursue their interests in a way that can do much to counteract the high-risk nature of the business they are in. Their main interest is the pursuit of profit. To achieve this, corporations will team up with corporations against which they would normally compete in order to act jointly as advocates for their industry or sector. Their efforts to pursue profits can often prove detrimental to the interests of people as citizens, even if they give us more choice and control over our leisure time as consumers. As businesses, they also tend to support political and economic conservatism, often opposing attempts to achieve social justice. They provide a model for how cultural business should be carried out – one that is not always positive. Whether they support such interests in the texts that they produce is still an issue of controversy. But they certainly pursue such interests as lobbyists and in their business strategies.

Chapter 7 argued that, in spite of the uneven concentration and conglomeration noted in Chapter 6, control of creative work by cultural industry companies remains relatively loose, but the increasing prominence and prestige of marketing personnel in the cultural industries, particularly in the creative conception stage, represents a potential erosion of some of that creative autonomy. Journalistic autonomy is also threatened, in many contexts, by the commercial imperatives of owners, but remains resilient as a professional ethos and a defence against the demands of executives. Chapter 7 also noted that there has been little improvement in the rewards and working conditions of creative workers – in fact, there appears to be some evidence of deterioration. Symbol creators remain underpaid and underemployed for the most part, while the rewards for superstars continue to rise to disgraceful levels. There has been some movement towards greater awareness on the part of new entrants to cultural production about the dangers they face in undertaking creative work and there have been some improvements in contracts.

Chapter 8 examined internationalisation and found that there were still very few opportunities for producers from outside the 'core' areas of cultural production to gain access to networks of circulation. The geographical concentration of power remains remarkable, though it does not take the form that 'cultural imperialism' writers proposed. Chapters 9 and 10 showed that digitalisation and the internet have provided a serious challenge to certain cultural-industry corporations, but have not substantially threatened the idea of corporate power in itself. It has, however, created a new generation of IT giants based on internet as well as computer technologies, and these corporations (most notably Microsoft, Google, Apple, Amazon, and to a lesser extent Yahoo) compete with, and sometimes form partnerships with, cultural-industry corporations. Against the claims of digital optimists that digitalisation and the internet were substantially enhancing the ability of cultural production to contribute to culture, society and democracy, Chapter 9 outlined a number of problematic aspects of digitalisation and the internet: inequalities in access, skills and activity; control of circulation and concentrations of attention; and problems of commercialisation, surveillance and unpaid work. At the same time, some positive contributions of the internet to culture and communication were discussed, and in Chapter 10 too.

My analysis of changes in texts highlighted the problems of making rashly optimistic or pessimistic claims about textual transformation. Chapter 11 began by noting a marked feature of cultural production since 1980: a huge proliferation of texts. Is there greater diversity, though? Attempts to provide objective measures of diversity in liberal-pluralist communication studies and sociology have foundered. Equally, cultural commentary often descends into unsubstantiated assumptions about homogenisation. Diversity remains an elusive and difficult concept.

Much clearer are changes concerning the commercialisation of texts. Advertising and promotional materials have all increased – in my view, to the detriment of the societies that we live in. Advertising messages encourage the view that buying objects and experiences is the primary way of achieving happiness. Of course, the objects and experiences we purchase can enhance our lives in many ways, but such commercial messages, in the main, encourage us to accumulate wealth and money purely in order to acquire and this leads to stress, envy, misery, alienation, pollution and conflict. Hidden promotional messages relegate symbolic creativity to the needs of accumulation. Beyond this, however, it is difficult to say that texts are now more likely to favour the interests of the powerful than they ever were before. Compliance, conservatism and complacency coexist with scepticism, anger and utopianism. Popular culture continues to be riddled with contradictions. Although some see a decline in news standards, here, too, there is ambivalence, as the pomposity of some older styles of 'serious' journalism is displaced both by triviality and by efforts to speak to important private and emotional concerns.

Meanwhile, the speeding up of the tendency of audiences to shift and flit across different cultural experiences means that symbol creators can no longer rely on the guaranteed attentiveness of those audiences (if, indeed, they ever could). This restlessness also encourages a certain scepticism about the authority of the media. Historical comparisons of quality across the whole range of a cultural industry's output are so difficult as to be almost meaningless. Simple stories of transformation in texts are often to be found, but will rarely stand up to scrutiny.

Overall, any assessment of the cultural industries must register the complexity, ambivalence and contradiction noted by Miège (1989) as features of capitalist cultural production (see Introduction). The growth of the large corporations is significant, but they work in more subtle and complicated ways than the jeremiads of some political economy accounts suggest. To make such an argument does not represent a compromise with corporate capitalism. Rather, it is the outcome of a clear-headed analysis of the very real complexities involved in making capital out of culture. As Jason Toynbee (2000: 2) puts it, also employing Raymond Williams's historical sociology of culture to support his analysis, while much of 'culture belongs to capitalism, there is something antithetical to capitalism in it'. A key question, however, is whether or not the steady commodification of culture noted in Chapter 6 threatens that relative autonomy of culture. Among the threats identified in this book are the increasing exclusive ownership of rights in cultural works and its effects on people's cultural experiences, as well as the use of market research and audience ratings to threaten creative autonomy (discussed in Chapter 7).

EXPLAINING CHANGE/CONTINUITY

If the 'fundamentally irrational' process of symbolic creativity 'conflicts with the calculating, accumulative logic of modern capitalism' (Ryan, 1992: 104), this helps to explain the very tangled and contradictory dynamics we have observed throughout this book. A better way to think about this conflict for me is via issues raised in my discussion of the commodification of culture in Chapters 2 and 6, combined with the emphasis I have placed throughout on the conflicts between creativity and commerce in understandings of cultural practice. As capitalism developed, art came to be understood as a domain that ought to be protected from commercial imperatives. This also applied to certain kinds of information and knowledge. Such protection was never complete – commodification and culture were entwined. As the opportunities for profiting from culture have grown, the lines drawn around culture have been pushed back.

Cultural-industry companies pursue profit and use recurring strategies to do so. However, the internal dynamics of the cultural industries are by no means sufficient to explain the change and continuity in them. Chapter 3 outlined the major *external* contexts for understanding change. Avoiding reduction, I identified four types of factors driving change and continuity in the cultural industries during the period under consideration:

- Political-economic change, in the form of the neo-liberal reaction to the Long Downturn.
- Changing business strategies, in the form of shifts in investment towards service industries, internationalisation and organisational innovations.
- Sociocultural changes.
- Technological change, particularly the development of the computer and various consumer electronics devices.

As will have been apparent, I am suspicious of explanations that privilege the role of the latter factor, technology. Although technologies are important and have real effects, technological reductionism is a real danger in the present climate. I hope that I have shown there are many reasons to avoid it. Instead, I have outlined how the various types of determinant overlap. If the actions of cultural industry companies have been privileged above other dynamics, this is because I believe that their intentions have a great effect on cultural, economic and political processes. After all, this is a book about the cultural industries.

IMPLICATIONS FOR FUTURE STUDY

This book has insisted on **the importance of thinking about the cultural industries as producers of texts**. The cultural industries are those that are most directly involved in the production of social meaning because they make and circulate texts – artefacts that are primarily intended to inform and/or entertain. This is the key to understanding the particular role of the cultural industries in relation to economic, political, social and cultural power. The study of the cultural industries has to incorporate the consideration of texts and the study of texts has to take seriously analysis of the cultural industries.

The best critical political economy and sociological approaches recognise the importance of meaning, but very few writers have achieved a sustained engagement with textual meaning in relation to cultural production. A number of researchers have contributed impressive attempts to do so (Born, 2005; Gitlin, 1983; Gripsrud, 1995; Toynbee, 2000). By incorporating textual change into my assessment and explanation of change/continuity in the cultural industries, I have hoped to re-emphasise the centrality – in the study of media, popular culture and mass communication – of the relationship between symbolic artefacts and the financing and organisation of their production.

My use of the concepts of diversity, quality and pursuit of interests represents a way of thinking about texts that focuses on their functions in people's everyday lives in contemporary society. By trying to think carefully about the evaluative criteria people bring to texts, we can counter the sweeping generalisations that debilitate various forms of cultural criticism. It should be clear that I have no time for fatuous dismissals of entire swathes of cultural production on the part of high-minded analysts. Equally, it must be apparent that I do not think the cultural industries play an altogether progressive role in the contemporary world. There is no question of complacently celebrating popular culture. There are plenty of unimaginative, uninformative, uninteresting texts around and they need to be scrutinised, probed and even lambasted. In other words, to repeat the formula I borrowed from Bernard Miège very early on in this book, we need to recognise the complexity, ambivalence and contestedness of culture. What I am arguing for is **an open-minded attitude towards the kinds of pleasures that people may take from texts and towards the uses to which people may put them**. By open-minded, I simply mean having an attitude that does not judge or assume in advance that any text plays a negative role in society. Audience research on how and why people value texts is therefore a vital corollary of the approach that I have taken in this book. There has been no space for such audience analysis on my part here – researching decades of cultural production has been enough of a task in itself.

One of the main achievements of radical studies of the media and popular culture has been to argue effectively for the importance of ethical questions regarding questions of power and social justice in relation to cultural production. I have attempted to build on this by emphasising the advantages of a **historically informed analysis of contemporary culture**. The reasons for this are obvious enough to anyone who values historical study. Good historical analysis can help to undermine casual assumptions about the present and near future. It can help to put our own situation into perspective. It can also help us to understand how things came to be the way that they are and, therefore, how they may be changed for the better. By using Williams's historical sociology of culture, I have tried to bring a long-term perspective to bear on recent issues.

Media and cultural studies have generally had a very shallow attitude towards history (with notable exceptions, mainly in studies of film and broadcasting, many of which have been referred to ealier). However, this book has been constructed around historical questions concerning change and continuity. This is because the question 'how much have things really changed?' kept cropping up time and again in my experience of teaching and research and in general discussions with friends (and, indeed, strangers) about the cultural industries. The arguments about digitalisation and the internet in the 2000s have continued these debates (see the Preface to this edition).

Many people have an interest in exaggerating change in order to draw attention to themselves – no doubt this has helped put the question of social and cultural change on the agenda. It seems to me that one useful function of academic work is to scrutinise carefully such exaggerated claims. In disciplines that tend to be heavily focused on primarily synchronic research methods, such as ethnography and interviews, the question of change is one that might encourage more diachronic, historical thinking. Finally, it also seems to me that another valuable task of academic writers is to explain *why* they think things have happened in the way that they have – hence the emphasis on explanation in this book.

One of the key aspects of my approach – borrowed from the cultural industries approach, but also to some extent from empirical sociology of culture – has been to **focus on cultural workers**, and particularly the division of labour involved in the symbol making that is at the heart of cultural production. I commented in Chapters 1 and 2 on the surprising neglect of cultural workers in studies on the cultural industries. My primary focus has been on symbol creators, for reasons I explained in Chapter 7: because of my emphasis on the importance of thinking about the power of cultural industries to create products that are based on information, knowledge and meaning, and which therefore have major implications for the rest of society. I hope the considerable attention I have paid to cultural workers can encourage the formation of partnerships with organisations representing the interests of often exploited staff and build bridges between the goals of university researchers and non-university activists.

In the 1990s, the study of cultural production unjustly had a reputation among some researchers, teachers and students of being the dreary analysis of big corporations. Since the first edition of this book was published in 2002, there has been a boom in studies of cultural production and of cultural labour. This has made the revision and updating of the two later editions a demanding, extended, but fascinating process. Some of this twenty-first century wave of research shares my desire to address the relations between power, culture and production using a range of disciplines and perspectives. I hope this book will encourage researchers and other readers to address these relations in ways that will take into account the special place of symbolic creativity, knowledge and expression in human life.

Glossary

analogue Systems of broadcasting or recording based on the conversion of words, images, sounds and so on, into analogue signals. These signals are analogous to the original act of communication – that is, they resemble or correspond to it. Analogue systems have increasingly given way to *digital* ones.

autonomy Independence or freedom from external control or influence. In the context of the cultural industries, this term is usually applied to the relative independence of *symbol creators* or symbol-making organisations from such control or influence (for example, by owners, a parent company or managers acting on behalf of a company). Complete autonomy is impossible, but it is a goal towards which many symbol creators aspire, with important effects on the organisation of cultural production.

blockbuster syndrome The tendency for fewer products, often expensive to produce and market, to dominate a medium, or popular culture in general, thereby crowding out smaller-scale, less well-resourced types of production.

bullshitters According to philosopher Harry G. Frankfurt, bullshitters seek to convey a certain impression of themselves without being concerned about whether or not anything at all is true. They just quietly change the rules governing conversation (or writing) so that claims about truth and falsity are irrelevant. Some analyses of cultural production are full of bullshit – especially those concerned with predictions about future transformations.

circulation The stage of cultural production involving getting products to audiences. It involves marketing, publicity, distribution and/or transmission.

commodification of culture The historical process by which cultural objects and services are increasingly made to be bought and sold on capitalist markets extended over time and space. See also *industrialisation of culture*.

complex professional Both a form and period of cultural production. An adaptation of Raymond Williams's concept of the 'corporate professional' form of cultural production, whereby, starting from the early twentieth century, but increasing from the mid-twentieth century, the commissioning of works became professionalised and more organised, new media technologies appeared, advertising became increasingly important and larger numbers of people worked for cultural businesses than in the past.

concentration   Market or industrial concentration refers to the extent to which a market or industry is dominated by the largest businesses. This is often expressed numerically, by the percentage of market share achieved by the biggest four or five companies or by other related means. While some economists will distinguish between market and industrial concentration, the distinction is trivial for the purposes of this book. The terms *market concentration* and *industrial concentration* are sometimes also used to refer to the process of increasing domination of the largest businesses.

conglomerate, conglomeration   A *conglomerate* is a corporation that consists of a group of businesses dealing in different products or services. *Conglomeration* is the process by which an industry, sector or economy becomes more marked by the presence and influence of such corporations.

convergence   The idea that telecommunications, computers and media are increasingly merging. Sometimes this list is extended to include consumer electronics. Occasionally the idea is mooted that these various industries might merge into one.

copyright   'If a work is eligible for copyright, then the copyright owners are permitted to do a number of different things with the work which are not permitted to those who do not own the copyright (unless they have been licensed by the rights holder)' (Frith and Marshall, 2004: 7). These include the following exclusive rights: to copy the work, make adaptations of the work or make 'derivative works' using parts of it, issue copies of the work to the public, perform the work in public, and broadcast the work. Copyright, then, is best thought of as *a bundle of exclusive rights* associated with creative works, rather than a single right. See also ***intellectal property rights***.

creative cities   Cities with supposedly high levels of creativity within them. This was a term used by policymakers in the 1990s and 2000s to denote the idea that urban 'creativity' could make a key contribution to economic prosperity and social welfare.

creative clusters   Business clusters are groups of linked businesses and other institutions located in the same place (a city or region), which enjoy competitive success as a result of their interconnections. The term 'creative clusters' was used by policymakers in the 1990s and 2000s to refer to cultural industry versions of this supposed phenomenon.

cultural imperialism   A term used by critics of the cultural industries to refer to the negative effects of advanced industrial and 'Western' cultures on less developed, especially 'non-Western', countries.

creative industries   Used by many writers and policy-makers as an alternative to cultural industries, as a policy concept this term tends to group a very wide range of activities together, including commercial and non-commercial industries. Researchers who prefer this term tend to favour a pragmatic approach to policy and power – see Chapter 5.

deregulation   The removal of regulation. This was a term, often used by advocates of *neo-liberalism*, to describe policy changes of the 1980s, 1990s and 2000s. Such changes were often intended to advance the *marketisation* of cultural production.

determination   A word generally used in Marxist traditions to refer to the process by which objective conditions (such as certain economic or political factors) might fix causally what happens or, more usefully, might set limits on what might happen.

digital   Electronic storage and transmission that involves converting images, words, sounds and so on into binary code that can be read and stored by computers.

digital optimism   A term I borrow from Graeme Turner (2010: 126), though I'm not sure that Turner would claim to have invented it. In the context of this book, it refers to the view that digitalisation and the internet have democratised cultural production and consumption.

digital rights management   Measures used to control and/or restrict access to digital data.

digitalisation   The increasing use of *digital* storage and transmission in cultural production and circulation and the increasing use of such digital systems, as opposed to *analogue* ones.

fair use   Copyright law generally requires that copyright holders can choose whether to authorise use of their materials. 'Fair use' is the term used in the USA and elsewhere to refer to exceptions to this requirement – so that, for example, materials can be used without asking permission.

file-*sharing*   The practice of making digital files (containing music, films, television programmes and other cultural products) available on the internet and other networks for others to share.

financialisation   A 'pattern of accumulation in which profit making occurs increasingly through financial channels rather than through trade and commodity production' (Krippner, 2005: 174); or, more broadly, the increasing tendency for financial investment and speculation decisions to influence other sectors of the economy, such as manufacturing, retail, or the cultural industries.

flow logic or model A model of commodity production identified by Bernard Miège (1987, 1989) as characteristic of the production of radio, television and new media. Key features include a continuous flow of products based on daily contact and the central importance of a programme planner and/or scheduler. See also *publishing logic or model*.

format (1) An idea or concept for a series of television or radio programmes that is sold as an idea or concept. (2) In its more specialist use, a term developed by Bill Ryan (1992) to refer to the way that cultural industry companies, in order to minimise *risk*, provide links between sequences of products through the use of common elements. Stars, genres and serial form are the main means he identifies.

geocultural markets Markets for cultural products, spread over more than one nation state, linked by shared cultural features. These can include language, religion and ways of life.

globalisation A term used to refer to changes that have brought about greater interconnectedness between different parts of the world.

government policy See *policy*.

horizontal integration The process by which businesses buy up other businesses in the same industry or sector, usually resulting in less competition for audiences and audience time.

industrialisation of culture The introduction of significant capital investment, mechanised production and division of labour into the realm of cultural production. See also *commodification of culture*.

information society A term used to refer to contemporary or future societies by those who believe that information and knowledge are now (or will soon become) central, as never before, to the way that societies operate. Information society discourse is writing, speaking or thinking that is based on this view.

integration See *horizontal integration, multisector and multimedia integration* and *vertical integration.*

intellectual property rights Bundles of exclusive rights attached to various forms of expression of knowledge, ideas or artistic work. The main areas are patent, trademark and *copyright*.

internationalisation The process by which businesses based in one nation, or in one particular set of nations, will buy and partner companies in other nations. Also, the increasing presence of such links.

liberalisation   In the domain of policy, a term used to refer to the removal of restrictions (though the use of the term sometimes downplays that some 'restrictions' might ultimately enhance equality, freedom and other goods).

Long Downturn   The era of slowed or reduced growth in the global economy, following the supposed Golden Age of growth in the post-Second World War period. The Long Downturn is usually taken to have begun in 1973 and ended (perhaps temporarily?) in the mid-1990s.

long tail, the   The idea that commerce will be increasingly oriented towards providing goods for niche products of relatively small demand. The name comes from a graph showing a chart of sales figures, with the highest selling products on the left and then a 'long tail' of many thousands of products selling small amounts tailing off to the right. However, selling many products to these markets, it is argued, may help to sustain businesses, because digitalisation allows for lower distribution costs.

marketisation   In this book, the term refers to the process by which market exchange (the buying and selling of goods, services and rights) has increasingly come to permeate the cultural industries and related sectors. See also *deregulation*.

media mogul   An owner who exerts very strong control over his own media company. This could be her company too, of course, except that they're always owned by men.

multisector and multimedia integration   The processes by which cultural industry businesses buy into other related areas of cultural industry production, often to ensure cross-promotion. This is a particular type of *conglomeration*.

neoclassical economics   A variety of economic analysis that, from the late nineteenth century onwards, sought to move beyond earlier 'classical economics'. It tends to assume that consumers are economically rational individuals, and that competition leads to maximisation of well-being. Although there are many heterodox brands of economics, and there are internal divisions within the neoclassical paradigm, it remains dominant in the discipline.

neo-liberalism   'A theory of political economic practices that proposes that human well-being can best be advanced by liberating individual entrepreneurial freedoms and skills within an institutional framework characterised by strong private property rights, free markets, and free trade' (Harvey, 2005: 2).

peer-to-peer networks (P2P)   In peer-to-peer networks, each computer operates as both a client and server for other computers in the network. The internet is itself based on this idea, but peer-to-peer became of particular importance to the cultural industries when it became used for *file-sharing*.

policy Government or public policy refers to the laws and regulations adopted and undertaken by governments.

polysemy the ability of texts to be interpreted in a number of ways.

project team The group of individuals responsible for the creative stage in cultural production. This concept is important because it draws attention to the complex division of labour involved in making cultural goods, especially during the *complex professional* period.

public domain The body of knowledge and creativity that is in the public domain can be used freely by the public because it is not in private ownership. This includes works where the ownership rights have expired.

public service broadcasting (PSB) Broadcasting intended to provide a service for nations, regions and/or communities, it is usually non-commercial, and carried out by a government or government-related agency. This service has been conceived of in various ways (see Chapter 4), but public accountability, public finance, universal service and addressing audiences as citizens are common features.

publishing logic or model (or 'editorial model') A model of commodity production identified by Miège (1987, 1989) as characteristic of the production of books, records and films. Key features include the sale of texts on an individual basis to be owned, organisation of production by a publisher/producer, and the presence of many small- or medium-sized companies clustering around oligopolistic firms. See also *flow logic or model*.

reductionism When someone believes that a social theory, method or explanation excessively reduces complex processes to simple ones, he or she may say that the theory/method/explanation is guilty of reductionism. I prefer this term to 'determinism' (see Chapter 3).

regeneration In the context of urban and economic policy, the process by which cities and towns are supposedly improved. There are strong connotations of areas that had entered decline being brought back to life. However, attempts at regeneration can sometimes lead to new forms of exclusion and marginalisation.

risk In the context of businesses, the possibility of commercial loss. A key concept in the analysis of the cultural industries because, while all businesses involve risk, and the attempt to manage it, an argument can be sustained that the cultural industries are among the riskiest of all modern enterprises.

search engines Programs designed to find information on the internet.

social networking sites Online services that provide the means by which people can communicate with others about shared interests and activities.

symbol creators   Those who engage in *symbolic creativity*. (I prefer this term to 'artists' for reasons explained in the Introduction.)

symbolic creativity   The process, common to all human societies, by means of which symbols – mainly writing, sounds and images – are brought into being. (I prefer this term to 'art' for reasons explained in the Introduction.)

synergy   The principle by which two or more different elements of a business might work together, so that the sales or profits might exceed what would have been produced by the two elements working independently.

texts   This term is used in a specialist way in cultural analysis to denote objects, artefacts and events that are meaningful. Some analysts think of any object, artefact or event in the world as potentially being open to analysis and, therefore, as texts. I use the term here in a narrower but nevertheless broad sense, as a collective name for all the 'works' produced by cultural industries, such as television programmes, films, recordings, books and so on. The term is not used here in its older sense – the wording of something written or printed – but it can refer to printed artefacts.

vertical integration   The process by which businesses buy up other businesses involved in different stages of the process of production and circulation. A business might buy 'downstream', such as when an organisation involved in making films buys a distributor of DVDs, or 'upstream', when a business involved in circulation or transmission (such as a cable television company) buys a programme-maker.

References

References to articles from newspapers, magazines and trade journals are given in the main text, not here (except where an author's name is provided). Where two dates are given, the first date refers to the edition of the particular book, chapter or article I have used, the second to the original date of publication. My apologies to authors for, in almost all cases, leaving out their precious sub-titles. I did it for reasons of space.

Adorno, Theodor (2002) *Essays on Music,* new translation by Susan H. Gillespie. Berkeley, CA: University of California Press.

Adorno, Theodor and Horkheimer, Max (1977[1944]) 'The culture industry: enlightenment as mass deception', in James Curran, Michael Gurevitch and Janet Wollacott (eds), *Mass Communication and Society.* London: Edward Arnold. pp. 349–83.

Ahlkvist, Jarl A. and Fisher, Gene (2000) 'And the hits just keep on coming: music programming standardization in commercial radio', *Poetics,* 27(5–6): 301–25.

Aksoy, Asu and Robins, Kevin (1992) 'Hollywood for the 21st century: global competition for critical mass in image markets', *Cambridge Journal of Economics,* 16: 1–22.

Albright, Mark (2005) 'The season for synergy', *Campaign for a Commercial-Free Childhood,* 16 November, available at www.commercialexploitation.org (last accessed September 2006).

Alderman, John (2001) *Sonic Boom.* London: Fourth Estate.

Alford, Robert (1998) *The Craft of Inquiry.* New York: Oxford University Press.

Allan, Stuart and Thorsen, Einar (eds) (2009). *Citizen Journalism.* New York: Peter Lang.

Allen, Rod (1998) 'This is not television …', in Jeanette Steemers (ed.), *Changing Channels.* Luton: University of Luton Press. pp. 59–71.

Amezaga Albizu, Josu (2007) 'Geolinguistic regions and diasporas in the age of satellite television', *International Communication Gazette,* 69: 239–61.

Amin, Ash and Thrift, Nigel (eds) (2004) *The Blackwell Cultural Economy Reader.* Oxford: Blackwell.

Amin, Hussein (1996) 'Egypt and the Arab world in the satellite age', in John Sinclair, Elizabeth Jacka and Stuart Cunningham (eds), *New Patterns in Global Television.* Oxford: Oxford University Press. pp. 101–25.

Ampuja, Marko (2010) *The Media and the Academic Globalization Debate.* PhD dissertation, University of Helsinki.

Anand, N. and Peterson, Richard A. (2000) 'When market information constitutes fields: sensemaking of markets in the commercial music industry', *Organization Science,* 11(3): 270–84.

Andersen, Robin (2000) 'Introduction', in Robin Andersen and Lance Strate (eds), *Critical Studies in Media Commercialism.* Oxford: Oxford University Press. pp. 1–21.

Anderson, Chris (2006) *The Long Tail*. New York: Hyperion.

Anderson, Christopher (2007) 'Creating the twenty-first-century television network: NBC in the age of media conglomerates', in Michelle Hilmes (ed.), *NBC – America's Network*. Berkeley, CA: University of California Press, pp. 275–90.

Andrejevic, Mark (2008) 'Watching television without pity', *Television & New Media*, 9(1): 24.

Andrejevic, Mark (2009) 'Exploiting YouTube: contradictions of user-generated labour', in Pelle Snickars and Patrick Vonderau (eds), *The YouTube Reader*. Stockholm: National Library of Sweden. pp. 406–22.

Ang, Ien (1985) *Watching* Dallas. London and New York: Methuen.

Ang, Ien (1991) *Desperately Seeking the Audience*. London: Routledge.

Anjum, Zafar (2005) 'Hollywood's Indian adventures', *Asia Times Online*, 2 December, available at www.atimes.com (last accessed September 2006).

Armstrong, Philip, Glyn, Andrew and Harrison, John (1991) *Capitalism Since 1945*. Oxford: Blackwell.

Arsenault, Amelia and Castells, Manuel (2008) 'The structure and dynamics of global multi-media business networks', *International Journal of Communication* 2: 707–48.

Arthur, Michael B. and Rousseau, Denise M. (eds) (1996) *The Boundaryless Career*. New York and Oxford: OUP.

Arthurs, Jane (2003) '*Sex and the City* and consumer culture: remediating postfeminist drama', *Feminist Media Studies*, 3(1): 83–98.

Aufderheide, Patricia (1999) *Communications Policy and the Public Interest*. New York: Guilford Press.

Augarten, Stan (1984) *Bit by Bit*. London: Unwin.

Auletta, Ken (1997) 'American keiretsu', *The New Yorker*, 20 and 27 October, pp. 225–7.

Auletta, Ken (2010) *Googled*. London: Virgin Books.

Bagdikian, Ben H. (2000) *The Media Monopoly* (6th edn). Boston, MA: Beacon Press.

Bagdikian, Ben H. (2004) *The New Media Monopoly*. Boston, MA: Beacon Press.

Bailey, Michael (ed.) (2008) *Narrating Media History*. Abingdon and New York: Routledge.

Baker, C. Edwin (1994) *Advertising and a Democratic Press*. Princeton, NJ: Princeton University Press.

Baker, C. Edwin (2002) *Media, Markets, and Democracy*. Cambridge: Cambridge University Press.

Baker, C. Edwin (2007) *Media Concentration and Democracy*. Cambridge: Cambridge University Press.

Bakker, Piet (2005) 'File-sharing – fight, ignore or compete: paid download services vs. P2P networks', *Telematics and Informatics*, 22(1–2): 41–55.

Banet-Weiser, Sarah (2007) 'What's your flava? Race and postfeminism in media culture', in Yvonne Tasker and Diane Negra (eds), *Interrogating Postfeminism*. Durham, NC: Duke University Press. pp. 201–226.

Banks, Mark (2007) *The Politics of Cultural Work*. Basingstoke: Palgrave.

Banks, Mark and Hesmondhalgh, David (2009) 'Looking for work in creative industries policy', *International Journal of Cultural Policy*, 15(4): 1–16.

Barfe, Louis (2003) *Where Have all the Good Times Gone?* London: Atlantic Books.

Barker, Chris (1997) *Global Television*. Oxford: Blackwell.

Becker, Howard S. (1982) *Art Worlds*. Berkeley, CA: University of California Press.

Belfiore, Eleonora (2002) 'Art as a means of alleviating social exclusion: does it really work? A critique of instrumental cultural policies and social impact studies in the UK', *International Journal of Cultural Policy*, 8(1): 91–106.

Bell, Daniel (1974) *The Coming of Post-industrial Society*. London: Heinemann.

Benkler, Yochai (2006) *The Wealth of Networks: How Social Production Transforms Markets and Freedom*. New Haven, CT: Yale University Press.

Bennett, Tony (1998) *Culture*. London: Sage.

Bennett, W. Lance (2012) *News* (9th edn). New York: Longman.

Bennett, W. Lance, Lawrence, Regina G. and Livingston, Steven (2007) *When the Press Fails*. Chicago, IL: University of Chicago Press.

Benson, Rodney (2011) 'Public funding and journalistic independence', in Robert W. McChesney and Victor Pickard (eds), *Will the Last Reporter Please Turn Out the Lights*. New York: The New Press. pp. 314–19.

Benson, Rodney and Erik Neveu (eds) (2005) *Bourdieu and the Journalistic Field*. Cambridge: Polity.

Berwanger, Dietrich (1998) 'The Third World', in Anthony Smith with Richard Paterson (eds), *Television: An International History* (2nd edn). Oxford: Oxford University Press. pp. 188–200.

Bettig, Ronald V. (1996) *Copyrighting Culture*. Boulder, CO: Westview Press.

Bianchini, Franco and Parkinson, Michael (eds) (1993) *Cultural Policy and Urban Regeneration*. Manchester: Manchester University Press.

Bilton, Chris (1999) 'Risky business: the independent production sector in Britain's creative industries', *Cultural Policy* 6 (1): 17–39.

Biressi, Anita and Nunn, Heather (2005) *Reality TV*. London and New York: Wallflower.

Biskind, Peter (1998) *Easy Riders, Raging Bulls*. London: Bloomsbury.

Bloom, Allan (1987) *The Closing of the American Mind*. New York: Simon & Schuster.

Blumler, Jay G. (1992) *Television and the Public Interest*. London: Sage, in association with the Broadcasting Standards Council.

Blumler, Jay G. and Gurevitch, Michael (1995) *The Crisis of Public Communication*. London: Routledge.

Bolaño, César, Mastrini, Guillermo and Sierra, Francisco (2004) 'A Latin American perspective for the political economy of communications', *Javnost/The Public*, 11(3): 47–58.

Bolin, Göran (2009) 'Symbolic production and value in media industries', *Journal of Cultural Economy*, 2(3): 345–61.

Boltanski, Luc and Chiapello, Eve (2006) *The New Spirit of Capitalism*. London: Verso.

Bordwell, David (2000) *Planet Hong Kong*. Cambridge, MA: Harvard University Press.

Bordwell, David, Staiger, Janet and Thompson, Kristin (1985) *The Classical Hollywood Cinema*. London: Routledge & Kegan Paul.

Born, Georgina (1993) 'Against negation, for a politics of cultural production: Adorno, aesthetics, the social', *Screen*, 34(3): 223–42.

Born, Georgina (1995) *Rationalizing Culture*. Berkeley, CA: University of California Press.

Born, Georgina (2005) *Uncertain Vision*. London: Vintage.

Bouquillon, Philippe and Combès, Yolande (2007) *Industries de la culture et de la communication en mutation*. Paris: L'Harmattan.

Bourdieu, Pierre (1984) *Distinction*. Cambridge, MA: Harvard University Press.

Bourdieu, Pierre (1993) *The Field of Cultural Production*. Cambridge: Polity Press.

Bourdieu, Pierre (1996) *The Rules of Art*. Cambridge: Polity Press.

Boyd, Douglas (1998) 'The Arab world', in Anthony Smith with Richard Paterson (eds), *Television: An International History* (2nd edn). Oxford: Oxford University Press. pp. 182–7.

Boyd-Barratt, Oliver (1980) *The International News Agencies*. London: Constable.

Boyle, James (1996) *Shamans, Software and Spleens*. Cambridge, MA: Harvard University Press.

Brants, Kees and Siune, Karen (1992) 'Public broadcasting in a state of flux', in Karen Siune and Wolfgang Truetzschler (eds), *Dynamics of Media Politics*. London: Sage. pp. 101–15.

Braverman, Harry (1974) *Labor and Monopoly Capital*. New York: Monthly Review Press.

Brenner, Robert (1998) 'Uneven development and the Long Downturn: the advanced capitalist economies from boom to stagnation, 1950–1998', *New Left Review*, I(229): 1–267.

Brenner, Robert (2000) 'The boom and the bubble', *New Left Review*, 11(6): 5–43.

Bruns, Axel (2008) *Blogs, Wikipedia, Second Life and Beyond*. New York: Peter Lang.

Burgess, Jean and Green, Joshua (2009) *YouTube*. Cambridge: Polity.

Burkart, Patrick (2010) *Music and Cyberliberties*. Middletown, CT: Wesleyan University Press.

Burkart, Patrick and McCourt, Tom (2006) *Digital Music Wars*. Lanham, MD: Rowman & Littlefield.

Burke, Peter and Briggs, Asa (2009) *A Social History of the Media* (third edition). Cambridge: Polity.

Burnett, Robert (1992) 'The implications of ownership changes for concentration and diversity in the phonogram industry', *Communication Research,* 19(6): 749–69.

Burnett, Robert (1995) *The Global Jukebox*. London: Routledge.

Burnett, Robert and Marshall, P. David (2003) *Web Theory*. London: Routledge.

Burns, Rob (2004) 'German television', in John Sinclair and Graeme Turner (eds), *Contemporary World Television*. London: BFI. pp. 70–4.

Burns, Tom (1977) *The BBC*. Basingstoke: Macmillan.

Burston, Jonathan (1999) 'Spectacle, synergy and megamusicals: the global industrialisation of the live entertainment economy', in James Curran (ed.), *Media Organizations in Society*. London: Arnold. pp. 69–83.

Bustamante, Enrique (2004) 'Cultural industries in the digital age: some provisional conclusions', *Media, Culture and Society* 26: 803-20.

Calabrese, Andrew (2005) 'The trade in television news', in Janet Wasko (ed.), *A Companion to Television*. Malden, MA and Oxford: Blackwell. pp. 270–88.

Calabrese, Andrew and Sparks, Colin (eds) (2004) *Towards a Political Economy of Culture*. Lanham, MD: Rowman & Littlefield.

Caldwell, John Thornton (2008) *Production Culture*. Durham, NC: Duke University Press.

Canclini, Nestor García (1995) *Hybrid Cultures*. Minneapolis, MN: University of Minnesota Press.

Caraway, Brett (2011) 'Audience labour in the new media environment', *Media, Culture and Society,* 33(5): 693–708.

Carr, Nicholas (2005) 'The amorality of Web 2.0', *Rough Type* blog, 3 October, available at www.roughtype.com (last accessed September 2006).

Castells, Manuel (1989) *The Informational City*. Oxford: Blackwell.

Castells, Manuel (1996) *The Rise of the Network Society* (volume I of *The Information Age*). Oxford: Blackwell.

Castells, Manuel (2008) *Communication Power*. New York and Oxford: Oxford University Press.

Caves, Richard E. (2000) *Creative Industries*. Cambridge, MA: Harvard University Press.

Caves, Richard E. (2005) *Switching Channels*. Cambridge, MA: Harvard University Press.

Centre for Cultural Policy Research (CCPR) (2003) 'Baseline study on Hong Kong's creative industries'. Hong Kong: University of Hong Kong.

Chambers, Iain (1994) *Migrancy, Culture, Identity*. London: Routledge.

Chan-Olmsted, Sylvia M. and Chang, Byeng-Hee (2003) 'Diversification strategy of global media conglomerates: examining its patterns and determinants', *Journal of Media Economics,* 16(4): 213–33.

Christianen, Michael (1995) 'Cycles in symbol production? A new model to explain concentration, diversity and innovation in the music industry', *Popular Music,* 14(1): 55–94.

Christians, Clifford G., Glasser, Theodore, McQuail, Denis, Nordenstreng, Kaarle and White, Robert (2009) *Normative Theories of the Media* Urbana, IL: University of Illinois Press.

Christophers, Brett (2009) *Envisioning Media Power*. Lanham, MD: Lexington.

Christopherson, Susan (2011) 'Hard jobs in Hollywood: how concentration in distribution affects the production side of the media entertainment industry', in Dwayne Winseck and Dal Yong Jin (eds), *The Political Economies of Media*. London: Bloomsbury. pp. 123–140.

Christopherson, Susan and Storper, Michael (1986) 'The city as studio, the world as back lot: the impact of vertical disintegration on the location of the motion picture industry', *Environment and Planning D: Society and Space,* 4: 305–20.

Christopherson, Susan and Storper, Michael (1989) 'The effects of flexible specialization on industrial politics and the labor market: the motion picture industry', *Industrial and Labor Relations Review,* 42: 331–47.

Clark, Kenneth (1969) *Civilisation*. London: BBC.

Clifford, James (1988) *The Predicament of Culture*. Cambridge, MA: Harvard University Press.

Coase, Ronald H. (1974) 'The economics of the First Amendment', *American Economic Review,* 64(2): 384–91.

Coffey, Steve and Stipp, Horst (1997) 'The interactions between computer and television research', *Journal of Advertising Research,* 37(2): 61–7.

Cohen, Nicole (2008) 'The valorization of surveillance: towards a political economy of Facebook', *Democratic Communiqué,* 22(1): 5–22.

Cohn, Nik (1989[1969]) 'Awopbopaloobop Alopbamboom', in *Ball the Wall*. London: Picador. pp. 49–139.

Coleman, Stephen (2005) 'Blogs and the new politics of listening', *Political Quarterly,* 76 (3): 273–80.

Coleman, Stephen and Blumler, Jay (2009) *The Internet and Democratic Citizenship*. Cambridge: CUP.

Collins, Richard (1986) 'Wall-To-Wall "Dallas"? The US-UK Trade in Television', *Screen* 27(3–4): 66–77.

Collins, Richard and Murroni, Christina (1996) *New Media, New Policies*. Cambridge: Polity Press.

Commission of the European Communities (1984) *Television Without Frontiers: Green paper on the establishment of the common market for broadcasting especially by satellite and cable*. Brussels: COM (92) 480 final.

Commission of the European Communities (1994) *Europe and the Global Information Society: Recommendations to the EC* (The Bangemann Report). Brussels: European Commission, 25 May.

Compaine, Benjamin (1982) *Who Owns the Media?* White Plains, NY: Knowledge Industry Publications.

Compaine, Benjamin and Gomery, Douglas (2000) *Who Owns the Media?* (3rd edn). Mahwah, NJ: Lawrence Erlbaum.

Cooper, Mark (2002) *Cable Mergers and Monopolies*. Washington, DC: Economic Policy Institute.

Corner, John (2000) '"Influence": the contested core of media research', in James Curran and Michael Gurevitch (eds), *Mass Media and Society* (3rd edn). London: Hodder Arnold. pp. 376–97.

Coser, Lewis A., Kadushin, Charles and Powell, Walter W. (1982) *Books*. New York: Basic Books.

Couldry, Nick (2000) *Inside Culture*. London: Sage.

Couldry, Nick (2003) *Media Rituals*. London: Routledge.

Couldry, Nick (2010) *Why Voice Matters*. London: Sage.

Council of the European Communities (1989) *Directive of the Coordination of Certain Provisions Laid Down by Law, Regulation or Administrative Action in Member States Concerning the Pursuit of Television Broadcasting Activities*, 89/552/EEC, *Official Journal of the European Communities*, L298/23, 17 October.

Cowhey, Peter F. and Aronson, Jonathan D., with Abelson, Donald (2009) *Transforming Global Information and Communication Markets*. Cambridge, MA and London: MIT Press.

Coyle, Diane (1999) *The Weightless World*. London: Capstick.

Craig, David and Cotterell, Gerard (2007) 'Periodising neoliberalism?' *Policy and Politics*, 35(3), 497–514.

Creative and Cultural Skills (2009) *Creative and Cultural Industry Impact and Footprint*. London: Author.

Croteau, David and Hoynes, William (2002) *Media/Society* (3rd edn). Thousand Oaks, CA: Pine Forge.

Crouch, Colin (2011) *The Strange Non-death of Neo-liberalism*. Cambridge: Polity.

Cultural and Creative Skills (2009) *Creative and Cultural Industries, Impact and Footprint Presentation*. London: Creative and Cultural Skills.

Cunningham, Stuart D. and Higgs, Peter L. (2008) 'Creative industries mapping: where have we come from and where are we going'? *Creative Industries Journal*, 1(1): 7–30.

Curran, James (1986) 'The impact of advertising on the British mass media', in Richard Collins, James Curran, Nicholas Garnham, Paddy Scannell, Philip Schlesinger and Colin Sparks (eds), *Media, Culture and Society*. London: Sage.

Curran, James (1990) 'Culturalist perspectives on news organizations', in Marjorie Ferguson (ed.), *Public Communication: The New Imperatives*. London: Sage. pp. 114–34.

Curran, James (1998) 'Newspapers: beyond political economy', in Adam Briggs and Paul Cobley (eds), *The Media: An Introduction*. Harlow: Addison Wesley Longman. pp. 81–96.

Curran, James (2002) *Media and Power*. London: Routledge.

Curran, James (2010a) 'Entertaining democracy', in James Curran (ed.) *The Media and Society*. London: Bloomsbury. pp. 38–62.

Curran, James (ed.) (2010b) *The Media and Society*. London: Bloomsbury.

Curran James (2011) *Media and Democracy*. Abingdon and New York: Routledge

Curran, James and Michael Gurevitch (eds) (2005) *Mass Media and Society* (5th edn). London: Hodder Arnold.

Curran, James and Park, Myung-Jin (eds) (2000) *De-Westernizing Media Studies*. London: Routledge.

Curran, James and Seaton, Jean (2010) *Power without Responsibility* (7th edn). London: Routledge.

Curtin, Michael (1999) 'Feminine desire in the age of satellite television', *Journal of Communication*, 49(1): 55–70.

Curtin, Michael (2003a) 'Media capital: towards the study of spatial flows', *International Journal of Cultural Studies*, 6(2): 202–28.

Curtin, Michael (2003b) 'The future of Chinese cinema: some lessons from Hong Kong and Taiwan', in Chin-Chuan Lee (ed.), *Chinese Media, Global Contexts*. London: RoutledgeCurzon. pp. 237–56.

Curtin, Michael (2007) *Playing to the World's Biggest Audience*. Berkeley, CA: University of California Press.

Curtin, Michael and Shattuc, Jane (2009) *The American Television Industry*. Basingstoke: Palgrave Macmillan/British Film Institute.

Cvetkovski, Trajce (2012) *Copyright and Popular Media*. Basingstoke: Palgrave Mcmillan.

Dale, Martin (1997) *The Movie Game*. London: Cassell.

Davis, Howard, and Scase, Richard (2000) *Managing Creativity*. Milton Keynes: The Open University Press.

Dayan, Daniel and Katz, Elihu (1992) *Media Events*. Cambridge, MA: Harvard University Press.

DCMS (1998) 'Creative industries mapping document 1998'. London: UK Department for Culture, Media and Sport.

DCMS (2001) 'The creative industries mapping document 2001'. London: UK Department for Culture, Media and Sport.

DCMS (2005) 'Creative industries economic estimates'. London: UK Department for Culture, Media and Sport.

De Kloet, Jeroen (2010) *China with a Cut*. Amsterdam: University of Amsterdam Press.

De Peuter, Greig and Dyer-Witheford, Nick (2005) 'A playful multitude? Mobilising and counter-mobilising immaterial game labour', *Fibreculture*, Online.

Demers, Joanna (2006) *Steal This Music*. Athens, GA: University of Georgia Press.

DiMaggio, Paul (1977) 'Market structure, the creative process and popular culture: towards an organizational reinterpretation of mass-culture theory', *Journal of Popular Culture*, 11: 436–52.

Dowd, Timothy J. (2000) 'Diversificazione musicale e mercato discografico negli Stati Uniti, 1955–1990', *Rassegna Italiana di Sociologia*, 41(2): 223–63.

Dowd, Timothy J. (2004) 'Concentration and diversity revisited: production logics and the U.S. mainstream recording market, 1940–1990', *Social Forces*, 82(4): 1411–55.

Downey, John (1998) 'XS 4 all? "Information society" policy and practice in the European Union', in John Downey and Jim McGuigan (eds), *Technocities*. London: Sage. pp. 121–38.

Downey, John (2006) 'The media industries: do ownership, size and internationalization matter?' in David Hesmondhalgh (ed.), *Media Production*. Maidenhead and Milton Keynes, Open University Press/The Open University. pp. 7–48.

Downing, John (2001) *Radical Media*. London: Sage.

Doyle, Gillian (2002) *Understanding Media Economics*. London: Sage.

Drake, Philip (2008) 'Distribution and marketing in contemporary Hollywood', in Paul McDonald and Janet Wasko (eds), *The Contemporary Hollywood Film Industry*. Malden, MA and Oxford: Blackwell. pp. 63–83.

Driver, Stephen and Gillespie, Andrew (1992) 'The diffusion of digital technologies in magazine print publishing: organizational change and strategic choices', *Journal of Information Technology*, 7(3): 149–59.

Driver, Stephen and Gillespie, Andrew (1993) 'Structural change in the cultural industries: British magazine publishing in the 1980s', *Media, Culture and Society*, 15: 183–201.

Drucker, Peter (1992/1968) *The Age of Discontinuity*. New Brunswick, NJ: Transaction.

du Gay, Paul and Pryke, Michael (eds) (2002) *Cultural Economy*. London: Sage.

du Gay, Paul, Hall, Stuart, Janes, Linda, Mackay, Hugh and Negus, Keith (1997) *Doing Cultural Studies*. London: Sage.

Dunkley, Christopher (1985) *Television Today and Tomorrow: Wall to Wall* Dallas? Harmondsworth: Penguin.

Durham Peters, John (2005) *Courting the Abyss*. Chicago, IL: University of Chicago Press.

During, Simon (1993) *The Cultural Studies Reader*. London and New York: Routledge.

Dyer, Richard (1981) 'Entertainment and utopia', in Rick Altman (ed.), *Genre: A Reader*. London: Routledge & Kegan Paul. pp. 175–89.

Edwards, Lee and Hodges, Caroline (eds) (2011) *Public Relations, Society and Culture*. Abingdon: Routledge.

Eikhof, Doris and Haunschild, Axel (2007) 'For art's sake! Artistic and economic logics in creative production', *Journal of Organizational Behaviour*, 28: 523–38.

Einarsson, Ágúst (2005) *Cultural Activities and Creative Industries in Iceland*. Reykjavik: University of Iceland.

Einstein, Mara (2004) *Media Diversity*. Mahwah, NJ: Lawrence Erlbaum.

Elliott, Philip (1977) 'Media organizations and occupations: an overview', in James Curran, Michael Gurevitch and Janet Wollacott (eds), *Mass Communication and Society*. London: Edward Arnold. pp. 142–73.

Epstein, Edward Jay (2005a) 'Gross misunderstanding', *Slate*, 16 May, available at http://slate.msn.com (last accessed September 2006 – search by article title).

Epstein, Edward Jay (2005b) 'Concessions are for girlie men', *Slate*, 9 May, available at http://slate.msn.com (last accessed September 2006 – search by article title).

ERC Services Subcommittee (Workgroup on Creative Industries) (2002) 'Creative industries development strategy: propelling Singapore's creative economy'. Singapore: ERC Services Subcommittee.

Ettema, James S. and Whitney, D. Charles (1994) *Audiencemaking*. London: Sage.

Euromedia Research Group (1997) *The Media in Western Europe*. London: Sage.

European Commission (1997) *Green Paper on the Regulatory Implications of the Telecommunications, Media and Information Technology Sectors: Towards a common approach to information society services* (DGXIII). Brussels: European Commission.

Evans, David S. (2009) 'The online advertising industry: economics, evolution, and privacy', *Journal of Economic Perspectives*, 23(3): 37–60.

Evans, Graham and Shaw, Phyllida (2004) *The contribution of culture to regeneration in the UK*. London: London Metropolitan University.

Ewen, Stuart (1996) *PR!* New York: Basic Books.

Fejes, Fred (1981) 'Media imperialism: an assessment', *Media, Culture and Society*, 3(3): 281–9.

Feld, Steven (1994) 'From schizophonia to schismogenesis: on the discourses and commodification practices of "world music" and "world beat" ', in Charles Keil and Steven Feld (eds), *Music Grooves*. Chicago, IL: University of Chicago Press. pp. 257–89.

Feldman, Tony (1998) *An Introduction to Digital Media*. London: Routledge.

Fenton, Natalie (2011) *New Media, Old News*. London: Sage.

Feuer, Jane (1984) 'MTM Enterprises: an overview', in Jane Feuer, Paul Kerr and Tise Vahimagi (eds), *MTM 'Quality Television'*. London: BFI. pp. 1–31.

Feuer, Jane, Kerr, Paul and Vahimagi, Tise (eds) (1984) *MTM 'Quality Television'*. London: BFI.

Fiske, John (1987) *Television Culture*. London: Methuen.

Fiske, John (1990) *Introduction to Communication Studies* (2nd edn). London: Routledge.

Fitzgerald, Scott (2012) *Corporations and Cultural Industries*. Lanham, MD: Lexington Books.

Flew, Terry (2007) *Understanding Global Media*. Basingstoke: Palgrave Macmillan.

Flew, Terry (2009) 'The cultural economy moment?' *Journal of Cultural Science,* 2(1). Online.

Flew, Terry (2011) *The Creative Industries*. London: Sage.

Flichy, Patrice (1980) *Les industries de l'imaginaire*. Grenoble: Presse Universitaires de Grenoble.

Flichy, Patrice (1999) 'The construction of new digital media', *New Media and Society,* 1(1): 33–8.

Fligstein, Neil (1990) *The Transformation of Corporate Control*. Cambridge, MA: Harvard University Press.

Florida, Richard (2002) *The Rise of the Creative Class*. New York: Basic Books.

Florida, Richard (2005) *The Flight of the Creative Class*. London: HarperCollins.

Forester, Tom (ed.) (1985) *The Information Technology Revolution*. Oxford: Blackwell.

Forester, Tom (1987) *High-tech Society*. Oxford: Blackwell.

Fox, Elizabeth and Waisbord, Silvio (eds)(2002) *Latin Politics, Global Media*. Austin, TX: University of Texas Press.

Frank, Robert H. and Cook, Philip J. (1995) *The Winner-Take-All Society*. New York: The Free Press.

Frank, Thomas (1997) *The Conquest of Cool*. Chicago, IL: University of Chicago Press.

Frankfurt, Harry G. (2005) *On Bullshit*. Princeton, NJ: Princeton University Press.

Fraser, Nancy (1997) *Justice Interruptus*. London: Routledge.

Freedman, Des (2006) 'Internet transformations: "old" media resilience in the "new media" revolution', in James Curran and David Morley (eds), *Media and Cultural Theory*. Abingdon: Routledge. pp. 197–208.

Freedman, Des (2008) *The Politics of Cultural Policy*. Cambridge: Polity.

Freidson, Eliot (1990) 'Labors of love: a prospectus' in Kai Erikson and Steven Peter Vallas (eds), *The Nature of Work*. New Haven, CT: Yale University Press. pp. 149–61.

Frith, Simon (1978) *The Sociology of Rock*. London: Constable.

Frith, Simon (1981) *Sound Effects*. New York: Pantheon Books.

Frith, Simon (1991) 'Anglo-America and its discontents', *Cultural Studies,* 5(3): 263–9.

Frith, Simon (1993) 'Popular music and the local state', in Tony Bennett, Simon Frith, Lawrence Grossberg, John Shepherd and Graeme Turner (eds), *Rock and Popular Music*. London: Routledge. pp. 14–24.

Frith, Simon (1996) *Performing Rites*. Oxford: Oxford University Press.

Frith, Simon (2000) 'The popular music industry', in Simon Frith, Will Straw and John Street (eds), *The Cambridge Companion to Pop and Rock*. Cambridge: Cambridge University Press. pp. 26–52.

Frith, Simon and Marshall, Lee (2004) *Music and Copyright* (2nd edn). Edinburgh: Edinburgh University Press.

Frow, John (1997) *Time and Commodity Culture*. Oxford: Oxford University Press.

Fuchs, Christian (2008) *Internet and Society*. Abingdon: Routledge.

Fuchs, Christian (2011) 'The contemporary World Wide Web: social medium or new space of accumulation?', in Dwayne Winseck and Jin Dal Yong (eds), *The Political Economies of Media*. London: Bloomsbury. pp. 201–220.

Galperin, Hernán (1999) 'Cultural industries in the age of free-trade agreements', *Canadian Journal of Communication,* 24(1): 49–77.

Galperin, Hernán (2004) *New Television, Old Politics*. Cambridge: Cambridge University Press.

Gandy, Oscar H., Jr (1992) 'The political economy approach: a critical challenge', *Journal of Media Economics,* 5(2): 23–42.

Gandy, Oscar H., Jr (2000) 'Race, ethnicity and the segmentation of media markets', in James Curran and Michael Gurevitch (eds), *Mass Media and Society* (3rd edn). London: Arnold. pp. 44–69.

Gans, Herbert J. (1979) *Deciding What's News*. New York: Vintage.

Garfield, Simon (1986) *Expensive Habits*. London: Faber and Faber.

Garnham, Nicholas (1990) *Capitalism and Communication*. London: Sage.

Garnham, Nicholas (1996) 'Convergence between telecommunications and audio-visual: consequences for the rules governing the information market: regulatory issues'. Brussels: European Commission, Legal Advisory Board.

Garnham, Nicholas (1998) 'Media policy', in Adam Briggs and Paul Cobley (eds), *The Media: An Introduction*. Harlow: Addison Wesley Longman. pp. 210–23.

Garnham, Nicholas (2000) *Emancipation, the Media and Modernity*. Oxford: Oxford University Press.

Garnham, Nicholas (2001) 'Afterword: the cultural commodity and cultural policy', in Sara Selwood (ed.), *The UK Cultural Sector*. London: Policy Studies Institute. pp. 445–58.

Garnham, Nicholas (2004) 'Class analysis and the information society as mode of production', *Javnost/The Public*, 11(3): 93–104.

Garnham, Nicholas (2005) 'From cultural to creative industries: an analysis of the implications of the "creative industries" approach to arts and media policy making in the United Kingdom', *International Journal of Cultural Policy*, 11(1): 15–30.

Garnham, Nicholas (2011) 'The political economy of communication revisited', in Janet Wasko, Graham Murdock and Helena Sousa (eds), *The Handbook of Political Economy of Communications*. Malden, MA and Oxford: Wiley-Blackwell. pp. 41–61.

Garofalo, Reebee (1993) 'Whose world, what beat? The transnational music industry, identity, and cultural imperialism', *The World of Music*, 35(2): 16–32.

Gendelman, Irina and Aiello, Giorgia (2010) 'Faces of places: façades as global communication in post-Eastern Bloc urban renewal', in Adam Jaworski and Crispin Thurlow (eds), *Semiotic Landscapes: Language, Image, Space*. London: Continuum. pp. 256–73.

Geraghty, Christine (1991) *Women and Soap Opera*. Cambridge: Polity Press.

Ghemawat, Pankaj and Ghadar, Fariborz (2000) 'The dubious logic of global meg-amergers', *Harvard Business Review*, July/August: 65–71.

Gibson, Lisanne (2008) 'In defence of instrumentality', *Cultural Trends* 17, 4: 247–57.

Gibson, Chris and Robinson, Daniel (2004) 'Creative networks in regional Australia', *Media International Australia*, 112: 83–100.

Giddens, Anthony (1991) *The Consequences of Modernity*. Stanford, CA: Stanford University Press.

Gilder, George (1994) *Life After Television* (revised edn). New York: Norton.

Gill, Ros (2007) *Gender and the Media*. Cambridge: Polity.

Gillespie, Marie (1995) *Television, Ethnicity and Cultural Change*. London: Routledge.

Gillespie, Marie (ed.) (2006) *Media Audiences*. Maidenhead and Milton Keynes: Open University Press/The Open University.

Gillespie, Marie and Toynbee, Jason (eds) (2006) *Analysing Media Texts*. Maidenhead and Milton Keynes: Open University Press/The Open University.

Gillett, Charlie (1971) *The Sound of the City*. London: Sphere.

Gillmor, Dan (2004) *We the Media*. New York: O'Reilly.

Gilroy, Paul (1993) *The Black Atlantic*. London: Verso.

Gitlin, Todd (1983) *Inside Prime Time*. New York: Pantheon Books.

Gitlin, Todd (1997) 'Introduction', in Patricia Aufderheide, Erik Barnouw, Richard M. Cohen, Thomas Frank, Todd Gitlin, David Lieberman, Mark Crispin Miller, Gene Roberts and Thomas Schatz (eds), *Conglomerates and the Media*. New York: The New Press. pp. 7–13.

Gitlin, Todd (1998) 'The anti-political populism of cultural studies', in Marjorie Ferguson and Peter Golding (eds), *Cultural Studies in Question*. London: Sage. pp. 25–38.

Gitlin, Todd (1999) 'Public sphere or public sphericules?' in James Curran and Tamar Liebes (eds), *Media, Ritual and Identity*. London: Routledge. pp. 168–74.

Glasgow Media Group (1976) *Bad News*. London: Routledge & Kegan Paul.

Glyn, Andrew (2005) *Capitalism Unleashed*. Oxford and New York: Oxford University Press.

Goldberg, David, Prosser, Tony and Verhulst, Stefaan (eds) (1998) *Regulating the Changing Media*. Oxford: Clarendon Press.

Golding, Peter (2000) 'Forthcoming features: information and communications technologies and the sociology of the future', *Sociology*, 34(1): 165–84.

Golding, Peter and Murdock, Graham (2005) 'Culture, communications and political economy', in James Curran and Michael Gurevitch (eds), *Mass Media and Society* (4th edn). London: Arnold. pp. 60–83.

Gomery, Douglas (2005[1986]) *The Hollywood Studio System*. Basingstoke/London: Macmillan/BFI.

Goodwin, Andrew and Gore, Joe (1990) 'World beat and the cultural imperialism debate', *Socialist Review*, 20(3): 63–80.

Grabher, Gernot (2002) 'The project ecology of advertising: tasks, talents and teams', *Regional Studies*, 36(3): 245–62.

Grainge, Paul (2008) *Brand Hollywood*. Abingdon: Routledge.

Grant, Peter S. and Wood, Chris (2004) *Blockbusters and Trade Wars*. Vancouver/Toronto: Douglas & McIntyre.

Gray, Brandon (2011) '2011 previews: sequels – now, more than ever', available at http://boxofficemojo.com/news/

Gray, John (1998) *False Dawn*. London: Granta Books.

Gray, Jonathan (2006) *Watching with the Simpsons*. New York: Routledge.

Greco, Albert N. (1995) 'Mergers and acquistions in the US book industry, 1960–89', in Philip G. Altbach and Edith S. Hoshino (eds), *International Book Publishing: An Encyclopedia*. New York: Garland Publishing. pp. 229–42.

Greco, Albert N. (1996) 'Shaping the future: mergers, acquisitions, and the U.S. publishing, communications, and mass media industries, 1990–1995', *Publishing Research Quarterly*, 12(3): 5–16.

Greco, Albert N. (2005) *The Book Publishing Industry* (2nd edn). Mahwah, NJ: Lawrence Erlbaum.

Greco, Albert, Rodríguez, Clara, Wharton, Robert M. (2007) *The Culture and Commerce of Publishing in the 21st Century*. Stanford, CA: Stanford University Press.

Greenfield, Steve and Osborn, Guy (1994) 'Sympathy for the devil? Contractual constraint and artistic autonomy in the entertainment industry', *Media Law and Practice*, 15: 117–27.

Grindstaff, Laura (2002) *The Money Shot: Trash, Class, and the Making of TV Talk Shows*, Chicago: University of Chicago Press.

Gripsrud, Jostein (1995) *The Dynasty Years*. London: Routledge.

Gronow, Pekka (1998) *An International History of the Recording Industry*. London: Cassell.

Grossberg, Lawrence (1995) 'Cultural studies vs. political economy: is anybody else bored with this debate?', *Critical Studies in Mass Communications*, 12(1): 72–81.

Grover, Ronald (2005) 'The lion, the witch, and the franchise', *Business Week* online, 7 November, available at www.businessweek.com (last accessed September 2006).

Guback, Thomas H. (1985) 'Hollywood's international market', in Tino Balio (ed.), *The American Film Industry*. Madison, WI: University of Wisconsin Press. pp. 463–86.

Hafez, Kai (2007) *The Myth of Media Globalization*. Cambridge and Malden, MA: Polity Press.

Hafner, Katie and Lyon, Matthew (1996) *Where Wizards Stay Up Late*. New York: Simon & Schuster.

Halavais, Alexander (2008) *Search Engine Society*. Cambridge: Polity.

Hall, Stuart (1992) 'Cultural studies and its theoretical legacies', in Lawrence Grossberg, Cary Nelson and Paula Treichler (eds), *Cultural Studies*. London: Routledge. pp. 286–94.

Hall, Stuart (1994) 'Cultural identity and diaspora', in Patrick Williams and Laura Chrisman (eds), *Colonial Discourse and Post-colonial Theory*. Hemel Hempstead: Harvester Wheatsheaf. pp. 392–403.

Hall, Stuart (1997a) 'The centrality of culture: notes on the cultural revolutions of our time', in Kenneth Thompson (ed.), *Media and Cultural Regulation*. London: Sage. pp. 207–38.

Hall, Stuart (ed.) (1997b) *Representation*. London: Sage.

Hall, Stuart and Jacques, Martin (eds) (1990) *New Times*. London: Lawrence & Wishart.

Hallin, Daniel C. (1986) *The "Uncensored War"*. New York: Oxford University Press.

Hallin, Daniel C. (1994) *We Keep America on Top of the World*. London: Routledge.

Hallin, Daniel C. (2000) 'Commercialism and professionalism in the American news media', in James Curran and Michael Gurevitch (eds), *Mass Media and Society* (3rd edn). London: Arnold. pp. 218–37.

Hallin, Daniel (2008) 'Neoliberalism, social movements and change in media systems in the late twentieth century', in in David Hesmondhalgh and Jason Toynbee (eds.), *The Media and Social Theory*. Abingdon and New York: Routledge. pp. 43-58.

Hallin, Daniel C. and Mancini, Paolo (2004) *Comparing Media Systems*. Cambridge: CUP.

Hamelink, Cees (1983) *Cultural Autonomy in Global Communications*. London: Longman.

Hardy, Jonathan (2004) 'Safe in their hands? New Labour and public service broadcasting', *Soundings*, 27: 100–14.

Hardy, Jonathan (2008) *Western Media Systems*. Abingdon and New York: Routledge.

Hardy, Jonathan (2010) *Cross-Media Promotion*. New York: Peter Lang.

Hargittai, Eszter and Walejko, Gina (2008) 'The participation divide: content creation and sharing in the digital age', *Information, Communication and Society*, 11(2): 239–56.

Harrison, Bennett (1994) *Lean and Mean*. New York: Basic Books.

Hartley, John (1999) *Uses of Television*. London: Routledge.

Hartley, John (ed.) (2005) *Creative Industries*. Malden, MA: Blackwell.

Hartley, John and Cunningham, Stuart (2001) 'Creative industries: from blue poles to fat pipes', in Malcolm Gillies (ed.), *The National Humanities and Social Sciences Summit: Position Papers*. Canberra: Department of Education Science and Training.

Harvey, David (1989) *The Condition of Postmodernity*. Oxford: Blackwell.

Harvey, David (2005) *A Brief History of Neoliberalism*. Oxford: Oxford University Press.

Harvey, David (2010) *The Enigma of Capitalism*. London: Profile.

Hatch, Martin (1989) 'Popular music in Indonesia', in Simon Frith (ed.), *World Music, Politics and Social Change*. Manchester: Manchester University Press. pp. 47–67.

Hauser, Arnold (1962 [1951]) *The Social History of Art*. London: Routledge and Kegan Paul.

Havens, Timothy (2006) *Global Television Marketplace*. London: BFI.

Havens, Timothy, Lotz, Amanda D. and Tinic, Serra (2011) 'Critical media industry studies: a research approach', *Communication, Culture and Critique* 2,2: 234-53.

Havens, Timothy and Lotz, Amanda D. (2012) *Understanding Media Industries*. New York: Oxford University Press.

Haynes, Richard (2005) *Media Rights and Intellectual Property*. Edinburgh: Edinburgh University Press.

Healy, Kieran (2002) 'What's new for culture in the new economy?', *Journal of Arts Management, Law and Society,* 32(2): 86–103.

Hearn, Alison (2008) 'Variations on the branded self: theme, invention, improvisation and inventory', in David Hesmondhalgh and Jason Toynbee (eds.), *The Media and Social Theory*. Abingdon and New York: Routledge. pp. 194–209.

Held, David, McGrew, Anthony, Goldblatt, David and Perraton, Jonathan (1999) *Global Transformations*. Cambridge: Polity Press.

Henwood, Doug (2003) *After the New Economy*. New York: The New Press.

Herman, Edward S. and Chomsky, Noam (1988) *Manufacturing Consent*. New York: Pantheon.

Herman, Edward S. and McChesney, Robert W. (1997) *The Global Media*. London: Cassell.

Hermes, Joke (1995) *Reading Women's Magazines*. Cambridge. Polity Press.

Hesmondhalgh, David (1996) 'Flexibility, post-Fordism and the music industries', *Media, Culture and Society*, 15(3): 469–88.

Hesmondhalgh, David (1997) 'Post-punk's attempt to democratise the music industry: the success and failure of Rough Trade', *Popular Music*, 16(3): 255–74.

Hesmondhalgh, David (1999) 'Indie: the aesthetics and institutional politics of a popular music genre', *Cultural Studies*, 13(1): 34–61.

Hesmondhalgh, David (2002) *The Cultural Industries*. London: Sage.

Hesmondhalgh, David (2005) 'Producing celebrity', in Jessica Evans and David Hesmondhalgh (eds), *Understanding Media: Inside Celebrity*. Maidenhead and Milton Keynes: Open University Press/The Open University. pp. 97–134.

Hesmondhalgh, David (2006a) 'Bourdieu, the media and cultural production', *Media, Culture and Society,* 28(2): 211–32.

Hesmondhalgh, David (ed.) (2006b) *Media Production*. Maidenhead and Milton Keynes: Open University Press/The Open University.

Hesmondhalgh, David (2007) *The Cultural Industries* (2nd edn). London: Sage.

Hesmondhalgh, David (2009a) 'Politics, theory and method in media industries research', in Jennifer Holt and Alisa Perren (eds), *Media Industries*. Malden, MA: Blackwell. pp. 245–55.

Hesmondhalgh, David (2009b) 'The digitalisation of music', in Paul Jeffcut and Andy C. Pratt (eds), *Creativity and Innovation in the Cultural Economy*. London: Routledge. pp 57–73.

Hesmondhalgh, David (2010a) 'Media industry studies, media production studies', in J. Curran (ed.), *Media and Society* (5th edn). London: Arnold. pp. 145–63.

Hesmondhalgh, David (2010b) 'User-generated content, free labour and the cultural industries', *Ephemera: Theory and Politics in Organization*, 10(3–4): 267–84.

Hesmondhalgh, David and Baker, Sarah (2008) 'Creative work and emotional labour in the television industry', *Theory, Culture and Society* 25: 97-118.

Hesmondhalgh, David and Baker, Sarah (2011a) *Creative Labour: Media Work in the Cultural Industries*. Abingdon and New York: Routledge.

Hesmondhalgh, David and Baker, Sarah (2011b) 'Towards a political economy of creative labour', in Janet Wasko, Graham Murdock and Helena Sousa (eds), *Handbook of Political Economy of Communications*. Oxford and Malden, MA: Blackwell. pp. 381–400.

Hesmondhalgh, David and Toynbee, Jason (2008) 'Why media studies needs better social theory', in David Hesmondhalgh and Jason Toynbee (eds), *The Media and Social Theory*. Abingdon and New York: Routledge. pp 1–24.

Hill, Annette (2005) *Reality TV*. Abingdon: Routledge.

Hindman, Matthew (2009) *The Myth of Digital Democracy*. Princeton: Princeton University Press.

Hirsch, Paul M. (1990/1972) 'Processing fads and fashions: an organization-set analysis of cultural industry systems', *American Journal of Sociology*, 77: 639–59.

Hirsch, Paul M. (2000) 'Cultural industries revisited', *Organization Science*, 11(3): 356–61.

Hjarvard, Stig (2008) 'The mediatisation of society: a theory of the media as agents of social and cultural change', *Nordicom Review*, 29(2): 105–33.

Hobsbawm, Eric (1995) *Age of Extremes*. London: Abacus.

Hoffman-Reim, Wolfgang (1996) *Regulating Media*. New York: Guilford Press.

Holden, John (2004) *Capturing Cultural Value*. London: Demos.

Holt, Jennifer (2003) 'Vertical vision: deregulation, industrial economy and prime-time design' in Mark Jancovich and James Lyons (eds), *Quality Popular Television*. London: BFI Publishing. pp. 11–31.

Holt, Jennifer (2011) *Empires of Entertainment*. New Brunswick: Rutgers University Press.

Holt, Jennifer and Perren, Alisa (eds) (2009) *Media Industries*. Oxford: Wiley-Blackwell.

Horwitz, Robert B. (1989) *The Irony of Regulatory Reform*. New York: Oxford University Press.

Horwitz, Robert B. (2005) 'On media concentration and the diversity question', *The Information Society*, 21(3): 181–204.

Hoskins, Colin, McFadyen, Stuart and Finn, Adam (1997) *Global Television and Film*. Oxford: Oxford University Press.

Hoskins, Colin, McFadyen, Stuart and Finn, Adam (2004) *Media Economics*. Thousand Oaks, CA: Sage.

Hotelling, Harold (1929) 'Stability in competition', *Economic Journal*, 34: 41–57.

Howard, Philip (2010) *The Digital Origins of Dictatorship and Democracy*. New York and Oxford: Oxford University Press.

Howard, Toby (1998) 'Survey of European advertising expenditure, 1980–1996', *International Journal of Advertising*, 17(1): 115–24.

Howkins, John (2001) *The Creative Economy*. London: Allen Lane.

Huet, Armel, Ion, Jacques, Lefebvre, Alain and Miège, Bernard (1978) *Capitalisme et industries culturelles*. Grenoble: Presses Universitaires de Grenoble.

Hui, Desmond (2006) 'From cultural to creative industries: strategies for Chaoyang District Beijing', *International Journal of Cultural Industries* 9: 317–331.

Humphreys, Peter J. (1996) *Mass Media and Media Policy in Western Europe*. Manchester: Manchester University Press.

Hunter, Dan, Lobato, Ramon, Richardson, Megan and Thomas, Julian (eds) (2012) *Amateur Media*. Abingdon and New York: Routledge.

IDATE (2010) *TV 2010 Markets and Trends, Facts and Figures*. Montpellier: IDATE.

IJOA (1998a) 'Africa and the Middle East – focus on the smaller adspend regions', *International Journal of Advertising*, 17(4): 515–20.

IJOA (1998b) 'Adspend in the Americas – a tale of two regions', *International Journal of Advertising*, 17(3): 393–8.

IJOA (2000) 'World advertising expenditure', *International Journal of Advertising*, 19(1): 139–44.

Introna, Lucas D. and Nissenbaum, Helen (2000) 'Shaping the web: why the politics of search engines matters', *The Information Society*, 16: 169–85.

Iosifides, Petros (1997) 'Methods of measuring media concentration', *Media, Culture and Society*, 19: 643–63.

Iwabuchi, Koichi (2002) *Recentering Globalization*. Durham, NC: Duke University Press.

Iwabuchi, Koichi (2003) 'Feeling glocal: Japan in the global TV format business', in Albert Moran and Michael Keane (eds), *Television Across Asia*. London: Routledge. pp. 21–35.

Iwabuchi, Koichi (2010) 'Globalization, East Asian media cultures and their publics', *Asian Journal of Communication*, 20(2): 197–212.

Jackson, Peter, Stevenson, Nick and Brooks, Kate (2001) *Making Sense of Men's Magazines*. Cambridge: Polity Press.

Jackson, William (2009) *Economics, Culture and Social Theory*. Cheltenham: Edward Elgar.

Jakobsson, Peter and Stiernstedt, Fredrik (2010) 'Pirates of Silicon Valley: state of exception and dispossession in Web 2.0', *First Monday* [Online], Volume 15, Number 7 (7 July).

Jakubowicz, Karol (2004) 'Ideas in our heads: introduction of PSB as part of media system change in Central and Eastern Europe', *European Journal of Communication*, 19(1): 53–75.

Jarvie, Ian (1992) *Hollywood's Overseas Campaign*. Cambridge: Cambridge University Press.

Jayne, Mark (2004) 'Culture that works? Creative industries development in a working-class city', *Capital and Class*, 84: 199–210.

Jenkins, Henry (2000) 'Art form for the digital age', *Technology Review*, 103(5): 117–19.

Jenkins, Henry (2006) *Convergence Culture*. New York: NYU Press.

Jensen, Pia Majbritt (2007) *TV Format Adaptation in a Transnational Perspective*. PhD dissertation, Aarhus University, Aarhus.

Jhally, Sut and Livant, Bill (1986) 'Watching as working: the valorization of audience consciousness', *Journal of Communication*, 36(3): 124–43.

Jin, Dal Yong (2011) 'Deconvergence and deconsolidation in the global media industries: the rise and fall of (some) media conglomerates', in Dwayne Winseck and Dal Yong Jin (eds), *The Political Economies of Media*. London: Bloomsbury Academic. pp. 167–82.

Johnson, Richard (1986/7) 'What is cultural studies anyway?' *Social Text*, 6: 38–90.

Johnson, Steven (2005) *Everything Bad is Good for You*. London: Allen Lane.

Jones, Candace (1996) 'Careers in project networks: the case of the film industry' in Michael Arthur and Denise Rousseau (eds), *The Boundaryless Career*. New York and Oxford: OUP. pp. 58–75.

Jones, Geoffrey, Arora, Namrata, Mishra, Surachita and Lefort, Alexis (2008) *Can Bollywood Go Global?* Boston, MA: Harvard Business School.

Jones, Paul (2004) *Raymond Williams's Sociology of Culture*. Basingstoke: Palgrave Macmillan.

Jordan, Tim (1998) *Cyberpower*. Abingdon: Routledge.

Kahn-Harris, Keith (2007) *Extreme Metal*. Oxford: Berg.

Karagiannis, Thomas, Broido, Andre, Brownlee, Nevil, claffy, kc and Faloutsos, Michalis (2004) 'Is P2P dying or just hiding?', available at www.caida.org/outreach/papers (last accessed September 2006).

Kato, Hidetoshi (1998) 'Japan', in Anthony Smith with Richard Paterson (eds), *Television: An International History* (2nd edn). Oxford: Oxford University Press.

Kealy, Edward R. (1990/1974) 'From craft to art: the case of sound mixers and popular music', in Simon Frith and Andrew Goodwin (eds), *On Record*. New York: Pantheon. pp. 207–20.

Keane, John (1991) *The Media and Democracy*. Cambridge: Polity Press.

Keane, Michael (2004) 'Asia: new growth areas', in Albert Moran and Michael Keane (eds), *Television Across Asia*. London: RoutledgeCurzon. pp.9–20.

Keane, Michael, Fung, Anthony and Moran, Albert (2007) *New Television, Globalisation and the East Asian Cultural Imagination*. Hong Kong: Hong Kong University Press.

Keat, Russell and Abercrombie, Nicholas (eds) (1991) *Enterprise Culture*. London: Routledge.

Keen, Andrew (2007) *The Cult of the Amateur*. London and Boston: Nicholas Brealey.

Kelly, Mary, Mazzoleni, Gianpetro and McQuail, Denis (eds) (2004) *The Media in Europe*. London: Sage.

Kennedy, Helen (2011) *Net Work*. Basingstoke: Palgrave Macmillan.

Kerr, Aphra (2006) *Digital Games*. London: Sage.

Kittler, Friedrich (2011[2002]) *Optical Media*. Cambridge: Polity.

Kit-wai Ma, Eric (2000) 'Rethinking media studies: the case of China', in James Curran and Myung-Jin Park (eds), *De-Westernizing Media Studies*. London: Routledge. pp. 21–34.

Klein, Bethany (2009) *As Heard on TV*. Burlington: Ashgate.

Kleinsteuber, Hans J. (1998) 'The digital future', in Denis McQuail and Karen Siune (eds), *Media Policy*. London: Sage. pp. 60–74.

Kline, Stephen, Dyer-Witherford, Nick and De Peuter, Greg (2003) *Digital Play*. Montreal: McGill-Queen's University Press.

Klinenberg, Eric (2007) *Fighting for Air*. New York: Metropolitan Books.

KMU Forschung Austria (2003) 'First report on creative industries in Austria'. Vienna: KMU Forschung Austria.

Kot, Greg (2009) *Ripped*. New York: Scribner.

Kraidy, Marwan M. and Khalil, Joe F. (2009) *Arab Television Industries*. Basingstoke: Palgrave Macmillan/British Film Institute.

Kraidy, Marwan and Sender, Katherine (eds) (2010) *The Politics of Reality Television*. New York: Routledge.

Krippner, Greta (2005) 'The financialization of the American economy,' *Socio-Economic Review* 3:173–208.

Kulturdokumentation, Mediacult and Wifo (2004) 'An analysis of the economic potential of the creative industries in Vienna'. Vienna: Kulturdokumentation, Medicault and Wifo.

Küng, Lucy, Picard, Robert and Towse, Ruth (eds) (2008) *The Internet and the Mass Media*. Los Angeles and London: Sage.

Lacroix, Jean-Guy and Tremblay, Gaëtan (1997) 'The "Information Society" and cultural industries theory', *Current Sociology*, 48(4): 1–62.

Laing, Dave (1985) *One Chord Wonders*. Buckingham: Open University Press.

Laing, Dave (1986) 'The music industry and the "cultural imperialism" thesis', *Media, Culture and Society*, 8(3): 331–41.

Laing, Dave (1992) '"Sadeness", scorpions and single markets: national and transnational trends in European popular music', *Popular Music*, 11(2): 127–40.

Laing, Dave (2004) 'Copyright, politics and the international music industry', in Simon Frith and Lee Marshall (eds), *Music and Copyright* (2nd edn). Edinburgh: Edinburgh University Press. pp. 70–85.

Lampel, Joseph, Shamsie, Jamal and Lant, Theresa K. (2006) *The Business of Culture*. Mahwah, NJ and London: Lawrence Erlbaum.

Lanchester, John (2010) *Whoops*. London: Penguin.

Landry, Charles (2000) *The Creative City*. London: Earthscan.

Landry, Charles and Bianchini, Franco (1995) *The Creative City*. London: Demos.

Lane, Anthony (2003) *Nobody's Perfect*. London: Allen Lane.

Lane, Anthony (2005) 'New frontiers', *The New Yorker*, 12 December, available at http://www. newyorker.com/critics/content/articles/051212cri_cinema (last accessed October 2006).

Lash, Scott and Urry, John (1994) *Economies of Signs and Space*. London: Sage.

Lax, Stephen (2008) *Media and Communication Technologies*. Basingstoke: Palgrave Macmillan.

Leadbeater, Charles (2000) *Living on Thin Air*. London: Penguin.

Leadbeater, Charles and Oakley, Kate (1999) *The Independents*. London: Demos.

Lee, Chin-Chuan (ed.) (2003) *Chinese Media, Global Contexts*. London: RoutledgeCurzon. pp. 237–56.

Lee, David (2009) *Precarious Creativity: Working Lives in the UK Television Industry*. PhD thesis, Goldsmiths, University of London.

Lee, Micky (2011) 'Google ads and the blindspot debate' *Media, Culture & Society*, 33(3): 433–47.

Lent, John A. (1990) *The Asian Film Industry*. London: Christopher Helm.

Lent, John A. (1998) 'The animation industry and its offshore factories', in Gerald Sussman and John A. Lent (eds), *Global Productions*. Cresskill, NJ: Hampton Press. pp. 239–54.

Leong, Anthony C.Y. (2002) *Korean Cinema*. Bloomington, IN: Trafford.

Lerner, Preston (1999) 'Shadow force', *Los Angeles Times Magazine*, 7 November.

Lessig, Lawrence (2001) *The Future of Ideas*. New York: Random House.

Lessig, Lawrence (2008) *Remix*. New York: Penguin.

Levitas, Ruth (1998) *The Inclusive Society?* Basingstoke: Palgrave Macmillan.

Levy, Emanuel (1999) *Cinema of Outsiders*. New York: New York University Press.

Liebes, Tamar and Katz, Elihu (1993) *The Export of Meaning*. Cambridge: Polity Press.

Ling, Rich and Donner, Jonathan (2009) *Mobile Communication*. Cambridge: Polity.

Lister, Martin, Dovey, Jon, Giddings, Seth, Grant, Iain and Kelly, Kieran (2003) *New Media: A Critical Introduction*. London: Routledge.

Little, Matthew (2005) 'The Western connection', *The Epoch Times*, 19 March, available at www.theepochtimes.com/news/5-3-19/27189.html (last accessed September 2006).

Livingstone, Sonia (2010) *Children and the Internet*. Cambridge: Polity.

Lloyd, Richard (2006) *Neo-Bohemia*. New York and Abingdon: Routledge.

Lobato, Ramon and Fletcher, Lawson (2012) 'Prestige and professionalisation at the margins of the journalistic field: the case of music writers', in Hunter, Dan, Lobato, Ramon, Richardson, Megan, Thomas, Julian (eds), *Amateur Media*. New York and Abingdon: Routledge.

Lomax, Alan (1978/1968) *Folk Song Style and Structure*. New Brunswick, NJ: Transaction.

Looseley, David (2004) 'The development of a social exclusion agenda in French cultural policy', *Cultural Trends*, 50: 15–26.

Lopes, Paul D. (1992) 'Innovation and diversity in the popular music industry, 1969–1990', *American Sociological Review*, 57(1): 56–71.

Lorenzen, Mark and Taübe, Florian A. (2008) 'Breakout from Bollywood? The roles of social networks and regulation in the evolution of Indian film industry', *Journal of International Management*, 14: 286–299.

Lotz, Amanda D. (2004) 'Textual (im)possibilities in the U.S. post-network era: negotiating production and promotion processes on Lifetime's *Any Day Now*', *Critical Studies in Mass Communication*, 21(1): 22–43.

Lotz, Amanda D. (2007) *The Television Will Be Revolutionized*. New York: New York University Press.

Lovink, Geert and Rossiter, Ned (eds) (2007) *My Creativity Reader*. Amsterdam: Institute of Network Cultures.

Lowery, Shearon and DeFleur, Melvin L. (1995) *Milestones in Mass Communication Research* (3rd edn). London: Longman.

Lundby, Knut (ed.) (2009) *Mediatization*. New York: Peter Lang.

Lyotard, Jean-François (1984) *The Postmodern Condition*. Minneapolis, MN: University of Minnesota Press.

MacDonald, Dwight (1963) *Against the American Grain*. London: Victor Gollancz.

Magder, Ted and Burston, Jonathan (2002) 'Whose Hollywood? Changing forms and relations inside the North American entertainment economy', in Vincent Mosco and Dan Schiller (eds), *Continental Integration for Cybercapitalism*. Lanham, MD: Rowman & Littlefield. pp. 207–34.

Mancini, Paolo and Hallin, Daniel (2001) 'Italy's television, Italy's democracy', posted 19 July, *OpenDemocracy*, available at www.opendemocracy.net/media-publicservice/ article_59. jsp (last accessed September 2006).

Mankekar, Purnima (1999) *Screening Culture, Viewing Politics*. Durham, NC: Duke University Press.

Mann, Charles C. (2000) 'The heavenly jukebox', *Atlantic Monthly*, 286(3): 39–73.

Mansell, Robin (1993) *The New Telecommunications*. London: Sage.

Marchetti, Gina and Kam, Tan See (2007) *Hong Kong Film, Hollywood, and the New Global Cinema*. London: Routledge.

Marglin, Stephen A. and Schor, Juliet B. (eds) (1992) *The Golden Age of Capitalism*. Oxford: Clarendon.

Marr, Merissa (2005) 'Selling "Narnia" ', *The Wall Street Journal* online, 25 November, available at http://online.wsj.com (last accessed September 2006).

Marsh, David (2002) 'Pluralism and the study of British politics: it is always the happy hour for men with money, knowledge and power', in Colin Hay (ed.), *British Politics Today*. Cambridge: Polity Press. pp.14–37.

Marshall, Lee (2006) *Bootlegging*. London: Sage.

Martin, Ron and Sunley, Peter (2003) 'Deconstructing clusters: chaotic concept or policy panacea?' *Journal of Economic Geography*, 3(1): 5–35.

Maslow, Abraham (1987/1954) *Motivation and Personality* (3rd edn). New York: Harper and Row.

Mastrini, Guillermo and Becerra, Martin (2011) 'Media ownership, oligarchies, and globalization: media concentration in South America', in Winseck, Dwayne and Jin, Dal Y. (eds) (2011) *The Political Economies of Media*. London: Bloomsbury Academic. pp. 66-83.

Mato, Daniel (2009) 'All industries are cultural', *Cultural Studies*, 23(1): 70–87(18).

Matos, Carolina (2008) *Journalism and Political Democracy*. Lanham, MD: Lexington.

Mattelart, Armand (1991) *Advertising International*. London: Routledge/Comedia.

Mattelart, Armand and Mattelart, Michèle (1990) *The Carnival of Images*. New York: Bergin & Garvey.

Mattelart, Armand and Mattelart, Michèle (1998) *Theories of Communication*. London: Sage.

Maxwell, Richard (1991) 'The image is gold: value, the audience commodity and fetishism', *Journal of Film and Video*, 43:1–2 and 29–45.

Maxwell, Richard (ed.) (2001) *Culture Works*. Minneapolis, MN: University of Minnesota Press.

Maxwell, Richard (2003) *Herbert Schiller*. Lanham, MD: Rowman & Littlefield.

May, Christopher (2000) *A Global Political Economy of Intellectual Property Rights*. Abingdon: Routledge.

May, Christopher (2004) 'Capacity building and the (re) production of intellectual property rights', *Third World Quarterly*, 25(5): 821–37.

May, Christopher (2007) *The World Intellectual Property Organisation*. Abingdon: Routledge.

Mayer, Vicki (2011) *Below the Line*. Durham, NC: Duke University Press.

Mayer, Vicki, Banks, Miranda J. and Caldwell, John Thornton (eds) (2009) *Production Studies: Cultural Studies of Media Industries*. New York and Abingdon: Routledge.

Mazzoleni, Giuseppe (1995) 'Towards a videocracy: Italian political communication at a turning point', *European Journal of Communication*, 10(3): 291–319.

McAllister, Matthew P. (2000) 'From flick to flack: the increased emphasis on marketing by media entertainment corporations', in Robin Andersen and Lance Strate (eds), *Critical Studies in Media Commercialism*. Oxford: Oxford University Press. pp. 101–22.

McAllister, Matthew P. (2005) 'Television advertising as textual and economic systems', in Janet Wasko (ed.), *A Companion to Television*. Malden, MA and Oxford: Blackwell.

McChesney, Robert W. (1993) *Telecommunications, Mass Media and Democracy*. New York and Oxford: Oxford University Press.

McChesney, Robert W. (1999) *Rich Media, Poor Democracy*. Urbana and Chicago, IL: University of Illinois Press.

McChesney, Robert W. (2004) *The Problem of the Media*. New York: Monthly Review Press.

McChesney, Robert W. (2008) *The Political Economy of Media*. New York: Monthly Review Press.

McChesney, Robert W. and Nichols, John (2010) *The Death and Life of American Journalism*. Philadelphia, PA: Nation Books.

McChesney, Robert W. and Pickard, Victor (eds) (2011) *Will the Last Reporter Please Turn Out the Lights*. New York: The New Press.

McDonald, Paul and Wasko, Janet (eds) (2008) *The Contemporary Hollywood Film Industry*. Oxford: Wiley-Blackwell.

McGuigan, Jim (1992) *Cultural Populism*. London: Routledge.

McGuigan, Jim (1996) *Culture and the Public Sphere*. London: Routledge.

McGuigan, Jim (1998) 'What price the public sphere?', in Daya Thussu (ed.), *Electronic Empires*. London: Arnold. pp. 91–107.

McLeod, Kembrew (2001) *Owning Culture*. New York: Peter Lang.

McQuail, Denis (1992) *Media Performance*. London: Sage.

McQuail, Denis (2005) *McQuail's Mass Communication Theory* (4th edn.) London: Sage.

McQuail, Denis and Siune, Karen (eds) (1998) *Media Policy*. London: Sage. pp. 95–106.

McRobbie, Angela (1998) *British Fashion Design*. London: Routledge.

McRobbie, Angela (2002) 'Clubs to companies: notes on the decline of political culture in speeded up creative worlds', *Cultural Studies,* 16: 516–31.

McRobbie, Angela (2005) *The Uses of Cultural Studies*. London: Sage.

McRobbie, Angela (2008) *The Aftermath of Feminism*. London: Sage.

Meehan, Eileen (1991) '"Holy commodity fetish, Batman!" The political economy of a commercial intertext', in Roberta E. Pearson and William Urrichio (eds), *The Many Lives of the Batman*. London: BFI and Routledge, Chapman and Hall. pp. 47–65.

Meehan, Eileen (2000) 'Leisure or labor? Fan ethnography and political economy', in Ingunn Hagen and Janet Wasko (eds), *Consuming Audiences? Production and Reception in Media Research*. Creskill, NJ: Hampton Press. pp. 71–92.

Meier, Werner A. and Trappel, Josef (1998) 'Media concentration and the public interest', in Denis McQuail and Karen Siune (eds), *Media Policy*. London: Sage. pp. 38–59.

Menand, Louis (2005) 'Gross points: is the blockbuster the end of cinema?', *New Yorker*, 7 February.

Menger, Pierre-Michel (1999) 'Artistic labour markets and careers', *Annual Review of Sociology*, 25: 541–74.

Menger, Pierre-Michel (2006) 'Artistic labor markets: contingent work, excess supply and occupational risk management' in Victor Ginsburgh and David Throsbt (eds) *Handbook of the Economics of Art and Culture*. Oxford: Elsevier, pp. 765–812.

Merritt, Greg (2000) *Celluloid Mavericks*. New York: Thunder's Mouth Press.

Miège, Bernard (1979) 'The cultural commodity', *Media, Culture and Society*, 1: 297–311.

Miège, Bernard (1987) 'The logics at work in the new cultural industries', *Media, Culture and Society*, 9: 273–89.

Miège, Bernard (1989) *The Capitalization of Cultural Production*. New York: International General.

Miège, Bernard (2000) *Les industries du contenu face à l'ordre informationnel*. Grenoble: Presses Universitaires de Grenoble.

Miller, Daniel (2011) *Tales from Facebook*. Cambridge: Polity.

Miller, David (1998) 'Promotional strategies and media power', in Adam Briggs and Paul Cobley (eds), *The Media: An Introduction*. Harlow: Addison Wesley Longman. pp. 65–80.

Miller, David and Philo, Greg (2000) 'Cultural compliance and critical media studies', *Media, Culture and Society*, 22 (6): 831–9.

Miller, Mark Crispin (1997) 'The publishing industry', in Patricia Aufderheide, Erik Barnouw, Richard M. Cohen, Thomas Frank, Todd Gitlin, David Liebermann, Mark Crispin Miller, Gene Roberts and Thomas Schatz (eds), *Conglomerates and the Media*. New York: The New York Press. pp. 107–34.

Miller, Paul (2005) 'Web 2.0: building the new library', *Ariadne*, 45, October, available at www.ariadne.ac.uk/issue45/miller (last accessed September 2006).

Miller, Toby (2010) *Television Studies*. New York: Routledge.

Miller, Toby, Govil, Nitin, McMurria, John, Maxwell, Richard and Wang, Ting (2005) *Global Hollywood 2*. London: British Film Institute.

Mitchell, Tony (ed.) (2001) *Global Noise*. Middletown, CT: Wesleyan University Press.

Mommaas, Hans (2004) 'Cultural clusters and the post-industrial city: towards the remapping of urban cultural policy', *Urban Studies*, 41: 507–32.

Montgomery, Sarah S. and Robinson, Michael D. (1993) 'Visual artists in New York: what's special about person and place?' *Journal of Cultural Economics*, 17: 17–39.

Moran, Albert (1998) *Copycat TV*. Luton: University of Luton Press.

Moran, Albert and Keane, Michael (eds) (2004) *Television Across Asia*. London: RoutledgeCurzon.

Moran, Joe (1997) 'The role of multimedia conglomerates in American trade book publishing', *Media, Culture and Society*, 19: 441–55.

Morin, Edgar (1962) *L'esprit du temps*. Paris: Bernard Grasset.

Morley, David (1986) *Family Television*. London: Comedia.

Morley, David and Chen, Kuan-Hsing (eds) (1996) *Stuart Hall*. London: Routledge.

Morris, Meaghan (1992) 'The man in the mirror: David Harvey's "condition" of post-modernity', *Theory, Culture and Society*, 9: 253–79.

Morris, Nancy and Waisbord, Silvio (eds) (2001) *Media and Globalization*. Lanham, Maryland and Oxford: Rowman & Littlefield.

Mosco, Vincent (1996) *The Political Economy of Communication*. London: Sage.

Mosco, Vincent (2004) *The Digital Sublime*. Cambridge, MA: MIT Press.

Mosco, Vincent (2009) *The Political Economy of Communication* (2nd edn). London: Sage.

Mosco, Vincent and McKercher, Catherine (2009) *The Laboring of Communication*. Lanham, MD: Lexington.

Murdock, Graham (1982) 'Large corporations and the control of the communications industries', in Michael Gurevitch, Tony Bennett, James Curran and Janet Wollacott (eds), *Culture, Society and the Media*. London: Methuen. pp. 118–50.

Murdock, Graham (1978) 'Blindspots about Western Marxism: a reply to Dallas Smythe', *Canadian Journal of Political and Social Theory* 2(2): 120–9.

Murdock, Graham (1990) 'Redrawing the map of the communications industries: concentration and ownership in the era of privatization', in Marjorie Ferguson (ed.), *Public Communication: The New Imperatives*. London: Sage. pp. 1–15.

Murdock, Graham (2000a) 'Digital futures: European television in the age of convergence', in Jan Wieten, Graham Murdock and Peter Dahlgren (eds), *Television Across Europe*. London: Sage. pp. 35–57.

Murdock, Graham (2000b) 'Reconstructing the ruined tower: contemporary communications and questions of class', in James Curran and Michael Gurevitch (eds), *Mass Media and Society*. London: Arnold.

Murdock, Graham (2011) 'Political economies as moral economies: commodities, gifts, and public goods', in Janet Wasko, Graham Murdock and Helena Sousa (eds), *The Handbook of Political Economy of Communications*. Malden, MA and Oxford: Wiley-Blackwell. pp. 13-40.

Murdock, Graham and Golding, Peter (1974) 'Towards a political economy of the media', in Ralph Miliband (ed.), *Socialist Register 1974*. London: Merlin. pp. 205–34.

Murdock, Graham and Golding, Peter (1977) 'Capitalism, communication and class relations', in James Curran, Michael Gurevitch and Janet Wollacott (eds), *Mass Communication and Society*. London/Milton Keynes: Edward Arnold with The Open University Press. pp. 12–43.

Murdock, Graham and Golding, Peter (1999) 'Common markets: corporate ambitions and communication trends in the UK and Europe', *The Journal of Media Economics*, 12(2): 117–32.

Murdock, Graham and Golding, Peter (2004) 'Dismantling the digital divide: rethinking the dynamics of participation and exclusion', in Andrew Calabrese and Colin Sparks (eds), *Towards a Political Economy of Culture*. Lanham, MD: Rowman & Littlefield. pp. 286–306.

Myerscough, John (1988) *The Economic Importance of the Arts in Britain*. London: Policy Studies Institute.

Naficy, Hamid (1993) *The Making of Exile Cultures*. Minneapolis, MN: University of Minnesota Press.

Napoli, Philip M. (2001) *Foundations of Communications Policy*. New York: Hampton.

Napoli, Philip M. (2003) *Audience Economics*. New York: Columbia University Press.

Napoli, Philip M. (2011) *Audience Evolution*. New York: Columbia University Press.

Neff, Gina (2012) *Venture Labor*. Boston, MA: MIT Press.

Negroponte, Nicholas (1995) *Being Digital*. London: Hodder & Stoughton.

Negus, Keith (1992) *Producing Pop*. London: Edward Arnold.

Negus, Keith (1997) 'The production of culture', in Paul du Gay (ed.), *Production of Culture/ Cultures of Production*. Milton Keynes/London: The Open University/Sage. pp. 67–118.

Negus, Keith (1999) *Music Genres and Corporate Cultures*. London: Routledge.

Negus, Keith (2006) 'Rethinking creative production away from the cultural industries', in James Curran and David Morley (eds), *Media and Cultural Theory*. Abingdon: Routledge. pp. 197–208.

Neuman, W. Russell (1991) *The Future of the Mass Audience*. Cambridge: Cambridge University Press.

Nichols, Randy (forthcoming) Who plays, who pays? Mapping video game production and consumption globally', in Nina Huntemann and Ben Aslinger (eds), *Gaming globally: production, play and place*. New York: Palgrave MacMillan.

Nixon, Sean (1997) 'Circulating culture', in Paul du Gay (ed.), *Production of Culture/Cultures of Production*. Milton Keynes/London: The Open University/Sage. pp. 177–234.

Nixon, Sean (2011) 'From full-service agency to 3-D marketing consultants: "creativity" and organizational change in advertising', in Mark Deuze (ed.), *Managing Media Work*. Thousand Oaks, CA: Sage. pp. 199–209.

Noam, Eli M. (2001) *Interconnecting the Network of Networks*. New York and Oxford: Oxford University Press.

Noam, Eli M. (2009) *Media Ownership and Concentration in America*. New York and Oxford: Oxford University Press.

Norris, Pippa (2001) *Digital Divide*. Cambridge: Cambridge University Press.

Oakley, Kate (2006) 'Include us out—economic development and social policy in the creative industries', *Cultural Trends*,15(4): 255–73.

Oakley, Kate (2011) 'In its own image: New Labour and the cultural workforce', *Cultural Trends*, 20(3–4): 281–9.

O'Connor, Justin (2004) '"A special kind of city knowledge": innovative clusters, tacit knowledge and the "creative city"', *Media International Australia*, 112: 131–49.

O'Connor, Justin (2010) *Arts and Cultural Industries*. Canberra: Australian Council for the Arts.

O'Connor, Justin and Gu, Xin (2012) 'Shanghai: images of modernity', in Yudhishthir Raj Isar, Michael Hoelscher and Helmut K. Anheier (eds),*Cities, Cultural Policy and Governance*. London: Sage.

Ofcom (2006) *Media Literacy Audit: Report on Adult Media Literacy*. London: Ofcom.

Ong, Aihwa (1999) *Flexible Citizenship*. Durham, NC: Duke University Press.

Orlowski, Andrew (2009) 'We were so keen to believe that web 2.0 would make the world a fairer place that we rejected all evidence to the contrary', *New Statesman*, 30 April, available at http://www.newstatesman.com/business/2009/05/

O'Reilly, Tim (2005) 'Web 2.0: compact definition?', *O'Reilly Radar* blog, 1 October, available at http://radar.oreilly.com (accessed September 2006).

Osborne, Thomas (2003) 'Against "creativity": a philistine rant', *Economy and Society* 32,4: 507–25.

Ó Siochrú, Sean, Girard, Bruce and Mahan, Amy (2002) *Global Media Governance: A Beginner's Guide*. Lanham: Rowman & Littlefield.

Østergaard, Bernt Stubbe (1998) 'Convergence: legislative dilemmas', in Denis McQuail and Karen Siune (eds), *Convergence*. London: Sage. pp. 95–6.

Ouellette, Laurie and Hay, James (2008) *Better Living Through Reality TV*. Malden, MA and Oxford: Blackwell.

Padioleau, Jean G. (1987) 'The management of communications', *Media, Culture and Society*, 9: 291–300.

Page, Will and Garland, Eric (2009) 'The long tail of P2P'. London: PRS For Music.

Papathanassopoulos, Stylianos and Negrine, Ralph (2011) *European Media*. Cambridge: Polity.

Passman, Donald S. (1998) *All You Need to Know about the Music Business* (revised and updated edition). London: Penguin.

Patelis, Korinna (1999) 'The political economy of the Internet', in James Curran (ed.), *Media Organizations in Society*. London: Arnold. pp. 84–106.

Paterson, Chris (2011) *The International Television News Agencies*. New York: Peter Lang.

Paterson, Richard (1998) 'Drama and entertainment', in Anthony Smith, with Richard Paterson (eds), *Television: An International History*. Oxford: Oxford University Press. pp. 57–68.

Peacock Report (1986) *The Report of the Committee on Financing the BBC*. London: HMSO.

Peiperl, Maury, Arthur, Michael, Goffee, Rob and Anand, N. (eds) (2002) *Career Creativity*. Oxford: OUP.

Pendakur, Manjunath (1990) 'India', in John A. Lent (ed.), *The Asian Film Industry*. London: Christopher Helm. pp. 229–52.

Peoples, Glenn (2011) 'Business matters: 75,000 albums released in U.S. in 2010 – down 22% from 2009', *Billboard.biz*, 18 February.

Perren, Alisa (2011) 'Producing filmed entertainment', in Mark Deuze (ed.), *Managing Media Work*. Thousand Oaks, CA and London: Sage. pp. 155–64.

Peterson, Richard A. (1976) 'The production of culture: a prolegomenon', in Richard A. Peterson (ed.), *The Production of Culture*. London: Sage. pp. 7–22.

Peterson, Richard A. (1997) *Creating Country Music*. Chicago, IL: University of Chicago Press.

Peterson, Richard A. and Berger, David G. (1971) 'Entrepreneurship in organizations: evidence from the popular music industry', *Administrative Science Quarterly*, 16: 97–107.

Peterson, Richard A. and Berger, David G. (1990/1975) 'Cycles in symbol production: the case of popular music', in Simon Frith and Andrew Goodwin (eds), *On Record*. New York: Pantheon. pp. 140–59.

Peterson, Richard A. and Kern, Roger M. (1996) 'Changing highbrow taste: from snob to omnivore', *American Sociological Review*, 61: 900–7.

Picard, Robert (2002) *The Economics and Financing of Media Companies*. New York: Fordham University Press.

Piore, Michael and Sabel, Charles (1984) *The Second Industrial Divide*. New York: Basic Books.

Pool, Ithiel de Sola (1977) 'The changing flow of television', *Journal of Communication*, 27: 139–49.

Pool, Ithiel de Sola (1983) *Technologies of Freedom*. Cambridge, MA: Harvard University Press.

Poole, Steven (2000) *Trigger Happy*. London: Fourth Estate.

Porat, Marc (1977) *The Information Economy*. Washington, DC: US Department of Commerce.

Porter, Michael (1990) *The competitive advantage of nations*. London: Macmillan.

Powdermaker, Hortense (1951) *Hollywood: The Dream Factory*. London: Secker & Warburg.

Power, Dominic (ed.) (2003) 'Behind the music: profiting from sound: a systems approach to the dynamics of the Nordic music industry – Final report', The Nordic Industrial Fund.

Pratt, Andy C. (2004) 'Creative clusters: towards the governance of the creative industries production system?', *Media International Australia*, 112: 50–66.

Pratt, Andy C. (2005) 'Cultural industries and public policy: an oxymoron?', *International Journal of Cultural Policy*, 11(1): 31–44.

Press, Andrea and Williams, Bruce (2010) *The New Media Environment*. Oxford: Wiley-Blackwell.

Press, Joy (2004) 'Out of the box', *The Village Voice*, 11–17 August, available at www.villagevoice.com/news/0432, press, 55810, 1 html (last accessed September 2006).

Preston, Paschal and Rogers, Jim (2011) 'Social networks, legal innovations and the "new" music industry', *Info* 13,6: 8-19.

Prichard, James (2005) 'Christian stores capitalize on "Narnia" tie-ins', *MSNBC*, Associated Press article, 9 December, available at www.msnbc.msn.com (last accessed September 2006).

Prindle, David F. (1993) *Risky Business*. Boulder, CO: Westview Press.

Queensland Government (2005) 'Creative industries in Australia and Queensland'. Brisbane: Queensland Government.

Quinn, Eithne (2004) *Nothing But a "G" Thang*. New York, NY: Columbia University Press.

Raboy, Marc (ed.) (1997) *Public Broadcasting for the 21st Century*. Luton: University of Luton Press.

Raphael, Chad (2001) 'Untangling the web', in Richard Maxwell (ed.), *Culture Works*. Minneapolis, MN: University of Minnesota Press. pp. 197–224.

Raphael, Chad (2005) *Investigated Reporting*. Urbana, IL: University of Illinois Press.

Rawnsley, Gary and Ming-Yeh Rawnsley (eds) (2010) *Global Chinese Cinema*. Abindgon: Routledge.

Reynolds, Simon (2005) *Rip It Up and Start Again*. London: Faber and Faber.

Rheingold, Howard (1992) *Virtual Reality*. London: Mandarin.

Rice, Ronald E. (2008) *Media Ownership*. Cresskill, NJ: Hampton Press.

Rigby, S.H. (1998) *Marxism* and *History* (2nd edn). Manchester: Manchester University Press.

Ritzer, George and Jurgenson, Nathan (2010) 'Production, consumption, prosumption', *Journal of Consumer Culture*, 10(1): 13.

Robertson, Roland (1990) 'Mapping the global condition: globalization as the central concept', in Mike Featherstone (ed.), *Global Culture*. London: Sage. pp. 15–30.

Roberts, Ken (2004) *The Leisure Industries*. Basingstoke: Palgrave Macmillan.

Robins, Kevin (1997) 'What in the world's going on?', in Paul du Gay (ed.), *Production of Culture/Cultures of Production*. Milton Keynes/London: The Open University/Sage. pp. 11–66.

Robins, Kevin and Cornford, James (1992) 'What is "flexible" about independent producers?', *Screen*, 33(2): 190–200.

Robotham, Don (2005) *Culture, Society and Economy*. London: Sage.

Rønning, Helge and Slaatta, Tore (2011) 'Marketers, publishers, editors: trends in international publishing', *Media, Culture and Society*, 33(7): 1109–20.

Ross, Andrew (1989) *No Respect*. London: Routledge.

Ross, Andrew (ed.) (1998) *No Sweat*. London: Verso.

Ross, Andrew (2000) 'The Mental Labor Problem', *Social Text*, 63, 18 (2): 1–31.

Ross, Andrew (2003) *No Collar*. Philadelphia, PA: Temple University Press.

Ross, Andrew (2009) *Nice Work If You Can Get It*. New York: New York University Press.

Rowan, David (2005) 'Disney's marketing menagerie', *Times Online*, 19 December, available at www.timesonline.co.uk (last accessed September 2006). '"Subdued" $100 million promotional campaign for "Narnia" ', ICV2.com 22 November 2006, available at www.icv2.com (last accessed September 2006).

Ruskin, Gary and Schor, Juliet (2009) 'Every nook and cranny: the dangerous spread of commercialized culture', in Joseph Turow and Matthew P. McAllister (eds), *The Advertising and Consumer Culture Reader*. New York: Routledge. pp. 410–15.

Ryan, Bill (1992) *Making Capital from Culture*. Berlin and New York: Walter de Gruyter.

Sadler, David (1997) 'The global music business as an information industry: reinterpreting economies of culture', *Environment and Planning A*, 29: 1919–36.

Saha, Anamik (2011) 'Negotiating the third space: British Asian independent record labels and the cultural politics of difference', *Popular Music and Society* 34(4): 437–54.

Said, Edward W. (1994) *Culture and Imperialism*. London: Vintage.

Sakr, Naomi (2005) 'Media policy in the Middle East', in James Curran and Michael Gurevitch (eds), *Mass Media and Society* (4th edn). London: Arnold. pp. 234–50.

Sánchez-Tabernero, Alfonso and Carvajal, Miguel (2002) *Media Concentration in the European Market*. Navarra: Universidad de Navarra.

Sánchez-Tabernero, Alfonso, Denton, Alison, Lochon, Pierre-Yves, Mounier, Philippe and Woldt, Runar (1993) *Media Concentration in Europe*. Dusseldorf: The European Institute for the Media.

Sassen, Saskia (1998) *Globalization and its Discontents*. New York: The New Press.

Sassen, Saskia (2000) 'Digital networks and the state', *Theory, Culture and Society*, 17(4): 19–33.

Sayer, Andrew (2000) *Realism and Social Science*. London: Sage.

Schatz, Thomas (1996) *The Genius of the System*. New York: Henry Holt.

Schiller, Dan (1994) 'From culture to information and back again', *Critical Studies in Mass Communication,* 11(1): 93–115.

Schiller, Dan (1997) *Theorizing Communication*. Oxford: Oxford University Press.

Schiller, Dan (1999) *Digital Capitalism*. Cambridge, MA: Harvard University Press.

Schiller, Herbert I. (1969) *Mass Communication and American Empire*. Boston, MA: Beacon Press.

Schiller, Herbert I. (1976) *Communication and Cultural Domination*. White Plains, NY: International Arts and Sciences Press.

Schiller, Herbert I. (1981) *Who Knows*. Norwood, NJ: Ablex.

Schiller, Herbert I. (1989) *Culture, Inc.* Oxford: Oxford University Press.

Schiller, Herbert I. (1998) 'Striving for communication dominance: a half century review', in Daya Thussu (ed.), *Electronic Empires*. London: Arnold. pp. 17–26.

Schlesinger, Philip (1978) *Putting 'Reality' Together*. London: Methuen.

Schlesinger, Philip (2007) 'Creativity: from discourse to doctrine', *Screen,* 48(3): 377–87.

Schlesinger, Philip and Tumber, Howard (1994) *Reporting Crime*. Oxford: Clarendon Press.

Schlesinger, Philip and Waelde, Charlotte (2012) 'Copyright and cultural work: an exploration', *Innovation: The European Journal of Social Science Research,* 25: 11–28.

Schudson, Michael (1993/1984)_*Advertising: the Uneasy Persuasion*. London and New York: Routledge.

Schudson, Michael (2012) *The Sociology of News* (2nd edn). New York: Norton.

Scott, Allen (2000) *The Cultural Economy of Cities*. London: Sage.

Scott, John (1995) *Corporate Business and Capitalist Classes*. Oxford: Oxford University Press.

Scott, Michael (2009) New Zealand's pop renaissance: *a creative industry as after 'neo-liberal' social policy*. PhD thesis, Auckland, NZ: University of Auckland.

Segrave, Kerry (1997) *American Films Abroad*. Jefferson, NC: McFarland & Company.

Shim, Doobo (2006) 'Hybridity and the rise of Korean popular culture in Asia', *Media, Culture and Society*, 28(1): 25–44.

Shirky, Clay (2008) *Here Comes Everybody*. London: Penguin.

Sinclair, John (1996) 'Mexico, Brazil and the Latin world', in John Sinclair, Elizabeth Jacka and Stuart Cunningham (eds), *New Patterns in Global Television*. Oxford: Oxford University Press. pp. 33–66.

Sinclair, John (1999) *Latin American Television*. Oxford: Oxford University Press.

Sinclair, John (2004) 'Latin American and Spanish television', in John Sinclair and Graeme Turner (eds), *Contemporary World Television*. London: BFI. pp. 90–3.

Sinclair, John (2009) 'Latin America's impact on world television markets', in Graeme Turner and Jinna Tay (eds), *Television Studies After TV*. New York and Abingdon: Routledge. pp. 141–8.

Sinclair, John (2011) 'Branding and culture', in Janet Wasko, Graham Murdock and Helena Sousa (eds), *The Handbook of Political Economy of Communications*. Malden, MA and Oxford: Wiley-Blackwell. pp. 206–25.

Sinclair John and Turner, Graeme (eds)(2004) *Contemporary World Television*. London: BFI. pp. 90–3.

Sinclair, John, Jacka, Elizabeth and Cunningham, Stuart (1996) 'Peripheral vision', in John Sinclair, Elizabeth Jacka and Stuart Cunningham (eds), *New Patterns in Global Television*. Oxford: Oxford University Press. pp. 1–32.

Singelmann, Joachim (1978) *From Agriculture to Services*. London: Sage.

Sinha, Nikhil (1997) 'India: television and national politics', in Marc Raboy (ed.), *Public Broadcasting for the 21st Century*. Luton: University of Luton Press. pp. 212–29.

Sinha, Nikhil (2001) 'State transformation and India's telecommunications reform', in Nancy Morris and Silvio Waisbord (eds), *Media and Globalization*. Lanham, MD: Rowman & Littlefield. pp. 55–76.

Siune, Karen and Hultén, Olof (1998) 'Does public broadcasting have a future?', in Denis McQuail and Karen Siune (eds), *Media Policy*. London: Sage. pp. 23–37.

Skeggs, Bev and Wood, Helen (2008) 'Spectacular morality: "reality" television, individualisation and the remaking of the working class', in David Hesmondhalgh and Jason Toynbee (eds), *The Media and Social Theory*. Abingdon and New York: Routledge. pp. 177–93.

Slater, Don and Tonkiss, Fran (2001) *Market Society*. Cambridge: Polity Press.

Smith, Anthony with Paterson, Richard (eds) (1998) *Television: An International History*. Oxford: Oxford University Press.

Smith, Chris (1998) *Creative Britain*. London: Faber and Faber.

Smythe, Dallas (1977) 'Communications: blindspot of Western Marxism', *Canadian Journal of Political and Social Theory*, 12(3): 1–27.

Snickars, Pelle and Vonderau, Patrick (2009)*The YouTube Reader*. Sweden: National Library of Sweden.

Sparks, Colin (2000) 'Media theory after the fall of European communism: why the old models from East and West won't do any more', in James Curran and Myung-Jin Park (eds), *De-Westernizing Media Studies*. London: Routledge. pp. 35–49.

Sparks, Colin (2003) 'Are the Western media really that interested in China?', *Javnost/ The Public,* 10(4): 93–108.

Sparks, Colin (2004) 'The impact of the Internet on the existing media', in Andrew Calabrese and Colin Sparks (eds), *Towards a Political Economy of Culture*. Lanham, MD: Rowman & Littlefield. pp. 307–26.

Sparks Colin (2008) *Globalization, Development and the Mass Media*. London: Sage.

Spigel, Lynn and Olsson, Jan (eds) (2004) *Television After TV*. Durham, NC: Duke University Press.

Spivak, Gayatri Chakravorty (1988) *In Other Worlds*. London: Routledge.

Sreberny, Annabelle (1997) 'The many cultural faces of imperialism', in Peter Golding and Phil Harris (eds), *Beyond Cultural Imperialism*. London: Sage. pp. 49–68.

Sreberny, Annabelle and Khiabany, Gholam (2010) *Blogistan*.New York: I.B. Tauris.

Stahl, Matt (2009) 'Privilege and distinction in production worlds: copyright, collective bargaining and working conditions in media making', in Vicki Mayer, Miranda J. Banks and John Thornton Caldwell (eds), *Production Studies: Cultural Studies of Media Industries*. New York and Abingdon: Routledge. pp. 54–68.

Stahl, Matthew Wheelock (2006) *Reinventing certainties: American popular music and social reproduction*. PhD thesis, University of California, San Diego.

Starosielski, Nicole (2011) 'Underwater flow', *Flow,* 15(1), available at http://flowtv. org/2011/10/underwaterflow/

Steemers, Jeanette (ed.) (1998) *Changing Channels*. Luton: University of Luton Press.

Steemers, Jeanette (2010) *Creating Pre-School Television*. London: Sage.

Stein, Laura (2006) *Speech Rights in America*. Chicago, IL: University of Illinois Press.

Steinert, Heinz (2003) *Culture Industry* (trans. Sally-Ann Spencer). Cambridge: Polity.

Sterling, Christopher H. and Kittross, John M. (2002) *Stay Tuned* (3rd edn). Belmont, CA: Wadsworth.

Stevenson, Nick (1999) *The Transformation of the Media*. Harlow: Addison Wesley Longman.

Stokes, Lisa Oldham and Hoover, Michael (1999) *City on Fire*. London: Verso.

Straubhaar, Joseph D. (1997) 'Distinguishing the global, regional and national levels of world television', in Annabelle Sreberny-Mohammadi, Dwayne Winseck, Jim McKenna and Oliver Boyd-Barrett (eds), *Media in Global Context*. London: Arnold. pp. 284–98.

Straubhaar, Joseph D. (2004) 'Brazilian and Portuguese television', in John Sinclair with Graeme Turner (eds), *Contemporary World Television*. London: BFI. pp. 90–3.

Straubhaar, Joseph D. (2007) *World Television*. Los Angeles and London: Sage.

Straw, Will (1990) *Popular music as cultural commodity: the American recorded music industries 1976–1985*. Unpublished PhD thesis, Graduate Program in Communications, McGill University, Montreal.

Streeter, Thomas (1996) *Selling the Air*. Chicago, IL: Chicago University Press.

Streeter, Thomas (2004) 'Romanticism in business culture: the Internet, the 1990s, and the origins of irrational exuberance', in Andrew Calabrese and Colin Sparks (eds), *Towards a Political Economy of Culture*. Lanham, MD: Rowman & Littlefield. pp. 286–306.

Streeter, Thomas (2011) *The Net Effect*. New York: New York University Press.

Stringer, Julian (ed.) (2003) *Movie Blockbusters*. London: Routledge.

Sugimaya, Mitsunobi (2000) 'Media and power in Japan', in James Curran and Myung-Jin Park (eds), *De-Westernizing Media Studies*. London: Routledge.

Sun, Wanning and Zhao, Yuezhi (2009) 'Television culture with "Chinese characteristics": the politics of compassion and education', in Graeme Turner and Jinna Tay (eds), *Television Studies After TV*. New York and Abingdon: Routledge. pp. 96–104.

Tasker, Yvonne (1996) 'Approaches to the new Hollywood', in James Curran, David Morley and Valerie Walkerdine (eds), *Cultural Studies and Communications*. London: Arnold. pp. 213–28.

Teo, Stephen (2000) 'Hong Kong cinema', in John Hill and Pamela Church Gibson (eds), *World Cinema: Critical Approaches*. Oxford: Oxford University Press. pp. 166–72.

Terranova, Tiziana (2004) *Network Culture*. London: Pluto Press.

Théberge, Paul (1997) *Any Sound You Can Imagine*. Hanover, NH: Wesleyan University Press.

Thomas, Pradip N. (1998) 'South Asia', in Anthony Smith with Richard Paterson (eds), *Television: An International History*. Oxford: Oxford University Press. pp. 201–7.

Thomas, Rosie (1985) 'Indian cinema: pleasures and popularity', *Screen*, 26(3–4): 116–31.

Thompson, John B. (1995) *The Media and Modernity*. Cambridge: Polity.

Thompson, John B. (2005) *Books in the Digital Age*. Cambridge: Polity.

Thompson, John B. (2010) *Merchants of Culture*. Cambridge: Polity.

Thompson, Kristin (1999) *Storytelling in the New Hollywood*. Cambridge, MA: Harvard University Press.

Throsby, C. David (2010) *The Economics of Cultural Policy*. Cambridge: Cambridge University Press.

Thussu, Daya Kishan (1999) 'Privatizing the airwaves: the impact of globalization on broadcasting in India', *Media, Culture and Society*, 21(1): 125–31.

Toffler, Alvin (1980) *The Third Wave*. London: Pan.

Tomlinson, John (1991) *Cultural Imperialism*. London: Pinter.

Tomlinson, John (1997) 'Internationalism, globalization and cultural imperialism', in Kenneth Thompson (ed.), *Media and Cultural Regulation*. London/Milton Keynes: Sage/The Open University. pp. 119–53.

Towse, Ruth (1992) 'The labour market for artists', *Richerce Economiche*, 46: 55–74.

Towse, Ruth (ed.) (1997) *Cultural Economics*. Cheltenham: Edward Elgar.

Towse, Ruth (2002) 'Introduction', in Ruth Towse (ed.), *Copyright in the Cultural Industries*. Cheltenham: Edward Elgar. pp. xiv–xxii.

Toynbee, Jason (2000) *Making Popular Music*. London: Arnold.

Toynbee, Jason (2004) 'Musicians', in Simon Frith and Lee Marshall (ed.), *Music and Copyright* (2nd edn). Edinburgh: Edinburgh University Press. pp. 123–38.

Toynbee, Jason (2006) 'The media's view of the audience', in David Hesmondhalgh (ed.), *Media Production*. Maidenhead and Milton Keynes, Open University Press/ The Open University. pp. 91–132.

Toynbee, Jason (2008)'Media making and social reality', in David Hesmondhalgh and Jason Toynbee (eds), *The Media and Social Theory*. Abingdon and New York: Routledge. pp. 265–80.

Toynbee, Polly (2005) 'Narnia represents everything that is most hateful about religion', *The Guardian* online, Special Report: Religious Affairs, 5 December, available at www.guardian.co.uk (last accessed September 2006).

Tracey, Michael (1998) *The Decline and Fall of Public Service Broadcasting*. Oxford: Oxford University Press.

Trappel, Josef, Meier, Werner A., d'Haenens Leen, Steemers, Jeanette and Thomass, Barbara (2010) *The Media in Europe Today*. Bristol: Intellect.

Tremblay, Gaëtan (2011) 'Creative economy statistics to support creative economy policies', *Media, Culture and Society*, 33,2: 289-98

Tuchman, Gaye (1978) *Making News*. New York: Free Press.

Tumber, Howard (ed.) (1999) *News: A Reader*. Oxford: Oxford University Press.

Tunstall, Jeremy (1971) *Journalists at Work*. London: Constable.

Tunstall, Jeremy (1986) *Communications Deregulation*. Oxford: Blackwell.

Tunstall, Jeremy (1993) *Television Producers*. London: Routledge.

Tunstall, Jeremy (1994) *The Media are American* (2nd edn). London: Constable.

Tunstall, Jeremy (1997) 'The United Kingdom', in Euromedia Research Group/Bernt Stubbe Østergaard (ed.), *The Media in Western Europe*. London: Sage. pp. 244–59.

Tunstall, Jeremy (2001) 'Introduction', in Jeremy Tunstall (ed.), *Media Occupations and Professions*. Oxford: Oxford University Press.

Tunstall, Jeremy (2008) *The Media Were American*. New York and Oxford: Oxford University Press.

Tunstall, Jeremy and Machin, David (1999) *The Anglo-American Media Connection*. Oxford: Oxford University Press.

Tunstall, Jeremy and Palmer, Michael (1990) *Liberating Communications*. Oxford: Basil Blackwell.

Turner, Fred (2006) *From counterculture to cyberculture*. Chicago: University of Chicago Press.

Turner, Graeme (2004) *Understanding Celebrity*. London: Sage.

Turner, Graeme (2010) *Ordinary People and the Media*. London: Sage.

Turner, Graeme and Tay, Jinna (eds) (2009) *Television Studies After TV*. New York and Abingdon: Routledge.

Turok, Ivan (2003) 'Cities, clusters and creative industries: the case of film and television in Scotland', *European Planning Studies*, 11(5): 549–65.

Turow, Joseph (1997) *Breaking Up America*. Chicago, IL: Chicago University Press.

Turow, Joseph (2012) *The Daily You*. New Haven, CT: Yale University Press.

Turow, Joseph and McAllister, Matthew P. (eds) (2009) *The Advertising and Consumer Culture Reader*. New York: Routledge.

UNCTAD (2008) *Creative Economy Report 2008*. Geneva: United Nations Conference on Trade and Development.

UNESCO (1980) *Many Voices, One World* (The MacBride Report). Paris: UNESCO.

UNESCO (1982) *The Cultural Industries*. Paris: UNESCO.

UNESCO (1999) *UNESCO Statistical Yearbook*. Paris: UNESCO Institute for Statistics.

UNESCO (2005) *International Flows of Selected Goods and Services, 1994–2003*. Paris: UNESCO Institute for Statistics.

Uricchio, William (2009) 'The future of a medium once known as television', in Pelle Snickars and Patrick Vonderau (eds), *The YouTube Reader*. Stockholm: National Library of Sweden. pp. 24–39.

Ursell, Gillian (2000) 'Television production: issues of exploitation, commodification and subjectivity in UK television labour markets', *Media, Culture & Society*, 22(6): 805–25.

Vaidhyanathan, Siva (2001) *Copyrights and Copywrongs*. New York: New York University Press.

Vaidhyanathan, Siva (2011) *The Google-ization of Everything*. Berkeley: University of California Press.

Van Dijck, José (2009) 'Users like you? Theorising agency in user-generated content', *Media, Culture and Society* 31: 41–58.

Van Dijck, José (2012) 'Facebook as a tool for producing sociality and connectivity', *Television and New Media* 13: 160–76.

Van Dijk, Jan A.G.M. (2005) *The Deepening Divide*. London: Sage.

Van Leeuwen, Theo (1999) *Music, Speech and Sound*. Basingstoke: Macmillan.

Varis, Tapio and Nordenstreng, Kaarle (1985) *International Flow of Television Programmes*. Paris: UNESCO.

Vink, Nico (1988) *The Telenovela and Emancipation*. Amsterdam: Royal Tropical Institute.

Vogel, Harold L. (1998) *Entertainment Industry Economics* (4th edn). Cambridge: Cambridge University Press.

Vogel, Harold, L. (2011) *Entertainment Industry Economics* (8th edition). Cambridge: Cambridge University Press.

VSS (2003) 'Communications industry overview'. New York: Veronis Suhler Stevenson.

VSS (2005) 'Communications industry forecast'. New York: Veronis Suhler Stevenson.

Waisbord, Silvio (1998) 'Latin America', in Anthony Smith with Richard Paterson (eds), *Television: An International History* (2nd edn). Oxford: Oxford University Press. pp. 254–63.

Wasko, Janet (1994) *Hollywood in the Information Age*. Cambridge: Polity Press.

Wasko, Janet (2001) *Understanding Disney*. Cambridge: Polity Press.

Wasko, Janet, Murdock, Graham and Sousa, Helena (eds) (2011) *The Handbook of Political Economy of Communications*. Oxford: Wiley-Blackwell.

Wasserman, Todd (2005) 'Tie-ins: big lists for Disney's Little and Narnia', *Inside Branded Entertainment*, 3 October, available at www.insidebrandedentertainment.com (last accessed 14 February 2006).

Waterman, Christopher Alan (1990) *Jùjù*. Chicago, IL: University of Chicago Press.

Webster, Frank (2006[1995]) *Theories of the Information Society* (3rd edition). London: Routledge.

Webster, James G. and Phalen, Patricia F. (1997) *The Mass Audience*. Mahwah, NJ: Lawrence Erlbaum.

Wells, Alan (1972) *Picture Tube Imperialism?* Maryknoll, NY: Orbis.

Wernick, Andrew (1991) *Promotional Culture*. London: Sage

Whale, John (1977) *The Politics of the Media*. London: Fontana.

Wicke, Peter (1990) *Rock Music*. Cambridge: Cambridge University Press.

Willens, Michelle (2000) 'Putting films to the test', *The New York Times*, Section 2, 25 June.

Williams, Kevin (2005) *European Media Studies*. London: Hodder Arnold.

Williams, Raymond (1958) *Culture and Society*. London: Chatto & Windus.

Williams, Raymond (1961) *The Long Revolution*. London: Chatto & Windus.

Williams, Raymond (1974) *Television: Technology and Cultural Form*. London: Fontana.

Williams, Raymond (1977) *Marxism and Literature*. Oxford: Oxford University Press.

Williams, Raymond (1981) *Culture*. London: Fontana.

Williams, Raymond (1983) *Towards 2000*. London: Chatto & Windus.

Willams, Raymond (1989) *What I Came to Say*, London: Hutchinson Radius.

Williamson, Lucy (2011) 'The dark side of South Korean pop music', *BBC News*, available at www.bbc.co.uk/news/world-asia-pacific-13760064 (last accessed November 2011).

Willis, Paul (1990) *Common Culture*. Milton Keynes: The Open University Press.

Winseck, Dwayne (2011a) 'The political economies of media and the transformation of the global media industries', in Winseck, Dwayne and Jin, Dal Y. (eds) (2011) *The Political Economies of Media*. London: Bloomsbury Academic, pp. 3–48.

Winseck, Dwayne (2011b) 'Financialization and the "crisis of the media": the rise and fall of (some) media conglomerates in Canada', in Winseck, Dwayne and Jin, Dal Y. (eds) (2011) *The Political Economies of Media*. London: Bloomsbury Academic, pp. 142–66.

Winseck, Dwayne and Jin, Dal Y. (eds) (2011) *The Political Economies of Media*. London: Bloomsbury Academic.

Winston, Brian (1998) *Media Technology and Society*. London: Routledge.

Wolf, Michael J. (1999) *The Entertainment Economy*. London: Penguin.

Wolff, Janet (1983) *Aesthetics and the Sociology of Art*. Basingstoke: Macmillan.

Wolff, Janet (1993 [1981]) *The Social Production of Art* (2nd edn). Basingstoke: Macmillan.

Wyatt, Justin (1994) *High Concept*. Austin, TX: University of Texas Press.

Wyatt, Justin (1998) 'From roadshowing to saturation release: majors, independents and marketing/distribution innovations', in Jon Lewis (ed.), *The New American Cinema*. Durham, NC: Duke University Press.

Yoon, Hyejin and Malecki, Edward J. (2009) 'Cartoon planet: worlds of production and global networks in the animation industry', *Industrial and Corporate Change*, 19(1): 239–71.

Yúdice, George (2003) *The Expediency of Culture*. Durham, NC: Duke University Press.

Zhao, Yuezhi (2003) 'Transnational capital, the Chinese state, and China's communication industries in a fractured society', *Javnost/The Public*, 10(4): 53–73.

Zhao, Yuezhi (2008) *Communication in China*. Lanham, MD: Rowman & Littlefield.

Zhao, Yuezhi, and Schiller, Dan (2001) 'Dances with wolves? China's integration with digital capitalism', *Info*, 3(2): 137–51.

Zimmer, Michael (2005–2006) 'The value implications of the practice of paid search', *ASIS&T Bulletin*, December/January, available at www.asis.org/Bulletin/ Dec-05/zimmer.html (last accessed September 2006).

Zoellner, Anna (2010) *Project Development in Independent Documentary Production*. PhD thesis, University of Leeds.

Zukin, Sharon (1995) *The Culture of Cities*. Oxford: Blackwell.

Index

Page numbers in *italics* refer to boxes and tables.

active audience theory 275–6
Adorno, T. and Horkheimer, M. 23–5
advertising/marketing
 and commercialism 375–81
 internet 333–4
 and market research 233–43
 personnel 78
 target marketing 389
alliances/networks 108–9, 212–14, *215*
Andersen, R. 376, 377
Anderson, C. 10, 30, 199, 330, 348
Andrejevic, M. 335
Arab world
 impact of digitalisation and internet 327
 journalism *292–3*
Arsenault, A. and Castells, M. 213–14
artifical scarcity 31
audience autonomy 352–3
audience maximisation 30–1
audience research 233–42, 392–3
 digital age 242–3
Auletta, K. 213, 333
Australia: marketisation of broadcasting
 144–5
autonomy
 audience 352–3
 creative 32–3, 79–81, 231–2, 263, *263–4*
 digital technologies 318
 journalistic 243–8
 see also control

Bagdikian, B.H. 204–5, 247
Baker, C.E. 208–9, 376
Banks, M. 256–7
 and Hesmondhalgh, D. 255
Becker, H. 47, 48, 55
Benkler, Y. 10, 318
Bennett, T. 57
book publishing
 impact of digitalisation 356–8
 quality issue 395–8

borderline and problem cases 18–20
Bordwell, D. 301
Born, G. 7, 240–2
Bourdieu, P. 22, 27, 49, 235
Brenner, R. 97–9, 100, 189
broadcasting
 as national/limited resource 129–30, 131–2
 power of 130, 132
 see also marketisation in
  telecommunications and broadcasting;
  public service broadcasting (PSB)
bureaucracies, types of 230–1
Burns, T. 241
Burston, J. 251
business ownership *see* ownership
business strategies 102–9

cable/satellite technology 142–3
 transnational television 284–7
Castells, M. 96, 103, 108–9, 193, 213, 320–1,
  327–8, 330–1, 332, 369–70
 Arsenault, A. and 213–14
Caves, R.E. 40, 254, 262, 264–5, 358
change
 agents 8–10
 and continuity 2–4, *65*, 407–10
 extent of 402–7
China 178–9, 217–18
 Hong Kong film industry 298, 299–301
 marketisation 147, 149–50
Chinese-language television 287–9
Christopherson, S. 256
circulation
 creativity and 229–33
 production and 4–6
citizen journalism 386, 387
co-opting 30–1
Coarse, R.H. 40
colonialism, legacy of 52
commerce and creativity, relationship
  between 28–9, 81–3

commodification 68–71, 221–5
communication studies 40–2, 50–1
comparative advantage, theory of 86–7
complex professional era 67, *67–8*, *73–4*,
231–2
concentration of ownership 30–1, 204–9
conglomerates/conglomeration 71–5,
195–200
consumer electronics 18–19, 114
content analysis 50
contracts *257–8*, 262–3
control 243–53
creativity and circulation 229–33
and interests in organisations 75–7
internet 321, 327–30
see also autonomy
convergence 113–14, 151–3, 313–14,
318–19, 320
homogenisation through 370
copyright 159–65
and contracts *257–8*, 262–3
core and 'peripheral' cultural industries *17*,
18, 21–2
corporate strategic alliances 108
costs, production and reproduction 29
creative autonomy 32–3, 79–81, 231–2, 263,
263–4
creative cities and creative clusters 170–4
creative industries analysis 57
creative managers 78, 84, 260–1
creativity
in creative industries policy *170–1*
and knowledge management 6–8
role in new economy *173*
see also symbol creators/symbolic
creativity
creativity and commerce, relationship
between 28–9, 81–3
critical political economy approaches 42–4
cross-media promotion and secondary texts
378–9
cultural determinism/reductionism 94–5
cultural economics 38–40
cultural economy 58
cultural imperialism *see under*
internationalisation
cultural industries
core and 'peripheral' *17*, 18, 21–2
definitions 16–18
and alternative terms 22–3
borderline and problem cases 18–20
objections and assumptions 20–2
distinctive features 26–33
importance of 4–10
singular and plural concept of 23–5

cultural industries approach to political
economy 44–5
vs Schiller-McChesney tradition 45–7
cultural labour *see* labour
cultural policy
definition *166*
see also policy changes
cultural production *see* production
cultural studies
achievements and limitations 51–4
media industries and production 54–8
theoretical and methodological
issues 60–1
vs political economy approaches 58–60
culture
commodification of 70–1
definition of 16, 95
Curran, J. 244, 247–8, 353, 382, 386
and Seaton, J. 373–4
Curtin, M. 371–2

Davis, H. and Scase, R. 229–32
determinism/reductionism 93–5
digital audiences *336–7*
research 242–3
digital divides 321, 323–7
digital games industry 358–61
digital optimism 56–7
criticisms and dilemmas 321–39
key claims 313–21
digital rights management
(DRM) 343
digitalisation 311–13
see also internet; new media
discourse 53
diversity
choice and multiplicity 365–75
newspapers 373–4
popular music 367–9
television 371–3
division of labour *see under* labour

East Asian television 287–92
Eastern Europe: marketisation 147, 149
ebooks 356–8
economic determinism/reductionism 61, 94
Eikhof, D. and Haunschild, A. 251–3
entrepreneurism 209–10
equality issues *see* digital divides; social
justice
Euro-pop 306
European Union (EU)
copyright legislation 63, 162
telecommunications and broadcasting
policy 155–6

Facebook 334, 338–9, 380
fashion 20
Federal Communications Commission (FCC),
    USA 134, *135*, 136, 211
file-sharing 343
film and film industry
    consumption 366–7
    cross-media promotion and secondary
        texts *378–9*
    independence and niche markets 398–400
    internationalisation 293–301
    see also Hollywood
Fiske, J. 7, 50
Florida, R. 172–3, 216
foreign direct investment (FDI) 105–6
formatting of cultural products 31–2
Fortune Global 500 List 220–1, *222–3*
Foucault, M. 57
Fowler, M. 40, 136
France: marketisation of broadcasting 143–4
free labour (internet) 334–5, 338–9
Frith, S. 55, 249
    and Marshall, L. 160
Frow, J. 69, 70–1

games industry 358–61
Garnham, N. 26, 27, 29, 30, 31, 44, 45, 51, 60,
    104, 140, 142, 153, 167, 174–6, 207–8,
    217, *294*
genres 32
Germany: marketisation of broadcasting 144
Gitlin, T. 49
global corporations 219–21
global policy 177–9
globalisation *see* internationalisation
Golding, P.
    and Murdock, G. 43, 324
    Murdock, G. and 323, 324
Google 19, 198–9, 214, 328–9, 333
Greater London Council (GLC) 166–7

Hall, S. 52, 110, 275
Hallin, D.C. 387–8
Hargittai, E. and Walejko, G. 325
Harvey, D. 9, 96, 97, 102, 105, 392
Havens, T. 290
Hearn, A. 380
Held, D. et al. 105, 107, 274, 294
Herman, E.S. and McChesney,
    R.W. *273–4*
Hesmondhalgh, D. 50, 60, 338
    and Baker, S. 234–5, 256, 257
    Banks, M. and 255
Hindman, M. 329–30
Hirsch, P.M. 30, 31, 47–8

Hollywood
    domination *73–4*, 293–4
    and independent cinema 398–9, 400
    marketing *235–6*, *237–8*
homogeneity
    assertions of 369–71
    and diversity 373–4
    through convergence 370
Hong Kong film industry 298, 299–301
Howard, P. 327
Howkins, J. 179, 216
Humphreys, P.J. 127, 138, 140–1, 373

identity 53
income, disposable 111
independent cinema 398–400
India
    film industry 295–7, 300–1
    marketisation of telecommunications and
        broadcasting 147–8
industrialisation and commodification,
    distinction between 68–9, 70
information society 100–2, 113, 123–4, 125–6
information technology 19, 112–14
integration 30–1, 200–4
intellectual property
    TRIPS agreement 160, *161–2*
    types 159
    see also copyright
interests
    in organisations 75–7
    and social justice 89–91
internationalisation 105–7
    cultural imperialism
        and globalisation 272–7
        and popular music 301–7
    film industry 293–301
    key aspects 277
    policy bodies 153–6
    and US domination 85–7, 270–2
    see also television
internet 313
    advertising/marketing 333–4
    commercialisation/surveillance 321, 330–9
    control/power issue 321, 327–30
    copyright legislation 162
    free labour 334–5, 338–9
    Google 19, 198–9, 214, 328–9, 333
    industries 19
    journalism 386–7
    uses and elements *322–3*
    Web 2.0 *317*
    see also social networking sites
Introna, L.D. and Nissenbaum, H. 328–9
Iranian election (2009) 327

Japan: marketisation of broadcasting 145–6
Jenkins, H. 56–7, 318–20, 360
journalism
    Arabic television and Al-Jazeera *292–3*
    autonomy 243–8
    professional and citizen 385–8
    see also newspapers

Klein, B. 250–1
Klinenberg, E. 211
knowledge management, creativity and 6–8
Korea: popular music *303*

labour
    division of labour
        and creative autonomy 78–83
        terms and conditions in different roles
            258–65
        and working conditions 83–5, 253–8
    free (internet) 334–5, 338–9
Lacroix, J.-G. and Tremblay, G. 68–9
Lash, S. and Urry, J. 9, 96, 201, 220, 407
Latin America
    marketisation of broadcasting 147, 150
    television drama 280–4
Levy, E. 398, 399–400
liberal-pluralism 41–2, 50–1
local and urban policy 167–70
Long Downturn 96, 97–9
'long tail' thesis 30, 330, 348
Lotz, A.D. 372

McChesney, R.W. 205, 385
    Herman, E.S. and *273–4*
    and Nichols, J. 385, 386–7
    see also Schiller-McChesney
        tradition
magazines 88–9, 235, 356
marginalised groups 381–4
market professional era 66
market segmentation and social
    fragmentation 388–92
marketing *see* advertising/marketing
marketisation in telecommunications and
    broadcasting
    deregulation and re-regulation 126–8
    dismantled rationales and 131–2
    policy 122–6
    state involvement 128–30
    waves 132–4
        advanced industrial states 137–40
        convergence and internationalisation
            151–6
        transitional and mixed societies 146–51
        US 134–7

Marx, K. 69
Mayer, V. et al. 55–6
media industries and production 54–8
media moguls and control of news *245–6*
media studies/radical media sociology 48–50
mega-corporations 192–4, *195*
Menger, P.-M. 254–5
mergers and acquisitions 187–92
Miège, B. 25, 44, 45, 51, 76, 84, 254, 359, 409
Miller, M.C. 395–8
Miller, T. et al. 260, 267
Mommaas, H. 171–2
Mosco, V. 44, 88, 366
Murdock, G. 38, 71, 75, 213
    see also and Golding, P.
music industry *see* popular music and music
    industry
MySpace 214, 347

Napoli, P.M. 237, 242–3, 348, 352
national growth 216–19
national policy 174–7
Negus, K. 20, 55, 197–8, 238
neoclassical economics 38–9, 40
    theory of comparative advantage 86–7
neoliberalism 39–40, 99–102
    see also marketisation in
        telecommunications and broadcasting
network organisation 230
networks/networking 108–9, 212–14, *215*
    see also social networking sites
Neuman, W.R. 27, 28, 94–5, 389
new economy, role of creativity in *173*
new technologies/media 87, 310
newspapers
    homogenisation and diversity 373–4
    impact of digitalisation 356
    unethical practices 388
Nixon, S. 240
Noam, E.M. 19, 23, 124, 153, 204, 206–7

Oakley, K. 177, 255, 256
O'Connor, J. 173–4
    and Gu, X. 178–9
offsetting misses against hits 30
organisation(s)
    ideal types 230–1
    and management 77–83
    and management studies 47–8
    structure and size *see under* ownership
ownership
    organisational structure and size 71–7, 107–9
        concentration 30–1, 204–9
        conglomeration 71–5, 195–200
        growth 216–21

ownership *cont.*
   integration 30–1, 200–4
   mega-corporations 192–4, *195*
   mergers and acquisitions 187–92
   networks/alliances 108–9, 212–14, *215*
   small companies 73, 209–11, 212
   popular music 304–7

participatory citizenship 42
patronage and artisanal era 66, *67–8*
'peripheral' and core cultural
      industries *17*, 18, 21–2
Peterson, R.A. 50
   and Berger, D.G. 367–8
   and Kern, R. 384
pleasure 53
policy changes
   copyright 159–65
   creative cities and creative clusters 170–4
   cultural policy, definition *166*
   global 177–9
   Greater London Council (GLC) 166–7
   local and urban 167–70
   national 174–7
   see also marketisation in
         telecommunications and
         broadcasting
political economy approaches 44–7
   critical 42–4
   and cultural studies 58–60
   and radical media sociology 48–50
political homogenisation 373–4
political-economic change: Long Downturn
      96, 97–9
political-regulatory change 99–102
politics of entertainment 381–4
polysemy 50
Poole, S. 359–60
popular music and music
      industry 249–51
   authenticity *vs* hybridity 302
   contracts and copyright 262–3
   impact of digitalisation and
         internet 341–8
   internationalisation 301–7
   interpretation 302–4
   measurement of diversity 367–9
   ownership 304–7
power relations 50
   see also autonomy; control
primary creative personnel 78
print-based media
   impact of digitalisation 356–8
   see also magazines; newspapers
problem and borderline cases 18–20

production
   change and continuity *65*
   and circulation 4–6
   and consumption: political economy
         approaches 46
   eras 66–8
   media industries and 54–8
   and reproduction costs 29
   stages 79, *80*, 81
   studies 55–6
profits *see* risks
project teams: roles and
      functions 77–9
public service broadcasting (PSB)
   case studies 140–6
   characteristics 137–8
   social and cultural role 140
   variations 138–40

quality issue 89, 392–400

radical media sociology/media studies 48–50
reality television 380, 392–5
reductionism/determinism 61, 93–5
regeneration and culture 176, 177
regulatory change *see* marketisation in
         telecommunications and broadcasting;
         neoliberalism
representation 52–3, 56
risks 27–30
   and risk minimisation 30–3
Rosen, J. 386
Ross, A. 178, 179, 257
Russia: marketisation of
         broadcasting 149
Ryan, B. 31, 32, 77–9, *80*, 232–3, 260, 410

Sassen, S. 331, 332
satellite technology *see* cable/satellite
         technology
Schiller-McChesney tradition 44, 51, 75, 208
   vs cultural industries approach to political
         economy 45–7
Schudson, M. 375–6
secondary texts, cross-media promotion and
      378–9
semi-public goods 29–30
semi-skilled/unskilled labour 79, 259–60
serials 32
service industries, investment in 102–5
Sinclair, J. 281, 282, 284, 286
   et al. 279–80, 406
small companies 73, 209–11, 212
social fragmentation, market segmentation
      and 388–92

social justice
  advertising and commercialism 375–81
  politics of entertainment 381–4
  role of journalism 385–8
social networking sites 327, 332–3, 334–5, 346
  Facebook 334, 338–9, 380
  MySpace 214, 347
  YouTube 198–9, 320, 333, 335, *351–2*
sociocultural change 109–11
sociology
  of culture and organisational/management
      studies 47–8
  radical media/media studies 48–50
sport 20
Sreberny, A. 272
star system 31–2
state involvement *see* marketisation in
      telecommunications and broadcasting;
      policy changes
Streeter, T. 113, 151–2, 160
subjectivity 53
Sunday Times 347, 353
symbol creators/symbolic creativity 6–8,
      20–1, 261–5
  loose control of 32–3, 81
  market and corporate professionals 66–7
  political economy approaches 46–7

target marketing 389
technical workers 78, 81–2, 84, 260
technological determinism/reductionism
      93–4
technologies, dominant 87
telecommunications
  and computers (convergence) 113–14,
      313–14, 318–19, 320
  and internationalisation 107
  as public utility 129, 131
  see also marketisation in
      telecommunications and broadcasting
telenovelas 281–4
television
  Arabic *292–3*
  East Asian 287–92
  and geo-cultural markets 277–87
  impact of internet and digitalisation 348–55
  market segmentation 390–1, *391–2*
  reality 380, 392–5
  textual diversification 371–3
  US: vertical integration *202–3*
  worldwide revenues *288*
Terranova, T. 334–5
texts
  assertions of homogeneity 369–71
  choice, diversity and multiplicity 365–75
  implications for future study 411–13
  internationalisation of 277

texts *cont.*
  market segmentation and social
      fragmentation 388–92
  problem of 50–1
  production and circulation of 4–6
  quality issue 89, 392–400
  and social justice issues 375–88
  see also specific types
textual change 88–91
theatre 251–3
theoretical perspectives
  communication studies 40–2
  cultural economics 38–40
  see also cultural studies; political economy
      approaches; sociology
Thompson, J.B. 357–8
Throsby, C.D. 21–2
time, leisure *vs* working 111
Times 347
Tomlinson, J. 276
Towse, R. 164, 254
Toynbee, J. 7, 210, 237, 409
Trade-Related Aspects of Intellectual
      Property Rights (TRIPS) agreement 160,
      161–2
Tunstall, J. 42, 83, 84, 85, 86, 112, 136, 142, 152,
      278, 283, 290
  and Machin, D. 144
Turner, G. 54, 291–2, 394
Turow, J. 334, 389

United Kingdom (UK)
  marketisation of broadcasting 142–3
  newspapers 373–4, 388
United States (US)
  copyright legislation 162–3
  domination 85–7, 270–2, 277–9
  Federal Communications Commission
      (FCC) 134, *135*, 136, 211
  marketisation of broadcasting 134–7
  television: vertical integration *202–3*
  see also Hollywood
unskilled/semi-skilled labour 79, 259–60
urban and local policy 167–70

vertical integration 30, 31, 200–4

Web 2.0 *317*
Williams, R. 16, 21, 66–8, 94, 95, 130, 409
Winseck, D. 192
working conditions 83–5, 253–8
working *vs* leisure time 111
world cinema *299*
world music 306–7
World Trade Organisation (WTO) 160, *161–2*
Wyatt, J. *235–6*, 237–8

YouTube 198–9, 320, 333, 335, *351–2*